Money, Ban
Public Finance

By the same author:

HISTORY OF ECONOMIC THOUGHT
17th Edition

RAJASWA KE SIDDHANT
14th Edition

MACROECONOMIC THEORY
10th Edition

MONETARY ECONOMICS
10th Edition

ARTHIK VICHARON KA ITIHAS
10th Edition

MONEY AND BANKING
1st Edition

MONEY, BANKING AND INTERNATIONAL TRADE
8th Edition

COOPERATION: PRINCIPLES, PROBLEMS AND PRACTICE
7th Edition

SAMASHTI ARTHASHASTRA
2nd Edition

Money, Banking and Public Finance

(8th *Edition*)

T.N. Hajela, Ph.D
Formerly Joint Secretary
University Grants Commission
New Delhi

Ane Books Pvt. Ltd.

New Delhi ♦ Chennai ♦ Mumbai
Bangaluru ♦ Kolkata ♦ Thiruvananthapuram ♦ Lucknow

Money, Banking and Public Finance

T.N. Hajela

First Edition : 1984
Eighth Edition : **2009**

Published by

Ane Books Pvt. Ltd.
4821, Parwana Bhawan, 1st Floor, 24 Ansari Road,
Darya Ganj, **New Delhi** - 110 002, India
Tel.: +91(011) 23276843-44, Fax: +91(011) 23276863
e-mail: kapoor@anebooks.com, Website: www.anebooks.com

Branches

- Avantika Niwas, 1st Floor, 19 Doraiswamy Road, T. Nagar,
Chennai - 600 017, Tel.: +91(044) 28141554, 28141209
e-mail: anebooks_tn@airtelmail.in
- G-012, Ground Floor, Jui Nagar Railway Station Building, Jui Nagar (East),
Navi Mumbai - 400 705, Tel.: +91(022) 27720842, 27720851
e-mail: anebooksmum@mtnl.net.in
- 38/1, 1st Floor, Model House, First Street, Opp. Shamanna Park,
Basavannagudi, **Bangaluru** - 560 004, Tel.: +91(080) 41681432, 26620045
e-mail: anebang@airtelmail.in
- Flat No. 16A, 220 Vivekananda Road, Maniktalla,
Kolkata - 700 006, Tel.: +91(033) 23547119
e-mail: anekol@vsnl.net
- # 6, TC 25/2710, Kohinoor Flats, Lukes Lane, Ambujavilasam Road,
Thiruvananthapuram - 01, Kerala, Tel.: +91(0471) 4068777, 4068333
e-mail: anebookstvm@airtelmail.in

Representative Office

- C-26, Sector-A, Mahanagar, **Lucknow** - 226 006
Mobile - +91 93352 29971

ISBN (10) : 81-8052-161-3
ISBN (13) : 978-81-8052-161-4

Printed at: Gopaljee Enterprises, Delhi

Preface to the Eighth Edition

A composite book on 'Money and Banking, International Trade and Public Finance' was published in 1984. In its seventh edition published in 1998, the portion on Public Finance was dropped owing to the change in the syllabi in Economics of most of the Universities. During the last one decade, the syllabi of the Universities in Economics both at the undergraduate and postgraduate levels have been reorganized, particularly after the circulation of the Model Curriculum by the UGC in 2002-03. Accordingly now the original book has been trifurcated into (I) Money and Banking, (II) Money, Banking and International Trade and (III) Money, Banking and Public Finance to fulfil the needs of students of various Universities in India.

The present volume has been prepared for the students of undergraduate and postgraduate courses in Economics of the Indian Universities. It would also be of use to those appearing in competitive examinations. The text has been prepared to the topics recommended by the Unversity Grants Commission in the Model Curriculum circulated to the Universities and adopted by them w.e.f. 2002-03. The language used is simple and the matter provided is concise and to the point. Consequently, it is not bulky and costwise, it is cheap.

The book has Two Portions. Portion one contains three parts, namely, Money, Banking Theory, and Banking in India, comprising 25 chapters. Portion two relates to Public Finance comprising 22 chapters.

In preparing the book, I have freely used the matter from the works of the original thinkers and writers. I acknowledge my debt to them.

I am thankful to Shri Sunil Saxena of Ane Books Pvt. Ltd. for the fine get up and excellent printing of the book and for keeping its price within the reach of students in these days of rising costs.

I shall welcome suggestions for the improvement of the book.

— T.N. HAJELA

Preface to the First Edition

This is a textbook on money and banking, income and employment, international trade and public finance which combines within its fold a systematic discussion and objective analysis of theory and policy concerning these fields in India. It is addressed to the teachers and students at Master's and B.A./B.Com. honours' levels of Indian Universities. The selection of topics and their discussion have been primarily guided by their relevance to contemporary Indian experience and planning needs.

The book has been designed to serve as a University-level text, keeping in view the syllabi of different universities. The book has become rather bulky since the objective has been to cover as large a portion of the syllabus of as many Universities as possible. although the courses in India do not follow a uniform pattern, it is felt that this book should cover most of the topics of any well-thought-out course in the subject. Appropriate selection of chapters, or even sections can also be made to suit the requirements of individual Universities.

While writing the book special care has been taken to make the discussion reasonably self-sufficient and easily intelligible without sacrificing the quality of treatment. I shall consider my efforts well paid if the book serves the needs of teaching the subject in Indian Universities.

Several friends and colleagues have prompted me to write this book. Several others have helped me in the actual writing of it. My thanks to each one of them. In writing a book of this type, one draws upon the contributions of so many writers and thinkers that separate acknowledgement of each one of them, apart from some references, is an impossible task. I make no attempt at it. All the same I owe a debt to all of them.

—T.N. HAJELA

Preface to the First Edition

[illegible]

Contents

MONEY AND BANKING

PART ONE : MONEY

PART TWO : BANKING THEORY

PART THREE : BANKING IN INDIA

PUBLIC FINANCE

Money and Banking

PART ONE
MONEY

Chapter 1

Evolution and Functions of Money

1. The Origin of Money : The Barter System and Its Defects

The importance of money for the smooth functioning of the modern complex economies can hardly be exaggerated. True, that more primitive societies of the past were able to function without it, it is difficult to visualize today an economic system, be it capitalistic or socialistic, which can function without money. How money reached this stage is quite interesting to know. It was not invented overnight. It is the result of a process of evolution through several hundred years. In the most primitive form of society, man procured goods not produced by him through force. After some time, he realized that this sort of practice was not socially desirable. He, therefore, started exchanging goods and services directly for goods and services. This system was known as barter. With the growing civilization and extension of economic activities people found the barter system normally deficient for meeting their growing exchange requirements. They found number of defects in the system, *viz*., (*i*) the defect of 'double coincidence of wants'; *i.e.* the difficulty of bringing two such persons together, each of whom would accept the commodities offered by the other; (*ii*) the defect of 'settling on terms'. This defect arose because of the absence of a common measure of value, *i.e.* the rate at which one commodity could be exchanged for the other; (*iii*) the defect of division of commodities—some time it was impossible to exchange a part of a commodity with a part of another commodity. For example, if one buffalo could be exchanged for two maunds of wheat the owner of wheat would not accept half of the buffalo for one maund of wheat; (*iv*) some commodities are more expensive than others, and one who wishes to dispose of this commodity may be unwilling to accept in exchange a large amount of the less expensive commodity; and (*v*) the difficulty in storing wealth—since most of the commodities lack sufficient durability people could not think of storing a commodity to provide for future contingencies. In a simple or primitive form of economy where people had too few and simple requirements of life, barter system was very convenient. But with every new development of commerce, with every fresh division of labour, with the extension of trade, barter became more and more difficult and inconvenient. As social organisation became more complex, the inconveniences of barter became all the more pressing. These difficulties and inconveniences motivated people to find out a suitable medium of exchange. Consequently, money was invented.

2. The Evolution of Money

In its earlier stages of development, commodities like spears, skins, stones, axes, tea, shells, tobacco, precious stones, etc. were used as money. The choice of such commodities was determined by factors like location of the community, climatic conditions, stage of cultural and economic development, etc. In primitive agricultural communities animals were the most obvious form of wealth and consequently, cattle were used as money. But this type of money (commodity money) lacked standardization. Its supplies were uncertain, it was indivisible too, it could not be stored and it also involved expenditure upon its own maintenance. Furthermore, it used to be bulky and unportable.

As society progressed, the character of commodity money also changed. Metals came into use in place of animals and other rough commodities. Gold and silver were the two metals which were first used as money. These metals, because of their certain attractiveness began to be in large demand and in course of time came to be regarded as 'natural money'. In order to give recognition to such metallic money central coinage was introduced.

But even metallic money was not free from defects. It was not safe to take metallic money while going out to make purchases and therefore, people took with them written documents like the traveller's cheque issued by reputed financiers as evidence of their command over certain quantity of money specified on the face of these documents. These documents, a mere substitute for actual money, were the first stage in the history of the development of paper money. People accepted them because they knew that these could be readily exchanged for money on demand. Thus, the letters of credit which were simply bank's promise to pay money came to be regarded as money. This is the second stage in the development of paper money. As people gradually became more used to bank notes, which contained an obligation for conversion into gold or silver, they were regarded as actual money, and this was the third stage in the history of the development of paper money. Today these notes circulate as a full-fledged money even without any obligation for conversion. Thus, gold and silver as money metals have been finally replaced and there is hardly any country in the world today where metallic coins circulate, except in the form of token coins.

3. How was Money Invented?

It is thus clear that the use of money arose out of the inconveniences of barter: although in the international sphere barter continued to be practised for a long time. A feature of a transaction involving money is that direct exchange gives way to indirect exchange. In a barter transaction giving and taking are both comprised in a single act; the use of money separates these two processes, since first a commodity is sold out for money, and then subsequently, at a later time the money so obtained is used to make the desired purchase. Let us add a word about the way money has been invented. As soon as people realised the difficulty of double coincidence of wants and that of exchanging commodities, which if divided would lose their quality, they first used a commodity as a unit of account or as a standard of value.

In the earliest stage, as already stated, commodities were used as standard of value and unit of account; in the second stage metallic money was used and in the final stage the paper money is in use. Now with the help of this unit of account, values of different goods and services could be expressed and compared. This led to the extension of area of exchange and to the emergence of the pricing system. Economic calculations became more rational and individual choice-making became easier. This also extended the scope of markets, and provided ample opportunities for specialization and division of labour. Now goods came to be brought and sold independently. At the same time the dependence of one person on the other was completely done away with. The use of time and efforts was substantially economized. When money came to be accepted as a common measure of value and a medium of exchange, its storage became easier and hence, money also started functioning as a store of value. This was the final stage in the invention of money. As Crowther has pointed out: "Money is one of the most fundamental of all man's inventions. Every branch of knowledge has its fundamental discovery. In mechanics it is the wheel, in science it is the fire, in politics it is the vote. Similarly, in economics, in the whole commercial side of man's social existence, money is the essential invention on which all the rest is based."[1]

But, to say that the barter system has been completely eliminated is wrong. In less developed countries it still reigns supreme in the rural areas. Even today, in the field of international trade, owing to the problem of international liquidity and scarcity of foreign exchange more and more countries are resorting to bilateral trade agreements which are nothing but a modified form of the old barter system.

1. G. Crowther, *An Outline of Money,* Revised Edition, p. 4.

4. Definition of Money

It is not easy to define money. Even economists of repute stood vexed at this issue. Consequently, there are as many definitions of money as there are economists. Some of these definitions are too wide, while others are extremely narrow. For example, Walker says that "Money is what money does, that which does the money work is the money thing."[2] This definition is not satisfactory because money performs many functions which can be performed by other articles as well, and from this point of view delimitation of money becomes rather difficult. Similarly, Karl Helfferich says that "we understand, therefore, by the term 'money' the complex of those objects which in a given economic area and in a given economic system have as their normal purpose the facilitation of economic intercourse (or the transfer of values) between economic individuals."[3] On the other hand, there are definitions which are extremely narrow, *e.g.* the definition given by Robertson according to which "Money is a commodity which is used to denote anything which is widely accepted in payment for goods, or in discharge of other kinds of business obligation."[4]

The different definitions of money have also been grouped together into three categories according to their characteristics. In the first category all those definitions have been included which are based on *general acceptability.* According to these definitions, any commodity can be used as money which has been accepted by people generally, provided that: (1) it should be acceptable to the general people as money; (2) its acceptance should be optional and without any fear; and (3) that it is not acceptable only for the present transactions or payments but also for deferred payments. The definitions given by Walker, Marshall, Robertson, Cole, Ely, Kent and Pigou fall in this category. For example, Ely says: "Anything that passes freely from hand to hand, as a medium of exchange and is generally received in final discharge of debts is money." According to Marshall money includes "all those things which are generally current without any special enquiry as means of purchasing commodities and services." In the words of Robertson, money is "a commodity which is used to denote anything which is widely accepted in payment for goods or in discharge of other kinds of business obligation." Cole defines money as "the purchasing power—something which buys things." From these definitions, it would be observed that all of these lay emphasis on general

---

2. F.A. Walker, *Money in Its Relations to Trade and Industry,* p. 1.
3. K. Helfferich, *Money,* Vol. 1, p. 281.
4. D.H. Robertson, *Money,* pp. 2-3.

acceptability. But we cannot include hundies or pronotes or credit instruments in this category and hence, the deficiency of these definitions.

In the second category are included all those definitions which emphasize the legal and constitutional aspects of money. According to these definitions, it is necessary for a commodity to function as money, to have legal recognition. The main exponents of this idea were Prof. Knapp and Hawtrey. According to Hawtrey, "First of all, it has to provide the means for the legal discharge of a debt; secondly, by supplying the standard of value, it has to correct the instability of credit." Thus, Hawtrey has highlighted two aspects of money: first, money acts as a means for the legal payments of all debts; secondly, it corrects the instability of credit by acting as a standard of value. Colbourn, however, does not agree with this view because according to him these definitions only highlight the lawyer's point of view about money which is a very narrow view. He points out that exchange is entirely optional and if anything is accepted under the pressure from the government then that transaction cannot be considered as exchange in true sense of the term. Besides, during period of inflation when the value of money falls down tremendously, even the pressure from the government does not make people to accept that money as had happened in Germany after the World War I and in 1944 in Hungary. Therefore, the acceptability of any commodity as money depends on the trust that people have in that money, and not on the pressure that is put by the government.

Then there are descriptive definitions or those definitions which highlight the functions of money. In this category we include the definitions given by Hawtrey, Withers, Sidgwick and Whittlesy. These definitions, as a matter of fact, describe money, they do not really define it. A proper definition must indicate the genus, as well as the factors which differentiate it from others of its own category and so these definitions are not scientific.

A proper definition of money, thus, is one which signifies the various functions performed by it. From this point of view Crowther's definition seems to be proper. He says, "For most purposes money can be defined as anything that is generally acceptable as a means of exchange (*i.e.* as a means of settling debts) and at the same time acts as a measure and as a store of value."[5]

There are economists like Edwin Cannan, according to whom there is no need of giving a definition of money. But this sort of attitude is not correct because for a scientific study of any subject it is necessary to define it. Actually speaking, a definition is a sort of introduction to the subject concerned; without definition one would not be able to delimit the subject of study and also

5. G. Crowther, *op. cit.*, p. 20.

determine its scope and subject-matter. Hence, definition of any subject of study is an essential pre-requisite.

In passing, we may also refer to the different view points adopted by people in defining money. Johnson and Feige have listed *four approaches*, namely, the conventional approach, the Chicago approach, the Gurley-Shaw approach, and the Central Bank approach. According to the first approach, money is looked upon as a medium of exchange and it includes only currency and demand deposits. These definitions emphasize the functional importance of money. The approach adopted by the Chicago School, of which Prof. Milton Friedman is the leader, includes not only currency and demand deposits but also time deposits and savings deposits of the commercial banks. The Gurley-Shaw approach includes currency, demand and time deposits and also such deposits and claims of financial institutions which can be used as instruments of payments. In the central bank approach money includes the credit created from all types of sources.

The modern approach, however, takes a broader view of money and includes all those assets which are liquid. This approach was mainly adopted by Radcliffe Committee appointed by the UK Government in 1957. The main exponents of this view are British economists Sayers and A.K. Cairncross and German economist Schmolders. John G. Raulett defines liquidity as "the ability of an asset to be converted into spendable form promptly without any risk of loss to its holder." While currency notes and coins are, as we know, liquid assets and also the deposits in current and savings accounts, short-term securities, shares of joint stock companies, etc. Treasury bills, savings certificates, fixed deposits receipts, etc., are not as liquid as the short-term government securities are, because it takes time in converting them into money, and also one has to suffer a financial loss in getting them discounted. But, we can call them as quasi-money, although these are not money in the legal sense, in practice, they are like money. It may also be noted that the amount of the quasi-money in circulation also influences the supply of actual money in the economy. Keeping all these things in view, we may conclude that so far as money in circulation in an economy is concerned, it not only includes actual money but also liquid assets as well as quasi-money. But Professor Chandler is not in favour of the inclusion of quasi-money in the category of money in circulation.[6]

5. Classification of Money

Different authors have classified money differently, emphasizing its different aspects. Broadly speaking, these classifications have been made on the basis

6. L.V. Chandler, *The Economics of Money and Banking,* 4th Edition, p. 16.

of: (*i*) the account maintained in a country; (*ii*) its legal recognition; and (*iii*) the matter of which the money is made.

Money of Account and Actual Money

So far as the first basis is concerned, money has been divided into two classes: Money of Account and Actual Money. While the former is a theoretical form, the latter is its practical form. Money of Account is that money in terms of which the accounts in a country are maintained. Actual money is different from money of account in the sense that while it is under active circulation, money of account is only used for accounting purposes. For example, in our country, the unit of account is the rupee while the actual money has undergone changes during the course of years. Similarly, in the UK, the Pound Sterling continues to be the unit of account but actual payments are made in paper currency and coins.

Prof. Seligman, on the same lines, has classified money into Ideal Money and Actual Money. Ideal Money for him is the same as the unit of account. Benham has also divided money into Unit of Account and Unit of Currency which are the same as Money of Account and Actual Money. The most important classification has been given by Keynes in his *A Treatise on Money*. According to him money is of two types, *i.e.* Money Proper and Money of Account. In his own words, "Money of Account is the description, or title and money is the thing which answers to that description."[7] He has further classified Money Proper into Commodity Money and Representative Money. Commodity Money is the full-bodied money; its face value is equal to its intrinsic value; it acts as a medium of exchange as well as a store of value. Representative Money, on the other hand, is the money which is also in circulation and acts as a medium of exchange, but is just a representative of commodity money and is convertible into it. All paper money issued in a country is put under this category. The representative money is also of two types: convertible and inconvertible; the former can be converted into commodity money while the latter cannot.

Legal Tender Money and Optional Money

So far as the second basis of classification of money is concerned, money has been divided into: (*i*) legal tender, and (*ii*) optional. Legal tender money is one which is, generally, accepted by people as' a means of payment. It has a legal sanction behind it and everyone within the geographical boundaries of a country is bound to accept it. Legal tender money can be: (*i*) Limited Legal Tender, and (*ii*) Unlimited Legal Tender. Limited Legal Tender means that

7. J.M. Keynes, *A Treatise on Money,* Vol. I, pp. 3-4.

money can be accepted only up to a certain limit which is fixed by law. For example, in our own country, small coins of 1 paisa, 5 paisa, 10 paisa, 20 paisa and 25 paisa are legal tender only up to a sum of Rs. 25 beyond which one is free to refuse to accept them. Unlimited Legal Tender is that money which anyone has to accept within the country up to any limit. For example, in India, 50 paisa coin and above and paper notes of all denominations are Unlimited Legal Tender. On the other hand, optional money has no legal sanction behind it but is accepted because of the high credit of the person putting that money in the market. All forms of Cheques, Bank Notes, Bills of Exchange, Promissory Notes, Hundies, etc. are optional money.

Metallic Money and Paper Money

The third and the most popular classification is one which is based on the material of which money is made. From this point of view, money is of two kinds: (*i*) Metallic Money, and (*ii*) Paper Money.

(*i*) Metallic Money

The money which is made of some metal is called metallic money. Metallic money has been further classified into: (*a*) Standard Money, (*b*) Token Money, and (*c*) Subsidiary Money.

(*a*) Standard Money. Standard money or coin is one whose face value is equal to the value of the standard metal contained in it; for example, the Indian Rupee which was in circulation between 1835-1893. Generally, a standard coin is made of precious metals like gold and silver. These coins have a well-defined weight and fineness. The standard money is, therefore: (*i*) the main coin of the country; (*ii*) its face value is equal to its intrinsic value, *i.e.* it is a full-bodied money; (*iii*) its coinage is free, *i.e.* the people are free to take gold or silver to the mint and get the coins in exchange on the payment of a fee. May be, in some cases the mint may not charge any fees; (*iv*) finally, it is unlimited legal tender.

(*b*) Token Money. Token money is a coin whose face value is higher than its intrinsic value. It is, generally, made of inferior and lighter metals. In fact, it is a subsidiary of the standard money and is generally used for small payments. The chief characteristics of such a money are: (*i*) its coinage is not free: (*ii*) its face value is higher than its intrinsic value; (*iii*) it is a limited legal tender, and (*iv*) it is a subsidiary of the standard money.

Status of the Indian Rupee. There has been some confusion about the status of the Indian rupee, whether it is a standard coin or a token coin. Undoubtedly, it was a standard coin before 1893. Today, the situation is entirely different. The Indian rupee is neither a full-bodied coin nor its coinage is free and that is why people prefer to call it a token coin. There are some people who would like to give it the status of a standard coin because: (*i*) it is the principal coin of the country and all prices are fixed in its terms and it is the money of account; (*ii*) the prices of foreign currencies are also expressed in its terms, and (*iii*) it is also an unlimited legal tender. But as a matter of fact, the Indian rupee is in a peculiar position in the sense that it possesses characteristics of both token as well as standard coins and that is why it has been considered better to give it the status of a standard token coin.

(*c*) Subsidiary Money. The subsidiary money consists of very small coins used to facilitate very small payments. Their chief characteristics are: (*i*) they are low valued coins and are made of extremely light metals like aluminium; (*ii*) they facilitate the transactions in low priced commodities and services; (*iii*) they are not subjected to free coinage; (*iv*) they are token coins; (*v*) the relationship of such coins with the standard coin is defined and determined by law; and (*vi*) they are a limited legal tender.

(*ii*) Paper Money

Paper money is made of paper. It is of two kinds: Currency Money and Bank Money. The former is the paper currency notes used within the country and the latter is the credit money issued by banks. Paper currency is issued by the central bank of the country or by any other bank authorized by the government of the country. For example, in India the Reserve Bank is the authority to issue paper notes.

Paper currency has been further sub-divided into four classes, *viz.* (*i*) Representative Paper Money, (*ii*) Convertible Paper Money, (*iii*) Inconvertible Paper Money, and (*iv*) Fiat Money.

(*i*) Representative Paper Money. As the name itself suggests, it represents the standard money of the country. In other words, it is fully backed by gold and silver reserves. Under such form of paper currency, everyone has the right to get the currency converted into gold or silver from the mint or the government. This arrangement is made only to gain confidence of the people in the paper currency. The chief purpose for adopting such a currency is to save the wastage of precious metals.

(*ii*) Convertible Paper Money. This system is a sort of improvement of the Representative Paper Money. In such a system, instead of cent per cent backing of metallic reserves, a certain percentage of its total value is kept in the form of metallic reserves and the currency all the time remains convertible into precious metals. Under this system, a "fixed percentage of the value of the currency in circulation is kept in the form of metallic reserves and the remaining part of the currency is covered by government securities". The part of the currency which is fully covered is known as Covered Issue while the other part is called as Fiduciary Issue. This system of paper currency was adopted by England and France in 1925 and India in 1927.

***(iii)* Inconvertible Paper Money.** Under such a system, the entire paper currency is not backed by metallic reserves and, therefore, it is not convertible. The notes are not convertible into any metal and circulate only due to the stability of the government. In the beginning, this type of currency was brought into circulation only during emergency but now it has become a regular feature.

***(iv)* Fiat Money.** Fiat money, generally, used at times of crises and is the same as the inconvertible paper money; the only difference being that it is issued during emergencies like war, while inconvertible paper money is used during normal times. According to Keynes, "Fiat money is Representative (or Token) Money, *i.e.* something, the intrinsic value of the material substance of which is divorced from its monetary face value now generally made of paper except in the case of small denominations—which is created and issued by the State but is not convertible by law into anything other than itself, and has no fixed value in terms of an objective standard."[8]

Credit Money

Credit money is created by commercial banks. The basis for the creation of this type of money is the demand deposits made by the persons who hold their accounts in the bank. In a sense, the money deposited by the depositors in a bank is transferred by the commercial bank to other persons in the form of a cheque or draft. These cheques or drafts are credit money created by the bank. It is also known as bank money. Although, it is not a legal tender, it is generally accepted by people as a means of payment. It is, however, not universally acceptable. And, no one can be forced to accept it. In advanced industrialised countries, this type of documents holds a very important position, almost as important as the notes issued by the government or the central bank of the country.

6. Money or Near Money

As stated above, cheques and drafts issued by the commercial banks are just a substitute for money, chiefly because they function as the medium of exchange. These instruments are issued by the banks on the basis of demand deposits which are for short term only. The banks do not allow the use of such instruments in the case of long-term deposits or time deposits which are made by people for a, fixed period. If the people wish to withdraw their deposits partially or wholly, they will require to give an advance notice to the bank and also incur penalty. So, the time deposits are not money in the real

8. *Op. cit.,* p. 7.

sense of the term. However, they can be converted into cash or demand deposits at the sweet will of the depositors concerned. But, they are 'near money' because they can be converted into real money at a short notice. Such money, does serve the purpose of store of value temporarily and can be converted into a medium of exchange at short notice without any loss in its face value. Such money assets are also found in circulation in the market in the form of bonds, debentures, insurance policies, securities, bills of exchange, treasury bills, etc. These are negotiable instruments and have a market and can be converted into real money.

We can now distinguish between money and near money. The former is a legal tender while the latter is not; the former provides immediate liquidity to the possessor; the latter does not. Near money is almost a substitute for money as it serves as a store of value; it possesses moneyness and is superior to real money since it yields income. Near money also brings about economy in the use of real money. Since, near money is safe to carry or to handle it is preferable to real money or cash. It has been estimated that about 80 per cent of near money in the USA is held by individuals.

7. Theoretical and Empirical Definitions of Money

Some textbooks attempt to classify these definitions on the basis of their empirical and theoretical emphasis. But, this sort of exercise does not seem to be fair. Some definitions can certainly be termed as narrow and others as broad; some may have greater theoretical implications, while others may have greater empirical significance. No definition can be labelled as purely theoretical or purely empirical. Milton Friedman has rightly said, "The definition of money is to be sought for not on grounds of principle, but on grounds of usefulness in organising our knowledge of economic relationships." Since money is purchasing power, the empirical results will finally be determined by the nature of assets included in the definition of money. That is why, in a later study, Friedman and Schwartz have emphasized that, "The selection of a specific empirical counterpart to the term money seems to us a matter of convenience for a particular purpose, not a matter of principle."

That is why we notice a wide variation in these definitions. And, it is natural too. The traditional economists and later Keynes considered currency and demand deposits as money. Friedman and his followers regarded currency plus all adjusted deposits in commercial banks, as money. The Radcliffe Committee included currency notes and bank deposits in money. Gurley and Shaw even included assets held by financial intermediaries and the liabilities of non-bank intermediaries in money, *viz.* bonds, insurance reserves, pension funds, savings and loans, shares, etc. Pesek and Saving included currency issued by the government and demand deposits of banks as money. They would exclude time and saving deposits from bank money, so long as these do not pay interest. But as soon as these deposits start paying interest, they will start to serve as money.

8. Functions of Money

The importance of money for modern economies is known by the functions that it performs. As a matter of fact, it is difficult to think of all economy these days which may work without the use of money. Kinley has classified the functions of money into three groups: (*i*) essential or primary; (*ii*) derived or subsidiary and (*iii*) contingent. We presume that the students are very well acquainted with these functions and, therefore, our discussion here would be rather brief.

(*i*) Primary Functions

Primary functions have also been called as fundamental functions. These are functions which money has been performing since its inception; it is a different matter that the form of money has changed from time to time.

1. Money as a Medium of Exchange. The first and the most important function of money is to act as a medium of exchange. According to Benham, "Money must act as a medium of exchange or currency, with which business can be carried. A country requires both a unit of account and a medium of exchange. Prices are expressed in terms of the unit of account but commodities and services are exchanged for money. Money overcomes the difficulties of barter by serving as a general medium of exchange, or means of payment."[9] The use of money completely eliminates the difficulty of double coincidence of wants and also that of the divisibility of commodities. Money is acceptable to all, while it is not necessary that all goods and services may be accepted by everyone. In this connection, Benham says, "A person will accept money in payment, not because he necessarily wants money for its own sake but because he knows that other people in turn will accept it from him in return for the goods and services which he himself requires."[10] It is because of this reason that money has been defined as 'generally acceptable purchasing power'. In short, the use of money has facilitated exchange and in a competitive economy it facilitates the fixation of prices thereby avoiding waste of time in bargaining.

2. Money as a Measure of Value. The second important function of money is that it acts as a measure of value, *i.e.* it measures the value of all goods and services or in other words, prices of all commodities and services

9. F. Benham, *Economics,* p. 353.
10. *Ibid.*

are expressed in terms of money. Thus, the difficulty faced under the barter system regarding the settlement of terms is removed with the use of money. Benham has expressed like this, "The use of money as a measure of value immensely facilitates economic calculation. A consumer with a certain money income is confronted with money prices, and these enable him to decide which assortment of goods and services he wants to buy. The changes in the demands of consumers affect prices and thereby induce entrepreneurs to produce more of the goods for which demand has increased and fewer of the goods for which demand has decreased. An entrepreneur knows the market price of each factor of production. He can, therefore, plan the location of his establishment, the size of his output, and his methods of production in such a way as to maximize his profits. This means that the factors are directed towards those uses in which their products have the greatest value."[11] During recent decades, especially after the Great Depression of the thirties, the difficulty which has earlier faced in the barter system has again come to the forefront. This difficulty has arisen chiefly because of the frequent changes in the value of money used. Since money is a common measure of value and if its value is not itself stable, it is obvious that the prices of other commodities and services would also not be stable.

It may not be out of place to mention here that these two functions are closely related to each other. They are performed simultaneously and it cannot be said that such and such function is performed first while the other one is performed later. Unless the value of commodities is measured in terms of money, money itself cannot act as a medium of exchange. Similarly, if money is not acceptable to people as a medium of exchange it would be impossible for money to act as a collective measure of value. It shall be a different situation altogether if simultaneously two currencies are in use, one of which if a foreign currency. Such a situation can arise when the domestic currency loses its credit in the international market. For example, this is what exactly happened after the World War I in Germany. Owing to unprecedented wartime inflation, the German Mark depreciated rapidly in value and, therefore, the people started entering into contract with each other in terms of foreign currencies because they were more stable in value than the Mark. The people for their long-term contracts made use of Dollars and other foreign currencies while they continued using the Mark as a medium of exchange for day-to-day or short-term transactions.

11. *Ibid.,* p. 354.

(ii) Subsidiary Functions

Under the second group fall a number of functions of money like: (1) standard of deferred payments, (2) store of purchasing power, and (3) a means of transferring purchasing power.

1. Standard of Deferred Payments. Money has successfully performed the function of a standard of deferred payments because, first, its value is relatively more stable than that of other commodities; secondly, the element of durability is higher as compared to other commodities; and finally, it possesses the quality of general acceptability. In the absence of money, lending would be difficult, rather impossible. It may, however, be mentioned in this connection, that as a standard of deferred payments also, money suffers from certain drawbacks and the main drawback is that its value is not wholly stable. Obviously, when the value of money itself depreciates or appreciates, it would be a source of great shock to the parties entering into lending and borrowing business. Moreover, since this function of money is not in any way separate from its function as a measure of value, Robertson does not consider it necessary to assign a separate place to it.

2. Store of Purchasing Power. Since money acts as a medium of exchange and is capable of discharging economic obligations, every individual and firm would like to hold a certain amount of money in reserve against future payments. Some payments are quick while others are distant. There are other payments which cannot be foreseen like payments during illness or due to sudden request from relatives or due to the miscalculation of the patience of the creditors, etc. To obviate all those situations, people try to keep some money in reserve as a liquid purchasing power. Again, this function of money is possible only because its value is more stable than that of other commodities. That is why Turner has said: "When we speak of value being stored in money, we do not imply that value is something intrinsic in money, we mean that money is a durable thing and that it is always saleable."[12]

3. Transferer of Purchasing Power. Finally, money also acts as a means of transferring purchasing power. With the extension of trade between distant lands it became necessary to transfer purchasing power from one place to another; and this was successfully done by money. Since money is, generally, acceptable to people, a person can sell his property at one place and purchase property at another place. This also leads to the use of idle money lying with one person and thus it facilitates the lending and borrowing activities and also to its use for more productive purposes. Hence, the importance of money in the socio-economic life of the community can hardly be exaggerated.

---

12. Turner, *Introduction to Economics*, p. 262.

(*iii*) Contingent Functions

Apart from the above functions, Prof. Kinley has enumerated four more functions, *viz.*, (*i*) it facilitates the distribution of national income. Thus, its productive activities are, generally, undertaken not for direct consumption but to sell the goods in the market. Again, the modern process of production is made possible by the collective effort and co-operation of the various factors of production. Whatever, therefore, is produced, does not belong to a particular individual but to the whole society and, therefore, the need for its distribution, among various factors contributing to it, arises. This part is successfully played by money; (*ii*) money helps in equalizing the marginal utility and marginal productivity. By the use of money, every producer is able to divide his expenditure on various factors of production in such a way that the marginal productivity of each factor of production becomes almost equal. This is the state of maximum production. Similarly with the use of money, every consumer is able to distribute his income on various items of expenditure in such a way that the marginal utility derived from each of them becomes almost equal. This is the point of maximum satisfaction. Money plays an important role in equalizing these marginal productivities or satisfactions; (*iii*) credit is the soul of modern business and commerce. That is why, during modern times the importance of banking in an economy has increased tremendously. The credit created by these banks and other financial institutions is based on money. Without the use of money, credit instruments cannot circulate. For example, we cannot issue cheques without having a bank balance. Similarly, the Central Government of a country cannot issue notes without having adequate reserves and the commercial banks cannot create credit without having adequate cash reserves. Thus, money is the foundation on which the superstructure of the modern credit system rests; (*iv*) lastly, money increases the productivity of capital; it is the most liquid type of capital. It can be put to any use. It is because of the liquidity of money that capital can be easily transferred from less productive uses to more productive uses and it is because of this fact that mobility of money has enormously increased during recent times.

(*iv*) Other Functions

As a matter of fact, all these functions are derived functions, *i.e.* these have been derived from the primary functions. Some writers have also enumerated certain other functions, *viz.*, (*i*) money helps in the maintenance of the repaying capacity. This is also a derived function in the sense that it is based on the quality of general acceptability of money. Since money is a liquid capital and is, generally, acceptable to all, every firm keeps some amount in reserve just for maintaining its repayment capacity. That is why, all financial institutions and government institutions have to keep some cash or liquid money to maintain their repaying capacity; (*ii*) money represents general purchasing power. When purchasing power is stored in terms of money, it can be put to any use. If money has been saved only with a specific object in view and if at a later date it becomes essential to use it for any other purpose which is more urgent under the circumstances, then the shift in its use can be easily made; (*iii*) money provides liquidity to capital. We have already dealt with this. According to Keynes, it is essential to keep capital in a liquid form because of: (*a*) income motive, (*b*) transactions motive, (*c*) speculation motive, and (*d*) precautionary motive. We shall deal with these motives in some detail later.

Prof. Graham has counted one more function and that is, that money is a bearer of option. In fact, this is the same function as we have discussed earlier in connection with the money being representative of the general purchasing power. Prof. R.P. Kent has mentioned money as a guarantor of solvency. As we know, this function is derived from the characteristic of money relating to liquidity.

Static and Dynamic Functions of Money

According to Paul Einzig, there are two broad classifications of the functions of money, *viz.*, (*i*) static, and (*ii*) dynamic. Static functions are those which help the operation of the economy but these do not create movement in the economy. In this respect the functions of money like medium of exchange, measure of value, store of value and measure of deferred payment are the static functions of money because these functions do not create any movement in the economy. The static functions are also known as passive, traditional, fixed or technical.

Such functions of money which influence the level of economic activity in the economy are known as dynamic functions. In modern times, the most important function of money is that of influencing the price level in the economy. It is because of the changes in the price level that changes in the level of employment, output, income, etc. are created. With the expansion of money, people get increased purchasing power, which leads to increase in prices and which ultimately causes an increase in the level of output, employment and income. If the supply of money is less than its demand, it becomes necessary for the maintenance of level of economic activity in the economy to increase it. If the rate of increases in the money supply is more rapid, inflation is caused in the economy. It is because of these dynamic functions of money that various governments are required to change their monetary policy from time to time. Paul Einzig has stated that it is with the help of money that the government frames deficit budgets and undertakes various programmes of high economic and social significance. The functions of money relating to: providing liquidity to capital or providing a basis for creation of credit, are also dynamic functions because they also influence the level of economic activity in the economy. Money also plays an important role in the re-distribution of income and property. Hence, the dynamic functions of money are also as important as its static functions are.

There are economists who believe that if changes in the supply of money and value take place too frequently, it will not be possible for money to perform its static functions and therefore, Paul Einzig stresses that for the successful performance of static functions, it is essential that the value of money is kept stable. But, it would not be wrong to say that slight changes in the value of money and price level are in fact, more conducive to the health of the economy. Of course, money cannot be allowed to run amuck and for this purpose it is essential to keep money under proper control.

According to Prof. Chandler, the most important function of money is to act as a great wheel of circulation and as a great instrument of commerce. Most of the economists are of the view that the most fundamental function of money is to act as a medium of exchange because this function is the foundation of all other functions. This is what Hansen believes. But it would be more correct to say that each and every function of money is important in its own place and the modern economic system cannot do without it.

From the above discussion it is clear that money plays an important role in the functioning of an economy. Trescott has said that "money may be compared to a Chemical Catalyst, which makes a reaction take place efficiently but it is not contained in the final compound."[13] Prof. Pierson has compared money with a railway engine engaged in shunting of wagons and coaches and to put them on the right track so that they are in a position to reach the right destination but the engine itself does not leave the station.

9. Nature of Money

It would, thus, be seen that money is only a means and not an end in itself. It is well-known that whatever goods and services are purchased by an individual or a firm are necessarily meant for satisfying the present needs and wants. No goods or services can be purchased without money. Thus, money is an instrument of satisfying human wants. If it did not possess this quality, it would have no value. We need money and it helps us in satisfying our wants. This is the true nature of money and it is this fact that provides supreme importance to it.

13. Paul B. Trescott, *Money, Banking and Economic Welfare,* p. 3.

Exercises

1. What is barter? Why was pure barter exchange inappropriate for economic growth and efficient functioning of the economy?
2. Define money and explain its evolution from the beginning to the present time.
3. What is barter system? Discuss the principal difficulties faced by a barter economy.
4. Describe the various types of money and explain their merits and demerits.
5. Distinguish between money and near money. Explain the importance of near money.
6. Discuss the nature and functions of money.
7. Discuss the role of money in modern times.
8. Discuss the functions of money. What are its disadvantages?
9. What are the distinguishing characteristics of money and what justifies its special place in economic theory?
10. "From the point of view of its demand function, it is essential to maintain a stable value of money." (Einzig) What are the functions of money and is its stability of value essential to their fulfilment?
11. Discuss the static and dynamic functions of money.

●●●

Chapter 2

The Role of Money

1. Introduction

The significance of money for the modern world can hardly be exaggerated. Money is omnipotent in all walks of life, in all types of economies, whether capitalist or socialist or planned. Almost every economic activity is undertaken with a view to getting some income in the form of money with which one can satisfy one's wants for goods and services either for consumption or for production. It permeates every walk of life. There is no aspect of life of the individual or society which has not been influenced by money.

The classical economists believed in the neutrality of money. They considered it as a harmless commodity, sterile or barren. It did not in any way influence the functioning of the economy. They regarded it only as a medium of exchange. It is useful so long as it possesses purchasing power, it becomes useless the moment it loses its purchasing power. They, therefore, considered monetary disturbances in the economy only as temporary and rare. And whenever they took place they were automatically corrected. According to them, money is just like a machine helping the increase in the pace of economic activity. Its introduction does not interfere with the operation of the law of value since the value of any commodity or service is determined by its demand and supply.

This attitude of the classical economists can be attributed to the fact that they believed that the money always helps the smooth functioning of the economy and does not have an independent influence of its own. It may be because their analysis was always related to long-term phenomena and that is why they argued that since in the long run the supply of money always adjusts itself to its demand, no monetary problem arises in the long period.

But, today the situation is entirely changed and the classical view does not hold true. We have become accustomed to the use of money so much that we cannot even think of undertaking any activity whether of consumption or of production or of exchange without its use. Not only that, money is today an engine of social and economic reforms. The system of exchange has undergone tremendous changes with the change in the form of industrial life. And the system of exchange prevalent at any particular time reflects the stage of economic development of a country. Thus, the development of money and mechanism of exchange reflect the development of industry and trade. No trade can take place, no industrial production, no consumption can be possible if the institution of money is not fully developed.

That is why the highly industrialised countries have the most developed economies. The use of money helps the division of labour on which depends the modern system of production. The use of machinery is also permitted by the use of money. The industry and trade are dependent on capital whose accumulation is also possible only with the existence of money. Thus, the modern world can hardly exist without money.

2. Role of Money in a Capitalist Economy

1. Lubricant of Economic Life. Money is the greatest and the most useful lubricant of economic life; with its help the function of the economy becomes smooth and easy. It is difficult to imagine how an economy can function at all without the aid of money, be it a capitalist economy or a socialist economy. The money has not only been responsible for helping the mass production of goods, it has also made possible the distribution and consumption of these goods which permeates our life. The extension of markets, division of labour, the large-scale production have all been facilitated by money. A very large proportion of the total volume of production is meant for the market and involves a long chain of productive and distributive processes. Each process is carried out by specialised groups of persons. Each member of these groups is paid for the contribution that he makes to the production of the commodity. In the absence of money, such payments would be made in kind and thus would entail much waste and inconvenience. Again, specialisation in any area on a significant scale is possible only if there exists a suitable machinery for exchanging the specialised products of the different groups and this facility is provided by money. Furthermore, the modern system of production depends very largely upon the savings of persons being made available to those who can productively use them. Savers do so in the expectation of a price which is paid in money. Thus, the existence of money is a condition for the development of credit money which is the backbone of a capitalist economy. It would not be wrong to say that the introduction of money and the growth of the money economy made possible the growth of economic liberalism. As Marshall has said, "The breaking up of old traditions, no doubt, destroyed some defences with which custom had covered the conditions of the 'inferior' orders of the people. Some of its immediate effects were injurious; but it was a necessary step toward their liberation from servile or semi-servile conditions. Its chief instrument was the substitution of values expressed in terms of money for obligations expressed in terms of customs."[1] Pigou is right when he remarks: "In the modern world 'industry' is closely enfolded in a garment of money."[2] Stating the conditions of money to the business world, Moulton remarks: "Money is the indispensable pre-requisite to the assembling of the concrete instruments of production. The businessman uses money, or its equivalent, to purchase materials for the construction of his factory; he uses his money in buying the supplies and materials necessary for its equipment; he bids competitively in the markets of the world for the raw materials used in the process of manufacturing; and he employs money as a means of attracting to his organisation, the requisite labour force and corps of administrative officials."[3] Money helps the process of market-pricing which induces the producers to produce the goods required by the consumers. It helps the consumers to economise their limited resources. This process of market-pricing evens out the conflicting decisions of millions of people in the economy without any central direction. "Just as our sensory organs receive impressions from the outside world and transmit them to the brain, where they become meaningful sense perceptions, the price system registers economic changes and converts them into price variations."[4]

Money is not only important for the business community and for economic calculations but it is also important for non-economic matters. In this connection, it would be enough to quote Davenport. He says: "It is almost past belief how far both in degree and direction, money valuations pervade all our thinking. Cheapness is prone to be synonymous with ugliness, richness with beauty, elegance with expensiveness. No one can tell for himself where the really aesthetic begins and the sheer pecuniary ends. In the field of morals also, cash register conscience is an actual thing. And one might go still further and note that almost all great political issues, and almost all absorbing social problems, and almost all international complications rest upon a pecuniary standard."[5]

2. The Dynamism of Money. The modern economic life is full of dynamism, which has been made possible by the use of money. As we all know, the most important characteristic of modern economic life is the unending flow of money payments which are circular in nature. The payment

1. Alfred Marshall, *Money, Credit and Commerce,* p. 264.
2. A.C. Pigou, *Industrial Fluctuations,* p. 117.
3. H.G. Moulton, *The Financial Organisation of Society,* Third Edition, p. 3.
4. P.B. Trescott, *Money, Banking and Economic Welfare,* p. 11.
5. H.J. Davenport, *Economics of Enterprise,* pp. 22-23.

made by the consumers for the goods and services, they purchase, is passed on through various types of traders ultimately to the consumers in the form of wages, interest and profit which they receive as owners of factors of production. There may be some leakage in this process of circulation, for example, some amount may be paid to the government in the form of taxes but the bulk of this amount runs through an unending circle. The smoother the circular flow of money, the easier and smoother would be the operation and stability of the economic system. The great depression of the thirties was caused mainly because of the disruption of this circular flow. And again, during the period following World War I, the enormous increase in the money supply was responsible for the debacle of many economies, especially the German economy. It does not mean that even during the course of the normal function of money, the problems would not be faced by the economy but such problems are created by natural forces and occurrences like floods, droughts, earthquakes, etc. Thus, there is a flow of money payments as people get wages and salaries from their place of work and when they use it for purchasing the commodities and services that they want. With the introduction of money, a single transaction is split into two separate transactions. Thus, in an exchange economy, two unending flows run in opposite directions, one flow is the stream of final goods and services which are produced and distributed by the people. The other stream is that of money payments which start when people are paid for their productive efforts and who pay others for their work. When these two flows are; in balance, the price level would be considered stable, and the growth of economy would be considered desirable. But if any of these flows increases without a corresponding increase in the other flow then there would either be inflation or deflation. So it is necessary that these two flows are kept in balance in such a way that the money supply is just adequate for the production of goods and services required by the economy at a particular point of time. Deflation means depression in the economy which leads to mass unemployment, low level of income, under-utilisation of economy's resources, etc. Through an injection of money in such a state of affairs, the economy can be brought to life since additional purchasing power would create demand for idle resources in the economy which would generate accumulative upward trend leading to the rise in the level of employment and income.

But to maintain a balance in these two flows is not an easy task. The production of goods and services and the stream of their supply can never be stable in a growing economy. This is because of the fact that while the raw material is produced in a particular part of the year, the finished product is sold throughout the year, or the finished product is sold out in particular part of the year, its manufacture is spread almost over the whole year. In short, the flow of goods and services is subject to seasonal variations which also affect the stream of money payments. Natural calamities like floods and droughts, social disorders like strikes and lockouts, international problems like war, all cause substantial disturbances in the production of goods and services as well as in the flow of money payments. Besides these, we are also free to make choice of goods and services and use our disposable income in an undisturbed fashion. Our decisions as free consumers influence the decisions of the traders, manufacturers and producers because they are guided by us. This might cause a shift in the production of goods and services; the production of old goods might be done away with and the production of new goods might be undertaken. Then, there is the technological factor which also causes considerable changes in the flow of goods and services and the payments. The R&D activities of the big industrial firms lead to technological changes in the methods of production, in the production of new goods, in the change of the shape and design of the commodities, etc. And these technological changes also influence the two flows. If the economy is to be kept at a stable level it is necessary that the flow of money payments must adjust to the changes which take place in the flows of goods and services over time, which means that the money supply should be flexible or elastic. The flow of money payments depends on two factors: first, the supply of money and secondly, the rate of spending, and therefore, merely changing the money supply will not solve the problem. It is also necessary that the rate of spending is also kept under control. Nowadays, almost all governments have realised the implications of over-spending or under-spending, over-supply or under-supply of money and therefore the control over the supply of money and its regulation is one of the means by which a government, accepting responsibility for the maintenance of full employment, attempts to influence the level of production. By taking steps to increase the volume of purchasing power in the hands of consumers or by making consumer's credit more readily available, a government may hope to stimulate demand and this supplemented by other measures may consequently, prevent a fall in prices and a decline in the level of check economic activity. The reverse policy may be adopted if it is thought that the level of consumers' demand is too high for the economic resources of the country to satisfy. Money carries out its active function through its influence on prices and money can do this whether the motivation comes from the state itself or a state-controlled institution or a body acting independently of the state. Thus, the role of money is really dynamic.

3. Role of Money in a Socialist or Collective Economy

So far, we were talking about the role of money in a *laissez-faire* economy. Some of the socialist writers like Marx and Lenin were extremely hostile towards the presence of money since they believed that it was money which makes possible for the capitalists to exploit the workers. Marx, in fact, thought that the surplus value accrued to the capitalist because of the existence of money and, therefore, he conceived of an economy where money would be abolished and commodities would be exchanged for commodities. It would, however, be wrong to believe that a socialist economy can function without money. The experience of the Bolshevists in Russia after 1917 for abolishing the use of money through extensive direct controls and free distribution of goods is before us. How miserably they failed, need not be spelt out. Subsequently, Lenin frankly admitted that the Bolshevists had made the greatest mistake of their career. Trotsky also emphasised that money was indispensable in socialist planning. Consequently, in the New Economic Policy of 1921, the slogan regarding the abolition of money was dropped. Russia faced unprecedented inflation up to 1924, and when government adopted central planning to establish a collective economy, the system of money and banking was assigned an important place. True, that production and distribution were being controlled by the State in the USSR, the income transactions were being carried on with the help of money. Money wage rates were serving as important guide to occupational choices for the workers. Thus, through the pricing system was under the control of the central planning authority and did not, quite unlike the capitalist system, govern the production of goods and allocation of resources between different uses, money performed the primary functions, *viz.* of the medium of payments and standard of value. According to Lerner and Lange, money is indispensable for a socialist economy because it serves as an efficient guide to economic activity and adds to the efficiency of the functioning of economy. To quote Halm: "Even if the aims of production should be determined by a dictator, the allocation of resources according to these aims would have to be the result of the working of a pricing process by means of which it is possible to compare the usefulness of the available resources in different fields of employment."[6]

4. Role of Money in a Planned Economy

In a planned economy, the functions assigned to money are more or less similar to those assigned by the Mercantilists then by the Classical economists. In planned economies, money provides the necessary stimulus to economic activities but with a difference. Paper money takes the place of gold and silver. Mercantilists regulated trade so as to induce a steady flow of gold and silver into the economy. But a modern planned economy does not require bullion from other countries for creating employment. It can itself create money by

---

6. G.N. Halm, *Monetary Theory,* Second Edition, p. 13.

printing currency notes or by creating bank credit. Thus, whatever may be the form of money, for a planned economy also, money is extremely essential.

5. Role of Money in Less-developed Economies

For underdeveloped or less-developed economies, money's role is really commendable, provided the objective is to achieve a rapid rate of growth. If an underdeveloped economy wants to raise the living standard of her people through economic planning, it will necessarily have to provide adequate monetary resources. As we all know, there is no dearth of natural resources in these economies; the only thing wanting is the monetary resources. That is why, the governments of all such countries gather monetary resources from all possible sources, *i.e.* by increasing taxation, by resorting to public borrowing, by courting loans from other countries and by deficit financing.

To understand the real significance of money, one has to keep the following points in mind:

1. According to Halm, "The use of money divides the market into buyers and sellers and splits barter into market supply and demand. Supply and demand determine the market prices which are exchange values in units of money. The direction of production is determined according to the existing and expected prices; the prices of the means of production—the businessman's expenses—and the prices of the finished goods. The difference between these two sets of prices means profits or losses to the producer. According to expected profit or losses, production is expanded or contracted."[7]

2. "Money is an indispensable condition for the development of a credit market. It is possible to borrow goods in a barter economy against the promise to give these goods or other goods back after a certain period. In that case, there are as many credit markets as there are different kinds of goods which may be subjected to borrowings. The development of money is the precondition of the formation of a uniform price for the uniform service and that is the object of credit transactions. Loans find their expression in money and it is the monetary economy alone in which it is possible to express price of loanable funds in the form of an interest rate."[8]

3. Money provides freedom to the people for making choiçes, of course, within limits. Since money provides the purchasing power to the people, it necessarily gives the freedom of choice to the people.

4. Money serves as a common denominator for subjective valuations on the assumption that the amount of purchasing power spent on the purchase of a commodity measures objectively the relative satisfactions to the purchaser.

---

7. *Ibid.*, p. 8.
8. *Ibid.*

But, since the money incomes of different people are never equal, this sort of assumption does not hold good.

5. The price level in an economy changes due to the fluctuations in the volume of money in circulation, and these changes in the price level bring about economic effects which are of immense importance to the society. Thus, by controlling the volume of money in circulation, the desired changes, economic as well as social, can be brought about.

6. The growth of money tells the history of the development of man's activity. It has brought, to a considerable extent, stability to trade and commerce, production and consumption and to the economy as a whole, and it is a very important index of the stage of development of the economy.

7. Since money serves as a standard of value, it has, by encouraging the division of labour, led to specialisation and development of markets.

8. Money provides social freedom. When money was not invented, all kinds of payments were made in the form of services. Consequently, some factors of production, like labour, were solely dependent on another factor of production like capital. The mobility of labour was very low. The use of money has provided this independence to the workers.

In short, we can say that money is an important tool of development of all sorts of economies, whether capitalist or socialist. In fact, it lubricates the economic system and provides the necessary freedom to the people to choose their own profession, to buy the goods and services required by them at any time or place they like; it provides the necessary spurt to economic activities and accelerates the rate of economic growth in less-developed economies.

6. Money—A Trouble Monger : Defects of Money

But there is a dark side of this picture as well. When on the one hand, money brings many advantages to the individual as well as to the economy, it can be a source of havoc and destruction to the economy as well. By facilitating the lending and borrowing activities, a stage has reached when people have started borrowing and lending of money for things which are not really in existence at all or would never come into existence. This sort of situation has given rise to speculative activities which influence the price level of a country to the detriment of the people and the economy.

Since the value of money means purchasing power and since it never remains stable, any change in the value of money leads to re-distribution of the real income of the society between various groups. With a view to bringing about desired distribution of the real wealth, the quantity of money as well as its velocity of circulation have to be strictly controlled. A slight oversight may bring about a catastrophic result. Not only that, besides adversely influencing the distribution of income, the changes in the value of money also affect adversely the creation of real wealth because it threatens the economic basis of contract and business expectations whose stability is very important for the smooth functioning of the economy. This fact can very well be substantiated by the historical evidence that is on record. During the inter-war period, a number of countries experienced enormous inflation as well as severe depression which were chiefly because of the mismanagement of money. In fact, money is a very good servant; it behaves nicely when it is under control. The problems of the inter-war period were mainly because of the mismanagement of money or because of the fact that the governments created money, without any fear, to finance their war activities. But even in those times when this facility of the printing of paper notes did not exist, when gold and silver used to serve as medium of exchange and when the money supply was not determined by the needs of trade and commerce, trade and industry suffered the consequences of the fluctuating supply of precious metals. Even then one witnessed the serious abuses of debasement, clipping and counterfeiting of coins. Hence, there is a need to control money. This control need not be very rigid. Money should be controlled with a view to keeping the economy stable. As already pointed out, the government will have to control the quantity of money in circulation as well as the power of people to spend, because the total money supply in an economy includes both these things. In good old days when the life of our predecessors was very simple, when the money was not in use, the problems were also less. And now when money has provided us with all conveniences and comforts, we find that we have completely subjected ourselves to the dictates of money and our problems have become enormous. Robertson is right when he says that "Money, which is a source of so many blessings to mankind, becomes also, unless we can control it, a source of peril and confusion."[9]

Exercises

1. Explain: "money by itself cannot produce anything but helps in the production and distribution of wealth."
2. Comment: 'Money makes specialised production and the generalised consumption possible'.
3. "The importance of money essentially flows from its being a link between the present and the future." (Keynes) Comment.
4. Define money and discuss its social significance.
5. Explain the following:
   "The institution of money is an extremely valuable social instrument making a large contribution to economic welfare. Money is not merely a veil or a garment or wrapper."
6. Discuss the following: Money is a good servant but a bad master.

---

9. D.H. Robertson, *Money,* p. 15.

•••

Chapter 3

The Circular Flow of Money

1. Meaning

The circular flow of money refers to all those transactions, that is, payments and receipts which take place between the different sectors of an economy through time. Such transactions can be of various forms, *viz.* saving, investment, taxation, imports, exports, loans, government purchases, etc. All these transactions flow in a circular fashion in the economy, since the income of one sector is the expenditure of another sector and *vice versa*, whatever is spent or invested is an injection into the circular flow and whatever is saved or not spent is a leakage from it.

2. Circular Flow of Money in a Two-sector Economy

The classical economists believed in an economy: (*i*) where total income is equal to total expenditure, (*ii*) the government interference is zero, and (*iii*) the economy has no links with the outside world. And, therefore, the circular flow of money in such an economy takes place from the business sector to the household sector, as payments to productive factors, in the form of wages, rents, interests and profits and from the household sector to the business sector. There are no leakages and hence no complication. In this section, we will try to explain the process of the circular flow of money in such a hypothetical economy.

The business sector comprises of producers who produce commodities and sell them to the consumers, that is, the household sector. So, in the first place money flows in the form of payments of rent, wages, etc. from the business sector to the household sector, for the services of the factors of production which are in its ownership and which are required for the production of goods needed for consumption by the household sector. The household sector, in turn, spends this income to purchase the commodities produced by the business sector. Money thus, flows between the two sectors in a circular fashion as depicted in Fig. 3.1.

The above analysis of the circular flow of money is based on the following assumptions:

1. That the entire income of the household sector is spent on the purchase of goods and services produced by the business sector.

2. That all goods produced by the business sector are sold out to the household sector and there is no balance of unsold goods.

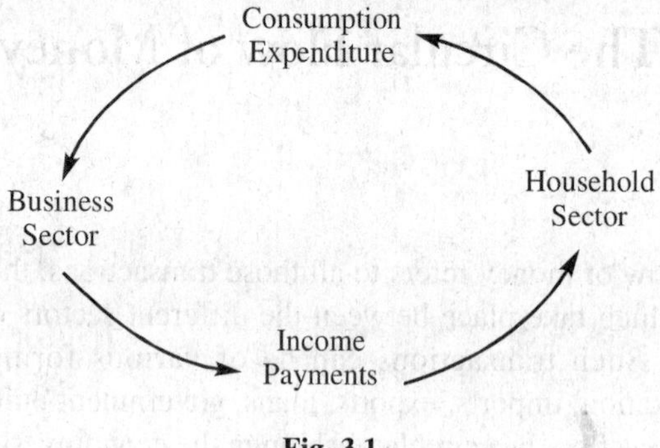

Fig. 3.1

3. That the business sector spends its entire income by way of payments to the factors of production owned by the household sector and no money is kept as reserve.

Needless to say that these assumptions are unrealistic, since the actual working of the economy does involve some sort of leakages from the income flow and injections in the expenditure flow which will certainly affect the circular flow of money.

3. Circular Flow of Money with Savings and Investments

In such a simple economy leakages take place in the form of savings and injections take the form of investment. Neither the household sector spends its entire income on the purchase of goods and services nor does the business sector spends its entire money income derived from the sale of goods on the purchase of the services of the factors of production. The household sector does have some savings while the business sector does have some undistributed profits. Some part of the savings of the household sector is invested in the capital market in the purchase of bonds, shares, debentures, etc. These are a type of flow into the capital market. The business sector borrows funds from the capital market for making investments. In this way the savings are taken away by the business sector for investment and the circular flow of money is maintained. The inclusion of savings and investments means that the expenditure has now two directions, one, directly through consumption of the household and the other, indirectly through investment expenditure by the business sector. The circular flow, therefore, takes place through the capital market which coordinates the activities of both the sectors as shown in Fig. 3.2.

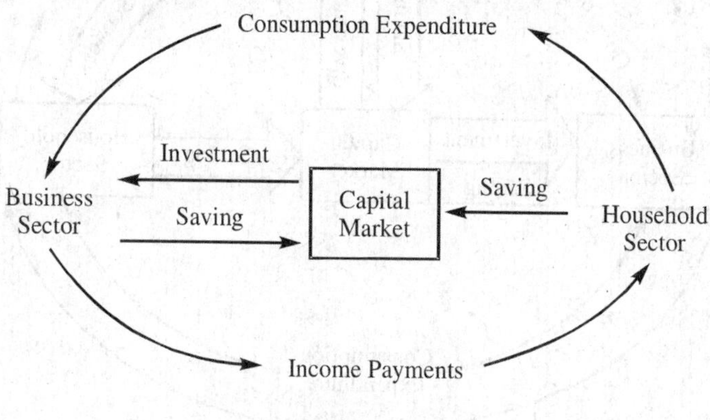

Fig. 3.2

4. Circular Flow of Money with Taxation and Government Expenditure

The simple economic model so far used may now be extended so as to include taxation and government expenditure. Since taxation is a leakage from the flow, it acts upon the circular flow of income like savings. Government expenditure, like investment acts as an injection into the circular flow of money. The national product consists of the production of consumer goods, investment goods and goods and services required by the government. Thus, the circular flow of money takes the course as shown in Fig. 3.3.

Now after adding the government expenditure and taxation, *i.e.* the government sector, we have a three-sector closed model. We first take the circular flow of money between the household sector and the government sector. Income and commodity taxes paid by the household sector to the government sector are leakages from the circular flow. The government in its turn pays to the householders for their services like salaries, pensions, unemployment relief, sickness benefits, etc. and also spends to develop human resources in the form of social services such as education, health and hygiene, housing, water supply, etc. The government expenditure is thus an injection into the circular flow of money.

In the circular flow of money between the business sector and the government sector all taxes paid by the business sector are leakages and all

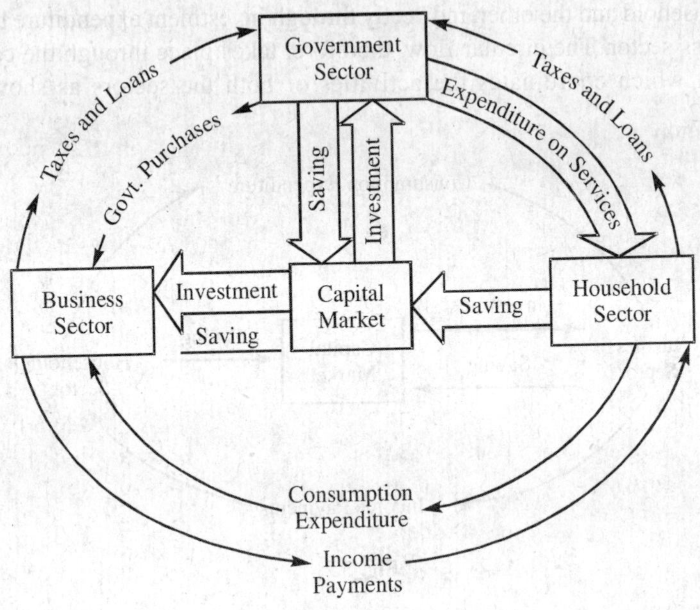

Fig. 3.3

government expenditure on purchases from the business sector, subsidies paid to them, etc. would be injection into the circular flow of money.

Now taking all the sectors together we find that since taxation is a leakage from the circular flow, it tends to reduce consumption of the household sector, which in turn reduces the sales and income of the business firms. Taxes paid by the business firms tend to reduce their investment and production. These leakages are offset by the government by purchasing goods from the business sector and services from the household sector, equal to the amount of the taxes paid by them. Thus, sales and production, and money income and expenditure are equal to each other. If government purchases exceed net taxes then it will incur a deficit in the budget to the extent of the difference between the two. The deficit is covered by the government by obtaining loans from the capital market which receives funds from the household sector in the form of savings. If net taxes exceed government expenditure, the government will have a surplus in its budget. In such a situation the government will reduce the public debt and supply funds to the capital market which are received by the business sector.

5. Circular Flow of Money with Foreign Trade

Keeping aside the government expenditure and taxation, let us explain the process of circular flow of money by introducing imports and exports into the simple economic model. Imports are another leakages from the circular flow of money as they drain out the current income without generating home production or income. Exports act as an injection into the domestic circular flow of money, increase production at home and generate new income. The circular flow is shown in Fig. 3.4.

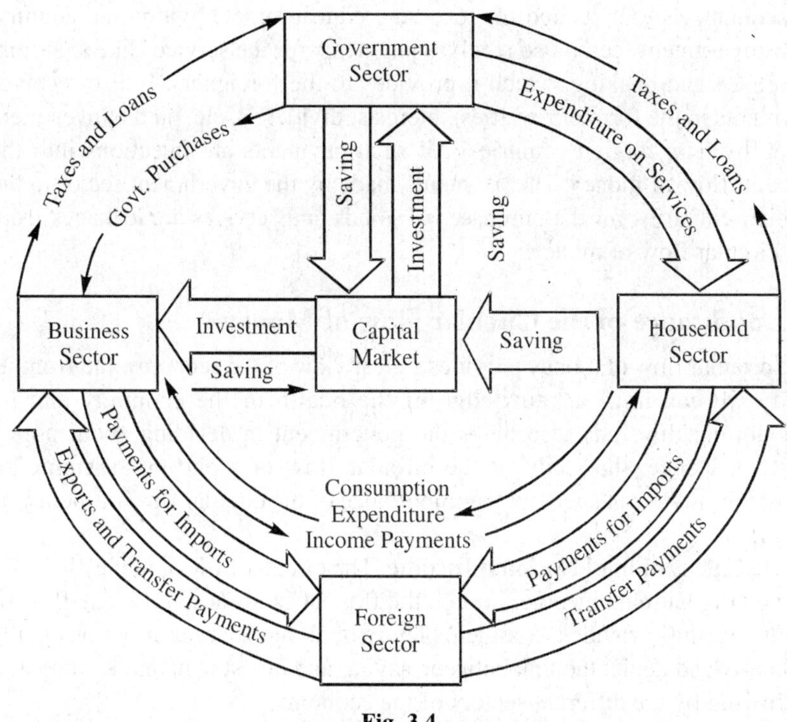

Fig. 3.4

Now taking income and expenditure of the household, business and government sectors in relation to the foreign sector, the process of circular of flow would be like this. The household sector purchases the goods imported from outside and makes payment for them which is, as said earlier, a leakage from the circular flow of money. The householders receive payment from the foreign sector for the services provided to them. The business sector receives income by exporting goods to foreign countries and all such payments are, as explained earlier, an injection in the circular flow of money. The business sector provides many services to other countries like insurance, banking, shipping, etc: for which it receives payments. The business sector also receives payments in the form of royalties, interests, dividends, profits, etc. for the investment made in other countries. It also makes payments to the foreign countries for the import of capital goods, machineries, raw materials, etc. and services obtained from them. All such payments are leakages from the domestic circular flow of money. The government sector also exports and imports the services and lends and borrows from foreign countries. The Government sector receives payments for all exports made by it to the foreign countries. The government sector also receives payments from foreigners when they visit the country as tourists and for receiving education, etc. within the country. The government sector also receives payments for the services like shipping, insurance and banking, which it provides to the foreigners. It also receives payments in the form of royalties, interests, dividends, etc. on the investment made by it in foreign countries. All such payments are injections into the circular flow of money. The payments made by the government sector to the foreign countries for the purchases of goods and services are leakages from the circular flow of money.

6. Importance of the Circular Flow of Money

The circular flow of money provides a clear view of the economy and from its study we can have a knowledge of the health of the economy and its functioning. Its study also helps the government in deciding about policy matters. Hence, the study of the circular flow of money is of immense importance. We can spell out the importance of the circular flow of money as under:

1. Calculation of National Income. The circular flow of money helps in calculating national income through the flow of funds accounts. The flow of funds accounts provide a complete picture of all monetary transactions in the economy and depict the link between saving and investment and lending and borrowing by the different sectors of the economy.

2. Formulation of Trade Policies. A study of the circular flow of money helps the government in working out a strategy for the promotion of exports and for controlling imports, since imports are leakages and exports are injections into the circular flow of money. The government can introduce changes in its trade policy by adopting measures which may increase exports and decrease imports.

3. Creation of Markets. The circular flow of money explains the links between the producers and consumers. With the help of money, producers purchase the factors of production whose owners, in turn, purchase goods and services from them. The producers and consumers can, therefore, conveniently create markets for their goods and services, with the help of study of circular flow of money.

4. Role in Monetary Policy. A study of the circular flow of money explains the importance of the monetary policy in establishing an equilibrium between saving and investment. The government controls the capital market through its monetary policy. Excess of savings over investment causes deflation, while excess of investment over savings causes inflation. The government can control these situations by regulating investment through its monetary policy.

5. Role in Fiscal Policy. The study of circular flow of money also highlights the importance of fiscal policy. The circular flow of money is in equilibrium when savings plus taxes are equal to investment plus government expenditure. Savings plus taxes represent leakages from the circular flow of money which must be equal to the injections of investment plus government expenditure into the circular flow of money. Excess of savings plus taxes over investment plus government expenditure will cause deflation which can be controlled by making changes in the fiscal policy, *i.e.* by reducing taxes and by increasing government expenditure. Excess of investment plus government expenditure over savings plus taxes will create inflation which can be controlled by promoting savings and increasing taxation.

6. Level of Economic Activity. Leakages from and injections in the circular flow of money cause disturbances in the functioning of the economy. If savings increase, the circular flow of money is depressed, which means that the level of employment, income and prices would fall and a deflationary process will start. If injections increase in the circular flow of money then the situation will be reversed and an inflationary tendency will develop in the economy. If leakages are more than the injections, the total supply of money would become less than the total output. Consequently the level of employment, income, output and prices would fall. If injections are more than the leakages, then the money supply would increase causing an upward movement of the level of employment, income, output and prices.

From the above, it is clear that a study of the circular flow of money is of great theoretical and practical importance for studying the functioning of an economy.

Exercises

1. Explain the meaning of circular flow of money with the help of a diagram.
2. What is meant by the circular flow of money? Explain its significance in an economy.
3. Explain the circular flow of money in an economy including the foreign sector. Use diagrams to illustrate your answer.

●●●

Chapter 4

The Demand for Money

Money is a stock variable. Its stock refers to its quantity in the economy as a whole at a particular point of time. The demand for money arises from the fact that it is an asset for its holders. Since it is acceptable to all, people hold it, not only for paying debts, but as a particular form of asset—one which is easy to be converted into other goods and services. Thus, money is a 'perfectly liquid' asset. This quality is not found in any other form of wealth. Moreover, other assets will also need to be changed first into money—which involves waste of time, cost and perhaps a capital loss. There is, therefore, a demand for money 'to hold' assets in the form of cash and current deposits. As such, the demand for money comes from the general public (excluding of course its producers).

1. Constituents of Demand for Money

What are the constituents of the demand for money? and why there is a public demand for money? A number of explanations have been put forward in this regard.

Nominal and Real Cash Balances

Before taking up these explanations or theories it would be helpful to clarify the distinction between nominal and real cash balances. Nominal cash balances are money or the current purchasing power of a unit of money (say, a rupee in the case of India, or a dollar in the case of USA or a pound in the case of UK). Real cash balances are money of some base year's purchasing power. A nominal unit of account (a rupee or a dollar or a pound) is always a unit of account: but it varies from time to time in its purchasing power, owing to the changes in the general price level. Hence, the real value, that is, the purchasing power, of a nominal unit of account keeps on changing over time. Real value comparisons, therefore, involve the selection of a base year with the wholesale price index number as hundred. A unit of account during that year had a certain amount of purchasing power at the prices prevailing during that year. The average value of the index number of the year for which the changes in the price level are to be found out is to be calculated. If the average value of index number has risen as compared to the base year then the real value of the unit of account would decrease and if it has gone down then the real value of a unit of account will increase, in comparison to the base year. Technically speaking, real cash balances mean the nominal cash balances divided by the price level. Symbolically, if M is the nominal money and P is the price level then the real cash balances will be M/P. Whenever P changes the distinction between nominal and real cash balances would be more relevant. The importance of P as a determinant of the nominal demand for money has been explained while discussing the quantity theory of money.[1]

2. Theories of the Demand for Money

We now take up the theories of the demand for money. We can divide these theories into four categories: (*i*) classical, (*ii*) neo-classical, (*iii*) Keynesian and (*iv*) post-Keynesian. We shall first take up the classical theory of the demand for money.

(*i*) Classical Theory of Demand for Money

The classical theory of demand for money or the quantity theory of money was propounded by Fisher. According to this theory, the demand for money arises for the fact that money is a medium of exchange. People spend their incomes on transactions and therefore, the demand for money is determined by the total quantity of goods and services, transacted during a given period. Again, the total demand for money also depends upon its velocity of circulation, that is why, Fisher expressed this in the form of the following equation:

$$PT = MV$$

Thus the Fisherian explanation was very simple.

(*ii*) Neo-Classical Theory of Demand for Money

The neo-classical theory, or the Cambridge approach, as it is known, has been put forward by Cambridge economists, Marshall and Pigou. According to this approach the demand for money is symbolically explained as under:

$$Md = KY$$

where Md = Amount of money demanded

Y = Money value of the national income

and K is a constant.

K refers to the demand for money per unit of account (say a rupee) of

1. Please *see* Chapter 6.

'income per unit time' or $K = Md/Y$. In other words, K indicates the proportion of money income the public likes to hold in the form of money, Y is income flow per unit of time (say per year), whereas Md is a stock at a point of time. Md has no *time* dimension while K has. For illustration, suppose Md is Rs. 5,000 crore and money income is Rs. 20,000 crore per year then K will be a quarter year which means that the public likes to hold one-fourth of its annual income in the form of money. This can also be explained with the help of Fig. 4.1.

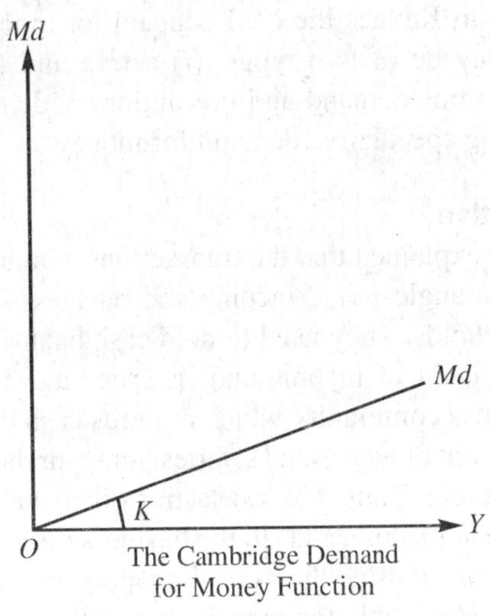

The Cambridge Demand for Money Function

Fig. 4.1

In Fig. 4.1 Md has been shown as a linear function of Y. It goes through the origin. The tangent of the angle which it makes with the horizontal axis = $Md/Y = K$.

According to this equation, the demand for money is the function of money income only and no other factor intervenes. The Cambridge approach emphasises the importance of money as a store of value. These economists held that people want to hold money for various motives. They, therefore, held that the demand for money was for cash balances which is influenced by a variety of factors, like, (*i*) the need for carrying on transactions, that is, for the exchange of goods and services; (*ii*) making future secure against uncertainty; (*iii*) income and wealth of the individual; (*iv*) opportunity cost of holding money as opposed to other assets. For the Cambridge economists the opportunity cost of holding money consists of the yield of real capital, the rate of interest and the expected rate of inflation; and (*v*) habits of the individual, system of payments prevailing in the society, availability of money substitutes, system of communication, etc. In the Cambridge equation the value of K has been assumed as stable. K is just the reciprocal of V in Fisherian equation.

(*iii*) Keynes' Theory of Demand for Money

Keynes theory is contained in his book, *The General Theory of Employment, Interest and Money.* According to him the demand for money arises because of its liquidity or 'liquidity preference' as he calls it.

As explained elsewhere this demand for money arises for three motives: (*i*) transactions motive, (*ii*) the precautionary motive, and (*iii*) the speculative motive. According to Keynes the total demand for money means total cash balances which may be of two types: (*i*) active and (*ii*) idle; the former comprising transactions demand and precautionary demand for money and the latter comprising speculative demand for money.

Transactions Motive

Keynes has further explained that the transactions demand for money can be looked at from two angles; *viz.*, income and business. The income motive relates to the households. They need to hold cash balances to cover the time gap between the receipt of income and its spending. The business motive relates to the business community which requires cash balances for meeting expenses like, payment of wages and salaries, rent, purchase of raw materials, payment of interest, etc. Thus, the transactions demand for money depends upon: (*a*) the personal income, and (*b*) the business turnover. The demand for money for transactions motive thus varies proportionately to the changes in the money income. The higher the money income the greater the demand for money and *vice versa*. The rate of interest has no role to play in determining the transactions demand for money. It is assumed to be a constant and stable function of income because the proportion of income to be held for transactions purposes is determined by institutional and technological factors influencing the payment and receipt of money, which do not change in the short period.

Precautionary Motive

People also hold some cash for meeting contingencies such as unemployment, sickness, accidents, etc. This is known as a precautionary motive. In the case of households the decisions are affected by these factors. Similarly, in the case of business firms the decision is influenced by the element of uncertainty of the future, *i.e.* economic fluctuations.

According to Keynes both the transactions and the precautionary motives are fairly stable and constant function of income and both are interest-inelastic. The money balances under these two motives are referred as 'active balances' by Keynes. This amount varies from one individual to the other and from one business firm to another. It will depend upon the frequency of income, credit arrangements, conversion of assets into money, degree of insecurity and uncertainty of future. But, these factors do not normally change in the short period. Relationship between the demand for active balances and money income is, therefore, proportionately positive.

Speculative Motive

Speculative motive is the third motive for which people hold money balances. Keynes calls such balances as 'idle balances'. Speculative demand for money is thus, the demand for holding cash for making speculative gains from the purchase and sale of bonds and securities owing to changes in the rate of interest/dividend. Obviously, this demand is determined by the rate of interest and bond prices. The rate of interest and the bond prices are inversely related. High bond prices indicate low rate of interest and low bond prices indicate high interest rate. For deciding, whether wealth should be held in the form of money or bonds, an individual investor compares the current rate of interest with the future rate of interest or the normal interest rate as called by Keynes. If people expect the future rate of interest to rise, they will anticipate capital losses, for avoiding which they will sell their bonds and keep cash holdings to lend it in future at a higher rate of interest, because when the rate of interest is low the bond prices are high and when the rate of interest is high the bond prices are low. When people expect the future rate of interest to fall in comparison with the current rate of interest, their demand for money for speculative motive decreases for buying bonds and sell them in future to make capital gains.

For deciding whether to hold cash or bond an individual investor would want to know about the net yield from a bond, *i.e.* interest earning from the bond plus or minus the capital gain or loss. If the net yield is greater than zero the individual will hold bonds and if it is less than zero then he will sell the bonds and if it is zero then the individual would be indifferent between bonds and money.

Hence, there is an inverse relationship between the speculative demand for money and the current rate of interest. When the interest rate rises the speculative demand for money falls and when it falls then the speculative demand for money rises.

Liquidity Trap

Liquidity trap represents the subjective minimum level of interest rates. An important characteristic of the speculative demand for money is that when the current rate of interest becomes very low people have no desire to lend money but they want to keep the whole money with them. This is the minimum critical level of the current rate of interest at which everybody becomes a money holder instead of a bond holder. In fact in such a situation the yield of bonds becomes so low and the risk becomes so high that the people do not want to keep bonds and decide to sell them for cash. To quote Keynes, "When the price of bonds has been bid up so high that the rate of interest is, say, only 2 per cent or less, a very small decline in the price of bonds will wipe out the yield entirely and a slight further decline would result in loss of the part of the principal."

This phenomenon of liquidity trap is full of a number of important implications. These are:

1. It will not be possible for the monetary authority to influence the rate of interest even by adopting a cheap money policy.

2. The rate of interest cannot fall to zero for a very long time, because some sort of compensation is necessary to offset the cost, and inconvenience involved in making investment in bonds and hence, the rate of interest has to be positive.

3. In the presence of a perfectly elastic liquidity preference any policy of a general wage cut cannot be effective. Such a policy will certainly cause wages and prices to decline and release money from transactions to speculative purpose. But, the rate of interest would not be affected because people would not like to part with their money due to the uncertainty prevailing in the money market. Finally, any increase in the money supply, instead of being invested, would be kept by people in bank or safe deposit vaults. Hence, the level of income will not be affected. So, the monetary policy has a very small role to play in affecting changes in the level of economic activity under conditions of absolute liquidity preference.

(*iv*) The Total Demand for Money

According to Keynes cash balances held for transactions and precautionary motives are primarily determined by the level of income $L_T = f(Y)$, and the speculative demand for money is determined by the rate of interest $L_s = f(r)$. In this way, the total demand for money is determined by both income and interest:

$$L_T + L_s = f(Y) + f(r)$$

$$L = f(Y) + f(r)$$

$$L = f(Y, r)$$

where L is the total demand for money.

Diagramatically, the demand of money can be shown as in Fig. 4.2:

In Figure 4.2 number (1) shows *OT,* the transactions and precautionary demand for money at *Y* level of income and different rates of interest. Number (2) shows the speculative demand for money at different rates of

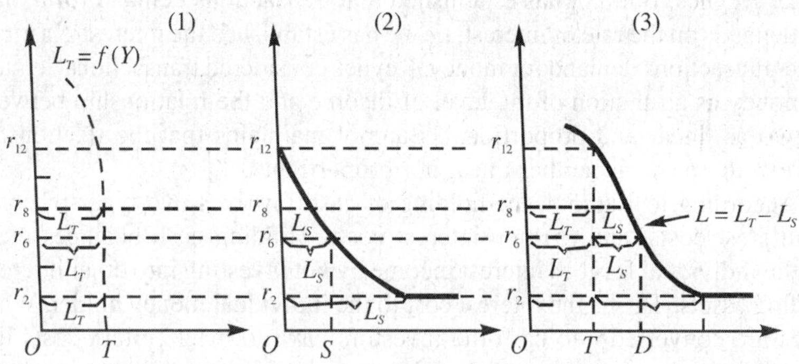

Fig. 4.2

interest. It is an inverse function of the rate of interest (at r_6) the rate of interest is *OS* and when the rate of interest falls to r_2, the L_s curve becomes perfectly elastic. Number (3) shows the total demand curve for money *L* which is a lateral summation of L_T and L_s curve. So, $L = L_T + L_s$ (at r_6 rate of interest the total demand for money is *OD* which is the sum of transactions and precautionary demand *OT* plus the speculative demand *TD, OD* = *OT* + *TO*. At r_2 interest rate the total demand for money curve also becomes perfectly elastic, indicating the situation of liquidity trap.

3. The Post-Keynesian Approaches (Portfolio Balance Approach)

The division of aggregate demand according to motives by Keynes has led to certain reactions from the modern economists. Keynes established a direct relationship between money-holding and income for determining transactions demand. According to him the speculative demand for money is determined by the relative yield on assets in an individual's portfolio. He has limited his analysis only to two assets, *i.e.* bonds and money. Thus, this combination of demand motives with two different approaches has been responsible for the criticisms at the hands of William Baumol and James Tobin on the one hand and Milton Friedman on the other. Baumol and Tobin have applied the portfolio analysis to the transactions demand, while Friedman has tried to remove the distinction between the motives for holding cash balances. We now take up these approaches.

Baumol's Analysis[2]

Unlike Keynes, Baumol has established that transactions demand for money also depends on the rate of interest, *i.e.* he has established the interest-elasticity of the transactions demand for money. Keynes considered transactions demand for money as a function of the level of income and the relationship between the two as linear and proportional. Baumol maintains that the relationship between these two is neither linear nor proportional.

According to Baumol, the holding of cash involves two types of costs: (*a*) interest costs, and (*b*) non-interest costs. Holding cash balances mean that the individual forgoes interest income by not investing into other interest-yielding assets. This is the interest cost to the individual money holder. When bonds are converted into cash the investors have to meet certain costs like brokerage fee, postal charges, etc. These are known as non-interest costs.

According to Baumol "a firm's cash balance can usually be interpreted as an inventory of money which its holder stands ready to exchange against purchase of labour, raw materials, etc." People hold cash because there is a time gap between income and expenditure and both do not take place simultaneously. But it is rather expensive to hold cash because this money could otherwise be used profitably elsewhere in the firm or invested in securities. Thus, an alternative to holding cash is investment in bonds which brings interest income. Accordingly, a firm would always strive for keeping the minimum balances for transactions and earn maximum interest from its investment into assets. The higher the rate of interest on bonds the lesser would be the transaction balances which a firm would like to hold. Supposing that a firm can invest in interest yielding assets and can also have cash, and assuming further that there is a fixed cost involved in the exchange of bonds with cash; the problem would be as to how a firm should decide about holding of assets. Whenever a firm holds transaction balances it incurs interest costs as well as non-interest costs. If the rate of interest on bonds rises, it would be profitable for the firm or individual to invest in bonds and if the rate of interest on bonds falls, it would be profitable for the individual and the firm to maintain higher optimal cash balances. When an individual or a firm makes large investment in bonds, it would be left with small cash balances and *vice versa*. But every investment in bonds will mean non-interest costs to the individual firm. The individual or a firm has, therefore, to maintain a balance between the income to be forgone through fewer bond purchases against the expenses to be incurred by making large investments in bonds. The higher the rate of interest, the larger the expenses a firm can bear in making bond purchases. Another important factor which will affect this decision will be the amount of money involved in these transactions, because the brokerage fees are relatively fixed. When the money involved in transactions is larger, the smaller will be the brokerage fees. The larger the total amount involved, the less significant will be the brokerage fees, because of the operation of economies of scale.

This means that at higher levels of income the average cost of transactions is lower. With an increase in the level of income the transactions demand for money also increases but this increase would be less than the increase in income. Since Baumol takes the income elasticity of demand for money as one half the demand for money will not increase proportionately to the increase in income. In any case, an increase in income would lead to larger investments in bonds and the investor will enjoy the economies of scale. Baumol also emphasises, in this connection, the importance of demand for real balances. According to Baumol the demand for real balances "is proportional to the square root of the volume of transactions and inversely proportional to the square root of the rate of interest". Hence, the relationship between price level and the transactions demand for money is direct and proportional. If the price level doubles, the money value of the transactions will also be doubled. When all prices double, brokerage fees will also be doubled. So people would like to hold high cash balances and avoid investments and withdrawals and the brokerage costs which they would otherwise incur. Hence, the increase in the money value of transactions and in brokerage fees brings about a rise in the optimal demand for money in exactly the same proportion as the change in the price level.

Is Baumol's Analysis Superior to the Classical and Keynesian Approaches?

Baumol's approach is superior to earlier approaches in the following respects:

1. Earlier approaches assumed the relationship between the transactions demand and the level of income as linear and proportional. Baumol held that transactions demand does increase with the increase in income, but less than proportionately.
2. Keynes held that the transactions demand for money is interest-inelastic, while Baumol has established that it is interest-elastic.
3. While analysing the transactions demand for money Baumol has emphasized the absence of money illusion.
4. Finally, Baumol's analysis integrates the transactions demand for money with the capital theory approach by including assets and their interest and non-interest costs.

Tobin's Analysis[3] (The Risk Aversion Theory of Liquidity Preference)

According to Tobin, Keynes theory suffers from two major defects: one, it points out that liquidity preference is determined by the inelasticity of expectations of future interest rates and two, that individuals hold either money

3. James Tobin, "Liquidity Preference as Behaviour Towards Risk," Feb. 1958, Reprinted in M.G. Mueller (ed.), *Readings in Macroeconomics*, 2/e, 1971.

or bonds. Tobin's analysis removes both these defects. His analysis is based on the assumption that the expected value of capital gain or loss from holding interest-bearing assets is always zero. It also explains that the individual's portfolio contains both money as well as bonds and not either of these at a time. He, therefore, starts his analysis with this assumption. According to him, money neither brings any income nor does it impose any risk on the individual asset holder. Bonds do yield interest and bring about income. It is, however, uncertain and involves a risk of loss or gain. The greater the investment in bonds, the higher is the risk of capital loss. An individual investor can court this risk provided he gets an adequate return from bonds.

According to Tobin, there are three types of investors. First, those who love to take risk and put all their wealth into bonds. They are like gamblers and speculators. The second category comprises of those investors who are plungers, *i.e.* they will either put all their money into assets or hold cash balances. In the third category fall those, who are risk averters or diversifiers. A majority of such investors prefer to avoid risk of loss and invest in bonds only when they expect adequate additional return. Such investors always diversify their portfolios and hold both money and bonds. For finding out different averters' preference between risk and expected return Tobin has used indifference curves having positive slopes, indicating that the risk averters expect greater returns in order to bear more risk. This is illustrated in Fig. 4.3.

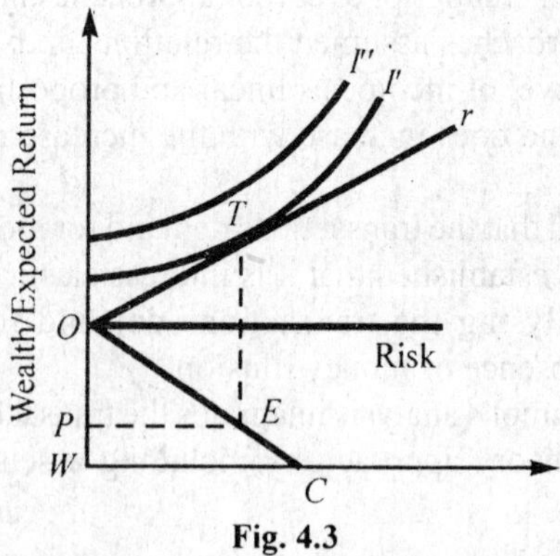

Fig. 4.3

In Fig.4.3 the horizontal axis measures risk while the vertical axis measures the expected returns. *Or* is the budget line of the risk averter. This line shows the various combinations of risks and expected returns on the basis of which he arranges his portfolio consisting of money and bonds. I' and I'' are indifference curves which means that the averter is indifferent between all combinations of expected returns and risks that each point on

2. W.J. Baumol, *The Transactions Demand for Cash: An Inventory Theoretic Approach*, *Quarterly Journal of Economics,* Vol. 66, No.4, Nov. (1952), pp. 545-56.

these indifference curves represents. Combinations shown on I' curve are preferred to those of I'' but the averter will achieve equilibrium at the point where his budget line is tangent to the indifference curve. This equilibrium point is T on the budget line which is tangent to I' curve.

In the lower portion of the diagram the vertical axis shows the wealth held by the risk averter in his portfolio and the line OC shows the risk as proportional to the share of the total portfolio held in bonds. Point E on OC line represents the portfolio mix of money and bonds that is OP (bonds) and PW (money). Hence, the risk averter diversifies his total wealth OW by putting partly in bonds and partly in cash. In any case, he has a preference for liquidity which can only be offset by higher rates of interest. At higher rates of interest, the demand for money will be lower and the incentive to invest into more bonds will be greater. The opposite will happen in the case of lower interest rates.

Is Tobin's Analysis Superior to Keynesian Analysis?

Tobin's analysis is superior to the Keynesian analysis of demand for money in the following respects:

1. Tobin[4] considers his theory as a 'logically more satisfactory foundation for liquidity preference than the Keynesian theory', because he does not depend on inelasticity of expectations of future interest rates but starts with the assumption that the expected value of capital gain or loss from holding interest-bearing assets is always zero.

2. It is more akin to practical life because it explains that individuals and firms diversify their portfolios and hold both money and bonds and not money or bonds.

3. While agreeing with Keynes that the demand for money is dependant on rates of interest and also inversely related to them, he does not agree with the view that at very low rates of interest the demand for money is perfectly elastic. In this respect he is more practical than Keynes.

4. Lastly, according to Laidler, the importance of Tobin's analysis is in "not what it tells directly about the aggregate economy, but rather it represents an interesting approach to the problem of relating demand for money to the existence of uncertainty an approach that probably has scope for considerable development in the future".[5]

Friedman's Approach

We have already discussed in detail Friedman's wealth theory of demand for

---

4. James Tobin, *op. cit.*
5. David E.W: Laidler, *The Demand for Money: Theories and Evidence,* 1972, Part Two.

money. So, here our treatment would be very brief. Friedman's analysis of the demand for money is based on the general theory of demand. It is more in conformity with the real life situation. According to him, the demand for money depends on three factors:

1. Total wealth to be held in the form of different assets;

2. Relative price of and return on one form of wealth as compared to other forms; and

3. Tastes and preferences of the wealth holders.

The cost of holding cash balances is influenced by: (*a*) the rate of interest, and (*b*) expected rate of change in the price level. Various forms of wealth, as used by Friedman in his demand function of money analysis, are discussed below:

1. Total Wealth. Total wealth comprises of different assets possessed by an individual. In actual life estimates of total wealth are hardly available and therefore Friedman says that income may be taken as an index of total wealth. Permanent income (Y) has, therefore, been substituted by Friedman for wealth.

2. Human and Non-Human Wealth. Total wealth comprises of both human and non-human wealth, but there are certain legal and institutional constraints in converting human wealth into non-human wealth. To avoid this difficulty Friedman has used the ratio of non-human to human wealth (W) as a variable in the demand function.

3. Money. Since money is primarily a medium of exchange, its real yield depends upon the price index (P) because it is the level of prices which governs the ability of money to command goods and services.

4. Bond. Bond is a perpetual source of money; Its yield (r_b) consists of the sum of its coupon plus expected capital gain or minus expected capital loss due to the expected variations in the market rate of interest.

5. Equity. Equity is like a bond, but it yields an income stream which maintains constant purchasing power. The yield on equity (r_e) comprises three components: (*i*) its coupon value; (*ii*) expected capital gain or loss due to variations in rates of interest; and (*iii*) expected changes in the general price level.

6. Commodities. Possession of physical goods provides an income to the owners in kind (utility) which is not measurable. But, their real return varies with the changes in the price level. Friedman uses the nominal yield of commodities (r_c) to consist their expected rate of price change per unit of time.

7. Human Capital. Since there is no market price for human capital, the rate of return on this form of wealth cannot be calculated.

8. Other Variables. Friedman uses u to indicate other factors which influence individual's tastes and preferences for money.

Taking above variables into account Friedman has given the following equation for the demand function of money:

$$M = f(Y, W, P, r_b, r_e, r_c, u)$$

We have already explained in detail Friedman's demand for money function in another chapter.

Exercises

1. Is it the liquidity preference satisfying the speculative demand for money alone which is interest-elastic, or other preferences also? Give reasons for your answer.
2. What are the motives for holding cash balances according to Keynes? Give the motivations introduced by modern economists.
3. Analyse the inventory theory approach to the tansactions demand for money. What is its relationship with the rate of interest?
4. What is 'liquidity trap'? Discuss its implications from the point of view of monetary policy aiming at full employment?
5. What is demand for money? Explain the factors which determine it.
6. Define the term 'liquidity preference'. What are its determinants?
7. The 'demand for money' is a demand for cash balances. Discuss.
8. Discuss the quantity theory approach to the demand for money and critically evaluate it.
9. Explain Keynes' theory of speculative demand for money.
10. Write a detailed note on Baumol's and Tobin's contributions to the theory of demand for money.
11. Discuss the portfolio selection approach to the speculative demand for money. How is it superior to Keynes' liquidity preference approach?

•••

Chapter 5

The Supply of Money

1. Introduction

In the literature on monetary theory, economists have used the term 'supply of money', 'stock of money', 'money stock' and 'quantity of money' as synonyms. In common parlance, supply of money means the total quantity of money available with the public for spending. Individuals and business firms operating in the economy are included in the term public. Thus, the governments, the central bank and commercial banks are not public and therefore the cash balances held by them are not included in the money supply.

Money supply is a stock concept when viewed with reference to a particular point of time. It is a flow concept when viewed over a period of time. As a stock, it comprises of the total currency notes, coins and demand deposits with the banks, held by the public. Since money supply can be used and spent several times during a period of time it becomes a flow. The number of times a unit of money changes hands during a given period of time is its velocity of circulation. Thus, for a given period of time, the flow of money supply can be known by multiplying the given stock of money by its velocity of circulation.

2. Components of Money Supply

Economists have not been in agreement about the components of the money supply. Broadly speaking, there are two views on this subject. The classical and neo-classical economists included in the money supply: (*a*) currency and legal tender money, and (*b*) demand deposits with the commercial banks. The modern economists however, include the whole spectrum of liquidity in the assets portfolio of the individual in the money supply. Thus, it includes: (*a*) currency, (*b*) demand deposits with the commercial banks, (*c*) time deposits with the banks, (*d*) financial assets with non-banking financial intermediaries, (*e*) bills (treasury and exchange), and (*f*) bonds and equities. These two approaches are clearly indicative of the fact that while the classical and neo-classical economists defined money supply on the basis of their acceptance of money as a medium of exchange, the modern economists give more importance to the store of value function of money.

Coins and paper notes, in totality, are known as currency. It is a legal tender money and is therefore called high-powered money (*H*). Currency is generally issued by the central bank of the country but there may be some variations from country to country. In India, one rupee note and coins are issued by the Ministry of Finance, Government of India, while all other notes and coins are issued by the Reserve Bank of India. The management and regulation of the currency take place in accordance with the system of note-issue adopted by a country in accordance with the law. Broadly speaking, the supply of currency and coins at any point of time, is determined by the requirements of the economy which are determined by a number of factors, namely: (1) physical volume of trade and transactions; (2) the nature of trade, whether wholesale or retail; (3) method of payment in use in the economy; (4) the general price level; (5) banking habits among the people; (6) distribution of income; (7) other factors like volume of demand deposits with the bank, government's taxation policy, monetary policy of the central bank, etc.

Demand deposits held by the commercial banks are another important constituent of the total money supply of the economy. It is generally called the secondary money while the currency issued by the government/central bank is known as primary money. The relative proportion of these two components of money supply depends upon the development of the banking system and the banking habits of the people. In highly industrialised advanced countries bank money constitutes the major proportion of the total money supply while in less-developed countries, the proportion of currency money in the total supply is much higher. The reason for a high proportion of bank money in advanced countries is that people are used to make payments through cheques while it is not so in the less-developed countries.

3. Approaches to the Measures of Money Supply

Broadly speaking, there are four alternative approaches regarding the measures of money supply. These are given below:

1. Classical and Neo-Classical Approach

This approach was based on the basic function of money as a medium of exchange and therefore, only currency and demand deposits with banks were included in the total money supply. This is considered as a narrow definition of money supply but it is analytically superior because it provides the most liquid and exact measure of money supply and also because the central bank can have a better control over it.

2. Monetarist Approach

Milton Friedman and his disciples have included currency, demand deposits and time deposits in the total money supply. They have included fixed deposits with the commercial banks in the money supply because they yield a fixed rate of interest to the depositors. Fixed deposits can also be withdrawn before the expiry of that period by paying a penal rate of interest and in this sense they possess liquidity like currency. This approach is based upon the importance of the function of money as a store of value and is therefore a broader definition of money supply.

3. Gurley and Shaw Approach

Gurley and Shaw have further widened the scope of money supply by including the liabilities of non-banking intermediaries, *i.e.* the saving bank deposits, shares, bonds, etc. which are close substitutes to money.

4. Radcliffe Committee Approach

It is the widest definition of money supply. It is based on the general liquidity of the economy. According to this approach money supply covers the whole liquidity position that is relevant to the spending decisions. It, therefore, includes cash, all types of bank deposits, deposits with non-banking financial institutions, near-money assets and the borrowing avenues available to the public. The difficulty with this kind of approach is that it is not easy to measure the money supply because of the vast variations in the degree of liquidity of different components of money supply. Besides, the central bank will have no control over a major portion of the money supply and hence it will not succeed in effectively implementing its monetary policy.

4. Velocity of Circulation of Money

The total money supply in an economy is affected to a very large extent by the velocity of circulation of money. An increase in the velocity of circulation of money will increase the money supply and a decrease in it will decrease the money supply. The concept of velocity of money equally applies to the growth of credit money, particularly in the short period. If M is the total amount of money at a particular moment of time, MV gives a measure of money supply over a period of time (V stands for the velocity of circulation of money). The velocity of circulation of money can be of two types: (*i*) transactions velocity, and (*ii*) income velocity. The number of times a unit of money is used in effecting total transactions is referred to as transactions velocity. In Fisherian equation V stands for transactions velocity. It can be arrived at by dividing the market value of all goods and services transacted by the total supply of money.

The number of times a unit of money is used in making payments for final goods and services, is known as income velocity of circulation of money. Income velocity of circulation of money is the ratio of market value of the final goods and services (Py) and the supply of money. Thus,

$$V = Py/M = Y/M$$

where Y is the real money.

The transactions velocity of circulation of money would be larger than the income velocity of circulation of money because the former relates to the transactions of all types of goods—finished and intermediate and the latter relates to the transactions of only final goods.

Factors Affecting the Velocity of Circulation of Money

The following factors affect the velocity of money:

1. Supply of Money. If the supply of money is more than the requirements of the economy, the velocity of circulation of money will be higher and, when the supply of money is less than the requirements of the economy, the velocity of money in circulation would be lower.

2. Credit Facilities. The growth of credit institutions also affects the velocity of circulation of money. If the lending and borrowing facilities expand, then the velocity of circulation of money increases.

3. Growth of Trade. Any increase in the volume of trade will lead to an increase in the number of transactions and hence the velocity of circulation of money will increase.

4. Changes in the Price Level. During inflation the velocity of circulation of money increases because people like to part with their money as soon as possible. On the contrary, during deflation the velocity of circulation of money decreases because people like to keep money with them.

5. Business Conditions. Velocity of circulation of money increases during a period of prosperity and decreases during slump conditions.

6. Payment System. If the settlements of the bills for goods takes place frequently and if the payment of wages of labour is made frequently then the velocity of circulation of money will increase.

7. Business Integration. The velocity of circulation of money will be low if business is vertically integrated.

8. Propensity to Consume. The higher the propensity to consume, the higher will be the velocity of circulation of money and *vice versa.* Lower propensity to consume means higher savings, which affect the velocity of circulation of money. Higher the savings, the lesser would be the velocity of circulation of money.

9. Regularity of income. If people receive their income at irregular intervals, the velocity of circulation of money would be very low, because people would like to hold more cash with them to meet unexpected expenditure.

10. Distribution of Income. If the distribution of income is equal, the velocity of circulation of money would be higher because the propensity to consume in the case of poor people is greater. If the distribution of income is unequal then the velocity of circulation of money will be low, because rich people have a low propensity to consume.

11. Liquidity Preference. If people have greater preference for keeping cash balances, the velocity of circulation of money would be low and if their preference for cash balances is low then the velocity would be high.

12. Means of Transport and Communications. The more developed are the means of transport and communications, the more quick would be the trade transactions and higher will be the velocity of circulation of money and *vice versa*.

13. Size of Population. Larger population will lead to an increase in the velocity of circulation of money and *vice versa*.

5. Theory of Money Supply

It is generally believed that the supply of money is created, regulated and controlled by the monetary authority of the country. But this is not correct. Money supply, in any country, is determined by all the players of the game, *viz.* the central bank, the commercial banks, the government and the public. The recent trend is also, to include financial intermediaries, other than commercial banks, as a source of money supply. Changes in the money supply, therefore, are brought about by the actions of all these players—treasury and the central bank creating the legal tender money or currency and commercial banks and other financial intermediaries creating demand deposits.

6. Constituents of Money Supply

Legal tender money, comprising of paper notes and coins, is the most important constituent of the total money supply. This is known as common money. Its proportion to the total money supply with the public, is very large in less-developed economies, because the people are not in the habit of making or receiving payments through cheques. The authority to issue paper notes and coins generally rests with the central bank (in India one rupee notes and coins are issued by the Ministry of Finance, Government of India). The monetary authority has, therefore, complete control over the supply of legal tender money. Paper money is issued by the monetary authority according to the requirements of business and trade. The expansion or contraction of paper currency, therefore, largely depends upon the actual needs of the economy, *i.e.* the financial needs of the government, business community, households and the general business outlook.

In advanced industrialised economies, owing to the developed banking habits of the people, a major portion of the total supply of money is in the form of deposit money, *i.e.* demand deposits in banks. Demand deposits can be either primary or derived. Deposits created out of cash deposited by individuals in their bank accounts are primary deposits, while those created by the banks through the advance of loans, investments, etc. are derived deposits. An increase in the demand deposits does not increase the total money supply because the cash available with the people is merely transferred to the bank in the form of deposits. The primary deposits can certainly form a basis for the expansion of credit by banks, *i.e.* for the creation of derived deposits. In this way, the derived deposits certainly lead to increase in the money supply.

To conclude, we can say, that the money supply in an economy is determined by three factors, *viz.*, (*i*) size of the monetary base, (*ii*) people's choice to hold cash or demand deposits in the bank, and (*iii*) the ratio between bank reserves and deposits. We explain these in turn in the following paragraphs.

The monetary base is comprised of the monetary gold stock, other types of money issued by the government and the amount of the central bank credit outstanding. The relative importance of these in bringing about variations in the monetary base differs from one monetary system to the other. In the gold standard, the gold stock, for example, was the most important determinant of the size of monetary base. Under managed currency standard, the size of the monetary base depends to a very large extent on other types of government money and central bank credit. The monetary base (B) is generally considered as the high-powered money (P), which is the total of the quantity of paper currency and coins in the hands of the people (C) + the actual bank reserves (R). Thus, $B = C + R$.

The relative amount of cash and deposits that the people wish to hold is another determinant of the money supply in the economy. If the people want to hold a larger portion of their wealth in the form of deposits then a larger portion of the monetary base will be passed to the banks and they will create more deposits by giving loans and advances. Thus, the total money supply would increase. However, people's choice for holding larger cash or larger deposits will depend upon the stage of development of the banking system in the country, banking habits among the people and the degree of monetisation of the economy.

The ratio between bank reserves and deposits is another determinant of the money supply in the economy. The higher the ratio of reserves and deposits, the smaller would be the amount of demand deposits to be supported by a given quantity of reserves.

A little while ago we mentioned about ordinary money and high-powered money. Let us explain these in a little more detail.

Ordinary money (*M*) is the sum of total currency and coins (*C*) held by the community and demand deposits of banks (*DD*). Therefore, $M = C + DD$. High-powered money (*H*) is the money produced by the government/central bank and held by the community and banks. It is, therefore, the total of: (*i*) currency held by the community (*C*); and (*ii*) cash reserves of banks which are of two types, *viz.* required reserves (*RR*) and excess reserves (*ER*). Thus, $H = C + RR + ER$.

An understanding of the difference between *M* and *H* is of vital importance for understanding the theory of money supply. Demand deposits are money, like currency. These are created by banks. For creating these deposits banks have to maintain reserves which are a portion of *H* and provides *H* the power of forming the basis for the creation of demand deposits. That is why, *H* is also known as 'base money' and *H*—theory of money supply as the money-multiplier theory of money supply.

We have seen that currency (*C*) is common to both *M* and *H,* the only difference being that whereas demand deposits are a component of *M,* reserves are a component of *H.* Since demand deposits are a certain multiplier of reserves, which are the component of *H,* money-multiplier ratio is the ratio of *M* to *H.* The relationship between *M* and *H* can be explained symbolically:

$$M/H \ = C + D/C + RR + ER$$

Banks' demand for reserves depends largely upon the volume of their deposits. It is affected by the same factors which affect the demand for currency. If in the above equation we divide each denominator and numerator by *D* then

$$\frac{M}{H} = \frac{\frac{C}{D}+\frac{D}{D}}{\frac{C}{D}+\frac{RR}{D}+\frac{ER}{D}}$$

Since the demand for reserves and demand for currency are both affected to a very great extent by the same factors, *viz.* the level of income and the rate of interest, besides other factors, it can be safely assumed that the two demands are highly co-related. The demand for *H* can thus, be expressed as a function of *D* and two behaviour ratios namely ratio of demand for currency to deposits ($C/D = Cr$) and the ratio of reserves to deposits of banks ($R/D = RRr + ERr$).

Substituting *Cr* for *C/D, Rr* for *RR/D, ERr* for *ER/D,* the above equation can be written as follows:

$$M/H = Cr + 1/Cr + RRr + ERr.$$

On the basis of the above equation we can now express M and H as follows:

$$M = \frac{Cr + 1}{Cr + RRr + ERr} \times H$$

$$H = \frac{Cr + RRr + ERr}{Cr + 1} \times M$$

It is therefore, clear that the money supply is determined by H, Cr, RRr and ERr.

If the volume of Cr, RRr and ERr is low, the volume of money supply would be higher and if it is high then the volume of money supply would be lower. A high volume of H will mean a higher volume of M. So, the value of the money multiplier (m) can be derived at

$$m = \frac{Cr + 1}{Cr + RRr + ERr}$$

7. Variations in the Money Supply

The changes in the money supply can obviously be made by those who create and also by those who use it. We can, therefore, analyse the factors affecting the money supply under two heads, the government or the government sector and the community, the foreign sector or the private sector. We can now look, at them in turn, as to how they influence the money supply.

The government influences the money supply through its budget. In the case of deficit budget, the government can borrow from the central bank or sell securities to the banking system. These transactions would lead to an increase in the financial assets of the banking system and cause an increase in the money supply. The government can also meet the deficit by drawing its balances from the central bank. This will also increase the money supply. The government can also draw upon the balances in the treasuries but this will also have the same effect as drawing the balances from the central bank. The government can also meet the deficit by printing more notes or by resorting to deficit financing. It also leads to an expansion of currency which will increase the deposits in the bank and lead to further expansion of money supply. A surplus budget of the government will affect the money supply in the reverse direction.

The government sector's transactions with the foreign sector can also affect the money supply. If the government has a deficit in its external transactions then some of the measures adopted for meeting this deficit will have no effect on the money supply but some others may produce some effect. If the government draws upon its balances with the central bank for purchasing foreign exchange the total money supply will not be affected. If the deficit in external payments occurs on private account the government will sell foreign exchange to the private importers, which will reduce the amount of currency held by the people and the total money supply will be reduced.

The private sector can influence the supply of money in three ways: (*i*) through purchase/sale of shares and securities from/to the banks; (*ii*) through variations in loans and advances from banks; and (*iii*) through variations in the net non-monetary liabilities of banks by purchasing/selling government securities. If the private sector takes more loans and advances from the banks or sells shares and securities to the banks then the total money supply would increase. The opposite will happen in the reverse position. The central bank can influence the money supply by changing the reserve requirements of the commercial banks and by using various credit control methods. But the central bank can succeed only when the money market is well-developed and well-organised and all the financial institutions are under its control.

It is thus clear that the transactions of the banking system with the government sector, or the domestic sector and the foreign sector can create changes in the total money supply in the economy.

Exercises

1. Explain the concept of money supply. Distinguish between total cost of money and total supply of money.
2. Discuss the various approaches to the definition of money supply.
3. Discuss the relation between money supply and high-powered money.
4. Explain the determinants of high-powered money.
5. What do you mean by the term velocity of circulation of money? Describe various factors that determine the velocity of circulation of money in a country.
6. Write notes on: (A) money base, (B) money multiplier, (C) cash reserve ratio.
7. Explain the concept of money supply function.
8. The supply of money is determined by many factors some of which are endogenous while some others are exogenous. Do you agree?
9. Explain the true position of the determination of the supply of money in an economy.

●●●

The central bank can influence the supply of money in many ways. (a) [illegible] of [illegible] securities in the open market [illegible] the [illegible] bank [illegible] of banks [illegible] [illegible] the reserve [illegible] banks the [illegible] [illegible] increase. The [illegible] will happen in the [illegible]. The central bank can influence the money supply by altering the reserve requirements of the commercial banks, or by [illegible] [illegible]. But the central bank can succeed only when the money market is well developed and [illegible] [illegible] of the financial institutions are under its control.

It is thus clear that different agencies in the banking system, with the government [illegible] or the [illegible] [illegible] [illegible] the total money supply in the economy.

[illegible]

2. [illegible] in the determination of money supply.
3. [illegible]
4. [illegible]
5. [illegible]
6. [illegible]
7. [illegible]

Chapter 6

The Determination of Value of Money—Transactions Approach

1. Introduction

In ordinary speech, the words 'value' and 'price' are often used as if they are synonymous. We often speak of the value of a thing when we mean its price. The act of valuation is a subjective process and consequently, value which is just the amount of satisfaction to be derived from a thing cannot be measured. That this is so, is clear from the fact that the same thing can at the same time have different values for different people or different values even for the same person on different occasions. This is also a feature of the value of money. Thus, the value of money is the same as the value of any other commodity. But the most important characteristic of money which distinguishes it from other commodities is that it is never demanded for its own sake but because it has the capacity to command goods and services in the market.

Since the value of money can be seen only through the value of other things, it has a separate value for every commodity or service. Elaborating this point Keynes states that, "Since the purchasing power of money in a given context depends upon the quantity of goods and services which a unit of money will purchase, it follows that it can be measured by the price of composite commodity made up of the various individual goods and services in proportion corresponding to their importance as objects of expenditure."[1] So we talk of the general value of money or the general purchasing power. In this connection, Fisher says that the purchasing power of money, "is the reciprocal of the level of prices, so that the study of the purchasing power of money is identical with the study of price level."[2] It will then mean a number of different values of money according to its uses. Therefore, Crowther says that "the only practical way of getting over this difficulty is arbitrarily to

1. J.M. Keynes, *A Treatise* on *Money,* Vol. I.
2. Irving Fisher, *The Purchasing Power of Money,* p. 14.

establish certain standard values of money."[3] He mentions three such standards. The first is with reference to wholesale prices of goods and services, and is known as wholesale value. The second is with reference to retail prices of goods and services which enter in consumption; this is the retail value of money. And the third is with reference to rate of wages payable to workers and this is the labour value of money. But economists like Kinley do not accept the type of approach adopted by Crowther and believe that the value of money is "the capitalised value of the service rendered in marginal exchange".[4] And similarly, Anderson believes in the absolute value of money. Economists like Hayek consider the concept of the general value of money as abstract.

The term 'value of money' is also used in other meanings. It is sometimes used to mean its command over a definite weight and fineness of gold or silver as was the case under gold and silver standards, *i.e.* its intrinsic value. But it is the exchange value of money in terms of gold or silver, it is made of. It is sometimes used to mean the units of foreign currency, it can purchase. In other words, a national currency has internal as well as external value. The internal value of a currency refers to the purchasing power of that currency in terms of domestic goods and services, while its external value is its foreign exchange rate, *i.e.* the domestic price of a foreign currency. This too depends upon the purchasing power of money in a country and its proportion to another currency having a command on some assortment of goods and services. In essence, in both the cases price aspect comes in. But for purposes of analysis these two aspects must be treated separately.

Thus, the concept of value of money is inseparable from that of prices. It has already been mentioned that value of money is just the reverse of price. If the price of a commodity goes up it will mean that the value of money in terms of that commodity has gone down. But a rise in value of every commodity is a contradiction in terms because value as explained earlier is relative, *i.e.* it means that one unit of a thing is worth so many units of another commodity. Therefore, the term 'value of money' should be used cautiously and not in a general way.

A further ambiguity arises from the use of the words 'price' and 'value' as if they were synonyms. The price of money is the payment for the use of a sum of money for a specified period, *i.e.* the interest payable on a loan. The price of money, therefore, is the rate of interest.

3. G. Crowther, *An Outline of Money,* p. 85.
4. D. Kinley, *Money,* p. 135.

Determination of Value of Money

Now we take up the question of the determination of the value of money. Broadly speaking, three theories have been propounded for explaining the determination of the value of money, *viz.*, (*i*) the commodity theory; (*ii*) the quantity theory; and (*iii*) the income theory.

2. The Commodity Theory of Money

According to the earliest version, the value of money depends upon the value of the material of which it is made; this is the commodity theory of money. In earlier times when money consisted of metallic coins, this theory was largely true. But in our times it is not applicable. According to the theory, the value of money is governed or determined by the real value of the metal of which it is made. But, would gold or silver of which a coin is made not be required for ornaments or for use in arts and industry and, therefore, not have value? It shall certainly have, even if it is not used for coinage.

Critical Evaluation of the Theory

Critics of the theory have pointed out that the contention of the commodity theorist is not wholly true. There is no doubt that there is a great demand for gold for non-monetary purposes, but this demand is still less than the demand for monetary reserves or for satisfying the growing requirements of international liquidity and also because gold is easy to store. As a matter of fact, the value of gold like any other commodity is determined by its demand which is derived from two sources and not one as suggested by commodity theorists. These sources are: (*i*) the use of gold for monetary purposes, and (*ii*) gold required for arts and industry.

Modified Version

Accordingly, a modified version of the theory has been put forward by certain economists of whom Robertson is the most prominent. According to him, "Once more we can keep on the right line if we start by remembering that money is only one of many economic things. Its value, therefore, is primarily determined by exactly the same two factors as determine the value of any other thing, *viz.* the conditions of demand for it and the quantity of it available."[5] Thus, according to this version of the theory, the value of money is determined by the amount of gold which it represents or in other words by the relation between the general price level and the cost of producing gold.

5. D.H. Robertson, *Money*, p. 28.

Criticism of the Modified Version

This theory has also been criticised. According to the critics, any fall in the price level would certainly reduce the cost of production of gold and, therefore, would increase its production but it would also encourage the mining of lower grade ores. But this will not in any way reduce the price of gold in the market because the price of gold is fixed by the government. It would not be correct thus, to say that the price of gold is determined by the free forces of demand and supply in the market. Secondly, there is a time lag between the change in the production of gold and the change in the price of gold that takes place owing to the increased or decreased production of gold, and *vice versa*. In short, we can say gold is not like other commodities in all respects and its short-run price elasticity of supply is very low. Thirdly, is it not true that the current output of gold is just a small proportion of the total gold stock available, and hence, any increase or decrease in the current output will hardly exert any influence on the current price of gold or on its supply? Lastly, if the gold were not demanded for monetary purposes, its price would have been substantially low. In view of these criticisms, we may conclude that the commodity theory does not really explain the factors which cause changes in the value of money and, therefore, cannot be a dependable source of guidance to the monetary authority in formulating the national policy.

3. Quantity Theory of Money

It is believed that the idea regarding the determination of the value of money by the supply of money was first mooted in the 15th century. According to some writers, a positive statement about the theory was given by Devanzatti, a bullion writer in the 16th century. Subsequently, the theory was enlarged and improved upon by Locke, David Hume, Mill and other classical writers in the UK. A number of writers have tried to prove that English Mercantilists before Locke did not have any idea about the quantity theory. Jacob Viner believes that although Locke is mentioned as having first formulated clearly the quantity theory, many of the Mercantilist writers before Locke from the beginning of 17th century onwards presented rather a very simple version of the quantity theory.[6] David Hume elaborated the theory in his essay "Of Money" in his monumental work, *Political Discourses.* Hume's version of the theory holds an important position in the classical economics. This version was, however, different from the quantity equation approach and also from the cash balance approach.[7] In the earlier version of the theory a relationship between the quantity of money and the price level was established, it was not

6. Jacob Viner, *Studies* in *the Theory of International Trade,* p. 40-41.
7. A.H. Hansen, *Monetary Theory and Fiscal Policy,* 1st Edition, p. 48.

suggested that the changes in the price level were necessarily proportionate to the changes in the quantity of money. The position of the early theorists can be explained by pointing out that they really believed in the increase in output over time owing to the improvement of technology; they also thought that the velocity of money could also change because of the changing nature of monetary institutions. And that is why the early quantity theorists did not assert that proportionate changes would take place in the price level owing to the changes in the money supply. So, according to the earliest version of the theory, the price level (*P*) changes with the changes in the quantity of money (*M*) in such a way that the price level increases with the increase in the quantity of money or decreases with the decrease in the quantity of money. In other words, the money elasticity of price level is always greater than zero. Even Marshall and Pigou assumed that the demand curve for money had a uniform unitary elasticity and, therefore, was a rectangular hyperbola.

In the United States, the theory was developed by Irving Fisher and Kemmerer. The theory was further modified by Cambridge economists. In the 20th century it was reinterpreted by Keynes and Patinkin and restated by Friedman. We now very briefly take up the various approaches adopted during the course of the last three centuries in developing the theory and giving the various equations used for explaining it. For the sake of convenience we can divide these approaches into: (*i*) transactions approach, (*ii*) Cambridge approach, (*iii*) real balance approach, (*iv*) income approach, and (*v*) Chicago approach.

Fisher's Transactions Approach

The equation of exchange or the quantity equation has been formulated in a number of ways. The most important is the cash-transactions version, *i.e.* $MV = PT$. This equation was presented by Irving Fisher in his book entitled *The Purchasing Power of Money* in 1911. In this equation *M* represents the average amount of money in circulation at any given time period; *V* is the average velocity of money during that period of time; *P* is the general price level (it is the weighted average of the sale price of all individual goods and services transacted by the community at any given time period) and *T* is the volume of trade or demand for money during that time period.

According to Fisher, the value of money or its purchasing power is dependent on the quantity of money as related to the amount of goods and services purchased by it. The *MV* side of the equation represents the supply of money or the total money expenditure at a given time incurred by the community. And the *PT* side represents the demand for money or the money value of all the goods and services bought during a given period of time. Fisher presupposes that the money is essentially required for transaction purposes or as a medium of exchange. And, therefore, the demand for money is equal to the total value of all goods and services transacted during a given period of time. This equation is known as the *Cash Transactions Equation.* It can also be expressed as

$$P = \frac{MV}{T}$$

Fisher later on expanded his equation of exchange by including credit money since in the original equation M represented the primary money, *i.e.* the currency money in circulation. He realised that in trade and commerce, banks' demand deposits or credit money is also used to a very great extent and therefore, he amended the equation as follows:

$$MV + M'V' = PT$$

or

$$P = \frac{MV + M'V'}{T}$$

where M' represents the credit money and V' is the velocity of circulation of M'. Fisher has, with the help of his equation, tried to prove that the price level or the value of money is essentially determined by the supply of money or the value of money is the function of the supply of money provided other things remain constant. In this way, Fisher established a direct relationship between the quantity money and its value.[8]

This can be explained with the help of diagrams as under:

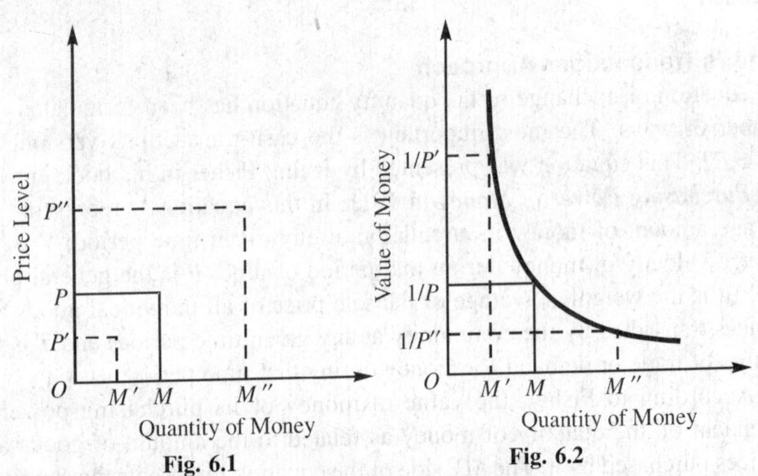

Fig. 6.1 **Fig. 6.2**

8. It is generally believed that the transactions approach was first adopted by Sidney Newcomb and Irving Fisher but it can be traced in the writings of early economists including J.S. Mill. According to Mill, "The value of money, other things being the same, varies inversely as its quantity; every increase of quantity lowers the value and every diminution raising it in a ratio exactly equivalent." (*Principles of Political Economy,* Vol. II, p. 55). David Ricardo considered an increase in the volume

Fig. 6.1 shows the effect of changes in the quantity of money. When the quantity of money is doubled from *OM* to *OM″* the price level is also doubled from *OP* to *OP″* and when it is halved to *OM′* then the price level is also halved to *OP′*.

Fig. 6.2 shows the inverse relationship between the quantity of money and the value of money. At *OM* quantity of money, its value is 1/*P*, when the quantity of money is doubled from *OM* to *OM″* the value of money is halved from 1/*P* to 1/*P″*. When the quantity of money is halved from *OM* to *OM′* the value of money is doubled to 1/*P′*. The downward sloping curve also shows this inverse relationship between the quantity of money and its value.

Assumptions of Transactions Approach

Fisher's equation of exchange is based on a number of assumptions which are as follows:

1. In the equation *P* is supposed to be passive, *i.e.* while it is determined by other elements in the equation, it itself remains passive or it does not influence other elements. Thus, the relation between the price level and other elements is one-sided.

2. Fisher assumes that *V* remains constant, *i.e.* it is neither affected by other factors nor it affects them.

3. It is also assumed that fluctuations do not take place, in *T* in the short period and if any change takes place in *T* then it is totally independent of the other factors in the equation. It is possible that *T* may be influenced by *P* but according to Fisher such condition would be abnormal.

4. The assumption that *T* remains constant is also based on another assumption that full employment exists in the economy and no idle resources are available to expand the production of goods and services.

5. Fisher has further assumed that the ratio of credit money to legal tender money remains constant. To conclude we can say that Fisher assumes

---

of money as causing a proportionate decrease in its purchasing power. He not only looked at money as an independent variable but also regarded the velocity of money as an institutional datum. In the United States, Taussig also stated the theory in a somewhat similar fashion. He says, "Double the quantity of money and other things being equal, prices will be twice as high as before and the value of money one half. Halve the quantity of money and other things being equal, prices will be one half of what they were before and the value of money double." (*Principles of Economics,* Vol. I, p. 205). In the words of Robertson, "Given the condition of demand for money, the relation between its value and the quantity of it available is of this peculiar kind: the larger the number of units available, the smaller, in exactly the same proportion, is the value of each unit." (*Money,* p. 31). In the words of Fisher: "The so called 'quantity theory', *i.e.* that prices vary proportionately to money has often been incorrectly formulated but (overlooking cheques) the theory is correct in the sense that the level of price varies directly with the quantity of money in circulation provided the velocity of circulation of that money and the volume of trade which it is obliged to perform are not changed." (*The Purchasing Power of Money,* 2nd Edition, 1920, p. 14).

P as a passive factor and considers other elements such as *M, V, V′* and *T* as constant. He establishes a direct proportional relationship between the supply of money and its value. The supply of money is an independent variable and the price level changes owing to the changes in the supply of money. To quote him again: *"One of the normal effects of an increase in the quantity of money is an exactly proportional increase in the general level of prices.* We find nothing to interfere with the truth of the quantity theory that variations in money (*M*) produce normally proportional changes in prices."[9]

Critical Appraisal of the Transactions Approach

1. The assumptions of Fisher's equation that *V* and *T* remain constant and that is why any increase or decrease in *M* causes a decrease or increase in *P* are not supported by facts. Experience shows that *V* varies with *T;* that *M* may increase without influencing *P,* if *T* also increases. Similarly, any increase or decrease in *M* may not produce proportional changes in *P.* Germany experienced hyperinflation after the World War I not so much due to the increase in the supply of money but due to the increase in *V.* An increase in money supply is also possible without any increase in price provided *V* declines. This has been proved by the occurrences in the domain of currency which took place in Germany when the currency was reformed; *V* was reduced by the issue of new 'renten mark' backed by the land of the country which helped in regaining the confidence of the people in the new currency. In this way, a decrease in *V* allowed accommodation for additional supply of money without any increase in *P.* The American boom of 1923 also proved that a considerable increase in *T* can cause an increase in *M* without causing any rise in the price level. Fisher himself realised that *V* varies with *T.* But he considered these as merely transitory. Hence it would be seen that the quantity equation is hardly of any help in explaining the price changes during the transition period. Thus, we may conclude that the theory only explains the long-term phenomenon.

2. The theory does not also explain the causes why prices and production behave in a different fashion in a trade-cycle. Despite an injection of additional dose of money in circulation during depression, prices behave very obstinately and instead of rising, fall further. This is not explained by the quantity equations but can be explained with the help of the fact that during the period of slump the rapid fall in *V* more than offsets the increase in *M.* As already stated, the Fisher's equations do not explain the short-run changes in the price level in all cases.

3. Fisher's equations also suffer from certain inconsistencies as pointed out by Halm. He explains that no useful purpose would be served by over-

9. Irving Fisher, *op. cit.*, pp. 157-58.

emphasising the importance of equation of exchange. He says, "We have to note that M refers to a point of time, whereas V refers to the turnover of money during a period of time; consequently, the expression MV would involve the inconsistency of multiplying non-comparable factors unless the assumption is made that M is an average amount of money in circulation during the period in question or is the same amount during the whole period. But these assumptions are not compatible with all possible purposes of the equation."[10]

4. Again, the transactions approach is based on the assumption that other things remain constant. Other things never remain constant and changes in anyone factor cause changes in other factors as well. An increase in M may or may not be followed by an increase in M', and there may be some time lag; it may also not be accompanied or followed by an increase or decrease in V of M and M'; and therefore; a rise in prices may take place only by a rise in T.

5. The equation of exchange concludes that with constant V any increase in M will lead to a rise in P. If the entire increase in M is absorbed by the transactions which do not involve exchange of goods, the price level of commodities may remain unchanged or may even fall. Such transactions which do not involve the exchange of goods may be, for example, the payment of wages, salaries, professional fees, the transactions of land and buildings or securities, etc. Again, it is difficult to have complete information about the "money-to-money" transactions which the banks conduct. Moreover, T itself may not reflect total transactions because the total sales only include the sale of the current output and not those of the existing stocks or bonds or second-hand cars, television sets, scooters, etc. and this makes the preparation of an accurate price index rather impossible. Hence, the futility of the equation.

6. The criticisms of Marget and Hayek are worth quoting. According to Marget, "The quantity equations, themselves are nothing more or less than short-hand expressions designed to indicate nature of the variables whose operations can be shown to influence prices. Each of the variables in these equations is merely a chapter-heading, a rubric for detailed analysis designed to explain why the variable in question will be of a different magnitude under different circumstances, and to indicate the circumstances under which, and the sequence in which, changes in the magnitude of one variable may be expected to be associated with changes in other variables."[11] Similarly, Hayek points out that the equation concentrates too much on general magnitudes: it establishes an unrealistic causal relationship between M and V, T and P, without realising that monetary factors can influence the economy only through many single price-making processes. He further says that the equation does not explain the changes in the structure of relative prices caused by monetary factors. Chandler has also objected against the equation on the same basis.

10. G.N. Halm, *op., cit.* p. 22.
11. A.W. Marget, *The Theory of Prices,* Vol. I, p. 81.

7. The equation does not provide adequate tools for analysing the factors which cause changes in the value of money.

8. According to the equation of exchange, the price level can be controlled by the monetary authority merely by changing *M*. But the depression of the nineteen thirties proved otherwise. In America, the Federal Reserve Banks engaged themselves in large scale open market operations to increase the supply of money in circulation in 1932. It was again adopted in 1933. But the bank loans did not increase and to the great disgust of the authorities the price level fell. This proves that the price level is not influenced by *M* and *M′* alone but by various other factors as well and among these factors non-monetary factors may be stronger than the monetary factors.

9. According to Crowther, the theory only explains the how and not why of the fluctuations in the value of money especially in the long period. It does not explain why an increase in *M* will cause a rise in prices at certain times and not at all times. In short period, the changes in the quantity of money are not the sole cause of changes in the price level; this is extremely misleading. According to the theory, the changes in the price level are all important, that all fluctuations in the level of business activity are caused by the changes in the price level or in other words, the changes in the price level are the root cause of trade cycles. This is not wholly true because prices fall or increase due to the fall or increase in the demand and both prices and demand fluctuate under the influence of some other common factor.

10. With the qualifying phrase, "other things remaining constant," the equation becomes static and unrealistic. It cannot explain the phenomenon of business cycles in real life. Human behaviour, legal framework, etc. undergo changes which influence an economy. Similarly, it does not explain the process through which prices are determined. Price making is a continuing process. Present prices are influenced by the past prices which also influence the future prices and, therefore, to assume, as has been done in the theory, that prices are solely influenced by the supply of money, will not be correct.

11. The equation of exchange has been further criticised on the ground that it has divorced the theory of the determination of the value of money from the general theory of value, which, with the help of the tools of supply and demand, can easily explain how the value of money is determined. Hence, there was no need for a separate theory of money.

12. The equation treats money only as a medium of exchange and overlooks the other important functions of money. The quantity theorists believe that money is demanded because people have to conduct transactions, but they ignore that money is also required because it is a liquid asset, that it can be stored in the form of securities. Had the quantity theorists integrated the transactions demand with speculative demand for money, their approach would have been more meaningful and realistic.

The Cambridge or the Cash-balance Approach

The Cambridge economists, especially Marshall, Pigou, Robertson and Keynes adopted the cash balance approach which had earlier been advocated by Adam Smith, Petty, Locke, Cantillon, etc. In this approach, the demand for and supply of money have been considered in reference to a particular point of time rather than a particular period of time. Again, instead of emphasising the supply side, it emphasises the demand side—the demand for money arises not for transactions but because of its being a store of value. The theory states that the real demand for money arises not because people want to exchange it for commodities and services but because they want to hold it on account of various motives. All these economists tried to show that the determination of the value of money could be a part of the general theory of value and the value of money could be determined by the forces of demand and supply. The Cambridge approach which is also known as the cash-balance approach has been summarised by Patinkin like this: "In its cash-balance version—associated primarily with the names of Walras, Marshall, Wickshell and Pigou—neoclasical theory assumed that, for their convenience, individuals wish to hold a certain proportion, K, of the real volume of their planned transactions, T, in the form of real money balances. The demand for these balances thus equals KT. Correspondingly, the demand for nominal money balances is KPT, where P is the price level of the commodities transacted. The equating of this demand to the supply of money, M, then produced the famous Cambridge equation, $M = KPT$. In the transactions version—associated primarily with the names of Newcomb and Fisher—the velocity of circulation V, replaced its reciprocal, K, to produce the equally famous equation of exchange, $MV = PT$. These equations were the parade-grounds on which neo-classical economists then put the classical theory of money through its paces."[12]

Marshall's Version

According to Marshall, the version of the theory is like this: "In every state of society there is some fraction of their income which people find it worthwhile to keep in the form of currency; it may be a fifth, or a tenth or a twentieth. A large command of resources in the form of currency renders their business easy and smooth, and puts them at an advantage in bargaining, but on the other hand it locks up in a barren form resources that might yield an income or gratification if invested, say, in extra furniture; or a money income, if invested, in extra machinery or cattle. A man determines this fraction after balancing one against another, the advantages of a further ready command, and the disadvantages of putting more of his resources into a form in which

12. Don Patinkin, *Money, Interest and Prices* (1956), p. 97.

they yield him no direct income or other benefit...let us suppose that the inhabitants of a country, taken one with another (and including, therefore, all varieties of character and of occupation) find it just worth their while to keep by them on the average ready purchasing power to the extent of a tenth part of their annual income, together with a fiftieth part of their property; then the aggregate value of the currency of the country will tend to be equal to the sum of these amounts."[13] Thus, according to Marshall, the demand for money is a stable function of income and property. His equation is $M = KY$, where M is the quantity of money and K is that proportion of money income (Y) which people want to hold in the form of cash or ready purchasing power. K is the reciprocal of velocity. If PO (price level time output) is substituted for Y, then

$$M = KPO$$

or

$$P = \frac{M}{KO}$$

Pigou's Version

This equation has been expressed by Pigou, which is also known as the Cambridge equation as:

$$P = \frac{KR}{M}$$

where P represents the value of money; K represents the proportion of total real income to be held in cash, R represents the total real income and M is the total quantity of money. According to Pigou when K and R are taken as constant, the above equation would be the equation of a rectangular hyperbola. Subsequently, this equation was modified after taking into consideration bank deposits because some people like to hold cash in the form of bank deposits as well. The enlarged version, therefore, is like this:

$$P = \frac{KR}{M}[c + h(1-c)]$$

or

$$M = \frac{KR}{P}[c + h(1-c)]$$

where c denotes the proportion of cash, people hold in actual legal tender, $(1 - c)$ is the proportion of that form of income which people keep in the form of bank deposits and h is the proportion of actual legal tender that bankers keep in cash against deposits held by their customers.

According to Pigou when K, R, c and h are treated as constants, this is also the equation of a rectangular hyperbola. This needs a little more

13. A. Marshall, *op. cit.*, I, *iv*, *iii*, p. 33.

elaboration; because in the first equation as given by Pigou, K and R are constant while in the second equation, both K, R, c and h are treated as constant, so what is meant by saying that equations are those of a rectangular hyperbola. In Pigou's equation P is not the price level but the purchasing power of money. To express it in terms of cash-balance equation, $M = KPT$ or $M = KPY$ where P is the price level, the equation would be as:

$$\frac{1}{P} = \frac{M}{KR\{c+h(1-c)\}}$$

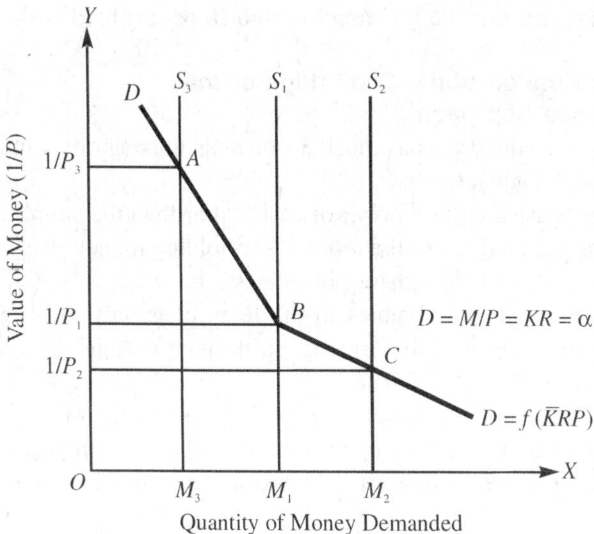

Fig. 6.3

In the above equation, K, c, h are all positive constants such that each one of these is less than unity but greater than zero. A rectangular hyperbola is a curve which is locus of a point, the product of whose distances from its asymptotes is a positive constant α^2. In Fig 6.3 demand curve of money, which in the cash-balance equation is a function of KRP, slopes negatively because the purchasing power of the money unit is less in terms of goods and services if people choose to hold more money in cash. The supply curves for money S_1M_1, S_2M_2 and S_3M_3 are vertical lines drawn on the assumption that money supply is independently determined by the government. According to the diagram when the money supply increases from OM_1 to OM_2, the value of money measured as inverse of the price level P, *i.e.* $1/P$, falls from $1/P_1$ to $1/P_2$. And when the quantity of money decreases from OM_1 to OM_3; the value of money increases from $1/P_1$ to $1/P_3$. The demand curve for money *DD* is the function of *KRP* or $DD = f(KRP)$ which is a rectangular hyperbola.

A rectangular hyperbola thus approaches the two asymptotes but never meets them. Walras, Marshall, Pigou and others assumed that the demand curve for money was a rectangular hyperbola simply because they believed that doubling of the money stock doubles the price level.

Prof. Robertson has given a somewhat different equation:

$$M = PKT \text{ or } P = \frac{M}{KT}$$

where *P* represents the price level, *T* is the total amount of goods and services (like *R* of Pigou), *K* is the function of *T* which people hold cash.

Critical Evaluation of the Cambridge or the Cash-Balance Approach

The Cambridge equation is as much a truism as the quantity equation, but, it has a number of advantages:

1. In emphasising the holding of cash rather than the supply, it is nearer to the Keynesian analysis of the motives for holding money (we shall study it later) and so to the modern theory of interest.

2. It points out that changes in the level of money income can come about through changes in the price level, through changes in real output or through both at once.

3. It indicates the importance of *K*. An analysis of the factors responsible for fluctuations in *K* offered scope for the study of many important problems like uncertainty, expectations, rate of interest, etc. which were not considered earlier.

4. It lays stress on the subjective valuations and human motives which are the basis of all economic activities. Nevertheless, as a theory, it is still inadequate.

5. According to Keynes, "The chief inconvenience of the Cambridge Quantity Equation really lies in its applying to the total deposits considerations which are primarily relevant only to the income deposits, and in its tackling the problem as though the same sort of considerations which govern the income deposits also govern the total deposits.[14] Keynes further holds that the significance attached to *K* (the proportion of bank deposits to the community's income) when extended beyond the income deposits, becomes misleading. The emphasis laid on the point that the amount of real balances that the people hold is determined by the comparative advantages of holding resources in cash, and in alternative forms, so that a change in *K* will occur because of a

14. J.M. Keynes, *op. cit.*, Vol. I.

change in these comparative advantages, is useful. But resources, as interpreted by Pigou, cannot be identical with current income. Keynes also holds that the equation is not able to solve the equation of the measurement of price level, since Pigou measures the quantity of real balances in terms of wheat. Again, the equation does not explain the disturbances caused by a change in the proportion of deposits held for different purposes, like savings, investment, etc. It is also not able to analyse the disturbances which occur in the price level owing to disparities between the rates of saving and investment.

6. The theory does not take note of speculative demand for money which is a very powerful factor in determining the demand for money in modern times. This means that the link connecting the theories of interest and level of income through the demand for money is missing. Further, while the theory includes the level of income, it ignores elements like productivity, thrift, liquidity preference, which are very essential for making the theory of the value of money, a comprehensive one. It also does not help in analysing the dynamic behaviour of prices in the economy, since it does not explain the magnitude of change in the price and output owing to a change in the money supply in the short period. It does not, also, highlight the important role that rate of interest plays in causing variations in the price level consequent upon a change in the money supply.

7. The assumptions that K and T remain constant and that the elasticity of demand for money is unity, make the theory unrealistic.

Comparison between the Transactions and Cash-Balance Equations

Robertson has pointed out that the two equations, *viz.*, the transactions equation and the cash-balance equation are just different observations of the same phenomenon; the cash-balance approach being concerned with "money sitting" while the transactions approach being concerned with "money on the wings". In other words, while the transactions approach treats money as a flow, the cash-balance approach treats money as a stock; while the transactions approach emphasises the role of V, the cash-balance approach emphasises the importance of K; while the transactions approach emphasises the value of money over a period of time, the cash-balance approach explains the determination of the value of money at a point of time. Mathematically, if we substitute $1/V$ for K and $1/K$ for V then the two equations would be identical. It would not, therefore, be wrong to say that apparently there is no fundamental difference between the two approaches.

However, there are economists who do not agree with this point of view. For example, Prof. Hansen holds that, "The Marshallian version of the quantity theory, $M = KY$ represents a fundamentally new approach to the problem of money and prices. It is not true, as is often alleged, that the "cash-balance" equation is merely the quantity theory in new algebraic dress. Substituting PO (price-level times output) for Y, the Marshallian equation becomes $M = KPO$. *Arithmetically,* K is therefore simply the reciprocal of V in the equation $MV = PO$. But it does not follow from the mere fact that $V = 1/K$ is an arithmetical identity, therefore, the Marshallian *analysis* is in fact the same thing as the Hume-Fisher analysis. To assert this is to miss entirely the significance of the K in the Marshallian equation."[15] Thus, while in the cash-balance equation, P represents the price-level, that is, the price of everything which enters into a transaction carried out by money, in the cash-balance equation P is concerned with the prices of only those commodities which enter into the community's real income, that is, it does not include those things which people buy to sell again or which people hold to use them not for consumption but for production.

While emphasising that the two equations stress differently on the effect of changes in the price-level, Keynes has stated as follows: "In terms of the Marshallian approach, sudden and rapid *shifts* in the desire of the public to hold money may profoundly affect prices even though the monetary authority successfully maintains a high stability in the money supply. The desire of the public to hold cash balances—'liquidity preference'—enters as a powerful factor. Drastic and sudden shifts in the desire to hold money, reflected in a change in K, may produce large and quickly moving changes in the level of income and prices. Shifts in public psychology, in expectations, must be taken into account no less than changes in the money supply. In the Marshallian analysis a shift in K may start an upward or downward movement. It is K not M that holds the stage."[16]

The concept of V in transactions equation is highly mechanistic in nature as contrasted with the concept of K in the cash balance equation. K necessarily emphasises human motives which are important dynamic variables. This concept is really important in the sense that it has led to further studies in regard to the analysis of the determinants of K and of the forces responsible for the changes in K, in the field of monetary theory after World War II.

It is also pointed out that the cash-balance equation is more useful because it is more easy to know the total cash balances held by the people than to know the total money spent on transactions. It also helps in comparing the relative advantages of holding cash and those of spending or investing, which the concept of velocity in fact implied. This shift in emphasis has certainly led to important developments in monetary and price theories. The cash-

15. A.H. Hansen, *Monetary Theory and Fiscal Policy,* First Edition, p. 49.
16. J.M. Keynes, *A Treatise on Money,* Vol. I, p. 133.

balance equation analyses value of money as a function of its supply on the one hand and of the demand on the other. The emphasis on *K*, as pointed out by Marshall himself, is more significant than *V*. Because it helps in understanding the occurrence of business cycles; it explains how fluctuations in the value of real balances cause cyclical changes in the price level. When people lose their trust in the currency of the country, they are not willing to hold it, prices rise and *vice versa*.

Again, the cash balance equation also represents a shift in emphasis from institutional and technological factors to psychological factors in the determination of the demand for money.

Further, the cash balance equation has led to the development of the concept of liquidity preference which has helped the development of income and employment theories during recent years and also to the explanation that the monetary authority has only limited powers to control crises. It may, however, be pointed out that the introduction of *K* did not lead to any different conclusions because *K*, like *V*, is also a stable factor undisturbed by autonomous variations affecting the price level independently of the quantity of money.

Patinkin's Views

Don Patinkin severely criticised the cash-balance approach of the Cambridge economists, because they failed to understand the true nature of the quantity theory as is obvious from the dichotomy that they maintain between the goods market and the money market. An increase in the stock of money is assumed to cause an increase in the price-level but not to have real influence on the goods market. His main attack is on the nature of demand curve for money, which according to him, is assumed by the Cambridge economists, to be a rectangular hyperbola with constant unit elasticity of demand for money, as is evident from the statement that doubling the stock of money leads to a doubling of the price level. He says that this approach ignores the real balance effect and assumes the absence of money illusion under the 'homogeneity postulate' (implying that the demand functions in the real sectors are insensitive to the changes in the absolute level of money prices). This could be true in a barter economy, but in money economy, the concept of absolute price level is meaningless and the non-existence of money illusion is unthinkable. According to Patinkin, the dichotomy of money and the level of relative prices is determined by the real demands (tastes) and real supplies (production conditions) and the absolute price level is determined by the demand for and the quantity of money—leads to two separate theories of prices, *i.e.* of relative prices and of absolute level of prices. He has reconciled the two theories by making the demand and supply functions depend on real cash balances as well as on relative prices. The gist of his argument is contained in the following paragraphs:

"Once the real and monetary data of an economy with outside money are specified, the equilibrium values of relative prices, the rate of interest, and the absolute price level are simultaneously determined by all the markets of the economy. It is generally impossible to isolate a sub-set of markets which can determine the equilibrium values of a sub-set of prices...it is fatal to succumb to the temptation to say that relative prices are determined in the commodity market and absolute price in the money market. This does not mean that the value theory cannot be distinguished from the monetary theory. Obviously, there is a distinction, but it is based on a dichotomization of effects, not on a dichotomization of *markets.* More specifically, both monetary theory and value theory consider all markets of the economy simultaneously. But, in each of these markets, value theory analyses individual experiments which measure the substitution effect and that part of the wealth effect which does not stem from changes in real balances; and monetary theory, individual experiments which measure the real-balance effect.

"Correspondingly, value theory analyses market experiments which do not (significantly) affect the absolute price-level and hence, do not generate real balance effects; and monetary theory, market experiments which do not (significantly) affect relative prices and hence do not generate substitution and non-monetary wealth effects. Thus, shifts in tastes, changes in technology and the like are in the domain of value theory. Changes in the quantity of money and...shifts in liquidity preference are in the domain of monetary theory.

"If we now examine this classificatory scheme, we will discover the grain of truth in the intuitive feeling that in some sense value theory is connected with the determination of relative prices and monetary theory with the determination of absolute prices. In particular, assume that by a *tatonnement* involving all prices and all markets the equilibrium values of money prices have been reached. We can now make use of this information to take a step backwards and approach the equilibrium position once again, but this time by a restricted *tatonnement.* For example, holding the absolute price level constant at its already determined *equilibrium* value, we can arbitrarily shift relative prices from theirs, and then study the nature of the dynamic forces that—working simultaneously in all markets—return the economy to its original equilibrium position. By the very definition of this procedure, such a return can be accomplished without any change in the absolute price level. Hence, the restricted *tatonnement* by which the equilibrium relative prices are thus redetermined need involve only these prices, need accordingly generate only substitution and non-monetary wealth effects, and can, therefore, be studied entirely within the confines of value theory.

"Similarly, we can define a restricted *tatonnement* which—starting from a knowledge of the *equilibrium* values of relative prices and interst—works simultaneously through *all* the markets of the economy to redetermine the equilibrium value of the absolute price level. Such a *tatonnement* can clearly succeed without requiring any changes in relative prices and interest; that is, it need generate only real balance effects. Hence, it can be studied entirely within the confines of monetary theory.

"This decomposition of the overall *tatonnement* into two components is a convenient expository device.... It can be used safely provided we are clear in our own minds that it separates out effects and not markets. In particular we must guard against the apparent tendency to slip over from this valid device into the invalid proposition of the false dichotomy that, starting with an absolute price level held constant at an *arbitrary* level, a *tatonnement* of relative prices in the *commodity markets alone* can determine these prices; that holding these relative prices constant at the value so determined, a *tatonnement* of the absolute price level in the *money market alone* can then determine this level; and that the absolute price level so determined, together with the relative prices determined by the first *tatonnement* in the commodity markets, must necessarily preserve the first equilibrium necessarily achieved in these markets. Clearly, this last statement will generally not be true unless the excess-demand equations of the commodity markets are actually independent of the absolute price level.

"This is the crucial point. The dynamic grouping of the absolute price level towards its equilibrium value will—through the real balance effect—react back on the commodity markets and hence, on relative prices. And it is precisely the constant failure to find this point explicitly recognized—and, indeed, the constant sensation of being just on the verge of having it explicitly contradicted—that is the basis of our original contention that the roots of the invalid dichotomy are to be found in the neo-classical analysis of Walras, Fisher, Pigou and Cassel." Patinkin's analysis is a real improvement on the traditional quantity theory and its value lies in the integration of commodity and money markets through the real balance effect. But it is incomplete. Archibald and Lipsey hold that the analysis is inadequate to the extent it is restricted to the impact effect of a change in a price and does not go through the long-period equilibrium. And if the analysis is extended to an infinite number of periods, general long-term equilibrium is found to be perfectly consistent with a unitary elastic demand curve for money—the real balance effect disappears. Patinkin conceded this defect in his analysis in the second edition of his book. But the big question whether the quantity theory refers to a short-term equilibrium or long-term equilibrium still remained unsolved.

Exercises

1. Critically examine Fisher's quantity theory of money.
2. Compare Fisher's version with the Cambridge version of the quantity theory of money. Which of these two do you regard superior and why?
3. Give the similarities and dissimilarities between the quantity theory of money and Cambridge cash balances theory.
4. Critically examine Fisher's version of quantity theory of money and assess its validity.
5. "The quantity theory of money in its earliest crude form is useless and misleading as no economist now believes in any fixed and automatic relationship between the quantity of money and the general level of prices". Examine this statement.
6. "The modern tendency in economic thinking, indeed, is to discard the old notion of the quantity of money as a causative factor in the state of business and a determinant of value of money and to regard it as a consequence." (Crowther) Discuss.
7. "The quantity equations remain the most illuminating summary of the forces determining the general theory of prices." Discuss.
8. "The cash balance equation is not the quantity theory in a new algebraic dress, it represents a fundamentally new approach to the problem of money and prices." Discuss.
9. State the equations of exchange given by Fisher and Pigou to explain the quantity theory of money. Explain the fundamental differences and similarities between these equations.

•••

Chapter 7

The Determination of Value of Money—The Keynesian Approach

1. Introduction

In the preceding chapter we have evaluated the two versions of the quantity theory of money. One can easily conclude that the quantity theory of money hardly affords a satisfactory explanation of the determination of the value of money and the factors that cause fluctuations in it. As an explanation to the changes in the price level, both versions are incomplete because they do not include all the factors that determine the price level. They, at best, include only those factors which determine the price level immediately. For example, there are several factors, institutional, psychological, technical, etc. which produce changes in the price level but in both the versions they do not find any place. Secondly, both the versions apparently suggest that price level stability can be achieved merely by regulating the supply of money. But the history of this century fully explains that this cannot be possible under all circumstances. Thirdly, the equations used in both versions do not expose the process by which the value of money or price level is determined. They only discuss the final results and avoid the *how* of the entire question. Fourthly, in both the equations it has been stated that the changes in the price level cause fluctuations in the level of economic activity in the economy but the fact is that the price level is changed by the changes in the economic activities of the people and so there is some confusion between the cause and effect relationship. Fifthly, the role of interest in the determination of the price level has not been given any importance, in both the equations. Some economists have pointed out that the value of money is determined by the level of income of the people and not by the total volume of money in circulation. In other words, it is the income, and not the supply of money which determines the value of money. Finally, both the versions fail in providing us with a suitable explanation of how to deal with short-term fluctuations in the price level.

2. Real Balance Approach

Not being satisfied with the cash-balance approach, Keynes, to start with, approached the whole question from the point of view of real balances. He held that a holder of money requires a quantity of real balances which is in appropriate relationship with the quantity of real transactions upon which those balances are spent. He measured real balances by consumption units and concluded that if this relationship remains intact, then the amount of cash balances which he would need would be equal to the amount of real balances as determined by the above relationship and, therefore, he formulated the following equation:

$$n = p(k + rk)$$

where n denotes the total quantity of cash, r is the proportion of banks' cash reserves to their deposits, p is the price level of consumption units, k represents the amount of real balances held in cash and k' stands for the real balances held in bank deposits. The proportion between k and k' is determined by the banking arrangements of the public and their absolute value is determined by the habits of the people. The value of r would depend upon the practices followed by the banking system regarding maintenance of reserves. So long as these values remain constant, a direct relation between the quantity of cash (n) and the price level (P) remains an evident fact.

Critical Evaluation of Real Balance Approach

Keynes equation suffers from a number of defects and he had to face a lot of criticism. First, P measures only the price level of consumption goods while we know that money is used for a vast number of purposes, business and personal. Thus, p in the equation does not measure the purchasing power of money. As pointed out by Keynes himself, "The possible causes of a variation of k' were limited to those which can be properly described as change of habit on the part of the public. This use of language was not as formally incorrect but it is misleading insofar as it is intended to include, for example, a change in the proportions of the total deposits represented by savings-deposits, business-deposits and income-deposits respectively due to a change in bank rate or in the business situation as a whole. In short, I was applying to the cash-deposits as a whole, conceptions which were only appropriate to the income deposits."[1] Again, the relationship between n and p is not correct at least in the short period because the changes in n cause changes in k, k' and r.

1. J.M. Keynes, *A Treatise on Money*, pp. 223-24.

3. Income Approach or Saving-Investment Theory of Keynes

Keynes admitted this fact and later on, made changes in his equation. In the light of his savings-investment theory, he connected the rate of interest and the stock of cash with the determination of price level and tried to explain how a disequilibrium between saving and investment disturbs the price level.

In this connection, he formulated two fundamental equations:

$$P = \frac{E}{O} + \frac{I' - S}{R} \qquad ...(1)$$

where P is the price level of consumption goods, E represents the total earning of the community during a given period, O stands for the total number of units produced in the same period, I' stands for the cost of production of new investment goods, S for the amount of total savings of the community in the same period and R for the consumption units produced.

$$\pi = \frac{Y}{O} = \frac{E + Q}{O} + \frac{I - S}{O} \qquad ...(2)$$

where π is the price level, O is the output, Y is the income, E is the income of factors of production, Q is the windfall profits due to the appreciation of the value of capital assets, I is investment and S is savings.

This can be explained in the following manner:

For the society as a whole, the total expenditure on the purchase of goods and services is equal to the total income of the society, *i.e.*

$$\pi O = Y \text{ or } \pi = \frac{Y}{O}$$

The total income of the society consists of two parts, namely, (1) the earnings of the factors of production including normal profits of the business community, and (2) windfall profits, *i.e.* extra profits accruing to the entrepreneurs due to the appreciation of the value of capital assets. So,

$$Y = E + Q$$

The value of the capital assets appreciates when the demand for investment is in excess of supply of new investment, which is limited by the current savings of the society. Hence, the owners of capital assets get a windfall profit. According to Keynes, windfall profits are the excess of investment over savings. Thus,

$$Q = I - S$$

Hence, the second fundamental equation as given by Keynes is:

$$\pi = \frac{Y}{O} = \frac{E + Q}{O} + \frac{I - S}{O}$$

Keynes has attached certain hypotheses to some of the variables in order to study the process of price movement. In the quantity equation, to avoid the problem of any counteraction of the movement in the quantity of money, by the corresponding changes in velocity of circulation of money (V) or transactions (T) or both, he has assumed that V and T remain constant. Keynes also implicity assumes that in the short run O remains constant. He also assumes that the ratio E/Q (rate of earnings of the factors of production per unit of commodity) remains stable. Q varies according to the changes in the market and natural rate of interest. Natural rate of interest is the expected profit on new capital investments, while the market rate is the rate of interest charged on borrowed money. If the natural rate is higher than the market rate, then people will borrow more and invest more in the new capital assets. Consequently, the demand for capital assets will rise, their value will appreciate and windfall profits will rise. If the two rates are equal then Q will be equal to zero and it will be less than zero when the natural rate is less than the market rate. From these hypotheses it may be concluded that the price level fluctuates around a rather stable equilibrium value, E/Q, in response to the variations of market rate around the natural rate of interest and causes fluctuations in the profit variable, Q. Since $Q = I - S$, the process of price variation can be expressed in terms of the relative behaviour of S and I.

The fundamental equations of Keynes indicate that there is a functional relationship between the quantity of money and the price level of goods and services (P) and that of output as a whole (n) in ideal conditions of equilibrium. According to Keynes this relationship is "of such a character that if the quantity of money were double, the price level would be double also".[2] The pivot of the whole analysis is, therefore, the relationship between S and I. As Keynes has himself said that S and I are not identical processes, but since savings facilitate investment, it is necessary to maintain equilibrium in such a way that $I' - S/R$ and $I - S/O$ are zero, because if S is higher than I or I', then prices would decline, losses would ensue and output will fall and *vice versa*.

Critical Evaluation of Keynes' Fundamental Equations

1.It has been pointed out that Keynesian equations are more or less similar to the quantity equations. Keynes himself stated that under ideal conditions of equilibrium, the relationship between the quantity of money and the price level is such that if the quantity of money were double, the price level would also be double. The conditions of equilibrium between I, I' and S as envisaged by him refer to a situation of full employment. Thus, to establish such sort of stability, it is enough to bring these three variables into equilibrium. But this reasoning is in conflict with his later approach in the General Theory where he shows that these variables remain in equilibrium even during depression.

2. J.M. Keynes, *op. cit.*, pp. 146-47.

2. These equations are based upon the unrealistic assumption of fixed output and this defect was recognised by Keynes himself in his General Theory.

3. Again, while Keynes claims his equations as dynamic, these hold true only under static conditions. According to these equations the rate of interest plays a dominant role in determining the business activity and the price level and by manipulating it the fluctuations in the business activity and the price level could be controlled. But in the General Theory he suggests that the volume of business activity depends not so much on the rate of interest as on the marginal efficiency of capital.

4. It has also been pointed out that these equations do not provide a satisfactory explanation of the fluctuations in the price level.

Income Theory of Money

The classical quantity theory of money assumes full employment of resources in the economy. Consequently it establishes direct and proportional relationship between the quantity of money and the price level. It also asserts that a change in the quantity of money does not bring about any change in the aggregate output. Income theory of money on the other hand states that the changes in the quantity of money can bring about changes in the price level only indirectly through changes in volume of aggregate expenditure, and consequently in total output. It, thus, attempts to integrate monetary theory and the general theory of income, output and employment. According to this theory, it is not the supply of money but the money income and the volume of expenditure which influence the level of prices as well as the output. The process is like this: an increase in the total money income means that the remuneration received by the factors of production in the form of rent, wages, interest and profit, will increase. Consequently, the total expenditure will increase which will lead to an increase in the total output and employment. Increased total expenditure will increase the prices only to the extent to which the production is inelastic due to certain factors impeding the production process. Finally, when the full employment is reached any further increase in total expenditure would lead to a proportionate increase in the price level, without altering total output. Thus, income theory of money is a reaction against the assertion of the classical economists that there is a direct relationship between money and prices.

The genesis of this theory can be traced to the book entitled *An Inquiry into the Currency's Principle,* written by Thomas Tooke published in 1844. After Tooke, Wicksell and Aftalion made meaningful contributions in the development of this theory. Finally, Keynes fully developed it. Keynes has analysed the determination of output and prices in both situations: full employment and less than full employment. The Keynesian theory can be looked at from two angles: (*i*) Income-Expenditure Approach, and (*ii*) Saving-Investment Approach. In fact, both these approaches are the same, but for the sake of clarity we will discuss both the approaches separately.

Income-Expenditure Approach

The Keynesian theory proposes as under:

1. That money income is equal to the money value of aggregate real output. Money income comprises of the remunerations received by the factors of production during a given period. It is also the money value of aggregate real output during that period. Real income is the total volume of goods and services produced during that period. Money value of the real income (*i.e.* total volume of goods and services multiplied by the price level) is the money income. Hence, money income is equal to the money value of the aggregate real output.

Symbolically, if Y represents money value, P represents the price level and O represents the total volume of goods and services then $Y = PO$.

2. Price level is determined by the ratio of money income and real income. If money income rises faster than the real income, prices will tend to rise and if real income rises faster than money income, prices will tend to fall. Symbolically

$$P = \frac{Y}{O}$$

3. Money income is either spent or saved. People spend their income either on the purchase of consumer goods and services or save. That portion of income which is not spent is saved. Symbolically

$$Y \text{ (Income)} = C \text{ (Consumption)} + S \text{ (Saving)}$$

4. Real income (O) is determined by aggregate demand or aggregate expenditure. Real income, *i.e.* the volume of goods and services produced by the community depends on the availability of real resources and their use in the process of production. In a capitalistic economy volume of production is determined by profits. Goods and services will be produced only to that extent and the labour force will be employed to that level which is most profitable. This will depend on the aggregate demand (AD) or expenditure (E) of the community on goods and services. Thus aggregate supply equates itself to aggregate demand *i.e.* AS (Aggregate Supply) = AD (Aggregate Demand). Symbolically, $O = AD = E$

5. Total expenditure (E or AD) is equal to consumption (C) and investment (I). Aggregate expenditure is incurred on consumer goods. Expenditure on consumer goods is determined by the real income and propensity to consume of the consumer concerned. The volume of investment goods will depend on

the marginal efficiency of capital and the current rate of interest. By marginal efficiency is meant the profitability of the capital. So symbolically

$$AD = E = C + I$$

6. Total money income is equal to total spending or expenditure. This is because one person's expenditure is another person's income. It is through their circular flow that income end expenditure determine and multiply each other. In short, expenditure creates income and income further creates expenditure and so on.

Symbolically, $Y = C + I$

7. Money income is the variable which determines output and prices. The aggregate expenditure depends upon money income. An increase in the money income will provide more purchasing power to the people who will use it for procuring more quantity of goods and services. The demand for goods and services will, thus, increase. It can happen in three ways:

(*i*) If the production is perfectly elastic an increase in aggregate demand will increase the volume of output and employment without altering the price level. (*ii*) If the production is relatively less elastic due to the shortages either of raw materials or labour force, an increase in the aggregate demand will affect both production and prices. It means that both production and prices will rise. (*iii*) If the production is perfectly inelastic, *i.e.* the economy's resources are fully employed, the increase in aggregate demand will increase the price level proportionately without any effect on the level of output.

It will, thus, be seen that there is no link between the supply of money and the aggregate expenditure and therefore the quantity theorists' approach of linking the two was wrong. The income theory has established that the quantity of money and its velocity of circulation are determined by the flow of expenditure on goods and services. It, however, does not mean that money has no role to play. The increase in money supply can increase aggregate spending but not directly, provided: (*i*) Investment is interest elastic, (*ii*) the consumption of the people is interest-sensitive, and (*iii*) liquidity preference of the people is interest-elastic.

We may now briefly state the main propositions of the income theory of money as under:

1. The price level and output are determined by the money income and the volume of expenditure and not by the money supply.

2. The price level will vary according to the change in the volume of expenditure but the extent of this variation would depend upon the degree of elasticity of production: (*i*) If it is perfectly elastic it will increase only output proportionately, (*ii*) if it is relatively less-elastic it will partly increase output and partly prices and (*iii*) if it is perfectly-inelastic, it will increase the prices proportionately without affecting the output.

Saving-Investment Approach

Saving-investment approach is another way of looking at Keynes' income theory. Whatever is left after consumption (C) out of the income (Y) is saving (S) and whatever is invested after meeting the consumption needs is the total investment (I) of the community. So both saving and investment are the excess of income over consumption.

Symbolically, $Y = C + I$ *or* $Y - C = I$

$Y = C + S$ or $Y - C = S$

Therefore $S = I$

In this way Keynes established an equality between saving and investment. This equality is derived from the equality of aggregate demand and aggregate supply. According to Keynes the economy is in equilibrium when the level of saving is equal to the level of investment. It means that what the community is taking out of the income stream in the form of saving, it adds exactly the same amount by undertaking investment. In such a situation, the entrepreneurs hardly have any incentive to change the level of output and employment. Keynes held that in the situation of disequilibrium between saving and investment (which can be possible because the decisions regarding saving and investment are taken by two different groups of people in the economy), equilibrium between these is restored not through the changes in the rate of interest as was upheld by the classical economists but through changes in the level of income. When saving exceeds investment, the level of profits of the entrepreneurs falls short of their expected profits. Consequently, they will reduce their investment and hence the level of employment and income in the economy will also fall down. When income falls saving also falls, reducing thereby the gap between investment and saving. The level of employment and income will continue to fall until investment and saving are in equilibrium. The fall in employment and income causes a fall in the price level. When investment exceeds saving, the process will be reversed.

How Far the Keynesian Approach is Superior to the Classical Quantity Theory of Money?

The income-expenditure approach of Keynes has been considered superior to the quantity theory of money in a number of ways. We explain these in the following paragraphs:

1. While depending on the changes in velocity of circulation of money, the quantity theory of money does not explain the causes which bring about changes in the velocity of circulation of money. This shortcoming is removed in the Keynesian approach. According to this approach, when saving exceeds investment, it implies that people are hoarding more and spending less money. Obviously the velocity of circulation of money will be reduced. The position

will be reversed when investment exceeds saving. So, it is the relationship between saving and investment that brings about changes in the velocity of circulation of money.

2. The quantity theory of money simply states that the changes in the quantity of money bring about proportionate changes in the price level. It, however, fails to provide an explanation for the changes that occur in the prices during the upswing or downswing phases of a trade cycle. It is unable to explain why an excess of money during depression is unable to revive the economy or the shortage of money is incapable of stopping a boom. The income theory provides explanations to all these. Mere increase in the money supply is not adequate to revive the economy. It is 'only when businessmen's expectation of profit or the marginal efficiency of capital starts rising that investment is encouraged and revival of the economy starts. So, an increase in investment and decrease in saving can revive the economy from depression. Similarly, an increase in saving and decrease in investment can control the boom.

3. The quantity theory of money assumes that there is full employment in the economy and therefore the quantity of money and the price level are in a direct and proportional relationship with each other. The income-expenditure approach is superior because it analyses the effects of changes in the quantity of money on the price level in both the situations, namely, full employment and unemployment.

4. The quantity theory of money explains only long-term changes while the Keynes theory explains short-run changes in the price level (value of money) which is more realistic.

5. The quantity theory of money does not provide satisfactory explanation for the causes which affect the price level due to changes in the quantity of money. Income-expenditure approach of Keynes does not only show that there is no direct relationship between the two but also shows that this relationship is indirect and disproportionate and the changes in the quantity of money affect the price level because of a disequilibrium between saving and investment. The income-expenditure approach also makes it amply clear that the changes in the quantity of money will not affect the price level so long as unemployment exists in the economy and as soon as the resources are fully employed there will be proportionate changes in the price level with changes in the quantity of money.

6. The Keynesian approach is superior in another respect as well. It takes into account both the monetary and real factors for the determination of the value of money, while the quantity theory of money takes into consideration monetary factors only. It neglects factors such as saving, investment, aggregate output, etc.

7. Since the quantity theory of money dwells only on the monetary factors, its importance is only for the monetary policy. But, since it does not identify the role played by the aggregate income and expenditure in affecting the level of economic activity, it cannot help in formulating policies commensurate with the needs of the time. In this respect the income-expenditure approach of Keynes is superior because it also points out the importance of fiscal measures for stabilising the economy.

4. The Keynesian Theory of Money and Prices

Disagreeing with the Cambridge economists about the direct and proportional relationship between quantity of money and prices, Keynes presented his own formulation of the quantity theory of money, in his *General Theory.* While doing so he has changed the monetary theory of prices into a monetary theory of output. He has also integrated the monetary theory with the value theory and merged the theory of interest with the monetary theory. Keynes lamented at the attempt of the classical economists to create a dichotomy between the relative price level and absolute price level. Keynes held that there is no direct relationship between the changes in the money supply and the prices. He considered money as a link between the present and future and therefore he did not accept the version of the classical economists regarding the neutrality of money.

According to Keynes, changes in the money supply affect the prices through the rate of interest. If the marginal efficiency of capital remains the same, at a particular point of time a fall in the rate of interest will increase the level of investment in the economy. An increase in the level of investment will raise the level of effective demand through multiplier effect, ultimately leading to an increase in income, output and employment. When unemployment prevails in the economy, the supply of factors of production is perfectly elastic and these factors are available at a constant rate of remuneration. The law of constant returns operates and prices do not rise with the increase in output. In such situation, output and employment will increase in the same proportion as the effective demand which will also increase in the same proportion as money supply. As soon as the point of full employment is reached, output will not increase with the increase in the money supply and effective demand: The elasticity of supply of output thus becomes zero and every change in the money supply will affect the prices which will rise in the same proportion as the effective demand. To sum up we can say that so long as there is unemployment in the economy any change in money supply will produce proportional changes in the output, without any effect on the prices; but as soon as the full employment is reached, changes in the money supply will produce proportionate changes in the prices. This reformulated quantity theory of money by Keynes can be illustrated with the help of Fig. 7.1.

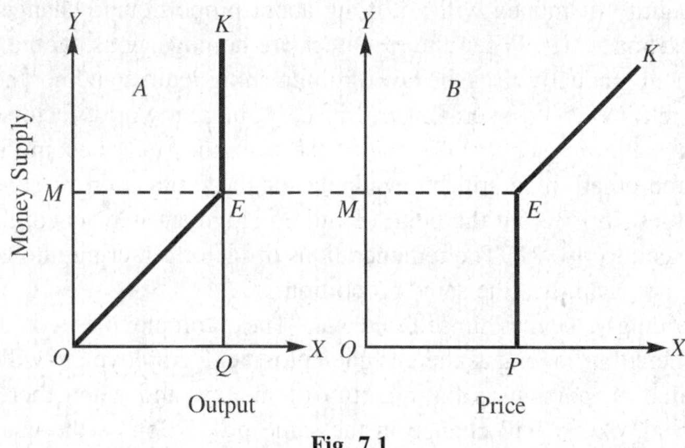

Fig. 7.1

Fig. 7.1 has two panels *A* and *B*. In panel *A* it has been shown that as soon as the money supply increases from *O* to *M*, the level of output also rises along the *OE* portion of the *OEK* curve. As the money supply reaches *OM* level, full employment output will be *OQ*. But after point *E* the output curve becomes vertical because any further increase in the money supply will not raise the output beyond *OQ*.

In panel *B* the relationship between money supply and prices has been shown. So long as economy is facing unemployment the increased money supply does not affect the prices. They start rising only after the full employment is reached. The figure shows that the price level *OP* remains constant with the money supply *OM* and corresponds with the full employment output *OQ*. An increase in the money supply above *OM* raises the prices in the same proportion as the money supply, this has been shown by the *EK* portion of the price curve *PEK*.

Assumptions of Keynesian Theory

The theory of Keynes is based on the following assumptions:

1. In a situation of unemployment all factors of production are perfectly elastic in their supply.
2. All unemployed factors are homogeneous and are interchangeable.
3. Law of constant returns is in operation and therefore prices do not alter with an increase in the output.
4. So long as there is unemployment, effective demand and quantity of money change in the same proportion.

Keynes was himself sceptical about these assumptions. He had realised that the real world was so complex that these simplified assumptions will not hold good. A number of complexities can arise. These can be: (*i*) The changes in the quantity of money will not bring about proportionate changes in the effective demand. (*ii*) When the resources are homogeneous, as the level of employment gradually rises the law of diminishing returns and not the law of constant returns would operate. (*iii*) Since, in the real world, factors are not interchangeable the supply of some of the resources may become inelastic while some others may still be available for the production of some other commodities. (*iv*) Before the point of full employment is reached, the wage unit will tend to rise. (*v*) The remunerations of factors entering into marginal cost may not change in the same proportion.

Accordingly, Keynes himself said that, "These complexities would qualify the statement that so long as there is unemployment, employment will change in the same proportion as the quantity of money, and when there is full employment, *prices* will change in the same proportion as the quantity of money."[3]

Critical Evaluation of Keynes' Theory

The Keynesian theory of money and prices has faced lot of criticism at the hands of the monetarists. According to them the theory suffers from the following shortcomings:

1. According to monetarists one shortcoming in the Keynesian theory is that, since it takes the prices as fixed one gets the impression that it analyses the effects of money, in terms of quantity of goods traded rather than in terms of their average price. This approach is an indirect one. Keynes has analysed the effects of monetary changes on economic activity through bond prices, interest rates and investment. But the monetarists feel that the monetary changes produce direct effects.

2. Milton Friedman, on the basis of empirical data, has established that the demand for money is highly stable, but according to Keynes monetary changes were largely swallowed by changes in the demand for money.

3. Keynes believed that money can be exchanged for bonds only, whereas, the monetarists believed that money can be exchanged for many other types of assets besides bonds like securities, physical assets, human wealth, etc.

4. Friedman has also criticised the Keynes theory on account of his argument that money hardly has any effect on income. According to Friedman the contraction of money supply leads to deflation or depression and therefore, it is wrong to say that money does not affect national income.

---

3. J.M. Keynes, *The General Theory of Employment, Interest and Money,* 1936, pp. 296-97.

Is the Keynesian Reformulation Superior to the Classical Quantity Theory of Money ?

Keynesian theory has been considered as superior to the classical quantity theory of money in a number of respects:

1. Unlike the classical economists Keynes does not consider the relationship between quantity of money and prices as direct and proportionate. He, therefore, establishes an indirect relationship between the two. While doing so, Keynes made the theory more realistic. His theory is not a pure monetary theory of prices like the quantity theory of money but it is a monetary theory of output and employment. His theory is thus an integration of both monetary theory as well as the theory of value. Not only this, it is also an integration of the monetary theory with the theory of output and employment. In other words, Keynes has integrated the monetary theory and theory of value through the theory of output in which the rate of interest has been allotted a predominant role. The Keynesian theory, thus, is superior to the classical quantity theory of money.

2. The classical theory of money is based on the assumption of full employment of resources which does not conform to the real life. On the other hand, Keynes holds that full employment is only an exception and in real life the economy operates below the level of full employment. Therefore, an increase in the quantity of money will cause proportionate increase in the level of output and employment, without any change in the price level. Hence, the Keynesian theory is superior to the classical quantity theory because it treats the relationship between the quantity of money and prices both in the unemployment and full employment conditions.

3. According to the classical quantity theory of money, every increase in the supply of money will lead to inflation. Keynes has established that so long as unemployment exists in the economy, the increases in the quantity of money will raise the price level only gradually and will not lead to inflation. It is only after the level of full employment is reached that the increases in the supply of money will lead to inflationary conditions.

4. Lastly, Keynes' theory of prices, as compared to the quantity theory of money, is of great importance for policy making. Increase in quantity of money, through deficit financing will be useful to wipe out unemployment from the economy.

Exercises

1. "So long as there is unemployment, *unemployment* will change in the same proportion as the quantity of money, and when there is full employment, *prices* will change in the same proportion as the quantity of money." (Keynes) Discuss.
2. The saving-investment theory can explain a number of things about the behaviour of money that the quantity theory cannot. Explain this statement.
3. Explain Keynes' analysis of the effects of changes in the quantity of money on the price level as presented in his *General Theory* and compare it with the Cambridge version of the quantity theory of money.
4. Discuss the view that price changes are better explained by Saving-Investment Theory than by the Traditional Quantity Theory of Money.
5. What are the shortcomings of the quantity theory of money? How does the income-expenditure approach is an improvement over it?
6. "The value of money, in fact, is a consequence of the total income rather than of the quantity of money." Discuss.

•••

Chapter 8

Friedman's Reformulation of Quantity Theory of Money

1. Introduction

The Chicago School under the leadership of Milton Friedman challenged the pure Keynesian view by arguing that an addition to the money supply will not be fully absorbed in idle balances. Instead, it may spill over into the market for goods and services, and thus have an immediate effect on the price level. This approach does not only revive the quantity theory but also has policy implications—so far as checking of inflation by controlling the rate at which money is being injected into the economy is concerned. We may now describe in brief the quantity theory as formulated by Friedman and his followers.

They maintain that wealth can be held in five broad forms, *viz.* money, bonds, equities, physical goods and human wealth. Each of these has distinctive characteristics and each offers some return in money or in kind. Money may yield a return in the form of money; for example, interest on deposits. But it is assumed that money yields its return solely in kind in the usual form of convenience and security, etc. It will make matters rather simple and will also not involve any loss of generality. So, the quantum of this return in 'real' terms per nominal unit of money clearly depends upon the volume of goods that unit corresponds to or on the general price level, which may be designated as *P*. If *P* falls, money appreciates and represents a capital gain in real terms which must be added to the nominal yield; and if *P* rises the real capital losses must be deducted from the nominal yield.

Bonds are those assets which yield a perpetual income stream of constant nominal amount. Their yield can be of two types: (*i*) the annual income, and (*ii*) any change in the price of bond over time—a return which can be positive as well as negative. If the rate of interest on the bonds is r_b, the nominal rate of return can be approximated by $r_b - (1/r_b)\, dr_b/dt$, where $(1/r_b)dr_b/d$ measures the rate of capital appreciation owing to changes in the rate of interest and *t* stands for time. This sum together with P defines the real return from holding of wealth in the form of bonds.

Equities are assets which yield a perpetual income stream of 'constant real' amount. The nominal return on equities can be in the form of either: (*i*) the constant nominal amount accuring annually in the absence of any change in P; or (*ii*) the increment or decrement to the nominal amount by way of adjustment to changes in P; or (*iii*) any change in the nominal price of the equity over time due to changes either in the interest rates, or in the price level. The nominal rate of return on equities can be approximated by $r_e + 1/p\ (dp/dt) - 1 r_e\ (dr_e/dt)$. This sum together with P is the real return from equities.

Physical goods are similar to equities, the only difference being that the annual stream they yield is in kind rather than in money. If we suppose that P applies equally to the value of these physical goods, then the nominal rate of return on them can be approximated as $1/p\ (dp/dt)$. Together with P, this sum would be the real return from holding wealth in the form of physical goods.

Human wealth is the discounted value of the expected stream of earned income. Since the market of human capital is a limited one, it is very difficult to define in market prices the terms of substitution of human capital for other forms of capital. Some substitution is always possible, say for example, people can sell assets in order to pay for training which will enhance their future income. The substitution of human capital for other forms of wealth takes place mainly through direct investment and disinvestment in the human agent. Regarding this form of capital therefore, the obstacles obstructing the alternative composition of wealth available to an individual cannot be expressed in terms of market prices or rates of return. Nevertheless, there is certainly, some rough division between human and non-human wealth in his portfolio of assets at any point of time and he may change this over time, but for the sake of simplification it may be treated as given at a point of time. Let w be the ratio of non-human to human wealth or of income from non-human to human wealth. The ultimate wealth owning unit is considered as dividing his wealth among the other forms so as to maximise utility subject to whatever restrictions affect the possibility of converting one form of wealth into another, This implies that he will seek an apportionment of this wealth such that the rate at which he can substitute one form of wealth for another is equal to the rate at which he is willing to do.

For determining the form of demand function, it would be appropriate to assume that the tastes and preferences of wealth owning units for the service streams arising from different forms of wealth are constant over considerable stretches of space and time. Explicit provision can, however, be made for some changes to the extent these are related to objective circumstances. For example, other things being equal, people want to hold a larger portion of their wealth in the form of money when they are moving around geographically or subject to unusual uncertainty than otherwise. Let u be any such variable. By combining all the factors described above we can obtain the following demand function for money:

$$M = f\left(P, r_b - \frac{1}{r_b} \times \frac{dr_b}{dt}, r_e + \frac{1}{p} \times \frac{dp}{dt} - \frac{1}{r} \times \frac{dr_e}{dt}, \frac{1}{p} \times \frac{dp}{dt}, w \frac{y}{r}, u\right)$$

where $\frac{y}{r}$ is the total wealth (it includes broadly all sources of income or consumable services). From this point of view, rate of interest expresses the relationship between the stock which is wealth and the flow which is income, so that if y be the total flow of income and r the rate of interest, the total wealth $w = y/r$.

Friedman holds that the most important factors influencing the demand for money are the rates of return from the different forms of wealth, the level of permanent income and the ratio of non-human to total wealth. For example, an increase in the expectation of inflation would cause a fall in the demand for money holdings, that is, a rise in velocity. Thus, velocity instead of being constant (as was assumed by classical and neo-classical writers) would now be affected by changes in the above variables. But these variables are generally subject to only slow change over time while the supply of money may undergo sudden changes. If this is so, then it means that the demand for money is independent of its supply. In other words, there is complete independence between the money stock and its velocity—which is an important element in the reformulated theory. It also means that the changes in the value of money are almost always determined by supply. Another important postulate of the theory is that the demand for money is normally insensitive to changes in the interest rate. Had the demand for money been substantially interest-elastic, then any change in the money stock could be absorbed by a comparatively small change in the interest rates inducing people to extend their demand for money to match the supply. In such a situation, a change in the money stock would be of no significance. On the other hand, if the demand for money was substantially interest-elastic, people instead of holding an additional money would spend on goods and services influencing the level of money incomes in the economy. Thus, interest rate insensitivity implies that the transactions motive dominates the assets motive in the total demand for money. It is because money as an asset, is able to act as a temporary abode of purchasing power, that the relationship between changes in the monetary variable and increased expenditures is more indirect and more complex than assumed by the classical economists. That is why, modern economists do not consider monetary policy as a viable counter-cyclical measure.

Friedman has made use of the fundamental principle of the theory of capital, that income is the yield of capital, and capital is the present value of income, in his analysis, which is the most important contribution to the development of monetary theory. Its theoretical significance lies in the conceptual integration of wealth and income as influences on behaviour. Although Keynes completely ignored the influence of wealth even in short-term analysis, the subsequent economists, following his tradition, have however, re-introduced it. But they have generally followed the Cambridge pattern of restricting wealth to non-human property—which treats wealth and income as entirely independent influences on behaviour. Consequently, this has led to faulty theoretical reasoning making it entirely redundant from the application point of view.

Friedman's analysis has one more important implication and that is related to the nature of the concept of income relevant to monetary analysis. He uses 'income' as the expected yield of wealth and not as is generally used in computing national income.

2. Basic Constituents of Friedman's Theory

We give below the basic constituents of the Friedman's quantity theory of money:

1. Wealth Theory of Demand for Money. Friedman's quantity theory of money is neither a theory of the price level nor that of money income or output. It is a wealth theory of demand for money. Friedman has used the term wealth in a very broad sense. Anything which can generate an income stream is wealth. That is why he includes even human capital into wealth. According to him as already stated above, wealth can be found in five forms, namely, (*i*) money, (*ii*) bonds, (*iii*) equities, (*iv*) physical assets, and (*v*) human capital. Money according to him is "durable consumer goods held for the services it renders, and leading a flow of services proportional to the stock". Therefore, the demand for money arises because it is an asset or capital.

2. General Demand Theory. Friedman has applied the general demand theory for consumer goods, to the demand for money. As in the case of general theory of demand Friedman assumes that the tastes and preferences of people who want to held money are constant over a long time. Accordingly the households, which are the wealth-holders consider money as a durable consumer good. Friedman further assumes that with an increase in the stock of money held, its marginal service yield diminishes in comparison to the yield of other assets. Thus, the law of diminishing marginal rate of substitution applies to money.

3. Determinants of Demand for Money. According to Friedman the demand for money depends on three major factors: (*i*) wealth held in various forms of assets; (*ii*) relative price of and return on different forms of wealth and (*iii*) tastes and preferences of the wealth-holders. People's desire to hold cash balances is determined and affected by: (*a*) the rate of interest, and (*b*) the expected variation in the price level. An increase in these would make the cash balances to fall while a decrease will make the cash balances to increase.

Demand for Money Function

Friedman has given the following equations for explaining the demand for money function:

$M = f(Y, W, P, r_b, r_e, r_c, \text{u})$

$M =$ aggregate demand for money; $Y =$ total flow of income;

$W =$ ratio of non-human to human wealth; $P =$ price level;

$r_b =$ market bond interest rate; r_e, equity yields; $r_e =$ expected rate of change of prices of commodities and u = utility determined variables which tend to influence tastes and preferences.

In the above equation the demand for money function is independent of the normal units used for measuring money variables which means that the demand for money changes in proportion to the changes in the unit in which prices and money income are indicated. It thus expresses that if price level and money increase to λ times their original level, demand for money also increases to λ times its original quantity, this can be expressed as follows:

$$\lambda M = F(\lambda Y, W, \lambda P, r_b, r_e, r_e, \text{u})$$

In this equation λ is replaced by $\frac{1}{Y}$, it adopts the form of the quantity theory of money as follows:

$$\frac{M}{Y} = f\left(W, \frac{P}{Y}, r_b, r_e, r_c, \text{u}\right) = \frac{1}{v\left(W, \frac{Y}{P}, r_b, r_e, r_c, \text{u}\right)}$$

$$Y = f\left(W, \frac{Y}{P}, r_b, r_e, r_c, \text{u}\right), M$$

Thus, according to Friedman, a change in the stock of money brings about changes in the same direction in the price level or income or both. So long as the demand for money remains stable, a change in its supply will bring about change in the price level. The money supply also affects the real value of national income and economic activity, only in the short period. Friedman firmly holds that as long as the demand for money remains stable the effects of changes in the money supply on total expenditure and income can be predicted. If the economy is operating at less than full employment, an increase in the supply of money will increase the level of output and employment through an increase in aggregate expenditure. But this will apply only to a very short period, because other factors will come into operation to bring the economy back to less than full employment level. That is why Friedman and his followers believed that the supply of money does not affect the real variables in the long run. When the economy is operating at full employment level an increase in the supply of money will raise the price level.

Fig 8.1 explains Friedman's quantity theory of money:

In Fig.8.1 income (*Y*) has been shown on the vertical axis and the demand and supply of money (*M*) have been shown on the horizontal axis. *ODm* (45° line) is the demand curve of money and *MS* is the supply curve of money. *Dm* curve varies with income, while *MS* curve is perfectly income-inelastic. These curves intersect at *E* and therefore, *OY* is the equilibrium income. When the supply of money rises, the *MS* curve shifts to the right to *M′S′*. Consequently the supply of money exceeds the demand, the total expenditure increases and the new demand and supply

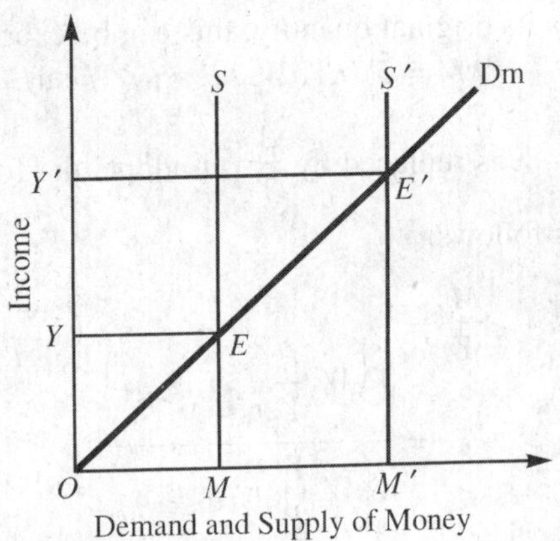

Fig. 8.1

of Money equilibrium is established at *E′* between *Dm* and *M′S′* curves. The income increases from *OY* to *OY′*.

3. Importance of Friedman's Theory

The importance of Friedman's theory lies in the following:

1. The Role of Price Level. Friedman and his followers have given prime importance to the price level in the demand function of money. It is the price level which establishes an equilibrium between its demand and supply. It is the link between money and inflation.

2. The Changes in Income Velocity. According to Friedman, cyclical changes in income velocity are caused by cyclical changes in the current income as related to permanent income, as against Keynesians, who believed that cyclical movements bring about changes in the interest rate. Consequently, during a period of boom the demand for money increases in proportion to an increase in the permanent income but less than proportionate to an increase in the current income because the rise in permanent income during the period of business expansion is less than the current income. It means that during a period of prosperity the income velocity rises. During recession the permanent income and demand for money change proportionately to each other, but less than proportionately in comparison to current income, and therefore, the income velocity declines.

3. Stability of Demand Function. By stability of demand function Friedman means that it is stable in terms of the variables which determine its value. It does not mean a constant velocity. Therefore, any increase in velocity during inflation or decrease in velocity during deflation is consistent with functional stability.

4. Marginal Role of Rate of Interest. Friedman considers that the rate of interest has very little role to play in influencing the demand for money.

5. Expected Inflation. Friedman holds that the expected rate of inflation is an important variable which affects the demand for money.

6. Importance of Monetary Policy. Friedman holds that since the demand for money remains stable, the monetary authority can only control its supply, and therefore the monetary authority should concentrate only on monetary policy to stabilise the economy. This is because Friedman assumes that the demand for money is interest-inelastic while Keynes and his followers assume a very low interest-elasticity of the investment function.

4. Criticisms of Friedman's Reformulated Quantity Theory of Money

Friedman's theory has been criticised on a number of counts as given below:

1. Friedman in his definition of money includes not only currency and demand deposits, but time deposits with commercial banks as well. This means that the demand for money will not be very much interest-elastic. If the interest

on time deposits increases, their demand will rise. But, at the same time the demand for currency and demand deposits will fall. So the effect of the rate of interest on the demand for money would be just very little. Again, Friedman does not make a choice between long and short-term rates of interest because in practice, for demand deposits a short-term rate will be preferable and for the time deposits a long-term rate will be preferable. Hence, such a rate of interest structure will definitely influence the demand for money.

2. Friedman, in his demand for money function prefers wealth variables to income. He holds that both wealth and income variables operate simultaneously, which is not correct. According to Johnson, "Wealth is the present value of income which is the return on wealth."

3. By including time deposits in the arena of money Friedman has considered money as a luxury good, most probably because he found that in the United States the trend rate of the money supply was higher than the income. But it is not so with every economy.

4. According to Friedman money supply is exogenous, because it is changed by the monetary authorities in an exogenous manner. His findings are based on the data collected from the United States. The neo-Keynesians who have verified the data hold that even in the USA the money supply is not exclusively exogenous; it contains lot of endogenous element in it.

5. Friedman has failed to recognise the importance of factors like prices, output, rate of interest, etc. in affecting the money supply.

6. Professor Kaldor[1] has found no evidence in support of a positive correlation between money supply and money GNP established by Friedman. According to Kaldor, in Britain, the best correlation is to be found between the quarterly variations in the cash holdings of the public held in the form of currency notes and coins and corresponding changes in personal consumption at market prices.

7. Friedman has not indicated the length of the period of time to which his theory would be applicable.

The validity of these criticisms can hardly be questioned. But, Friedman's contribution to the theory of money can also not be pushed aside.

Johnson[2] has rightly said that, "Friedman's application to monetary theory of the basic principle of capital theory is probably the most important development in monetary theory since Keynes' *General Theory.* Its theoretical significance lies in the conceptual integration of wealth and income as influences on behaviour."

1. N. Kaldor, "The New Monetarism", *L.E.R.,* July 1970.
2. H.G. Johnson, "Recent Developments in Monetary Theory", *I.E.R.,* Feb., 1963.

5. Friedman and Keynes—A Comparison

Both Friedman and Keynes have used the demand for money function in their analysis, but there is a vast difference between the concept of demand for money function used by both the economists. These differences are given below:

1. Friedman considers money as an asset or capital good serving as a temporary abode of purchasing power. People hold it because it provides a stream of income or consumable services. On the other hand, Keynes includes in money, only demand deposits and non-interest bearing debt of the government. Thus, Friedman has used a much wider definition of money than Keynes for explaining the demand for money function.

2. In Friedman's analysis the demand for money is a function of many variables, for example, the yield on money, the yield on bonds, the yield on securities, the yield on physical assets and the yield on other assets. In the Keynesian system the demand for money is confined to bonds only where the rates of interest indicate the cost of holding it.

3. Both economists have explained differently the effects of changes in the quantity of money on the economic activity. While Keynes held that changes in money supply affect economic activity indirectly through prices of bonds and rates of interest, in the Friedman's system monetary changes directly affect prices and production of all goods and interest rates have only a marginal role to play.

4. According to Friedman people hold money balances for a variety of purposes and in different forms, like cash money, physical assets, total wealth, human wealth, etc. But, according to Keynes money balances are held by the people only for three motives, namely, transactions, precautionary and speculative motives.

5. Lastly, while Friedman has drawn a distinction between permanent income and nominal income and has used it in his theory, Keynes has not made any such distinction. According to Friedman, permanent income is that "which a wealth-holder can consume while keeping his wealth intact and nominal income is one which is measured in the current units of currency, and is determined by both prices and quantity of goods traded."

Exercises

1. Discuss briefly Milton Friedman's version of the quantity theory of money. In what way is it superior to the classical quantity theory of money?
2. Examine critically the statement that the revised version of the quantity theory of money is that there exists a stable demand function for real money holdings.
3. Explain the contribution of Milton Friedman to the quantity theory of money.
4. Explain Friedman's reformulation of the quantity theory of money. How does it differ from that of Keynes?

•••

Friedman and Keynes—A Comparison

Exercises

Chapter 9

Measurement of Changes in the Value of Money

1. Introduction

In the previous chapters we have analysed various theories propounded from time to time for the determination of the value of money. Now we take up the problem of the measurement of the value of money. Although Crowther tried to tide over this difficulty by indicating three standard values of money, for example, the wholesale prices of goods and services, the retail prices of goods and services and the rate of wages payable to labour, the difficulty however remained unsolved. Regarding the wholesale prices of goods and services it may be said that it is not any easy task to club various commodities into a class or group. Similarly, the variations in the retail prices of commodities and services are so rapid and frequent that to find out an average or mean of these changes is really a hard nut to crack. Likewise, the rate of wages payable to labour also changes from time to time and cannot be regarded as a standard measure of the value of money; especially these days when the trade unions are so strong. It would, therefore, be appropriate to say that there is no absolute measure of the value of money. Actually what we are really concerned with is the changes in the value of money as related to other periods. Theoretically, the value of a commodity like gold makes no difference to anyone, because, it does not matter to the world whether the general level of prices is high or low, but what does matter is the process of rising or falling of the general level of prices, that is to say, the change from one general level of prices to another. Theoretically, again, even this should not matter if all prices rise or fall simultaneously and proportionately all around, because no one would be in any way worse or better. But that is just what does not happen. We are thus interested not in measuring the absolute value of money but only in knowing the rate of fluctuations. The changes in the value of money bring changes in the distribution of real income which bring different effects on various sections of society and various sectors of the economy. These changes are important to all people who are in receipt of money incomes and to those who are engaged in the buying or selling of commodities or services. Let us for the moment not take into account those persons who are paid in kind. For example, transport employees, certain sections of the government employees, hotel employees, railway servants are provided with uniforms; domestic servants, hotel employees and workers in hospitals receive free board and lodging; railway employees enjoy also a certain amount of free travel, etc. To the extent wages are paid in kind, a measure of immunity is provided from fluctuations in the value of money. The foremost and most important drawback in the use of money as a medium of exchange or a unit of account or store of value is that it is not a stable measure like a yard or a pint or a litre; it is always changing in value. Another drawback is that its value in terms of different commodities and services does not change to the same extent nor always in the same direction. When these changes are gradual and hardly noticeable, they are of little importance. But when they are on a large scale, they can have serious consequences as has been experienced during the 20th century. Changes in the value of money make their effects felt in two main directions: (*i*) on the level of production and employment, and (*ii*) on the distribution of income.

2. Effects on Production and Employment

Let us first consider the effects of the changes in the value of money on the level of production and employment. In the event of falling prices, there would not be at any particular point of time a proportionate fall in the prices of all commodities and services. The prices of finished products used for immediate consumption will fall almost immediately, and in the case of primary products, like foodstuffs and raw materials, prices may even fall quite sharply. But the cost of production in the case of almost all commodities will not fall proportionately; in other words, in some the fall may be very little while in others it may be very high. For example, rent and rates and other fixed charges will remain fixed for some time; the prices of raw materials, contracts for the purchase of which have already been entered into will not fall. Wages are likely to fall very slightly. Since the cost of production is generally incurred at the time of starting production which if begun at a higher level of prices than those prevailing at the time when the commodity is offered for sale in the market, obviously the profit margin will be less than was anticipated, and in the case of a steep fall in prices, the entrepreneur may even incur a loss. It would thus, be seen that in the event of falling prices, there is a greater risk involved for the entrepreneur and it will be natural on his part to be more cautious and to restrict output. This sort of caution on his part would undoubtedly increase the level of unemployment and the concomitant result would be that the general level of total demand will fall. This assumes the shape of a circle and leads entrepreneurs to have pessimistic estimates about future and curtail their production further; and the circle goes on. In short, we can say that falling prices check business activity' and increase unemployment and that is why the growth economists do not favour a policy of deflation or falling prices. While falling prices may be detrimental to the interests of the economy as a whole, certain sections do benefit by them. They are to the advantage of creditors who in real terms receive more value of their money than what they had at the time of advancing the loan. The consumers are also benefited as the unit of money they spend fetches more quantity of commodities and services. But, on the other hand, the debtors suffer because they have to pay more in real terms than what they had received at the time of accepting the loan; the government too finds it more difficult to balance its budget in these circumstances, since its income from taxes will fall, while much of its expenditure remains unchanged.

The effect of rising prices on production is just the opposite. Since costs do not rise as rapidly as prices, profit margins are generally greater than were anticipated. This creates a feeling of optimism among the entrepreneurs who are encouraged to expand their production and consequently the level of employment and total demand is further stimulated. Until full employment is reached, the rise in prices will generally be only of moderate extent, but if demand continues to expand beyond this point the prices will begin to rise more rapidly. If the prices are increasing gradually then production will be stimulated. To maintain a high level of employment, a rising price level seems to be essential, especially gently rising price level. That is why most of the modern economists have agreed that for the maintenance of economic growth and development there should be controlled inflation. In a period of high employment, a reduction in the total volume of purchasing power through a contraction of credit is generally effective in checking a further fall in the value of money but the result is curtailment of production. An attempt to stimulate production through an expansion of the volume of purchasing power may not always be successful; the result may be an increase in the demand to hold money instead of an increase in consumers' demand. In recent decades, however, it has not only stimulated production but has also led to inflation. From the social point of view, a prolonged period of rising or falling prices tends to bring speculation and sometimes boom of business activity comes to crash like the great crash of Wall Street.

3. Effects on Redistribution of Incomes

In the field of distribution, the changes in the value of money bring far reaching effects. A society is generally composed of a number of classes of people, for example: (*i*) people with fixed incomes; (*ii*) people whose incomes though fixed in the short period can be adjusted to changes in the value of money like lawyers, doctors, etc.; and (*iii*) people whose incomes vary with the changes in the value of money, for example, businessmen and entrepreneurs. But this sort of classification is not rigid and any number of persons can be covered under one or more of these groups.

The most serious effect of a change in the value of money is that it brings about an arbitrary redistribution of incomes. When the value of money is falling, some people may receive the same income as before, many others may find that although their incomes have increased, they have not kept pace with the rise in prices; and on the other hand, some people may find that their incomes have increased more than the rise in the prices of commodities and services. People with fixed incomes find that their real incomes fall when the value of money falls and rise when the value of money rises. This group includes old people who have retired from work and who are living on fixed pensions; people who are still engaged in some kind of jobs—there are many whose salaries are fixed or are subject to revision only at longer intervals. There are many salaried workers, too, whose salaries are adjusted only if a considerable change in the value of money has taken place. As a result, all those people who are on fixed incomes find that their real incomes fall considerably with rise in prices. In our country, until recently pensions received by the retired people were in the form of annuities which remained fixed in amount whatever happened to the cost of living. However, in the UK and other European countries pensions in general are reviewed annually and increases are awarded according to the rise in the cost of living. National Insurance pensions are also reviewed annually, many firms in private industry, for example, banks and insurance companies, periodically adjust the pensions of retired employees. Nevertheless, there is often quite a considerable time lag between a fall in the value of money and increase in pensions. Thus, a fall in the value of money or a rise in prices adversely affects a large number of people in the society.

People who derive their incomes chiefly from the profits of industry or whose incomes consist of fees based on current prices are generally benefited by rising prices. Since all costs of production do not immediately increase, or at least to the same extent, profits rise with the rise in prices. Rising prices, too give a boost to production which also raises the margin of profits, unless the government in its attempt to check inflation restricts the distribution of dividends as a part of an income policy. Increased turnover resulting in greater profits will, too, more than compensate the owners of many small businesses for the rise in prices. However, when the value of money is increasing or when the prices are falling, the incomes of this group of people will probably fall to a greater extent than prices; since production will be checked and profits more than proportionately reduced. Since, however, the long-term tendency is for prices to rise, and in recent decades to rise rapidly, the periods when profit-receivers gain are likely to be more frequent than those when they suffer from changes in the value of money.

In between those with fixed incomes and the profit-receivers or the entrepreneurs are the wage-earners. A fall in the value of money may not always be immediately followed by a rise in wages but a rise in the cost of living has always been put forward as a strong argument in support of a rise in the existing level of wages. Although, during periods of rising prices the entrepreneurs generally feel inclined to meet demands for higher wages, there has always been a short time-lag between the two events. This time-lag would be more pronounced if there is considerable unemployment before the rise in prices begins and the wages are not likely to rise much until the unemployed people have been absorbed. When, however, full employment has been reached, both prices and wages will tend to move upwards more rapidly. Once inflation is in its full swing the demand for labour will exceed the supply and wage demands will become more insistent. Competition among employers for the available workers would also tend to raise wages. Since the rising demand for labour will not be equally spread over all occupations, wages in those industries where trade union is the strongest or where the work is not to the liking of the workers, either on account of its unpleasantness or because of the awkwardness of the working hours, will rise more than the average. And if the period of inflation is quite long then wages may even rise more than the rise in prices. In times of pronounced inflation, wages of unskilled workers also tend to rise relatively to the wages of skilled workers.

In some circumstances, there would be a time-lag between the increase in the value of money and fall in the wages and so in such periods, the real wages of workers will tend to rise. Since, however, in these circumstances, the level of production will also fall, many workers will be thrown out of job and so only those who are able to retain their jobs benefit from the increase in the value of money. Recent experience has shown that reduction in the wages of workers in manufacturing industries has become increasingly difficult owing to the growing strength of trade unions and consequently, falling prices have tended to reduce the total amount paid in wages through an increase in unemployment rather than through wage reduction. In agriculture, however, wage reductions under such conditions are more severe, but there is less unemployment. Some of the governments may follow a severe deflationary policy and may adopt extreme measures to reduce the incomes of salaried people, as happened in 1931 in the UK when a supplementary budget was brought in to reduce the pay of civil servants, local government employees, teachers, members of parliament, armed forces and the unemployed. During the 19th century in the ups and downs of trade cycles, the wage earners were generally worse off during periods of rising prices and better off during periods of falling prices, but in a prolonged period of high employment as happened since World War II wage earners have increased their real wages in spite of rising prices. The time-lag in the case of salaried workers used to be much more pronounced and since unemployment in their case is much rarer, their real incomes used to rise and fall in the reverse ratio to the rise and fall in the value of money.

4. Other Effects of Changes in the Value of Money

Let us make a passing reference to some other effects of changes in the value of money. Since all prices do not change in the same proportion and all people do not purchase the same assortment of goods, the extent to which a particular individual or family is affected will depend on the fluctuations in the prices of those commodities which they are accustomed to use. This may aggravate or alleviate the effect of the redistribution of income brought about by the general price changes. If the redistribution of income is in favour of the lower paid groups of workers, there will be a tendency for the prices of the commodities they use to rise as a result of increase in total demand. There is likely, too, to be less saving, since the real incomes will be less than formerly and also that the declining real value of past savings will act as a deterrent to future savings. A fall in the value of money provides benefit to all debtors including the government, which finds the burden of the interest payments on the national debt reduced. The limited companies would find the burden increased, householder with a heavy mortgage on his property and the man who has bought goods on the hire-purchase system would be at a disadvantage. When debtors gain, creditors lose and vice versa. Periods of rising and falling prices associated with the trade cycle alternated with one another with great regularity during the 19th century, and so both periods when some people were gaining while others were losing were not only relatively short but to some extent cancelled out, though not quite because of the long-term tendency for prices to rise.

The government may also adopt the redistribution of incomes as a deliberate policy. It may be desirable when the inequalities of incomes are great. But to resort to redistribution of incomes through changes in the value of money is fraught with danger. It may be arbitrary and in some circumstances may actually accentuate inequality. So, if at all the government thinks that redistribution of incomes is necessary, it should adopt other means. From the point of view of personal income, reasonable stability in the value of money is desirable but since a generally rising price level appears to be necessary for maintaining full employment, it has become necessary to try to mitigate the hardships imposed on some sections of the community by these conditions. Thus, wages and salaries nowadays have a tendency to run ahead of prices. In our country, most people in receipt of pensions have during recent years been awarded periodic increases. It is, therefore, gradually being realised that the incomes of retired people should be increased not merely to keep pace with a rising cost of living but to enable them to share with others the benefits of economic growth. Finally, it may be stated that during recent years, due to the prolonged period of rising prices, the government securities have depreciated and people have realised that fixed-interest stocks offer no protection against inflation for their savings, an increasing number of people have now turned to unit trusts as a hedge against the continued depreciation in the value of money.

5. Measurement of Changes in the Value of Money

Though the value of money cannot be measured, attempts have been made to measure the changes in the value of money with the help of index numbers. As we all know, the prices of all commodities and services do not register a rise or fall simultaneously; the prices of some commodities and services fall when the prices of others rise. Prices of some commodities and services rise in greater proportion, while those of others rise in smaller proportion. The prices of certain commodities may not change at all and so, if we find out the average of the fluctuations in the prices of various commodities and services, we can generally know whether the general price level has risen or fallen. This averaging of the prices of various commodities and services on which money is spent is called the price-level and a series, of price-levels is called the index number. Index numbers are numbers which represent the price of chosen commodity or group of commodities at a selected date which is used as a standard with which we may compare the prices of the same commodity or group of commodities at a subsequent date. They are figures of price-levels arranged in a tabular form with a view to showing the changes in the prices of goods and services for the purpose of indicating the fluctuations in the value of money. Index numbers show, at a glance, variations in the prices of articles with the corresponding changes in the value of money. In the construction of index numbers, a large number of goods in general use are selected, the price of a certain quantity of a particular quality of each commodity is ascertained. Later on, say at intervals of months or years, the price of the same quantity of each of the commodities is again taken, and the new figure in each case is compared with that formerly recorded. The difference is calculated as a percentage, and the total of these percentages indicates the movement of the general level of prices.

Index numbers are to be constructed for some specific purpose. Broadly speaking, index numbers are constructed to give an idea of the general price level of the itmes included in the list for the construction of index numbers. We have earlier mentioned that from the point of view of value of money some standard for the determination of its value has to be taken. Crowther and Robertson talk of wholesale prices. Keynes, on other hand, is in favour of the use of index numbers of retail prices. He says: "An index number of the purchasing power of money should include directly or indirectly, once and once only, all the items which enter into final consumption."[1] Some economists have used wage index numbers to measure changes in the value of money. In all cases, the principle is the same: a base year is selected and the prices of a group of commodities in that year are noted. The index number for the base year is 100 and changes are shown as a percentage variation from the base. Thus, a rise of 10 per cent in prices is compared with the base year would give an index number of 110 and a fall of 5 per cent an index of 95, the value of money, of course, changing in inverse proportion to the index number. Since the value of money can be calculated with perfect accuracy only in terms of a single commodity or service, the smaller the group selected and the greater its homogeneity, the more accurately will the index number reflect price changes. It was partly for this reason and partly due to the absence of data for constructing other types of index numbers that the earliest index numbers were for wholesale prices. Even if all these index numbers of wholesale prices had the same base year, the resulting index numbers would not be the same, since they did not cover exactly the same group of commodities. Moreover, wholesale prices relate mainly to raw materials and do not include services which are an important source of changes in the level of prices in the long periods. Again, wholesale prices are subject to wide variations during short periods due to the specialised nature of such articles. It was not until the early years of the twentieth century that an attempt was made to compile an index of retail prices. In this case the difficulty of selecting the items to be included was much greater than with wholesale prices, since at that time to a greater extent than today there was wide variation in the size of incomes, with even greater variations in the ways in which they were spent. Again, there is no combination of goods and services which must be considered as representative for even the same class of people under different circumstances. Crowther has rightly pointed out: "Strictly speaking, everybody has a particular selection of goods which he is interested in and even this individual price average changes with alternations in his circumstances like tastes, income and surrounding."[2] Not only this, lack of uniform level of

1. J.M Keynes, *A Treatise on Money,* p. 57.
2. G. Crowther, *op: cit.,* p. 87.

consumer's goods prices which vary from place to place and even from one shop to another in the same place, makes the selection of prices a difficult task.

The construction of wage index numbers has been advocated due to the fact that wages enter into the prices of all the commodities. But, there are different kinds of labour and we cannot get an average price of labour wages. Moreover, wages tend to be 'sticky' and there is always a time-lag between the rise and fall in prices and the fall and rise in wages. Thus, there is great difficultly in selecting some standard through which changes in the value of money may be measured. It has, therefore, been considered desirable to use different types of index numbers for different purposes. If the purpose is to measure the changes in the value of money with reference to wholesale dealers or market then wholesale prices are taken as standard; and if the purpose is to measure fluctuations in the value of money with reference to real income of the people, the consumers index numbers or the retail price index numbers are used.

6. Methods of Preparing Index Numbers

The primary principles for constructing an index number are given below:

1. Purpose. As stated earlier, the type of index number is to be determined according to the purpose which it is required to serve. If the purpose is to study the effects of the changes in the value of money on the workers and consumers, then a retail price index number is to be constructed, and if we propose to study the effects of the changes in the value of money on entrepreneurs and traders, then we have to use the wholesale price index number. It would be worthwhile to quote Haberler in this connection. He says "The general price level is not a given, self-evident fact, but a theoretical abstraction. It is a scientific tool which has to serve for certain scientific and practical purpose.... An economically relevant definition of price level cannot be independent of the purpose in mind, and for each purpose a separate index number must be computed."[3]

2. Selection of Commodities. After having decided the purpose of constructing an index number we have to select the number and kinds of the commodities. The commodities selected should be representative of the tastes, habits and customs of people, should be cognizable and unlikely to vary in quality. If the purpose is to construct the index number for measuring the value of money for the entire country, it is necessary to select commodities which are representative of the entire country because it is impossible to include

3. G. von Haberler, "The Meaning and Uses of a General Price Index", *Quarterly Journal of Economics,* 1928, pp. 435-36.

the prices of each and every commodity and service available at a particular point of time. If we want to know the changes that the fluctuations in the value of money have caused in the cost of living of the working classes, then we must select only those commodities which are generally consumed by the workers. Mitchell, however, pleaded that the number of commodities chosen was not of great importance, if our objective is to indicate broad movements of prices. But he did say that the number of commodity groups should be large enough to present a comprehensive picture of the economy.

3. Selection of the Base Year. An appropriate year has then to be selected in terms of which the price change in other years shall be expressed as percentages. This particular year will be known as the base year. While selecting the base year, care must be exercised towards selecting neither too prosperous nor too depressed years from the point of view of economic conditions in general. So, the base year should be such that prices by and large in such a year must have been normal. According to Crowther, "Any period will do, but it is necessary to have some base to which later prices can be compared, just as every map maker must have a datumline to which he can refer altitudes."[4] This base year may be: (*a*) fixed base, or (*b*) chain base. In the fixed base method, the average price of a particular year is taken as the base; alternatively average of prices during several years, say, a period, is taken as the base price. A base period is superior to the base year in the sense that it is less affected by chance variation and is more representative. Under the chain base or shifting base method, the prices relative for each year are calculated upon the prices of the preceding year.

4. Collection of Price Data. The selection of prices of commodities and services is also very important. The easiest method could be to collect market quotations from journals, newspapers, etc. but, it is necessary to ensure that the prices quoted therein are representative of the large volume of transactions, otherwise there is likelihood of an error. In case the index number relates to the workers' cost of living then the prices should be collected from markets where the workers make bulk of their purchases. It is, therefore, necessary that proper care is taken to collect price data from right sources so that the index number does not present a distorted picture.

5. Averaging. After determining the purpose and selecting commodities, base year and the prices, the final act is to find out the average of prices both in the base year as well as in the subsequent year. The price of each commodity during the base period is treated as equal to 100 and that for the period under enquiry is stated as a percentage of the price during the base period. This is known by dividing the price of the period under enquiry by the base price and

4. G. Crowther, *op. cit.*, p. 87.

multiplying the whole by hundred. For instance, the price of wheat during a base period is Rs. 10 a kilogram and that for the period under enquiry is Rs. 15 a kilogram, the percentage figure will be $\frac{15}{10}\times 100 = 150$. And finally, the average of such numbers is obtained which gives the required index number.

The following is the specimen of an index number of retail prices:

Index Number of Prices of Certain Commodities in 1997 Base Year = 1983

Articles	*Prices in Base Year*	*Indices of Base Year*	*Prices in 1997*	*Indices for 1997*
Wheat	Rs. 50 per qtl.	100	Rs. 150 per qtl.	300.00
Rice	Rs. 125 per qtl.	100	Rs. 625 per qtl.	500.00
Cloth	Rs. 2.00 per metre	100	Rs. 8.00 per metre	400.00
Sugar	Rs. 100 per qtl.	100	Rs. 300 per qtl.	300.00
Ghee	Rs. 5.00 per kilo	100	Rs. 26.25 per kilo	525.00
Milk	Re. 1.00 per lt.	100	Rs. 3.00 per lt.	300.00
		100		2325.00
				Average = 2325 ÷ 6 = 387.50

According to the above table, there has been a rise of 287.50 per cent in the prices of the commodities concerned in 1997 as compared to prices in 1983. This means that the value of money has gone down by more than 2/5 of what it was in 1983.

7. Weighted Index Numbers

The above method for the construction of index numbers gives equal importance to all commodities. In practical life, we attach different importance to different items of consumption. In order to give proper places to various items concerned, taking in view their importance in consumption, weights are attached to commodities in proportion to their relative importance. For example, if the general people spend a major portion of their income on wheat, cloth and milk, then these commodities will be given greater weight and if generally speaking, people give less importance to items like sugar, *desi ghee*, then smaller weight is to be given to these commodities in the index number. After attaching weights, the current indices of each item are multiplied by the respective weights which gives the weighted indices of the commodity for the period under enquiry. The weighted indices are then added up and divided by the total of weights which gives the index number required. The following table is a specimen of weighted index number.

Weighted Index Number of Prices of Certain Commodities in 1997 Base Year = 1983

Arti-cles	*Wei-ghts*	*Base Year Prices*	*Indices of Prices in Base Year*	*1997 Prices*	*Indices of 1997 Prices*
Wheat	4	Rs.50 per qtl.	100 × 4 = 400	Rs. 150 per qtl.	300 × 4 = 1200
Rice	1	Rs.125 per qtl.	100 × 1 = 100	Rs. 625 per qtl.	500 × 1 = 500
Cloth	2	Rs.2.00 per metre	100 × 2 = 200	Rs. 8.00 per metre	400 × 2 = 800
Sugar	1	Rs.100 per qtl.	100 × 1 = 100	Rs. 300 per qtl.	300 × 1 = 300
Ghee	1	Rs.5.00 per kilo	100 × 1 = 100	Rs. 26.25 per kilo	525 × 1 = 525
Milk	1	Re.1.00 per litre	100 × 1 = 100	Rs. 3.00 per litre	300 × 1 = 300
Total	10		1000		3625
Average			1000 ÷ 10 = 100		3625 ÷ 10 = 362.50

By attaching weights to the same items in above example, the index number shows that the prices have gone up by 262.50 per cent instead of 287.50 per cent as shown by simple index numbers.

8. Difficulties in the Construction of Index Numbers

The construction of index numbers is full of difficulties—theoretical as well as practical. Theoretically, one finds that index numbers are mere approximations and can be interpreted in more than one way. Secondly, international comparisons become difficult on account of different bases, different sets of commodities or differences in their quality or quantity. Thirdly, comparisons between different times and places are also not easy and are rendered invalid as several commodities are replaced by others. Fourthly, it is not easy to ascertain whether relative expenditure has remained the same or changed and if so, to what extent. Among the practical difficulties, the foremost one is in regard to obtain reliable data about prices. We all know that collection of statistics of prices is not only costly but is also difficult to manage. It is easy to obtain the prices of goods in organised markets but for commodities sold in the retail market, it is rather impossible to get reliable data. Consequently, the index number constructed to measure changes in the cost of living is bound to be defective either because the prices of goods are not real or because the commodities selected are not representative of the entire people. The second difficulty arises from the fact that it is not possible to decide about the selection of commodities and about attaching weights to them. Different persons have different incomes and buy different commodities and therefore each person is affected differently by the change in the prices of commodities. A cost of living index number constructed on the basis of the commodities consumed by a typical working class family at any point of time may not be very relevant to a middle class family whose consumption pattern may be entirely different. Moreover, changes do take place in tastes and habits of people. Therefore, comparison of the price changes of the two different years may not be very relevant. Most serious is the fact that the selection of different weights will yield different results. Where some prices are rising and others falling, one set of weights will show a rise in the index number and another a fall. Comparison over fairly long periods may be possible in the case of wholesale prices, if no changes are made in the composition of the commodities covered. But in the case of retail prices, this is a more serious difficulty. The selection of commodities is based on a survey of the actual expenditure of a group of people at a certain time but the way in which these people distribute their expenditure is liable to change with the passing of time for a number of reasons: demand may change as their standard of living rises or as the distribution of population within the various age groups changes; tastes or fashions may undergo a change or new commodities may come on to the market; changes in quality may occur without any price changes. And, therefore, no comparison of retail prices can be even approximately accurate except for very limited periods. Comparison is also not possible for a further reason and that is, the composition of the groups, upon whose expenditure the weights are based may not be the same in all cases. The higher the standard of living of the people included in these enquiries, the less accurate is the index likely to be as a mirror of the distribution of expenditure of particular sections within the group. The reason for this is that as the standard of living rises, the percentage of income spent on necessaries tends to fall and additional expenditure falls on a widening range of other things where individual choice has a more significant effect.

How significant this weighting is, depends on the purpose to which an index number is put. If the preliminary survey on which the weights are based is intended only to depict how people within a certain range of income spend their money the result may be of interest to social workers and some others. But if it is used for bringing about changes in the wage rates, then it cannot be considered as a very satisfactory device. It is quite possible that commodities which fall within the range of people in the higher income group may rise in price, while other prices remain fairly steady, and yet this would raise the index number and in industries, such as building and cotton textiles, where wages are linked to the Index of Retail Prices, would result in higher wages to some people on the ground that the cost of living had risen, whereas in fact no change in their cost of living may have taken place at all.

It would, thus, be seen that index numbers are not a very satisfactory method of measuring the changes in the value of money. If measurement of changes in the purchasing power of money within the borders of a single country presents so many difficulties, it shows how much more difficult it is to attempt to compare the purchasing power of money in different countries.

9. Advantages of Index Numbers

Despite the difficulties and limitations of index numbers as given above, it cannot be denied that they have been playing a very useful role in providing us an instrument for comparing the economic conditions of different people at different times and for measuring the changes in the relative economic conditions of different sections of people in the country during any given period of time. The social reformists have made considerable use of index numbers. The economists have taken help of index numbers to alleviate the standards of lower income group people. The governments have made judicious use of index numbers in formulating their economic and social policies relating to population control, price control, rationing, food control, taxation, etc. During recent years, some of the difficulties faced in the construction of index numbers have been removed to a considerable extent. The limitation of index number in regard to the non-comparability has been removed with the help of "reversal tests" when the base periods are reversed and the so-called 'ideal' index numbers have been constructed. The chain index is an improvement on the earlier simple index number; although it is also not free from defects. However, we cannot say that index numbers are redundant and useless. We cannot undertake an objective and realistic study of social and economic phenomena through time without the help of index numbers. Take for example, the difficulties created by the great depression of the thirties and the post-war inflation for the people would not have been known to us in the absence of index numbers. The achievements of planning would not have been available to us without the help of various types of index numbers. These are, in fact, most important tools by the help of which we can judge the performance of the economy over time. Product indices may help us in finding out which type of political system is better from the point of view of rapid economic growth of a country. In short, by making use of index numbers we can measure quantitative changes in the wages, imports, exports, employment, industrial activity, production of raw materials, major food grains, changes in the area of cultivation, population, etc. And, therefore, they are a useful guide to an understanding of economic problems and indicate general tendencies which are very important for formulating the social and economic policies in the country.

Exercises

1. What are simple index numbers? How are they constructed? Give their uses.
2. How are changes in the value of money measured? What are the defects in the system of index numbers? To what extent can they be remedied?
3. What is an index number? How is it constructed? What are the uses and limitations of index numbers?

Chapter 10

Inflation, Deflation and Reflation

1. Introduction

Stability of the price level is a prime objective of monetary policy. Changes in the price level or value of money are important to all people who receive money incomes and to all those who are engaged in the buying and selling of goods and services for money. In an advanced modern economy, this means that fluctuations in the price level affect all and sundry, although a small section of people still receive part of their incomes in kind, say, for example, policemen, hotel, and hospital employees are provided with uniforms, or railway employees get a certain amount of free travel and so on. To the extent the wages are paid in kind, a measure of immunity is provided from fluctuations in the value of money. A great drawback of the use of money is that unlike other measures like yard or a litre or a minute, it is not a stable measure, its value has always been changing. A second drawback is that its value in terms of goods and services does not change to the same extent or always in the same direction. When these changes are small and gradual they are not harmful but when they are steep and vast they can be of serious consequence as experienced in the last century. In this chapter, we take up the problems connected with the variations in the value of money in terms of goods and services or the price level. We shall consider changes in the general price level and their effects on the economy. We have stated already that the value of money and price level move in opposite directions. A rise in the price level means a decline in the value of money and *vice versa*. We have seen that the changes in the price level can be measured by constructing an index number of retail prices and that this is the measure generally recognised and used by the governments everywhere in the world.

Fluctuations in the Price Level

Frequent variations in the price level are not desirable for the smooth functioning of an economy and its constituents. An upward movement of it is generally known as inflation, while its downward movement is known as deflation. We have discussed the effects of changes in the price level on production, employment and distribution in a separate chapter. We now deal here with the causes of such fluctuations and policies that may be formulated to deal with them. First, we take up inflation.

2. Definition of Inflation

Inflation is commonly understood to be a situation in which the prices of goods, services and all other commodities go on rising substantially and at a fast pace. Economists are, however, divided about the origin, causes and effects of inflation. There has also been no unanimity among them regarding its definition. Some consider it as a phenomenon of rising prices, while some others consider it as a monetary phenomenon. In the first category, fall economists like Johnson, Crowther, etc. Crowther defines inflation as a "state in which the value of money is falling, *i.e.*, the prices are rising". Harry G. Johnson says that, "I define inflation as substantial rise in prices." According to Gardner Ackley, "inflation is a persistent and appreciable rise in the general level or average of prices."

In the second category are included economists like Pigou, Kemmerer, Coulborn, Hawtrey, etc. Prof. A.C. Pigou held that if money incomes expand more than in proportion to income earning activity, there is inflation. Similarly, Hawtrey defined inflation as that state of economic life in which "there is the issue of too much currency". Kemmerer likewise defines inflation as "too much money and deposit currency in relation to the physical volume of business being done". According to Coulborn, inflation is a situation of "too much money chasing too few goods".

The one common element in all these definitions is the evidence of disequilibrium which causes a rise in the price level. In fact, inflation is not a single definitive phenomenon capable of being described precisely. Whatever definitions have been given are just an enumeration of the factors that cause its development and continuation. To the quantity theorists inflation meant an increase in the quantity of money; while rise in the price level was considered to be its effect.

Keynes' View

Keynes held that inflation was a phenomenon of full employment. It is synonymous with an excess of aggregate demand over aggregate supply in conditions of full employment, while the rising prices are just an indication of the existence of the above fact. According to him, true inflation starts only after full employment. Keynes also accepts that prices may rise even before full employment due to the existence of certain obstacles in the expansion of output. But rise in prices which is really threatening to the economy is in the situation of true inflation. However, excess demand need not necessarily cause an upward movement in the price level, since in an open economy the situation could be met by expanding imports. Moreover, it is not always due to an excess demand that an upward movement in the price level occurs. There are many other causes and a rise in prices under their impact should surely be an inflation. So, perhaps it may be desirable to define inflation as a situation in which the price level generally tends to rise upward.

Modern Economists' View

The modern economists consider inflation as a comprehensive and unified phenomenon. They also relate the rising price level with the changing level of unemployment. According to the analysis of inflationary phenomenon as provided by the modern economists there are only two types of inflation: (*i*) demand-pull inflation; and (*ii*) cost-push inflation. In the former, inflation and falling unemployment exist together while in the latter, inflation and rising unemployment exist together.

During the late 1950s A.W. Phillips put forward a thesis that a permanent long run trade-off existed between inflation and unemployment. It implies that less inflation means more unemployment and high inflation means less unemployment.

In the decade following the Phillips thesis, Milton Friedman and his followers advanced the argument that a trade-off between inflation and unemployment was only a short-run phenomenon. In the long run both inflation and unemployment exist together and rise together. These economists also treated inflation as one integrated phenomenon which combined both demand-pull and cost-push inflation. According to these economists "inflation" is a unified phenomenon of which demand and cost elements are integral parts and in which expectations of future price level changes play a dominant role.

3. Forms of Inflation

Inflation has been called by different names depending upon its degree or rate of price rise and nature and government interference.

1. Degree of Price Rise

According to the degree of price rise, inflation has been named as creeping, walking, running and galloping or hyper inflation.

(*a*) **Creeping Inflation.** Creeping inflation is the mildest form and is conducive to economic progress and growth. In this form, the prices rise imperceptibly over a long period. In fact, some economists have pleaded strongly for the existence of a creeping inflation in the form of secular rise in prices to save the economy from secular stagnation. There are, however, other economists who are opposed to the idea because they feel that creeping inflation is dangerous for the overall stability of the economy. According to them, it is a sort of conception which when once takes place goes on increasing until the baby is delivered. With the passage of time, the infant instead of creeping starts walking, running and galloping.

(*b*) **Walking Inflation.** When creeping inflation gets help from some other factors and price rise becomes more marked, the situation is known as that of walking inflation.

(*c*) **Running Inflation.** If the price rise becomes more rapid and the prices rise by fits and starts, the situation is that of running inflation.

(*d*) **Hyper Inflation.** In hyper inflation the prices rise every moment, in fact, limitlessly. Philip Cagan has concluded that hyper inflation begins when prices start rising at the rate of more than 50 per cent a month. After the First World War, Germany has passed through various periods when prices not only rose by 50 per cent a month but doubled every week and on certain occasions they doubled everyday. It was really a startling situation and firms during those days started paying wages to their employees thrice a day. It is the most dangerous situation and economists have been scared of this type of inflation.

2. According to Scope

Inflation can be comprehensive and partial.

(*a*) **Comprehensive.** It is comprehensive or economy wide when prices of commodities rise throughout the economy without any exception.

(*b*) **Partial.** Partial inflation is of a sporadic or sectional nature. It takes place when the prices of some goods rise owing to a temporary shortage due to physical conditions. For example, a rise in the price of food grains due to crop failure, or due to floods or a rise in the price of general goods due to a railway or bus strike is such a situation in view. Thus, in a sporadic inflationary situation the rise in prices is not due to the shortage caused by distortions in the price structure, *i.e.*, either due to the rise in the price of raw materials or due to an increase in the wage rates but due to the restrictions imposed by physical conditions on the smooth supply of goods and commodities. The shortages of current production are further aggravated by a backlog of demand. Consequently, market prices shoot high and any increase in prices does not help in restoring the supply to meet the increasing demand.

3. According to Government Interference

According to the degree of interference by the government, inflation can be open or suppressed.

(*a*) **Open.** When government interference is nil, and prices rise freely, it is a situation of open inflation. When prices are prevented from rising or when the rate of increase has been slowed down by the government through certain measures like price control or rationing, it is a situation of suppressed inflation. In the opinion of Milton Friedman open inflation is an "inflationary process in which prices are permitted to rise without being suppressed by government price control or similar techniques". The post-war hyper inflations faced by Germany, Austria, Russia, etc. during the twenties or by Hungary and China during the forties of the last century are the examples in view.

(*b*) **Suppressed.** Suppressed inflation is, in fact, the result of policies of the government relating to price control and rationing under which the prices are prevented from rising at least for some time, but they rise vigorously as soon as these controls are lifted. Wartime controls are an instance of suppressed inflation. The word 'suppression' implies: (*i*) the postponement of the present demand to future; and (*ii*) the diversion of demand from one type of goods to another. Suppressed inflation is full of disadvantages: firstly, it creates enormous difficulties for administration; an hierarchy of price controllers and supply officers is created to check the rise in prices. If these people are not efficient, and if their integrity is not of a high order and if they do not have the experience required for administering such difficult situations, the price control and rationing machinery is bound to be unsuccessful. We have ample experience of such an inefficient and corrupt machinery during the first and second World Wars. We found that because of their corrupt practices and inefficiency, a parallel black market developed and the rationed and price-controlled goods were sold there. This sort of situation ultimately develops into a hidden price inflation, which is more harmful than open inflation. According to Halm, "Once the population finds that it cannot even buy its modest rations, blackmarket operations become the preoccupation of everybody. Where one such blackmarket transaction earns more money than a week's or a month's hard work, productivity will decline enormously."[1]

Suppressed inflation also leads to a wasteful diversion of productive resources of the economy from the production of essential goods whose prices are statutorily fixed to the production of those commodities which are not essential and whose prices are not statutorily fixed. Obviously, this would not amount to the optimal use of community's productive resources and will thus be detrimental to the economic and social welfare of the community. Milton Friedman considers suppressed inflation worse than the open inflation. Citing the example of Germany he concludes that the result of suppression was that the output in Germany was curtailed to one-half of the pre-war level. The

1. G.N. Halm, *The Economics of Money and Banking*, p. 417.

price mechanism which efficiently allocates scarce resources into productive uses was not allowed to function; the workers worked for only 2-3 days in a week and were paid in kind; they bartered their commodities which they received as wages with other simple articles and farm products. We need not spell out the inefficiency of the barter system insofar as the organised and productive use of the resources is concerned. In short, in open inflation owing to the functioning of the price mechanism the resources are allocated most efficiently, while in suppressed inflation the price mechanism is not allowed to function leading to the wasteful use of productive resources of the economy; and hence the former is better than the latter.

4. Other Forms

There could be other types of inflation as well. For example, profit-induced inflation, deficit-induced inflation, wage-induced inflation, mark-up inflation, ratchet inflation and stagflation. Profit-induced inflation is that situation in which due to a reduction in the costs, the price start declining but the government does not allow this to happen. Consequently, the prices although remain the same, due to a fall in the cost of production, the margin of profits of the producers goes on increasing. Keynes has named this inflation as profit-induced inflation. Deficit-induced inflation takes place when the government fails to step up its income to meet the increased expenditure and consequently it is forced to cover the deficit by resorting to printing of paper currency. This leads to a rise in the price level. Wage-induced inflation occurs when the workers organise themselves into strong trade unions and force the employers to increase their wages leading to an increase in the cost of production and rise in prices. Mark-up inflation is a result of the manipulations of the big and monopolistic business organisations. These organisations calculate their production costs and they add a certain mark-up to them to yield the pre-decided rate of profit on their capital investment. This sort of practice is quite common in the USA and this has been one of the most important factors causing inflationary pressures. The higher the demand for a commodity, the greater is the size of the mark-up. Study of price mark-ups during the five post-war recessions from 1947–70 in the USA conducted by Professors Howard M. Wachtel and Peter D. Adelsheim revealed that the big business corporations tend to increase price when total volume of sales falls, to maintain the profit margins at existing levels. This is in contradiction to the economic theory that for combating inflation it is necessary to create unemployment to control demand and reduce the price rise. Ratchet inflation is a situation in which the prices in certain sectors are not allowed to fall even when there are strong reasons for the prices to fall. In certain circumstances the sectoral distribution of aggregate demand is not uniform; in certain sectors it is high while in others it is low. In those sectors where the demand is high, the prices should rise while in sectors where it is low the prices should fall. But in these sectors the prices are not allowed to fall owing to the strong resistance put up by the industrialists and trade unions. The net result is that there is a rise in the general price level; such a situation is known as that of ratchet inflation. During recent times a new term has been coined, which is known as stagflation, which is a sort of situation where inflation is accompanied by stagnation on the development front or a situation in which high prices exist with high level of unemployment. In the western world almost in every country we find that the economy is in the grip of stagflation today. Less developed countries which have adopted economic planning as an instrument of their economic development are also faced with this type of inflation and the Keynesian economists have failed to answer a solution for such a situation.

4. Inflationary Gap

The concept of inflationary gap was originated by Keynes in his pamphlet *How to Pay for the War?* published in 1940. Although Keynes chiefly referred to the phenomenon of inflationary gap caused by an increase in government's expenditure on war, it could also cover cases where under full-employment conditions, increase in public investment outlays is not offset by a corresponding decline in the aggregate private consumption outlays. It represents an excess of the aggregate demand for goods and services over their total supply at constant price, under conditions of full employment. The gap, therefore, is between the increasing purchasing power and the failure of the current rate of production to keep pace with the increasing purchasing power. This gap, according to Klein, "is the difference between what the population will try to consume out of the income (which is determined by the interaction of consumption function and the level of government expenditure) and the amount available at pre-inflation prices". According to Kurihara, inflationary gap can be defined as "an excess of anticipated expenditure over available output at base prices".[2] Thus the gap is the difference between anticipated effective money demand of the people for consumption output and the supply of the consumption output at pre-inflation prices. How this gap helps in price rise can be illustrated with the help of an example. Let us assume that in a given period of time national income distributed to the factors of production is Rs. 100 crore. Out of this Rs. 20 crore are collected in the form of taxes. The 'disposable' income available to the community then remains Rs. 80 crore. On the other hand, let us also assume that the value of the national product at pre-inflation prices available for public consumption

2. K.K. Kurihara, *Monetary Theory and Public Policy,* p. 41.

(after paying for government expenditure inclusive of transfer items), is Rs. 60 crore. Therefore, inflationary gap becomes Rs. 80 crore minus Rs. 60 crore or Rs. 20 crore. Thus, inflation is caused by the fact that people have Rs. 80 crore to spend over goods valued at Rs. 60 crore at pre-inflation prices. If the production of consumption goods is increased to the same extent, the gap will disappear. Since it is not possible to increase production in short periods and in an economy which is already operating at full employment level, any attempt to increase the supply of goods, will only result in an increase in the factor prices which would lead to an increase in the aggregate money incomes without any corresponding increase in the production of consumer goods.

Factors Causing Inflationary Gap

Inflationary gap is generally caused by two types of factors, *viz.*, (*i*) those which affect increase in money incomes; and (*ii*) those which cause a decline in the level of production of consumer goods.

1. Increase in Money Incomes. So far as the increase in money incomes of the members of a community is concerned, it could be affected by a number of factors:

(*a*) The policy of the government to expand credit may lead to inflation. Such a policy implies an excessive issue of paper currency or an excessive creation of bank deposits. Bank rate policy of a country can change the credit structure. Generally a reduction in the bank rate leads to an expansion of credit which in its turn may bring about inflation, *i.e.*, a state of rising prices.

(*b*) Increase in the velocity of circulation of money due to an increase in the propensity to consume or in the schedule of marginal efficiency of credit or from a reduction in the liquidity preference, may lead to inflationary conditions. In Germany, there was too much of such inflation after the World War I and the Deutschemark became unacceptable to the people. If a shopkeeper got it he made his man run as fast as he could to an exchange bank in the street corner to get it exchanged for some foreign currency which had a higher value. Such a state is described as a 'flight from currency'.

(*c*) Natural causes like the discovery of new mines of gold or silver may lead to inflation. This inflation is technically called 'metallic inflation'. This type of inflation has now become out of question as there is practically no country which is on metallic standard.

(*d*) Deficit financing resorted to by a country is some times responsible for creating inflationary trends in prices. Budgetary disequilibrium can be adjusted by this process which may lead to partial inflation.

(*e*) Banks may also create inflation on their own behalf by expanding the loans. This may take place in two circumstances: (*i*) when there are sufficient borrowers, and (*ii*) when they possess enough of cash. Once credit expansion takes place, it continues for sufficiently long time. Banks by lowering their cash ratio also can create inflationary conditions. They generally keep an adequate cash reserve and something more by way of margin. They have to keep this margin intact even when they create credit.

2. Factors Affecting Supply of Consumer Goods. A fall in the volume of production without a corresponding reduction in the money supply will raise prices and create inflationary conditions. The factors which may bring about a reduction in the volume of production are many but the most important are: (*i*) If the industries have reached such a state beyond which the laws of diminishing returns are likely to operate, every successive unit of capital and labour if applied in production will bring forth diminishing returns. At this stage, if production and cost of production remain constant, partial inflationary conditions would ensue. (*ii*) If trade unionism is strong and workers can get their grievances redressed by force, production may decline and partial inflation may follow. Due to the efforts of trade unions, purchasing power of the workers may go up without any corresponding increase in production. Thus shorter hours, holidays with pay,. higher wages, etc. unaccompanied by a proportionate increase in production may lead to inflationary trends. Under such conditions, price increase will be inflationary, (*iii*) Natural catastrophies may also bring about inflationary conditions by decreasing the volume of production. Floods, earthquakes and other natural calamities of the kind will decrease the production and will bring inflationary effects. Apart from these, there are other factors as well which cause inflation. For example, rapid changes in population which cause inflation through changes in production. A rapid rise in population will increase the output less, than proportionately and this will lead to a rise in price. Again, the financing of a war by printing paper notes also leads to inflation. During war, capital is diverted from productive channels to unproductive industries causing shortage of consumer goods which leads to a rise in their prices and hence inflationary conditions.

Removal of Inflationary Gap

Inflationary gap can be reduced by natural forces; but it would be better if deliberate measures are adopted to reduce aggregate expenditure. The general price level rises because of this inflationary gap, but the rise in the price level does not directly narrow down the inflationary gap. However, price rise indirectly creates such effects which tend to reduce this gap. These indirect effects of price rise are:

1. Wealth Effect. A rise in the general price level reduces the real wealth held by the people which may cause a reduction in their consumption expenditure.

2. Trade Effect. Rising prices discourage exports and encourage imports; hence the aggregate spending in the economy would be reduced.

3. Keynes Effect. When the money supply remains constant or increases in proportions less than the rise in prices, then the rate of interest will increase causing a reduction in the investment expenditure.

4. Fiscal Effect. Higher tax collections relative to the rise in prices reduce the real disposable income and, thus, reduce consumption expenditure. Again, transfer payments made in money become less in real terms owing to a rise in prices and thus reduce the consumption expenditure. Similarly, if the government budgets are fixed in money terms the real government purchases will also decline by rising prices. Hence the government expenditure relative to rise in prices will be reduced.

5. Price Expectation Effect. If people expect that the rise in prices is only temporary, they will defer the purchase of consumer durables and investment in plant and machinery. This will also lead to the reduction of the inflationary gap.

6. Redistribution Effect. The entire price increase will go to the entrepreneurs as profits of the money wage rates are fixed. Since the profit earners have a lower propensity to consume than wage earners, a redistribution of income of this sort will reduce the aggregate demand and the inflationary gap would be narrowed.

7. Money Illusion Effect. If some persons suffer from money illusion and if they spend a fixed portion of their income in money terms, then rise in prices will reduce the real value of such expenditure and will narrow the inflationary gap.

Significance of Inflationary Gap

The significance of the concept of inflationary gap can be known by the following:

1. Effect on national income and prices. The inflationary gap can directly affect the national income and prices. When it occurs at full employment it increases money income of the people, without increasing the output because the resources are already fully employed. This leads to a rise in prices.

2. Non-monetary inflation. While recognising that demand-pull inflation is chiefly caused by flow of expenditures, the Keynesian analysis provides the possibilities of the existence of non-monetary inflation. Keynes held that the effect of excessive growth of money stock may be uncertain because it will lead to inflationary rise in prices indirectly first, through its impact on the rate of interest and then on aggregate spending.

3. Anti-inflationary measures. Inflationary gap gives directions to the monetary authority and the government for adopting suitable measures for controlling inflationary pressures. These measures may be in the direction of influencing the propensity to consume, to save, and to invest, which together determine the price level.

Limitations of Inflationary Gap

The concept of inflationary gap is static in nature and therefore suffers from the following limitations:

1. Time lags. There are time lags between the adjustment of wages and rising prices and also between the receipt of income and its spending. The larger the time lags the milder will be the effect of inflation. If it were not so, then inflation during and after the two World Wars would have had more disastrous results. Keynes himself was of this view when he said, "It is these time lags and other impediments that come to our rescue. Wars do not last for ever."

2. Current flows. Inflationary gap is related to current flows of income, expenditure, consumption, investment, saving, etc. But rise in prices does not affect only the current output. It also affects the output produced earlier and is currently being sold in the market.

5. Causative Factors of Inflation

We now take up the causative factors of inflation. Inflation is caused either by an increase in demand or by an increase in the cost of production; the former is known as demand-pull inflation and the latter is called cost-push inflation. We deal with these in the following paragraphs:

Demand-pull Inflation

When the rise in the general price level is due to an increase in the demand for goods and services in excess of their supply at current prices, the situation is known as demand-pull inflation. By demand, we mean aggregate real demand for output and by supply of goods and services we mean maximum feasible or potential or full employment output at current prices. Thus, the supply of goods relate to the ability of an economy to produce goods and services and make available for disposal at the current prices in the market. When the aggregate demand for these goods and services exceeds the supply of these goods and services, the upward shift in the price level, is known as demand-pull inflation.

Factors Causing Demand-Pull Inflation

Regarding the factors responsible for the situation of demand-pull inflation, we come across two streams of arguments put forward by: (*i*) the quantity theorists or the monetarists, and (*ii*) the Keynesians.

Arguments of the Monetarists. The arguments given by the monetarists for the occurrence of demand-pull inflation are based on the quantity theory of money, that is, given the velocity of circulation of money any increase in its supply will increase the total money expenditure. Since, there is full employment in the economy, the increased demand will push the prices upward. In a static economy with a given level of output and velocity of money being constant, increase in the supply of money is alone responsible for increase in the price level, which is proportionate to the increase in the money supply. Since money supply is controlled by the monetary authority, the rate of inflation also becomes policy determined. In a dynamic economy the real demand for money grows over time. Similarly, the real national income also grows over time. According to the Cambridge economists, the growth rate of national income as well as of the real demand for money is equal, because the income elasticity of demand for money is unity. The increase in the money supply in excess of the real demand for money leads to an increase in prices which ultimately become inflationary.

Arguments of the Keynesians. According to the Keynesians demand-pull inflation occurs because of an increase in the aggregate demand (*AMD*) at the point full employment.

According to Keynes, inflation occurs because of an increase in the aggregate demand (*AMD*) at the point of full employment. Such an increase in the price level can be illustrated with the help of Fig. 10.1.

Suppose *AMD* is represented by *D* curve and aggregate supply by *Z*. The economy is at full employment at *N* output and the price level is *AN*/*ON*. If the *AMD* increases to *D′* the price level will rise to *BN*/*ON*. If the *AMD* rises to *D′* the price level will rise to *CN*/*ON*.

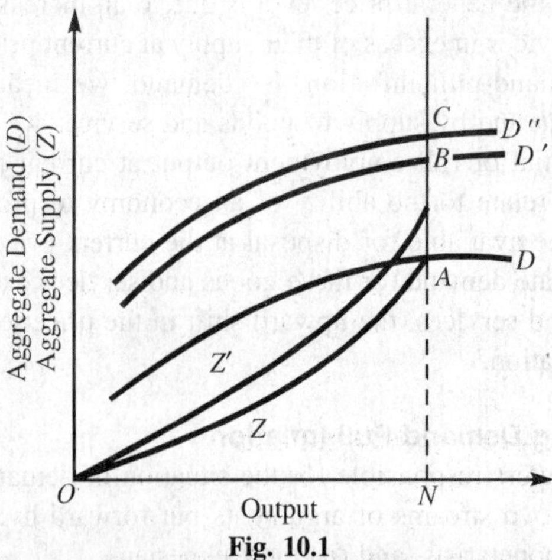

Fig. 10.1

The Keynesian approach, however, assumes that by simply raising the level of *AMD* it would be enough to establish full employment. It ignores the possibility that price rise may generate further increase in *AMD* and thus lead to further price rises. If this happens, then inflation is not a simple static condition of excess demand, or even a series of isolated events. It is rather a process which starts before full employment is reached.

In Fig.11.1, if wage rates rise, costs of production rise and the supply curve shifts upwards to *Z′*, we have the inflationary spiral, higher demand increasing costs, increased costs leading to higher demand. From the Figure it can be seen that if the *D* curve shifts up less than the *Z* curve each time wage-rates are increased, the process will be a diminishing one. Eventually, the *D* and *Z* curves will cut at the full employment output, but at a much higher price level. In other words, the aggregate demand now equals the aggregate supply and hence there is equilibrium. This can happen because of the following reasons:

(1) Some income groups cannot secure increases in income when prices rise. Suppose, some inflation occurs in an economy, initially in equilibrium at full employment. As prices rise, workers and entrepreneurs can increase their money incomes, whereas rentiers' money incomes would remain fixed. In such a situation, the process of inflation can continue until workers and entrepreneurs have regained their original level of real incomes. On the other hand, rentiers, because of the increased price level, suffer a fall in real income. In other words, equilibrium is established by a redistribution of income. The time taken to reach a new equilibrium, and the way in which redistribution occurs, will depend largely on institutional factors, *e.g.*, the strength of organised labour, and the proportion of rentiers' income to total income. The larger the proportion, the smaller will be the price rise necessary to bring the inflation to a stop.

(2) Certain income groups may be able to secure only a part increase in income as prices rise. Rentiers' money income need not be absolutely fixed. Inflation will eventually work itself out if one group does not try, or is not strong enough, to maintain fully its real income by increases in money income. Thus, the 'money illusion' may mean that labour does not seek full increases to maintain real wages, while salary-earners may not be able to press their claims. Eventually, such groups will have lagged so far behind in increases in money wages that the stronger groups will have maintained their real income at the expense of the weaker.

(3) Expected price rises are less than actual price rises. This again will damp down the amount by which the *D* curve rises, allowing the *Z* curve to catch up.

(4) Import prices do not rise as incomes and aggregate demand increase.

In this case, there is no need for incomes to increase in the same proportion, as the prices of home-produced goods in order to maintain real income, but only in proportion to the general price level including imports.

(5) The propensity to consume may fall as prices rise. This may occur through:

(*a*) A redistribution of real income, *e.g.*, from wage-earners to profit-earners.

(*b*) A time-lag in increasing real consumption. Where increased real incomes go to profits, companies may be slow to increase dividend distribution. Although such profits are usually retained for future investment, a period of time may elapse before this actually takes place, *e.g.*, through bottlenecks in the capital goods industries. Some expenditure, too, may be fixed in money terms, past higher purchase commitments.

(*c*) A 'Pigou effect'. The rise in prices lowers the real value of cash balances, and people may maintain this real value by reducing consumption.

(*d*) Real disposable income may fall because of progressive taxation. This would mean increased real saving by the government provided it does not increase its money expenditure accordingly.

(6) There may be no increase in the supply of money. In such a situation the extra demand for active balances will cause a rise in the rate of interest with some effect on the level of investment.

The above analysis suggests, that although, in the absence of fresh 'shocks', inflationary pressure eventually works itself out, the effect on the price level may be considerable, especially on the passive groups in the economy and relatively small, or if there is little decrease in the real consumption as money incomes and prices rise. It is likely, therefore, that the government will have to intervene to check the price rise.

Factors Causing an Increase in Aggregate Demand

Aggregate demand may increase due to a number of factors:

1. Deficit Financing. In times of war or under other abnormal situations requiring a huge increase in government spending, the government for meeting this expenditure may resort to deficit financing which increases the money supply in the hands of the people, thereby increasing their demand for goods and services. In most of the developing countries, the governments have to obtain funds for executing the development plans through deficit financing and this has led to a situation of inflation.

2. Increase in the Velocity of Money. During periods of boom and prosperity, owing to an increase in the *MEC* and *MPC,* the velocity of circulation of money increases.

3. Expansion of Credit. The expansion of credit may be resorted to either as a matter of policy by the government or by the commercial banks of the country. The central bank can expand credit by lowering the bank rate or by purchasing government securities. The commercial banks can expand credit by lowering the cash reserves. Expansion of credit is generally resorted to in periods of increasing economic activity and once it starts, it continues for a sufficiently long period of time.

4. Increase in Public Expenditure. Aggregate demand may also increase as a result of an increase in public expenditure either for meeting the requirements of defence, or of economic development or for boosting the level of economic activity in the economy.

5. Expansion of Exports. If the export of commodities increases, less goods are available for domestic consumption. This would make the existing demand at home excessive of the available quantity of goods leading to an increase in their prices.

6. Increase in Population. Increase in the population of the country raises the general level of aggregate demand of the people for goods and services. As Prof. Coulborn states, "If population increases rapidly, while the aggregate volume of money remains stable, the consequent rise in the velocity of circulation is likely to outweigh the countervailing decrease in the volume of money per head; further, a rapid increase of population may increase output less than proportionately—another factor tending to raise prices."[3]

7. Trade Union Activities. These days trade unions are very strong. They continuously agitate for higher wages, shorter hours of work, more holidays with pay and other amenities. In a democratic country, the government is often compelled to accede to the unreasonable demands of the workers. The increase in wages increases the purchasing power of the workers and hence the aggregate demand.

Tests to Indicate the Presence of Demand-Pull Inflation

(1) It is not at all easy to find a direct means of measuring the level of excess demand over any specific period. Lengthening waiting lists for manufactured capital and consumer goods, may, therefore, be taken as symptomatic of excess demand.

(2) Since manufacturers endeavour to meet unsatisfied demand by expanding their output which involves the employment of more people, a more reliable indicator may, therefore, be the level of unemployment which can be used as a 'proxy' measure for the state of final demand. As the economy moves closer to its maximum possible output under the presence of unsatisfied demand, competition for the available labour becomes more intensive, costs increase and are passed on in the form of higher prices.

---

3. W.A. Coulborn, *A Discussion of Money,* p. 159.

(3) Further evidence indicating the presence of demand-pull inflation can be obtained from rising earnings drift. It means that besides the increase in the national wage rates, the employers may be willing to give additional bonuses, revise piece-work rates, or provide the opportunity for artificially created weekend or overtime working, to increase the average earnings of employees so that the employers can get and keep the labour that they require. This suggest that the employers do not want to get their production disrupted owing to labour disputes and hence they are conciliatory when they have buoyant demand for their products.

(4) A rising level of business profitability per unit of sales may be yet another possible indicator of the existence of demand-pull inflation. This again suggests that profit margins can be increased because of a high level of demand. However, profit figures are likely to be only a retrospective indicator of the level of demand since increased demand may only be reflected in more profitable operations with a considerable time lag. Company managements also often work to constant 'mark-ups' on costs and do not necessarily raise profit margins, even when they have excess demand for their products.

(5) An analysis of the movements in the value of imports may provide evidence of demand-pull inflation. If total expenditure on imports, especially on manufactured goods, is rising due to increasing imports, this may be taken as evidence of demand diversion; that is, buyers are substituting imported goods for home products they would have preferred had they been immediately available.

(6) Devaluation may also cause excess demand, especially if there were few unemployed resources before it. If foreign demand for exports is price elastic, devaluation should lead to a significant expansion of export orders. If, at the same time, home demand for imported manufactured goods is also price elastic, demand diversion to home produced substitutes should also take place. Such an increase in aggregate demand without adequate resources to meet it may prove highly inflationary unless the government acts to cut down the level of domestic spending.

Cost-push Inflation

This sort of inflation emanates from changes which arise on the side of supply or cost of production, independently of any excess demand in both final goods and factor markets. As the level of unemployment decreases, certain income groups may put pressure to seek money income increases, *e.g.*, producers may seek higher real profit margins and the trade unions may exert pressure for increasing the wage rates. We thus have cost-push inflation—either due to profit push or due to wage push. The market power of these factor inputs is increased, when resources are fully employed. But, even in a situation of less than full employment, the fact that the government is committed to full employment may encourage employees' organisations, especially, if well organised, to press pay increase claims aggressively. Since rates of wages are negotiated collectively for an industry, the cost of all firms in the industry rise owing to the increase in wage rates. Other industries also follow suit and therefore costs rise throughout the economy and are recouped in higher prices. These increases provide additional purchasing power and so the level of aggregate demand increases further.

Since subsequent price increases erode the initial benefits gained from their pay increase, they provide the incentive for the next pay claim. Moreover, each group does not want to lag behind other groups and so the chain of pay claims continues. The process of cost-push inflation can be self-perpetuating, provided increase in the money supply or income velocity of circulation enables the rising price level to be financed. The pay increases result in higher prices and also generate higher money incomes which sustain the real level of aggregate demand. In the absence of any growth in the economy, real incomes remain constant, though the imperfections of the pay negotiating machinery may result in a redistribution of real income, the more militant groups gaining at the expense of less aggressive ones.

The costs of home products may also rise, if a country is heavily dependent on imported raw materials whose prices are increasing owing to inflation in the exporting country.

The process of cost-push inflation is illustrated in Fig. 10.2.

An increase in wage rates shifts the *Z* curve upwards followed by a rise

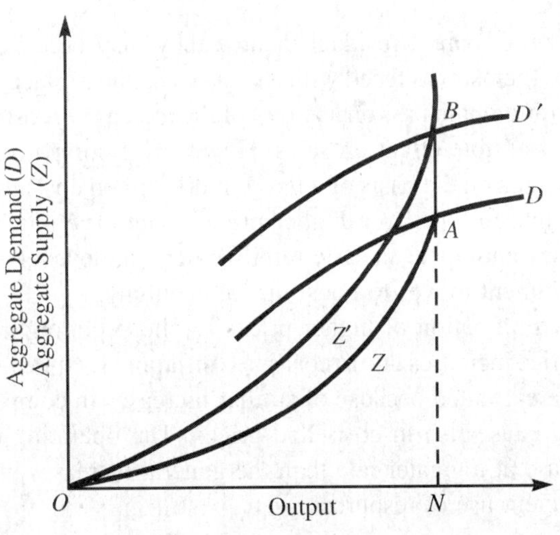

Fig. 10.2

in the *D* curve, even though there is no excess demand to start with. In the above figure at equilibrium output *ON* the price level is *AN*/*ON*. A rise in wage-rates shifts the aggregate supply curve up to *Z′*; consequently, the aggregate demand curve moves upwards to *D′*. There is thus a higher price level *BN*/*ON*, which leads to further wage increases and another rise in the *Z* curve. Now, will this process come to an end? In the figure the process is likely to continue indefinitely since the *Z* and *D* curves have shifted up to the same extent. Where aggregate demand shifts up less, some unemployment will result. This may produce a moderating effect on wage demands. The process may come to an end for the reasons given when we discussed demand inflation.

It should be noted that both demand-pull and cost-push inflation are inter-related in the inflationary process. Both types of inflation need an increase in the aggregate demand to keep them going; that is, demand influences are always present in inflation. They differ in that they have a different motivating force, a difference which is important from the point of view of policy.

Tests to Indicate the Presence of Cost-Push Inflation

The following may be suggested as indicators of the presence of cost-push inflation:

(1) Devaluation and tax increases or the adoption of new taxes are clearly identifiable external causes, which lead to a significant rise in the cost and hence prices of commodities. These exert both a cost-push and demand-pull influence at the same time. Higher value of imports, especially of raw materials, semi-finished products, and capital equipment, exert a major influence on industrial costs.

(2) Since profits are a residual income they may be expected to fall if companies find themselves faced with rising costs, due to slack demand. They are reluctant to attempt to pass on any part of the increase in costs to consumers for fear of the possible effect on sales. However, if company managements price their products on the basis of a fixed 'mark-up' on costs they may prefer a reduced volume of sales at a higher price to preserve unit profit margin, especially if they anticipate an early improvement in the level of demand as a result of government moves to boost up the economy.

(3) The determination of higher prices by the declining industries is an indication of price increases due to cost-push inflation. Despite falling demand, pay increases are granted because of similar increases in comparable rates of pay, and these cause rise in costs and prices. The operating costs are also likely to increase at a greater rate than the general increases in prices owing to the less efficient use of resources.

Factors Leading to Shortfall in Supply

1. Hoarding of Goods. It has been witnessed that during a period of shortages and rising prices, people have a tendency, particularly the businessmen and the trading class, to hoard essential commodities for earning profits in future. This creates artificial scarcity in the market and raises the prices of these goods further.

2. Attitude of the Trade Unions. During rising prices trade unions also adopt an antagonistic posture. They indulge in strikes and intensify their demand for higher wages. On the one hand, the output level goes down and on the other a rise in wages increases the cost of production. Consequently, the inflationary spiral is further intensified.

3. Scarcity of Factors of Production. The supply of the factors of production is generally inelastic. For example, labour, equipments and raw materials cannot be increased on demand. Consequently, when the demand for goods and services goes up, it is not possible to increase the output to the extent of the increase in demand.

4. Natural Calamities. Sometimes natural calamities like floods, earthquakes, etc. create conditions in which the supply of goods and services declines. Even if the demand remains stationary a decrease in supply leads to the increase in the prices.

5. Increase in Exports. Sometimes the supply of goods and services in the country is reduced by an increase in the exports of such commodities and services. This causes an increase in the inflationary pressure.

6. Operation of Law of Diminishing Returns. The supply of goods and services may also slow down because of the operation of the law of diminishing returns. The law operates when production is sought to be increased by employing more units of variable factors with fixed factors and given technology. Consequently, the cost per unit goes on increasing and the result is a rise in prices.

7. War. During a war owing to an increase in demand for military requirements the supply of essential commodities and services falls short of requirements of civilian population and therefore there is a rise in prices.

8. Global Rise in Prices. Inflation may also occur because of the shortage of basic materials which are generally imported from other countries. If there is a rise in the prices of such basic materials, the prices of final products are bound to increase. This is what has been happening in the developing countries.

Conclusion

We may therefore conclude that of the two types of inflation the cost-push inflation is more difficult to control than the demand-pull inflation. It can be possible to control demand-pull inflation by proper monetary and fiscal policies; but it is not easy to reduce the cost of production with the help of these policies; for example, wages once increased cannot be brought down. Again, rise in prices is a combined effect of both demand-pull and cost-push inflation. The demand-pull inflation occurs because of an increase in money supply and aggregate expenditure while the cost-push inflation arises mainly due to increase in wages, profits and the cost of the raw materials.

6. Demand-cum-Cost Inflation

In the real life situation it is very difficult to assess whether the price rise is due to the demand-pull factors or cost-push factors. This sort of dichotomy seems to be far away from the real world situation. So, in the actual world, it is demand-cum-cost inflation. Both demand-pull factors and cost-push factors are inter-related in the inflationary process. Both types of inflation need an increase in the aggregate demand, to keep them going. They differ in that they have a different motivating force, a difference which is important from the point of view of policy.

The demand-pull inflation tends to generate forces of cost-push inflation. When prices rise due to an excess increase in aggregate demand, the workers ask for higher wages owing to a rise in the cost of living. Similarly, the cost-push inflation gives rise to demand-pull inflation; when the workers' monetary demand for consumption goods increases due to a rise in their wages. That is why, H.G. Johnson has stated that, "The two theories are, therefore, not independent and self-contained theories of inflation but rather theories concerning the mechanism of inflation in monetary environment that permits it."

7. Inflation and Developing Economies

Do We Need a Separate Theory of Inflation for Developing Economies?

During recent decades it has been held by various economists that the theories of inflation applicable to the developed economies cannot be made to apply to developing economies. These economists hold that for developing countries a separate theory of inflation need to be evolved because such countries are structurally backward, unbalanced and highly fragmented due to market imperfections. Consequently, resources are generally under-utilised, the national income is low, the rate of capital formation is low and such countries are pitiably poor. Therefore, the traditional aggregative analysis of aggregate demand and supply, which is appropriate for the developed economies where markets are efficient and integrated, does not suit to the conditions of developing countries. For these countries, we need a disaggregated sectoral analysis which can focus on the structural and sectoral bottlenecks responsible for generating inflationary tendencies. The economists who hold these views are Myrdal and Streeten in the main, besides several other Latin American economists. To sum up, therefore, we can say that in the developing economies: (*i*) inflation occurs as a result of the developmental effort and the resultant structural changes, and (*ii*) the causes and nature of inflation are determined by the socio-economic-political structure which determines the sectoral demand and supply gaps and bottlenecks that emerge in the process of development and impede it. We now discuss these gaps in the following paragraphs.

Gaps Impeding the Development Process

1. Resource Gap. The developing countries generally do not have adequate resources to embark upon a programme of economic development. Generally these countries depend for their development on the public sector. But the government is not able to raise adequate resources from taxes, public borrowing and profits of the public sector undertakings to execute the various development programmes. Consequently, the government has to take recourse to deficit financing which gives rise to inflation. Further, the private sector also, is short of resources because of low rate of savings and high costs and therefore pressure for expansion in the money stock and bank credit is ever mounting which further intensifies the inflationary spiral.

2. Foodgrains Gap. The developing countries, in general suffer from agricultural backwardness, owing to defective land tenure system, out-dated methods of cultivation, lack of irrigational facilities, growing pressure of population on land, etc. Consequently, the agricultural output falls very much short of the needs of the growing population. This gap between the demand and supply of foodgrains raises the prices of foodgrains which affect the entire structure of prices.

3. Foreign Exchange Gap. The developing countries have been having a perpetual disequilibrium in their balance of payments. They are in dire need to import capital goods, essential raw materials and semi-finished goods, and in many cases foodgrains and other consumer goods. They have a very small exportable surplus and consequently low export earnings, particularly because of the trade restrictions imposed against them by the developed countries, and their low competitive power. As a result they have a wide foreign exchange gap. They cannot increase the domestic supply of goods either through domestic production or through imports. And therefore, the prices of goods increase leading to a rise in the general price level.

4. Infrastructural Gap. Most of the developing countries suffer from inadequate infrastructural facilities particularly in the field of power supply and transport services. This stultifies the growth and development in other sectors and also leads to under-utilisation of productive capacity of the economy. Consequently, the increase in money supply is not fully absorbed in the productive process and therefore leads to inflation.

5. Resource Utilisation Gap. Such countries suffer from various imperfections like immobility of the factors of production, rigidity of prices, lack of knowledge of market conditions, rigidity of social and institutional structures, lack of training and education, etc. Consequently, optimum allocation and utilisation of resources have not been possible in these countries. Therefore, the output does not increase with an increase in the money supply which increases the inflationary pressure all the more.

6. Capital Gap. The major characteristic of these economies is the low rate of capital formation, which arises from as well as leads to poverty in these countries. Therefore, an increase in money supply instead of breaking the vicious circle of poverty, intensifies the inflationary spiral.

7. Entrepreneurial Gap. Such countries also suffer because of lack of entrepreneurial skill and adventurous spirit. Most of the business people are merchants and traders; and very few are real manufacturers and producers of capital as well as consumer goods. They do not strive to adopt innovative techniques and methods. They spend a very low proportion of their capital on R&D activities and therefore, are unable to increase real output. The increase in money supply leads to a rise in prices.

8. Labour Force Gap. The existence of disguised unemployment in these countries does not allow the increased money supply to increase the level of employment and output and therefore, the inflationary pressure is increased.

8. Inflation and Economic Development

From the foregoing analysis we can say that generally the developing countries are inflation prone. Now, the most important question is whether in such countries, inflation is a source of strength or weakness. Whether inflation promotes economic development or retards it? What is the role of inflation in the process of economic development? In this connection, we find two approaches: Keynesian approach and the quantity theory approach.

Keynesian Approach

According to Keynes inflation promotes economic growth in two ways—first, by redistributing income from wage earners to the profit earners. The former have a low propensity to save while the latter have a high propensity to save and invest. Second, inflation raises the nominal rate of return on investment as compared to rate of interest and hence promotes investment which leads to economic growth. These arguments are based on the assumption that profit earners are able to anticipate inflation while others are not. However, these arguments are not supported by facts.

Quantity Theory Approach

This approach believes that: (*i*) during long inflationary periods the behaviour of all sectors of economy gets adjusted to the expectations of inflation and therefore, (*ii*) the effect of inflation leads to redistribution of income from holders of money stock to the monetary authority and not to the redistribution of income from wage-earners to profit-earners as Keynesians hold. The transfer of money balances to the money issuing authority means that 'inflation tax' is imposed on holding of money which implies that the holders of money have to forego the real resources in order to restore the real value of their money holdings.

Inflation tax. Inflation tax consists of the real resources which are passed on by the holders of money stock to the monetary authority, as a result of inflation. If these resources are invested to execute the development programmes an inflationary policy may lead to repudiate the process of economic growth. So long as the real income is constant, each dose of the new currency to finance a government budget deficit will raise the prices proportionately. For example, if the government issues new currency worth Rs. 1 crore and if the real balances are of the order of Rs. 5 crore the nominal supply of money will rise to Rs. 6 crore and so there will be an increase of 20 per cent in the prices. This rise in prices will make the real value of money stock to fall to Rs. 5 crore and the original stock of money will now be able to purchase only goods and services worth Rs. 4 crore. Thus, the new issue of Rs. 1 crore takes away an equivalent amount of purchasing power from the existing money stock. It therefore appears that the government has confiscated 20 per cent of the existing stock of money.

It may however be mentioned that inflation tax may not always contribute to the growth of process, at least, in the initial stages of the introduction of an inflationary policy for economic development. In the initial stages the advantages of an inflationary development policy may be outweighed by waste of resources or by evasion of taxes or by a high collection cost of a tax, etc. All these would cause a waste of real resources and a reduction of real income.

Does Inflation Promote Economic Development?

The controversy regarding the contribution of inflation to economic development has led to the expression of opposite views, by two schools of thought, *viz.*, the Keynesians and the monetarists.

(A) The Keynesian View

The Keynesians believe that inflation promotes economic development while the monetarists hold just the opposite view. The arguments put forward by the Keynesians are as follows:

1. Inflation Increases Profits. Inflation increases the profits of the profit earners, that is, the entrepreneurs. Since the entrepreneurs have a high propensity to save, the savings in the economy increase which are used for the purposes of investment. With increase in investment the level of income, output and employment goes up.

2. Inflation Creates Optimistic Outlook. During inflation, prices rise faster than the costs, profits increase and the businessmen are encouraged to invest more and more in new productive enterprises. Therefore inflation creates an optimistic outlook in the investors.

3. Inflation Leads to Optimal Use of Resources. Inflation raises the level of aggregate demand which, in turn, leads to the maximum use of manpower and other resources and to the achievement of the goal of full employment.

4. Increase in Demand for Money. Deficit financing is inevitable for implementing the development projects, and also for the mobilisation of resources and their utilisation. It also helps in meeting the continuously growing demand for money during the early stage of development. Monetary expansion through deficit financing leads to increase in investment and hence aggregate output. It transforms the non-monetised sector into the monetised sector. It also results in increasing the level of income. All these factors result in the growing demand for money.

It is, therefore, clear that inflation promotes economic development. It is a continuing process; inflation helps economic development which, in turn, results in further inflation.

(B) The Monetarist's View

The monetarists led by Friedman have held that inflation retards economic growth. In this connection, they argue as under:

1. Retards the Process of Saving. Rising prices discourage people from maintaining the previous rate of saving and therefore the saving habits of the people are distorted and the rate of capital formation slows down.

2. Discourages Foreign Capital. Foreign governments and entrepreneurs are discouraged from investing further funds during the phase of inflation in the developing countries. Hence, the inflow of foreign capital is checked. Sometimes inflation may even lead to the withdrawal or diversion of foreign capital already invested in the economy.

3. Discourages Investment. The qualitative composition of investment is distorted because inflation discourages investment in key industries and infrastructural services in which either the prices are controlled or the gestation period is longer.

4. Increases the Cost of Development Projects. Rising prices lead to the increase in the cost of the development projects; the completion of which is not only delayed but the burden of such projects on the general public is also increased. Moreover, it requires injection of more money into the projects through deficit financing which further leads to rise in prices.

5. Leads to Speculation. Inflation encourages speculative investment in inventories. The businessmen, for earning more profits, speculate in scarce commodities instead of increasing their output.

6. Aggravates Balance of Payments Problem. Developing countries already do not have a happy position regarding their balance of payments. Inflation further aggravates the problem. Rising prices retard exports and increase imports. An increase in domestic incomes and prices further encourages people to import more from abroad.

7. Creates Uncertainty in Future Expectations. Inflation leads to the creation of uncertainty in future expectations and thereby distorts the entrepreneurs' investment decisions. Moreover, rising prices further activate workers movement for an increase in their wages. There are strikes and lock-outs. All these vitiate the atmosphere and retard investment.

Conclusion

We may therefore conclude that: (*i*) inflation is inevitable for economic development. It may, however, have to be ensured that the rate of inflation is kept within limits. (*ii*) The financing of economic development programmes, resulting in inflation do have a possibility of retarding the process of economic growth by: (*a*) distorting the allocation of resources, (*b*) wasting inflation-generated resources on consumption, (*c*) creating uncertainties, (*d*) discouraging innovations and improvements and (*e*) promoting inefficiency due to a system of protection and exchange control.

9. Effects of Inflation

Inflation is considered to be helpful so long as it leads to an increase in the level of income, output and employment. If it is unable to achieve this objective, it becomes dangerous to the economy. Inflation has, therefore, wide ranging effects on the economic, social, moral and political life of the country. These effects are as follows:

(A) Economic Effects of Inflation

1. Effects on Production. It is generally believed that rising prices boost up the profit expectations of the entrepreneurs. They are encouraged to increase their investments and hence output and employment. Keynes was of the view that so long as the economy does not reach the level of full employment, moderate or creeping inflation will have a beneficial effect on the economy. Hyper or galloping inflation is dangerous because it creates uncertainties, which is not good for production. Inflation is harmful for production because it interrupts the smooth operation of the price mechanism, and distorts allocation of resources. Further, it retards saving and capital accumulation by reducing the purchasing power of the people. Inflation dampens the inflow of foreign capital in the country, as already explained before. It encourages hoarding of essential commodities leading to exorbitant rise in prices and black-marketing of goods. It encourages speculative activities among the entrepreneurs. The entrepreneurs, instead of increasing their profits through genuine activities, resort to speculation and make quick profits. Inflation reduces the volume of production by slowing down the process of capital accumulation and by creating business uncertainties. Inflation leads to the diversion of resources from the production of essential commodities to the production of non-essential commodities, because the incomes of the rich increase phenomenally and consequently their demand for luxury goods increases rapidly. Finally, inflation leads to the deterioration in the quality of goods and materials. Since the chief objective of the producers is to earn high profits, the consideration of maintenance of quality is relegated to the background.

2. Effects on Distribution. Inflation results in distorting the distribution of income and wealth in the economy. Since rising prices mean a fall in the value of money or a fall in the purchasing power of money, inflation leads to a situation in which the distribution of income and wealth becomes more favourable to people with flexible incomes like businessmen, traders, merchants, speculators, etc. and it becomes unfavourable for people with fixed incomes like labourers, salaried persons, teachers, interest and rent earners, etc. Hence, people with flexible incomes gain during a period of rising prices, while people with fixed incomes lose. Inflation, thus, increases the economic burden of those sections of the society which are not in a position to bear it. That is why, inflation has been called as 'unjust'. Its effects on different sections of the society are discussed below:

(*i*) *Business and Trading Community.* During a period of inflation the business and trading community gains because its members earn windfall profits, since the cost of production of their goods does not increase as fast as the prices; and being the borrowers of money they return less, in terms of, purchasing power to their creditors.

(*ii*) *People with Fixed Income.* During inflation the fixed income groups suffer the most because, while their incomes remain fixed the real value of their incomes goes down.

(*iii*) *Debtors and Creditors.* During inflation the debtors gain and the creditors lose. The debtors gain because they had borrowed the money when the purchasing power of money was high and they repay their debts when the purchasing power of money is low. The creditors lose because they get back their money when it can purchase less quantity of goods and services as compared to the time when they had lent money when it was purchasing more quantity of goods and services.

(*iv*) *Investors.* Those investors who have invested their money in equities stand to gain in inflation because of rise in profits; while those investors who have invested their money in debentures and fixed income bearing securities, are losers because their income remains fixed.

(*v*) *Farmers.* Farmers are generally the gainers during inflation because of a faster rise in prices of farm products, than the cost of production.

(B) Non-economic Effects of Inflation

The Non-economic effects of inflation on the social, moral and political life of the people are more serious.

1. Social Effects. Inflation is inequitable because it makes the distribution of wealth more favourable for the rich. The gap between rich and the poor is widened, and the class conflict in the society is intensified.

2. Moral Effects. Inflation erodes the morality and ethics of the business class. It promotes black-marketing and increases the greed of the businessmen and trading community to reap high profits by adopting undesirable and unethical means, by resorting to the creation of artificial scarcity and adulteration in their products.

3. Political Effects. Inflation adversely affects the political life of a country. It increases corruption among the politicians, and erodes the political discipline. There is a growing feeling of discontentment among the people which results in the loss of faith in the government. The mass discontentment sometimes results in political upheavals, which may even result in the fall of the government.

It has been rightly remarked that inflation is economically unsound, politically dangerous and morally indefensible. Therefore, as far as possible inflation should be avoided and even if it is resorted to, should be kept under check.

10. Measures to Control Inflation

The policy of most of the governments in the world to combat rising prices has been along the following lines:

(A) Monetary Measures

Monetary measures are adopted by the central bank of the country to influence the supply of money and credit in the economy. These measures are discussed as follows:

1. Bank Rate. Bank rate is the rate at which the central bank lends money to the commercial banks. When the central bank increases the bank rate, the commercial banks have also to increase their lending rate and when the central bank lowers the bank rate, the commercial banks, in turn, have to decrease their rate of interest. In the period of inflation the central bank increases the bank rate which leads the commercial banks to increase their rate of interest, which in turn dampens the enthusiasm of the businessmen and consumers to obtain loans from the bank. The result is that the money supply in the economy is reduced.

2. Open Market Operations. During the period of inflation the central bank sells government securities to the commercial banks in the open market. This reduces the cash reserves of the commercial banks. Consequently, the banks are compelled to reduce their lending capacity. This results in the reduction of money supply in the economy.

3. Minimum Reserve Ratio. During a period of rising prices the central bank increases the minimum reserve ratio which implies that the commercial banks are required to keep larger reserves with the central bank. Consequently, their deposits decline, the power of the banks to create credit is restricted and thus further expansion of money supply is checked.

4. Selective Credit Control. The central bank adopts selective credit control measures to influence certain sectors of the economy. This practice is more prevalent in developing countries. Through such measures the central bank can divert the flow of credit from unproductive and inflation-prone sectors to the productive and growth-oriented sectors. First, measures are taken to curb consumer spending, particularly on consumer durables (by reducing loan facilities for instalment purchasing), and second, by raising the margin requirements for the purpose of giving loans. Margin requirement is the difference between the market value and the maximum loan value of a security. For example, if a bank was advancing a loan of Rs. 10,000 on a security worth Rs. 12,000, raising the margin requirement would mean that the bank would lend Rs. 8,000 or 9,000 or less against the security worth Rs. 12,000. In this way, the supply of money gets reduced.

Limitations of Monetary Measures

It is not necessary that the monetary measures may succeed in controlling the money supply in the economy. A dear money policy has no doubt noble objectives, but it has its own limitations, which are as follow:

(1) If the commercial banks possess excess reserves they will not have to curtail their lending activities even if the central bank increases the minimum reserve ratio.

(2) In the event of cost-push inflation, monetary measures will not succeed in controlling the factors responsible for increasing the cost of the commodities.

(3) If the inflation has been generated by the scarcity of commodities, monetary measures will not be of much help in increasing the output and hence the supply of commodities in the market.

(4) If the inflation has been generated by deficit financing, monetary measures will be hardly of any use to check it.

(5) In almost all economies large quantities of near moneys are in circulation in the market which possess high liquidity. Therefore, merely by controlling the money supply inflation cannot be controlled.

(6) According to Prof. Galbraith, there are three reasons for the failure of dear money policy to check rise in prices: (*i*) high earning investments are not affected at all by changes in the rates of interest; (*ii*) the government generally fails to have a complete control on the real investment, and (*iii*) the monetary measures are implemented with such softness that they fail to make much dent on inflation.

(B) Fiscal Measures

Fiscal measures include taxation, public expenditure and public borrowing adopted by the government of the country. During a period of rising prices the government's anti-inflationary policy includes the following fiscal measures:

1. Increase in Taxation. The objective of an anti-inflationary taxation policy is to restrict demand for goods and services without affecting their production. The objective is to curtail the purchasing power of the people. That is why, progressive direct taxes are preferred because on the one hand they reduce the disposable income of the people and on the other they are appropriate from the point of view of social equity. Excise duties, sales tax, etc. are such taxes which can be made use of aggressively during a period of price rise.

2. Reduction in Public Expenditure. During a period of rising prices the level of effective demand is very high because of the increase in public and private spending. It is, therefore, necessary that the government should check its unproductive expenditure. Since public expenditure is autonomous, its reduction will have a multiplier effect on the total expenditure of the economy. But it has also its limitations, for example, it is not possible to reduce public expenditure in all sectors, for example during war times the defence expenditure cannot be reduced or even during tension on the borders it may not be easy to reduce defence expenditure. Again, in a developing economy heavy reduction in expenditure may adversely affect long-run investment programmes.

3. Public Borrowing. The government may resort to excessive public borrowing to control inflation. Through this measure, the government takes away excess purchasing power from the people which reduces the aggregate demand and hence the price level. In inflationary conditions, public borrowing has necessarily to be compulsory, which means that the government may deduct compulsorily a certain percentage of wages or salaries in exchange for saving bonds, which may be redeemable after a few years. But it may always be not easy for the government to do so for the simple reason that it involves an element of compulsion on the people. Moreover, it may frustrate poor people who are not in a position to contribute anything.

4. Control of Deficit Financing. A deficit budget means excess of government expenditure over its revenue. To meet this deficit, the government may resort to deficit financing which means printing of new currency notes. For controlling inflation the government should reduce deficit financing to the maximum possible extent. The budget deficits, if at all necessary, can be met through saving or taxation. The government can also issue bonds for being purchased by non-banking investors like insurance companies, which will take away the extra spending power from the public and thus help in controlling inflation.

Limitations of Fiscal Measures

Anti-inflationary fiscal measures also have limitations, which are as under:

(1) Curtailment of government spending may also lead to the curtailment of several welfare schemes meant for the poor people.

(2) The government may lack efficiency in administering fiscal measures and therefore their proper implementation may not be possible.

(3) The success of fiscal measures depends on stability in the political system, strong will of the government and public co-operation, which may not be available.

(4) Fiscal measures alone may not succeed in controlling inflation and therefore a combination of fiscal and monetary measures may be required.

(C) Direct Controls

Direct controls have been used to curb consumption and investment and hence reduce the excess demand. These include rationing of consumer goods, price control, hire purchase restrictions, building licences, industrial licences, wage freeze, etc. Price controls and rationing have not been found to be very effective because of lack of a competent administrative machinery, specially in developing countries, and have often led to black-marketing and corruption. Keynes did not favour price control, because it fails to bring about equilibrium between the purchasing power and available output. Prof. Kurihara also does not support price control because of administrative difficulties. Keynes was also not in favour of rationing because it is wasteful. Kurihara has only supported rationing for "diverting consumption from particular articles whose supply is below normal," rather than for "controlling aggregate consumption".

In spite of these, direct controls are considered more effective than monetary and fiscal measures. In the modern world they seem to be inevitable because they are easy to apply and are quick in their effects; they are more selective and discriminatory; and the intensity of their operations can be varied from time to time according to the requirements of the situation.

(D) Other Measures

Besides the measures stated above there are some other measures as well which could be taken for checking price rise. These measures are:

1. Raising the Level of Output. One of the major causes of inflation is the shortfall in aggregate output relative to aggregate demand. Although it is not possible to increase the output of all the commodities in a general way, because the resources already stand utilised fully, it could, however, be possible to increase the output of certain essential consumer goods, *i.e.*, food, clothing, etc. For increasing the production of such commodities, the resources will have to be diverted from the production of luxury goods. Such re-allocation of resources will help the increase in output and check the rise in prices.

2. Proper Wage Policy. Increase in wages and profits is another reason for rise in prices. It will therefore be helpful for checking inflation if a ceiling is fixed on these, so that the disposable income is kept down and the cost-push inflation is checked. If an increase in wages seems to be inevitable, the government could link wage increase to productivity increases. This would ensure that increase in wages will not lead to increase in cost and hence increase in prices.

3. Population Control. An ever growing population is another cause for bringing about an increase in demand for goods and services and thus creating a short-fall in the supply of these commodities. It is, therefore, necessary that population is kept under control by suitable programmes and measures to check the increasing pressure on general demand for goods and services. This will help to check the rise in prices.

4. Over Valuation. Sometimes over valuation of domestic currency in terms of foreign currency may also help in controlling inflation. First, since the domestic goods will become costlier it will check exports and make available goods and services in the domestic market. Second, by encouraging imports it will add to the domestic stock of goods and services. Third, since the raw materials from abroad would be imported at a lower price, goods could be made available to the domestic market at a lower price. This will check the cost-push inflation.

5. Promotion of Savings. The government should try all possible measures to promote savings among the people. Savings reduce the purchasing power and thus disposable income of the people and check the rise in prices. Efforts should be made to control wages and profits through appropriate economic policies. If need be, wages should be freezed or linked with productivity. Such a measure will not permit the costs and prices to rise.

11. Is Inflation Bad?

Inflation in its early statge is not bad, it is rather, conducive to economic growth. Inflation which has continued over a quarter century or more at varying rates—hyper inflation—is really bad and it is this type of inflation most of the governments are confronted with. In the past hyper inflation has been caused by war. In recent years, the root cause is usually a sizeable and prolonged excess of government expenditure over tax yield.

The government cannot acquire resources indefinitely by printing notes. When the price level rises at such a fast rate that the public loses faith in the stability of the monetary unit, trade will no longer be carried on with money. Such a flight from currency implies that exchange of goods and services will take place on a purely barter basis. Since the government has nothing to barter, it must resort to outright requisition. Hyper inflation can produce a demoralising effect on the business community and impair production. A merchant will not sell his goods for money if he expects a price rise by the afternoon. Unless he is given a physical unit of some commodity he will prefer to hold his stock of goods rather than make the exchange. Production also suffers during inflation. Since workers are paid in money they have no incentive to work so that production breaks down except in a few areas where it is possible to make compensation in kind.

Looking to the social effects of hyper inflation, these are no less terrifying than the economic effects. Debtors payoff their debts in worthless currency and the creditors suffer. The earnings of fixed income groups are wiped out. The value of accumulated liquid savings disappears. Some sections of the society are defenceless. Thus, the entire society is set against itself and political institutions are under strain. Industry and thrift are replaced by hoarding and speculation. Normal economic activity is completely paralysed.

Even creeping inflation carries to some extent the danger of producing similar effects, though less drastic. If the long-run outlook is for a rising price level, the inducement to save may be impaired. Interest rates will rise owing to a fall in real savings and because of expected price increases. Investment and growth may be retarted. Creeping inflation may affect small savers adversely. Government bonds, insurance policies, saving deposits, pension rights, and other forms of fixed-interest-bearing assets decline in real value.

There is very little evidence to show that fairly mild sort of inflation has impaired economic efficiency and saving-investment decisions seriously. Anti-inflationists, however, tend to emphasise its re-distributive consequences, the fact that a mild sort of inflation, if continued for long, escalates into hyper inflation and that inflation creates balance of payments problems as long as fixed exchange rates are maintained.

So far, about the bad effects of inflation. But, is it not better to have one's income eroded by rising prices than not to have any income at all? Obviously, it is not possible for society to enrich itself by restricting output and creating unemployment. Knowing this fact, we even then attempt every time to combat inflation by inducing recession through tight money policies and restrictive budgets. The resultant loss of output and increase in unemployment easily outweigh the cost of the inflation itself. Again, people fail to appreciate the benefits of productive gains and high employment and the way these benefits are transmitted throughout the economic system.

Perhaps the chief source of anti-inflation bias lies in the fact that we are not able to measure inflation properly. The most common method of measuring price level is the use of consumer price index, which is not an index of prices but rather a measure of the cost of living for a particular representative group. Usually, such indices are constructed by taking a weighted sum of quantities multiplied by their prices in a base year. But such indices are difficult to construct properly. They contain built-in biases that make them poor measures of price changes in a growing economy.

12. Deflation

Deflation is the reverse of inflation. It is associated with a contraction of bank credit and the volume of purchasing power. If a country is on the gold standard then the bank credit and the volume of purchasing power will contract following upon an outflow of gold from the country. Off the gold standard there is never another compulsion upon a country to deflate. Since a deflationary policy will tend to raise the value of money, and thereby check production and increase unemployment, the term has acquired a somewhat sinister connotation. Deflation still tends to be associated with the Great Depression of 1930s.

Paul Einzig defines deflation as "a state of disequilibrium in which a contraction of purchasing power tends to cause, or is the effect of a decline in the price level". In fact, it means an excessive fall in prices due to contraction of currency or due to greater demand for currency. Deflation thus implies a condition in which the value of money rises.

According to Crowther, "Deflation is that state of the economy where the value of money is rising or the prices are falling." Just as every price rise is not inflation, similarly every fall in prices is not deflation. When prices fall due to the declining level of employment, output and income then it is a situation of deflation.

Causes of Deflation

Deflation usually comes after inflation. Sometimes the government or the central bank may aim at pre-war economic conditions to return and this is achieved through deflation. Moreover, the desire to maintain gold standard is often evolved by a policy of deflation. In the deflation period, the total quantity of money is not less than before, but the velocity of circulation falls. When deflation begins once, it continues for some time. The optimists lose more heavily because they become bankrupt. The pessimists lose the least. They buy small stocks of goods and postpone the dates for renewal of plants, etc. They borrow from the bankers as minimum as possible. There is a curtailment of activity everywhere. This causes deflation to go on. The slump is intensive and prolonged. When deflation comes, excessive losses take the place of windfall gains, and the effort of everyone to hold as small stocks as possible brings industry to a standstill. Unemployment takes the place of profiteering and there is a gloom over the business world. This is the vicious circle of deflation.

But will contraction go on until everybody becomes bankrupt? The answer is no. This is because people do not reduce their standard of living below a certain minimum. Past savings are spent and then the reflationary process begins. But the poor people have no savings or their savings are so low that they will be quickly exhausted. In this way, second reflationary force begins. At this stage, state comes forward and helps such people, in various ways. The state may borrow, if unemployment is acute, such borrowings are spent in creating new avenues of employment. Thus the economic system is set for reflation.

We have discussed the evil effects of deflation in a separate chapter. The deflation can be cured only by raising the level of aggregate demand in the economy. To raise the level of aggregate demand it is essential to raise the level of aggregate consumption and aggregate investment in the economy. The level of aggregate consumption or propensity to consume can be raised by adopting such measures which may induce people to spend more, *i.e.*, the government may impose direct taxation at progressive rates on people of higher income groups and grant subsidies to the poor. The level of aggregate investment could be raised by reducing the rate of interest, providing business tax reliefs and by other such measures which may increase the marginal efficiency of capital in the private sector. In the public sector, the government should undertake a massive programme of public works. Thus, the public works programme should go side by side with the measures adopted for improving the marginal efficiency of capital in the private sector. This implies that the government under the public works programme, should undertake only those projects which are either too big or which are least profitable so that they cannot be undertaken by the private sector. The manner of financing the public works programme is also very important. If the public works programme is financed through taxation, then it will not be as effective in giving a boost to the economy as much as it is financed through public borrowing or through the creation of more money, that is, by deficit financing. The most important fact, however, is that any programme of public works should be properly planned, timed and executed.

Effects of Deflation

Effects of deflation may be worse than the effects of inflation. Like inflation, it affects all and sundry. We discuss the effects of deflation as follows:

(A) Effects on Different Sections of Society

1. Producers. During the period of deflation producers suffer because of the following:

(*i*) prices fall more rapidly than the cost of manufacturing goods;

(*ii*) the time gap between the purchase of raw materials and other inputs and the delivery of final goods makes. all the difference. While producers purchase raw materials and the other inputs at higher prices, they sell the finished goods at a time when the prices have gone down because of deflation;

(*iii*) there is a fall in demand because of deflation. Consequently, profits decline, goods remain unsold and therefore there is over-production and over-supply in the market.

2. Traders and Businessmen. The traders and business people are also adversely affected, they suffer loss because they purchase their stock at higher prices but they have to sell the products at lower prices due to the trend of falling prices.

3. Investors. Deflation affects all types of investors in the society but all the investors are not equally affected. The fixed income investors are gainers because incomes remain constant while the prices decline, others with variable incomes lose because with the fall in prices their incomes decline.

4. Fixed Income Class. During the period of falling prices the wage earners and salaried persons gain because their wages and salaries remain stationary while their purchasing power goes on increasing with the falling prices.

5. Consumers. During deflation the consumers generally gain because the purchasing power of their money increases. But if there are consumers whose income declines with a fall in prices then they will be losers during deflation. Such a case may be of those whose income depends on profits.

6. Creditors and Debtors. The creditors gain during deflation because in terms of purchasing power of money they get more if the debts are repaid during the period of deflation and the debtors lose because they have to repay more in terms of purchasing power of money.

(B) General Effects

Since deflation means a general rise in the purchasing power of money it has far reaching effects on the economy of the country, which are given below:

(1) During deflation prices and profits decline, the level of output falls; some businesses are closed and the concomitant result is that the general level of employment goes down.

(2) The real burden of the tax-payers is increased because of a fall in prices and a rise in the value of money.

(3) Due to general recession in the economy the bank business also suffers since the loan advancing activity of banks stands very much reduced.

(4) The real burden of public debt increases during deflation.

(5) The pace of economic growth declines during deflation.

(6) There is a general decline in the profits of the public sector undertakings, even resulting into losses during deflation due to a fall in prices.

(7) Finally, deflation creates industrial unrest in the economy due to a rise in the number of industrial disputes.

Control of Deflation

For an effective control of deflation it is necessary that measures which may raise the level of aggregate demand in the economy should be taken. The level of aggregate demand can be raised only by means of upward shift of the level of aggregate consumption and aggregate investment in the economy. The level of aggregate consumption or propensity to consume can be raised only by adopting such measures as may induce people to spend more. Following measures can be taken to increase the level of aggregate demand in the economy:

1. Public Works Programme. In the public sector, the government should undertake a massive programme of public works. The public works programme should go side by side with the measures adopted for improving the marginal efficiency of capital in the private sector. This implies that the government under the public works programme, should undertake only those projects which are either too big or which are less profitable, so that, they cannot be undertaken by the private sector.

2. Financing of Public Works Programme. The manner of financing of the public works programme is also important. If the public works programme is financed through taxation, then it will not be as effective in giving a boost to the economy as it is financed through public borrowing or through the creation of more money, *i.e.*, by deficit financing. Deficit financing will make available to the government adequate resources for executing its developmental projects without creating an adverse effect on the level of investment in the private sector.

3. Reduction in Taxation. The government should introduce measures to reduce the burden of various taxes levied on the income of the people as well as on commodities. A reduction in taxes will increase the purchasing power of the people. Similarly, tax relief should also be provided to businessmen to encourage investment.

4. Repayment of Public Debt. The government should repay the old public debts during the period of deflation, so that the purchasing power of the people is increased and they spend more on the purchase of goods and services.

5. Redistribution of Income. The government should also take such measures which may cause a redistribution of income in favour of the poor, since their marginal propensity to consume is high.

6. Cheap Money Policy. To fight deflation the monetary authority should adapt a cheap money policy so that the interest rates are reduced and investment is stimulated. This will raise the level of economic activity in the economy.

7. Credit Expansion. As a general policy the central bank should reduce its bank rate and the commercial banks should be helped to adopt a policy of credit expansion to promote business and industry in the economy. Bank loans should be made expeditiously available to the entrepreneurs for productive activities.

8. Foreign Trade Policy. To combat deflation the government should also radically change its foreign trade policy, so that exports are promoted and imports are reduced. Such a step will solve the problem of over-production. Besides, production in the economy should be regulated in such a fashion that the over-production in the economy is reduced.

13. Which is Good—Inflation or Deflation?

Inflation and deflation are two opposite situations and both of these are necessary evils of the present day economic order. We have seen that they affect different classes of society differently. Inflation is advantageous to business, trade and industry while deflation is useful for people with fixed incomes. In other words, inflation is beneficial for production while deflation for the distribution of wealth but only when these remain within manageable limits. Whether in peace time or in war time, inflation or deflation leading to violent fluctuations in the value of money is undesirable. As Keynes remarked, "Inflation is unjust and deflation is inexpedient; of the two deflation is worse." When Keynes showed his preference for inflation, he meant that inflation is a lesser evil than deflation. Keynes never preferred inflation after the level of full employment is reached in the economy. He was against deflation because it not only redistributed wealth in an arbitrary fashion as inflation does, it also hinders the creation of new wealth in the economy. In deflation people stand more demoralised than inflation because while inflation makes it extremely difficult for people to meet their essential requirements, deflation on the other hand makes people paupers and places them in a position where they cannot meet even their essential needs, by causing mass unemployment in the economy. Deflation diminishes the productive capacity of the workers. While inflation boosts up the morale of the entrepreneurs, deflation depresses the morale of the workers and encourages the unproductive 'rentier class'. That is why, Keynes showed a preference for inflation, as he has himself said, "It is worse, in an impoverished world, to provoke unemployment than to disappoint the rentier."[4] But as Keynes has further stated that "it is not necessary that we should weigh one evil against the other. It is easier to agree that both are evils to be shunned."

14. Reflation and Disinflation

Both these terms have been invented to obviate the use of the more usual terms inflation and deflation. In the 1920s by inflation was meant what we now call hyper inflation, and it would have been difficult to persuade a government to pursue a deliberate policy of mild inflation and hence the use of the term reflation. Similarly, in recent years when it has been experienced that the only way to check hyper inflation is to adopt a mild measure of deflation, the association of the word with mass unemployment deterred governments to make use of it and so a new term disinflation had to be invented. Reflation is a moderate degree of controlled inflation. When prices have come down abnormally low so that economic activity ceases to be profitable, the monetary authority may adopt measures to put more money into circulation with a view to raise prices and encourage economic enterprise. This is one of the remedies to meet depression suggested by those who think that money

4. J.M. Keynes, *A Tract on Monetary Reform,* pp. 44-45.

factor is the primary cause of such depressions. In the words of Paul Einzig, "Reflation indicates deliberate expansionary efforts to prevent a fall in prices or to stimulate a recovery of prices following upon their fall." Disinflation is a mild form of deflation. It refers to a process of bringing down prices, when they have risen abnormally due to inflation, by contracting currency.

Exercises

1. Give a critical assessment of any one theory of inflation and give reasons for selecting that particular theory.
2. "Inflation is an excess of aggregate demand over aggregate supply." Discuss and analyse the factors which cause inflation.
3. What is inflation? What are the types of inflation?
4. What are the effects of inflation and how can inflation be controlled?
5. "Inflation widens inequalities while deflation narrows them down." Do you agree with this statement?
6. What is inflationary gap? How does it arise and how can it be removed from the economy?
7. Explain the demand-pull inflation and cost-pust inflation.
8. "Inflation is unjust and deflation is inexpedient; of the two deflation is worse." Comment.
9. Distinguish between demand-pull and cost-push inflation. Why is it difficult to separate one from the other?
10. How do you account for inflation in an under-developed country?
11. Is inflation harmful for economic development?
12. "Inflation is inevitable in a developing economy." Discuss.
13. "The distinction between cost-push and demand-pull inflation is unworkable, irrelevant and even meaningless." Do you agree? Give reasons for your answer.
14. Discuss the theory of structural inflation.
15. Is inflation purely a monetary or purely a non-monetary or an institutional phenomenon? Give your answer keeping in view the inflationary conditions prevailing in a developing country.
16. Write notes on: (*a*) open and suppressed inflation, (*b*) mark-up inflation, (*c*) stagflation, and (*d*) sectoral inflation.
17. How do you account for inflation in developing countries? Is inflation harmful for economic development?
18. Explain the meaning and consequences of deflation. How will you use the monetary and fiscal policies to combat the evils of deflation?

•••

Exercises

Chapter 11

Phillips Curve and Stagflation

1. Introduction

Both Keynes and Mrs. Robinson foresaw a possibility of attaining simultaneously the dual objective of full employment and price stability without the help of either price control or wage control. However, the experience of many countries with strong producer pressure groups shows that a fall in the level of unemployment increases pressure on prices and when the price level is stable, unemployment crosses the level which is considered 'socially tolerable' by countries committed, in principle, to achieve full employment.

2. Phillips Curve[1]

This has also been substantiated by research into the relationship between money wage-rates and the level of unemployment in UK, between 1861 and 1957 carried out by Prof. A.W. Phillips. From it is obtained the 'Phillips Curve' which depicts this relationship and is shown in Figure 11.1.

The research made by Prof. Phillips appears to support the hypothesis that the rate of change of money wage-rate can be explained by the level of unemployment and the rate of change of unemployment. The relation between the rate of change of money-wage rates and unemployment is likely to be curvilinear and not linear. Phillips has used this curve to determine that for the UK a rate of 5.5 per cent unemployment is needed if wages are to be held steady and a rate of 2.5 per cent unemployment is needed if prices are to be held steady. This means that wages would rise by the same percentage as increase in productivity which is estimated to be 2 per cent per year. In other words, wages will rise when unemployment is low and wages will fall but slowly because of the downward rigidity of wage rates, when unemployment

1. A.W. Phillips, The Relation between Unemployment and the Rate of Change of Money Wage Rates in the United Kingdom, 1861-1957, *Economica,* November 1958, pp. 283-99.

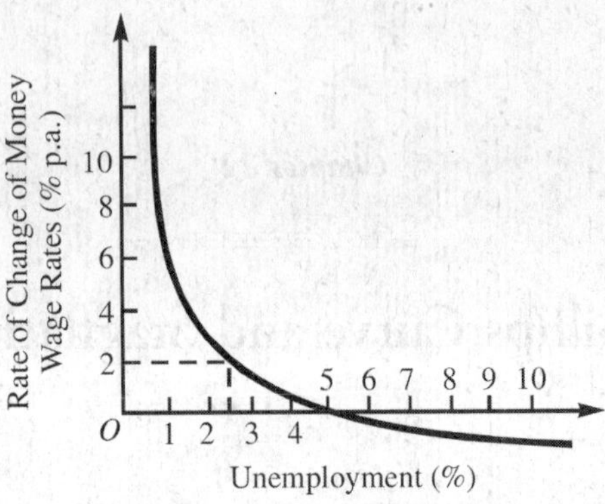

Fig. 11.1

is high. This inverse relationship between the rate of change of money wages and the rate of unemployment has come to be known as Phillips' Curve.

It appears that Phillips' main argument was demand-pull in nature. The low level of unemployment reflects the excess demand because excess demand in the labour market causes wage inflation and also determines its speed. During periods of low unemployment labour scarcity causes an upward rise in wages. Similarly, during periods of high unemployment the excess supply of labour causes wages to move downwards.

Samuelson and Solow[2] have estimated a similar curve for the USA and have found more optimistic figure of 2.5 per cent unemployment necessary for price stability assuming that productivity increases at 2.5 per cent per annum.

3. Lipsey's Analysis[3] of Phillips Curve

The statistical relationship established by Phillips in the wage inflation and unemployment has been further analysed by Prof. Lipsey. In this connection, he has pointed out two behavioural relationships: (*i*) a positive relation between the rate of change in the money wage-rates and the magnitude of excess demand for labour; and (*ii*) an inverse non-linear relation between excess demand for labour and unemployment. These two relationships are found in single micro labour market.

Lipsey assumes that wage inflation is the increasing function of the proportionate excess demand for labour. He further maintains that the relation

2. Samuelson and Solow, Analytical Aspects of Anti-Inflation Policy, *American Economic Review,* May 1960, pp. 174-94.
3. R.G. Lipsey, "The Relation between Unemployment and the Rate of Change of Money Wage Rates in the United Kingdom 1862-1957: A Further Analysis", *Economica,* February 1960.

between excess demand for labour and the rate of unemployment is negative and non-linear which implies that the greater the excess demand, the lower will be the level of unemployment and the lower the excess demand the higher will be the level of unemployment. When the excess demand is zero, the labour market will be in equilibrium, but this does not mean that there will not be any unemployment. Lipsey measures the excess demand for labour by only the excess of number of vacancies over the number of unemployed persons. Thus, excess demand for labour can be zero only when the unemployment rate is positive. The unemployment compatible with zero excess demand is called frictional unemployment, which arises because of the lack of instantaneous matching of vacancies with unemployed workers.

The non-linear relationship means that while the unemployment rate will fall below frictional level because of the positive excess demand for labour, it can never fall below zero, however high the level of excess demand may be.

4. Policy Implications of Phillips Curve

Phillips curve analysis aroused considerable interest among the policy makers particularly because of the implications of its relationship with price inflation. Changes in the price level were first related to the changes in the money wage rate and that is why Phillips curve expressed the inverse relationship between the rate of price inflation and the rate of unemployment. The policy makers, therefore, interpreted Phillips curve as a relation between price inflation and unemployment. Thus Phillips curve enables the policy makers to choose a given rate of unemployment (or inflation) and bear the cost of a necessary rate of inflation (or unemployment). It means that inflation can be reduced only at the cost of higher unemployment or it can be increased only at the cost of lower unemployment.

5. Criticisms of Phillips Curve

(1) The explanation provided by Prof. Phillips has not been accepted by all the economists. According to some economists changes in the price level are at least as important in determining changes in the wage-rates as unemployment, which have been ignored by Prof. Phillips.

(2) The 'money illusion' among workers as suggested by Keynes is largely absent in today's bargaining because wage earners would make every effort to retain their share of national income if this has been eroded by rise in prices.

(3) Prof. H.G. Johnson has raised doubts about the applicability of the Phillips curve to the formulation of economic policy. In this connection he says, "On the one hand the curve represents only a statistical description of

the mechanics of adjustment in the labour market resting on the simple model of economic dynamics with little general and well tested monetary and value theory behind it. On the other hand, it describes the behaviour of the labour market in a combination of periods of economic fluctuation and varying rate of inflation, conditions which presumably influence the behaviour of the labour market itself, so that it may reasonably be doubted whether the curve would continue to hold its shape if an attempt were made by economic policy to pin the economy down to a point on it."[4]

Johnson[5] has further criticised the Phillips curve analysis on two grounds: (*i*) it does not provide any basic theoretical principle which can be verified by his study. And so it is only a statistical description; and (*ii*) it is the crudest explanation of the dynamics of economic market.

(4) According to Milton Friedman[6] relationship between the volume of employment and the rate of change in money prices is fallacious, because it implies a relationship between real and nominal magnitudes.

(5) The Phillips curve has virtually no practical value because it is unstable and not permanent. Relationship between inflation rate and unemployment rate as observed by Prof. Phillips is neither stable through time within a country nor across the countries.

(6) The powerful role played by trade unions in the determination of wage rates in the labour market and thus in influencing the wages has also been ignored.

(7) Wages and prices are influenced by each other. Wages first influence prices through the increase in the cost of production and then prices influence wages through their effect on cost of living. The Phillips curve only considers the effect of wages on the prices and ignores the effect of prices on wages.

(8) The Phillips curve analysis is based on the assumption that inflation is an internal phenomenon of a country but in fact inflation now is an international phenomenon.

(9) The Phillips curve analysis fails to provide an explanation of the existence of stagflation, that is, existence of high rate of inflation with high rate of unemployment, found in all the highly industrialised countries of the world.

6. Stagflation

Stagflation is a situation in which prices and unemployment grow simultaneously. In other words, when high rate of inflation exists with high

4. Harry G. Johnson, *Essays in Monetary Economics,* London, 1967, pp. 132-33.
5. Harry G. Johnson, *Inflation and Monetarist Controversy,* 1972, pp. 58-59.
6. Milton Friedman, The Role of Monetary Policy, *American Economic Review,* March 1959.

rate of unemployment the situation is termed as stagflation. This phenomenon of stagflation has been witnessed since 1967 onwards by the major industrialised countries of the world. It proves that the prediction of Phillips curve has been untrue and wrong, because Phillips observed that with high rate of inflation the level of unemployment will be low.

Causes of Stagflation

We come across with a number of views about the phenomenon of stagflation. The most prominent of these are the explanation of stagflation provided by the followers of Keynes, the other is the view expressed by supply side economists and the third is the view expressed by the monetarists. These views are given as follows:

1. Keynesians View. The Keynesians hold that the phenomenon of stagflation causes an upward shift in the Phillips curve which indicates that the given level of unemployment is associated with a higher rate of inflation. This upward shift is caused primarily by an increase in the cost of production. An increase in the cost of production is caused by various factors such as the global increase in the prices of crude oil, increase in wages under the pressure of trade unions or due to an increase in the cost of living due to rise in prices and changes in the composition of demand for labour.

2. Supply-side View. According to the supply side economists, stagflation has been caused by a rise in the cost of production and a shortfall in the aggregate supply of goods and services created by the various measures adopted by the government, for example, minimum wage legislation, social security measures, high tax rates, etc. Higher tax rates reduce the after-tax pay of the workers, after-tax interest earnings of the savers and after-tax return of the investors. Consequently, saving, investment and work effort, all are discouraged which adversely affect the level of output and employment and increase prices in turn.

3. Monetarists View. The monetarists hold that stagflation is caused by the changes in inflationary expectations. The monetarists view is best explained by the Friedman-Phelps model which explains that an expansionary monetary policy can raise the level of employment at the cost of inflation only when the workers are enabled to anticipate correctly the rate of inflation. Such a policy will never be able to reduce the employment. It can succeed only in the short period so long as the government is able to befool the labour by maintaining an actual inflation rate higher than that expected by labour. In the long run, when the labour is able to correctly anticipate the rate of inflation which is actually higher, the unemployment rate will return to its natural level. And so, in the long run both the price level and the rate of unemployment will increase as a result of the expansionary monetary policy.

Principal Causes of Stagflation

From the above views it is clear that the main cause of stagflation is the reduction of aggregate supply, due to which the levels of output and employment fall and the level of prices rises. This shortfall in the aggregate supply is caused by a number of factors, which are:

1. Restricted Supply of Labour. The supply of labour may be restricted by a rise in money wages under the pressure from trade unions, a rise in legal minimum wage and an increase in marginal tax rate, adversely affecting workers' work effort.

2. Increase in Indirect Taxes. Higher commodity taxes increase cost and prices and cause a decline in the level of output and employment.

3. Global Increase in the Prices of Essential Raw Materials. A rise in the prices of essential raw materials, like crude oil, at the international level increases the costs and prices of domestic products and thus restricts output.

4. Increase in Money Wages. Due to an increase in money wages there is a rise in the cost of production. Money wages do not rise because of a rise in the prices but because of the variations in the expectations of prices to rise. The labour force, therefore, makes an attempt for the restoration of the same level of real wages which prevailed prior to the inflationary expansion in demand.

Measures to Control Stagflation

The following measures can be adopted to control stagflation:

1. Anti-inflationary Income Policy. An anti-inflationary income policy adopted by the government is not aimed at affecting the prices and incomes of specific commodities and groups of people but to check or to slow down a rise in the general price level and level of money incomes. If the income policy succeeds in controlling prices and wages, not only would the current rise in prices be checked but the expected rate of inflation would also be reduced. So, the basic objective of an anti-inflationary income policy should be to couple the increase of money wages with the increase in productivity, and both should be properly aligned. Additionally, the prices in different industries will also have to be increased or decreased or stabilised according to the productivity growth. In industries having productivity growth rate above national average rate, prices should be reduced; in industries having productivity growth rate below the national average rate the prices should be increased and in industries where the productivity growth rate is equal to the national average rate the prices should be stabilised.

The chief difficulty of an income policy is that an effective control of wages and prices is possible only in the short run. Such controls actually aggravate the problem of inflation after the termination of income policy due to pent-up liquidity. And, therefore, the income policy to be effective in reducing inflationary expectations, must be combined with a policy of restricting the rate of monetary inflation in accordance with the inflation target, after allowing margin for output growth and secular change in the velocity of circulation of money.

2. Reduction in the Marginal Tax Rates. We have already stated the view of the supply side economists that higher marginal tax rates lead to a decline in the supply of labour, saving and investment and therefore lead to an upward shift in the aggregate supply curve. If that happens, then stagflation can be checked by reducing the marginal tax rates.

3. Manpower Policies. There is general agreement among the economists that proper manpower policies can provide a real solution for keeping inflation and unemployment under check on a long-run basis. Such manpower policies can be:

(*i*) *Reduction in the Frictions in the Labour Market.* The frictions can be reduced by minimising the time and cost of collecting information about employment opportunities and vacancies.

(*ii*) *Removal of Barriers.* Barriers which limit the entry into a profession or artificially maintain wages at high rate, should be removed.

(*iii*) *Manpower Training.* Proper manpower training programmes should be initiated to ensure the mobility of labour.

(*iv*) *Improvement of Skills.* Proper programmes for the improvement and upgradation of skills and competence of the workers; should be undertaken to bring about a change in the pattern of supply of labour.

(*v*) *Composition of Labour Demand.* Measures should be undertaken to increase the employment opportunities so that the composition of labour demand is favourably influenced.

7. Friedman-Phelps Model of Stagflation

Milton Friedman and E.S. Phelps[7] have tried to explain the phenomenon of stagflation and thus to prove the instability of the Phillips curve, in terms of inflationary expectations. According to this model: (*i*) the excess labour demand affects real wage and not the money wage and therefore Phillips curve is wrong; (*ii*) the trade-off between money wage inflation and unemployment can exist only in the short run, so long as both buyers and sellers of labour remain confused about the identity of money wages and real wages and are unable to anticipate correctly the rate of inflation. Since, in the

7. M. Friedman, "The Role of Monetary Policy", *American Economic Review,* Vol. 58, March 1968, pp. 1-17; E.S. Phelps, "Money Wage Dynamics and Labour Market Equilibrium", *Journal of Political Economy,* Vol. 76, pp. 678-711.

short period both the buyers and sellers of labour confuse money wage changes with real wage changes and wrongly interpret inflation, the changes in the money wage rates can offset the rate of unemployment. To explain it further, when the monetary authority adopts an expansionary policy, the economy experiences both price and wage inflation. The rise in money wages will be wrongly interpreted by the buyers of labour as a reduction in the real wage and by the supplier of labour as an increase in real wages. And therefore, in the short run both employment and inflation will rise. Hence, the prediction of the Phillips curve appears to be true. But this will be only short lived. Ultimately both the buyers and suppliers of labour will correctly assess the rate of inflation which is actually higher and will incorporate the same into new labour contracts and consequently the unemployment rate will return to its old natural level. Hence, there is no trade-off between inflation and unemployment in the long run.

From the policy point of view the implication of this model is that the monetary policy can influence both employment and output only in the short run and not in the long run.

Criticisms of the Friedman-Phelps Model

This model has been criticised on the following counts:

1. Persistence of Unemployment. This model does not properly explain the reasons for the persistence of unemployment below or above the equilibrium level. The model attributes unemployment persistence to the delays in the availability of information generated endogenously in the model by the inflationary or deflationary shocks. But, this delay is not generated endogenously by the model and therefore it is difficult to precisely know its length. It is therefore not possible to know the extent of change in unemployment due to inflationary or deflationary shocks.

2. Degree of Adjustment to Inflation. The model leans heavily on the assumption regarding the extent of adjustment of expected inflation to actual inflation. There can be three positions: (*i*) If the adjustment is full then it would mean that the expected inflation has been fully absorbed into the current wage changes, so that there is no money-illusion and there is no trade-off between inflation and unemployment in the long run. (*ii*) If the degree of adjustment is nil, then it means that the workers suffer from money-illusion and therefore there is a trade-off between inflation and unemployment as predicted by Phillips curve. (*iii*) Finally, if the adjustment is less than full then it means that workers have been only partially compensated for anticipated inflation. It implies that there is some trade-off between inflation and unemployment and the workers do have money-illusion, even in the long run.

3. Empirical Evidence. Empirical evidence suggests that the degree of adjustment between expected and actual inflation ranges between .3 and .8. It means that people do adjust to inflation and are subject to some degree of money-illusion and therefore the adjustment is not complete, as suggested by Friedman-Phelps model.

4. Implication about Money-Illusion. The degree of adjustment being nearly zero or sufficiently less than unity does not necessarily mean that people are subject to money-illusion. If wages are settled through collective bargaining, the workers may not be able to fully incorporate their inflationary expectations into their contracts.

5. Assumption regarding Expectations. The model assumes that current expectations are equal to the weighted average of past rates of inflation. This has been challenged by the concept of rational expectations. According to this concept expectations are formed rationally on the basis of an economic model of the determination of the variable concerned and not according to the weighted average of the past values of the variable.

6. Rational Expectations Hypothesis. According to the model the real variables can be influenced by monetary policy only in the short run and not in the long run. But the rational expectations hypothesis states that the monetary policy aiming at stabilisation cannot lead all people to estimate the rate of inflation correctly. Some of the people will underestimate and others will overestimate. It thus means that the stabilisation policy cannot succeed to affect the output and employment levels even in the short run.

7. Concept of Natural Rate of Unemployment. The critics have pointed out that the concept of natural rate of unemployment, on which the model is based, has not been defined in specific terms and therefore it is vague.

Exercises

1. Discuss the theory of the Phillips curve and bring out its apparent policy implications.
2. Explain the relationship between inflation and unemployment.
3. What is Phillips curve? Discuss its utility as a tool of economic analysis.
4. How does the Phillips curve explain the trade-off between unemployment and inflation? Discuss its policy implications.
5. Examine the factors which cause shifts in the short run in Phillips curve.
6. Explain the phenomenon of stagflation. Suggest measures to control it.
7. Examine Friedman-Phelps model of stagflation.

●●●

Chapter 12

Theories of Trade Cycles

1. Introduction

The predominantly private enterprise economies, have over the last one century, faced fairly regular fluctuations in the level of economic activity. Up to the World War-I these fluctuations followed a pattern in which the average period of the cycle from peak to peak or trough to trough was five to eight years and the average fluctuation in the level of output was from five to ten per cent. Between two World Wars the same pattern could be discerned, but the fluctuations took place in unusually depressed conditions. Since 1945, however, fluctuations have been much less marked mainly because of the counter-cyclical policies adopted by the governments. These periodical fluctuations in aggregate economic activity, particularly in employment, output, income, prices, etc. which occur with a certain regularity have been named as trade cycles or business cycles.

2. Definitions of Trade Cycles

Trade cycles have been defined differently by different economists. Let us cite a few definitions.

According to W.C. Mitchell, "Business cycles are a species of fluctuations in the economic activities of organized communities: The adjective 'business' restricts the concept to fluctuations in activities which are systematically conducted on a commercial basis. The noun 'cycles' bars out fluctuations which do not recur with a measure of regularity."[1]

According to Keynes, "A trade cycle is composed of periods of good trade characterised by rising prices and low unemployment percentages alternating with periods of bad trade characterised by falling prices and high unemployment percentages."[2]

1. W.C. Mitchell, *Business Cycles.* Vol. I, p. 468.
2. J.M. Keynes, *A Treatise on Money.* Vol. I, p. 78.

To quote Gordon: "Business cycles consist of recurring alternation of expansion and contraction in aggregate economic activity, the alternating movements in each direction being self-reinforcing and pervading virtually all parts of the economy." Frederic Benham defines a trade cycle as "a period of prosperity followed by a period of depression. It is not surprising that economic process should be irregular, trade being good at some time and bad at others."[3]

Tinbergen views a trade cycle as the "inter-play between erratic shocks and an economic system able to perform cyclical adjustment movements to such shocks."

According to Ragnar Frisch, "Impulses from outside operate upon the economy, causing it to move in a wave-like manner, just as an external shock will set a pendulum swinging. But it is the 'inner structure of the swinging system' which determines the length of the wave movement. The oscillations of the system may have a high degree of regularity, even though the impulses which set it going are quite regular in their behaviour."

Hansen defines a trade cycle as, "Peculiarly a manifestation of industrial segment of the economy from which prosperity or depression is redistributed to other groups in the highly inter-related modern system."

From the above definitions it is clear that a trade cycle is characterised by a period of good trade, rising prices and low level of unemployment, alternating with a period of bad trade, falling prices and high level of unemployment. It is a very complicated economic phenomenon. Economists have not been able to arrive at a unanimously agreed conclusion regarding the nature and the period of a trade cycle.

3. Features of Cyclical Fluctuations

Describing the characteristics of these cyclical fluctuations, Estey writes, "These cyclical fluctuations are characterised by alternating waves of expansion and contraction. They do not have a fixed rhythm, but they are cyclical in that the phases of contraction and expansion recur frequently and in fairly similar patterns. These patterns are most marked in those countries which are built upon 'business' rather than agriculture and have been particularly notable in England and the United States for over one hundred years."[4] All fluctuations in the economy are therefore not cyclical. Cyclical fluctuations have the following features:

1. Synchronic. A trade cycle is synchronic. The entire business of an economy acts like an organism. Any happening on the economic front affects

---

3. Frederic Benham, *Economics.* p. 341.
4. James Arther Estey, *Business Cycles,* p. 11.

the entire economy and through the mechanism of international trade, the entire world.

2. Recurrent. Cyclical fluctuations are wave-like movements and are recurrent in nature. A trade cycle is characterised by alternation of expansion (prosperity) and contraction (depression) in economic activity. They are repetitive and rhythmic. The period of prosperity is followed by depression which is followed by a period of prosperity.

3. Cumulative. The process of expansion and contraction is of a cumulative self-reinforcing nature. Each upswing or downswing feeds on itself and generates further movements in the same direction, until its direction is reversed by external forces.

4. Self-generating. A trade cycle contains self-generating forces, *i.e.*, it can terminate the period of prosperity and start depression. Thus, there cannot be either an indefinite depression or an unending prosperity.

5. Not-identical. The periods of trade cycle are not identical, although they recur with great regularity. Some are mild while others are quite severe. In some, the upswing is longer than the downswing and in others it is just the reverse.

6. Asymmetrical Movements. The peak and trough in a trade cycle are not symmetrical. The movements from upward to downward is more sudden and violent than that from downward to upward. The downturn is sharp and steep. In statistical terms it is relatively narrow at its peak and flatter at its trough.

Considerable variations in the frequency and amplitude of cyclical movements have been found and therefore, no two cycles have been alike or symmetrical. This may have been firstly, due to the various external factors like wars and political changes, advances in technical knowledge, changes in consumers' preferences, floods and droughts, etc. upsetting the pattern, and secondly, because not one but innumerable cycles operate concurrently. All these cycles do not move in harmony; some lead the overall picture, some lag behind it. As Stanley Bober describes it, "In one sense a business cycle is not a 'real' phenomenon but a way of describing the net effect on the economy of short run cyclical movements in individual activity."

4. Types of Trade Cycles

Trade cycles have been classified differently by different economists. J.A. Schumpeter distinguished three types of cycles: the *Short Kitchin Cycle* of approximately forty months' duration, the longer *Juglar wave* averaging nine and a half years' length and the very long *Kondratieff Wave* taking more than fifty years to run its course. Subsequently, Kuznets distinguished 'secular swing' of 16-20 years which has been described as 'so pronounced that it dwarfs the 7-11 years cycle into relative insignificance.'

5. Phases of Trade Cycle

One of the tasks of economic analysis is to look behind the general cycle, at the large number of individual cycles comprising it. It follows then, that although an analysis of trade cycles will provide us with clues for predicting the future course of events, no cycle is likely to be identical with its predecessors; the forces leading to expansion in one cycle phase may be quite differently apportioned from the forces which led to expansion in a preceding phase. A single comprehensive theory of cyclical fluctuations is, therefore, really unattainable. Consequently, large number of theories have been set forth, some attributing cycles to wholly *exogenous* causes, such as variations in climatic conditions, others asserting them to be generated *endogenously* through the inner nature and motion of the economic system itself. Before

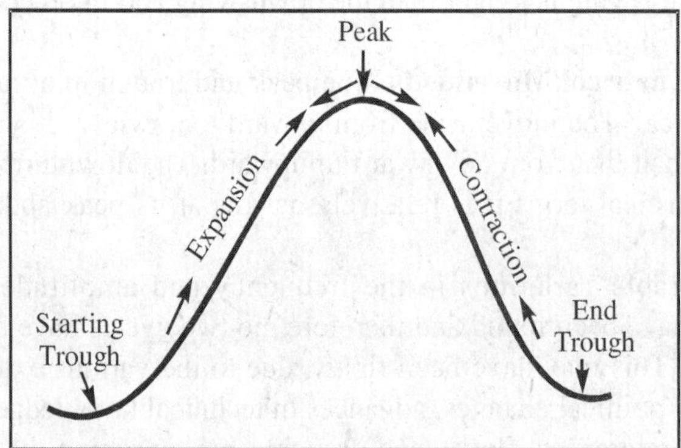

Fig. 12.1

taking up the various theories of trade cycle, let us briefly describe the various phases of a trade cycle. According to the analysis given by Burns and Mitchell there are two major phases of a trade cycle, *viz*., expansion and contraction; the two critical mark-off points being peak and trough. The expansion phase extends from trough to peak while the contraction phase extends from peak to trough. Apart from these phases, there are also two turning points, *i.e.*, upper and lower turning points whose duration is relatively short. The lower turning point leads to the revival of the economy which rapidly grows into the expansion phase while the upper turning point leads to recession that soon throws the economy into depression. Thus, there are four phases of a trade cycle according to this analysis, *viz*., (*i*) revival, (*ii*) expansion, (*iii*) recession, and (*iv*) contraction. They have also divided a complete cycle from trough to trough into nine stages.[5] Figure 12.1 gives an idea of these stages.

However, this analysis was not acceptable to Schumpeter. He held that a trade cycle, should be marked of from equilibrium to equilibrium. According to him a trade cycle could be either of two phases or of four phases. In a two-phase cycle, the economic activity is either above the equilibrium level or below it. There are four equilibrium points and the equilibrium areas cluster around them. Figure 12.2 shows the operation of a two-phase cycle.

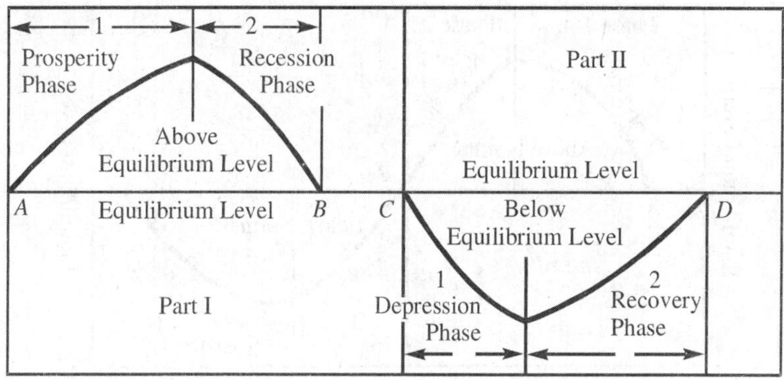

Fig. 12.2

Part I of the above Figure shows the two-phase cycle in which economic activity is above the equilibrium level while Part II shows that the economic activity is below the equilibrium level during the entire period of the cycle. Thus, there are four equilibrium points and the equilibrium areas cluster around these points. In Part I, beginning from the equilibrium point *A* and ending at the equilibrium point *B,* the economy has been functioning above normal level. The period between these two points could be regarded as 'good'. This period could be divided into: (*i*) the prosperity phase, and (*ii*) the recession phase. In Part II the trade cycle operates in the reverse direction. Here, the economy is operating below normal level. Thus, this period of the trade cycle may be called as 'bad'.

Schumpeter divided the four-phase cycle as follows: (*i*) the prosperity phase, (*ii*) the recession phase, (*iii*) the depression phase, and (*iv*) the revival phase. This cycle is just a combination of the two phases of the above normal activity and below normal activity cycles. In Fig. 12.3 the first half of the cycle is divided into two phases, *viz*., the prosperity phase characterised by an increase in the level of employment and the recession phase when the

5. A.F. Burns, and W.C. Mitchell, *Measuring Business Cycles,* NBER, New York, 1946.

employment is on the decline. When the economy reaches the point *B*, the second half of the cycle starts which again has two phases, *i.e.*, the depression phase characterised by the falling employment and the recovery or revival phase characterised by increasing employment.

Broadly speaking, a trade cycle has four phases, *viz.*, boom or the upswing, recession or the upper turning point, depression or the downswing and recovery or the lower turning point. We describe, very briefly, the chief features of each of these as follows:

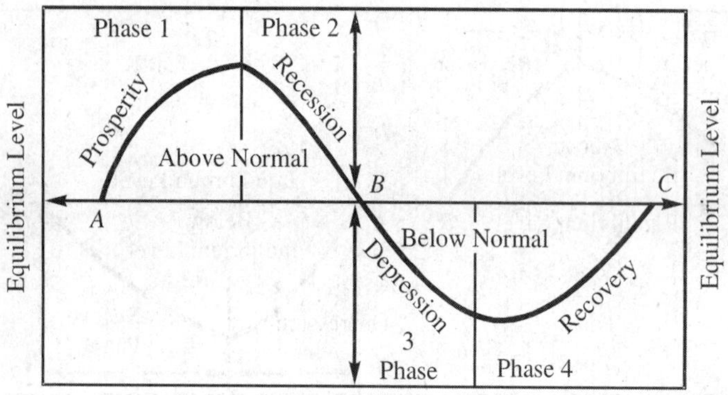

Fig. 12.3

Boom

In this period there is all round prosperity. The business outlook is extremely optimistic. The economy operates at full capacity. The level of employment is high; the volume of output is large; the price level tends to be rising; interest rates tend to increase; speculative activities are at high pitch; investment spending is at a high level; total income of the country increases and credit expansion is at its height. In short, the economic activity is at its pinnacle and the idle resources or unemployed workers are very few.

Recession

As soon as the near full-employment is reached, the equilibrium is disturbed by shortage of investment funds leading to an increase in lending rates, and shortage of factors leading to an increase in their prices, finally resulting in increased costs and high prices. Consumer spending falls, leading to a decline in sales and hence revenues. With a view to liquidating their stocks, the firms start selling their goods at a low price and hence most of the firms suffer losses. Investment spending declines and unemployment starts, leading to a fall in the aggregate demand. A wave of pessimism sweeps the entire economy. The turning point from optimism to pessimism or the point where the period of boom ends, is called the point of recession. In fact, as Professor Lee has remarked, "A recession once started, tends to build upon itself much as forest fire, once underway, tends to create its own draft and gives internal impetus to its destructive activity."[6]

Depression

The period of recession is rather short because depression sweeps the economy very soon. It is just the opposite of boom. In the words of Haberler, "Depression means a state of affairs in which real income consumed or volume of production per head and the rate of employment are falling or are sub-normal in the sense that there are idle resources and unused capacity, especially unused labour."[7] The entire economic activity becomes slack. The level of unemployment rises, rates of interest and wages and profits tend to fall, the national income, production, investment and the price level—all show a declining trend. The level of aggregate demand reaches the lowest point.

Recovery

But the forces causing depression reinforce the economic activity. The same forces rejuvenate the economy. During depression, the businessmen postpone replacement of their equipment and the consumers defer their spending on the purchase of durable goods. When prices crash, they start purchasing capital goods and so the level of output increases, which increases the level of employment and hence the level of aggregate demand. The process of recovery once started takes the economy to the peak of prosperity and the cycle is completed repeating itself at frequent intervals.

6. Theories of Trade Cycle

In view of limited space, it is not possible to discuss in detail each and every theory propounded so far and therefore, we describe some of the more important theories here:

(1) The Sunspot Theory

This theory was propounded by W.S. Jevons, the noted British economist, in 1875 and is the oldest theory on the subject. He contended that variations in the atmosphere of the sun as evidenced in the frequency and the magnitude of the sunspots influence the climate and hence the rainfall. These occurrences have a very profound influence upon harvests which in turn influence the level of business activity. A bad climate leads to crops failure which gives an

---

6. M.W Lee, *Economic Fluctuations* (Homewood, 1955), p. 42.
7. G. Haberler, *Prosperity and Depression,* p. 259.

unusual depression and enwraps the whole economy. Good climate brings boom and prosperity to agriculture and to trade and industry. These periods of good and bad agricultural production alternate with each other and hence boom and depression follow each other. They are actually rhythmic in nature. In this respect Jevons appears to have drawn inspiration from the suggestions of Sir William Herschel. According to him the business cycles occur with a 10 or 11 year cycle in the sunspot activity. In the recent past, an American economist, H.L. Moore, also pointed out that there was a marked cycle in rainfall in the major agricultural regions of the USA which was the cause of the business cycle. He was also of the view that there was some relation between the rainfall cycles and the planet Venus, which passes every 8 years between the earth and the sun. Thus, according to Moore business cycle is a natural phenomenon and, the meterological influences are transmitted through agriculture to other sectors of the economy. The protagonists of this theory emphasise that the Great Depression of the nineteen thirties was also caused by the climatic changes in the predominantly agricultural countries which ultimately spread to industrial countries as well.

However, the theory does not have many supporters today. It is not easy to prove that trade cycles are exclusively the result of climatic changes; if these were, then trade cycles would never occur in highly industrialised countries which are not dependent on agriculture. But facts do not support this. We can believe at the most that meteorological influences are one of the many factors that cause the occurrence of the trade cycle.[8]

(2) The Psychological Theory

This theory has been developed by a number of economists like J.S. Mill, Beveridge, Marshall, Pigou, Lescure, Keynes, etc. It is a group of theories which attribute the occurrence of trade cycles to psychological and emotional reactions of the business community to the changing conditions of the economy. The tendency of the business class to react quickly to any change, may be, in the rates of interest or the government policy relating to imports and exports, or a change in situation due to war or failure of crops, etc. causes cyclical fluctuations. All the economists, whose names have been mentioned above had almost the same view. Beveridge, in his work *Unemployment: A Problem of Industry,* published in 1909, stressed the important part played by

8. To many economists this theory is a mere pedagogic exercise. J.M. Clark, in this connection says, "This does not mean that agriculture has no effect on the business cycle. ... It simply means that agriculture is not a regularly acting force tending typically and regularly to help initiate recovery or stimulate the revival or in any other way to play habitually the same role in at least a predominant number of cycles." J.M. Clark, *Strategic Factors in Business Cycles* (1935), p. 62.

psychological factors in the occurrence of a trade cycle and held them exclusively responsible for its occurrence. According to him the tendency of the business class to react excessively to the changing conditions of the economy is responsible chiefly for the cyclical fluctuations. The same year Lescure presented a psychological explanation for the occurrence of the trade cycle. He held that the actual cause. of alternately occurring waves of over-production and under-production lies in the fluctuations in the profit expectations of the business community. Pigou also treated the occurrence of the industrial fluctuations solely to psychological factors—over-pessimism and over-optimism of the business class. Their over-optimism during periods of brisk trade causes over-production and leads to over-valuation of capital assets. As Keynes pointed out, "It is an essential characteristic of the boom that investments which will in fact yield, say 2 per cent in conditions of full employment are made in the expectation of a yield of 6 per cent, and are valued accordingly.[9] Since the supply exceeds the demand, the products remain unsold, businessmen suffer losses and immediately they grow pessimistic and reduce their productive activities. To quote Keynes again, "When disillusion comes, this (optimistic) expectation is replaced by a contrary 'error of pessimism' with the result that investments which would in fact yield 2 per cent in conditions of full employment are expected to yield less than nothing; and the resulting collapse of new investment then leads to a state of employment in which the investment, which would have yielded 2 per cent in conditions of full employment, in fact yields less than nothing."[10] According to Pigou, "The extent of the revulsion towards pessimistic error, which follows when optimistic error is disclosed, depends, in part; upon the magnitude of the preceding optimistic error....But it is also affected by what one may call the detonation which accompanies the discovery of a given amount of optimistic error. The detonation is greater or less according to the number and scale of the legal bankruptcies into which the detected error explodes."[11] In short, the theory states that industrial fluctuations are caused by the psychological reactions of the industrial community.

The psychological theory, no doubt, states only a part of the truth and neglects the part played by various exogenous factors and monetary factors that influence the psychology of the entrepreneurs. The theory does not explain the how and why of the start of recovery and depression. It also does not explain the causes which. give rise to optimism and pessimism. Moreover, it fails to explain the periodicity of a trade cycle. Schumpeter does not consider

---

9. J.M. Keynes, *The General Theory of Employment, Interest and Money* (London, 1936), p. 321.
10. *Ibid.*, p. 322.
11. A.C. Pigou, *Industrial Fluctuations* (London, 1929), p. 94.

it worthy of reliance. He says: "And since individual errors cannot convincingly be held to produce *big* disturbances, unless they are overwhelmingly one way, we may put our trust in 'waves of optimism and pessimism,' a version that was quite common and later on, was to appeal to such authorities as Pigou and Harrod. There are many other variations of this theme, none of which is entirely devoid of a modest element of truth and all of which are unequal to the burden put upon them."[12]

(3) Theory of Innovations

This theory was formulated by Schumpeter. He states that cyclical disturbances are caused by innovations carried out in industrial and commercial organisation. By innovations, Schumpeter means, "Such changes of the combinations of the factors of production as cannot be affected by infinitesimal steps or variations on the margin. They consist primarily in changes in methods of production and transportation, or in changes in industrial organisation, or in the production of a new article, or in the opening up of new markets or of new sources of materials. The recurring periods of prosperity of the cyclical movements are the form progress takes in capitalistic society."[13] When the innovators start investing in the application of their ideas, the cyclical upswing starts. The process may start with a few leading entrepreneurs, but very soon it gets going and followed by others. The innovating activity is helped by the banking system's readiness to advance loans. The demand for productive resources increases, but there being no idle resources, competition among the entrepreneurs raises their prices. Thus, money incomes increase and a positive rate of interest emerges. The demand for consumer goods also increases and hence the revenue of the businessmen goes up. The innovational activity induces a second economic wave which is superimposed on the primary wave. Additional consumption spending induces old firms to raise their output. Speculative activity gets boosted up and new borrowing starts. The secondary wave covers a much wider area and is more important than the first one. In the early stages of the upswing the proportion of production goods in the total output is greater than the consumption goods. But as soon as the new plants begin to operate, new goods start flowing into the market.

But this process of expansion cannot continue indefinitely. It contains the seeds of self-destruction in addition to several accidents and incidents. Firstly, the entrepreneurial activity characteristically starts off in a definite direction and does not spread itself equally over the entire economy. There are limits to which a particular industry can advance without a corresponding

---

12. J.A. Schumpeter, *History of Economic Analysis* (1954), pp. 1133-34.
13. J.A. Schumpeter, *The Explanation of the Business Cycle, Economica,* December (1927), p.295.

development of other industries. Secondly, innovations disturb the existing equilibrium, leading to a constant revision of value of different elements in the system with a view to adjusting with the temporary situations. The estimation of costs and receipts becomes very difficult. Uncertainty increases the element of risk in the new enterprises. Before embarking on new innovations they wait for the equilibrium to be established again. Thus, innovational activity comes to a halt not because new innovations are not available, but because the climate is not favourable for them. Moreover, as the innovations start bearing fruits, entrepreneurs repay the loans to banks, which causes deflationary effects. Consequently, this leads to lowering of prices and money incomes, thus intensifying the adjustment process. It is just a recession, a temporary phase, because soon after, the economic conditions again become favourable for further entrepreneurial activity. Depression actually starts with the stoppage of innovational activity in the secondary wave as major portion of the investment is of a speculative nature, which collapses at the slightest fall in prices. Again, in the secondary wave most of the enterprises that develop are fraudulent, which cannot withstand the test of adjustment during recession. Consequently, with a slight fall in prices, the debt structure starts shaking, leading to liquidation and a further fall in prices. Thus, the vicious spiral of falling prices and contraction starts, and this leads to depression. After the depression has run its course, the system works itself through a new point of equilibrium which is not the same as before. The return from depression to new equilibrium is known as 'Recovery'. According to Schumpeter, there are possibilities that the process of depression may peter out owing to depression in business, that is, the events like bankruptcies, breaks in individual markets, shut-downs, etc. which cause depression, lose momentum with the spread of their effects. Further, some firms go bankrupt and close down creating facilities for others to expand. This spells not only actual and potential losses, but also actual and potential gains. But this invariably does not happen and therefore, in such cases, help from outside the economic system is necessary for reversing the process of depression and bringing back recovery. Once the new equilibrium is established, the conditions become favourable for the application of new innovations and the cycle repeats itself.

A critical appraisal of this theory reveals that it has a number of lacunae, *e.g.*, (*i*) it presupposes the existence of a typical institutional framework of the society; (*ii*) it considers innovations to be the only factor responsible for generating cyclical fluctuations; (*iii*) it exclusively relies on financing of innovations by bank credit and ignores the part played by voluntary savings in financing innovations; and (*iv*) it assumes that the economy is already operating at full employment point, *i.e.*, all the factors of production including labour are already fully employed. But this does not mean that innovations play a major role in causing industrial fluctuations or ups and downs in the level of business activity. Since most innovations are self-financed by the firms out of their development reserves, the theory is an inadequate explanation of the occurrence of the trade cycle in the modern business world.

(4) Under-Consumption or Over-Saving Theory

This theory originates from the rejection of Say's Law by Malthus, Sismondi, Lauderdale, Marx and others. These writers attribute the creation of crisis to low consumption of workers owing to a fall in wages, leading to accumulation of goods, fall in prices, increase in unemployment and a crisis. Although these writers explained the occurrence of crisis in their own way, it was Hobson, who sharply criticised the Say-Ricardo-Mill thesis about the non-occurrence of a general glut in the market as every supply creates its own demand—and stated that the trade depression occurs due to 'over-saving since it impoverishes the community, throws labourers out of work, drives down wages, and spreads the gloom and frustrations through the commercial world which is known as depression in trade...' Hobson states the process like this: "Many individuals produce more than what they consume. They thus do not match their individual share of total demand for production with their individual share of total supply of production. In a money economy, it is necessary that a seller of goods may simultaneously and to an equal extent be a buyer of goods. The act of creating the supply gives the supplier the power to create demand but this does not necessarily mean that the owners of the power will use it entirely by consuming as much of goods as they have produced. In other words, demand need not necessarily be equal to supply and hence some saving can always take place;"

According to Hobson the modern society is characterised by great inequalities of income. A large portion of the total wealth is owned by a small class. In times of prosperity, producers share larger part of increased income than the wage-earners. The recipients of larger incomes have larger savings and invest them in productive enterprises, leading to an increase in the production capacity of the economy and the volume of goods available for consumption for which the effective demand is inadequate at the prevailing prices. These goods can be sold out only at reduced prices. A decline in prices leads to a decline in producers' incomes and purchasing power. This further depresses the economy.

Hobson's ideas can merely be treated as an explanation of the occurrence of crises and not a theory. Though his arguments are not cogent, his explanations are very much near the Domar-Harrod analysis. Domar has praised Hobson for his keen observations and considers him superior to Keynes in that he clearly visualises that any increase in investment would increase the productive capacity of the society. According to Domar, "Even though both Keynes and Hobson were students of unemployment, they actually addressed themselves to two different problems. Keynes analysed what happens when savings (of the preceding period) are not invested. The answer was unemployment, but the statement of the problem in this form might easily give the erroneous impression that if savings were invested, full employment would be assured. Hobson, on the other hand, went a step further and stated the problem in this form: Suppose savings are invested, will the new plants be able to dispose of their products? Such a statement of the problem was not at all, as Keynes thought, a mistake. It was statement of a different and possibly also a deeper problem. Hobson was fully armed with σ[14] effect of investment, and he saw that it could be answered only by growth. His weakness lay in a poor perception of the multiplier effect and his analysis lacked vigour in general. He gave a demonstration rather than a proof. But the problem to which he addressed himself is just alive today as it was fifty and twenty years ago.[15]

The critics point out that the theory is based on the assumption that the savings are automatically invested. But this is not the case always. Investment of savings depends upon the prospects of earning profits. The theory does not explain the process of return from depression to recovery. It is also pointed out that the tendency of under-consumption or over-saving can only explain the under-employment equilibrium and not the occurrence of industrial fluctuations. Finally, the theory states that depression starts with the over-production of consumer goods, which means that their prices fall, but observed facts have shown that depression starts with the fall in the prices of capital goods followed by a decline in the prices of consumer goods at the end.

(5) Professor Hicks' Theory of Trade Cycles

Economists have made use of the concepts of the multiplier and the accelerator to explain the occurrence of trade cycle. According to them, the interaction between the multiplier and the accelerator provides a possible explanation to the fluctuations occurring in a capitalist economy in the field of business activity. Hicks, Hansen, Harrod, Samuelson and Kurihara are such economists who attribute the occurrence of business fluctuations to the cumulative effect of the multiplier and the accelerator. We have explained in detail these two concepts earlier. Let us for the present see how this happens. Whenever there is a new investment in the economy, the income expands several times greater than the original investment merely because of the operation of the principle

14. The Greek letter σ (sigma) indicates the increase in the productive capacity of the economy which results from each rupee invested. It is the ratio of output to capital.
15. E.D. Domar, *Essays in the Theory of Growth* (1957), p. 104.

of the multiplier. The income so increased accelerates the demand for consumption goods on account of an increase in the aggregate propensity to consume. When the demand for consumption goods increases, it induces investment in a much larger measure, on account of the operation of the accelerator. Increased investment brings out an increase in incomes and hence in the demand for consumer goods. This cycle goes on and the interaction between the multiplier and the accelerator lands the economy in the upswing of the trade cycle. The amount of this leverage would depend on the values of the multiplier and accelerator coefficients. If these values are high, then the leverage would be very large and it can generate a situation of hyper inflation. But in actual life, the values of the multiplier and the accelerator are never high and hence the leverage is not also very big and therefore, upswing in business activity is moderate. But this upswing does not continue for long or indefinitely. As Keynes has stated, the marginal propensity to consume declines with an increase in income which brings upswing in business activity to an end. This can be understood like this. A decrease in the propensity to consume results in a greater decrease in investment because the accelerator starts operating in the opposite direction. A decline in the level of investment decreases income owing to the operation of the multiplier in reverse direction. This causes further decline in the level of consumption and hence a further decrease in the level of investment. And so, the working of the accelerator and the multiplier in the reverse direction leads to the downswing of business activity or deflation, throwing the economy into depression. But the fall in income during depression is not followed by a proportionate fall in the propensity to consume which means that by and by the demand for capital goods increases, the level of investment starts picking up, which through the combined effect of the multiplier and the accelerator removes the slackness in the business activity and starts another upswing of the trade cycle. This is how we explain the upswing and downswing of a trade cycle in terms of multiplier-accelerator interaction.

According to Hicks, "The theory of the multiplier and the theory of the accelerator are the two sides of the theory of fluctuations just as the theory of demand and the theory of supply are two sides of the theory of value."[16] Besides the multiplier and the accelerator, the concept of the warranted rate of growth also plays an important part in the theory. The warranted rate of growth is that rate of growth which will maintain itself. It is the rate which is consistent with the level of equilibrium between the saving and investment. It means that when the rate of real investment is equal to the rate of real saving in the economy, the economy grows at a warranted rate of growth. The interaction

---

16. J.R. Hicks, *A Contribution to the Theory of Trade Cycle,* p. 38.

between the multiplier and the accelerator moves around the warranted rate of growth. Prof. Hicks has followed, in this respect, Robertson who treats consumption as a function of income of the previous time period. If consumption in any given period is '*t*' and if the income of the previous time period is '*t* – 1' and if current consumption is the function of the previous time period, then $Ct = f(Yt - 1)$. We thus find that this approach is different from the one adopted by Harrod, who treats current consumption as a function of current income, *i.e.*, $Ct = f(Yt)$.

There are certain other important elements in the theory which need highlighting. Hicks assumes the existence of both autonomous and induced investments. According to him autonomous investment is determined independently and is not influenced by the changes in the level of output or national income. It is an exogenous factor arising from technological change caused by an increase in pupulation or from public investment; it is not a function of change in the level of output. In the words of Hicks, "There can be little doubt that quite a large proportion of the net investment which goes on in normal conditions has been called forth, directly or indirectly, by past changes in the level of output, there is certainly some investment for which this effect is so small as to be insignificant. Public investment, investment which occurs in direct response to invention, and much of the 'long range' investment which is only expected to pay for itself over a long period, all of these can be regarded as *autonomous investment* for our purposes."[17] It is the autonomous investment which starts an increase in the level of employment and output. Its force is reflected through the multiplier.

Induced investment, on the other hand, is a function of the past changes in the level of income or level of output or of consumption; in other words it is determined by the changes in the aggregate demand or aggregate consumption. It is an endogenous factor. The concept of induced investment is the centre of Hicks' explanation of the trade cycle because its force is reflected through the accelerator. Hicks regards that an increase in the output from the period to the next causes a 'hump' of investment (induced investment) which later on interacts with the multiplier; this is the concept of accelerator as used by Hicks. Thus, autonomous investment through the multiplier, and induced investment through the accelerator, cause cyclical fluctuations in the business activity.

Like the multiplier Hicks has also used the accelerator with a lag which means that induced investment like consumption also reacts to the changes in the level of output with a time lag. He also assumes that the ratio between the changes in the output and the changes in the level of induced investment is a

17. *Ibid.*, p. 59.

fixed one, or in other words he assumes a fixed marginal capital-output ratio. He, thus, assumes that the numerical value of the multiplier and the accelerator does not change and therefore he assumes that the multiplier is active throughout the different phases of the cycle while accelerator remains inactive only during depression. During the upswing of the trade cycle both the accelerator and the multiplier work simultaneously and therefore, the expansion is cumulative in nature. An increase in autonomous investment causes increase in income and consumption expenditure through the multiplier which induces an additional investment outlay through the accelerator. During all this process no change takes place in the capital-output ratio insofar as the autonomous investment is concerned.

Let us also throw light on the Hicksian explanation of the upper and lower turning points. Hicks treats the lower turning point as a primary function of the autonomous investment because during the downswing phase of the trade cycle the induced investment is negative. During the period of contraction some production certainly takes place, although the level of production will definitely be lower than the existing production capacity, which means that the total capital stock in the economy is not being used fully or is greater than what would have been adequate to produce the total output demanded for consumption. But, during the process of production, the productive equipment wears out and to maintain the existing plant capacity, the worn-out plant must be replaced. This is taken care of by the surplus plant capacity that exists in the economy, which means that the worn-out equipment will not be replaced by a new one and the plant capacity which is lying idle will be put to use and so at the end of each time period, the surplus plant capacity would be less than what it was at the beginning of the period. A point would definitely reach when there would be no surplus plant capacity and to maintain the productive capacity of the economy intact, the worn-out equipment (*i.e.*, autonomous investment) would act as lever for the economy during the depression phase of the trade cycle. This would cause an increase in the net investment expenditure and thereby an increase in income and expenditure in a multiplier fashion, which is further strengthened by the force of the accelerator. The interaction between the multiplier and the accelerator leads to cumulative expansion.

Hicks considers the analysis of the upper turning point as more difficult. For explaining this, he has used the concept of natural rate of growth as given by Harrod. He starts like this: trade cycles have weak endings as well as strong endings; those with weak endings are 'free' cycles and those with strong endings are 'constrained' cycles. A free cycle that occurs with the combined action of the multiplier and the accelerator is not adequate to push the economy to the level of production which is determined by the natural growth rate. The upper turning point occurs in such a cycle. A constrained cycle occurs when the combined action of the multiplier and the accelerator pushes the economy up until the terminal point of expansion as set by the production ceiling is reached and it strikes against it. No, further expansion takes place thereafter. Hicks calls it a constrained cycle because further expansion is dependent on the production ceiling; once the ceiling is reached, expansion cannot take place faster than the rate at which the ceiling itself is growing and the rate of growth of ceiling is determined by the size of population, the rate of technological developments, the available stock of capital, etc. After the production ceiling is reached, the force of the multiplier and the accelerator becomes inadequate to maintain the rate of expansion, as stated above: But according to Hicks, "This is not a thing which it is able to do, so long as it is operating under pressures we are describing; or rather it cannot keep to this track for more than a very limited time. When the path has encountered the ceiling, it must (for a little) bounce off from it and begin to move in a downward direction."

It can thus be concluded from what Hicks has stated that in a capitalist country contraction is bound to follow expansion. He has also emphasised that if technological developments do not take place, if the population does not grow, if the capital stock does not increase and if the other growth factors do not increase, the economy is bound to plunge into depression for a long period: firstly, because without technological developments autonomous investment may not rise over time and therefore accelerator will remain inoperative and the level of investment will remain static so long as the need for replacement of worn-out equipment does not occur; and secondly, in the absence of technological developments, replacements will be definitely slow.

The main shortcoming of Hicks' theory is that it assumes that both the multiplier and the accelerator have fixed values during different phases of the trade cycle or in other words he assumes the multiplier and accelerator as constant. The multiplier is a function of marginal propensity to consume and further studies on the subject have proved that the marginal propensity to consume is not constant in relation to cyclical changes in income, although permanent consumption is a stable function of permanent income. As the economy passes from one phase of the cycle to another, multiplier changes. Moreover, the distribution of income also changes from one phase of the cycle to the other and therefore, the changes in the marginal propensity to consume are bound to take place depending of course, upon whether the distribution of income has taken place in favour of the poorer or the richer classes. The assumption that the accelerator has a fixed value is also not correct. The capital-output ratio is bound to change over time. Moreover, the ratio will be different for the different sectors of the economy which certainly does not depend at a uniform rate. Not only that, the gestation period for different types of capital projects is bound to be different. This means that the expansion of output will invoke different investment responses and therefore to assume the capital-output ratio as constant is not correct. According to Kaldor, the use of the principle of accelerator made by Hicks is rather crude. He says, "It must necessarily assume that investment generated by a change of output is some coefficient of the change of output that is independent of the absolute size of the change. In reality, however, the rate of expansion of firms is confined by the financial resources (quite independently of the behaviour of the market rates of interest), which means that they cannot take advantage of large investment opportunities as quickly as of small ones....This is not because the financial resources of the firm may be adequate for the one but inadequate for the other. It is also because expectations are far less likely to be elastic with respect to large changes than small ones."

(6) Theory of Long Waves

We now discuss, in brief, an important theory which explains the occurrence of long trade cycles. Siberling, an American economist, holds that long trade cycles are caused by major wars. A major war like the First World War or the Second World War is accompanied by monetary expansion due to increase in public expenditure which necessitates increased taxation, expansion of public debt and finally the expansion of money supply. This leads to inflation and allround prosperity in the country during the war. When the war comes to an end, there is a sudden decline in the level of public expenditure causing a fall in the price level. The extractive industries are more adversely affected than manufacturing industries, there is a general slackness in the economic activity which may be called as a primary post-war recession but this is short-lived because the wages of the industrial workers do not, fall in proportion to the fall in the prices. Their real wages move up, they are able to satisfy their demand for durable consumer goods, especially the luxury goods which they could not purchase during the war. This increase in demand compensates to some extent, the manufacturing industries which had suffered owing to the stoppage of orders from the government during the war. Thus, the immediate post-war recession is short-lived. But, the extractive industries do not gain, and so the imbalance between them and the manufacturing industries disturbs the equilibrium of the economy and causes a long wave of depression which may last for decades.

(7) The Keynesian Approach

Keynes did not formulate a separate theory of trade cycle and his views on the subject can be gathered from his General Theory. Moreover, there was no need of developing a theory on trade cycles, since the *General Theory* is quite comprehensive. Nevertheless, his book has a separate chapter which contains his ideas on the subject. But, it cannot be treated as a theory—it is simply an explanation of the level of employment quite independently of the cyclical nature of change in employment. It neither provides an account of the different phases of the trade cycle nor does it examine closely the empirical data of cyclical fluctuations.

We have earlier examined in detail the Keynesian theory of prices and we have described fully the Keynesian views on inflation and deflation. According to the Keynesian theory of interest and money the level of income and employment in an economy is determined by *MPC,* liquidity preference and *MEC.* In the short run, the first two factors are quite stable. It is the *MEC* (since it is governed by the expectations about future yield) which is the sole disturbing factor. It determines the investment function which determines the level of employment and thus plays a crucial role in cyclical fluctuations. The collapse of the *MEC* leads to the down-swing of the trade cycle and its revival leads to the upswing of the cycle. Since these points have been dealt with in other chapters, we do not propose to repeat them here. However, we would like to produce here a summary of the discussion of trade cycle by Keynes, as given by Hansen.

1. The cycle is caused primarily by the fluctuations in the level of investment.

2. Variations in the level of investment are caused mainly by the variations in the marginal efficiency of capital.

3. Variations in the rate of interest have indeed at times played an important role, but, more typically, changes in the liquidity preference schedule, induced by fluctuations in the *MEC,* reinforce and supplement the primary factor, *i.e.*, *MEC.*

4. Variations in the *MEC* are due to: (*a*) changes in the prospective yields of capital goods, (*b*) changes in the replacement cost of capital goods. Variations in the cost of capital goods are caused by the changes in the level of investment produced in a given period; in other words, by the extreme pressure placed upon the capital industries during the boom. Variations in costs are secondary and supplementary to the primary initiating factor, which is the fluctuation in the prospective yields of new capital goods.

5. Towards the end of a boom, the prospective yield of capital declines because of the growing abundance of capital goods—which induces a wave of pessimistic expectations so that the anticipated yield, once the turning point is past, is usually lower than the facts justify.

6. In the absence of more thoroughgoing measures (*e.g.*, fiscal policy), a variable rate of interest may be useful to stabilise the cycle. Keynes, however

prefers a maintained low rate of interest in conjunction with other more radical measures designed to regularise the cycle.

7. Keynes did not agree with those who advocated the choking off of the boom by an increase in the rate of interest. He, therefore, suggested a programme of sustained full employment.

Prof. Metzler holds that Keynes has been responsible for introducing at least two fundamental changes in the theory of trade cycle. The first change relates to the definition of the 'normal' or 'equilibrium' level of economic activity—this is the level of income at which intended savings are equal to non-intended investment. The second change relates to the explanation of turning points of the cycle. None before him provided a satisfactory explanation of these. It was Keynes who with the help of his consumption function provided a satisfactory explanation of these. Again, with the help of the concept of multiplier Keynes has explained the cumulative nature of expansion and contraction. Keynes also explained the observed periodicity of the boom and depression.

The Keynesian analysis has been criticised sharply by Hazlitt, Moore and others. According to Hazlitt, the concept of the *MEC* is vague and has been used in different senses. At one time it means the actual present yield of capital assets, at another time it means the expected future yield of the capital assets and at still another time it means merely the outlook for business profits, regardless of the specific return to a specific capital asset. Again, it does not explain the periodicity of cycle, which is very important. Further, Keynes has stated that the duration of downward movement lies between three and five years, but no statistical evidence has been provided in its support. Similarly, he has not produced any statistical evidence in support of his conclusion that the duration of the slump has a definite relationship to the length of durable assets and also to the carrying costs of surplus stock. Hazlitt further points out certain contradictions in his ideas. He says: "The interest according to him (Keynes) should be low in the depression, low in boom and, low in crisis. His (Keynes') remedy to keep the boom going by encouraging over-investment and malinvestment and then, when the boom cracks, to keep the boom going by lowering the rate of interest, still more to encourage still more over-investment and malinvestment."

(8) The Self-Generation Theory

W.C. Mitchell, who is the author of this theory, is of the view that the pace of economic activity in an economy, slackens or quickens under the influence of internal political conditions, changes in monetary and banking systems, war or peace, new industrial methods, international relations, etc. Trade crisis is just one feature of a recurrent cycle which is expected to be followed by depression, then recovery, then prosperity, then crisis and so on. Trade cycles differ from each other in their duration and effects and prominence of their phases. Each phase of a cycle generates the other. Mitchell also believes that different parts of the economy are inter-linked and any maladjustment started in one part spreads throughout the economy. According to him instability is an essential feature of a business economy. Economic activity in a free enterprise economy depends upon income and profits. Profits are determined by the cost-price relationship which might turn out to be different from what the producers had expected while undertaking investment. And hence the instability in a business economy.

According to Mitchell depression sows the seeds of a new upswing. During depression costs are reduced, profit margins eventually improve, inventories are low and eventually require restocking, weak firms are weeded out, banks become more willing to lend as excess reserves accumulate and so on. The revival then starts. Once the revival starts, the economy grows in a cumulative manner. Now, increase in production leads to increased incomes of the factors of production, sales expand and worn-out equipment and depleted inventories are replaced. The business optimism generally improves. Prices start rising and expectations of further price increases stimulate business further. Profits increase rapidly, business investment expands and all these react and act on each other and rise further in a cumulative manner. Ultimately, cost-price relationship becomes unfavourable and profit margin starts declining. Overhead costs do rise ultimately, but immediately. the operating costs rise rapidly owing to the pressure of output on capacity, rising wage rates, decreasing labour efficiency and rising costs of raw materials. Other stresses like, depleting bank reserves, tightening bank credit and growing cost of new constructions and equipment also are created. Under these stresses, some industries discover that their profits were declining. Deteriorating profits coupled with contraction of credit induce firms to reduce their output. The lenders seek repayment of old debts and thus the process of liquidation starts. Since the different parts of the economy are inter-dependent, the liquidation process spreads to other firms also. This leads to a decline in the general level of production, income and employment. The process of decline continues until the economy builds up corrective forces strong enough to start a new recovery.

According to Mitchell the phenomenon of trade cycle is an extremely complex one and cannot be explained in terms of a few aggregative variables. He states: "But, despite these advances theorists who sought to explain business cycles were insufficiently informed about the phenomena with which they were dealing, and had to reason for the most part from untested assumptions. The complexity of economic organisation suggested to ingenous minds an embarrassing array of plausible hypotheses. No one could determine which among these jostling competitors was least inadequate, or whether any combination of them would account for what happens."

Despite the good points the theory has, it fails to analyse the underlying real factors which cause turning points. The theory depends chiefly on the errors of optimism and pessimism and the possibility of horizontal maladjustments, but these can only help in explaining relatively mild savings in the investment activity. These are not adequate to explain wide variations in the level of investment activity which cause the turning points of the major cycles. It would be interesting to know what Prof. Knight has to say about the theory. He says: "The theory likens the economic mechanism to a perpetual motion machine. And no machine will run indefinitely on the power which originally sets it into motion unless, like a clock, it is periodically rewound. It will run down because of friction. The cycles of the economic machine like the revolutions of clock would become successively weaker if no fresh facts are imparted to them."

(9) The Cobweb Theory

The theory explains cyclical fluctuations in dynamic terms, whereas the earlier theories were static in nature in the sense that they assumed that the adjustments between supply and demand take place simultaneously and ignored the time lag. According to this theory, the supply takes time to adjust itself to changes in demand. Thus, the supply of goods in any given period is the function of the price prevailing in the period preceding it, whereas the demand depends upon the price which prevails in the current period. The theory has its major application in the field of the agricultural products, the supply of which can be varied only after a certain time lag. In the case of wheat or rice it can be one year while in the case of rubber or tea it can be five years. Generally speaking, if it takes H months to produce and market a commodity, the quantity now supplied would be a function of price H months ago and the cycle would necessarily be $2H$ months' duration.

Tinbergen has extended the application of the theory to durable goods, since their supply also takes time to adjust itself to changes in demand. Perishable goods are consumed in a single transaction and hence their supply will be the result of the price prevailing H months ago. But, since the durable goods continue giving service for some time, the previous price does not determine their supply, but only determines additions to the total stock. Hence, the rate of increase of the stock depends on the total stock some time ago. Tinbergen shows that this could cause oscillations of a duration longer than $2H$ because of the durability of the goods.

The cobwebs have been divided into: (1) converging type, (2) diverging type, and (3) continuous type. In the continuous type of cobwebs, the fluctuations in price and output continue rotating around the equilibrium at the same level. In the converging type, the economy, when distributed from equilibrium position has a tendency to regain it through a series of oscillations. Each oscillation is more damped than the preceding one. The amplitude of the fluctuations narrows down when the slope of the supply curve is steeper than that of the demand curve. In the diverging type, the amplitude of the fluctuations increases with the passage of time. Once disturbed from the equilibrium position, the economy moves away cumulatively into serious disequilibrium. This happens when the slope of the supply is less steep than that of the demand curve.

Figure 12.4 shows the series of reactions when the elasticities of both demand and supply are equal to each other. In the initial period the quantity (Q_1) is large resulting in a relatively low price, where it intersects the demand curve at P_1. This low price calls for a low supply (Q_2) in the next period. The short supply leads to a high price P_2 which results in increased production (Q_3) in the third period with a corresponding low price (P_3). Since this low price in the third period is identical to that of the first period, the production and price in subsequent periods will continue rotating around the path Q_2, P_2, Q_3, P_3, etc.

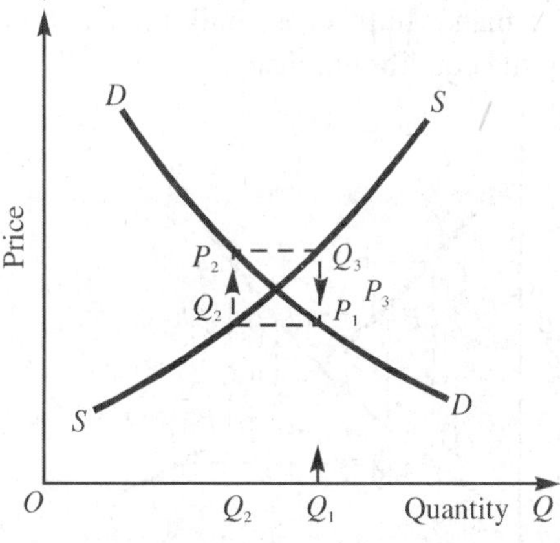

Fig. 12.4

Figure 12.5. depicts the series of reactions when the elasticity of supply is greater than the elasticity of demand. In the initial period the supply is moderately large (Q_1) and with price P_1 and the series of reactions is traced by the dotted line. In the next period, there is moderately reduced supply (Q_2) with a corresponding high price (P_2). High price leads to an increase in supply

(Q_3) in the third period resulting in a considerable reduction in price (P_3). In the next period the supply is sharply reduced (Q_4) with a corresponding high price (P_4). In the fifth period supply again increases to Q_5 and so on. Thus, the situation might continue to remain unstable until either the price falls to zero or production is completely stopped or a limit is reached to available resources so that production can no longer increase.

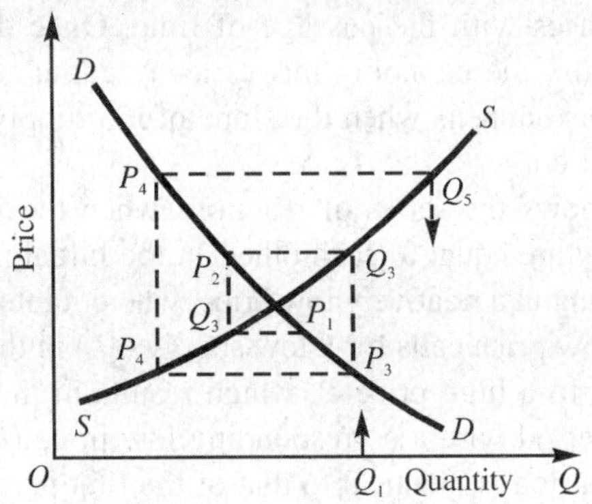

Fig. 12.5

Figure 12.6 represents a series of reactions when the elasticity of supply is less than that of demand. In this case only the reactions take place in the manner assumed by the equilibrium theory.

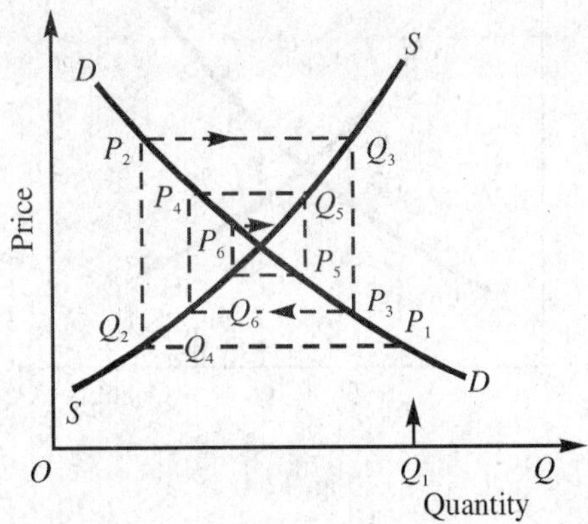

Fig. 12.6

This theory also has serious deficiencies. First, the course of reactions indicated by the theory will not apply to an economy where the price or output of commodities is determined by administrative decisions. Second, the theory is of limited application only even in the case of commodities which nearly fulfil all the assumptions. For example, in agricultural or cattle rearing, once the farmers make initial commitment in acreage sown or cattle bred they cannot certainly increase the supply, but they can definitely reduce the supply (by ploughing up portions of the crop or by slaughtering breeding stock) until the product is finally marketed. Thus, there is some elasticity in supply in the downward direction. Third, weather conditions impose another limitation on the application of the theory. Natural variations may cause unduly high or low production and thus, set a new cycle of response in reaction. Fourth, the theory assumes that the supply in the current period is determined by the price of the commodity prevailing in the preceding period. But this is not wholly true, because producers' decisions are influenced not only by prices in the preceding period but by the prices expected in the next period, prices of the inputs, and estimation about the strength of their competitors. Fifth, the price of a commodity is not only determined by its supply, but also by the changes in the supply of competing products, changes in the income of the consumers and changes in the factors affecting their markets, like tariff quotas, freight rates, weather conditions, and even changes in the tastes and fashions. Finally, in actual practice neither the diverging cobwebs type of reactions (unending cycle) nor the constant type of cobwebs can continue indefinitely as shown in Figs. 12.5 and 12.6. However, the theory is useful in providing a technique to demonstrate the process of change over time.

Monetary Theories

1. Hawtrey's Theory. R.G. Hawtrey holds that industrial fluctuations are caused by monetary factors. The upward phase of the trade cycle is caused by an expansion of money and bank credit and also by an increase in the velocity of circulation of money, while the downward phase is caused by a contraction of these things. Cyclical fluctuations are the result of the factors which cause variations in the circular flow of money and the changes in the supply of bank credit cause variations in the income-expenditure flow.

The prosperity phase of a trade cycle starts with the expansion of bank credit leading to a fall in the rate of interest—grant of loans by banks on easy terms and expansion of inventory holdings by the merchants. Consequently, the merchants place large orders with the producers, for the execution of which the producers expand production by employing more resources. This results in raising the level of income and employment and hence further increase in the demand for goods and services. With the expansion of business and full employment of the factors of production, prices further rise leading to inflationary conditions. The prosperity phase ends with the contraction of credit by banks owing to the depletion of their cash reserves. The contraction of credit exerts a deflationary pressure on prices and profits, on consumers' income and outlay. And the cycle now moves in the reverse direction. It is the decline of effective demand reflected in reduced outlay by consumers and increased holdings of cash balances owing to credit contraction which starts the vicious circle of deflation leading to depression. During depression, the traders for repaying bank loans want to sell their stocks of goods at whatever price they get. With the repayment of loans the cash reserves of banks swell up. Their credit creating capacity increases. and to utilise their idle funds, they stimulate borrowing by lowering their lending rates. This induces the traders to increase their inventories and the process of expansion again sets in.

Hawtrey admits that non-monetary factors, like inventions, bumper harvests, etc. do influence productive activity, but believes that their effects are synchronised with the monetary effects. According to him, the periodicity of trade cycles is due to monetary effects and not due to non-monetary effects, and this can be overcome by a suitable monetary policy. He holds that the flexibility and inherent instability of bank credit seize on fluctuations in business and turn them into rhythmic changes. If this is eliminated by a suitable banking policy, the trade cycle would not occur.

Hawtrey's theory has been challenged on a number of counts. First, changes in inventories are not the sole initiator of the cumulative movement in the economic activity. At the most, such changes can only create minor cycles, which cannot be considered as trade cycles. Second, monetary inflation and deflation are not the causes but the results of trade cycles, since credit expansion follows business expansion and credit contraction follows business contraction. Third, changes in the rate of interest are not generally a cause but the result of the crisis, since in actual practice it has been seen that a rise in the rate of interest occurs after the crisis and not before it. Fourth, the contention of Hawtrey that expansion of money supply leads to expansion of business activity is not wholly true. It has been found in actual practice that a cheap money policy does not always lead to expansionary movements. Actually, many a time the money supply adjusts itself to changed conditions resulting from non-monetary causes. Fifth, Hawtrey has exaggerated the role of wholesalers and has relegated the capital goods industries and other constituents of the economy to the background. Wholesalers do not always finance their inventories by borrowing but with their own funds as well. When they bank on borrowings they do not bother for a high or low rate of interest. Again their decisions about their inventories are generally guided not by changes in the rate of interest but by expectations about price changes, cost of storage, etc. Finally, as Haberler points out, "His contention that reasons for the breakdown of the boom are always monetary ones and that the prosperity could be prolonged and depression stayed off indefinitely, if the money supply were inexhaustible, would certainly be challenged by most economists."

2. Hayek's Theory. F.H. Hayek, who is the best exponent of the monetary over-investment theory of trade cycle holds that trade cycles are caused by the shortening and the lengthening of the process of production which are the results of the expansion of money supply, leading the market rate of interest to decline below the natural or equilibrium rate of interest.[18] During depression, which is caused by the shortening of the process of production, the market rate falls below the natural rate as banks increase the supply of money in excess of the supply of voluntary and real savings. This stimulates investment activity. The monetary investment exceeds the real savings, the difference being financed by the new bank, credit. The increase in investment lengthens the process of production. According to Hayek, this lengthening of the process of production not financed by voluntary savings cannot be sustained and must necessarily be followed by shrinkage in the process of production which must cause depression.

An increase in the supply of money ultimately ends in depression. This happens because if the increased supply of money is made available to the producers, it will ultimately reach the consumers in the form of income of factor owners. The entrepreneurs first increase their investment. This lengthens the process of production. Consequently, the demand for capital goods relates to prices and profits of consumer goods. Resources are, therefore, diverted from consumers goods industries to capital goods industries. The supply of consumer goods declines and on the other, demand for them increases from those workers who are employed in capital goods industries. Thus, the prices and profit on consumer goods rise and attract the producers' attention. The consumer goods industries now start competing with capital goods industries for obtaining resources. Consequently, the factor prices go up. The cost in capital goods industries increases and profit margins decline. In the meantime the banking system decides to reduce the rate of credit expansion and the market rate of interest rises above the natural rate and investments decline. Due to shortage of capital, producers try to replace labour for capital, *i.e.*, they try to produce more consumer goods by shortening the process of production. And thus recession begins, leading to depression. The increased money supply reaches the consumers directly, it will lead to an increase in the demand for consumer goods. This would increase their prices and profits on them. The producers would increase their output of consumer goods by using methods which yield quick results, though these may not be the most efficient

18. The natural or equilibrium rate of interest is the rate at which the demand for loanable funds just equals the supply of voluntary savings. And the market rate of interest is that which prevails in the market and is determined" by the supply of and demand for money.

methods. Thus, the process of production would be shortened leading to depression. It may be noted that in this theory boom ends because of the shortage of savings or capital funds. When the banks decide to stop credit creation, the investments financed through credit must fall unless there is a large volume of savings. Since the volume of savings can never be large, shortage of capital arises, interest rates go up, investment falls and depression starts. Since the trade cycles are caused by the failure of the banking system to keep the supply of money neutral, Hayek suggested that the supply of money be kept constant except for such changes which may be necessary to offset the changes in the velocity of money.

Hayek's theory has been criticised on a number of scores: First, the theory is based on the assumption that the utilisation of resources for investment would encroach upon the resources required for the production of consumer goods. But, when resources are not fully employed (and this is always the case), investment and consumption are complementary and not competitive. Second, the assumption that saving and investment are in equilibrium and that the equilibrium is disturbed by the banking policy does not hold good. Third, the assumption that factors of production can be shifted from consumer goods industries to capital goods industries and from capital goods industries to consumer goods industries as and when desired is not correct. Fourth, the assumption that an increase in demand for consumer goods causes a shortening of the process of production and a decline in the investment in capital goods industries is not correct, because the increase in the demand for consumer goods would raise the marginal efficiency of capital which, instead of discouraging would encourage investment. Fifth, it considers the rate of interest as the sole determinant of the volume of investment and ignores other factors like technological changes, innovations, etc. Finally, the theory does not at all explain the major phases of the trade cycle.

3. Friedman's Theory. Prof. Milton Friedman and Schwartz[19] on the basis of their study of the behaviour of the US economy, concluded that business cycles originate from the changes in the money stock which themselves have a cyclical behaviour. According to them, a change in money stock influences different economic magnitudes, some of which adjust more quickly than others, causing distortions in economic activity and ultimately giving rise to business cycles. These lags are very important in so far as the occurrence of the phenomenon of business cycle is concerned. According to their estimate, during the seven cycles between 1927 and 1970 peaks in the rate of change in the money stock precede reference cycle peaks (in economic activity series) before downturns by 20 months on an average and troughs in

19. M. Friedman and A.W. Schwartz, "Money and Business Cycles", *RES.* (Supplement), 1963.

the rate of change of the money stock precede troughs by about 11 months on an average before upturns. The lag of economic activity appears to be shorter for troughs than for peaks. During these decades there have been strong secular changes in the money stock. In deep depressions a greater fall in money stock has taken place. There has been a reduction in the growth rate of money stock in mild depressions, instead of any actual decline in it. A cycle, usually consists of the contraction phase, in which economic activity declines to the trough of the cycle, followed by expansion and finally reaching the peak. These phases are super-imposed over a long run secular growth path, as shown in Fig.12.7.

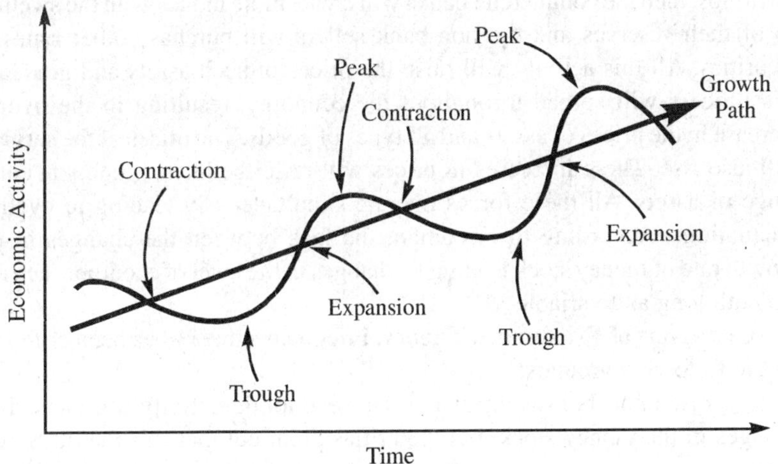

Fig. 12.7

While explaining the causal relationship between the money stock and economic activity, they have stated that: (*i*) changes in economic activity have always been caused by changes in money stock; (*ii*) almost every major change in the money stock has been accompanied by changes in economic activity; and (*iii*) changes in the stock of money have been caused by a specific type of exogenous factors rather than by changes in economic activity.

Friedman and Schwartz have therefore concluded that first, appreciable changes in the growth rate of money stock are adequate and essential for causing appreciable changes in the growth rate of economic activity; second, this holds good both for long secular changes and also for changes over periods roughly of the length of business cycle. They also hold that a secular change in the growth rate of money stock leading to longer period changes in the growth rate of economic activity is reflected through changes in the behaviour of the price level rather than in the growth rates of output. However, short period changes in the growth rate of money stock also cause an appreciable effect on the growth rate of output. They believe that substantial increases in the money stock over short periods have been a major cause of inflation of prices and substantial contractions in the money stock over short periods have been responsible for serious economic contractions.

Explaining the transmission mechanism they start with a state of moving equilibrium in which real per capita income, the stock of money and the price level are changing at constant annual rates. In such a situation, if the central bank increases the money stock by purchasing securities in the open market, first the commercial banks and other non-bank sellers will adjust their portfolios, then the commercial banks will create more money with the swelling up of their reserves and the non-bank sellers will purchase other types of securities. All this activity will raise the prices of such assets and gradually this process will spread throughout the economy, resulting in the overall increase in the prices of assets and all types of goods. The prices of the services will also rise. These increases in prices will raise the interest rates on entire range of assets. All these forces operate simultaneously leading to cyclical fluctuations. According to Friedman, the lags between the changes in the growth rate of money stock leading to changes in the level of economic activity are both long and variable.

Criticisms of Friedman's Theory. Friedman's theory has been criticised on the following grounds:

(1) Friedman holds that changes in economic activity are caused by changes in the money stock, but the critics point out that it is the other way round.

(2) According to Friedman changes in the money stock are the principal reason for business cycles. But in fact, business cycles are caused by a number of factors, including monetary changes.

(3) According to Friedman the time lags are both long and variable; but Culbertson considers this as incorrect because: (*i*) it relates turning points in one series in the money stock to turning points in economic activity; and (*ii*) it implies that changes in money stock is an exogenous variable and that monetary changes cause economic changes. In fact this causal process runs in the other directions as well.

Non-Monetary Theories

Spiethoff, Cassel and Robertson are the chief architects of the non-monetary over-investment theory. According to these writers, cyclical fluctuations are caused by over-investment. But they do not consider the money system as a causative factor of the process of trade cycle. We now describe their views one by one.

1. Spiethoff's Theory. According to Spiethoff, there are four sectors in an economy, *viz.*, (1) Non-durable consumer goods industries; (2) Durable and semi-durable consumer goods industries; (3) Durable capital goods industries; and (4) Industries producing materials supplied to capital goods industries. He holds that these sectors are so inter-linked that expansion and contraction take place through movements within and among these sectors of an economy. The upswing starts with the opening of new investment opportunities in the sector 3. This results in the disproportionate expansion of capital goods industries and the shortage of consumer goods in the early expansionary period. Expansion of sector 3 leads to an expansion of sector 4 also. The level of employment and income in these sectors goes up. Consequently, consumption spending increases and expansion also starts in sectors 1 and 2. But, when more and more plants start production, the prices of consumer goods start falling and over-investment in capital goods industries is experienced. The prospecting comes to an end. During depression no investment is made in sectors 3 and 4 as there already exists an excess capacity in sector 3. Consequently, production in these sectors reaches a low level causing a fall in the level of employment and income in the economy leading to a contraction in sectors 1 and 2.

2. Gustav Cassel. The approach of Cassel is the same as that of Spiethoff, the only difference being the question of expansion turning into contraction. According to Cassel, the cause of upswing turning into a downswing is not over-investment in consumer goods, as held by Spiethoff, but general over-investment which is not warranted by the volume of total real savings available in an economy.

3. Robertson. Robertson has synthesised the two approaches—non-monetary and monetary. While non-monetary factors cause trade cycles, money system also makes its contribution. According to him some fluctuations are definitely desirable for economic growth, but when these desirable fluctuations invoke excessive responses which cause destabilising fluctuations in the economy the problem really becomes serious. The situation arises due to the existence of 'indivisibility' in certain investments. Certain projects require huge investment and once it is undertaken, the amount becomes excessive in relation to the existing demand for the output of such investment. Since such investments are of an indivisible nature, a smaller amount of investment would not serve the purpose. Not only that, such investments are also time consuming. They have a long 'gestation period'. It obscures the amount of realised investment, the results of which are not within sight. In the meantime, in a competitive economy, other investors go ahead with their own projects which eventually result in over-investment leading to a glut of new goods in the market. Regarding the role of non-monetary factors, Robertson says that they may give further stimulus to these fluctuations. Any additional supply of money in circulation will only further the existing state of imbalance. It will first cause the prices to rise, which will mislead the producers leading to further investment and hence will deepen the crisis.

The theory, however, does not provide a complete explanation of the causes of the lower turning point in a trade cycle.

7. Control of Trade Cycles

However, it cannot yet be said that there is a universal agreement on the explanation provided by anyone theory, though in recent decades the area of disagreement has undoubtedly narrowed down. Now very few economists accept the view that trade cycle is a monetary phenomenon, a view which was so strongly held until 1930s. It is now felt that cyclical fluctuations must be controlled through active government intervention. There is also a fairly general agreement on the point that fluctuations are to be regarded as an integral part of the process of long-term economic growth.

Some are of the opinion that full employment can be established only if the government assumes a responsibility for a deliberate slow inflation so that consistently rising prices may attract adequate investment. These people argue that labour, business and firms are so effectively organised sectors of the market that they are in a position to maintain prices and wages at levels higher than those consistent with maximum sales and production and therefore, the government cannot maintain full employment without expanding the supply of money and deliberately inflating prices. But to imagine that the government would be able to contain inflation at a moderate level would be wrong. Those who fear that moderate inflation might develop into hyper inflation hold that the government should stabilise the price level without inflation. It has, however, been observed in actual practice that for achieving full employment and rapid economic development, some inflation is necessary. And so, now it has been realised that stability of the price level is not as important as maintenance of a high level of employment and a satisfactory rate of growth.

It has been found that with the expansion and contraction of income certain stabilising forces start operating automatically. For example, (1) As income expands, more money is required for transactions and precautionary motives and hence the rate of interest tends to rise. With the rise in prices, the Pigou effect comes into play, for the real value of cash holdings falls, and so the people reduce their consumption to restore the value of their cash holdings to former level in real terms. (2) The overall distribution of income is so altered in boom and depression that the *MPC* alters in the desired direction. Then, there may be a time lag in adjusting consumption to changes in income, because in the short term consumers find it difficult to change their living standards. Again, the business firms adopt divided equalisation policies irrespective of the level of profits and thus business saving increases. There is a diminishing *MPC,* so that expansion and contraction of income comes to an end. (3) In the domain of investment, the accelerator, which is a destabiliser, eventually works in the reverse direction, because the rate of increase in consumption is not maintained. Again, the growth in the public sector of the economy limits bullish and, bearish expectations and thus produces a stabilising effect. (4) As we shall see later, with expansion of incomes, exports decrease and imports increase owing to the income and price effects. But these income effects ultimately stabilise either exports or imports. (5) Fiscal measures like progressive taxation, social security measures, etc. all produce stabilising influence. It is true that these automatic stabilisers do exert some influence but it is not sufficient to stabilise the level of economic activity and if the level of income is to be maintained at the full employment point, a more positive action is required.

Any positive action towards economic stabilisation would involve maintenance of an effective balance between aggregate demand and aggregate supply. It is only the government to which this task can be assigned for a number of reasons. First, the government can effectively influence the aggregate purchasing in the economy by using the tool of taxation. Second, it can change the trend of private expenditure by varying its own expenditures. Third, the government can frame a monetary policy which can influence all the sectors of the economy uniformly. Fourth, if these tools do not bring about the desired effect then the government has the capacity and power to introduce certain direct control measures like price controls, wage freeze, rationing, allocation of materials, credit squeeze, etc. Finally, if the commitment of the government to a policy of full employment is known to people, then much of the uncertainty from which cyclical fluctuations start will be eliminated. Moreover, the government can assume and exercise powers of coercion, especially for collecting statistics and information required for effective planning.

The government can alter the level of consumption spending by influencing the level of disposable income and the marginal propensity to consume. So far as the level of disposable income is concerned, social security programmes, more particularly, unemployment insurance, have a special role to play. Social security contributions by employers and employees rise and fall along with the rise and fall in the level of employment. Social security payments by government, move inversely with the fluctuations in the volume of unemployment. During periods of declining economic activity, the government can increase payments to the unemployed at a time when its social security collections are falling because fewer people have full-time jobs. A liberal and widespread programme of unemployment benefits can be an important tool to stimulate personal incomes during periods of declining economic activity. Similarly, through progressive taxation the government can produce an automatic stabilising influence on the level of economic activity. During recession income-tax payments will decline relatively faster than aggregate personal incomes if the government grants personal exemptions, and during boom income tax collections will rise relatively faster if the government makes the rate of taxation more progressive. This would stabilise disposable income and also the level of consumption. Similar stabilising effect can be produced by corporate income tax. Since corporate profits fluctuate very widely, these effects can be obtained without changing the tax rate. If the government wishes to enlarge them it can reduce exemptions and raise the rate during booms and follow a reverse policy during depressions.

The government can change the level of *MPC* by changing the distribution of income. Since the poor spend a larger portion of their income on consumption than the rich, any step taken to equalise personal incomes will raise the general propensity to consume of the whole economy. This is, however, not a practical way of moderating cyclical fluctuations. The most direct way can be to change incomes through taxation. But frequent changes in the tax structure are neither practicable nor desirable. Besides having political and social repercussions, they would create uncertainty and decrease the volume of private investment. However, they may prove beneficial in dealing with long-term trends. But much will depend on how progressive the taxation already is. If the tax structure is already highly progressive, then the possibilities of achieving the desired result are very few—because any increase in the level of consumption would be offset by a reduction in savings and investment. The distribution of income can also be changed by changing the division of national income between wages and profits. An increase in wages at the expense of profits would tend to increase the *MPC*. But this may also reduce the level of investment. Still another way is to tax consumption and savings at different rates. For example, Friedman and Poole suggest the levy of a special tax on consumption expenditure in addition to the regular income tax. Slichter suggests that a part of person's savings should be exempted from income tax which would provide greater incentive to save. James Tobin has suggested the introduction of a scheme for compulsory savings whereby the taxpayers may be required to deposit a certain percentage of their income with the government to be repaid at some stipulated time in future.

The control on private investment is very necessary but it is the most difficult task. To stimulate investment during period of depression is not so difficult as it is to curtail it during period of boom and the desired results can be achieved by withdrawing all concessions, by levying an investment tax, by directly controlling the floatation of new securities and by using direct controls as is often done during wars.

The government can also use monetary policy as an instrument of economic stabilisation. This has been used by several governments to manage their economies, since the nationalisation of central banks. Such a policy implies the influence of the level and composition of aggregate demand by manipulating rates of interest and volume of credit. The transitional instrument of monetary policy is bank rate, supplemented by open market operations, where necessary. Since the end of last World War, certain other methods of control have been developed, and demand has been made to make monetary policy more effective and more selective in its impact on the economy. We have discussed all these measures in detail in a separate chapter.

We are well aware of the shortcomings of the monetary policy; but the general view is that it does and can play an important part in achieving stable growth—contributing through high employment and stable prices. In mixed economies, monetary policy is used as a general measure of control. It does not allocate resources for particular uses, it does not even attempt to divert resources from one use to another, which would raise the rate of growth of the economy. On the other hand, it simply exercises general control over aggregate demand, stimulating it or restraining it with a view to achieving full use of resources leaving their location to be determined by the free interplay of market forces. Nevertheless, it does influence the distribution of total spending between capital goods and consumer goods simply because its impact on demand varies from one sector to the other; of course, this is just its incidental effect. A monetary policy designed to divert resources from a less desired use to a more desired use can no doubt be successful in achieving the objective and hence in achieving potentially more rapid rate of growth. But in a mixed economy, like India, such a policy cannot be used without coming into conflict with the objectives of full employment and price stability and without curtailing the sphere of activity of the free enterprise system.

Since monetary policy alone has not been able to check cyclical fluctuations, it has been suggested that it should be supplemented by suitable fiscal measures. Keynesians have recommended a policy of compensatory finance in this connection. This has been advocated chiefly on the ground that the circle of the government's economic activity has, during recent decades, expanded to such an extent that it is now in a position to influence the level of output in a country. And so, the government should regulate its activities in such a way that it offsets the cyclical fluctuations. The chief instruments of fiscal policy are taxation, public spending and public debt. The government can make use of these instruments as and when required. For example, during a downswing phase of a trade cycle, the government should not levy new taxes and rather reduce the rates of existing taxes substantially so that more money is available to the people to spend on consumption goods which would offset the falling demand and economic activity. Not only this, the government can itself undertake massive spending programme on public works projects to stimulate the level of economic activity. The funds required to finance these projects should be obtained either by creating new money or by borrowing from the banks. Whatever may be the case, the aim of the government should be to inject more money in the economy with a view to offsetting the deflationary effect of the declining level of economic activity. This may also be called as policy of deficit spending. On the contrary, the government during the upswing phase of a trade cycle can follow a policy of surplus budgeting which would imply levying of new taxes, reduction of expenditure on public works, withdrawal of money from circulation and thus checking the rate of inflation. These two policies would help the government to maintain the level of economic activity at a stable point.

Fiscal measures can be of two types: first, to stabilize the level of economic activity without any direct attempt on the part of the government; such measures have been called as automatic stabilizers or built-in stabilizers, for example, progressive taxation. Under progressive taxation a part of the increased income of the people would go to the government and hence the purchasing power of the people would be proportionately reduced. Similarly, when the income of the people falls, the revenue of the government would also be proportionately reduced. This is the automatism of the measure. Other types of measures can be used at the discretion of the government. Such measures can be: (*a*) to change the level of public expenditure while keeping the rates of taxes stable, (*b*) to keep the public expenditure stable while changing the rates of taxes and (*c*) to co-ordinate the changes in the rates of taxes and public expenditure in a suitable manner. The first would be appropriate during depression while the second type of measures would be more suitable for checking inflation and the third one is useful for correcting depression as well as inflation. In short, we can say that it is for the government to decide what particular policy it would like to adopt for correcting a particular situation. It has generally been seen that fiscal measures have been effective only when a suitable monetary policy had been adopted simultaneously.

So far we discussed measures which were indirect in nature. There can be measures which produce direct effect on the economy by controlling the effective demand. Such measures can be price control, rationing, industrial licensing, control of wages of workers, etc. All these measures aim at controlling the level of economic activity in different areas, but their success generally depends upon the administrative competence and efficiency and the co-operation of all classes of society.

The measures for controlling trade cycles about which we spoke earlier are such that their implementation would require lot of care and caution on the part of government as well as administrative competence, efficiency of the staff and co-operation of the people. It has been seen that success has not been achieved by most of the governments in controlling trade cycles and therefore, most of the economists are of the view that under the existing economic order trade cycles are unavoidable. We can only delay or reduce their severity with care. Economists are also not unanimous in the choice of the methods that can be used successfully to check trade cycles. In fact, we need two types of measures: (*i*) which prevent the occurrence of business fluctuations, and (*ii*) which can cure the situation of boom and depression. The first type of measures may be called as preventive measures, while the second type of measures can be called as curative measures. It is well-known that the type of the remedy will differ according to the symptoms of the disease. The influence of climatic factors and natural calamities upon trade cycles cannot be ruled out altogether. So, the best course would be to reduce the dependence of the economy on nature as far as possible. In a country like ours, for example, dependence on monsoons should be reduced or minimised. Then there exists lack of equilibrium between the demand and the supply in the economy which can be rectified by collecting and disseminating correct and up-to-date statistical information on the conditions of crops, employment, imports, and exports prices and cost of living, per capita income, etc. Moreover, the nationalisation of industries and government spending with a definite purpose can also remedy the situation to a considerable extent. And finally, there can be a well-regulated monetary and banking policy by the government so that it may help in controlling the crises.

Curative measures are adopted to soothen the trade cycle rather than to eradicate it. Some of the important methods can be: (*i*) programme of public works during depression, (*ii*) a planned production in the country so as to co-ordinate the needs and the output of the country and in this respect nationalisation proves to be very effective, (*iii*) elastic public expenditure to meet finance requirements; this would require proper expending and sound budgeting, and (*iv*) a sound monetary and fiscal policy to fight crisis. During the period of depression the central bank may decide to sell its securities, thereby mopping up the purchasing power of the people and influencing the quantity of money in circulation. The reverse may be adopted during times of boom. Which of the above measures would be appropriate to control fluctuations in economic activity is difficult to say. The fact remains that a set of measures after proper permutation and combination would have to be decided by the government keeping in view the situation prevailing at a particular point of time in the economy. No one single measure has been or would be or can be effective to control trade cycles. Moreover, it is neither possible nor feasible to maintain complete economic stability. The most feasible thing would be to regulate the level of economic activity in the best interest of the country and its people.

Exercises

1. "Business cycles are a monetary phenomenon." Discuss this statement in the light of Friedman's views.
2. How monetary changes affect business cycles? Explain it with reference to empirical evidence provided by Friedman.
3. Critically examine Prof. Hicks' theory of trade cycles.
4. What is a trade cycle? Explain the expansion and contraction phases of a trade cycle.

Chapter 13

Post-Keynesian Developments in Trade Cycle Theories

1. Introduction

Economists have made use of the concepts of the multiplier and the accelerator to explain the occurrence of trade cycle. According to them, the interaction between the multiplier and the accelerator provides a possible explanation to the fluctuations occurring in a capitalist economy in the field of business activity. Hicks, Hansen, Harrod, Samuelson and Kurihara are such economists who attribute the occurrence of business fluctuations to the cumulative effect of the multiplier and the accelerator. We have explained in detail these two concepts earlier. Let us for the present see how this happens. Whenever there is a new investment in the economy, the income expands several times greater than the original investment merely because of the operation of the principle of the multiplier. The income so increased accelerates the demand for consumption goods on account of an increase in the aggregate propensity to consume. When the demand for consumption goods increases, it induces investment in a much larger measure, on account of the operation of the accelerator. Increased investment brings out an increase in incomes and hence in the demand for consumer goods. This cycle goes on and the interaction between 'the multiplier and the accelerator lands the economy in the upswing of the trade cycle. The amount of this leverage would depend on the values of the multiplier and accelerator coefficients. If these values are high, then the leverage would be very large and it can generate a situation of hyper inflation. But in actual life, the values of the multiplier and the accelerator are never high and hence the leverage is not also very big and therefore, upswing in business activity is moderate. But this upswing does not continue for long or indefinitely. As Keynes has stated, the marginal propensity to consume declines with an increase in income which brings upswing in business activity to an end. This can be understood like this. A decrease in the propensity to consume results in a greater decrease in investment because the accelerator starts operating in the opposite direction. A decline in the level of investment decreases income owing to the operation of the multiplier in reverse direction. This causes further decline in the level of consumption and hence a further decrease in the level of investment. And so, the working of the accelerator and the multiplier in the reverse direction leads to the downswing of business activity or deflation, throwing the economy into depression. But the fall in income during depression is not followed by a proportionate fall in the propensity to consume which means that by and by the demand for capital goods increases, the level of investment starts picking up, which through the combined effect of the multiplier and the accelerator removes the slackness in the business activity and starts another upswing of the trade cycle. This is how we explain the upswing and downswing of a trade cycle in terms of multiplier-accelerator interaction.

2. Hicks' Model of the Trade Cycle

Prof. J.R. Hicks has also formulated his model on the basis of the principle of multiplier-accelerator interaction. According to him it is an interaction between multiplier and the accelerator which leads to the path of economic fluctuations around the warranted rate of growth. So, Hicks' model has five ingredients:

1. Warranted rate of growth,
2. The consumption function,
3. Autonomous investment,
4. Induced investment function, and
5. Multiplier accelerator relation.

The warranted rate of growth is consistent with saving-investment equilibrium. When real investment and real savings grow at the same rate, then it is the warranted rate of growth. Hicks holds that it is the interaction between the multiplier and the accelerator which prepares the path of economic fluctuations around warranted growth rate. The consumption function can be expressed as $Ct = \alpha Yt - 1$.

The consumption in period '*t*' is regarded as a function of income (*Y*) of the previous period ($t - 1$). Thus consumption is less than income and the multiplier is considered as a lagged relation. Autonomous investment is not in any way related to the growth of the economy and is therefore not affected by the variations in the level of output. Induced investment is affected by the changes in the level of output and is therefore a function of the growth of the economy. In the Hicks' model the accelerator is based on induced investment which together with the multiplier brings about an upturn. Hicks defines accelerator as a ratio of induced investment to the increase in incomes. The values of the multiplier and the accelerator remaining constant, economic fluctuations are caused by 'leverage effect'.

Assumptions of Hicks' Model

Hicks has formulated his model on the following assumptions:

(1) The model assumes a progressive economy in which autonomous investment grows at a constant rate and so the system is in a state of moving equilibrium.

(2) The model further assumes that the values of the multiplier and the accelerator are constant and provide a strong tendency to instability as a reaction to any disturbance, so that any upward displacement from equilibrium will not be self-correcting but will cause a continuing movement of the explosive variety away from equilibrium.

(3) The model also assumes that there is no scope for the economy to expand beyond the full employment level of output.

(4) The operation of accelerator in the downturn of the cycle provides an indirect check to the downward movement of the economy.

(5) The model assumes that the relation between the multiplier and the accelerator is lagged because consumption and induced investment operate with a time lag.

(6) Finally, the model assumes that the average capital-output ratio is greater than unity and that gross investment does not fall below zero. Hence the cycles are inherently explosive but are controlled by ceilings and the floors of the economy.

The Model

According to Hicks, "The theory of the multiplier and the theory of the accelerator are the two sides of the theory of fluctuations just as the theory of demand and the theory of supply are two sides of the theory of value." Besides the multiplier and the accelerator, the concept of the warranted rate of growth also plays an important part in the theory. The warranted rate of growth is that rate of growth which will maintain itself. It is the rate which is consistent with the level of equilibrium between the saving and investment. It means that when the rate of real investment is equal to the rate of real saving in the economy, the economy grows at a warranted rate of growth. The interaction between the multiplier and the accelerator moves around the warranted rate of growth. Prof. Hicks has followed, in this respect, Robertson who treats consumption as a function of income of the previous time period. If consumption in any given period is 't' and if the income of the previous time period is '$t - 1$' and if current consumption is the function of the previous time period, then $Ct = f(Yt - 1)$. We thus find that this approach is different from the" one adopted by Harrod, who treats current consumption as a function of current income, *i.e.*, $Ct = f(Yt)$.

There are certain other important elements in the theory which need highlighting. Hicks assumes the existence of both autonomous and induced investments. According to him autonomous investment is determined independently and is not influenced by the changes in the level of output or national income. It is an exogenous factor arising from technological change caused by an increase in population or from public investment; it is not a function of change in the level of output. In the words of Hicks, "There can be little doubt that quite a large proportion of the net investment which goes on in normal conditions has been called forth, directly or indirectly, by past changes in the level of output, there is certainly some investment for which this effect is so small as to be insignificant. Public investment, investment which occurs in direct response to invention, and much of the 'long range' investment which is only expected to pay for itself over a long period, all of these can be regarded as *autonomous investment* for our purposes." It is the autonomous investment which starts an increase in the level of employment and output. Its force is reflected through the multiplier.

Induced investment, on the other hand, is a function of the past changes in the level of income or level of output or of consumption; in other words it is determined by the changes in the aggregate demand or aggregate consumption. It is an endogenous factor. The concept of induced investment is the centre of Hicks' explanation of the trade cycle because its force is reflected through the accelerator. Hicks regards that an increase in the output from the period to the next causes a 'hump' of investment (induced investment) which later on interacts with the multiplier; this is the concept of accelerator as used by Hicks. Thus, autonomous investment through the multiplier, and induced investment through the accelerator, cause cyclical fluctuations in the business activity.

Like the multiplier Hicks has also used the accelerator with a lag which means that induced investment like consumption also reacts to the changes in the level of output with a time lag. He also assumes that the ratio between the changes in the output and the changes in the level of induced investment is a fixed one, or in other words he assumes a fixed marginal capital output ratio. He, thus, assumes that the numerical value of the multiplier and the accelerator does not change and therefore he assumes that the multiplier is active throughout the different phases of the cycle while accelerator remains inactive only during depression. During the up-swing of the trade cycle both the accelerator and the multiplier work simultaneously and therefore, the expansion is cumulative in nature'. An increase in autonomous investment causes increase in income and consumption expenditure through the multiplier which induces an additional investment outlay through the accelerator. During all this process no change takes place in the capital-output ratio insofar as the autonomous investment is concerned.

Let us also throw light on the Hicksian explanation of the upper and lower turning points. Hicks treats the lower turning point as a primary function of the autonomous investment because during the downswing phase of the trade cycle the induced investment is negative. During the period of contraction some production certainly takes place, although the level of production will definitely be lower than the existing production capacity, which means that the total capital stock in the economy is not being used fully or is greater than what would have been adequate to produce the total output demanded for consumption. But, during the process of production, the productive equipment wears out and to maintain the existing plant capacity, the worn-out plant must be replaced. This is taken care of by the surplus plant capacity that exists in the economy, which means that the worn-out equipment will not be replaced by a new one and the plant capacity which is lying idle will be put to use and so at the end of each time period, the surplus plant capacity would be less than what it was at the beginning of the period. A point would definitely reach when there would be no surplus plant capacity and to maintain the productive capacity of the 'economy intact; the worn-out equipment (*i.e.*, autonomous investment) would act as lever for the economy during the depression phase of the trade cycle. This would cause an increase in the net investment expenditure and thereby an increase in income and expenditure in a, multiplier fashion, which is further strengthened by the force of the accelerator. The interaction between the multiplier and the accelerator leads to cumulative expansion.

Hicks considers the analysis of the upper turning point as more difficult. For explaining this, he has used the concept of natural rate of growth as given by Harrod. He starts like this: trade cycles have weak endings as well as strong endings; those with weak endings are 'free' cycles and those with strong endings are 'constrained' cycles. A free cycle that occurs with the combined action of the multiplier and the accelerator is not adequate to push the economy to the level of production which is determined by the natural growth rate. The upper turning point occurs in such a cycle. A constrained cycle occurs when the combined action of the multiplier and the accelerator pushes the economy up until the terminal point of expansion as set by the production ceiling is reached and it strikes against it. No further expansion takes place thereafter. Hicks calls it a constrained cycle because further expansion is dependent on the production ceiling; once the ceiling is reached, expansion cannot take place faster than the rate at which the ceiling itself is growing and the rate of growth of ceiling is determined by the size of population, the rate of technological developments, the available stock of capital, etc. After the production ceiling is reached, the force of the multiplier and the accelerator becomes inadequate to maintain the rate of expansion, as stated above. But according to Hicks, "This is not a thing which it is able to do, so long as it is operating under pressures we are describing; or rather it cannot keep to this track for more than a very limited time. When the path has encountered the ceiling, it must (for a little) bounce off from it and begin to move in a downward direction."

It can thus be concluded from what Hicks has stated that in a capitalist country contraction is bound to follow expansion. He has also emphasised that if technological developments do not take place, if the population does not grow, if the capital stock does not increase and if the other growth factors do not increase, the economy is bound to plunge into depression for a long period: firstly, because without technological developments autonomous investment may not rise over time and therefore accelerator will remain inoperative and the level of investment will remain static so long as the need for replacement of worn-out equipment does not occur; and secondly, in the absence of technological developments, replacements will be definitely slow.

Criticisms of the Hicks' Model

The Model constructed by Prof. Hicks has invited criticisms from various economists. These criticisms are summarised below:

(1) Hicks assumes that autonomous investment continues throughout different phases of the cycle at a steady pace which is unrealistic. Autonomous investment does decline during the financial crises. Moreover, autonomous investment may also be subject to variations due to technological innovations as suggested by Schumpeter.

(2) Hicks considers growth as dependent on variations in autonomous investment. According to him it is a burst of autonomous investment from the equilibrium path which leads to growth. Prof. Smithies[1] is, however, of the view that Hicks' model does not provide a complete explanation of the cycle by imputing growth to an unexplained extraneous factor. According to him the source of growth should lie within the system itself.

(3) It is not possible to draw a distinction between autonomous and induced investment. In this connection Prof. Lundberg points out that in the short run every investment is autonomous and in the long run a major amount of autonomous investment becomes induced. He also points out that of the total investment a particular part may be induced and the remaining may be autonomous. Hence the distinction between the two is of doubtful validity.

1. A. Smithies, "Economic Fluctuations and Growth", *Econometrica,* January 1957.

(4) Objection has also been raised against the explanation given by Prof. Hicks of the ceiling (upper limit) of the cycle. According to Duesenberry, the ceiling (upper limit) does not provide adequate explanation of the onset of depression. At the most it can impede growth and not cause a depression. Paucity of resources cannot cause investment to decline suddenly and thus bring depression. Even Hicks has admitted that monetary factors may also lead to the onset of depression even before reaching the level of full employment.

(5) Economists are also not satisfied with the explanation given by Hicks of the lower turning point (floor) of a cycle. Hicks holds that increase in autonomous investment at the bottom leads to the lower turning point. However, Harrod is not convinced that autonomous investment would increase at the bottom of the depression. According to him depression may retard autonomous investment rather than encourage it.

(6) In the Hicksian Model it has been assumed that the average capital-output ratio is greater than unity for a time lag of one year or less. It means that explosive cycles are in-built in the model. But empirical evidence shows that change in output causes a change in investment spread over many periods and consequently there have been damped cycles and not explosive cycles.

(7) According to Hicks the full employment ceiling is not affected by the path of output. It has been pointed out by the critics that the full employment level is determined by the magnitude of the resources available to the country. The capital stock is one such resource. When the capital stock is increasing during any period, the full employment ceiling is raised.

(8) The critics also point out that Hicks does not appear to be very clear about the role of monetary factors in the trade cycle. According to him the downswing might start even before reaching the full employment ceiling, if banks follow a contractionary monetary policy. Elsewhere, he holds that the protracted length of the contraction from 1922-23 was mainly due to monetary crisis. Again, at another place he says that monetary factors may cause the downturn, but he traces the fundamental causes of the downturn to the real factors rather than to monetary factors.

(9) Critics also point out that since Hicks' analysis is based on the multiplier-accelerator interaction in rigid form, it provides a mechanical explanation of the trade cycle and there is no place for human judgment, decisions and business expectations.

(10) Hicks has also been criticised for emphasizing that the contraction phase of a cycle is longer than the expansion phase. But the actual behaviour of the post-war cycles has indicated that the expansion phase of a cycle has been longer than the contraction phase.

Notwithstanding these shortcomings of the Hicksian model, it will have to be admitted that this model is much superior to the earlier models in so far as the explanation of the turning points of the trade cycle is concerned.

3. Samuelson's Multiplier-Accelerator Interaction Model of Trade Cycle

Prof. Samuelson has constructed a model on the basis of multiplier-acceleration interaction for explaining the occurrence of trade cycles. In this model he assumes one period lag and different values of the *MPC* (α) and the accelerator (β) which bring about changes in the level of income. This model is as follows:

$$Yt = Gt + Ct + It \quad \text{...(1)}$$

where Y is national income, G is government expenditure, C is consumption expenditure, I is induced investment and t represents time.

$$Ct = \alpha Yt - 1 \quad \text{...(2)}$$

$$It = \beta(Ct - Ct - 1) \quad \text{...(3)}$$

Substituting equation (2) in (3)

$$It = \beta(\alpha Yt - 1 - \alpha Yt - 2)$$

$$It = \beta\alpha Yt - 1 - \beta\alpha Yt - 2) \quad \text{...(4)}$$

$$Gt = 1 \quad \text{...(5)}$$

Substituting equations (2) and (5) in (1),

$$Yt = 1 + \alpha Yt - 1 + \beta\alpha Yt - 1 - \beta\alpha Yt - 2 \quad \text{...(6)}$$

$$= 1 + \alpha(Yt - 1 + \beta Yt - 1) - \beta\alpha Yt - 2$$

$$= 1 + \alpha(1 + \beta)\, Yt - 1 - \beta\alpha Yt - 2 \quad \text{...(7)}$$

In the words of Samuelson, "If we know the National Income for two periods, the national income for the following period can be simply derived by taking a weighted sum. The weights depend, of course, upon the values chosen for the marginal propensity to consume (*MPC*) and on the relation (*i.e.*, accelerator)." Samuelson, after assuming the value of the *MPC* as greater than zero and less than one and the value of the accelerator as greater than zero, explains five types of cyclical fluctuations as given in the following table:

Case	*Values*	*Behaviour of the Cycle*
1.	$\alpha = .5, \beta = 0$	Cycleless Path
2.	$\alpha = .5, \beta = 1$	Dumped Fluctuations
3.	$\alpha = .5, \beta = 2$	Fluctuations of Constant Amplitude
4.	$\alpha = .5, \beta = 3$	Explosive Cycles
5.	$\alpha = .5, \beta = 4$	Cycleless Explosive Path

In the above table, *Case* 1 shows a cycleless path because the accelerator does not play any part and only the multiplier is effective as shown in Fig.13.1.

Case 2 shows the damped cyclical path fluctuating around the static multiplier level and slowly subsiding to that level as shown in Fig. 13.2.

Case 3 shows fluctuations of constant amplitude repeating around the multiplier level, as shown in Fig.13.3.

Case 4 shows explosive cycles as shown in Fig.13.4.

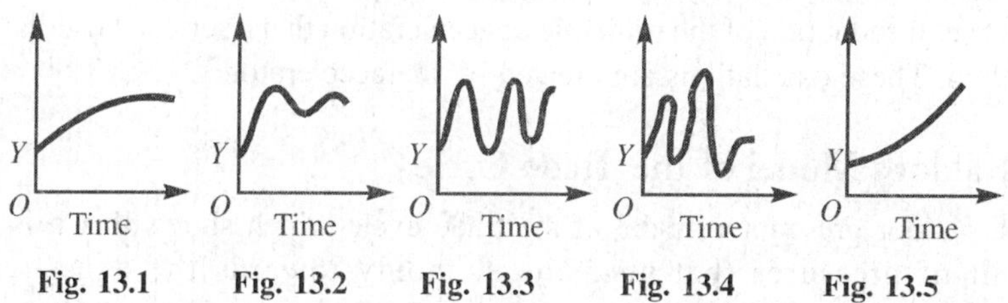

Fig. 13.1 **Fig. 13.2** **Fig. 13.3** **Fig. 13.4** **Fig. 13.5**

Case 5 relates to a cycleless explosive upward path finally approaching a compound rate of growth as shown in Fig. 13.5.

Experience has, however, revealed that only 2 cases of damped cycles have been witnessed. Case No.2 of damped cycles has been experienced in an irregular fashion in a milder form. Such cycles have occurred chiefly because of exogenous factors like wars, innovations, etc., which may be called erratic shocks. But their magnitude is not possible to be measured. Case No.3 is also cyclical in nature but such cycles have not been experienced. Case No.4 has also not been experienced because such cycles can occur only in the absence of endogenous economic factors, which limit the swings.

Limitations of Samuelson's Model

Samuelson's Model suffers from the following limitations:

(1) It does not say anything about the length of period of the different cycles explained by him.

(2) It is based on the assumption that *MPC* and the accelerator are constant but in real life they change with the change in the level of income. Hence this is applicable only to the study of small fluctuations.

(3) The cycles explained in the Samuelson's model swing around a stationary level in a trendless economy which is not real because an economy is not trendless, but is in a process of growth.

Merits of the Model

Despite these limitations, the model has the following uses:

(1) It is a useful tool for explaining business cycles as also a guide for the formulation of a policy to stabilise the economy, as pointed out by Prof. Kurihara.

(2) Again, the model also succeeds in explaining that the cyclical fluctuations take place because of the combined effect of the multiplier and the accelerator. The greater the value of the multiplier the greater would be the chance of cycleless path. By itself, the multiplier cannot produce any cyclical fluctuations from any given impulse but only a slow increase to a constant level of income determined by the propensity to consume. It is only after the introduction of the principle of acceleration that a series of oscillation resulted. These oscillations are created by the accelerator.[2]

4. Kaldor's Model of the Trade Cycle

Prof. Kaldor presents a model of the trade cycle which shows that it is the result of pressures that push the economy towards the equality of ex-ante saving and investment. According to Kaldor it is the difference between the two that gives rise to a cycle. Kaldor explains the stability and instability conditions with the help of the following linear diagrams (Figs. 13.1 and 13.2).

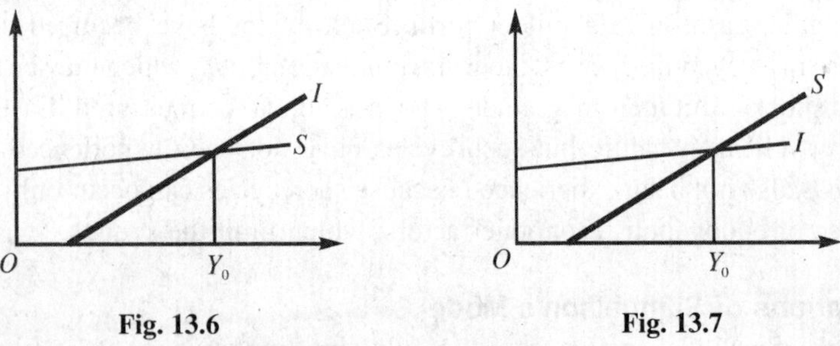

Fig. 13.6 **Fig. 13.7**

In these figures there is a single equilibrium position where investment and saving are equal at the level of income Y_0. In Fig. 13.6 I is greater than S and there is an unstable equilibrium position beyond Y_0 because such a situation will lead to limitless expansion, to full employment and hyper inflation. In Fig. 13.7, S is greater than I which means that there is a downward movement to the left of Y_0 which will lead to zero output and employment and to the collapse of the economy. Since these diagrams depict linear saving and investment functions and do not produce a cycle, Kaldor has adopted non-linear saving and investment functions. A non-linear investment function is shown in Fig. 13.8.

As the economy moves into the expansion phase, shown by the movement from the left along the I curve, the curve is almost flat. It implies that there is excess capacity at a low level of income and the net investment is zero.

---

2. J.A. Estey, *Business Cycles,* 1956.

Contrarywise in the case of a high level of income when the economy moves into the contraction phase, the I curve is again flat and the net investment is small, because the increasing costs and increasing difficulty of borrowing discourages entrepreneurs from expanding their business still faster. This slows down the rate of increase in output. It means that the existing capital stock and the capacity are in excess of the current output. Consequently further investment declines, income falls and the ultimate effect is that the economy moves into the contraction phase.

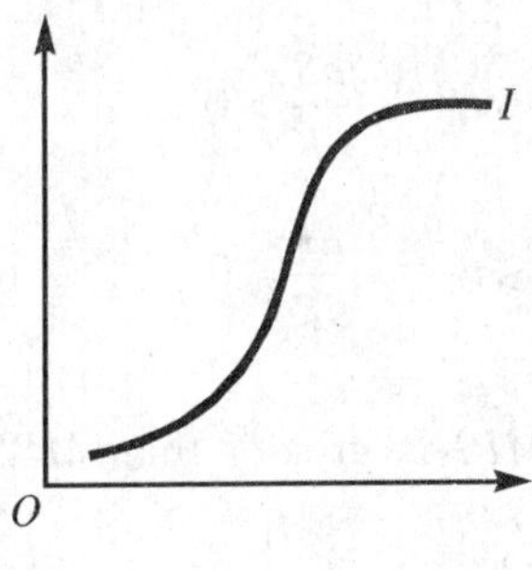

Fig. 13.8

Likewise, a non-linear saving function is shown in Fig. 13.9.

When the non-linear saving and investment curves are brought together the cycle appears as shown in Fig. 13.10.

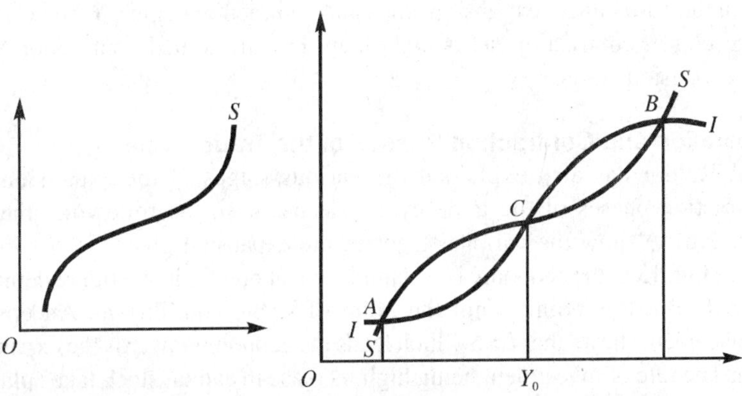

Fig. 13.9 **Fig. 13.10**

In Fig. 13.10 multiple equilibrium points, *i.e.*, *A*, *B* and *C* have been shown. Of these *A* and *B* are stable positions and *C* shows the position of instability. Between *C* and *B* and below *A*, investment is greater than saving ($I > S$). It implies that there is a rise in the level of income. Between *A* and *C* and above B, saving is greater than investment ($S > I$) which means that there is a fall in income.

A and B are positions of stability only in the short run. It is only in the long run that they become unstable and the path of the cycle is visible. For this, Kaldor introduces the capital stock as another variable that affects the relationship between saving and investment. He takes both saving and investment as functions of Income (Y) and capital stock (K) so that:

$$S = f(Y, K)$$
$$I = f(Y, K)$$

and

$$\frac{dS}{dY} > 0, \quad \frac{dS}{dK} > 0$$

$$\frac{dI}{dY} > 0, \quad \frac{dI}{dK} < 0$$

and $\frac{dI}{dY} > \frac{dS}{dY}$, that is MPI is greater than MPS over the expansion or contraction phase of the cycle.

The relationship $MPI > MPS$ shows the instability of the economy which will move either towards expansion or contraction. In the above figure, A and B are "switch points" in the long run, in which the economy changes its direction either towards expansion or contraction. Point C is unstable in both directions. When C and B come closer, the expansion phase of the cycle starts. When they are joined, expansion stops and contraction begins. When C and A come closer, contraction starts and when they are joined contraction stops and expansion starts.

Expansion and Contraction Phases of the Trade Cycle

Prof. Kaldor has also explained the various stages of the expansion and contraction phases of the trade cycle. He has used the following diagram (Fig.13.6) to show the various stages of the expansion phase.

In Fig. 13.6, the economy is in equilibrium at point C in the figure depicting stage 1. But this point is not the point of stable equilibrium. An upward displacement shows that $I > S$ which leads the economy towards the expansion path. The rate of investment being high increase in capital stock takes place at a fast pace. With the increase in the capital stock, the MEC declines and investment curve shifts downward. Simultaneously, with the increase in the capital stock of the economy, the income goes up and savings also rise. Consequently, the saving curve shifts upward. Hence, the downward shift of the investment curve I and upward shift of the saving curve S bring the point C closer to B as depicted in figure of stage 2. This process continues till the points C and B coincide as shown in figure of stage 3. But, at this stage $S > I$ in both directions. It means that this is a position of an unstable equilibrium in the downward direction and from here onwards the downward movement of the economy starts till point A is reached in stage 3.

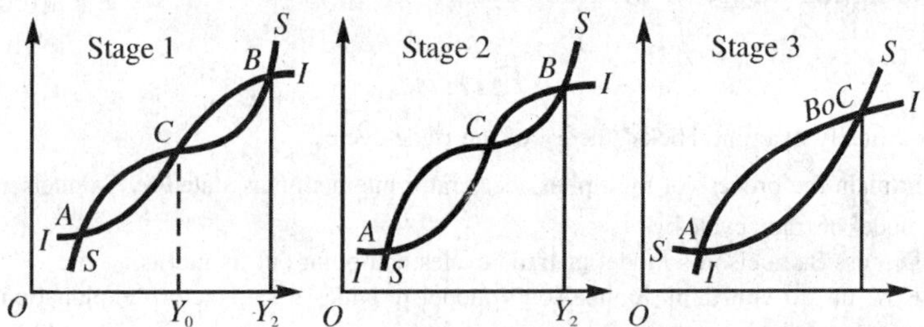

Fig. 13.11

Kaldor has used the following diagram (Fig. 13.12) to depict the stages of the contraction phase of the trade cycle.

The contraction phase has also 3 stages. Point A in stage 4 of Fig. 13.12 is the point of short run stable equilibrium but at a very low income level. We start from this point. In the long run due to a low level of income the capital stock decreases and the investment curve I shifts upward. Consequently saving falls and the saving curve moves downward. Thus, the shifting of the I curve upward and of the S curve downward bring A and C closer as shown in Fig. 13.12 of stage 5. This process continues till I and S curves are tangential and points A and C coincide as shown in the stage 6 of Fig. 13.12. But this $A + C$ position at Y. Income level is unstable in the upward direction because $I > S$. The expansionary process starts and continues till the economy reaches the higher level of income Y_2 at point B. From B, the I and S curves gradually reach the positions as shown in stage 1 Fig. 13.11 of the expansion phase and again the cyclical process starts. In this way, Kaldor's cyclical process is self-generating.

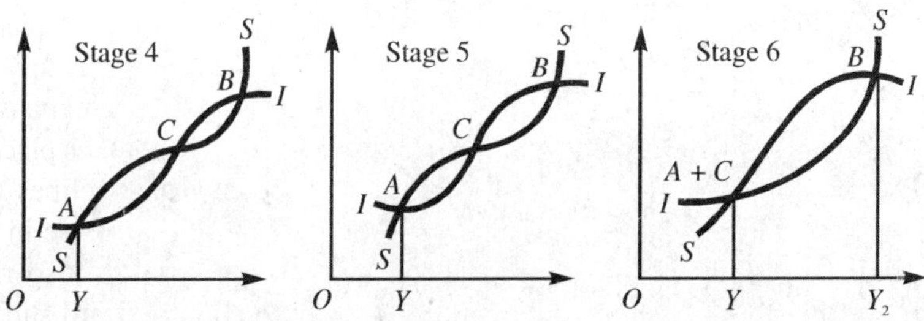

Fig. 13.12

From the above analysis it is clear that in Kaldor's model the cycles are not necessarily of the same length and duration. Expansions and contractions are also not necessarily symmetrical. It has also been pointed out that Kaldor has neither used the acceleration principle nor the monetary factors in explaining his theory of the trade cycle.

Exercises

1. Critically examine Hicks' theory of the trade cycles.
2. Explain the process of multiplier-accelerator interaction as stated by Samuelson in his model of trade cycles.
3. Discuss Samuelson's model of trade cycles and point out its merits.
4. How far do you think Samuelson's model provides a satisfactory explanation of the trade cycle?
5. Write an explanatory note on Kaldor's model of the trade cycle.
6. Describe the expansion and contraction phases of the trade cycle as explained by Kaldor and use diagrams.

●●●

PART TWO
BANKING THEORY

Chapter 14

Money and Capital Markets

1. The Money Market

Meaning and Features

The money market plays a vital role in the development .of an economy; it is rather its integral part. It is a special type of organisation where the credit and capital are supplied. Let us not take it to be as any particular place where the activities concerning the supply of credit and capital are carried on; it is the whole area over which activities of the borrowers and lenders of money are spread. In such a market people deal in short-term loans; the price at which the money is bought and sold is called the rate of interest. It is extremely helpful in stabilising the prices by facilitating the transfer of capital and floating funds from time to time and place to place according to their demand and supply. The essential feature of the money market is that it is the market for short-term loans, the providers of the loans generally being the commercial banks, which lend at "call or short notice" to the members of the discount market. The efficiency of a money market, thus, is determined by the extent to which it can supply money and control and regulate its volume according to the requirements of industry, trade and commerce as well as by its capacity to mobilise surplus funds from one section of community to another where it can be put to more efficient use. The demand for such funds arises from businessmen and governments for their various operations. The supply comes from the banks which obtain it from the people in the form of deposits. Money market is considered to be tight when the supply of money falls short of the demand and the rate of interest increases, and it is cheap or easy when the supply of money exceeds its demand and the rate of interest falls. When the commercial banks wish to increase their holdings of cash they call back some of these loans and the central bank then enters the money market as lender of last resort. The discount houses in some of the countries came into existence as dealers in bills of exchange and it is to provide themselves with funds for the discounting of bills that discount houses and bill brokers borrow for short terms from the commercial banks or in times of monetary stringency from the central bank. The activities of the members of the money market and the discount market overlap to such a considerable extent that nowadays the term "money market" is taken to include the combined business of the two markets. In recent decades the money market has widened the scope of its business and the variety of its institutions. The world's highly developed money markets are the London Money Market and the New York Money Market. And so, the money market can be concrete and real and its operations can be witnessed in the Lombard Street, London or the Wall Street, in New York. The various instruments which constitute the money market are more or less standard and any type of personal relationship between the lender and the borrower is of no importance. Both the parties are brought in contact with each other through the dealers. Banker's acceptances' market is a very important constituent of a money market. Money market also comprises the commercial paper market, the short-term treasury bill market and also the call money market. While the bankers' acceptances' market and the commercial paper market utilise short-term funds for financing domestic and foreign trade, the treasury bill market employs funds to finance the short-term requirements of the government. The call money market carries on trading in existing securities or the issue of new securities before they reach the ultimate investor. According to Crowther, it is the "collective name given to the various firms and institutions that deal in the various grades of near-money". The Reserve Bank of India has, however, given a more elaborate definition which runs: "A money market is the centre for dealings, mainly of short-term character, in money assets, it meets the short-term requirements of borrowers and provides liquidity or cash to the lenders. It is the place where short-term surplus investible funds at the disposal of financial and other institutions and individuals are bid by borrowers, again comprising institutions and individuals and also the government itself."

Functions of a Money Market

A money market performs the following functions in an economy:

1. Profitable use of surplus funds. It enables banks and other financial institutions and non-financial business corporations and governments to make use of their surplus funds in a profitable manner in the short period.

2. Helps economic development. By providing short-term funds to various institutions for their working capital requirements a money market promotes the development of commerce, industry and trade. This is done by the discounting of trade bills through commercial banks, brokers, acceptance houses, and discount houses, etc.

3. In the aid of banks. Due to the existence of a money market the commercial banks can call in some of their loans instead of borrowing from the central bank. This saves them from paying a higher interest rate to the central bank.

4. In the aid of government. The government can also raise short-term funds at low interest rates by issuing treasury bills instead of borrowing from the central bank or issuing paper currency. This would also not cause any inflationary rise in the price level.

5. Promotes savings and investments. A money market promotes savings and investments by increasing liquidity and safety of financial assets.

6. Equilibrium between demand and supply of funds. A money market allocates/allows resources to be used in a rational way through channelisation of savings into investments and thus establishes equilibrium between the demand and supply of loanable funds.

7. Effective implementation of monetary policy. It is only through a well-developed money market that the central bank can effectively control the banking system and provide a direction to the development of commerce and industry through its monetary policies. The money market, thus, helps in the effective implementation of the monetary policies of the central bank.

8. Economical use of cash. Since a money market deals in near-money assets, it helps the economical use of cash. As the funds can be conveniently and safely transferred from one place to another, a money market helps the growth of commerce and industry.

Sectors of a Money Market

We have said earlier that money market deals in short-term funds. Since there are different types of credit transactions, for each of these types there is a specialised sub-market which is a constituent of the money market. These sub-markets are:

1. Call Money Market. It is the most important constituent of the money market dealing in extremely short period loans, say, for a day or for a maximum period of 7 days to brokers and dealers of stock exchanges. These loans are provided by the commercial banks without any collateral security. These are known as call loans because they can be called back by the lending bank as and when it requires. Such types of loans undoubtedly meet the short-term requirements of liquidity, but are not profitable.

2. Collateral Loan Market. In this section of the money market, loans are provided on the basis of securities, stocks and bonds, etc. which are returned to the borrower as soon as he repays the loan. In case the loan is not repaid by the borrower, the collateral becomes the property of the lender. The period of such loans is a few months. These loans are generally taken by brokers and dealers in stocks and shares.

3. Bill Market or Discount Market. This is also known as short-term commercial paper market; it specialises in the sale and purchase of commercial bills like the bills of exchange and the treasury bills. A bill of exchange is an unconditional written order signed by the seller requiring the buyer to whom it is addressed to pay on demand or at a fixed date in future a specific amount of money to the order of the seller or to the bearer. The bill of exchange, thus, is a sort of written agreement between the buyer and the seller. The seller after having sold the goods to the buyer draws upon him a bill requiring the buyer to pay a definite sum of money to the order of the seller either on demand or at a subsequent date. This bill is then sent by the seller to buyer for acceptance and no sooner the buyer indicates his acceptance then it becomes a legal document. The bill is then returned to the seller who may either retain it until the date of maturity or may get it discounted by a bank in case he needs the funds immediately. The bank charges some commission for discounting such bills. While the bills of exchange are issued by private parties, the treasury bills are issued by government. A treasury bill is a type of short-term security, generally of 91 days duration, issued by the government and sold by the central bank on its behalf. These are sold in auction to the highest bidder in the market. Since these are issued by the government, they do not involve any risk for the purchaser. And that is why commercial banks treat them as the best investment. In short, the commercial paper market or the businessmen market deals only in short-term bills of exchange and government securities.

4. The Acceptances Market. It is a market which deals with bankers' acceptances, which are a sort of draft drawn by a firm upon a bank and accepted by it whereby it is required to pay to the order of a specified party or to the bearer the amount of money indicated therein at a specified date. Such acceptances arise out of commercial transactions both within the country as well as outside the country. Since these papers carry the banker's signatures, these can be easily designated in the money market.

Constituents of a Money Market

The following organisations constitute a money market:

1. Commercial Banks. These form the most important constituent of the money market. They provide an outlet for short-term investments. They also undertake investment by discounting the bills of exchange and treasury bills. While lending their funds, they have to ensure that their funds remain as liquid as possible and also bring the maximum possible profits.

2. Non-Banking Financial Institutions. In this group come the insurance companies and business corporations which have surplus short-term funds and which provide the same to the borrowers in the money market.

3. Acceptance Houses. Such houses are very important in the UK. They specialise in the acceptance of commercial bills and exchange bills on behalf of their customers. When these bills are accepted by Acceptance Houses, they are easily designated by the discount houses.

4. Central Bank. The central bank is the apex of the monetary and banking structure in the country. It controls and regulates the activities of commercial banks and financing institutions. It is the lender of last resort and, therefore, all other financing agencies which are members of the money market obtain loans and advances from the central bank. It regulates the activities of the money market in a number of ways. In the highly industrialised countries, the central bank's task is extremely easy because the money market is highly developed but in less developed countries, the money market not being well organised and developed, the regulation and control of the central bank on the money market is not so effective.

Instruments of the Money Market

The money market operates through a number of instruments.

1. Promissory Note. The promissory note is the earliest type of bill. It is a written promise on the part of a businessman to pay to another a certain sum of money at an agreed future date. Usually, a promissory note falls due for payment after 90 days with three days of grace. A promissory note is drawn by the debtor and has to be accepted by the bank in which the debtor has his account, to be valid. The creditor can get it discounted from his bank till the date of recovery. Promissory notes are rarely used in business these days, except in the USA.

2. Treasury Bill. But the major instrument of the money markets is the treasury bill which is issued for varying periods of less than one year. They are issued by the Secretary to the Treasury in England and are payable at the Bank of England. There are also the short-term government securities in the USA which are traded by commercial banks and dealers in securities. In India, the treasury bills are issued by the Government of India at a discount generally between 91 days and 364 days. There are three types of treasury bills in India—91 days, 182 days and 364 days.

3. Bill of Exchange or Commercial Bills. Another instrument of the money market is the bill of exchange which is similar to the promissory note, except in that it is drawn by the creditor and is accepted by the bank of the debtor. The creditor can discount the bill of exchange either with a broker or a bank. There is also the foreign bill of exchange which becomes due for payment from the date of acceptance. The rest of the procedure is the same as for the internal bill of exchange. Promissory notes and bills of exchange are known as trade bills.

4. Inter-bank Term Market. This market is exclusively for commercial and cooperative banks in India, which borrow and lend funds for a period of over 14 days and upto 90 days without any collateral security at market-determined rates.

5. Call and Notice Money. There is the call money market in which funds are borrowed and lent for one day. In the notice market, funds are borrowed and lent upto 14 days without any collateral security. But deposit receipt is issued to the lender by the borrower who repays the borrowed amount with interest on call. In India, commercial banks and cooperative banks borrow and lend funds in this market but mutual funds and all-India financial institutions participate only as lenders of funds.

6. Commercial Paper (CP). Commercial papers are issued by highly rated companies to raise short-term working capital requirements directly from the market instead of borrowing from the banks. Commercial paper is a promise by the borrowing company to repay the loan at a specified date, normally for a period of 3 months to 6 months. This instrument is very popular in the USA, UK, Japan, Australia and a number of other countries. It has been introduced in India in January 1990.

7. Certificates of Deposits (CD). Certificates of deposits are issued by commercial banks at a discount on face value. The discount rate is determined by the market. In India, the minimum size of the issue is Rs. 25 lakh with the minimum subscription of Rs. 51akh. The maturity period is between 3 months and 12 months.

Working of the Money Market

The money market consisting of commercial banks, discount houses, bill brokers, acceptance houses, non-bank financial institutions and the central bank operates through the bills, securities, treasury bills, government securities and call loans of various types. As the money market consists of varied types of institutions dealing in different types of instruments, it operates through a number of sub-markets.

First, the money market operates through the call loan market. It has been defined as "a market for marginal funds, for temporarily unemployed or unemployable funds". In this market, the commercial banks use their unused funds to lend for very short periods to bill brokers and dealers in stock exchange. In developed countries, even big corporations lend their dividends before distribution to earn interest for a very short period. The central bank also lends to commercial banks for very short periods. Such loans are mostly for a week, even for a day or a night and can be recalled at a very short notice. That is why a short period loan is known as call loan or call money. Bill brokers and stock brokers who borrow such funds use them to discount or purchase bills or stocks. Such funds are borrowed at the "call rate" which is generally one per cent below the bank rate. But this rate varies with the volume of funds lent by the banks. If the brokers are asked to pay off loans immediately, then they are forced to get funds from large corporations and even from the central bank at high interest rates.

Second, the money market also operates through the bill market. The bill market is the short-period loan market. In this market, loans are made available to businessmen and the government by the commercial banks, discount houses and brokers. The instruments of credit are the promissory notes, internal bills of exchange and treasury bills. The commercial banks discount bills of exchange, lend against promissory notes or through advances or overdrafts to the business community. Similarly, the discount houses and bill brokers lend to businessmen by discounting their bills of exchange before they mature within 90 days. On the other hand, government borrows through the treasury bills from the commercial banks and non-bank financial institutions.

Third, the money market operates through the collateral loan market for a short period. The commercial banks lend to brokers and discount houses against collateral bonds, stocks, securities, etc. In case of need, commercial banks themselves borrow from the large banks and the central bank on the basis of collateral securities.

Finally, the other important sub-market through which the money market operates is the acceptance market. The merchant bankers accept bills drawn on domestic and foreign traders whose financial standing is not known. When they accept a domestic or foreign trade bill, they guarantee its payment at maturity. In recent years, the commercial banks have also started the acceptance business.

Money Market in Less Developed Countries (LDCs)

One of the important characteristics of all under-developed or less developed countries is the existence of an unorganised or under-developed money market. It would be more pertinent to say that in such economies two types of money markets exist side by side. Since a vast population in these countries reside in the rural areas and is poor, the money market in such areas consists of indigenous bankers, money-lenders, traders, landlords, pawn brokers, etc. and is under-developed. On the other hand, in the urban and semi-urban areas there is a sort of developed money market which consists of the central bank, the commercial banks, brokers, discount and acceptance houses, etc. We now describe the characteristics of these two markets in the following paragraphs:

Characteristics of an Under-developed Money Market

(1) The lenders and the borrowers are in close touch with each other.

(2) The loan transactions are generally very flexible. The borrower can obtain loan according to his requirements depending, of course, on his goodwill with the lender or the nature of security which he is willing to provide.

(3) No single individual sticks to money lending alone. It is one of the many activities that people generally are engaged in. Most of the people do the business of money lending along with other economic activities.

(4) In this type of money market, a number of interest rates prevail. They are neither uniform nor fixed. They vary from person to person and situation to situation, and depend largely on the purpose for which the loan is required and the security offered for obtaining that loan. In the case of urgent requirement the interest rate charged is generally higher and exorbitant.

(5) In such a market formal accounts are never maintained. Formal receipts are not issued either for the payment of interest or for the repayment of the principal amount by the borrowers. The accounts are maintained in the most secretive fashion and are not open to inspection or check by any authority.

(6) Such a market has no link with the developed money market. Consequently, the value of monetary transactions is very small and profitable and productive use of savings is prevented.

Characteristics of a Developed Money Market

(1) It is a well-organised market with the central bank at the top. The central bank is the controlling authority in the field of monetary and banking matters. It is the leader of the money market, which controls, regulates and directs the activities of the entire money market. It generates financial liquidity and acts as the lender of the last resort for the various constituents of the money market.

(2) The money market comprises of a number of specialised sub-markets each dealing in a separate credit instrument; for example, call loan market, the bill market, the treasury bill market, the acceptance market, the foreign exchange market, etc. The state of development of the money market depends upon the number of sub-markets as well as the number of dealers and the integration of the various sub-markets.

(3) The commercial banks constitute an important segment of the money market. As a matter of fact they are the hub of all the activities of the money market. The commercial banks are an important link between the borrowers and the central bank. They are an important source for the supply of short-term funds. It is therefore, necessary that the entire banking system should be integrated and well-knit.

(4) We have already stated that, a money market deals in near-money assets, for example, bills of exchange, promissory notes, securities, bonds, debentures, treasury bills, etc. The larger the number of such assets the more developed would be the money market.

(5) A developed money market possesses an integrated interest rate structure. Without an integrated interest rate structure the central bank will never be able to make effective use of the bank rate policy.

(5) A developed money market easily mobilises financial resources both from within and outside the country. It can also provide easy and cheap remittance facilities from one market to another globally.

2. The Capital Market

Meaning and Features

A capital market deals in stocks, shares, debentures of corporations, bonds and securities of govemments on a long-term basis and thus provides fixed and working capital to industry. The individuals and other institutions existing in the market provide loanable funds. The various institutions participating in the capital market are, the merchant bankers, the commercial banks and the non-bank financial intermediaries like insurance companies, mutual funds, investment houses, unit trusts, leasing finance companies, building societies, etc.

There are also issuing houses which do not provide capital but simply under-write the shares and debentures issued by joint stock companies. The demand for funds for meeting working and fixed capital requirements emanates from joint stock companies, governments, improvement trusts, port trusts, etc. The capital market carries all its activities through a stock exchange. A stock exchange facilitates transactions in the sale and purchase of shares, stocks, bonds, securities and debentures. It not only deals with secondary securities but also in the new issues. In short, the capital market pools medium and long-term funds through a variety of institutions and mechanisms and makes them available to various individuals, governments and business houses.

Functions of a Capital Market

(1) By mobilising savings and channellising them into productive investments the capital market encourages capital formation and promotes economic growth of the country.

(2) It brings together the savers (as lenders) and investors (as borrowers) who are known as 'surplus units' and 'deficit units' respectively. It, therefore, acts as a bridge between the two. It facilitates the use of resources more productively and profitably.

(3) The capital market promotes economic growth through rational allocation of resources. The various constituents of the capital market direct the flow of funds into more productive channels. In the absence of a developed capital market surplus funds are generally used for wasteful and unproductive purposes and are hoarded in the form of gold, jewellery, real estates, or spent on conspicuous consumption, etc.

Difference between Money Market and Capital Market

(1) While the money market deals in short-term funds (generally for a period of less than one year), the capital market deals in long-term funds (generally for a period of up to 25 years).

(2) The money market uses short-term securities like promissory notes, bills of exchange, treasury bills, etc. whereas the capital market uses long-term securities like shares, debentures, bonds and securities of the government.

(3) The central bank, commercial banks, non-bank financial intermediaries and bill brokers are the main constituents of a money market, while stock exchanges, mutual funds, investment banks and trusts, insurance companies, leasing companies, etc. are the constituents of a capital market.

Relationship between Money Market and Capital Market

Both the markets are closely linked with each other. The constituents of both the markets actively participate in the activities of both the markets. So, both the markets are interlinked. The lenders may make available their funds to both the markets depending upon the quantum of such funds, the rate of return and their investment criteria. Borrowers may obtain funds from both the markets according to their convenience and requirements. Financial institutions and corporations may participate in both the markets by transacting in short-term and long-term instruments. All long-term securities become short-term instruments when they reach near-maturity stage and hence they become money market instruments. Inter-market flow of funds can also take place whenever the treasury finances maturing bills with treasury securities or whenever a bank gives a short-term loan to a firm out of the proceeds of a maturing loan. A change in the rate of return in the money market may lead to change in the rate of return in the capital market and *vice versa*. A decline in short-term interest rates in the money market is likely to be followed by a decline in the long-term interest rates in the capital market. In any case the money market interest rates are prone to change more quickly than the long-term interest rates in the capital market.

Exercises

1. What is a money market? Explain its functions.
2. Define money market and describe its working.
3. What do you understand by the capital market? Distinguish between money and capital markets.
4. What is a money market? Explain its importance. How are the money and capital markets related?
5. What is money market? What are the characteristics of a developed money market?

•••

Chapter 15

Organisation and Structure of Commercial Banks

1. Introduction

The importance of commercial banks to modern economic life can hardly be exaggerated. With extreme specialisation and division of labour grown over the years the spell of isolated life of the old good days stands completely broken and now individuals as well as nations seem to have become completely dependent on each other. Consequently goods and services are now being produced on a large scale, a process which is full of complicacies and extremely roundabout in character. Obviously, this requires an intensive use of capital which cannot be available unless savings are made in the society. Savings lead to capital which facilitates production and generates income which means further savings. This process is facilitated by commercial banks. Each one of us, whether a producer or an investor or a consumer must obtain the services relating to "the stimulation of saving, the gathering together of the amounts saved, the promotion of productive investment and of the rapid utilisation of the resulting capital implements". All these services are rendered by the commercial banks.

2. Definitions

Etymologically, the term 'bank' is said to have been derived from the term 'banco'. Some attribute the origin of the word 'bank' to 'bancus' or 'banque' or 'bane'. All these terms, however, mean a bench upon which the medieval European money-lenders or money changers used to carry on their monetary transactions. These derivations, however, give one the impression that banking in Europe was started during the middle ages. But the origin of banking is much more antiquated and no define dates of its origin can be determined.

To define a bank is not an easy task. There are so many definitions that one feels lost in them and the curiosity of the reader is turned into confusion. The term 'bank' or 'banking' is generally used in a very broad sense including the capitalist, the financiers, the stock brokers, the banking corporations and what not. Thus, even the best authorities have found a devil and deep sea problem to define the scope and functions of a bank. Mostly, the term 'banker' has been either defined in the negative or in such a manner as to lay itself open to debate. For example, the Negotiable Instruments Act, 1881 (India), lays down that the term includes persons or a corporation or a company acting as "bankers". This is the definition which does not at all help one to know anything about banking as a business, or bank as an institution. Even the Bankers Books Evidence Act, 1891 and the Indian Stamp Act, 1899 have failed in this respect. Not only this, even the English Law has not been successful in giving us a satisfactory definition. The earliest attempt to provide a definition was however, made by the legislators in the USA. They said: "By 'banking' we mean the business of dealing in credits and by a 'bank' we include every person, firm or company having a place of business where credits are opened by the deposit or collection of money or currency, subject to be paid or remitted on draft, cheque or order, or money is advanced or loaned on stocks, bonds, bullion, bills of exchange, or "promissory notes or where stocks, bonds, bullion, bills of exchange, or promissory notes are received for discount or sale". This is more a description than a definition of a bank.

The *Oxford English Dictionary* defines a 'bank' as "an establishment for the custody of money received from or on behalf of its customers. Its essential duty is to pay their drafts on it, its profits arise from the use of the money left unemployed by them." This definition, too, is not satisfactory because it does not lay down the fundamental principles of the working of a bank. According to the Bills of Exchange Act, 1882, "a banker includes any body of persons whether incorporated or not who carry on the business of banking". This definition neither explains the correct meaning of the term 'bank' nor points out the nature of banking as a business and hence it does not serve our purpose.

According to Dr. Hart, "a banker is one who in the ordinary course of his business honours cheques drawn upon him by persons from and for whom he receives money on current account." This definition also is not complete because a bank does not only honour cheques of those who have money on current account but also performs many other functions which have not been mentioned therein.

According to Sir John Paget, "no person or body corporate or otherwise can be a banker who does not take deposit accounts, take current accounts, issue and pay cheques and collects cheques, crossed or uncrossed, for his customers". Similarly, the Indian Companies Act, 1936, lays down that "Banking Company is a company which carries on as its principal business the accepting of the deposits of money on current account or otherwise, subject to withdrawal by cheque, draft or otherwise." In the words of Hilton Young Commission 1926, "the term Bank or Banker should be interpreted as meaning every person, firm or company using in its description or title 'bank' or 'banking' and every company accepting deposits of money subject to withdrawal by cheque, draft or order." All these definitions emphasise the acceptance of deposits as the primary function of a bank. Thus, they have clearly omitted the agency functions performed by a modern bank from the scope of banking. Sayers has defined a bank as "an institution, whose debts are widely accepted in settlement or other people's debts to each other". Similarly, Crowther says, "a banker is a dealer in debts—his own and other people's". Kinley too, has defined bank as "an establishment which makes to individuals such advances of money or other means of payment as may be required and safely made and to which individuals entrust money or means of payment as may be required and safely made and to which individuals entrust money or means of payment when not required by them for use". According to Gautier, "the word bank expresses the business which consists in affecting on account of others receipts and payments, buying and selling either money or gold and silver or letters of exchange and drafts, public securities and shares in industrial enterprises—in a word—all the obligations whose creation has resulted from the use of credit on the part of states and societies and the individuals". According to Findlay Shirras, "a banker or bank is a person, firm or company having a place of business where credits are opened by deposit or collection of money or currency...or where money is advanced or loaned". These definitions bring us somewhat nearer to the actual meaning of a banking institution and also explain the various functions performed by banks. But certainly and undoubtedly the definition given by Horace White, a "manufacturer of credit and a machine for facilitating exchange", is short but precise.

3. Classification of Joint-Stock Banks

Various joint-stock banks have been classified on the basis of functions performed by them. Broadly speaking, there are following types of banks:

(1) Commercial Banks

These banks generally advance short-term loans to businessmen and traders, because their deposits are only for a short period. Generally, these banks give loans for a period extending from three months to six months. These banks do not give loans on long-term basis to industries. In our country, the majority of joint-stock banks are commercial banks which finance trade and commerce.

(2) Industrial Banks

These are special types of banks, as the name itself suggests. They extend long-term loans to industries. They also help industrial firms in selling and purchasing debentures and shares. They even underwrite the debentures and shares of big industrial houses. Broadly speaking, these banks perform three types of functions:

(*a*) They accept long-term deposits.

(*b*) They meet the credit requirements of industries. Generally, the credit requirements of industries are of two types: firstly, they require capital to purchase land, erect buildings and for the purchase of heavy machinery. Secondly, the industries require short-term loans to buy raw materials and to meet their day-to-day needs. So, far as short-term requirements are concerned, they are generally met from the loans received from the commercial banks. But for their long-term requirements, the industries have to depend on the industrial banks.

(*c*) Finally, the industrial banks tender advice to big industrial houses regarding the sale and purchase of their shares and debentures.

These banks play a very important role in the advanced and highly industrialised countries. In our country, owing to the absence of industrial banks, the governments at various, levels have set up Industrial Finance Corporations for providing long-term finance to industries.

(3) Agricultural Banks

For meeting the requirements of agricultural community, special types of banks have been set up in predominantly agricultural countries. The agriculturists and peasants require short-term loans to purchase various inputs like seeds, fertilisers, plough, etc. for carrying on their agricultural operations. Secondly, the farmers require long-term loans to purchase land, to effect permanent improvements on the land, to buy machinery and to provide irrigation works. To fulfil these requirements of the farmers, various types of agricultural banks have been set up in various countries. In our country, these are: (*i*) Agricultural Co-operative Banks, and (*ii*) Land Development Banks. The former provide short-term finance to the farmers while the latter extend long-term loans to the agriculturists.

(4) Foreign Exchange Banks

These banks specialise in financing foreign trade by making international payments through the purchase and sale of foreign exchange bills. Foreign trade involves the problem of converting the currency of one country into that of another. The foreign exchange banks solve this problem. These banks have in stock the currencies of various countries and for this purpose they open branches in different countries. In our country, all the foreign exchange banks are controlled by foreigners. In the post-independence period, the monopoly of foreign banks has to a great extent ended and now some of the commercial banks in India have also started dealing in foreign exchange business. But even now the foreign exchange banks hold an important position.

4. Organisational Set-up of Banks

Although the activities undertaken by various types of joint-stock banks 'are almost the same throughout the world; the organisational set-up is, however, different in different countries. From the organisation point of view, various banks have been divided into two types, *viz.*, (1) Branch Banking, and (2) Unit Banking. From the ownership point of view, these banks have also been classified into: (1) Chain Banking, and (2) Group Banking. From the point of view of lending practices, banks have been further divided into: (1) Pure Banking, and (2) Mixed Banking.

A. Unit Banking vs. Branch Banking

Unit banking refers to that type of banking where the business is carried out through a single office. In branch banking, it is done through more than one office. The former is also called the 'localised banking' and the latter 'delocalised banking'. Unit banking is a speciality of American banking system. There it is no doubt supplemented by 'correspondent bank system' which combines the advantages of branch banking as well. In this system, a country bank in America can open accounts with bigger banks and carry on several transactions through them enjoying, thus, the advantages of branch banking without incurring any expenditure on the maintenance of a separate branch office. The unit banks do not stand by themselves alone, but are connected with the correspondent bank system. To simplify the matter, we can say that unit banking refers to small scale banking while branch banking refers to large scale business. Branch banking is very popular in the United Kingdom, Canada, Australia and India. Following are the merits of branch banking or demerits of unit banking because the merits of one are the demerits of the other.

Merits of Branch Banking

1. Economies of Scale. Branch-banking enjoys the economies of large scale production. Banks with branches are capable of collecting huge resources and hence applying the principle of specialisation more effectively than the unit banks, by employing better staff, distributing the work in a way so as to spare more efficient people for controlling and supervising the policies of bank management, for example, laying down of the banking policy, selecting the securities devoid of risks of investment, finding out means to improve methods of organisation and account-keeping of the bank, proper distribution of banks' assets among various items, recruitment of the staff and their management and other jobs of similar nature connected with the policy-making of the bank. All this can be possible in branch banking because of the large resources of the banks. In unit banking the resources being limited, the applicability of the principle of specialisation is comparatively limited.

2. Low Cost of Remittance of Funds. In branch-banking, the remittance of funds from one place to another is possible at a lower cost than in the unit banking. Naturally, people are attracted more towards that bank whose services are comparatively cheaper.

3. Risk Minimised. The element of risk is very much reduced by dividing its assets geographically in branch banking. By distributing their assets at different places, they minimise the possibilities of risk. Thus, in this system, all the eggs are not placed in one basket. A bank without branches is not capable of diffusing its risks. In the event of business going down in a particular locality the assets of a unit bank may depreciate in value and the bank may be faced with a serious crisis. During the Great Depression of the 1930s, British banks showed greater stability than the American banks. The British banks with their branches could meet the crisis all right while the smaller American banks were washed away by the depression. The same thing happened in India during the time of partition.

4. Economy in Maintaining Cash Reserves. In branch-banking, cash reserves are economised to a large extent. Each branch office can maintain lower cash reserves. In times of emergency, one branch can draw upon the other in order to replenish its reserves. In the correspondent banking system, even a unit bank can derive this advantage, by drawing upon its deposits with the correspondent bank but it may not prove to be remunerative as the deposits with the correspondent bank do not generally yield appreciable return.

5. Uniformity in Rates of Interest. Branch-banking brings about uniformity in the rates of interest in the market. It mitigates the disparities in the rates of interest prevailing in different localities by mobilising capital from one branch to another. It is only in the absence of the movement of funds that rates of interest differ from place to place. And if this difficulty can somehow be overcome by quickening the movement of capital, the rate of interest will tend to be uniform. This can be done through branch-banking only because it arranges for the movement of funds to a place where they are tight from the place where they are in abundance and hence its superiority over the unit banking.

6. Better Utilisation of Funds. In branch-banking, funds are better utilised than in unit banking. The free movements of funds add to the usefulness of banking operations. The funds of one branch may be sent to another where they are in great demand for the purpose of investment on a better return. Branch-banking thus leads to a quicker and more profitable seasonal mobilisation of funds from the surplus areas to tight areas. It, thus, finds out an outlet for better utilisation of and better returns for idle funds, which the unit banks are incapable of.

7. Economical Functioning. Branch-banking is said to be more economical than unit banking. It can run more efficiently with a comparatively small staff with less 'pretentious building' and less expensive equipment than an independent unit bank. This view is, however, controversial. Who would deny the fact that the expenses of all the branches taken together would be many times more than an independent bank? And hence, a comparison between the two on this ground does not seem to be logical.

8. Wide Scope for Diversified Use of Funds. It is pointed out that branch-banking offers a wider scope for varied investments. It can effectively execute the policy once enunciated. Suppose that it is decided to invest money in government securities, then all the branches will carry out this policy. Again, it will be more convenient to implement such a policy through that office which is nearest to a Stock Exchange, as this would help in maintaining the safety and liquidity of the loans, in as much as the securities may quickly be disposed of, because of its nearness to the Stock Exchange. A unit bank can enter in comparatively limited number of advances than the branch-bank, taking the advances of all the branches together. A branch-bank can diversify its advances over several businesses which are independent of each other.

9. Diversification of Services. A branch bank can have a deeper knowledge of various economic problems of the people of different regions of the same country and of the people of different countries as well. It can have a complete picture of the habits, behaviour, customs and traditions of the whole country, because of its branches in different parts of the country. This knowledge helps the branch-bank in rendering diversified services according to the needs of the people of different regions.

10. Wider Scope for Training. Lastly, branch-banking offers wider scope for training those people who wish to make banking as their career. Different processes of banking can be learnt in different branches. Much groundwork can be learnt and undertaken and it is easier to trace the origin of the working of a bank and the various stages till its final disposal.

Demerits of Branch Banking

1. Success within National Boundries Only. Branch-banking can be successful only within national boundaries. After the national frontiers are crossed, it has to face serious difficulties arising out of the divergencies of law, customs, traditions, business conditions, monetary units, etc. from one country to another. These banking branches in foreign countries are not free from difficulties.

2. Difficulty in Co-ordination. Co-ordination of the working of various branches is a Herculean task. It is well-nigh impossible to exercise control and supervision over too many branches in an effective manner. And in the absence of efficient supervision, a branch bank may create havoc. Inefficient management is the greatest danger of unwieldy branch banking.

3. Costly Affair. Opening up of a new branch means an addition to the total expenses of the bank without any hope of additional business. The establishment and maintenance charges are bound to go up with the opening of new branches, shrinking the total profits thereof. Again, with an increase in the volume of business, the co-ordination and centralised control over branches become a costly affair.

4. Hiding of Weak Links. Under the unit banking system, the failure of a bank removes a weak spot forever. But under the branch-banking system, "a weak branch may be permitted to continue like a festering sore, which may gradually be eating into the vitals of a bank and may, without warning to the public, bring it slowly to the brink of virtual collapse. Thus branch banking acts as a smoke-screen for hiding the weak links instead of exposing them to the public eyes."

5. Disadvantages of Bureaucracy. Branch-banking suffers from all the disadvantages of bureaucracy. It suffers from red-tapism and even urgent matters are disposed of with delay, due to the reference to the Head Office. Even the funds may have to be transferred to headquarters without caring for the local interests.

6. Risk of Indiscriminate Branch Opening. Branch banking confers great benefits if it is kept within limits but, "when it overshoots its mark and degenerates into indiscriminate branch opening, it brings in its wake over-banking with its accompanying evils of cut throat competition, rate cutting, offering of excessively high rates for attracting deposits and propensities to risky investments".

7. Lack of Personal Contact with Customers. In unit banking, the manager develops his personal contact with the local businessmen and thus acquires a complete knowledge of their business integrity, creditworthiness and business morality and hence is in an advantageous position to judge the borrowing capacity of every businessman. This advantage is not available to a branch bank. But Sayers is of the opinion that even the branch bank can refuse credit to an unpleasant man without impairing his social contacts. In this respect, his position is better to a unit manager because he has to refer each proposal for sanction to his head office, and hence "if there is occasion to refuse a loan, he can always thrust the unpleasant onus to that remote abstraction, head office, without running so much danger of terminating his social contacts with the clients".

We can now conclude that branch-banking is more beneficial than unit banking and that is why in countries like the USA where unit banking had flourished in the past, branch banking has started gaining ground in recent decades. The reasons for the success of branch banking in the USA are not far to seek. Firstly, unit banks have been granted the right to open branches in neighbouring areas so that their business could increase and they could earn more profits. Secondly, the American banks have adopted the chain banking system, according to which an individual or a group of individuals can own a number of banks at the same time. These banks maintain their separate existence but their ownership is concentrated in the hands of one individual or a group of individuals. This helps in co-ordinating the activities of various banks in constituting the chain. Finally, as stated earlier, correspondent banks have been set up which render valuable advice to the unit banks, receive deposits from them, provide remittance facilities and give them loans in times of need.

B. Chain Banking vs. Group Banking

Under the chain banking system two or more banks are owned by one person or a group of individuals as explained above. This system of banking developed in the USA towards the middle of the last century but during the Great Depression almost all such banks collapsed. This system enjoys certain advantages; for example, financial resources can be fully utilised, better managerial services can be provided, higher profits can be earned, risks can be diversified, operational costs can be minimised and administrative control can be centralised. But the system is also not free from defects. For example, it suffers from lack of efficient management and supervision and lack of flexibility; it leads to corruption on the part of officers and employees, and these banks can also undertake speculative activities.

The group banking system was very common in the USA between 1925 and 1929. Under this system two or more banks are directly or indirectly controlled by an Association, Trust or Corporation. Before the Great Depression, there were in the USA as many as 300 groups controlling more than 2,000 bank branches. The system has a number of advantages, namely: (*i*) every bank retains its own identity and maintains its own board of directors. The central administrative office controls the various members of the group and takes steps to improve the level of efficiency in their day-to-day working. (*ii*) It ensures the liquidity of financial resources. (*iii*) It exercises economy in advertising expenditure. (*iv*) Being a big establishment it can easily acquire the services of experts in the management of the business of the member banks. (*v*) The stores are commonly purchased by a common purchasing organisation and therefore lot of economy is exercised in the store purchase. (*vi*) The group management also takes steps to secure new business for its constituents. This system also is not free from defects. Firstly, if one member bank of the group fails, it produces adverse effect on other member banks. Secondly, it will not be possible under the system to achieve a high level of efficiency because the central administrative office is generally not able to enforce codes of discipline on member banks. Finally, this system can also give rise to corruption because in the common purchase of stores the organisation may succumb to pressures exerted by unscrupulous and strong firms.

C. Mixed Banking vs. Pure Banking

Mixed banking is a system under which commercial banks advance short as well as long-term loans to businessmen and industrialists. Commerce requires short-term loans while industry requires short-term as well as long-term loans. When commercial banks give both these types of loans, the system is known as mixed banking. The German banking system is the best example of this type of banking in the world. The development of this sort of system in Germany has been the result of various historical factors. In Germany, industrialisation took place earlier than the development of trade and commerce and since there were no financial institutions which could finance the development of industries, the commercial banks took upon themselves the responsibility of financing the long-term requirements of the industries.

Pure commercial banking, as indicated before, deals with only short-term financing. This system has been first evolved in the UK. The British banks do not lend for more than six months; firstly, because they receive deposits only for short periods; and secondly, because of the historical reasons, that is, the industrial development of Britain took place after the development of trade and also that a large number of financial institutions specialising in giving loans to industries were set up earlier than the commercial banks. Needless to say that the system of pure commercial banking is safe and ensures the liquidity of the financial resources of the banks. But, only on this basis it would not be proper to deem the system of pure banking as a desirable one because if the commercial banks do not participate in the financing of industries, the industrial development of the country is bound to suffer.

In the pure commercial banking system, the banks develop self-reliance and are not affected by the fluctuations in the margin of profits of the industries. But in the mixed banking system, during depression, the banking system is always under threat of instability. That is why, during the Great Depression, a number of banks collapsed in Germany. Secondly, the locking up of the bank resources in long-term investment is not at all a safe practice and it is, therefore, necessary that such an activity is undertaken only by specialised institutions.

In India, the banking system has been of the type of pure commercial banking. After the nationalisation of 14 major commercial banks in 1969, the nationalised banks have also started advancing long-term loans on easy terms to small scale industries. But it is clear that this sort of practice may not be conducive to the health of the banking system in the country. When there are specialised institutions like the Industrial Finance Corporation, the State Finance Corporations, the Industrial Development Bank, Industrial Credit and Investment Corporation, etc. the commercial banks should withdraw themselves from the field of long-term financing and should concentrate exclusively on meeting the short-term requirements of industry and trade.

D. Correspondent Banking

Correspondent banking is a unique feature of the US banking system. In a country of the size of the USA it is impossible for any single bank to open its branches in every nook and corner of the country. So, over the years a unique system has been developed in the USA. There are banks serving the requirement of the semi-urban and rural areas. There are city banks which operate in big towns. There are state banks in industrial and big towns having their branch offices in other towns and cities. The country banks deposit their surplus funds with the city bank and the city banks deposit their funds with the state bank. In the correspondent banking system, regional centres in big cities, like New York, for banking operations have been established where the country and city banks make deposits with big banks operating in more than one centre. A correspondent bank in one centre has correspondent relation with banks in other centres. It means that a big bank is a bank for small banks, which maintain their deposits with it. This big bank provides the small banks all kinds of banking facilities for extension of credit, foreign exchange transactions, cheque clearing and collection, purchase of securities, etc. These facilities are in addition to other services which they provide to small banks like, giving advice for portfolio management, supplying data on the health of the economy, etc.

Advantages of Correspondent Banking

Such a system has a number of advantages:

(1) Funds can be transferred easily, conveniently and quickly from one place to another. Cheques are cleared without involving much time which is a great facility to trading and business firms.

(2) By providing facilities for credit, foreign exchange transactions,

mobilisation of credit, etc. the correspondent city banks help the development of the economy through the development of trade and industry.

(3) By providing technical advice to the country banks the correspondent bank strengthens the banking system of the country and also smoothens the financial machinery of the country.

(4) By providing information to the country banks, the correspondent bank creates an awareness among them about the general trends of the functioning of the economy.

(5) By helping the country banks and by accepting deposits from them, the correspondent bank is able to swell its business and earn more profits. Not only that, these banks also serve as an important source for providing funds to the country banks.

(6) The correspondent banking system helps the overall growth of the economy. It prevents the establishment of monopoly by any single bank. Industry and trade benefit in a large way by easy and quick transfer of funds across the country as well as across the borders without much delay. The country banks can also provide to the general public those facilities which are being provided to them by the big barks.

Disadvantages of the Correspondent Banking System

Apparently correspondent banking does not suffer from any shortcomings; but sometimes, it is feared that the correspondent banks may in order to earn more profits throw the principles of safety and liquidity to the winds and advance loans on the basis of the deposits of country banks, much in excess of the desirable limits. This can jeopardize the safety of the entire banking system of the country.

Exercises

1. Discuss the relative advantages and disadvantages of unit and branch banking system.
2. What is mixed banking? Discuss its merits and demerits.
3. Discuss the salient features of the chain-banking and group-banking systems.
4. What is correspondent banking? Explain its role in the American banking system.

●●●

Chapter 16

Credit Creation by Commercial Banks

1. Functions of Commercial Banks

In its earliest stages, banking was mainly confined to money-changing. But now it includes so many functions and of such varied nature that it was even difficult to imagine about them in the 19th century. It is not possible to prepare an exhaustive list of these functions as the services that a bank provides these days are so diverse and varied and its responsibilities are so great and ever-expanding that its final stage can hardly be predicted. We discuss below some of the fundamental functions performed by a bank.

1. Bank as a Borrower

Banking implies borrowing and lending of money. The bank borrows money from some people and lends it to others. Bank is a borrower in the sense that it accepts deposits from people. Depositors are thus its creditors. The deposits can be accepted by a bank under three accounts, *viz.*, Current Account, Fixed Account and Savings Account. The deposits made in the current account can be withdrawn at any time. The bank does not pay any interest on the money deposited under this account to the depositor. Such account is generally maintained by businessmen and commercial firms. The bank levies certain charges on the customer for the services rendered by it. Money deposited in the 'fixed account' is for a certain fixed period of time and such deposits can be withdrawn only after the expiry of that period. These deposits are also known as bank's time liabilities. The rate of interest paid by the bank is the highest on the money deposited under this account and the longer the period, the higher is the rate of interest subject to a fixed rate of interest after a specified period of time. Deposits made in 'savings account' are subject to certain restrictions; for example, a depositor can withdraw only a specified sum of money in a week or he cannot withdraw more than two or three times a week or so on. The rate of interest allowed on such deposits is rather low. But such type of deposits, too, encourage small savings in the country.

2. Bank as a Lender

Banks canalise the accumulated funds or deposits received in various accounts as mentioned above into productive uses in the form of loans, advances, overdraft facilities and cash credits against approved securities. The bank has to apply great caution while investing its funds, for it is on the liquidity of these funds that the soundness of a bank depends. The bank, thus, selects such investments from where money can be easily called back. The bank after retaining a certain portion of its deposits, lends money to the parties who require funds for investment or other purposes in the form of loans. The loans can be ordinary in the sense that these are given for a specified period to a person or firm against some collateral security. The loan amount is credited to the account of the borrower who can withdraw it according to his requirements. The bank can recall such loans as and when it desires to do so. Then there can be cash credit facilities. Under this account, the bank gives loans to the borrowers against certain securities. The bank does not give the entire amount of loan at that time but it opens an account in the name of the debtor and allows him to withdraw the money from time to time up to a certain limit determined by the value of the stocks kept in the debtor's godown. The godown remains in the possession of the bank. The debtor cannot overdraw the amount and the bank charges interest only on the amount withdrawn from its account. Such loans are very popular in India. Then there are overdraft facilities granted by the bank to its customers who are reliable. Under this facility an account holder can overdraw the amount through cheques and has to pay interest on the amount overdrawn by him. Another type of lending facility which is very popular with modern banks in that of discounting the bills of exchange. If the holder of a bill of exchange requires money, he can get it discounted from the bank who after deducting certain commission pays the current price of the bill to him. The bank can secure its payment from the party concerned on the maturity of the bill.

3. Agency Functions of a Bank

Besides these two main functions, a bank performs several other functions like agency services, general utility services or miscellaneous services. The bank can perform the following agency functions:

(1) *Sale and purchase of securities.* Since banks are better informed about the market conditions than the people, they sell and purchase securities on their behalf on the most favourable terms and charge nominal amount for this service.

(2) *Remittance of funds.* Banks remit funds on behalf of their clients by draft or mail transfers or by telegraphic transfers.

(3) Banks collect and make payments of promissory notes, bills, cheques, coupons, subscriptions, rents, dividends or other periodical receipts or payments like insurance premia and levy charges on their customers for these services.

(4) Banks also act as trustees, executors and attorneys. They are better fitted to do these services because firstly, they can guarantee continuous existence which no other agency can. Secondly, they can claim better integrity than other agencies in view of their organisation; and lastly, they employ technically trained staff who possess lot of experience and business insight and are capable of administering such trust properties. They also appoint income-tax and sales-tax experts who prepare returns of their clients and help them in acquiring refund of income-tax and sales-tax in appropriate cases.

(5) Banks also carry on correspondence on behalf of their customers. They correspond with income-tax authorities, obtain passports, travellers tickets, secure passages for their clients and do such other jobs as desired by their customers.

4. Service Functions

There are other functions as well, which are for providing utility service and which the banks perform not as agents but as part of their banking business. These service-oriented functions are:

(1) Issuing of letters of credit, bank drafts, travellers' cheques, etc.

(2) Sale and purchase of foreign exchange.

(3) Underwriting loans to be raised by the government and other public institutions.

(4) Serving as a referee to the financial standing, business reputation and respectability of their customers. But they exercise great caution and care in collecting and passing on such information to others. They are the custodian of their customers' secrets, but because such information can be required for estimating the creditworthiness, it is also essential for them to supply such information, of course, with utmost secrecy. This is, however, not very much prominent in our country.

(5) Banks also supply important statistical and financial information regarding trade, commerce and industry. They publish such information which is immensely useful to the business world. Since the banks are fully acquainted with the latest economic situation in the country, they are in a position to render useful service to their customers by providing them advice on financial matters.

(6) Banks also maintain safe deposit vaults and lockers and receive valuables and securities for safe custody.

5. Creation of Credit

Through its functions of granting loans and accepting deposits, the bank creates credit. This activity is of extreme importance for any economy. We have made a passing reference in the above discussion that when the bank gives loan to its customers it retains with it some portion of the deposits received from its other customers and gives the remaining by way of loan. It only lends out a certain portion of the deposits received. Again, it does not pay the amount of loan in cash but only by opening an account in the name of the borrower. Thus, while giving a loan, it also creates a deposit or a loan against itself. And since the deposits of the bank are treated like money, the creation of such deposits leads to an increase in the total money supply of the economy. This is what is known in common parlance as the creation of money or credit by banks. And it is through this activity that the banking system plays a very crucial role in affecting the operational efficiency of the economy of a country. The subject is highly controversial and one comes across two types of extreme views. On the one hand there are some who believe that banks create credit while on the other there are some who strongly resent this view. Before taking up this controversy, let us try to know what is credit and what is the process of credit-creation.

(a) What is Credit?

The word 'credit' has originated from the Latin word, '*Credo*' which means 'I believe'. Credit is a matter of ıaith, faith in the person and no less than in the security offered. In the words of Cole, "Credit is purchasing power not derived from income; but created by financial institutions either as an offset to idle incomes held by depositors in the banks, or as a net addition to the total amount of purchasing power."[1] For a modern economy, credit is inevitable. In the advanced countries of the West, even for the purchase of consumer goods, credit is obtained by people and it is provided without much inconvenience to them by the banks. In fact, no economy can function without credit; all economic transactions are settled by means of credit instruments today. It is the very life-blood of the modern business and commercial system. One can know the importance of credit for the modern economic system by knowing the ways in which it serves the economy. We very briefly refer to these. Firstly, credit provides the most convenient and economic medium of exchange by either supplementing or superseding other forms of money. Secondly, it facilitates the production and exchange of goods and services. Thirdly, it increases the level of aggregate demand and level of consumption in the country. Fourthly, it promotes thrift by providing productive channels

1. G.D.H. Cole, *Money: Its Present and Future,* p. 308.

of employment for savings in the economy. Fifthly, it facilitates development of large scale enterprises and specialised industries. Sixthly, it facilitates the optimal use of the capital resources of the economy. Seventhly, it influences the level of output and employment in the economy by influencing the rate of capital formation in the country, especially during the periods of trade cycles. Eighthly, it provides the financial system with powers to render useful services to the economy in providing a system of exchange and a system of capital supply. Lastly, it benefits the society as a whole. And so, credit is indispensable for a modern economy. It is the life-blood of business and industry and banks are the institutions which are directly responsible for the creation of credit.

(b) Do Banks Really Create Credit?

Banks accept deposits from the public. All depositors do not withdraw what they deposit and so, the banks can safely lend a portion of these deposits. The bank earns a profit by borrowing at lower rate and lending at a higher rate. Thus, there are deposits which are received from the public and are known as cash deposits. There are credit deposits as well. Withers held that loans make deposits. According to him the major portion of deposits of a bank consisted of credit deposits created by the loans advanced by banks to the depositors. Bank does not advance loans in the form of legal tender money, but in the form of cheques. In other words, the amount of the loan instead of being paid in cash is credited in the books of the bank to the borrower who is allowed to draw it from time to time by means of cheques. The banks create deposits in two ways. Firstly, in a passive manner and secondly in an active manner. In the former, the bank creates passive deposits when it opens a deposit account in the name of a customer who brings cash or cheques to be credited in his account. These deposits are also known as primary deposits because these form the basis of the loan transactions undertaken by the bank; they provide funds to the bank for advancing loans. By its experience, the bank knows that the entire amount received as primary deposits is not going to be withdrawn at the same time. And so, after keeping a small percentage of these deposits in cash, the bank advances loans to its customers. The percentage so maintained is known as the cash reserve ratio. The active deposits are created by the bank in a more active manner by opening a deposit account in the name of the borrower. These deposits are created by the bank itself and, therefore, they are known as active or derivative deposits. For example, when a bank grants a loan of Rs. 50,000 to a customer against some collateral security, it opens an account in his name and credits Rs. 50,000 to it. The borrower may withdraw this amount either at once or in instalments according to his requirements. The important thing to be noted is that while advancing a loan, the bank has also created a new deposit in its books. And that is why, Withers said that loans make deposits. While primary deposits do not add to the total supply of money in the economy, the creation of active deposits does add to the total supply of money. When the loan is repaid by the borrower, the derivative deposit is completely wiped out and leads to a net decrease in the total supply of money in the economy.

The bank also creates active deposits when it purchases securities or other forms of assets from the public. When the bank buys these assets, it makes payment to the sellers by opening a deposit account in their name. The bank may also create active deposits when it purchases bills of exchange in a similar way. Active deposits are created by the banks only when the people want to get loans from them and, therefore, if there are no borrowers, there would be no active deposits.

(c) Process of Credit Creation

The process of credit creation is multiple in its nature. If we keep in view the entire banking system then an individual bank at best creates credit which is only a fraction of the total original money received by the entire banking system. At any given time, the credit multiplier would be greater than one and less than infinity. The process of multiple credit expansion would be like this. Suppose *X* borrows money from the bank, but the bank opens a deposit account and credits the amount to his account. Now *X* can pay to his creditors through cheques drawn upon his account with the bank. Suppose the creditor who has received the cheque from *X*, deposits that cheque in another bank in his account. The other bank now receives the primary deposit in the form of a cheque drawn upon the first bank. After keeping some cash, the second bank may create another active deposit by giving loan to *Y*. *Y* may make the payment out of his account to his creditor who has a deposit account with a third bank. This third bank will now receive the primary deposit in the form of a cheque drawn on the second bank. This process goes on repeating until the total volume of derivative deposits created by all the banks become a multiple of the initial amount created by the original bank. This is the process of multiple credit expansion in the entire banking system. But, if we take the process of credit creation by one single bank, we will find that the credit is created in a similar fashion. Suppose *X* bank gives loan to *A* by creating active deposits. *A* makes payment by issuing a cheque drawn upon the bank to his creditor *B*. *B* deposits that amount again in the bank and the bank on the basis of this primary deposit again advances a loan to another borrower *C*. And this creates an active deposit. *B* makes payment through a cheque to a creditor who in turn deposits the cheque to his account in the same bank which is again a primary deposit and the bank advances loan on the basis of this primary deposit to *D* which becomes an active deposit and so on. This process continues until the final amount of active deposits created by the bank is larger than the original deposit. Supposing under the law, the cash reserve ratio to be maintained by the banks is 10 per cent and if the bank has an original reserve of Rs. 200, it can create a total active deposit of Rs. 2,000. In the case of an individual bank, the bank can lose cash only to public and not to any other bank in the country. Because for meeting public demand it has already kept a cash reserve ratio of 10 per cent. But, taking the banking system as a whole any individual bank will have to lose the whole amount of its active deposits to other banks and therefore, it cannot create an amount of deposits greater than the original deposit. Thus, the banking system as well can create an amount of active deposit which is a multiple of the original deposit depending upon the cash reserve ratio to be maintained by the banks. The credit multiplier can operate forward as well as backward. When the bank receives primary deposits, it leads to multiple expansion of credit and when the bank loses a certain amount of cash, it leads to a multiple contraction of credit. Thus, in the former the multiplier moves forward and in the latter it moves backward.

So Hartley Withers was convinced of the potency of the banks to create credit. He asserted that initiative in the creation of credit was with the bank. The borrowers are free to withdraw their loanable funds or to transfer them to others as stated earlier. Thus, in every case, so long as a loan is due, a deposit to that amount will remain outstanding in bank. This is true in the case of loans only and not in the case of overdraft facilities. Sayers holds the same view when he says that "banks are not merely purveyors of money, but also, in an important sense, manufacturers of money". But Walter Leaf does not agree with him. He raises a serious objection against this view.[2] Dr. Cannan also held the same view.[3] According to these economists, the initiative in the creation of credit does not lie with the bank but with the depositors whose money has been loaned out by the bank. They further maintain that the depositors provide banks with the powers to lend money as they do not withdraw all the money at a time. And banks loan out unwithdrawn deposits. In this respect Cannan compares bank with a cloak room, where an evening party guests come and deposit their cloaks with the attendant. It is known that the party would not break before 9 p.m. Now if the attendant of the cloak room lets out 85 cloaks to be returned before 8.30 p.m. and keeps 15 with him with the idea that some guests may leave earlier, then we will not say that the

2. Walter Leaf, *Banking*, 1928, pp. 101-04.
3. E. Cannan, *An Economist's Protest*, 1907, p. 382.

attendant has created 85 cloaks. Similarly, banks do not create credit at all. Dr. Leaf analysed the balance-sheets of the 'Big Five', and found that while the advances had greatly increased during the first months of 1926, their deposits had decreased. This clearly proved that loans did not make deposits.

The Leaf-Cannan argument has been subjected to severer criticism because firstly, it is based on the analogy of an individual bank; they have not taken into consideration the banking system as a whole. While it is true that no individual bank can create an active deposit which is larger than its original deposit, the banking system as a whole can cause a multiple expansion of credit as explained already. Secondly, as Prof. Crowther points out that the reality of bank deposits can be easily understood when one compares them with the quantity of money in circulation and the cash reserves possessed by commercial banks. He explains like this:

In 1949, the total net deposits of commercial banks in the UK were £ 6 thousand millions. But the quantity of money in circulation at that time was £ 1,600 millions. And the cash reserves of the banks were about £ 250 millions. If the banks can merely lend to the extent of their cash reserves, then their deposits should have been only £ 250 millions. If the banks did not create money, where could the excess of £ 5,750 millions of deposits have come from? Hence, it may not be doubted that banks create money.

(d) Limitations on the Powers of Banks to Create Credit

Both the views given above are partially true. In other words, in the first instance, deposits make loans and then loans make deposits. Banks do not have limitless power to create credit. Their power to create credit is enormous in highly industrialised countries where people are in the habit of carrying on transactions through the banks alone and where people do not believe in hoarding. In less developed countries like India, the power of the banks to create credit is very much limited. Even otherwise, too, banks power to create credit is not absolute; it is subject to various limitations. These limitations are:

1. Total Volume of Cash in Circulation. Power of the bank to create credit is limited necessarily by the total amount of cash in circulation in a country. The total amount of primary deposits received from the public is dependent on the total volume of cash in circulation. With the increase in the actual amount of money in circulation, the volume of primary deposits will also increase which would enable the commercial banks to create a larger volume of active deposits. On the other hand, if the actual volume of currency in circulation decreases, the volume of primary deposits with the commercial banks will also decrease and consequently, the volume of active deposits created by the banks would also decrease.

2. Cash Reserve Ratio. The total amount of cash which a bank can keep in its possession is determined by the policy adopted by the central bank. The central bank has an absolute monopoly in note-issue and hence it can increase or decrease the total amount of notes in circulation at its discretion. Moreover, the central bank requires the commercial banks to maintain a certain cash-reserve ratio. If the central bank increases this ratio, the amount available to the bank for advancing loans will be proportionately reduced and *vice versa*.

3. Banking Habits of the People. The power of a bank to create credit is further limited by the habit of the people to use banks, *i.e.* whether people believe in the use of cheques or cash. The power of the bank is very greatly increased by the habit of people to use cheques and curtailed when people use cash for their day-to-day transactions. To elaborate this point further, when a bank issues loans to a person, he or she withdraws the amount by cheque and gets cash from the bank, reducing thereby the cash reserves of the bank and hence its power to create credit. In the event of people using cheques, the cash reserves of the banks remain intact and hence its power to create credit is not adversely affected.

4. External Drain. The term refers to the cash withdrawn from the banks by the borrowers. According to Prof. Whittlesey, the commercial banks' power of creating credit is limited by the existence of the external drain. As already explained, the commercial banks expand the volume of credit created by them on the basis of the excess reserves with them. Some of the borrowers are likely to withdraw part of their deposits in cash, which would automatically reduce the excess reserves of the banks and hence their power to create credit.

5. Banks Reserves with the Central Bank. Every bank is required to keep certain reserves with the central bank of the country. The central bank keeps on changing the percentage of these reserves from time to time. In the event of an increase in this percentage, the power of the commercial banks to create credit is reduced in the same proportion and in the event of its reduction, the power of the commercial banks is increased in the same proportion.

6. Availability of Good Securities. Every loan advanced by a bank is backed up by some kind of valuable collateral security like stocks, shares, bills, bonds, etc. If these securities are not available in adequate number, the banks cannot expand their lending activities and hence their power of creating credit becomes very much limited. In the words of Sayers, "The banks put this newly created money into the hand, not of everybody at once, but of those individuals who can offer to the bank the kind of asset which the bank thinks attractive."

7. Conditions of Trade and Business. The commercial banks' power to create credit is further determined by the conditions of trade and business in the economy. In a period of business prosperity when opportunities for profitable investments are greater, there is greater demand for bank loans from the business people. In such a situation, the banks are in a better position to create more credit. On the contrary, during a period of depression, the scope for profitable investment being limited, the demand for bank loans stands at a very low level and hence in such a situation, the bank's power of credit creation stands automatically diminished.

2. Utility of Modern Banking

The banking system plays a crucial role in maintaining the health of the economy. In fact, it is the centre of all economic activities. It lubricates the entire economic system and helps the community in a number of ways. The significance of the role played by the banking system in economic life is still greater in the industrially advanced countries of the West. The modern banking system not only supplies the community with a mechanism of exchange, it also canalises surplus funds of the community in the most productive channels. It does not only safeguard the savings of the community but also stimulates savings by inculcating among the people the habit of thrift. It economises the use of capital by the society. If the use of all the credit media were stopped then gold or silver alone would have to be used as the medium of exchange and one can imagine that the amount of gold that would be required for this purpose would be many times more than what is now in use. Moreover, its use as a medium of exchange would involve lot of hardship to people. Banking system supplies a cheap substitute to gold in the form of cheques, bills of exchange, etc. and this leads to an enormous saving in the direct use of precious metals.

The modern banking system provides funds to the business community in times of need. It mediates between the buyer and the seller and helps the movement of goods through the various processes of production. Not only that, it also assists the society to produce wealth, through its lending operations. It not only makes the productive utilisation of idle funds possible but also ensures their effective and optimal use. By discounting the bills of exchange, the banking system restores the control of wealth which has been released to others on credit. No only this, the bank can advance loans on personal security if the borrowers have proved themselves honest. The bank thus transforms honesty, skill and ambition into liquid capital rather the productive capacity itself is changed into capital. The greatest economic service performed by a bank is to serve the interests of the community when it charges the lowest price or rate of interest for its services. Uniformity of such rates is, however, not less desirable. Discrimination in rates is socially and economically undesirable so far as it affects the competitive powers of the individual producers in a competitive economy by affecting the cost of production. In short, we can say that the banking system is the most important constituent of a modern economy. It would not be wrong to say that for the sound economic health of a country, a sound system of commercial banking is extremely essential. The great industrial revolution of the 19th century would not have been possible without a proper banking system in Europe.

3. Role of Commercial Banks in a Developing Economy

The banking system is of more importance for the economic growth of less developed countries. A sound banking system mobilises savings of the people, channelises them into productive activities and boosts up the rate of capital formation in the economy. Secondly, through a network of branches in rural and backward areas, the banking system can accelerate the process of monetisation in the economy. Thirdly, the banking system can permit business innovations by providing cheap credit facilities to entrepreneurs, which would not be possible for want of adequate bank credit. Fourthly, the banking system can provide long-term finance to business and industry and that helps the development of commerce and industry in less developed countries. Fifthly, the banking system by adopting a cheap money policy can help the economic growth of such countries. Finally, the banking system can provide financial accommodation to priority sectors such as agriculture and small-scale industries. Thus, a well-developed commercial banking system can prove a boon for the economic development of less developed countries.

4. Nationalisation of Commercial Banks

Since the termination of the World War II, in a number of countries commercial banks have been nationalised. Nationalisation means state ownership or socialisation. It is argued that nationalisation of commercial banks increases the efficiency of the banking system because it is felt that under private ownership and management, the banks do not perform their duty of distributing loanable funds and transferring deposits as efficiently as a public institution should do. The protagonists hold that under government control, the banking system works with greater economy. As against this argument, it has been pointed out that "as soon as the banks pass into the hands of the Government, red tapism, bureaucracy, routine proverbial delay in the disposal of urgent matters caused by the requirement of the meticulous observance of technicalities, are bound to arise and as a result, efficiency will suffer". Efficient banking implies the quick disposal of things and it is and it has been a satisfactory feature of commercial banking in our country prior to 1969. But after 1969, *i.e.* after the nationalisation of 14 major banks in the country it has been experienced that the efficiency of the commercial banks has deteriorated considerably. In fact, our experience has been that public institutions have failed in carrying on this function successfully. The working of various industrial finance corporations also bears a testimony to this fact.

Again, it has been argued that the nationalisation of commercial banks leads to greater integration of the banking activities in the country. As against this, it can be pointed out that even if the commercial banks are not nationalised, a central bank can be equally effective in integrating the whole system, as in the event of nationalisation of commercial banks, because of the wide powers given to it after nationalisation. So the argument that under a nationalised central bank integration implies the nationalisation of commercial banking system does not appeal to a scientific mind.

Further, it has been pointed out that since the central bank has been nationalised because of its being a creator of money, why should then the joint stock banks be not nationalised for the same reason? But do the commercial banks really create money just as the central bank does? And if not, then the argument is fallacious. According to some, when socialism is the accepted creed of the day, what loss can there be from a nationalised banking system. It is rather essential, and in its absence, the process of transition from capitalist to a socialist form of economic organisation by nationalising the key industries might be hampered by the independent policies pursued by these private banks. The protagonists fear that "independent banks might sabotage socialisation by refusing to lend or at least discriminating against industries already socialised". But this sort of fear is baseless. It is well-known that government securities are the safest and the most liquid asset in which a bank can invest money. Why should then the private banks object in advancing loans to socialised industries when they are as safe as the government securities?

Nationalisation can, to a certain extent, check the tendency of private banks to open too many branches, out of sheer competition with other banks. As a matter of fact, the integration and co-ordination of the entire system would be better and more satisfactory than what it is today. The cut-throat competition would be stopped and much national waste would be saved. It may have to be accepted that nationalisation is not the only method to check the indiscriminate opening of branches. This objective can very well be achieved by giving wide powers to the central bank as provided under the Banking Companies Act of 1946 and 1949 in our country. The powers of the Reserve Bank are so wide that it now exercises greater control over the independent joint-stock banks in the country than what it was exercising before nationalisation.

To conclude, we may say that it is a highly controversial issue and we cannot arrive at any conclusion by arguing. In fact, Sayers has rightly said that to favour or oppose nationalisation is not a matter for economists but for the politicians to decide. If the government decides to nationalise the key industries, then there should not be any objection against the nationalisation of commercial banks. But the main problem would be then about the choosing of the time for nationalising the banking system. Bank nationalisation should only be undertaken when the economy has reached a stage where it can develop and grow under the government control.

Exercises

1. "Loans create deposits." Explain the statement and point out the limitations to credit creation by banks.
2. How do banks create credit? What are their limitations?
3. "Banks are not merely traders in money, but, in an important sense manufacturers of money." In the light of this statement explain the credit creation function of the commercial banks.
4. Distinguish between primary and derivate deposits of commercial banks. How does the creation of derivative deposits increase the total amount of purchasing power at the disposal of the community?
5. Discuss the mechanism of multiple expansion of bank deposits. What are the limitations of the banking system as a whole in regard to the creation of such deposits?
6. Commercial banks can only lend to the public to the extent that the members of the public have lent their money to them." Discuss.

•••

Chapter 17

Functions of the Central Bank

1. Introduction

England is considered to be the home of central banking. Although the Bank of England was established in 1694, it started functioning as a central bank only after 150 years of its existence. Among the existing central banks, the Riksbank in Sweden was the first to start but the Bank of England was the first to perform the fundamental functions of a real central bank. The concept of a central bank is an evolutionary one. It has grown with years. Central banking operations were never governed by any theoretical principles but were always guided by the temperament and discretion of individual operators.

By the end of the 19th century, almost every country in Europe had a central bank. But, the countries of the East, barring a few countries like Japan, Java and Egypt and of the New World were without a central bank. In the Western hemisphere, not even a single central bank was in existence in 1900. The Federal Reserve System in America was created in 1913 and the Bank of Canada was established in 1934. The 20th century witnessed a faster rate of development of central banks. The stimulus was, however, provided by the International Financial Conference held at Brussels in 1920. After the World War II, the establishment of the International Monetary Fund further boosted the development of central banking in Afro-Asian and Latin American countries and today almost every country of the world has a central bank.

2. Definition

To define a central bank is a ticklish issue. There has been a great diversity of opinion in regard to its definition. Each writer has defined it in his own way emphasising either one or more functions performed by it. According to Kent, it is "an institution which is charged with the responsibility of managing the expansion and contraction of the general public welfare".[1] Vera Smith says,

1. R.P. Kent, *Money and Banking*.

that "the primary definition of central banking is a banking system in which a single bank has either a complete or residuary monopoly in the note-issue. It was out of monopoly in the note-issue that were derived the secondary functions and characteristics of our modern central banking." According to Shaw, a central bank is a bank which controls credit and Hawtrey on the other hand holds that a central bank is the lender of the last resort. To quote Shaw: "The one true, but at the same time, all-sufficing function of a central bank is control of credit." The statutes of the Bank for International Settlement define a central bank as: "The bank in any country to which has been entrusted the duty of regulating the volume of currency and credit in that country." M.H. de Kock regards central banking as a science. He defines a central bank as "a bank which constitutes the apex of the monetary and banking structure of its country which performs as best as it can in the national economic interest, the following functions:

(1) The regulation of currency in accordance with the requirements of business and the general public, for which purpose it is granted either the sole right of note issue or at least a partial monopoly thereof.

(2) The performance of general banking and agency services for the state.

(3) The custody of the cash reserve of the commercial banks.

(4) The custody and management of nation's reserves of international currency.

(5) The granting of accommodation in the form of re-discounts or collateral advances to commercial banks, bill brokers and dealers or other financial institutions, and the general acceptance of the responsibility of lender of last resort.

(6) The settlement of clearance balances between the banks.

(7) The control of credit in accordance with the needs of business and with a view to carrying out the broad monetary policy adopted by the state."[2]

Similarly, Sayers has remarked that "the business of a central bank as distinguished from a commercial bank is to control the commercial banks in such a way as to promote the general monetary policy of the State". There are three fundamental points implicit in this:

(1) A central bank does not, as a commercial bank does, exist to make maximum profits, for its owners.

(2) It must have some means of controlling the commercial banks.

(3) It is subordinate to the State.[3]

---

2. M.H. de Kock, *Central Banking* (Third Edition), p. 21.

3. R.S. Sayers, *Modern Banking,* p. 71.

3. Need for a Central Bank

The need for a central bank arises from the vast expansion of monetary, fiscal and trade activities of the government and the people and the concomitant result of its activities produced on the economy. With the vast expansion of commerce and international trade, it has been necessary that commercial banks provide financial facilities for daily operations. The commercial banks perform this duty by creating credit. Indiscriminate expansion of credit or its contraction leads to fluctuations in the level of economic activity in the economy and all such fluctuations are bad for the health of the country's economy. Hence, some institutions must be there to exercise control on the credit creation activities of the commercial banks and this institution has been the central bank. Again, after the disappearance of precious metals from the currency system and after the adoption of the paper currency, it has become extremely essential that the issuing of notes is undertaken by a single authority. And this task has been assigned in all countries to the central bank. The central bank issues paper currency only according to the needs and requirements of the country. And since it is also a controller of credit, it can easily feel the pulse of the economy and withdraw notes issued in excess of requirement or issue more notes, whenever required. Thirdly, a central bank is also needed to help the commercial banks in times of need or economic crisis. And that is why, the central bank has been called as a lender of the last resort. And finally, the central bank is a hand-maiden of the government and carves out its policy piously and sincerely. This has been possible only because the central bank exercises full control over the banking system of the country.

4. Principles of Central Banking

Three main considerations govern the operations of a central bank; these are known as the fundamental principles of central banking. Firstly, the central bank is always motivated by the spirit of national welfare. The operations of the central bank must always be guided by the objective of maximising the welfare of the people or the nation and not by maximising the profits as is the objective of commercial banks. It does not, however, mean that the central bank should undertake activities without keeping in view their financial implications or results. As a matter of fact when de Kock said that the central bank should work exclusively in the interest of public welfare he meant that profit earning should be a secondary consideration for a central bank and the maximisation of public welfare should be its primary objective. Secondly, the central bank's operations should aim at maintaining the monetary and financial stability in the economy. And from this point of view, every central bank has been provided with wide powers for controlling the monetary and banking structure of a country and for achieving the objective. Thirdly, the central bank's activities should be free from all political considerations or influences. It should not be governed by the ideology of any particular political party. It does not mean that it should not work in unison with the government of the country. What it means is that it is not the ideology of political party in power that would decide its policy but the economic conditions of the country which should receive the foremost consideration from the central bank. Since the government is expected to solve the economic problems of the country and the central bank is also supposed to find out a solution for the economic problems of the country, therefore, both of these should work in co-operation with each other. Finally, a central bank should not compete with the commercial banks in the country or should not perform such banking transactions as accepting deposits from the general public and accommodate regular commercial customers with discounts or advances. In this connection de Kock has pointed out that "such operations might come into direct conflict with its functions as the bankers' bank, the lender of last resort and the controller of credit. It has, for example, come to be recognised over a wide range of countries that the success of a central bank depends largely upon the whole-hearted support and co-operation of the commercial banks, and that such co-operation can be effectively obtained only if it refrains from competing directly with them in their ordinary banking business, except when compelled to do so in the national economic interest."[4]

From the foregoing account it is clear that the central bank is an institution entirely different from other commercial banks. It is the top of the banking system and it regulates and controls the activities of commercial banks. It is an institution created and owned by the state. Its objective is not to maximise profits but to serve the interests of the people and nation, to promote the economic development of the country and create an environment of economic stability. It should not have any direct dealings with the public. It should not compete with the commercial banks because it has to function as a bankers' bank and lender of last resort. It possesses the monopoly of note-issue. It is the custodian of the foreign exchange reserves of the country. It is a banker to the government and finally it is a banker of all commercial banks in the country; it acts as a clearing house for them. And so, we find that a central bank is entirely different from a commercial bank and the principles governing central banking are also different from those governing commercial banking. But some general and broad similarities, no doubt, can be traced in the functioning of both these types of banks. For example, both these institutions deal in money in some form or the other. Both the institutions create credit. Both the

4. M.H. de Kock, *op. cit.*, pp. 22-23.

institutions do not extend loans against immovable properties. And finally, both extend short-term loans. These are no doubt similarities which are general in nature but so far as specific functions are concerned, it would not be wrong to say that the central bank's position in the banking system of the country is that of a friend, philosopher and guide.

5. Functions of a Central Bank

As already stated, there is complete lack of unanimity among monetary and financial experts about the functions of a central bank. In practice, a central bank performs not less than seven functions as enumerated by de Kock and stated earlier in the chapter and no one function can be singled out as the most important, as these are complementary to one another. While discussing the functions of a central bank we shall follow the chronological order as provided by history:

1. A Bank of Issue

This was the first function which was originally undertaken by the central banks and that is why until the beginning of 20th century, they were known as banks of issue. The issue of currency has always been a prerogative of the state, but the state thought it proper to hand over this function to banks. In some countries, this right was automatically acquired by banks which had been doing this since their inception. In other countries this right was entrusted to them owing to the heavy depreciation and the consequent loss of public confidence in notes issued by the state or because note issuing was considered more safe in the hands of banks. Whatever be the case, the commercial banks until the 19th century had the right of note-issue and the state introduced specific laws to regulate the note-issue granting partial or complete monopoly to one bank. The state might have been motivated in various countries for granting partial or complete monopoly to anyone bank because it found that there was no uniformity in the notes issued by various banks; or because the notes issued by them were in limited quantity because the size of the reserves for backing these notes was also limited or because sometimes these banks failed to convert these notes into cash. It has been recognised that this privilege was the primary factor in the development of central banking. Hawtrey may not consider the note issue function as an essential function; in practice; however, it has formed the edifice of the central banking structure, to the effect, that today every central bank has been given the sole or partial monopoly of note-issue in its country. If this responsibility is taken over by the state, then political considerations and the financial needs of the state, rather than considerations of a sound monetary system, may lead the government astray involving the risk of excessive issue and consequent depreciation. It also remains a fact, that a government may be free from ulterior motive, yet it will be incapable of adjusting the supply of paper currency to the varying needs of the community. So, neither the government nor the commercial banks were found to be suitable institutions for carrying out these responsibilities and that is why the central banks were given the exclusive right of note-issue. The Bank of England got complete monopoly of note-issue in 1884. By entrusting this responsibility to the Bank of England, the government could ensure: (*i*) uniformity in the monetary system, (*ii*) elasticity in the monetary system, (*iii*) effective control of credit creation, (*iv*) stability in the internal and external value of money, (*v*) a constant source of profit and strengthening of the confidence of the people in the monetary system. It is on account of these advantages that the right to issue notes has been given to the central banks in almost all countries of the world. However, the governments for regulating the issue of notes, have formulated laws.

2. A Friend, Philosopher and Guide to the Government

The central bank acts as a friend, philosopher and guide to the government. It is a banker, agent and adviser to the government. As a matter of fact, this was the first function performed by those institutions which were subsequently converted into central banks. It was later that the privilege of note-issue was granted to them in lieu of loans made to the state. As a government's banker, the central bank credits the banking accounts of its government, makes temporary advances to its government in anticipation of the collection of taxes or raises internal loans and makes extraordinary advances during emergencies like war, etc. and carries out government's transactions involving the sale and purchase of foreign exchange. It also acts as a financial agent as well as an adviser to the government. The central bank keeps the account of the government in the same way as commercial banks keep the accounts of their clients. The financial operations of the government are so huge that they entail an enormous amount of accounting, clerical work and expense. The government in some cases makes specific payment to the central bank directly according to the turnover or an agreed yearly amount or indirectly through an arrangement whereby the government has to maintain a maximum credit balance in its accounts with the central bank, even if it has to borrow from the latter at times in order to maintain the requisite balance. In other cases, the central bank performs all these functions free of charge.

The main reason for the central bank's performing this function does not lie in the fact that it is more convenient and economical, but in the fact that there is intimate relationship between public finance and monetary affairs. The state is the biggest borrower and the largest receiver of revenue. The central bank is charged with the responsibility of controlling credit. As the government's financial activities can disturb the money market and rates of exchange and counteract the credit policy of the central bank, the centralisation of government's banking operations in the central bank, gives the latter a better opportunity of keeping in close touch with the general financial conditions at any time, providing the best advice to the government and taking the necessary steps. The central bank, in its capacity of government's banker supplies the government with the foreign exchange required for meeting its external debt services or making purchases abroad. Further the central bank performs all the duties involved in the administration and management of national debt. It also provides agency services to the state. It administers the equalisation funds and clearing agreements whenever they have been introduced for stabilising exchange rates, by keeping separate banking accounts for these purposes and carrying out all the transactions in gold and foreign exchange connected therewith. It also grants advances to the government. It has been experienced that the governments have at times misused this facility and government borrowing has been the main factor leading to inflation and hyper inflation in various countries. That is why, the necessity of limiting advances to the government has been felt from time to time merely as an important prerequisite of a sound currency policy and resort has been taken to legislative enactment for this purpose. The Federal Reserve Act of the United States, 1913 is an example in view. In fact both the parties, the government and the central bank are responsible for the national economic welfare. The government is the ultimate authority for laying down the monetary policy and the monetary standard for the country and the central bank is responsible for carrying out this policy and maintaining this standard and safeguarding the national economic welfare thereby. The government should, therefore, not only consult the central bank, while framing the monetary policy but give a 'free hand' and assist in carrying out such monetary policy. The central bank, too, in its turn should co-operate with the government in times of emergency and acute economic depression. Thus, both of these institutions must have mutual consideration and full co-operation for each other's duties and responsibilities and that is how the public interest can best be served.

3. A Custodian of Cash Reserves

A central bank is also a custodian of the cash reserves of the commercial banks operating in the country. This function of a central bank has evolved through the passage of time and is closely associated with the other two functions discussed before. It is also because the central bank performs this function that it has been made the custodian of country's metallic reserves. The significance of a centralised cash reserve system can hardly be exaggerated; it is a source of great strength to the banking system of a country.

It enhances the element of elasticity in the credit structure of a country. It needs no explanation that bank reserves when concentrated at one place can fully and effectively be utilised during financial crises. Talking about the transfer of banks' reserves to the vaults of the Federal Reserve Banks, Burgess pointed out that it did not merely imply a change in the geographical location of the reserves but that it "made a change in the character and effectiveness of the reserves and enabled them to serve more adequately their original purpose."[5] He pointed out two emergencies which were to be met. Firstly, when only a few banks required additional funds, the reserves could be shifted to that bank, where the need was the greatest. Secondly, in case of a general requirement of funds, the centralised reserves could be utilised for increasing the total amount of funds available in the market.

By the centralisation of reserves, their use becomes economical, banking system becomes more elastic and the credit structure becomes more liquid. This elasticity and liquidity are acquired by the central bank's function of re-discount. In the absence of such a centralisation, the commercial banks will have to keep more cash to meet the emergencies than what they are doing now in the presence of a central bank and the centralisation of reserves. It further increases the capacity of the central bank to re-discount or create credit for meeting the cash requirements of the money market.

The statutory provision requiring the commercial banks to keep minimum credit balances with the central bank was, for the first time introduced in the USA and followed by others later. It was chiefly done "to strengthen the financial position of the central bank in general and its capacity to control credit in the common interest". The system travelled far and wide and was followed immediately by New Zealand, Australia and Sweden. Besides providing elasticity and liquidity to the banking and credit structure of the country, the centralised cash reserve system also provides the central bank with adequate funds to strengthen its financial position and thus enables it to carry on its re-discounting operations more easily and safely. It also provides moral obligation on the part of central banks not to enter into competition with commercial banks. Even otherwise, a central bank cannot afford to do so because firstly, it has to maintain a large reserve ratio to its liabilities than the commercial banks; secondly, if it enters into competition, by way of advances and discounts, the liabilities would go up while the reserve will remain as before, making the position of the central bank vulnerable; and lastly, it would increase the claims against the central bank for gold, which would either deteriorate the balance of trade position or lead to export of capital. The increased demand for foreign exchange would not only reduce the total amount

5. Burgess, *Reserve Banks and Money Market,* Revised Edition, Harper, pp. 26-27.

of reserves of the central bank, but its reserve ratio as well. All this is true, however, in the gold standard. But in the managed currency standard when the central bank is totally subordinate to the government the problems assume a different shape altogether. A greater co-operation and participation of the commercial banks in the scheme of credit control should, therefore, be maintained at all times. There should be greater co-operation between the central bank and commercial banks so that national economic welfare may be safeguarded properly.

4. A Custodian of Foreign Exchange

This function is a necessary corollary of the previous function. Metallic reserves are maintained against note issue as also against the entire credit structure, like deposits. The maintenance of adequate reserves is necessary to safeguard the monetary standard of the country. In gold standard, the central bank must maintain enough gold reserve; in inconvertible paper standard, the central bank should hold enough reserves of foreign exchange so that the external value of the currency might be maintained as desired. So long as the countries were on the gold standard, foreign exchange transactions were neither frequent nor important. Since World War I, a greater economy in the use of gold and greater elasticity in the monetary system resulted in the adoption of gold exchange standard, in which foreign exchange entered as a part of the statutory reserve against notes and deposits in countries like Germany, Belgium, Austria, Hungary, Romania, Bulgaria, Poland, India and many others.

The central bank was, thus, required to maintain a minimum reserve against both its notes and deposit liabilities. Its gold and foreign exchange were, therefore, not available for settling international accounts. The maintenance of two reserves was, therefore, required one internal reserve for covering the domestic note circulation and the other external reserve the main object being to maintain confidence in the domestic currency as well as international sphere and also setting a limit to the expansion of credit. As a disciplinary instrument, it has no equal but it should be flexible.

The foreign exchange operations of central banks have come to occupy an important place in the domain of central banking after the World War I. This function is performed through its open market operations to the extent that in recent years, due to monetary and exchange crises, central banks have played an increasingly important role in exchange operations. In this respect, the central bank also performs the function of an exchange bank. There has, however, been no uniformity so far as the manner and extent of these operations are concerned. For example, in England, after the suspension of the gold standard in 1931, the Bank of England carried on the work of exchange stabilisation till the establishment of the Exchange Equalisation Fund in 1932 and since then the Bank has been acting as an agent of the Fund. After the World War II, the Bank of England performed exchange operations more effectively as an agent of the treasury. Thus, this function has also evolved out of circumstances although later it received a statutory recognition. This is an overlapping function so far as central bank's functions of government's agent and bankers' bank are concerned. But this is a natural outcome of state control.

5. Lender of Last Resort

The centralisation of metallic reserves further increased the power of the central bank to create credit and thus to re-discount and act as a lender of last resort. Prior to the publication of Bagehot's *Lombard Street* in 1873, there was a great divergence of opinion regarding central bank's function as the lender of last resort. According to Bagehot, "Theory suggests, and experience proves, that in a panic the holders of the ultimate Bank reserve (whether one bank or many) should lend to all that bring good securities quickly, freely and readily. By that policy they allay a panic; by every other policy they intensify it. The public have a right to know whether the Bank of England—the holders of our ultimate bank reserve—acknowledge this duty, and are ready to perform it. But this is now very uncertain."[6] He further adds that "nothing, therefore, can be more certain than that the Bank of England has in this respect no peculiar privilege; that it is simply in the position of a bank keeping the banking reserve of the country; that it must in time of panic do what all other similar banks must do; that in time of panic it must advance freely and vigorously to the public out of the reserve".[7]

This function of the central bank has emanated from its re-discounting function. It implies that the central bank should be prepared to meet all reasonable demands for accommodation from commercial banks and other credit institutions subject to certain conditions which form the main tenets of the discount rate policy of the central bank. It does not, however, mean that for being the lender, the central bank must carry on re-discounting operations, otherwise it would not be that. A central bank may be a lender, without being a bank of re-discount, *e.g.* it may grant advances to the government or to the public in times of monetary stringency.

According to Willis, re-discounting is "the conversion of bank credit into central bank credit". Re-discounting implies the acceptance of the responsibility of endeavouring to guarantee the liquidity of the entire credit structure of the country and not merely that of the central bank itself. At the

6. Walter Bagehot, *Lombard Street* (1873), p. 85.
7. *Op. cit.*, p. 96.

end of the 18th century, the Bank of England, with great reluctance assumed this responsibility and it was only in 1873 that this function was given due recognition. After this year, the function of the lender of last resort was resumed automatically by all banks, and in the words of de Kock, "it came to be regarded as a *sine qua non* of central banking".[8]

The significance of re-discounting is very great. Firstly, it makes the credit structure more elastic and liquid. Secondly, it enables the commercial banks to have more funds as and when necessary by affording a ready medium for the conversion of some of the assets into cash. Finally, it makes use of cash reserves economical. In the absence of re-discounting facilities, the commercial banks will have to keep huge cash reserves for emergencies but with the central bank, having powers of re-discounting, such huge reserves need not be kept, thereby making the use of cash reserves more economical.

It may, however, be noted that this function is not free from abuses. It should be exercised with great caution. Firstly, the facility of rediscount could be abused by the commercial banks. They should not, therefore, have the privilege of seeking accommodation from the central bank at all times. A commercial bank does not become eligible to credit only because it has a legible paper, but also if its business is such as not to endanger the credit conditions. Secondly, the banks should not exercise economy in their reserves to such an extent as to necessitate accommodation even in normal times. In short, re-discounting facilities should not be treated as permanent capital, but should be availed of as and when necessary.

For the proper performance of this function, it is essential that the central bank must be equipped with very wide powers. It must be independent to exercise its judgement. But how it is that while functioning as the lender of last resort, the central bank seems to have neglected its responsibility as the controller of cash reserves. In fact, there are handicaps all right but only temporary. The central bank is all pervasive, so far as its functioning is concerned. As Sayers remarks, "fulfilment of its duty as lender of last resort, does not destroy the Bank of England's power over the banking system. Its function as a lender of last resort does mean that its powers over the aggregate supply of money are subject to some temporary handicaps; but as the ultimate source of cash can always exercise great influence over the prices at which the money is made available to the people who want to spend it."[9] Again, the central bank should not be legally restricted in the performance of this function. It should be a matter of great satisfaction both to commercial banks and the general public that the central bank grants accommodation at a time when the

---

8. *Op. cit.*, p. 99.
9. R.S. Sayers, *Modern Banking*, p. 114.

commercial banks fail to do so. The commercial banks must also realise that, in times of emergency, the central bank must have wide powers of lending and re-discounting so as to give them enough accommodation, so that they could, in their turn, give required facilities to their customers.

It may, however, be pointed out that this function occupied an important place in the domain of central banking operations, but during the thirties and the forties of the last century it badly suffered and was gradually replaced by open market operations and other methods of credit control.

6. A Bank of Central Clearance

Central clearance implies the settling of differences between the various banks by making transfers of account at the central bank. This is done either daily or weekly. The Bank of England adopted this function first and gradually it was adopted by other central banks. Some accepted it as an automatic function of a bankers' bank while for some it was introduced in their laws, *e.g.* the central banks of Chile, Columbia, Austria, Hungary, Australia, etc. In some countries, commercial banks have themselves set up their own clearing houses while in others this duty is performed by the central bank. In the former, the central bank is a member of the local clearing houses and performs only the functions of settling difference between banks at the end of each clearing.

Although, this function is not given any particular importance, it is considered as a natural function of a central bank. According to Shaw, "A central bank will operate as the clearing house for all its member banks as a mere matter of mechanism or of book-keeping."[10] It is, thus, the logical outcome of central bank's function as the custodian of the cash reserves of member banks. As Kisch and Elkin pointed out, it was but natural for the central bank "to set up an expeditious and economical machinery for the clearance of drafts and settlement of internal accounts," just because "as holder of the balances of the commercial banks, a central bank is specially qualified for this duty."[11] There are writers like Jauncey and Willis who consider the clearing function of the central bank as the most important one. According to Jauncey, "clearing is the main operation of central banking".[12] In the opinion of Willis, "The clearing function, with its ancillary elements...is among the most significant of central banking functions and is one for which only a very incomplete substitute may be found through resort to other expedients."[13]

---

10. W.A. Shaw, *Theory and Principles of Central Banking*, p. 155.
11. Kisch and Elkin, *Central Banks* (Fourth Edition), p. 144.
12. L.C. Jauncey, *Australia's Government Bank*, p. 166.
13. *Op. cit.*, p. 359.

It need not be emphasised that the clearing operations are no doubt simple but quite significant. They are of great convenience to the banking community. They also economise the use of money. Further, as Willis pointed out, "It is not only a means of economising cash and capital but is also a means of testing at any time the degree of liquidity which the community is maintaining."[14] He maintains that "the bank performs its characteristic function by determining what classes of goods are to be admitted to the field of exchange and the process of clearing indicates the extent to which the judgements which have thus been registered by the bank, have been sound, or at least in accordance with the judgements of other elements in the productive processes of the community".

7. A Controller of Credit

The functions of the central bank discussed in the preceding pages, though originally evolved independently, are the natural offshoots of the main function, namely the control of credit performed by the central banks these days. This function has assumed immense importance during modern times. During recent decades, there have been so severe fluctuations in the monetary field that the necessity of credit control has come to occupy a front position in the central banking operations.

6. Central Bank and Trade Cycles

It does not require any emphasis that periodical fluctuations in the price level are not conducive to the economic welfare of a nation and hence must be avoided at all costs. These fluctuations are termed as trade cycles. The phenomenon of trade cycle is very intricate and its effects are very dangerous. The central bank, as the monetary authority of the country, is responsible for controlling cyclical fluctuations in the price level. But, as these movements are caused by monetary as well as non-monetary factors, simply monetary action, however timely and effective, will have no effect and it is almost impossible for the central bank to control them. Nevertheless, it exercises certain amount of influence on the movements of these cycles.

In periods of boom and prosperity the business activity expands. Production, business and trade grow rapidly which has to be stopped because sooner or later the tide must turn. This can be in two ways: firstly, the undue expansion of trade and industry may lead to serious credit strain due to various factors, like the export of gold and thereby reduce the credit base due to unfavourable balance of trade, thus creating disequilibrium in the shape of

14. *Op. cit.*, p. 313.

low prices, contraction of production, income and employment. Secondly, as prices rise very rapidly than wages and other costs in the boom period, the supply of consumer goods is created without a corresponding increase in the amount of purchasing power so that certain groups do have the desire and capacity to consume while others do not. Yet, these groups may not be able to do so on account of higher prices. This process of disequilibrium is hastened if the banks decide to increase the rates of interest and contract credit. The crisis is also hastened by the strikes and industrial unrest arising out of the gap between wages and prices. If this gap is removed and the wages are increased, the costs of production would rise thereby reducing the margin of profits and thus leading to the slackening of the business activity. Whatever the case may be, whether under-consumption or over-production, the fact remains that such maladjustments between production and consumption bring about price fluctuations. The relationship of banking operations and cyclical fluctuations is thus, clear. In most cases, they are the effect and not the cause of such fluctuations. Though bank credit is not important as far as the financing of business is concerned, it is important to note that bank credit policy is based on the working capital of business concerns which form the bank deposits. Again, banks do not finance business on their own but advance loans after receiving applications for discounts. Thus, credit position depends upon business activity and not *vice versa*. A suitable credit policy for correcting these cyclical fluctuations, therefore, seems to be meaningless so long as bank credit is the effect and not the cause of cyclical movements. Hence bank credit alone cannot be used as the basis of trade cycle control, especially because the velocity of bank credit is a matter of common reactions and hence uncontrollable. Besides, there are many non-monetary factors which are at work. These factors are: (*a*) the unusual instability of demand for capital resulting from the losses and interruptions caused by war; (*b*) the changes in the established relationship between debtor and creditor countries owing to war debts; (*c*) the rapid rate at which technical changes in the field of manufacturing industries and agriculture are taking place; (*d*) the shifting character of demand resulting in a want of balance between the demand and supply of services as against manufacturing products; and (*e*) rigidity of money rates. In view of these non-monetary factors there cannot be any perfect credit control but there is no doubt that the central bank with the co-operation of commercial banks can reduce these fluctuations. The credit policy of the central bank must be a timely one, otherwise after the movements have gained speed, it becomes futile. The timeliness of such action depends upon the availability of statistical data, historical evidence, that is, past experiences and finally upon personal discretion and judgement. Before constituting such a policy, the central bank must also analyse the extent to which bank credit is responsible for a given situation at a particular time and then note the following factors before taking any step: (*i*) the exact time of action, (*ii*) whether the cyclical movement is due to monetary or non-monetary causes, and (*iii*) to check it at the time when its effect is most noted and not after. There are economists who emphasise that the total credit supply must increase with increase of population. But this method is too rigid and is not free from dangers.

Prof. Hayek is, however, of the opinion that controlling the business cycles by stabilising the bank credit involves the risk of retarding economic progress because the psychological initiative towards the progress will disappear. He, therefore, says that bankers have to exercise great caution before granting credit on an increasing scale. Thus, personal discretion seems to be the best policy although fundamentally the effectiveness of credit control would depend upon: firstly, the co-operation between the central bank and commercial banks, and secondly the co-operation between the central bank and the Treasury. The latter one is comparatively more important from the practical point of view as public finance and monetary affairs are intimately connected. Besides, this is necessary because of the prominence of the public works policy as a means to smoothen the business cycles and such a policy is laid down by the Treasury. This is known as "compensatory finance". Its importance was emphasised as early as 1909 by Bowley in his evidence before the Barlow Commission of England. According to him public works should be stopped during the boom period and started in the depression period. This was endorsed in 1919 at the First International Labour Conference in Washington. Lord Keynes in 1930 also stressed the importance of the method. According to Marriner Eccles, depression is caused by financial stringency as a result of contraction of credit in general, resulting in unemployment due to more of savings relative to investment and, therefore, the government must adopt compensatory finance to do just the opposite of what private business and individuals do by adopting deficit budgetary methods.[15] This method was adopted in countries like Sweden, USA, Finland, Norway, Great Britain, Canada and Australia. Modern economists especially Keynes lay greater emphasis on investment planning or control as an alternative to a monetary policy in a democratic society.

7. Role of Central Banks in Less Developed Economies

For less developed economies a central bank is more important than what it is for well-developed economies. In the highly industrialised economies where people are accustomed to using banking facilities, where the commercial

15. American Bankers Association Journal, 1937. This view has been later on supported by English economists like Mac Gregor, Salter, Cole, Henderson and Robbins.

banking system is fully developed, where the money and capital markets are well-organised, the central bank has all the conditions favourable for its efficient working. But, in less developed economies where the people have all financial transactions in cash, where the money and capital markets are not properly organised and where the commercial banking system is either in its infancy or does not exist at all; the central bank is required to play a more positive role. This role has to be in the direction of the development of the money and capital markets and the commercial banking system and also to provide banking facilities to the community.

In those countries where the central bank does not want to undertake directly the functions of the commercial banks, it can promote the development of an integrated commercial banking system, either by providing cheap and liberal re-discounting facilities to the commercial banks or by giving a subsidy to them. As a matter of fact, these two things can be done by the government and not by the central bank; the government can reduce the stamp duty on certain types of credit instruments and can also provide subsidy, of course, on the suggestion and advice of the central bank. Whereas in the highly advanced economies, the chief role of the central bank is that of controlling the credit, in less-developed economies its role is not only that of a central bank but also of laying down a dynamic economic policy for the rapid economic growth of the economy. It has to promote the development of various financial institutions which can mobilise savings and make available adequate investible funds for the development of agricultural, industrial and foreign trade sectors of the economy.

8. Nationalisation of Central Banks

The concept of central banking has undergone radical changes, especially after the World War I, owing to heavy strain on government finances, the urge for liquidity to meet emergencies and the increased requirement of foreign exchange and the growing emphasis on economic planning and full employment. It has been increasingly recognised that in the presence of an independent central bank, no govemment can carry out its monetary policy. England again took the lead and the Bank of England was the first central bank to be nationalised. We have said before that the success of a credit control policy depends entirely upon closer ties between the government and the central bank. The government, sometimes has to resort to deficit spending, for which rates of interest have to be kept stable. In the less developed economies, especially where a policy of economic planning and full employment has been adopted, the government and the central bank have to act in complete unison. Again, international co-operation on all matters of peace and prosperity of the world is being fostered and the success of such organisation depends upon the consent of respective governments to whom the advice is given by the central bank. So, the positive co-operation between the two has to be established by nationalising the central bank so that it may form an integral part of the public machinery of economic regulations in international as well as national affairs. Thus, central banks in Australia, New Zealand, Canada, Denmark and India were nationalised during the decade following the World War I. However, during recent decades the public opinion seems to be in favour of granting greater independence to the central banks and protecting them against undue political pressure. In Australia and New Zealand this has been given a practical shape. And it is justified too. The central bank cannot be made a tool in the hands of the government. It should be an independent authority in the government fold and it is the responsibility of the Parliament to see that an adequate degree of freedom is given to it in monetary and financial matters. Not only that, the central bank is equally responsible to the people and it is its duty to keep them informed about the implications of various monetary and fiscal measures.

Exercises

1. Trace the history of the growth of central banks. In what respects do the present- day central banks differ from the initial central banks?
2. What are the main functions of a central bank? Discuss the economic significance of a central bank serving as a bankers' bank.
3. What are the main characteristics of a central bank? How does the central banking differ from commercial banking?
4. Are the central banks universally necessary? Discuss the role of a central bank in a developing economy.
5. "A well-organised central bank controls the internal price level, stabilises the foreign exchange rate and prevents the occurence of financial and industrial crises." Discuss. How does a central bank do this?
6. Discuss the significance of central bank in the economic development of a country.

●●●

Chapter 18

Central Bank and Credit Control

1. Objectives of Credit Control

There is, no unanimity of opinion regarding the aims of credit control. Controversy has raged round the question as to whether the primary objective should be the stability of exchange rates or of the internal price level or of business activity and employment. The traditional objective of credit control was stabilisation of rates of exchange, either through the maintenance of monometallic standard or bimetallic standard. The gold standard was maintained throughout the world only with this objective. But the stabilisation of exchange rates in the gold standard was accompanied by short-term changes in the internal and world prices, and by an alternating series of expansion and contraction of economic activity. Some efforts were made during 1923-28 in the USA to control these business cycles, but it was unanimously accepted that the levels of prices, production and trade in a country were secondary to stabilisation of exchange rates. This policy was based on the belief that the economic welfare in the world was primarily dependent upon the maintenance of international confidence and the expansion of international trade which in their turn were dependent upon the stable rates of exchange based upon fixed gold parities.

But, since the breakdown of the gold standard, the traditional objective has been replaced by the stabilisation of the price level. The economic nationalism continued gaining ground and the people continued believing that the national economic welfare was dependent upon the stabilisation of domestic price level. Price fluctuations create serious disturbances in the economic relationships within a country and maladjustments between different countries and hence the need to stabilise the price level. Again, the stabilisation of exchange rates is at the mercy of the monetary policies of other countries, while that of the price level is independent of the monetary policies of other countries. Sweden, England and the USA practically followed such a monetary policy. There are some economists who would like the monetary authority to eliminate the business cycles, which according to them are not the outcome of price level changes. To them, economic stabilisation is the main objective of credit control. The most important recent trend in monetary policy is to combine both the stabilisation of exchange rates and the economic stabilisation, *i.e.* promoting and maintaining high levels of economic and real income. After the World War II, many nations declared the maintenance of full employment as the basic objective of their economic and financial policies, and more recently, the objective has become that of maintaining a stable rate of economic growth.

2. Methods of Credit Control

According to de Kock, there are nine methods of credit control which may be used by central banks.[1] These are:

(1) The lowering or raising of their discount and interest rates with a view to lowering or raising money rates generally and encouraging the expansion or contraction of credit.

(2) The buying or selling of securities or bills of exchange in the open market with a view to putting additional funds into the market or withdrawing funds therefrom and thus expanding or contracting credit.

(3) The rationing of credit as an alternative or an addition to raising discount and interest rates.

(4) The taking of 'direct action either in the form of coercive measures against any offending bank or other financial institution or in the form of directives to banks generally concerning their lending and investment operations, in order to assist the central bank in controlling the quantity of credit as well as securing a better qualitative distribution of credit.

(5) The lowering or raising of the minimum cash reserves to be maintained by the commercial banks, as an additional means of enabling the central bank to expand or contract their capacity to create credit.

(6) The imposition of minimum secondary reserve requirements to be maintained by the commercial banks in the form of government securities and other specified assets, in order to restrict their capacity to extend credit for general business purposes.

(7) The regulation of the terms and conditions under which credit repayable in instalments may be granted for purchasing or carrying consumers' durable goods, as a means of exercising some direct control over the volume of outstanding consumer credit.

(8) The regulation of margin requirements in connection with purchase

1. M.H. de Kock, *Central Banking,* Third Edition, pp. 125-126.

of stock exchange securities, as an instrument for exercising some direct control over the volume of credit used in the security markets.

(9) The use of moral suasion and publicity to achieve the desired objectives. We now discuss these methods, one by one, in the following paragraphs:

1. Bank Rate Policy

The first step, usually taken by the central bank is the raising or lowering of the bank rate, as and when required. Bank rate, in England refers to officially published rate at which the Bank of England is prepared to discount approved bills. The central bank through appropriate changes in the banking rates controls the volume of credit indirectly by influencing the rate of interest as a determinant of the volume of total loans and investment in the country. The principle governing the regulation of total credit in the country has been stated by Henry Thornton like this: "In order to ascertain how far the desire of obtaining loans at the bank may be expected at any time to be carried, we must inquire into the subject of the quantum of profit likely to be derived from borrowing there under the existing circumstances. This is to be judged by considering two points: the amount, first, of interest to be paid on the sum borrowed; and secondly, on the mercantile or other gain to be obtained by employment of the borrowed capital...We may, therefore, consider this question as turning principally on a comparison of the rate of interest taken at the bank with the current rate of mercantile profit."[2] According to Spalding, "In theory, if not in actual practice as far as our own money market goes, the bank rate is the minimum rate charged by the bank for discounting approved bills of exchange." But bank rate is different from discount rate. Discount means a deduction made while making payment of the amount of the bills of exchange by the commercial banks. This is what is known as the market rate of discount. Now as the central bank does not compete with commercial banks or undertakes banking operations with a profit motive, the bank rate is always lower than the market rate of discount. Bank rate as an instrument of controlling credit was for the first time used by the Bank of England in 1839. Before that year, rationing of credit was the usual method to control credit, mainly because the monetary structure was not so intricate then.

Theory of Bank Rate

The efficacy of bank rate changes to control credit by affecting the level of economic activity can hardly be over-emphasised. The opinions, however,

---

2. Henry Thornton, *An Enquiry into the Nature and Effects of the Paper Credit of Great Britain*, p. 267.

differ regarding the way in which it affects the level of economic activity. Hawtrey-Keynes controversy is quite well-known in this regard. According to Hawtrey, main changes take place through changes in the short-term rates while Keynes emphasised the importance of the changes in the long-term rates. Besides Hawtrey and Keynes, there were some traditional views which have been referred to by Keynes in his *Treatise on Money.* These views are:

(1) According to one school of thought, bank rate is an instrument of regulating the quantity of bank money. A rise in the bank rate will contract and a fall in it will expand the volume of money in circulation. But this view is, however, not universally true. A rise may not produce any effect on credit conditions under boom conditions and a fall in it may not expand bank money in period of depression.

(2) The second school of thought believed it to be a means of saving gold reserves by affecting the foreign exchange rates.

(3) The third school held that bank rate influences the rate of investment more than the rate of saving. Its rise will discourage and its decline will stimulate the rate of investment. But how bank rate does it is a matter of keen controversy between Hawtrey and Keynes. Though both of them agree with the fundamental thing that bank rate influences the volume of economic activity in the way, that it influences the cost of holding goods like warehouse charges, depreciation, insurance charges, etc. but the difference lies in the class of goods, the changes in the holding of which are considered more significant.

Hawtrey's Views

According to Hawtrey, a dealer, whether wholesaler or retailer, always holds stocks of goods mainly to meet consumers' demands, without making them wait and also to avoid the consequences of the variations of supply. This holding of stocks which acts as a sort of insurance to equate demand and supply is of some monetary value to the dealer which he balances against the cost of holding of stocks. It needs no explanation that the quantity of stocks held by the dealer varies with the cost of holding it and the elasticity of demand of the commodity hardly matters in this regard. Further, this cost of holding stocks varies with the changes in the short-term rate of interest. Now, the vicious circle goes like this:

A fall in the short-term rates of interest, reducing the cost of holding encourages the dealer to stock more, orders to manufacturers rise, output expands, employment increases, money incomes rise and the inflationary spiral with rising prices and production starts. Conversely, a rise in the short-term rates increases the cost of holding stocks, production falls, prices fall, unemployment increases and the deflationary spiral starts. This view depends on two factors, *viz.*, (*a*) the proportion of the interest charges to the cost of holding stocks, and (*b*) the elasticity of demand for the commodity.

As regards the first factor, there are certain charges like insurance, depreciation and the price itself, which varies from commodity to commodity. In bulky and perishable commodities, these costs will be more than the rate of interest, and as such, commodities cannot be held for long unless they are imperishable and their elasticity is high. Thus, interest rates have no bearing upon the holding of stocks. Hawtrey, therefore, says that as most of the commodities are bulky or perishable or susceptible to quick changes in prices, bank rate changes will have no great effect on business activity.

Keynes' Views

In the opinion of Keynes, bank rate affects the internal economic situation, through the long-term rates of interest, which are no doubt, always associated with variations in the short-term rates. Now, let us see the way in which the changes in the long-term rates are produced.

With a rise in the cost of borrowing, the individuals and firms who used to finance their business after borrowing from the bank will stop doing so and instead start selling their securities as yield from them will relatively fall. The sale of securities will thus, be stimulated. Secondly, individuals and firms, instead of investing their surplus funds into securities, will deposit them into the banks as the yield on time deposits will increase. This decline in demand and pressure to sell securities will reduce the prices of securities in the market. It is in this way, that the long-term rates will be affected by the changes in the short-term rates and as Keynes says, these movements of the long-term rates will affect the propensity of entrepreneurs to hold fixed capital goods. Low long-term rates by increasing the prices of securities will encourage the entrepreneurs to float new shares for the construction of new fixed capital goods. Keynes' view is more widely accepted than Hawtrey's. It may be noted that these two views are not mutually exclusive, for a decline in short-term rates may stimulate additions to stocks as well as, lead to a fall in long-term rates, which will stimulate investment in fixed capital. The difference is only that of emphasis. Hawtrey lays stress on the former and Keynes on the latter. It may also be worthwhile to note that while Keynes assigned an important role to the policy of interest rate in his *Treatise,* he subsequently seems to have changed his opinion in his *General Theory.* In the latter work, he points out that the downward changes in the interest rates are not so important as measures taken by the state to push up the level of investment in the economy in order to stabilize the level of business activity and the internal price level during depression.

Effects of Bank Rate Changes

Bank rate changes affect the internal economy of a country as well as the international balance of payments position. The effects of bank rate changes on the domestic economy may be: (*i*) direct, and (*ii*) indirect.

The direct or primary effects would be a fall in the prices of fixed capital goods and increase in savings. Investments will go down, production will fall and margin of profits will disappear. The prices of commodities and securities will also fall.

The indirect or secondary effect would be a fall in the prices of capital goods and hence a fall in their production. Unemployment in such industries will grow, money incomes will fall, demand for consumption goods will deteriorate and their prices will fall. So far as the effects of bank rate changes or the international balance of payments position are concerned, these are: (*i*) A rise in the bank rate may be helpful in correcting the disequilibrium in the exchange rates in the long run. In the event of unfavourable balance of payments position, a rise in the bank rate, in a gold standard country, will not only check the export of gold from the country but attract the inflow of gold, by way of foreign investments. The position would, thus, be reversed and the disequilibrium would be corrected. (*ii*) A rise in the bank rate starts a deflationary process involving contraction of credit investment and employment, leading to a fall in the domestic money incomes. Exports will increase and imports will decline. Balance of trade will thus become favourable. (*iii*) Falling prices would reduce the level of employment, wages would be lowered and cost of production would decline. Disequilibrium would, thus, be corrected.

We, thus, find that the bank rate policy is an effective weapon for correcting the exchange disequilibrium. This is one side of the picture. The case may be otherwise too. A continued inflow of gold due to stimulated exports would again create disequilibrium. The concomitant result would be inflation, cheapening of money, expansion of credit, speculation, all culminating in inflating the price level. Exports would decline and imports would rise. Outflow of gold would, therefore, start once again. The success of the bank rate policy would, therefore, depend upon two factors. Firstly, it should be applied immediately and at the desired time so as to produce its immediate effects on the money rate and credit structure; and secondly, the economic structure should be flexible so as to be quickly adjusted. In rigid conditions the bank rate policy is however, not effective.

Significance of Bank Rate

According to de Kock, the significance of the discount rate is of a three-fold nature.

"In the first place the official discount rate indicates the rate at which the public should be able to obtain accommodation on the specified types of papers. As the central bank regulates the monetary activity of the country, bank rate has come to be known as the standard rate of discount." "Secondly...discount rate represents the basis of the rates at which they can obtain central bank credit...." Thirdly, the psychological value of the discount rate is of importance to the central bank as an instrument of credit control. It is at last a reflection of its opinion on the credit situation and sometimes of the economic position generally."[3] As Gibson said, a rise in the discount rate may be regarded as "the amber coloured light of warning, of a robot system of finance and economics".[4] Or as Addis pointed out, "the danger signal, the red light warning, the business community of rocks head on the way in which they are engaged," while a fall in the discount rate may be looked upon as "the green light indicating that the coast is clear and the ship of commerce may proceed on her way with caution...." Burgess also emphasised the psychological value of the changes in the bank rate. He says: "The psychological value of the discount rate depends *inter alia,* on the prestige of the central bank and the degree of co-operation which it can obtain from the commercial banks and other credit institutions."[5]

"In the light of experience, this co-operation can best be secured by means of conventional relationship between the discount rate of the central bank and the various rates quoted by the commercial banks, somewhat on the lines of the traditional conventions observed by the English banks." Copland, while referring to the situation in Australia said that, "Clearly the most satisfactory arrangement is a system under which the leadership of the central bank is recognised in a set of conventions through which the banks implement the banking policy desired from time to time by the central bank."

Bank Rate Policy and Gold Standard

Prior to 1931 when most of the countries of Europe were on gold standard it was the responsibility of the central bank to safeguard the gold reserves of the country. Since the existence of the gold standard depended on the free movement of gold, *i.e.* free import and export of gold, it was the responsibility of the central bank to see that neither the import of gold was in excess nor its export was in excess. The central bank used for this purpose the instrument of bank rate. In the event of outflow of gold, the central bank increased the bank rate which ultimately led to an increase in the market rate of interest, in making the investments costlier and in causing a decline in the level of business activity

3. *Op. cit.,* pp. 166-171.
4. *London Bankers' Magazine,* April 1957.
5. *Op. cit.,* p. 230.

and internal price level. Obviously, the exports used to rise and imports used to decline, leading to a check in the outflow of gold. Similarly in the event of inflow of gold, the central bank reduced the bank rate and made the cycle to move in the reverse direction.

Conditions for the Success of the Bank Rate Policy

The success of the bank rate policy is governed by three conditions which are:

(*i*) There should be a close relationship between the bank rate and the various interest rates prevailing in the market. It is necessary because the market interest rates have to move in line with the bank rate, *i.e.* when the bank rate is increased, the market rates must also increase and then the bank rate is reduced, the market rates should also come down. But, such a relationship is possible only when the money market is fully developed and when the banking system of a country is well-organised and developed. In the countries of the West like the USA, the bank rate policy has been very successful but in less-developed countries like India it has not succeeded to that extent.

(*ii*) The second essential condition for the success of the bank rate policy is that the economic structure should be elastic. In other words, the price structure, the wage structure, and the cost structure should be elastic so that adjustment can take place easily and smoothly with the changes in the volume of credit caused by the changes in the bank rate. This elasticity was very well found in the economic structure of western countries like the UK, more particularly, before the World War I. After the World War I and especially after the Great Depression of the thirties, the economic structure in the western countries has lost that elasticity and has become quite rigid with the result that the bank rate policy is now not as effective an instrument of credit control as it used to be.

(*iii*) Finally the short-term funds market in the economy should be well-organised and developed. In less-developed countries like India, the market for short-term funds is highly underdeveloped and disorganised and consequently, the bank rate policy has been rather ineffective in controlling credit.

So, we can say that the bank rate policy has its own limitations and these are:

(*i*) The bank rate policy can be successful only when the three conditions indicated above are fulfilled.

(*ii*) As we have stated before, the success of the bank rate policy depends on the effects that the changes in the bank rate produce on the entrepreneurial activities. But it has been seen that in actual practice, the real entrepreneurial activities are not adversely affected by the changes in the market rates of interest because the chief factor influencing them is the margin of profit. It has officially been stated that in Great Britain and America, the activities of the entrepreneurs are influenced not by the changes in the rate of interest but by the changes in the margin of profit. And therefore, it has been stated by a number of economists that there cannot be any direct relationship between market rates of interest and the bank rate. Some economists have also stated after opposing Hawtrey that investments in the public sector are also not at all governed by the rate of interest as was assumed by him.

(*iii*) While the bank rate policy can be successful in checking inflation, it is hardly effective in curing deflation. The lowering of the bank rate during deflation, with the sole object of expanding the volume of credit and thus to induce the entrepreneurs and businessmen to take loans and intensify their economic activities, has hardly succeeded.

(*iv*) The changes in the bank rate may cause another embarrassing situation when in the event of its rise with a view to controlling domestic inflation it might also attract at the same time short-term funds from foreign countries into the country, thereby neutralising the effect of the rise in bank rate.

(*v*) It has been pointed out that one of the most serious limitations of the bank rate policy is that it does not make any distinction between productive and unproductive activities. Even if the objective of raising the bank rate is to curb speculation, the genuine productive activities are also discouraged.

(*vi*) It has also been found in practice that the commercial banks do not remain completely dependent on the central bank for acquiring resources since they themselves maintain ample liquid resources and consequently the bank rate policy has not been successful.

(*vii*) The bank rate policy has also not been able to correct disequilibrium in the balance of payments. The success of the bank rate policy in this field depends on the complete non-existence of any artificial restrictions on foreign exchange and the flow of capital between countries. These days we do not find any country which has not imposed artificial restrictions on the movement of capital to maintain stability in the rate of exchange. This has left the bank rate policy as utterly ineffective.

Declining Importance after World War I

The significance of the bank rate policy considerably declined after the World War I owing to a variety of reasons. Since we have mentioned these in the preceding paragraphs we can make here a passing reference only.

Firstly, the money market and the credit structure have radically changed and have become so rigid as not to be responsive to bank rate policy as much as they are to the open market operations.

Secondly, the increasing use of the direct methods of credit control, like open market operations, alteration of reserve ratio of the commercial banks, etc. have also been responsible for the decline of the bank rate policy as a weapon of credit control.

Thirdly, with the suspension of the international gold standard, the bank rate has virtually disappeared. These days the emphasis has shifted from exchange stabilisation to price stabilisation.

Fourthly, the cheap money policy as an objective to bring about business recovery by pulling down the rate of interest has also been responsible for this situation. Wagemann has rightly said that the bank rate policy, "presupposes an economic system in which the price, wage and interest levels—at least in greater part are readily movable and in which entrepreneurs work on a narrow margin and consequently react very sensitively to the slightest changes in costs and the profits basis... The more an economy is regulated in prices, wages, transportation charges, and the more the Government extends its influence over business, the more the influence of interest declines."

Fifthly, the methods of financing trade and commerce have changed considerably. Now the bills of exchange are not used for financing trade and that is why the commercial banks now do not have the necessity of obtaining re-discounting facilities from the central bank.

Sixthly, the control of the central bank on the commercial banks has also become relaxed. The commercial banks have been maintaining more liquid assets. They sometimes neutralise the effect of the increase in the bank rate by offering higher interest rates to their depositors.

Seventhly, the industrialists and entrepreneurs have now become less sensitive to changes in the rates of interest owing to the changes introduced in the taxation structure and productive cost structure.

Finally, the importance of bank rate policy has been relegated to the background especially because of the importance attached to the fiscal policy, especially after the Great Depression of the nineteen thirties.

However, during recent years, a revival in the significance of bank rate policy has been witnessed. Inflation is now a worldwide phenomenon and to fight inflation in almost all the countries of the world resort has been taken to the bank rate policy. It is no doubt true that along with the bank rate policy several other measures of credit control as well as use of fiscal measures has been made. It would, therefore, not be wrong to conclude with de Kock that "although it must again be admitted that present day conditions and Governmental policies do not afford much scope for independent discount rate action, there is good reason to believe that the official discount rate has nevertheless a useful function to perform in conjunction with other measures of control."[6]

2. Open Market Operations

Open market operations is another weapon available to the central bank for controlling credit in the economy. By open market operations we mean the buying and selling of eligible securities by the central bank in the money and capital markets. The chief constituents of the money market as we know are the institutions like banks, business corporations, financial intermediaries, etc. which deal in negotiable instruments either on their own behalf or on behalf of their clients. These instruments are freely discountable at the central bank and are more or less a substitute for high powered money. It may be noted that the dealing takes place only in those instruments which have a fixed maturity date. During a period of business prosperity, the central bank disposes of the eligible securities to reduce the supply of money in the market. These instruments are purchased by the various constituents of the money market. In the capital market transactions take place in instruments which have no fixed maturity date. The main participants are the insurance companies, the investment trusts, etc. The sale of these instruments by the central bank leads to a reduction in the cash reserves of the bank. Secondly, they are forced to reduce their advances and refuse further loans to their clients. The investment activity in the country gets slackened and the boom situation recedes.

Similarly, during a period of depression, the central bank purchases the eligible securities in the market. The individuals and institutions sell these securities and deposit money so received with the commercial banks whose cash reserves increase and are used by them ultimately for giving fresh advances. Consequently, the economic activity increases, leading to a rise in the level of investment, employment and prices.

The open market operations have assumed different forms in different countries. In the UK, the joint stock banks do not discount their bills with the Bank of England. When as a result of the sale of securities, their funds get depleted, they curtail their commitments and recall their advances. And, therefore, the economic system is so flexible that it functions automatically. In the USA, this is not the case. There, the joint stock banks discount their bills with the Federal Reserve Bank and the credit restrictions may not be enforceable and hence a limit is assigned to each member bank beyond which it cannot draw. With the exhaustion of the limit, each member bank for keeping its position intact curtails advances and recalls loans. Therefore, increasing use has been made of this method. It initiates the movements in rates and then

6. *Op. cit.*, p. 179.

the changes in the official rediscount rate come at the end of the process. In England, open market operations are undertaken by the Bank of England to make the existing official rediscount rate effective. Again, in the USA, the member banks have to maintain legal minimum cash reserves which are changeable according to circumstances. In England, the banks have to keep customary cash reserves. In Australia, open market operations have not been successful because the market for government securities has been very tight. During the World War II, open market operations were meant for maintaining interest rates and for supporting the price of government securities. In countries like Sweden and Argentina, this policy was meant for absorbing the surplus liquid funds in the money and capital markets. Now open market operations have become one of the potent devices for credit control.

Under the gold standard, this policy was adopted to sterilise or offset the movements of gold. The policy of open market operations is adopted to achieve the following objectives:

(1) As already stated, under the gold standard, the objective was to sterilise or offset the movements of gold. The inflow of gold in the country led to expansion in the volume of credit in the country and consequently a rise in the internal price level. If the central bank felt that the rise in the level of internal prices was not in the interest of the economy, then it used to reduce the volume of credit through sale of securities which ultimately resulted in a fall in the internal price level. In the event of outflow of gold from the country there was an automatic reduction in the volume of credit in the economy and thus a fall in the internal price level. In that situation the central bank purchased securities in the market to remove the shortage of credit money. This led to an increase in the cash reserves of the commercial banks which enabled them to increase the volume of credit in the economy and hence a rise in the price level.

(2) The second objective of this policy is to check the export of capital to other countries. If according of the central bank, the export of capital is not in the interest of the economy, it starts selling securities and thus, withdraws the surplus money from the money market.

(3) In the event of shortage of funds in the money market adversely affecting the business activity, the central bank starts purchasing securities and thus provides funds to the money market.

(4) It has been seen that in certain situations, the commercial banks are faced with the problem of withdrawal of deposits by the depositors under the influence of some rumour about the failure of the bank. In technical terms, such a situation is called as 'run on the bank'. In such a situation, the central bank comes to the rescue of the commercial banks and starts purchasing securities. This increases the cash reserves of the banks and enables them to

fulfil their commitments and meet the situation. The confidence of the public is restored in the bank and the bank is saved from going insolvent.

(5) Open market operations are also undertaken to supplement the effect of bank rate policy.

Limitations of Open Market Operations

This policy has been quite effective and popular because: (*i*) it produces a very direct and immediate effect on the credit conditions in the economy; (*ii*) Now its scope stands largely expanded owing to the increased availability of government and other eligible securities in the money market; and (*iii*) the bank rate policy has become ineffective owing to the changes in the economic structure of the various countries. But the success of the open market operations depends on the fulfilment of certain conditions. These conditions are:

(1) It is essential that the market for different types of securities should be well-organised and developed. In less-developed countries this condition is hardly fulfilled and that is why the open market operations policy has not been as successful as it has been in the countries of the west.

(2) The cash reserve ratio which the commercial banks are required to maintain must decrease or increase in accordance with the sale or purchase of securities so that corresponding changes take place in the volume of credit in the country. But, if the commercial banks maintain a higher cash reserve ratio than they are required to maintain, or if they maintain other types of secret reserves, then the policy will not be successful. In the countries of the west this policy has not been very successful because the commercial banks are generally accustomed to maintain higher cash reserve ratio with the central bank.

(3) The quantity of money in circulation and the cash reserves of the commercial banks may not increase in the event of the central bank's purchasing securities due to extraneous factors like the outflow of capital or an adverse balance of payments or hoarding by the people. Again, in the event of the central bank's selling securities the effect may be just reverse due to the inflow of capital or a favourable balance of payments and so on.

(4) When the central bank wants to increase the cash reserves of the commercial banks by purchasing securities the public might be withdrawing cash from the bank out of sheer panic. The desired result may thus not be achieved in such conditions.

(5) Even if the cash reserves of the commercial banks enlarge, they may accumulate the same for meeting an emergency. In such situation, the credit may not expand. Even if the commercial banks decide to expand credit, the entrepreneurs might feel indifferent towards this attraction due to an apprehension of depression.

(6) The policy can be successful only when the central bank possesses adequate open market securities for sale. If the central bank wishes to attract credit, it should have large investment in government securities. The timing too, of such a policy must correspond with a period of depression and when expansion of credit is a desired objective.

(7) The open market operations can be successful only when the commercial banks do not have a direct access to the central bank for financial accommodation. If the commercial banks have a direct access to the central bank then the reduction in their cash reserves through open sale of securities by the central bank will be neutralised by the commercial banks through borrowing from the central bank.

Similarly, as a result of open purchase of securities by the central bank, the additional funds available to the commercial banks are utilised by them for repaying outstanding loans of the central bank, then the object of credit expansion will not be achieved.

(8) It has been stated that the open market operations are more successful in controlling the expansion of credit rather than in stimulating expansion of credit. During a period of depression, the business prospects not being very bright, the entrepreneurs are hardly encouraged to borrow funds from the commercial banks in spite of the fact that they are available at much lower rates.

Which Policy is Better?

Bank rate or open market operations—which policy is better? From the foregoing discussion it would be seen that neither the bank rate policy nor the open market operations is by itself successful in achieving the desired objective. Each should be supplemented by the other, in order to be effective. The raising of bank rate alone will not be effective if the banks possess surplus funds unless the central bank also withdraws surplus funds, by selling securities. Similarly, if the central bank sells securities without raising the bank rate the member banks may replenish their reserves by re-discounting their bills with the central bank and thus avoid contraction of credit. That is why, economists are of the opinion that the bank rate policy should be adopted only to correct a permanent disequilibrium, while the open market operations may be undertaken to remove a temporary maladjustment. From the point of view of credit control, open market operations are, therefore, necessarily complementary to the bank rate policy.

The utility and adaptability of open market operations has been a subject of keen controversy particularly between Hawtrey and Keynes. The former was a champion of non-monetary theory of trade cycles while the latter was an advocate of an equilibrium between savings and investments. According to Hawtrey, "An addition to the outstanding quantity of money, the unspent margin in itself can accomplish nothing, since the supply of money is the flow of money spent on exchange of commodities, and since the release of cash by traders is indispensable condition of an increase in the consumers' income. So much so that an absorption of cash is inseparable from an equivalent reduction of consumers' income." Hawtrey has, thus, no faith in open market operations alone as instrument of credit regulation, and he considers that the use of discount rate is also essential. Keynes on the other hand believes that these operations, if undertaken skilfully and extensively, alone could achieve the objective provided that they are supplemented by a properly planned investment policy.

3. Other Methods of Credit Control

In addition to the methods of credit control stated above, the central banks in the various countries of the world have adopted other forms of credit control as well. Among these mention may be made of: (*i*) rationing of credit, (*ii*) direct action, (*iii*) changes in the cash reserves of the member banks, and (*iv*) changes in margin requirements on security loans. We now discuss these methods as follows:

1. Rationing of Credit. This is probably the oldest method of credit control. It was adopted by the Bank of England as early as the end of the 18th century. The Bank, however, discontinued rationing of credit since the Bank Act of 1844 and came to rely upon bank rate. This situation also developed in other countries. It was only under extreme abnormal conditions that this method was resorted to by the continental central banks from time to time. Germany adopted it in 1924. Under this method, the central banks used to impose a ceiling upon the discount for anyone bank or reject a proportion of each discount application whenever the total demand for loans was more than the amount it was prepared to discount on anyone day. After World War I, this method has been made use of to control the exceptionally difficult situation created by war and post-war inflation. These days, credit rationing by the central bank has become an important component of the general economic policy. According to de Kock, "Rationing of credit and capital is a logical concomitant of the intensive and extensive planning adopted by authoritarian states."

2. Direct Action. The central bank may refuse to rediscount the bills of those banks whose lending policy runs counter to its directives. The aim of this policy is to acquire qualitative control of credit. It is subject to two limitations: firstly, "the difficulty of deciding at any time and for any bank when there arises an increase of bank credit militating against sound credit conditions," and secondly, "the effect of such division on the part of central bank will be to make the commercial banks slacken their vigilance on their true position and shift to the central bank the onus of ascertaining the true position." This method has been most extensively used by central banks to implement their credit policies. It can take three forms, namely (*i*) the central bank may reject altogether any application for grant of discounting facilities to its member banks; (*ii*) it may refuse to sanction further financial accommodation to a member bank if its existing borrowings have exceeded its capital and reserves; and (*iii*) it may start charging penal rate of interest on loans taken by a member bank beyond the prescribed limit. It may be noted that the success of this method depends only on the strength of the central bank to enforce its directives on the member banks. To achieve the objective, in several countries, the central banks have been given statutory powers; they have also been given authority to lay down rates of interest to be charged on different types of loans and advances and also to regulate the flow of bank credit for particular purposes in the economy.

Selective Credit Control: At times, the central banks have also resorted to selective credit control, according to which loans are given on a selective basis; the selection being made in respect of either individual banks or in respect of individual commodities to check speculative activities in the economy. But the method of selective credit control also has certain limitations. These are: (*i*) it is not easy to make a distinction between productive and unproductive uses of credit. The object of selective credit control is generally to divert bank credit from less productive to more productive uses but it is very difficult for the commercial banks to make such distinction and therefore, the effectiveness of this method is considerably diluted; (*ii*) the effectiveness of this method is further reduced by the fact that the commercial banks cannot control the ultimate use of credit in the economy, because the loans are used exclusively by the borrowers; (*iii*) the method of selective credit control is generally applied to commercial banks alone and non-banking financial institutions which contribute substantially to the total volume of credit in the economy are left out. It has been seen that generally the policies of these financial institutions run counter to those of the central bank; (*iv*) under the method of selective credit control no restriction is imposed on clean credit and consequently, the measures like higher margin requirements are violated by the borrowers through securing clean loans from the commercial banks; (*v*) it has also been witnessed that at times the commercial banks have manipulated their accounts for advancing loans to their clients under different names for various uses which have been prohibited. This has made the method of selective credit control quite ineffective.

Moral Suasion. The moral suasion is psychological. It is not as offensive as the direct action, since it does not involve any compulsion or punishment.

Opinions, however, differ about the effectiveness of such a policy. In respect of the United States of America, Burgess opines that the "Reserve Banks may at times exercise an important influence on the general credit situation through the informal suggestions which they make to bankers." But writers like Clark believe that unless it has teeth, its efficacy is doubtful. While in the USA, it has not achieved any success, in Great Britain it has been very successful. Moral suasion includes the issue of directives by central bank to the member banks in clarification of the general banking policy and tendering advice about the nature of, and, the risks involved in various investments. It is through its warning and advice that the central bank influences the credit policy of its member banks. In our own country also, the Reserve Bank has been making use of such a method. Such cooperation between the central bank and its constituents can go a long way in stabilising the banking system of a country. But it has also its limitations. De Kock has rightly concluded that "while there is scope for the useful application by central banks of moral suasion, its limitations in various directions must be fully recognised. In countries where there are highly liquid monetary conditions and where the central bank either cannot undertake open market operations at all or cannot do so on a scale sufficient to counteract the undue liquidity, it is advisable, if not essential, for the central bank to use moral suasion as far as possible, in spite of its limitations. Its success would depend largely on the prestige and personal authority of the central bank; the technical means and statutory powers at the disposal of the central bank; the degree of co-operation between the central bank and the commercial banks as well as other financial institutions and make-up of the country's banking and credit structure:"[7]

3. Changes in the Cash Reserve Requirements. The central bank can also control credit by making necessary changes in the cash reserves to be kept with her by the commercial banks. This method is known as the method of Variable Cash Reserve Ratio and was for the first time suggested by Lord Keynes. For a long time this method was considered as indispensable for promoting the overall liquidity and the solvency of the banking system. It inspired greater public confidence in the competence of the commercial banks to meet their obligations to depositors. But, now the position stands considerably changed. It is now considered as a supplementary method for effective credit control. It was introduced for the first time in the USA in 1933, followed by New Zealand and Mexico in 1936, Sweden and Ecuador in 1937 and Australia in 1941. Now in almost all the countries of the world, the central banks make use of this method. The ratio, however, varies from country to country according to the nature of economic development and

7. *Op. cit.*, pp. 231-32.

industrial progress. During inflationary conditions, since the commercial banks have excessive cash reserves, they follow a policy of expansion of credit. The central bank considering this over-expansion as harmful, raises the cash reserve ratio and thus sterilizes a part of the cash reserves of the commercial banks and compels them to reduce the creation of credit in the economy. In times of deflation, the central bank lowers down the required ratio with a view to expanding the cash reserves of the commercial banks and thus enabling them to create more credit than before. An expansion in the volume of credit obviously creates a spurt in the economy and raises the level of economic activity. It is in this way that the central bank influences the creation of credit by changing the cash reserve ratio. Needless to point out that this method is quite effective not only theoretically but from the practical point of view as well. It affects the economy through the change in the size of credit multiplier. When the cash reserve ratio is raised, the size of the credit multiplier becomes small and when it is lowered, then the size of the credit multiplier becomes large. As a matter of fact this method appears to be more effective and powerful than the open market operations. But it has also some limitations. Changes in reserve requirements may not at times bring about corresponding changes in bank cash reserves and even if they are able to do so, the volume of credit may not correspondingly change since commercial banks do not always increase or decrease their investments according to changes in their cash or because the scope of demand for bank credit does not vary with the cash. De Kock is right in concluding that "while it is a very prompt and effective method of bringing about the desired changes in the available supply of bank cash, it has some technical and psychological limitations which prescribe that it should be used with moderation and discretion and only under obviously abnormal conditions".[8]

4. Secondary Reserve Requirements. This method was first used in the USA in 1945. According to this method the commercial banks are asked to invest, up to a certain minimum, their surplus funds, in short-term government securities and other liquid assets which means that they did not only consider it necessary to call upon member banks to maintain their minimum reserves with Federal Reserve Banks, but also insist upon them for minimum holdings of short-term government securities and other liquid assets with a view to limiting their opportunities for disposing of such assets in order to increase their loans for general business purposes. Such restrictions were subsequently imposed in France, Belgium, Mexico, India, Sweden, Norway, Holland and the Philippines. The motive behind this method is simply to restrict the lending capacity of the banks. In some countries it has been used as a valuable anti-

8. *Ibid.*, p. 237.

inflationary measure, and in others it has facilitated deficit financing by the government. According to de Kock, the method of secondary reserve requirements "can be made to play a valuable part in any positive disinflationary monetary policy under conditions of exceptional inflationary pressures caused by war, rearmament or other abnormal circumstances."[9]

5. Changes in Margin Requirements. This method was first adopted in the USA in 1934 chiefly to control speculative activities in securities. The Federal Reserve Banks have been empowered to lay rules and regulations regarding the amount of credit that could be extended by banks against securities and also regarding margins for loans by brokers to their customers. This method has proved to be quite effective. But like the changes in the reserve requirements, it also suffers from the drawbacks of throwing an enormous responsibility on the central bank and also tending to cause the latter to be singled out, for the role of 'arch scapegoat'. As Burgess has pointed out, "It will directly and immediately influence the profits and even solvency of considerable groups of people."[10]

6. Regulation of Consumer Credit. This method was first adopted in America in 1941. It was introduced by an executive order issued by the President empowering the Board of Governors of the Federal Reserve System to "regulate the terms and conditions under which credit repayable in instalments may be extended for purchasing consumer durable goods." The chief objective was, therefore, to reduce the demand for goods, the civilian supply of which already stood reduced because of the growing needs of the defence personnel. An increase in demand for these goods would have caused the price level to rise and would have also absorbed the materials increasingly required for defence purposes. This method is a supplementary instrument to be used along with the other methods and more basic fiscal tools used by the government in fighting inflation. This was primarily a war measure but it continued even after the war up to 1952. It was also adopted by countries like Canada, Great Britain, Australia, New Zealand and Belgium. But for less developed countries where there is no organised system of consumer credit, this method does not have much value.

7. Publicity. Quite a good number of central banks have used publicity as an instrument of credit control. They regularly publish statements of their assets and liabilities, reviews of credit and business conditions and reports of their own operations, general money market and banking conditions. It has been employed quite extensively in the USA. Some central banks use it as a matter of duty while others attach special importance to it. It may, however,

---

9. *Ibid.*, p. 241.
10. W.R. Burgess, *Reserve Banks and the Money Market,* p. 257.

be pointed out that this method is very useful for highly industrialised countries, but in less developed countries where the percentage of illiteracy is very high and where people are utterly ignorant about the significance of banking statistics, this method is hardly of any value.

3. Perfect Credit Control—A Myth

We have discussed above the methods of credit control adopted from time to time by the central banks. In practice, however, effective control is a hard nut to crack. The controlling authority should have access to all forms of credit, whether bank credits or non-bank credits, both of them are used for purchasing goods and services. John Stuart Mill, Leaf, Anderson and others are of this opinion. According to Prof. Lewinske, "A rise in prices is always in the first place accomplished without a resort to bank credit, the increased demand for goods being affected with the aid of book credits."[11] Further the control can be effective only when there is mutual co-operation between the central bank and the commercial banks on the one hand and between commercial banks themselves on the other. If the commercial banks do not have direct relations with the central bank in the matter of keeping reserves as in the USA, the control can hardly be effective. Again, if the credit is not used by the commercial banks for genuine trade purposes, but for speculative activities, the control cannot be effective. That is why de Kock feels the necessity of personal element in regard to credit control. Maclanghlu was right when he said that "the principal factor in credit is the state of mind and you cannot control credit until you control public opinion".[12]

Thus, control of credit can never be perfect. Price mechanism is so intricate and complex that it can hardly be made to work according to prefixed rules and pre-determined policies. Determined changes in the quantity of money cannot bring about the desired changes in the price level. In the absence of reliable indices, such a quantitative control can never be possible. Moreover, it is not definite that the changes in the price level are always due to the changes in the quantity of money in circulation. There may be other causes which are beyond the control of the central bank, for example: (*i*) prices may rise due to the scarcity of goods caused by natural calamities like floods, drought, crop failures, wars, etc.; (*ii*) bank credit is not the only form of credit used for the purchase of goods and services. Again, it is also not only used for the purchase of goods but of securities as well. Thus, at times, commodity prices instead of rising may decline. The efficacy of credit control, therefore, depends upon the correct diagnosis of the changes in the price level;

---

11. Lewinske, *Money, Credit and Prices,* p. 64.
12. American Bankers' Association Journal, August 1936.

(*iii*) again, changes in the velocity of circulation of money may also bring about changes in the price level. We cannot practically measure the changes in the velocity and hence credit control may also not be effective; and (*iv*) finally, the commercial banks may not co-operate with the central bank, even if it adopts all the methods simultaneously. They may hold large cash reserves and neutralise the efforts of the central bank.

Thus, a perfect control of credit is a myth. As Anderson pointed out, "The disturbance of economic equilibrium is responsible for depression and it is through price changes that a broken equilibrium is restored." A well-developed bill and money market and perfect co-operation between the central bank and the commercial banks can go a long way to make the credit control effective. A co-ordinated economic and monetary policy is also of vital importance. As de Kock has said, "The Central Bank should not follow an automatic policy, but only allow changes in the credit situation and the level of money rates and prices, if it observes a definite trend resulting from some disequilibrium in the domestic economic structure or from some external influence."

Exercises

1. Discuss the various methods and devices which are normally employed by a central bank to control credit in the country.
2. Explain clearly the process through which changes in the bank rate influence the price level in the country.
3. Discuss the efficacy of the bank rate and open market operations in controlling inflation in the country.
4. Discuss the main functions of quantitative credit controls and bring out their limitations.
5. What do you mean by selective credit controls? In what way are they superior to traditional monetary weapon?
6. "The selective instruments of credit controls are more effective than general instruments in an under-developed economy." Discuss.
7. Discuss the relative importance of quantitative and qualitative techniques of credit control in a developing economy.
8. How does a central bank seek to control the volume and directions of credit? What are the limitations to its power to do so?
9. Discuss the effectiveness of variable reserve ratio as a means of credit control. What are its limitations?
10. "From the stand point of credit control, open market operations are complementary to bank rate policy." Discuss.
11. Compare the views of Keynes-Hawtrey regarding the economic consequences of variations in the bank rate. What views have been held by the Radcliffe Committee in this regard?
12. Discuss the 'incentive effects' and 'general liquidity effects' of bank rate. Which of the two is more important?

•••

Chapter 19

Monetary Policy

1. Introduction

Monetary policy in its narrow sense, refers to the credit control of a central bank; in its broad sense, it means all those monetary and non-monetary measures which influence the cost and supply of money. Paul Einzig defines monetary policy, "as including all monetary decisions and measures irrespective of whether their aims are monetary or non-monetary, and all non-monetary decisions and measures that aim at affecting the monetary system".[1] Monetary policy as an instrument of economic stabilisation, has been used by various countries to manage their economies, especially since the nationalisation of central banks. Such a policy involves influencing the level and composition of aggregate demand by manipulating rates of interest and the volume of credit. The traditional instrument of monetary policy is bank rate, supplemented by open-market operations and selective credit control, where necessary. Since the end of the last world war, certain other methods of credit control have been developed and attempts have been made to make monetary policy more effective and more selective in its impact on the economy.

Although the place of monetary policy among public policies has always been important, it has never been so significant as it is today. Classical economists had a common tendency to regard monetary phenomenon as rather misleading reflections of real phenomenon, on the ground that money obscured otherwise transparent exchange relations. They, therefore, placed major emphasis on production, exchange and consumption of goods. According to them, monetary policy was simply used as a tool for the maintenance of cheap money policy. But the modern theory of money is almost the reverse of the traditional theory. The stability of money is no longer taken for granted, and yet the stabilisation of the value of money is brought into direct relation with

1. Paul Einzig, *Monetary Policy: Ends and Means*, p. 50.

the stabilisation of the levels of income, output and employment. In fact, monetary policy has a positive role to play in bringing about non-monetary reforms as an instrument to implement the economic policy of the state. Such a role has been only recognized by the governments of various countries after the World War II. This is due to: (*i*) the persistence of world-wide inflationary trends, (*ii*) the inability of the governments to check such trends and to bring about stabilisation through non-monetary measures, and (*iii*) the belief that the extent to which fiscal measures can be effectively used is limited by international and domestic political considerations and for successful fight against inflation available instruments of monetary technique must be put in active operation. It may be pointed out that before the Great Depression of the 1930s, monetary policy was considered to be as the most effective instrument of economic stabilisation but during the depression it lost its prestige and fiscal policy occupied its place. It was only after the outbreak of the World War II, owing to worldwide inflation that the monetary policy regained its lost prestige. These days, the governments have been making use of both monetary and fiscal policies in economic management.

2. Objectives of Monetary Policy

Broadly speaking, monetary policy has been used towards the fulfilment of these objectives: (*i*) exchange rate stability; (*ii*) price stability; (*iii*) neutrality of money; (*iv*) stabilisation of income; (*v*) full employment; and (*vi*) economic growth. We now discuss these objectives in the following paragraphs.

1. Exchange Rate Stability

Stability of exchange rates, as an objective of monetary policy, was the most important objective in the 19th century and during the early decades of the 20th century, but has now lost its significance, especially since the breakdown of the gold standard. The gold standard had an in-built mechanism for ensuring exchange stability owing to its automatic functioning. In the event of favourable balance of payments and inflow of gold, the monetary authority of the country used to expand currency and credit which obviously resulted in a rise in the internal price level making exports to fall and imports to rise. In the event of unfavourable balance of payments and the outflow of gold, the monetary authority took steps to contract the currency and credit proportionately which resulted in a fall in the internal price level and hence in the increase of exports and decrease of imports. The disequilibrium in the balance of payments was automatically corrected without any change in the exchange rate. Thus, it was through imports and exports of gold that the country on the gold standard removed the disequilibrium in the balance of payments and ensured exchange stability. In economically weak countries, constant fluctuations in the exchange rate caused a crisis of confidence and led to a large scale withdrawal of short-term funds and the flight of capital. This created an unusual strain on the limited foreign exchange reserves of the country. The experience of the financial crisis of the nineteen thirties has proved, how harmful were the effects of a fluctuating exchange rate on the economy of the country. Instability of exchange rates is not only harmful for foreign trade, but is also disastrous for domestic trade, particularly for countries which are largely dependent on foreign trade. For small nations like Denmark and England whose economic prosperity solely depends upon foreign trade, the exchange stability is highly desirable. Small countries can hardly afford a fluctuating exchange rate, especially if they are dependent on the flow of foreign capital. They must sacrifice domestic price stability as long as there are important countries having a fairly stable monetary system to which they can peg their monetary unit. Hence, exchange rate stability is very essential for maintaining stability in international economic relations. That is why, all the leading countries of the world attached more significance to the stability of exchange rates than to price stability. We now summarise the various arguments put forward in favour of exchange stability: (*i*) frequent fluctuations in the exchange rates give rise to speculation leading to further fluctuations in the exchange rates; (*ii*) they result in loss of confidence among the foreign investors and hence the flight of foreign capital from the country; (*iii*) exchange instability also leads to price instability; (*iv*) exchange instability also disturbs the international economic relations and can also have political repercussions; (*v*) exchange instability also disturbs the foreign trade of the country; and (*vi*) frequent exchange fluctuations also adversely affect international lending by the creditor countries. This difficulty may be enormous for less-developed countries which need foreign capital for the execution of their economic plans. In short, we can say that maintenance of exchange stability is of vital importance for a country which is interested in maintaining cordial economic and political relations in the international sphere and in promoting monetary co-operation and understanding among the various countries of the world.

Arguments have also been advanced against exchange stability as an objective of monetary policy. These arguments are: (*i*) Exchange stability is generally obtained at the cost of internal price stability. A fluctuating price level seriously hampers the economic progress of the country and, therefore, internal price stability is more important than exchange stability. (*ii*) Exchange stability also leads to an easy communication of inflationary or deflationary effect from one country to the other. A country, therefore, is always at the mercy of the other countries.

A policy of exchange stability can be useful for those countries: (*i*) whose foreign trade is quite sizeable, and (*ii*) who are largely dependent on foreign capital for their economic development. It may be recalled that after the World War II, the International Monetary Fund was specially set up to bring about stability in the exchange rates among member countries and since then price stability within the country has gained an edge over exchange stability as an objective of monetary policy. Since exchange stability is automatically provided by the IMF, the individual governments have not to bother about it. But during the seventies of the previous century, especially after the devaluation of the US dollar in 1973, the international monetary system completely collapsed and we again started facing a situation of fluctuating exchange rates. In that context, therefore, exchange stability again acquired added significance as an objective of monetary policy.

2. Price Stability

Price stability as an objective of monetary policy gained an edge over exchange stability after the Great Depression or to be more precise, after the establishment of the IMF. Among the foremost economists who supported domestic price stability as an objective of monetary policy, mention may be made of Gustav Cassel and J.M. Keynes. How much has price stability affected the economic, social and political life of different countries needs no explanation. The worst feature of price instability is that it is cumulative in nature. When started, it never stops and gets on becoming violent and more violent as time passes disturbing the entire economic, social and political set-up of the country. Ample instances can be found in the economic history of the world of such situations. In the USA, the New Deal policy accepted price stabilisation as its main objective. President Roosevelt had on that occasion said, "It is to the interest of the nation to have government help to private enterprise to gain sound general price levels and to protect those levels from wide perilous fluctuations." A number of advantages have been claimed for a policy of price stabilisation. These can be stated briefly as follows: (*i*) such a policy will render the trade cycle inoperative and will make the economy free from all cyclical fluctuations; (*ii*) it will help bring about stability in the economy because it will remove economic uncertainty which is very detrimental for promoting business activity; (*iii*) it will help money to perform its basic functions properly and smoothly; (*iv*) while inflation brings about artificial prosperity in the economy, a policy of price stabilisation will bring about prosperity in the real sense of the term and people would really be getting economic gains; (*v*) such a policy would ensure an equitable distribution of economic gains among the various sections of the society; and (*vi*) it will ultimately promote economic welfare of the community.

The policy has been criticised by a number of economists on the following grounds: (*i*) The concept is rather vague in the sense that it does not indicate which price level is to be stabilised, since there are always a number of price levels in an economy. To find out a standard price level is rather impossible, and when this policy is adopted, the selection of price level would be made arbitrarily by the monetary authority. (*ii*) Again, the concept does not indicate the prices which are to be stabilised, whether the wholesale prices or retail prices or consumer goods prices or producer goods prices are to be stabilised; (*iii*) such a policy is not likely to confer any substantial benefit on the economy since, firstly, price changes are caused by and do not lead to economic fluctuations in the economy; and secondly, the changes in the level of economic activity are caused not only by the changes in the price level but by a host of other factors and therefore, there is no guarantee that by stabilising the price level, the level of economic activity in the economy would be stabilised; (*vi*) in a capitalist set-up, price variations are considered very useful because of the operation of the price mechanism which is the soul of a capitalist economy. If the price level is stabilised, the allocation of resources between different industries and sectors would not be ideal and the price mechanism would be completely ineffective and useless; (*v*) it has been contended that such a policy will hamper the economic growth of the country because no incentive would be available to the entrepreneurs to increase production or to make fresh investments; (*vi*) such a policy also leads to economic inequalities. If rising prices benefit certain sections of the community like industrialists, businessmen, factory owners, shopkeepers, the declining price level also provides substantial benefits to certain groups of the community like the fixed income groups or the pensioners, etc. The benefit so accruing to the large proportion of the community would be denied if prices are stabilised; (*vii*) it has also been argued that this policy cannot be made practicable as it is not possible to bring about stability in the supply of money and credit on the one hand and the supply of output on the other; and (*viii*) price stabilisation as a general policy is not required to be adopted in all situations. Ample evidence can be collected in support of the fact that a slowly rising price level or a slowly falling price level has always led to greater economic gains to the community. Moreover, from the point of view of full employment stabilisation of price level is not the desired objective.

And so, on account of these difficulties it has never been considered as a laudable objective. Moreover, the prices vary from one sector to another quite considerably and exhibit different trends. Now, it is generally agreed that stabilisation of economic activity consistent with full employment and economic growth is more important than the internal price stability. However, there are some who hold that instead of the prices of commodities, the prices of factors of production should be stabilised. In fact, changing prices in different sectors of the economy in response to changes in demand or supply should be more helpful in correcting maladjustments in the economy than a stable price level. If it were possible to achieve both full employment and price stability simultaneously then it would be the best situation, otherwise the objective of price stability will have to be sacrificed. Price stability can be a suitable objective of monetary policy in those countries which are large in size, which are agricultural and in which the volume of foreign trade is quite insignificant. In addition to these theoretical objections there are also technical difficulties involved in controlling the volume of credit and the price level. It has been experienced that the banking system has always been more successful in checking a rise in prices than to stimulate them. Hayek has rightly pointed out that the objective of price stability ignores "the realistic requirements of a dynamic society.[2]

Alternative Price Policies

Since price stability as an objective of monetary policy, on account of its serious weakneses, has lost its position, various alternatives have been suggested by economists. These suggestions can be grouped under two heads, *viz.*, a policy of slowly rising prices and a policy of slowly falling prices. A policy of slowly rising prices has been recommended on two grounds: firstly, it tends to stimulate production and increase employment; and secondly, it reduces the real burden of money debt which has become an ordinary feature of our economic life. In spite of these advantages, such a policy suffers from certain defects. Firstly, it does not do justice to fixed income groups, as with the rise in the prices, the volume of goods and services over which a unit of money possesses the command diminishes; although it is pointed out that the effects of very gently rising prices would be spread over such a long period that no one will feel conscious of it. Secondly, by providing incentive to enterprise it provides shelter even to those who are utterly incompetent. Before a generally extra stimulus to entrepreneurs is provided, it becomes essential to know whether a particular enterprise stands in need of such stimulus. Not only this, if by providing stimulus through a rise in prices, cost factors also go up, the incentive would evaporate. Again, such a policy would discourage capital formation, may lead to deterioration in quality owing to over-production and may also encourage speculation. Therefore, before such a policy is adopted, all these factors need be taken into consideration.

On the other hand, there are some economists who have made a case for slowly falling prices as the objective of monetary policy. They have pointed

---

2. F.A. von Hayek, *Monetary Theory and the Trade Cycle,* pp. 18-22.

out a number of advantages of such a policy. Firstly, it keeps enterprise up-to-date and secures the benefit of scientific advancement to the society in the form of lower prices or greater purchasing power of money. If the price level falls by almost the same percentage as the increase in production, an automatic increase in the real earnings of the wage earners would be secured and they would share the national prosperity without any adjustment of money wages. It is also argued that falling prices bring proper relationship between savings and investment which brings business crisis. According to Robertson, "It is true that if prices fall, the real value of balances rises but that is mere automatic reflection of the increase in productivity....If you then inflate credit to keep prices stable, you are inflicting enforced savings, not transforming voluntary saving into industrial capital. There is all the difference in the world from this point of view between an increase of credit in proportion to population and an increase in proportion to production." So, on the one hand, when a policy of slowly falling prices promotes business efficiency, improves distribution, discourages incompetent entrepreneurs, provides large benefits to consumers and improves overall balance of payments position of the country, it has certain difficulties as well. For example, it discourages production and the levels of output, income and employment fall under the impact of falling prices; secondly such a situation may lead to depression and thirdly when once a deflationary spiral starts, it becomes very difficult to control it. "In a world full of imperfect and monopolistic competition and of monopolies and combinations, it is difficult to know in advance by how much prices would be falling after each unit of time. This is so, as the current rate of economic advancement cannot be known till it has taken place."

We have discussed above the different policies regarding price stability advocated by different economists. It seems to be a highly controversial issue. These policies are meant for long-term operation, while most of us are concerned with the short-term consequences or benefits, namely, mitigation of cyclical fluctuations in economic activity and maximum possible utilisation of resources. The best policy in regard to level of prices should be governed by the economic situation of the country. For that matter, any policy cannot become a permanent feature.

Exchange Stabilisation *vs.* Price Stabilisation

Like many other economic issues, in this field also we find economists differing with each other. It, however, is certain that it is possible to achieve both these objectives simultaneously. Under gold standard, exchange stabilisation was successfully achieved but at the expense of internal price stability. Both these objectives could be achieved even under gold standard provided that the rules of the game were not strictly observed. Besides, there could be situations in which both these objectives could be compatible. For example, in a situation where economy is operating at the overfull employment and the country is facing unfavourable balance of payments; it would be the best policy to control currency and credit and thereby to stabilise the rate of exchange as well as the internal price level. In another hypothetical case, if the economy is passing through a phase of depression and unemployment and if it is enjoying a favourable balance of payments, the expansion of currency and credit will simultaneously lead to the fulfilment of both the objectives. But these two situations are only hypothetical and can never be found in the practical world. It has also been pointed that it is also possible to achieve these objectives simultaneously if there is international monetary co-operation amongst the countries of the world; and a number of countries had reached a situation where both these objectives stood achieved with the establishment of the International Monetary Fund. But, since the breakdown of the International Monetary Fund system in the early 1970s, the situation again became precarious.

3. Neutrality of Money

Certain economists like Wicksteed, Koopmans, Hayek, Robertson, etc. advocate that the objective of the monetary policy should be to keep the money neutral, *i.e.*, to ensure that the quantity of money in circulation does not affect the prices. These economists believe that business fluctuations occur because of the changes in the quantity of money in circulation and if the disturbances caused by monetary changes could be controlled or eliminated, then instead of vigorous fluctuations, only smooth adjustments to changes in technology, consumers' preferences, or acts of God will take place in the economy. A neutral money policy thus, implies two things: first, the monetary authority will have to be given authority to counter balance changes in the velocity of circulation of money caused by hoarding and dishoarding by people. Second, unless basic changes in the structure of the economy, *viz.*, population, technology, etc. are compensated by changes in the quantity or velocity of circulation of money, there would be such disturbances as would be quite contrary to the neutral money theory. It should also be noted that changes in prices may even occur when money remains neutral, owing to the changes in the volume of transactions and improved productivity of the factors of production. This theory has, therefore, been criticised on a number of points: firstly, it is based on wrong premises, *i.e.*, it carries with it all the assumptions on which the quantity theory of money is based. Secondly, it is not easy to implement this policy because it is not possible to keep the supply of money constant in actual practice without which money cannot act in a neutral fashion. Thirdly, even after keeping the money supply constant at a particular level, it is not sure that the price level would be stable because other factors like technological improvements may cause changes in the level of output, which would certainly lead to a decline in the price level owing to a decline in the production cost. Fourthly, the policy appears to be self-contradictory, because on the one hand the protagonists of this policy advocate that the state should play a passive role or the state should not interfere in the economic affairs, on the other hand for maintaining a constant supply of money they expect monetary authority to make frequent adjustments with the fundamental changes in the economy. Fifthly, the policy is not practicable at all because the money supply cannot be kept constant permanently at a particular level. In the present day dynamic economic situation, money can never play a passive role. Thus, the neutral money theory has not been proved by empirical tests and has not therefore, advanced beyond the stage of academic discussion.

4. Stability in the Level of Income

Economists, like Hawtrey, who regard cyclical fluctuations as a purely monetary phenomenon advocate that the objective of monetary policy should be to stabilise level of income by avoiding the over-issue of credit at all costs. Income stabilisation also implies that in a situation of falling levels of income and investment owing to deflation or hoarding by people the monetary authority should expand credit so that the income is restored to its former level. But, this is not an easy objective to achieve. First, constant changes in the volume of credit, will definitely create an atmosphere of uncertainty in the economy which would dampen its growth. Second, the present distribution of national income is already not equitable and the maintenance of the present level would hardly be justified. Finally, for stabilising income, the level of employment will have to be stabilised first and the present level of employment is already so low that it cannot be considered satisfactory for stabilisation.

5. Full Employment

As already stated, nowadays achievement of full employment is considered to be the most important objective of the monetary policy. According to Keynes, "The object of a monetary policy should be to reduce the ebb and flow of the trade cycles, and bring about equilibrium between savings and investment at the level of full employment."[3] The object of a monetary policy should, therefore, be not only to cure the booms and depressions, when already occurred, as advocated by pre-Keynesian classical economists, but also to check the recessionary or inflationary tendencies in their initial stages. For achieving the full employment of available resources, the monetary policy

---

3. J.M. Keynes, *A Tract on Monetary Reforms,* 1923.

should aim at increasing the level of consumption and investment spending in the economy. In the short period, the consumption spending being more or less stable, the monetary policy should aim at raising the level of investment spending, by following a cheap money policy which will encourage borrowing for investment and which through multiplier-acceleration effect will raise the level of investment. Once the level of full employment is achieved, then the monetary policy can maintain it through the equalisation of saving and investment. But as soon as the point of full employment is achieved, this policy should be reversed. If this is not done, the economy will face a situation of hyper inflation. It would be more prudent for the state to pursue a policy of stable price level. Thus, it would be seen that a cautious policy objective of full employment should be integrated with the objective of price stabilisation, and also with the objective of exchange stabilisation because the maintenance of full employment cannot be possible without the maintenance of equilibrium in the balance of payments. In short, we can say that the full employment objective is the most ideal one because in its achievement, the other two objectives are automatically achieved.

6. Economic Growth

In recent years, the emphasis has been shifted from full employment to economic growth as the main objective of monetary policy. Modern economists view monetary policy as a long-term policy, because: (*i*) full employment in an economy cannot be possible without increasing the rate of economic growth; (*ii*) an increasing rate of economic growth is also necessary because of the desire among people of enjoying a high standard of living; and (*iii*) an ever-increasing rate of economic growth is essential for the survival of less-developed countries because of the intensive competition prevailing at present in the world. As a matter of fact, economic growth is now considered as the primary objective of monetary policy in the highly developed countries of the west. However, Prof. Howard Ellis has strongly objected to the pursuing of this objective by the less-developed countries because a developing economy is highly susceptible to inflationary pressures. But the fear entertained by Ellis has no valid ground and most of the economists have agreed that the monetary policy in a developing economy has to play a significant role in increasing the rate of economic growth. Economic growth implies a sustained increase in the real national income or per capita output. It means: (*i*) an increase in real output, (*ii*) the goods and services should be such as to satisfy consumer wants, and (*iii*) the process of growth should be achieved within the framework of economic system. For a sustained economic growth it is essential that firstly, the production capacity of the economy should continuously expand and secondly, the demand for those goods and services which are being produced under the impact of growth should correspondingly increase. This is necessary because if the production capacity of the economy exceeds the level of aggregate demand, the idle plant capacity would not be fully utilised and unemployment would be the ultimate result. Consequently, the process of growth would be stultified. If on the other hand, aggregate demand exceeds the production capacity of the economy, prices would ultimately rise. Consequently, speculative activities would be encouraged and inefficient conduct of business resulting into boom must ultimately end in recession. Such a sort of situation would hamper the process of economic growth. In short, for a sustained economic growth at higher rates it is necessary to maintain a proper balance between the production capacity of the economy and the level of aggregate demand. An important condition for a sustained economic growth is that the total demand should be increased to match total output resulting from growth. In this respect, monetary policy must be directed towards achievement of two objectives, *viz.*, (*i*) to establish a balance between the total money demand and the production capacity which, as already pointed out, means a restrictive monetary policy, when the total demand exceeds production capacity, and an expansionary policy when the total money demand is far below the production capacity of the economy; and (*ii*) to create favourable conditions for saving and investment which implies that the rate of capital formation must be very high. Since capital formation is not possible without saving and people cannot be encouraged to save unless the prices remain stable, a policy of price stabilisation becomes inevitable. Thus, the monetary policy can help the process of economic growth by: (*i*) minimising changes in the level of prices and economic activity, and (*ii*) maintaining high levels of saving and investment. It may, however, be noted that the success of the monetary policy in achieving the objective of economic growth depends essentially on two things—firstly, the monetary policy should be flexible, *i.e.*, if the aggregate supply of goods exceeds the aggregate money demand then the monetary authority should pursue a policy of credit expansion and in the reverse situation the monetary authority should pursue a restrictive monetary policy. The flexibility in the monetary policy is very essential for establishing an equilibrium between aggregate money demand on the one side and the aggregate supply of goods and services on the other. Secondly, it should be capable of promoting capital formation in the economy which can be possible only when the level of prices stands fairly stabilised. Again, it should also promote the inflow of foreign capital which is so essential for the economic growth of a country.

The growth objective is considered superior to other objectives, because: (*i*) the other objectives, such as, exchange stabilisation, price stabilisation or even full employment involve the concentration of the monetary authority on the short-term requirements only, and (*ii*) an ever increasing rate of economic growth is the fundamental requirement of every country. We may, therefore, conclude that the objective of economic growth cannot be achieved without achieving the objectives of price stabilisation and exchange stabilisation. And full employment of resources in an economy cannot be possible without an increasing rate of economic growth, and therefore, the growth objective appears to be the best objective of monetary policy because it enwraps other objectives as welt.

3. Targets of Monetary Policy

The policy tools available to the monetary authority do not influence directly the policy variables namely, growth, employment and prices. That is why they have to depend on intermediate targets which they feel can be reasonably controlled by the instruments available to them. But this will depend upon the mechanism through which the various instruments of monetary policy are expected to influence the final targets of economic growth, full employment and price stability. Any monetary policy can aim at achieving these targets by three instruments namely : (*i*) money supply, (*ii*) credit availability, and (*iii*) interest rates.

The monetary authority cannot control the level of output and prices directly, and therefore, it chooses the growth rate of money supply as an intermediate target. Friedman is of the view that the monetary authority should avoid creating inflationary and recessionary tendencies and should allow the money supply to grow at the rate of 3 to 4 per cent per year for a smooth growth of the economy.

Credit availability and manipulation of interest rates are other target variables of monetary policy. The monetary authority can influence the short-term interest rates. It can also change the credit availability and affect economic activity by rationing of credit or selective credit control, etc. It can also influence the level of economic activity through its expansionary or contractionary monetary policies through changes in the short-term interest rates. But these have their own limitations. First, it cannot be firmly predicted that the size and the timing of the effects of changes in the rate of interest and credit availability on the aggregate spending would be according to expectations and as desired. Second, regarding rates of interest, the real interest rate is more important than the nominal interest rate. While nominal interest rate can be controlled, the real rate of interest cannot, because of the difficulty in measuring the expected rate of inflation. If the monetary authority raises the nominal rate, the real rate will automatically rise. But this may not always happen. When the money interest rates are raised the expectations of price inflation may also grow simultaneously. In such a situation a rise in the nominal interest rate may lead to a fall in the expected real rate. Thus, the monetary authority cannot rely on changes in the nominal rate of interest as a target of monetary policy.

Changes in the credit availability cannot be a stable target of monetary policy, because the expected results may be offset by expansion of credit by the non-bank financial intermediaries.

So, money supply and rate of interest are the intermediate targets of monetary policy. But, both can not be adopted simultaneously. The monetary authority can either change the money supply or it can manipulate the rate of interest. If the monetary authority targets the money supply, it will lose control of the rate of interest and *vice versa.* Therefore, generally the monetarists favour the target of money supply. Because: (*i*) it can be measured. Since a variety of interest rates prevail in the market the adjustment of nominal rates to real interest rates is not easy; (*ii*) the linkage between the money supply and the nominal GNP is more direct and predictable than the link between interest and nominal GNP.

According to Tobin, market yield on equities can be a target variable. He suggests that the monetary authority should strive at equating the market yield on equities with the real return expected from the investment in physical capital. With the increase in the real rate of return on equities the value of existing capital equipment will decline and the purchase of new capital equipment would be discouraged. Tobin holds that this target is superior to others, because market value of equity capital can be easily observed and an index of market value can be compared with a price index of investment goods. But this has its own difficulties. It is not easy to compare the value of existing assets with that of newly produced assets. Besides, linking of investments with stock market changes is not possible.

The targets of monetary policy, as discussed above, are not easy to be relied upon singly by any monetary authority. A combination of these targets would have to be adopted according to existing economic and financial conditions. It may, however, be added that economists have not accepted Tobin's suggestion regarding the adoption of market yield on equities as a target of monetary policy.

4. Indicators of Monetary Policy

The targets discussed above are also the indicators of monetary policy. Money supply can be a good indicator of the monetary policy provided it is under the full control of the central bank. The money supply determines both the level of output and prices in the short period and the level of prices and nominal aggregate demand in the long period. The central bank can bring about changes in the money supply through open market operations and changes in reserve requirements. This is the contention of the monetarists. Money supply affects aggregate demand through effects on a wide range of assets. Keynes, however, held that money supply changes affect the aggregate demand through the changes in the prices of bonds only but the monetarists hold that the money supply changes affect changes in the level of aggregate demand through changes in the prices of a large number of assets and not of bonds only. In the first instance, increased money supply will be used to buy not only financial assets but real assets as well. Any fall in the interest rates owing to an increase in the demand for financial assets, will be only temporary. Interest rates will rise with a rise in the GNP, because money would be needed for meeting the requirements of day-to-day cash transactions owing to the expanding business. Firms will take more loans and consequently the rate of interest will rise. Rate of interest will also rise because of an expansionary monetary policy.

The lowering or increasing of rates of interest, after an expansionary monetary policy will depend on the speed and strength with which the GNP changes and on the expectations regarding future prices. The same will be the position regarding the lowering or increasing of interest rates after a contractionary monetary policy.

Regarding interest rate as an indicator of monetary policy, Keynesians and the monetarists hold different views. While agreeing that the rate of interest can not be a potent indicator because of lack of tight control of the central bank both of them differ regarding the transmission mechanism. The Keynesians hold that increase in money supply will reduce the rate of interest, if the demand for money does not become perfectly elastic. A reduction in the interest rate will raise the level of investment if it is not interest-inelastic. So, the interest rates will not rise with an increase in the money supply. On the contrary, the monetarists hold that the increase in money supply affects the rate of interest. It shall happen like this. The central bank proposes to increase the money supply through open market operations. This will cause a decline in the rate of interest by increasing the bank reserves, on the basis of which banks would expand their loans. Consequently, the rate of interest will fall but for a short period because the low interest rate will encourage investments, prices of investments goods will rise raising the demand for financial and real assets and ultimately their prices will go up. This process will lead to a rise in the rate of interest. Lastly, when lenders expect prices to rise they purchase interest-bearing securities. This will increase the interest rate. What will be the rate of interest, will depend on the rate of inflation caused by the increased money supply. That is why, Friedman asserts that instead of manipulating the rate of interest the monetary authority should control the money supply.

There is no consensus among the economists regarding the use of these indicators. The creation of an appropriate indicator will require a close look on the various problems that are to be solved. Firstly, the monetary authority will have to have a close look at the nature of money supply and then to find out appropriate measures to control it. So, the problem would be, as to what extent the money supply will respond to a change in the desired direction. Secondly, the monetary authority shall have to make sure that the money supply will affect the level of economic activity to the desired extent. Finally, the monetary authority will also have to take note of the proposed indicator's exogeneity relative to the economic variables that it decides to influence.

5. Monetary Policy During Depression (Expansionary Monetary Policy)

The chief characteristics of depression are falling prices, incomes, output and employment, low rates of interest and unusually high liquidity preference. The objective of monetary policy during depression is to increase the velocity of circulation of money, to satisfy demands of people for hoarding, (including precautionary and speculative motives), to strengthen the cash position of banking and non-banking institutions, to stimulate lending, to reduce the interest rates, etc. So, the aim of the monetary policy is to expand the supply of credit in the market so that the credit conditions become easy and there is an upward shift in the level of aggregate demand. It means that the monetary authority through open market operations purchases government securities, lowers the reserve requirements of member banks, reduces the discount rate and stimulates consumer and business credit through selective credit control. By taking such measures the central bank reduces the cost of credit and revives the economy. This process can be explained with the help of Fig. 19.1 by using *IS* and *LM* curves.

In panel A of the diagram when the money supply is increased in the economy, the *LM* curve moves to *LM′* which means that the income increases from *OY* to *OY′*. Due to an increase in the aggregate demand, the demand curve shifts from *D* to *D′* as shown in panel B. Consequently, the output increases from *OQ* to *OQ′* at a higher price level *P′*. If all goes well with the monetary policy the equilibrium can be established at *E′* which will represent the full employment situation. But this is very unlikely to happen because it has been witnessed during the depression of the 1930s when the monetary policy failed in stimulating the recovery of the economy from the depression. When the economy is passing through a phase of recession the revival becomes impossible because the business activity comes almost to a grinding halt and the businessmen do not feel inclined to borrow and build up inventories even at a very low rate of interest. They, rather prefer to reduce their inventories by repaying their loans. And, so, the question of further borrowing does not arise.

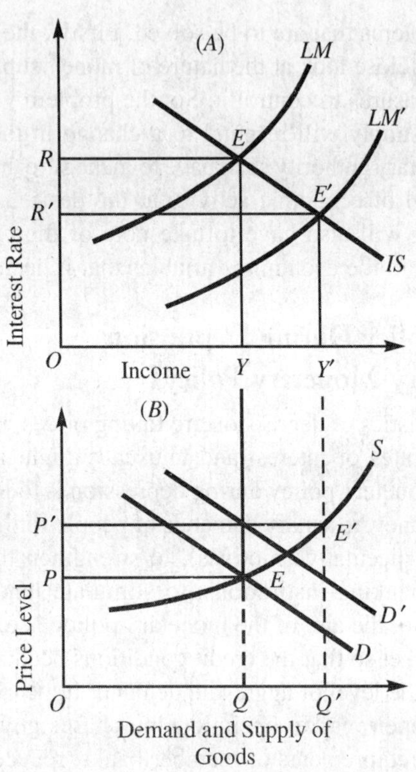

Fig. 19.1

Due to growing unemployment and reduction in incomes, the consumers also do not feel encouraged to borrow from the banks and purchase consumer durables. It is possible that in such a situation an expansionary monetary policy or a cheap money policy may not lead to the revival of the economy but it can surely prevent the situation from getting worse This is what Keynes has tried to explain in his *General Theory,* that is, in severe depression, a highly elastic liquidity preference schedule or the liquidity trap renders monetary policy utterly ineffective. But, a monetary policy can certainly prove effective if it aims to offset the liquidity preference of the people to the maximum possible by pumping reserves in the banking system so as to induce banks not to liquidate their earning assets, and supply cash to all sorts of lending institutions through open market operations. The central bank should try to develop confidence among the business community by lowering the rates of interest and by holding up bond prices. If this much is done successfully other forces will automatically be activised.

6. Monetary Policy During Inflation (Restrictive Monetary Policy)

During inflationary conditions the marginal efficiency of capital becomes very high owing to rising level of prices, income, output and employment. Consumption and investment spending are at their peak and business activity expands rapidly, credit goes on expanding and a stage is reached when the banks find it difficult to cope with the ever-increasing demand for credit. Under such conditions the objectives of monetary policy should be to reduce the velocity of circulation of money and squeeze credit so that the level of aggregate demand falls rapidly. This objective can be achieved by increasing the rates of interest, followed by open market operations. Margin requirements and consumer credit conditions could also be tightened. If even then level of aggregate spending does not fall appreciably then reserve requirements may be raised to curtail the power of the banks to expand credit. It is no doubt easier to check inflation than deflation with the help of monetry policy, but it is not without limitations.

7. Role of Monetary Policy in Developing Economies

The chief objective of the monetary policy in developing economies should be, obviously, to raise the rate of capital formation and economic growth. This can be done by adopting a policy of cheap money and to stimulate investment by lowering the rate of interest, directing investment into desired channels through selective credit controls (if investment is found to be misdirected) and by undertaking public investment on a large scale (since private investment may not be forthcoming in adequate amounts). In view of scarcity and shyness of capital, some economists have suggested a policy of high rates of interest for such economies. In their opinion, high rates of interest would channelise the scarce capital only to the most productive uses and would eliminate wasteful use of resources. It would stimulate savings and check inflation. It is true that a policy of high 'interest rates may be successful in doing all this but it may not be desirable to generally restrict investment just for keeping inflation under check. In fact, a mild dose of inflation helps in raising the level of investment. But, if the inflationary pressure continues mounting up, then the monetary authority would be required to use both direct and indirect methods of credit control. Of these measures, the open market operations cannot be of much help because in such economies the bill market is generally small and undeveloped. The central bank does not have a complete control over the commercial banks and therefore they maintain an elastic cash-deposit ratio. The commercial banks are also not encouraged to invest in government securities because of their low rate of interest, and they prefer to keep their reserves in liquid form. The commercial banks generally also do not borrow from the central bank.

Similarly, the bank rate policy can also not be effective because of: (*i*) lack of bills of discount, (*ii*) the small and undeveloped bill market, (*iii*) a large non-monetised sector, (*iv*) the existence of indigenous bankers, beyond the control of the central bank, (*v*) habit of the commercial banks to maintain large cash reserves, and (*vi*) a large unorganised money market.

However, it is believed that the use of variable reserve ratio can be more helpful than the bank rate policy or the open market operations. This is because the commercial banks keep large cash reserves. But this also has its limitations because the non-banking financial intermediaries are outside the control of the central bank. They do not keep their deposits with the central bank and therefore the central bank is unable to control them. Even among the commercial banks those which do not maintain excess liquidity will be affected more than those which maintain excess liquidity.

It is therefore held that qualitative credit control methods are more effective in such economies. In developing economies people generally tend to invest in gold jewellery, real estate, etc. instead of investing their money in productive channels. The selective credit control measures are therefore more suitable for controlling and limiting credit facilities for speculative and unproductive activities. The selective credit control methods, as already explained, may be: changing the margin requirements, regulating consumer credit and rationing of credit.

The monetary policy can create a favourable climate both for saving and investment in such economies. The shape of investment would, however, depend on the policy of credit institutions and the forms of credit control that are adopted. In most developed countries, the commercial banks provide only short-term credit which is chiefly used for carrying inventories, purchasing land and real estate and for financing the production of export crops. The government will have to make guarantees or provide rediscount facilities, if the commercial banks are to be induced to advance medium and long-term loans. Selective credit controls can also influence pattern of investment and production. The commercial banks can differentiate between different sectors and industries in matters of cost and amount of credit, the duration, the amount of collateral, etc. If the central bank has adequate control on the commercial banks, selective control could be exercised to indirectly influence the behaviour of banks by having different rediscount rates for different types of loans or by making exception in regard to reserve requirements on a selective basis, etc.

For correcting an adverse balance of payments, the monetary authority besides excercising direct control on foreign exchanges may make use of the bank rate. It is a well-known fact that developing countries suffer from serious imbalance in their balance of payments. They have to incur foreign loans to meet their planned targets of development, to develop their infrastructure like power, irrigation, transport, etc. to undertake direct productive activities in strategic sectors like iron and steel, fertilizers, chemicals, etc. and have to import huge quantity of equipment, machinery, raw materials, etc. Their exports do not keep pace with imports. Moreover the exports are high in prices due to inflation. Consequently, there is imbalance on their balance of payments. This imbalance can be narrowed down by raising the bank rate and the general structure of interest rates. High rates of interest will also attract the inflow of foreign funds and help in reducing the imbalance in the balance of payments.

It is also held that a policy of high rates of interest would induce people to save more, develop banking habits among them, speed up the monetisation of the economy and thus promote capital formation and economic growth. Again, it will channelise scarce capital resources to more productive uses. Since high rates of interest generally discourage investment, some economists are not in their favour. However, empirical studies have proved that in developing economies investment is interest inelastic, because interest is just a small fraction of the total investment cost.

For the success of the monetary policy in developing countries it is very essential that the currency and credit system of the country is reorganised along sound lines. Banking and credit facilities must be extended to all people, especially in rural areas. The monetary authority should promote branch-banking in rural areas particularly. The monetary policy can go a long way in doing all this. Again, the working of the central bank must be made more effective by bringing the non-monetised sector in its fold so that changes in the money stock or rates of interest may produce desired effects on economic activity, and develop a well-organised money market which is at present completely missing in these countries.

Finally, debt management is another area in which the monetary policy can play an effective role in such economies. The monetary authority can fix proper timing of issuing of government bonds, stabilise their prices and minimise the cost of servicing of public debt. In developing economies public borrowing is very essential for funding the plan projects and for controlling the money supply. But public borrowing must be at cheap rates. It is only then that the government bonds will be more attractive to the people and will also keep their burden low.

We now summarise below the main limitations of the monetary policy in the developing economies:

1. Unorganised money and capital market.
2. A large monetised sector.
3. A large number of NBFIs outside the control of the central bank.

4. Large cash reserves with the commercial banks.
5. Existence of foreign banks.
6. Large hoarding in the form of jewellery, gold, real estate, etc.

It is because of these limitations that the monetary policy in developing countries has not been able to play an effective role in the fulfilment of its objectives.

8. Assessment of the Role of Monetary Policy

We have discussed the merits and demerits of the various objectives of monetary policy and the instruments that are made use of by the central banks. To summarise, we can say that the central bank has a number of instruments for operating its monetary policy, *e.g.*, the bank rate policy, the open market operations, the changes in the banks' cash reserves or minimum requirements in respect of margins, selective credit control, etc. In addition to these instruments there are three other adjuncts to monetary policy, *viz.*, (*i*) physical controls, (*ii*) fiscal policy, and (*iii*) other instruments. On account of the failure of the bank rate policy, the governments in various countries had to adopt a policy of physical controls. Such controls have been made use of during war times, like the rationing of all consumer goods, the limitation and restriction of imports, the licensing of raw materials and building and the control of investment. In a democratic country, the decision for planning the investment and also for enterprise is taken by individuals while in a planned economy the government itself decides what shall be produced. A large measure of the central planning had no necessity to be introduced during the World War II, and this made it easier for a government which favoured physical controls. And even after the war was over, these controls continued for some time. In less developed countries, pledged to economic development, such controls are still being resorted to as a matter of general policy. It may, however, be noted that these controls do not get rid of the causes of inflation, they only succeed in suppressing them.

So far as fiscal policy is concerned, even before the World War II it was regarded as an alternative to bank rate. Since, as it was thought, a low bank rate had failed to stimulate business activity, it was suggested that this might be accomplished through an inflationary budget. This was the school of thought which favoured deficit financing in times of trade slump. In western countries many economists favoured a policy of deficit budgeting during slump conditions and a policy of surplus budgeting during inflationary conditions. Thus, the budget became a dynamic instrument of economic policy. In the countries of the West, fiscal policy however did not replace, but supplemented the physical controls which had been previously employed. Some economists have argued that the heavy taxation required to obtain the budget surplus is of itself inflationary in its effect in the environment of full employment. Additional direct taxation cannot be imposed on account of its disincentive effect on the workers with the result that production suffers, and so the higher taxation tends to fall on commodities, thereby raising their prices and cost of living and so stimulating further demands for wage increases which, in conditions of full or 'over-full' employment were likely to be granted. To permit a level of purchasing power in excess of that desired by the monetary authorities and then to remove this excess thorough taxation makes fiscal policy a rather crude device. For fiscal policy to be effective it must be applied quickly and not delayed until the next normal budget time.

During recent times, bank rate and fiscal policy have been frequently combined and supplemented by other instruments of policy. These have been termed as a 'package deal'. This term came to be applied to the use of a number of instruments of monetary policy in combination with one another at a particular time for the purpose of controlling inflation or correcting an adverse balance of payments. Instruments of monetary policy or their adjuncts have rarely been employed singly. In any particular situation it is not possible to say, therefore, precisely what influence each individual instrument of policy has had. Only the effectiveness of the 'package deal' as a whole can be judged.

Apart from the above, limitations of the monetary policy also arise on account of the time lag between the decision and its actual execution. It is, therefore, necessary that the monetary authority must have a fairly good idea about the time which would elapse between the formation and the implementation of the policy. This is one reason why Prof. Milton Friedman has criticised the flexibility of the monetary policy and has advocated that the central bank should increase the money supply at a fixed rate annually consistent with the annual rate of growth of the economy.

9. Operational Aspects of Monetary Policy

Thus far, a discussion on the general aspects of the monetary policy under different conditions. Now we describe in detail its operational results. As already stated, the chief objective of the monetary policy is to influence the level of total spending by varying: (*i*) the rate of interest, and (*ii*) the volume of credit. We take up these one by one.

1. Interest Policy

Since interest is the price of credit, a rise in its rate should contract the demand for credit and thus reduce the aggregate demand. The monetary authority can influence both the short-term and the long-term rates of interest. Variations in the short-term rate of interest can be introduced by (*a*) changing the bank rate, and (*b*) selling and purchasing treasury bills. Changes in bank rate may directly affect the rate of interest on bank loans and may influence other short-term rates, *e.g.*, money at call, bills discounted, etc. But it is doubtful whether such changes will affect investment or consumption expenditure to any appreciable extent. Small firms may have to cut down their inventories, and consumers may be discouraged, by the higher repayments, from taking personal loans from banks. This is not likely to happen as the interest charges form only a part of the cost of holding stocks or of .the total instalment repayment of a loan. Since most personal saving is now contractual, higher interest rates are also not likely to encourage personal saving. Since short-term interest changes do little to discourage spending, these might prove inflationary in nature because of a number of difficulties. First, these may increase difficulties in balance of payments on current account by increasing the cost of short-term borrowing from abroad. Second, these increase the cost of servicing the national debt. Third, the sale of treasury bills, by which bank rate policy is reinforced, does little to change the overall liquidity position of the banks, for it simply replaces cash by another liquid asset. Finally, the rise in the short-term rate may increase the long-term rate, since short-term loans are substitutes for long-term loans, there is bound to be a tendency for the rates of interest to move in the same direction. But the extent to which such a movement takes place depends upon people's expectations of the future long-term rate. However, a change in the short-term rate may or may not affect the long-term rate. If it does, it may not be in harmony with government policy. So, by influencing the long-term rate, the government may affect the level of aggregate demand. But this has also certain difficulties in its way. First, the long-term rate can be lowered by decreasing the demand for or by increasing the supply of money. The demand for money will decline if there is an appropriate change in attitudes to either active or speculative balances, though both are interdependent. Thus, the demand for active balances will decline if the government follows a deflationary policy, if incomes are paid at shorter intervals, if the liquidity of other assets is increased or if people are willing to suffer the inconvenience of meeting their requirements with smaller balances. The demand for speculative balances will depend on people's estimation about 'normal' rate of interest. If they estimate that it will fall then their demand will decrease. But, changing the long-term rate of interest by causing people to shift their demand for liquidity is not practicable. This aim can be fulfilled more easily by altering the supply of money—which will not only lower the rate of interest directly but will also lower it indirectly by increasing the liquidity of other assets. But in a period of depression when the rate of interest is already very low and the demand for money is infinitely elastic, any increase in money will be absorbed by adding to liquid hoards. It goes into the 'liquidity trap'. In other words, when bonds rise to a certain price, people are so convinced that the next move will be downwards, that the supply of bonds offered to the government is infinite at this price because people just want liquidity. The rate of interest, thus, cannot fall below a certain level unless a penalty is imposed on holding idle balances. This implies that the authorities are powerless to bring down the rate of interest for stimulating investment. The only method of expanding the income is either by improving the expectations of the entrepreneurs or by increasing the propensity to consume.

Second, even if the rate of interest is altered, it may have little effect on the aggregate demand because, firstly, investment may be interest-inelastic and hence changes in the rate of interest can do little directly to influence the level of investment spending; and secondly, the *MPC* may be relatively low, which means a small multiplier and hence any change in investment owing to a change in the rate of interest will not affect the level of income very substantially. Thus, the interest policy working through the effects which follow directly from a change in the price of borrowing, will be ineffective where investment is interest-inelastic or the *MPC* is low. If either of these conditions holds, the main effort must be directed to shifting the position of *IS* curve by playing on the expectations of entrepreneurs or by varying the propensity to consume. Such a change in the expectations of the entrepreneurs may result indirectly from interest policy. Thus, by lowering the rate of interest, the government may convince the entrepreneurs that it is committed to a policy of expansion. The chances of success in this direction are greater in the midway stage between boom and slump. When the boom is gathering momentum, a high rate of interest may not deter investment. In a depression when entrepreneurs are pessimistic, a low rate of interest may be ineffective in promoting a recovery.

Third, not only may interest policy be ineffective (except when it affects expectations), it may be undesirable, because: (*a*) a small change in the long-term interest rates may cause much larger changes in short-term rates, thus producing complications in the short-term market, because in a short-term security an early re-payment of the full nominal value being guaranteed, any fall in its price can only come about because there has been a general rise in interest rates and thus the yield to maturity of this particular security has correspondingly declined. To avoid this, the authorities must convince people that the change in the long-term rate is permanent. (*b*) A higher rate of interest increases the cost of borrowing from abroad, especially when there has been a considerable impact on the short-term market. This increases invisible payments on the current account of the balance of payments. (*c*) A higher rate of interest increases the cost of internal borrowing, thereby increasing the taxation burden of servicing the 'national debt.' (*d*) Interest policy does not discriminate between: (*i*) firms which export a high proportion of their output and firms which do not, and (*ii*) projects of high and low social value, *e.g.*, a slum clearance scheme and a gambling club. (*e*) Interest policy may increase instability. Unlike fiscal policy which contains an element of automatic stabilisation, interest policy requires a deliberate decision of the authorities. It may occur at the wrong time, for there is a large measure of uncertainty regarding the speed at which an interest change will work or the exact effect on the expectations of entrepreneurs. An error in timing may increase instability; for example, if a rise in the rate of interest coincides with the downturn in business activity.

Fourth, it may create difficulties for the government to manage public debt. The government borrowing by treasury bills has to be reduced if it puts too large a supply of liquid assets in the hands of the banks. A switch to long-term borrowing implies an addition to the supply of long-term bonds and thus a fall in their price *i.e.*, a rise in the long-term rate of interest. Can the authorities permit such a rise? The major holders of long-term government debt, owing to inflation will lose confidence in holding it, because of the erosion in its value. If it possesses a high degree of liquidity, they will be induced to hold such debt. This means that the holders must be convinced that its price is not likely to fall, *i.e.*, that the authorities will not allow the long-term rate to rise, at least in the near future. Any weakening here would result in a considerable rise in the cost of government borrowing, for people would be unwilling to purchase bonds except at an initial high rate of interest. In practice, however, this puts the government in a serious difficulty. If there are more sellers of bonds than buyers, the government will have to instruct its brokers to buy the surplus in the market in order to support the existing price. But, this would mean that the Central Bank is carrying out open market operations in the wrong direction—instead of tightening credit it is putting extra cash in the hands of the public and increasing the liquidity of commercial banks. The latter can be corrected by instructing the banks to restrict lending. The former presents few difficulties provided people simply add to their liquid balances in the bond market. But suppose, this Keynesian view does not prevail and as Friedman and others suggest, there is an overflow of the extra money directly on to the markets for goods and services, then the government's task of managing public debt as economically as possible directly clashes with the aim of controlling inflation. And, therefore, at times, it is considered desirable, to hold down the rate of interest, resort has to be made to restricting the volume of credit.

2. The Volume of Credit

Since the policy of a high long-term rate of interest is full of disadvantages, monetary authorities, since the World War II, have, as far as possible, fixed the rate of interest and carried out measures to maintain it. In practice, this means keeping the long-term rate below that which would be determined in the market by the demand for and supply of funds. And so, the demand for money has exceeded its supply. Consequently, since the World War II, advances have not been allocated by interest rates; instead, some kind of non-price 'rationing' has always had to be imposed by banks usually on requests from the government. Varying the availability of credit, therefore, simply means that the monetary authorities are changing the stringency of their 'rationing' terms. The policy takes three main forms, *viz.*, (1) changing the amount of liquidity in the economy, (2) direct controls over both the amount and type of credit, and (3) hire-purchase controls.

Liquidity in the economy is varied chiefly by influencing the liquidity of the banks. Since the rate of interest is 'controlled' below the market rate, the demand for bank loans exceeds their supply. Thus, curbing the supply of money does not cause the rate of interest to rise as much as it would have risen in a free market; it simply means that bank loans are reduced and the demand for credit exceeds their supply. Similarly, if the authorities increase the supply of money, advances can increase. But rationing is still necessary; it is simply less stringent.

Rationing of funds has two main effects: first, the Central Bank indicates the lines on which the banks have to operate their 'rationing' policy. This is known as 'moral suasion'. While the instructions of the Central Bank are faithfully carried out, most banks would prefer to work on their own estimate of the creditworthiness of borrowers. They do not like being placed in the awkward position where they have to grant a loan to one customer and refuse to another of equal financial standing. Second, the limitations imposed on the banks have merely led to the development of other sources of credit—'near money'. Thus, in the past the view of liquidity has been too narrow. Consequently, the traditional weapons of open market operations, bank rate and varying liquidity ratios are now not as effective in controlling the economy as was imagined. While they are still used as part of a 'package', they have to be supplemented chiefly by 'moral suasion' which can be more extensive and discriminating in its operation.

Consumption spending (and some short-term investment spending, *e.g.*, on machinery) is regulated by varying the conditions (the percentage deposit and time of repayment) upon which hire purchase credit can be obtained.

Direct monetary controls have the following merits:

(1) They can be introduced or changed quickly. Moreover, adjustments can, if necessary, be made by fine degrees, the Central Bank changing its pressure on the banks by the extent of its requests and selling of securities.

(2) The effects of change are quickly felt, because direct controls are

invariably negative. If it wished, the government could overnight reduce fixed investment to almost zero. Similarly, stiffer hire-purchase terms can reduce the consumption immediately.

(3) Direct controls can be discriminatory.

Direct monetary controls suffer from the following disadvantages:

(1) Controls over investment tend to prevent efficient firms from expanding and to inhibit innovations. Licences, permits and credit are granted on past performance, for the bureaucrats find it easier to decide on this basis.

(2) A cumbersome administrative organisation is required to operate them.

(3) Decisions regarding credit for investments may be taken on political and other considerations rather than on economic merit.

(4) Controls may prove very effective in limiting expansion. Removal of controls may not help expansion of activity.

(5) Certain controls tend to discriminate against small firms. Banks are the chief source of capital to small firms. When they have to ration loans, they tend to favour the larger firms whose creditworthiness is better. This is particularly hard on the small firms whose resources are not so big as those of the large firms.

(6) Controls over consumption fall exclusively on a narrow range of industries, chiefly consumer durables; not only is this unfair, but it tends to disrupt the flow of demand and output. Thus, spending on durable items tends to be bunched and firms find it more difficult to plan for future expansion.

(7) Controls in one sector of the industry increase the strain in other sectors and industries of the economy. Moreover, controls over investment cannot be contained indefinitely if a satisfactory rate of future growth is to be obtained.

(8) In course of time, all controls are circumvented. Legal experts find out ways to overcome the restrictions and to establish sources of finance outside the commercial banks. The borrowers do not find a perfect market; they are able to find other sources when the usual sources are blocked.

Thus, controls over the availability of credit may be useful in the short run and possess the merit of being discriminatory. They are merely useful as emergency measures designed to supplement and strengthen other weapons. They cannot be regarded as an alternative to such measures. We have seen that, in the long run, controls are not effective in limiting the total flow of consumption and investment spending. Borrowers can obtain funds from outside the banking system at higher rates of interest. When government borrows through treasury bills, it provides the liquid assets to the private sector. In short, no control of bank advances is likely to succeed for long in reducing spending unless it is accompanied by a general restriction of liquidity and a general rise in interest rates. Furthermore, borrowers whose requirements of credit are urgent, obtain loans even at higher rates. This implies that the interest policy affects the long-term investment plans and hence may take time to show effect. Thus, the attack on inflation must be broader-based, not relying on monetary policy alone, but extending it to fiscal policy. But even fiscal policy, to be successful, must be supported by an effective monetary policy.

Exercises

1. What are the principal objectives of monetary policy? Is there any conflict between these objectives? If so, how can these conflicts be reconciled?
2. Discuss the main objectives of monetary policy. Can monetary policy achieve them alone?
3. Discuss the relative merits of exchange stability and price stability as objectives of monetary policy.
4. Discuss the various targets of monetary policy.
5. What are the indicators of monetary policy?
6. Discuss the principal instruments of monetary policy. What are their limitations?
7. Discuss the role of monetary policy in a developing economy. What are its limitations?
8. Discuss the objectives of monetary policy. How far monetary policy is effective in controlling inflation?
9. Discuss the controversy over rules and discretion of monetary policy.
10. Distinguish between cheap and dear money policy. Explain their relative effectiveness.
11. Discuss the effectiveness of monetary policy.

●●●

PART THREE

BANKING IN INDIA

Chapter 20

Indian Money Market and Capital Market

1. Introduction

An economy is comprised of various markets such as, labour market, product market, financial market, etc. Financial markets are of two types: money market and capital market. Money market deals in short-term credit. It comprises of various firms and institutions dealing in short-term funds. In money market, relatively liquid and easily marketable assets are bought and sold. These assets are like short-term government securities, treasury bills, bills of exchange, etc. So the entire machinery which channelizes short-term funds is known as money market. Crowther defines money market as, "A collective name given to the various firms and institutions that deal with various grades of near money." Thus, the main constituents of a money market are the lenders and the borrowers of short-terms funds.

2. The Indian Money Market

The Indian money market is composed of : (*i*) the organised sector, and (*ii*) the unorganised sector. The organised sector comprises the Reserve Bank of India, the State Bank of India, the nationalised banks, other commercial banks, the foreign exchange banks, the cooperative banks and the land development banks; while the unorganised sector comprises the sahukars, mahajans, shroffs and other small scale moneylenders in the rural and semi-urban areas. Prior to the establishment of the Reserve Bank of India, the Indian money market was composed of loose-knit units, hardly related to each other. Each unit was self-contained in its respective sphere and followed an independent policy and thus produced a weakening effect upon the entire monetary structure. The Indian commercial banks were jealous of the privileged position enjoyed by the European dominated Imperial Bank of India. The relation between the cooperative banks and commercial banks was not at all regular. The indigenous bankers were like today not at all modern in their moneylending operatings. The exchange banks were purely European in character and managed and controlled the foreign trade of the country to a very considerable extent and competed with the Indian commercial banks in the internal trade of the country as well.

A. Characteristics of the Indian Money Market

Following are the chief characteristics of the Indian money market:

1. Two Sectors. The money market is divided into two sectors with hardly any relationship between them. Consequently, there is a wide disparity in the rates of interest in the two sectors. The financial institutions in the organised sector have been providing mostly long-term loans to indtistries. Their lending rates are also different from the general market rates. Besides, there are also financial intermediaries, such as call-loan brokers, stock brokers and underwriters.

2. Seasonal Monetary Stringency. The Indian money market suffers from seasonal monetary stringency. The seasonality of demand for money and credit follows generally the course of agricultural seasons. The period from end of October to end of April or the beginning of May is the busy season and the agriculturists require funds for financing the post-harvest movement of agricultural products to the final consumer, for financing the needs of seasonal industries like sugar, *khandsari, gur,* etc. and also for maintaining the higher tempo of economic activity after the rainy season. During the busy season the market is generally tight and the rates of interest are quite high, while in the slack season, the rates are quite low and the money market is very cheap. Consequently, there are wide variations in money rates between these two periods.

3. Lacks Elasticity. Another disquieting feature of the money market in India is that it lacks elasticity. The bill market not being fully developed or organised, the use of bills, which facilitates the money to expand or contract easily, quickly and automatically with the changes in the level of economic activity, is not very common in the country. But the development of a bill market definitely depends upon the development of bill-habit in the people which is rather absent in our country. The reasons for this sort of situation are not far to seek: firstly, the liquidity ratio of Indian banks being high, they prefer to invest their funds in government securities, to discounting of bills. Secondly, banks do not get enough encouragement from the Reserve Bank of India in so far as the rediscounting facilities in respect of these bills is concerned. Thirdly, the defective forms of hundies, further hinder the development of a bill market. From the forms it is difficult to distinguish whether the hundi is a purely finance bill or a genuine trade bill, since it is not supported by relevant documents like sale contracts, invoices, etc. Moreover, they are various in forms and are subject to divergent practices and for this very reason it is not always safe to purchase them. Finally, the advantages of cash-credit advances abandon the necessity for bill discounting. On account of the narrowness of the security market, the scope for making use of the open market operations in government securities to control credit is rather limited.

4. Unorganised Sector Lacks Homogeneity. The unorganised sector of the market is beyond the control of the Reserve Bank of India. The indigenous banker like the sahukars, the mahajans, the chettiars are completely free to carry on their transactions in any way they like; there is hardly any difference in short and long-term loans and there is wide disparity in the interest rates. Thus, the unorganised sector lacks homogeneity.

5. Lack of Discount Houses. Again, the Indian money market does not have discount houses and the reason is that there is an utter lack of commercial bills. Only few bills are discounted by the banks, that too is being done by foreign banks.

6. Inter-Bank Market. Finally, the existence of inter-bank market in the country is rather important and is the most sensitive sector of the Indian money market.

B. Constituents of the Indian Money Market

As already stated the Indian money market is divided into the organised sector and the unorganised sector. The organised sector comprises as already stated: (*i*) the Reserve Bank of India; (*ii*) the State Bank of India and its associate banks; (*iii*) the Indian commercial banks; (*iv*) the exchange banks, the cooperative banks; (*v*) special semi-governmental institutions which make their funds available to the money market through the banks; (*vi*) special institutions like the Industrial Development Bank of India, State Finance and Industrial Corporations; (*vii*) nationalised banks; and (*viii*) National Bank for Agriculture and Rural Development, etc. The unorganised sector is so known, because it is not controlled and coordinated by the Reserve Bank of India. It comprises of indigenous bankers and moneylenders. These two sectors are the main suppliers of funds in the money market.

The demand for short-term funds emanate from the borrowers which comprise : (*i*) the Central Government; (*ii*) the State Governments; (*iii*) local bodies; (*iv*) traders, industrialists, exporters and importers, farmers; and (*v*) general public.

C. Special Markets of the Organised Sector

The organised sector comprises of a number of special markets which are as follows:

1. Call Money Market

The call money market, also known as inter-bank call money market is the most important component of the organised sector. The funds or loans are given only for one day. Its chief features are:

(*i*) It provides facilities for making temporarily available the surplus funds of some banks to other banks which need these funds.

(*ii*) The banks are the main participants in the call money market and the State Bank of India is the main lender.

(*iii*) The main link between the borrowers and the lenders are the brokers.

(*iv*) Because of its highly sensitive and competitive nature, the call money market is the chief indicator of the position of liquid funds in the organised money market.

(*v*) The market is highly sensitive to the fluctuations in the demand and supply of funds. It very quickly reacts to the pressure of excess demand for and excess supply of funds. The market is a great leveller of the day-to-day changes in the reserve position of the individual banks and is thus responsible for improving the functioning of the entire banking system.

2. Treasury Bill Market

Treasury bills are the main instruments dealt with in this market. These bills are short-term bills and are the liability of the Government of India. They are initially issued to meet the short-term financial requirements of the government, but they become a permanent source of funds to the government because every year a portion of the treasury bills is converted into long-term bonds. These bills are of two types: ad hoc and regular. The former type of bills are only issued to the State Governments, semi-government departments and foreign central banks and are not available for the general public. They can also not be sold or bought in the market like the regular treasury bills, which are freely marketable and available to the banks as well as general public. Both these types of bills are sold by the Reserve Bank of India.

It may be noted that in this respect India is very much backward. The treasury bill market is highly limited and does not play any role in the open market operations, like the UK and the USA. There are no dealers and hence the Reserve Bank of India is the only supplier and purchaser of these bills. These bills are not popular with other non-banking financial institutions.

3. Commercial Bill Market

Bills issued by the business firms are known as commercial bills. Such bills are generally of three months maturity. It is a promise to pay the specified amount in the specific period by the purchaser of goods to the seller. The bilis become marketable only after the banks of the purchaser has endorsed it and written a word 'accepted' on it. The seller can only present the bill to his bank for discounting thereafter. In times of emergency the bank can also sell the bills to other banks or to the Reserve Bank of India. In India the bill market is not so developed as it is in the UK and the USA because of the non-existence of acceptance houses and discount houses.

4. Collateral Loan Market

The loans which are backed with securities are known as collateral loans. In this market the commercial banks provide short-term funds on the securities and shares or debentures of the government, etc.

5. Certificate of Deposits and Commercial Paper Market

It was in 1989 that the Reserve Bank of India introduced these instruments with a view to widening the range of money market instruments and giving greater flexibility for the deployment of short-term funds to the investors. So, these types of instruments are mainly traded in these markets.

6. Discount and Finance House of India (DFHI)

With its own resources. of Rs. 100 crore and the financial support of the Reserve Bank of India, the DFHI was established on 26 April, 1988, to: (*i*) bring the entire financial system comprising of all banks in the public sector, private sector, cooperative sector and foreign banks, all Indian financial institutions and non-banking financial institutions in the private and public sectors, within the ambit of the Indian money market; and (*ii*) to equilibrate short-term surpluses and deposits of these instruments at market related rates through inter-bank transactions, in the case of banks, and through money market instruments in the case of banks and others. The main instruments are: call funds, treasury bills, certificate deposits, commercial papers, term deposits and Central Government dated securities. The DFHI is both a borrower and a lender and its chief objective is to increase the liquidity of various money market instruments. Further, it aims at stabilising the call money market rates by building up a huge turnover. The Reserve Bank of India started extending liquidity support to DFHI in June 1996 in the form of "Reverse Repos Facility" in government dated securities and 91-day treasury bills, with a view to stabilising the call money rates. The Reserve Bank of India has, however, withdrawn the facility of providing refinance against treasury bills. Since March 1996, the DFHI has also become a primary dealer in government securities.

7. Securities Trading Corporation of India (STCI)

The Corporation was established in May 1994 with a fully paid-up capital of Rs. 100 crore. Its objective is to develop secondary market in government securities and treasury bills. It also undertakes ready forward transactions in these instruments which take place in Mumbai and are routed through the SGL accounts maintained by the Reserve Bank of India. It also borrows and lends in the call money market. It also gets liquidity support from the Reserve Bank of India like the DFHI. It has also become a primary dealer in government securities.

8. Primary Dealers

There are four other primary dealers, dealing in government securities since March 1996. These are the ICICI Securities, the SBI Gilts Ltd., the PNB Gilts Ltd., and the Gilt Securities Trading Corporation Ltd. These primary dealers also receive liquidity support from the Reserve Bank of India similar to the one available to the DFHI and the STCI.

9. Satellite Dealers (SDs)

The RBI has registered nine financial institutions and two banks to act as a second tier in the trading and distribution of government securities. These are known as SDs and have provided ready forward transaction facility in the government securities market. They can obtain advances from the RBI on their basis, like the primary dealers.

10. Inter-Bank Participations (IBP)

With a view to facilitating the adjustment of short-term liquidity within the banking system, the Reserve Bank of India has introduced the instrument called the Inter-Bank Participations. These instruments are of two types, one on risk sharing basis and the other without risk sharing. The former could be for 90-180 days at an interest rate to be fixed between the issuing bank and the participating bank subject to a minimum of 14 per cent, per annum. The aggregate amount of IBP under an account at the time of issue should not exceed 40 per cent of the outstandings in the account. The IBPs without risk sharing could be of a maximum of 90 days maturity at an interest rate to be fixed between the concerned banks subject to a ceiling of 12.5 per cent per annum. These instruments are considered as part of the demand and time liabilities of the borrowing bank and are subject to reserve requirements. The ceiling rate of 12.5 per cent has now been. removed.

11. Repurchase Agreements Auctions (REPOS)

With a view to levelling the interest rates in the call money market, the Reserve Bank of India on 10 December 1992, introduced the scheme of Repurchase

Agreements Auction (Repos) in the Central Government dated securities. These are repurchase agreements for the sale and repurchase of a security. It permits the holders of the security to raise cash using it as a collateral. Under Repos transactions, a part of one kind of asset is liquidated in order to buy it back. Banks could, however, substitute it either by cash or RBI balance for securities. Their period is 14 days. The Repos have been employed as an indicator of expected call rates in order to bring call money rates at feasible level. Repos transactions are allowed only in Mumbai through the Subsidiary Central Ledger (SCL) accounts maintained by the Reserve Bank of India.

12. Money Market Mutual Funds (MMMFs)

In 1992, the RBI also allowed commercial banks and financial institutions to set up Money Market Mutual Funds to invest their resources in money market instruments like treasury bills, government dated securities, corporate bonds and debentures, commercial papers, etc. But much progress has not been achieved and the number of active MMMFs stands reduced to three from eight.

D. Functions of Indian Money Market

Following are the main functions of the Indian money market:

(1) It facilitates the utilisation of surplus fund profitably for a short period.

(2) It facilitates the availability of short-term funds to the various public and private institutions and thus enables the development of commerce, industry and trade within the country as well as outside the country.

(3) It saves the commercial banks from borrowing from the Reserve Bank of India, whenever the banks are short of cash. The commercial banks are also saved from paying a higher rate of interest to the Reserve Bank of India.

(4) It helps the government in raising short-term loans at low rates of interest on the basis of treasury bills, without increasing inflationary pressure in the economy.

(5) It lends a helping hand to the Reserve Bank of India in the successful implementation of its monetary policy.

(6) It acts as an aid to the Reserve Bank of India in controlling the banking system and thus influencing the development of commerce and industry.

(7) It facilitates financial mobility by transferring funds from one sector to the other which is very essential for the development of commerce and industry in the country.

(8) It promotes savings and investments by providing liquidity and promoting safety of financial assets.

(9) It equilibrates the demand and supply of loanable funds and thus helps in the rational allocation of resources.

(10) It economises the use of cash by dealing in near money assets.

3. Defects of the Indian Money Market

1. Unorganised Sector still beyond Control

Now we proceed to take up the defects from which the Indian money market suffers today. We have earlier stated that the Indian money market suffers mainly because of lack of relationship between its different segments. Although, prior to the establishment of the Reserve Bank of India, the Indian money market was divided into various sections and units and all these units, say for example, the Imperial Bank of India, the foreign exchange banks, the joint-stock banks, the co-operative banks, etc. confined their activities to their own areas and to a particular class of business, their relations were more competitive than co-operative. After the establishment of the Reserve Bank, these separatist tendencies have no doubt, to a great extent disappeared, more particularly after the passing of the Banking Regulation Act, 1949. The co-operative banks have now also come within the jurisdiction of the Reserve Bank and so it can be said that the organised sector of the money market is now under the effective control of the Reserve Bank. The reliance of the commercial banks for rediscounting and borrowing facilities on the Reserve Bank has considerably increased. The Reserve Bank also undertakes regular inspections of the books of these banks and issues guidelines for their lending operations, from time to time. But the major drawback is the absence of control of the Reserve Bank on the unorganised sector. The indigenous bankers are even today outside the control of the Reserve Bank, despite frantic efforts made by it. Very recently, signs have started developing for the increasing control of the Reserve Bank of India on the indigenous bankers, since the bigger indigenous bankers have started forming themselves into joint-stock companies.

2. Competition within the Same Sector

Again, one finds that even in these two sectors, there is tough competition among the members of the same sector, *e.g.*, the State Bank of India and other commercial banks compete with each other. Similarly, the members of the unorganised sector compete among themselves. This sort of competition is not only wasteful but is also detrimental to the interests of the poor agriculturists, specially small and marginal farmers and also endangers the speedy economic development of the country.

3. Fragmentation

One also finds that the Indian money market suffers from fragmentation. In other words, it would not be correct to call the money market in India as an All India Market in the true sense of the term. There is hardly any contact between the money markets in smaller towns and those in the bigger towns like Mumbai, Kolkata, Delhi, Chennai, etc.

4. Large Variety of Money Rates

As a consequence of this competition between the various constituents of the money market and intrasectoral competition a large variety of money rates prevail in the country. This creates confusion and chaos. The confusion is worse confounded when one finds that there are different rates of interest in bigger and smaller towns, in rural and urban areas, in different localities of the same town and in different seasons in the country. Such sort of diversity in the rates of interest is hardly to be seen in any of the money markets of developed countries of the West. Nearly 50 years ago, the Central Banking Enquiry Committee had remarked: "The fact that a call rate of .75 per cent, a hundi rate of 4 per cent, a bank rate of 4 per cent, a bazar rate of small traders of 6.38 per cent and a Calcutta bazar rate for bills of small traders of 10 per cent can exist simultaneously indicates extraordinary sluggishness of the movement of credit between the various markets." And the situation has not changed much in these years. The result of such a situation is that changes in the bank rate do not produce the desired result.

5. Undeveloped Bill Market

As stated already, the existence of an undeveloped and unorganised bill market is the greatest defect of the Indian money market. In fact the Indian money market has not been able to function properly and effectively only because of this reason. Although, hundies have been in use since time immemorial, there is a general shortage of hundies in the market. That is why, the commercial banks have not been able to invest more than 6 per cent of their deposits in hundies. This can also be the reason for compelling the businessmen and traders to conduct their business in cash. Whatever may be the position, the absence of a developed bill market has certainly marred the efficient functioning of the Indian money market. It is, therefore, essential that the Reserve Bank of India should take steps to popularise the use of hundies among Indian businessmen and offer facilities for rediscounting them. The position now stands very much improved in this respect but it cannot be considered satisfactory at all. The steps taken by the Reserve Bank for developing the bill market, will be discussed later in this chapter.

6. Seasonal Variations in Interest Rates

Another defect from which the Indian money market suffers today is the lack of synchronisation between the demand for and supply of credit facilities during various seasons of the year. As already stated, during the busy season the supply of credit does not increase proportionately, while during the slack season there is a general fall in the demand for credit facilities. The supply of money being generally elastic, there is a wide variation in the rates of interest during these two parts of the year. Despite sincere efforts of the Reserve Bank, it has not been possible to eliminate these seasonal variations in the rates of interest. Ultimately, it affects the economic development of the country.

7. General Shortage of Capital

There is a general shortage of capital in the Indian money market. Firstly, the per capita income of the people in the country is quite low and therefore, the saving capacity of the people is rather limited. Secondly, the banking services in the rural areas are hardly adequate and hence the rural savings are not being mobilised, to the desired extent. Consequently, the rate of capital formation is low and mobility of the capital is also at a low ebb.

8. Lopsided and Unbalanced

The Indian money market is rather lopsided and unbalanced. The rural areas which cover the major portion of the country are inadequately served by commercial banks. The indigenous bankers are, therefore, in a very large number and they provide a large amount of credit to trade and business. It would not be wrong to say that in certain parts of the country, they enjoy monopoly in the moneylending business. On the other hand, one finds that specialised banking institutions are conspicuous by their absence. These specialized institutions are the industrial banks, discount houses, Indian-owned foreign exchange banks, etc.

The above defects have been considerably reduced during recent decades by the Reserve Bank. The different parts of the money market stand today very much interlinked, the discrimination between foreign and Indian commercial banks has virtually disappeared, the money rates in different parts of the country are not very much uniform; the seasonal monetary stringency stands very much reduced and the bill market in the country is now on its way to development. In this respect, the nationalisation of major commercial banks has no doubt been a great step in the direction.

4. Measures for the Improvement of Indian Money Market

We have seen that the Indian money market suffers from various shortcomings. A number of measures have been taken from time to time for the development of the Indian money market. The Reserve Bank of India has also taken several steps in this direction. It set up two committees, one Chakraborty Committee and the other Veghul Committee to explore the possibilities of enlarging the scope of money market and to make recommendations for evolving other suitable money market institutions. The Reserve Bank of India has taken action on some of the recommendations of these committees.

Steps Taken by the Reserve Bank of India

The Reserve Bank of India has adopted various measures for removing the defects of the Indian money market. Some of the important measures are given below:

1. The Reserve Bank of India introduced two schemes, one in 1952 and the other in 1970 for encouraging the use of bills in the banking system. The Reserve Bank of India has also enlarged the variety of bills.

2. For improving the working of indigenous bankers the Reserve Bank of India has taken the following measures: (*a*) compulsory registration, (*b*) maintenance and audit of accounts, and (*c*) providing financial accommodation through banks.

3. For coordinating and integrating the different components of the Indian money market in the organised sector, the Reserve Bank of India has evolved procedures and conventions.

4. The Reserve Bank of India under the Banking Regulation Act, 1949 provides equal opportunities to all the banks in the country in matter of licencing, opening of branches, raising of share capital, the type of loans to be given, etc.

5. For strengthening the money market the Reserve Bank of India has taken steps for the amalgamation and merger of weak banks into the few strong banks. It has also been encouraging the expansion of banking facilities in the country.

6. The Reserve Bank of India has also taken steps to minimise the differences in the interest rates between different sections as well as different centres of the money market. Now the structure has become more sensitive to changes in the bank rate.

The Reserve Bank of India has not succeeded in a large measure in improving the Indian money market. It is still facing difficulties in effectively controlling the money market. These difficulties are:

1. It has not been able to develop the bill market. Consequently, it is unable to withdraw surplus funds from the money market by disposing of bills.

2. It has not been able to bring the indigenous bankers under its effective control and thus integrate the money market.

3. The call money market has not been developed satisfactorily, with the result that commercial banks do not maintain fixed ratios between their cash reserves and deposits and the Reserve Bank of India has to undertake open market operations on a large scale to influence the operations of the commercial banks.

Further Suggestions for Improving the Indian Money Market

The following further suggestions are offered for improving the Indian money market:

1. Control over Non-Bank Financing Companies. During recent months a number of cases have come to light where public limited finance companies have cheated the general public by inviting deposits to the tune of crores of rupees. The Reserve Bank of India has not been able to protect the depositors from exploitation and cheating of such finance companies. Similarly, a number of chit funds have also been cheating the general public. The Reserve Bank of India should, therefore, insist on a uniform legislation for regulating the activities of chit funds and financing companies. The legislation should specially incorporate a provision that at least 25 per cent of deposits accepted from the public would be deposited by such companies with the State Bank of India or the Reserve Bank of India; and also that such companies will have to submit every quarterly a statement indicating the names of the depositors, the amounts of deposit and the period of such deposits to the Reserve Bank of India.

2. Standard Forms of Hundies. The Banking Commission (1972) recommended that standard forms of hundies should be prescribed and the Negotiable Instruments Act be made to apply to such hundies, but so far nothing in particular seems to have been done in this regard. It is a well-known fact that in the organised sector of the Indian money market large transactions are performed by discounting hundies by the indigenous bankers. The commercial banks, however, do not accept these hundies. It is therefore necessary, that suitable action may be taken immediately by the Reserve Bank of India to implement the recommendation of the Banking Commission.

3. Regulation of the Activities of the Indigenous Bankers. The situation of the banking services now available in the rural areas is far more improved than what it was in the early 1960s of this century. A number of branches have been opened by commercial banks, lead banks, regional rural banks and cooperative banks in the rural areas after 1969. Despite the expansion of banking facilities in the rural areas indigenous bankers continue to occupy an important position. As early as 1972 the Banking Commission had recommended the regulation of the activities of indigenous bankers through commercial banks but unfortunately no progress has been made in this direction so far.

4. Development of Bill Market. A developed bill market is very essential for the growth of Indian money market. Despite the efforts made in this direction by tne Reserve Bank of India the situation does not appear to have improved to a satisfactory extent. The government should, therefore, at least in its own departments and public sector undertakings make it compulsory that payments for all credit purchases should be in the form of bills which should be honoured on due date. Besides, Reserve Bank of India should lay down simpler procedure for rediscounting of bills. These steps will go a long way to develop bill culture in the country.

5. Development of Money Market in Other Centres. At present the money market is confined to four major cities in the country. For the proper growth of the money market it is necessary that adequate banking and clearing house facilities are provided on a large scale, discount and acceptance houses are established and cheap remittance facilities are extended throughout the country to facilitate the mobilisation of funds.

6. Creation of Secondary Market. For imparting adequate liquidity in the Indian money market it is essential that an active secondary market is created by developing new sets of institutions. This step will certainly improve the functioning and growth of the Indian money market.

5. Bill Market in India

The bill market essentially refers to the buyers and sellers of bills of exchange. It is not confined to any particular place. It covers all those organisations and individuals who deal in the bills of exchange. It need not be emphasised that the bills of exchange are essential for the smooth operation of business and commerce since by their use the transfer of cash becomes easy. A merchant need not carry with him cash to collect goods and he can make payment through the bills of exchange. The seller of goods presents a bill of exchange to the purchaser who after indicating his acceptance returns it to the seller which becomes a legal document and the purchaser stands committed to make payment to the seller of goods after the period specified in the bill is over. In case of emergency the seller can also get the bill discounted by some bank. Thus, the use of bills of exchange makes business operations very smooth and quick and therefore an organised bill market is a boon to the business community nay, to the entire banking system.

It is a pity that no attention was paid to the development of an organised bill market in the country by the British Government. A bill market could not develop even after the establishment of the Reserve Bank in 1935 because *firstly,* the Reserve Bank did not provide any incentive to the scheduled banks to do bill business. The scheduled banks were unwilling to discount bill with the Imperial Bank as that would have provided the Imperial Bank with an opportunity to know the position of their bill-portfolios. The Imperial Bank of India was the sole performer in the field of rediscounting of bills. *Secondly,* there was an acute shortage of bills. The major portion of Indian business comprised agricultural produce and in the absence of adequate warehousing arrangement it was not possible to create a large number of agricultural bills.

Again, in India the demand for funds is rather seasonal and therefore, the use of bills is not very much required. Another factor responsible for the shortage of bills was that the Indian commercial banks preferred gilt-edged securities and therefore, new bills could not be created. *Thirdly,* the existence of different types of hundies drawn in various regional languages and governed by different customs also proved to be a hindrance in the organisation and development of a bill market in India. *Finally* a high stamp duty on bills also proved to be a powerful deterrent to the development of the bill market. It was only in 1952 that the Reserve Bank of India paid some attention to it.

The Reserve Bank of India implemented a bill development scheme on 16th January, 1952. It may be helpful to mention here that prior to 1952 the Reserve Bank of India used to provide financial accommodation to the scheduled banks against approved government securities. With the implementation of the bill market scheme, the scheduled banks could secure financial accommodation from the Reserve Bank against usance promissory-notes which were essentially treated by the Reserve Bank as a security. It means that the Reserve Bank did not really rediscount these promissory-notes. Another condition was that the Reserve Bank did not accept promissory-notes which matured after three months, nor was it prepared to lend against the security of demand bills.

Initially the Bill Market Scheme was introduced in 1952 on an experimental basis. It was confined to the—

(1) scheduled banks with deposits of Rs. 10 crore and above;

(2) loans with the minimum limit of Rs. 10 lakh; and

(3) to the individual bills whose minimum value should be of Rs. 1 lakh.

Subsequently, the scope of the scheme was widened from time to time and finally the following changes have been incorporated—(*a*) bringing more banks within the fold of the scheme; (*b*) reducing the minimum eligibility value for bills; (*c*) reducing the minimum limit of advances; (*d*) extending the scheme to export bills with the minimum usance of 180 days. The scheme became popular, but it could not help the development of the bill market. As a matter of fact, it was a pseudo scheme in the sense that its objective was not the development of a genuine bill market but to extend financial accommodation to commercial banks by the Reserve Bank of India. The scheme was not based on the genuine trade bills but on the conversion of loans and advances of the banks into usance bills. It therefore could not impose the discipline of making payment on the due date and of supporting credit transactions with genuine trade transactions. The bill scheme on the other hand evolved a cash credit system of bank lending which was more convenient and elastic for the borrowers. The Dehajia Committee pointed out the abuses of the system and suggested the use of bill financing for supervising the loans given by the commercial banks.

The New Bill Market Scheme

The Bill Market Scheme 1952, therefore, was chiefly intended to enable the commercial banks to obtain refinance from the Reserve Bank of India by converting a portion of their cash credit advances portfolio. The question of enlarging the use of bills of exchange as an instrument for providing credit and the creation of a proper type of bill market in India was further examined by a Study Group under the Chairmanship of Shri M. Narasimhan constituted by the Reserve Bank of India in 1970. The Reserve Bank of India announced the New Bill Market Scheme in the light of the recommendations of this group, which came into effect in November 1970. In this Scheme there was no change in so far far as the drawing, accepting and discounting of the bills were concerned, but the only new thing was relating to the rediscounting of bills. According to the Scheme only certain types of bills were eligible for the purpose of rediscounting with the Reserve Bank of India. While the commercial banks would continue to discount and rediscount bills of other types, no rediscounting and refinancing facilities will be extended by the Reserve Bank of India against such bills.

Chief Features of the New Bill Market Scheme

Following are the chief features of the New Bill Market Scheme:

(1) All scheduled banks are eligible to offer bills of exchange for rediscounting to the Reserve Bank of India.

(2) Only genuine trade bills relating to the sale and purchase of goods are covered under the scheme.

(3) The bills are rediscounted by the Reserve Bank of India, but this facility is available at its offices at Mumbai, Kolkata, Chennai and New Delhi. If the number of small bills is very large then these shall have to be given in lots.

(4) The bill should be drawn on and accepted by the bank of the person who purchases the goods. If that bank is not a licensed one, the bill should also bear the signature of a licensed scheduled bank.

(5) The bills should have maximum usance of 90 days.

(6) The bills should bear at least two good signatures.

(7) Bills relating to the sale of goods to the government departments, quasi-government bodies, and statutory bodies are not to be covered under the Scheme. But later on, according to the modification introduced in the Scheme in 1971 these bills have also been covered under the Scheme.

(8) The bills of exchange drawn and accepted by the Industrial Credit

and Investment Corporation of India have also been covered under the Scheme with effect from April 1972.

Difficulties Faced by Trade and Industry

There are a number of difficulties in the development of the bill market. These difficulties are:

(1) A general reluctance on the part of industry, trade and government department to accept bills.

(2) Absence of specialised credit information agencies.

(3) Administrative work involved in handling invoices and scrutiny of documents of title to goods.

(4) Non-availability of stamp paper of required denomination.

(5) The requirement of affixing stamp on each bill and payment of stamp duty.

(6) Absence of an active secondary market for bills since rediscounting of bills is only permitted with the apex level financial institutions.

Remedial Action Taken by RBI

The Reserve Bank of India set up a Committee to Review the Working of the Monetary System in 1985, and the Working Group on the Money Market in 1986. They made important recommendations which were accepted and implemented by the Reserve Bank of India. These are as follows:

(1) The Reserve Bank of India has developed the treasury bills market of 91-days maturity. In 1986 it introduced 182-days Treasury Bills and in April 1992 these were replaced by 364-days Treasury Bills.

(2) The number of financial institutions eligible for rediscounting bills has been increased. Apart from the scheduled banks and selected urban cooperative banks 21 other financial institutions like LIC, UTI, GIC, NABARD, all development banks, all mutual funds, etc. have been included in the Scheme.

(3) For rediscounting commercial bills, treasury bills and government dated securities the Reserve Bank of India has established the Discount and Finance House of India (DFHI), as a major financial institution.

(4) For the development of secondary markets in government dated securities and treasury bills the Reserve Bank of India in May 1994 established the Securities Trading Corporation of India (STCI). It undertakes ready forward transactions in these instruments. It has become a primary dealer in government securities since March 1996.

(5) The Reserve Bank has introduced a Drawee Bill Scheme to enable the large scale units to secure finance from banks against bills accepted for payment to small scale units.

(6) For promoting bill culture the Reserve Bank had fixed the discount

rate at 15.5 per cent and the rediscount rate at 12.5 per cent, but with effect from May 1989, the rediscounting has been made entirely free.

(7) The ICICI Securities, SBI Gilts Ltd., PNB Gilts Ltd. and Gilt Securities Trading Corporation Ltd. have also been allowed by the Reserve Bank to operate as primary dealers in Government securities.

(8) The Reserve Bank removed a major administrative constraint when it introduced the scheme of derivative usance promissory note in October 1988. Now the banks can draw a derivative usance promissory note for suitable amounts with maturity up to 90 days on the basis of genuine commercial or trade bills discounted at their branches. The Reserve Bank, further, advised the banks to attain a ratio of bill acceptance to their inland credit purchases of 25 per cent as a bill discounting limit of the same order.

(9) The Reserve Bank of India allowed with effect from April 1993 the authorised dealers in India to rediscount export bills abroad at rates linked to international interest rates. This will enable the bill holders to derive the benefits of international competitive rates.

(10) In July 1992 the Reserve Bank of India advised the commercial banks as follows—(*i*) They should be cautious in discounting bills drawn by financial companies set up by large industrial houses on other group companies; (*ii*) they should not rediscount the bills discounted by non-bank financial companies; and (*iii*) they should ensure that the overall credit limit provided to finance companies and to hire-purchase and leasing companies should not exceed three times the net worth of such companies.

Weaknesses of the New Bill Market Scheme

The New Bill Market Scheme introduced by the Reserve Bank of India as been a right step, but its functioning over the years has not been found satisfactory. A number of weaknesses have been pointed out. These weaknesses are:

(1) The Scheme has not been able to develop a genuine bill market for the reason that the borrowers as well as the banks still have dealings in cash credit.

(2) The Scheme has not been able to cover the indigenous bankers and other constituents of the unorganised sector of the Indian money market.

(3) The Scheme has not been extended so far to the agricultural sector.

(4) Hundies which are used on a large scale in Indian trade and commerce have not been recognised by the Reserve Bank of India for rediscounting.

(5) The bill market is primarily restricted to derivative usance promissory notes rather than to genuine trade bills.

(6) The government, public sector undertakings and general industrial houses still do not accept bills for financing business.

6. Indian Capital Market

All those institutions and mechanisms through which medium and long-term funds are pooled and channelised to individuals, businesses and the governments constitute capital market. It deals in long-term securities of different types, which serve the requirement of purchasers and sellers of these instruments. The Indian capital market comprises of unorganised and organised markets. The unorganised market is composed of indigenous bankers, moneylenders, etc. who operate in the small industry sector, trade and agriculture. A major portion of private savings is invested by people in their own business. Many people also invest in the enterprises of their relatives and friends. Black money and wealth flow freely between the unorganised and organised sectors. The unorganised money market is, thus, most unsystematic. There is no uniform policy regarding interest rates, maturity of financial assets, etc. Despite the measures taken by the government and the Reserve Bank of India this sector is still out of their control.

The organised capital market comprises a number of financial institutions, like the UTI, IFCI, IDBI, IRBI, ICICI, LIC, GIC, SIDBI, Industrial Development Corporation, State Financial Corporation, merchant banker, leasing and financial companies, mutual funds, housing finance banks, Stock Holding Corporation of India, Discount and Finance House of India, besides the commercial banks. The organised sector of the Indian capital market is regulated by the Securities and Exchange Board of India (SEBI).

A. Instruments of the Capital Market

A number of securities or instruments of different maturities, interest rates, dividend, liability, ownership, voting rights, etc. are traded in the Indian capital market. The following instruments are dealt with in the Indian capital market:

(1) Corporate securities which include preference shares, bonus shares and right issue shares, stocks, bonds, convertible and non-convertible debentures, etc. and bonds of the public sector undertakings.

(2) Shares issued by mutual funds like UTI Master Shares, UTI Master Growth, Canshare, Cangrowth, SBI Magnums, GIC Growth Plus, Goldshare, Starshare, etc.

(3) Government bonds and securities, also known as gilt-edged securities, issued by the Central and State Governments and local bodies. A number of other innovative hybrid instruments have also been floated for attracting investors in new issues like warrants attached to convertible and non-convertible debentures, secured premium notes attached with warrants, deep discount bonds, accident insurance attached with warrants and non-convertible debentures with sale of '*khokhas*' to banks, zero-interest bonds, etc.

B. Divisions of Capital Market

The Indian capital market is divided into: (*i*) Gilt-edged market; and (*ii*) Industrial security market, according to the risk involved in the instruments. We shall now have a brief idea of these markets.

1. Gilt-edged Market. Gilt-edged market deals in government securities issued by the Central Government, State Governments and local bodies and arc backed by the Reserve Bank of India. These are long-term bonds for being sold to the public, banks and financial institutions. They carry low rates of interest as compared to the bonds issued by companies. Moreover, they provide a variety of tax incentives and rebates. From the point of risk, safety and liquidity, these bonds are more preferable to the industrial securities.

2. Industrial Security Market. This market deals in the purchase and sale of new and old shares and debentures issued by the corporate sector. It is divided into : (*i*) the primary market; and (*ii*) secondary market.

(*a*) *The Primary Market.* The primary market relates to new issues. These are issued by the public limited companies directly to the general public in the form of shares, fully convertible debentures, non-convertible debentures, preferential shares and debentures, rights issues, etc. Sometimes companies also issue shares through private placement. Such placement is made to specific group of investors such as friends, relatives and possessors of shares of the same company or institution.

(*b*) *The Secondary Market.* This market is also known as a stock market and deals in shares and debentures at the stock exchanges. In this market various types of shares and debentures are actively traded by brokers, mutual funds, Non-Bank Financial Institutions, like the UTI, LIC, GIC, etc. At present there are 22 recognised stock exchanges functioning in India.

C. Working of Indian Capital Market

At the time of the Partition of India there were only eight stock exchanges, at Bombay, Calcutta, Madras, Ahmedabad, Delhi, Kanpur, Hyderabad and Bangalore. The ordinary and preferential shares of the British Managing Agency Houses and of well established Indian companies, like the Tata Iron and Steel Company, in addition to Government securities were traded. Until the first half of the 1950s, the capital market in India was mainly responsible for the mobilisation of financial resources for the corporate sector. But the capital market suffered a setback after the nationalisation of Imperial Bank of India in 1955, Insurance Companies in 1956, establishment of development banks like ICICI, IDBI, IFCI, etc. and the nationalisation of commercial banks, since these institutions started providing subsidised credit to trade and industry. As a result, the companies had to issue shares at a discount, very much below the market value. Further, after the amendment of the Foreign Exchange and

Regulation Act (FERA), foreign companies were made to dilute their capital by issuing new shares either at par or at an approved premium to the Indian investors. Consequently, the FERA companies issued 40 per cent of their shares at low prices to Indians. When the government found that the importance of the capital market had substantially waned, it started taking various steps to promote demand and supply in the capital market. The government provided a number of incentives for the purchase of equity and debenture issues, such as, reduction in the corporate tax rate, higher rate of interest on debenture, etc. In the 1980s, the capital market started regaining health as a result of these measures. During the last 15 years the Indian capital market, due to the efforts of the government, has emerged as one of the important capital markets in the world and it continues to be the main source of finance for the private and public sectors.

7. Measures to Reform the Indian Capital Market

Despite the stimulation of the capital market by the government, it still suffers from a number of shortcomings. Before listing the defects of the Indian capital market, we shall spell out the various reformatory steps taken by the government to improve the Indian capital market. These are as under:

1. Securities and Exchange Board of India (SEBI)

The government setup the SEBI on 30 March, 1992 as an autonomous and statutory organisation. Further, the Office of the Controller of Issues was abolished w.e.f. 29 May, 1992. SEBI is now responsible for supervising the issue of new shares, protecting the interests of investors, promoting the development of the capital market and for regulating the functioning of stock exchanges.

2. Primary Market Reforms

With a view to removing the inadequacies and deficiencies in regard to the issue of shares, following measures have been taken:

(*i*) Companies have been given freedom to fix the prices and premium on shares and debentures after clearance from the SEBI. It may be noted that the SEBI does not vet the offer documents.

(*ii*) For public issues, minimum subscription for an individual has been fixed at Rs. 2,000 with effect from 1 November, 1996.

(*iii*) The minimum percentage of securities to be issued to the general public has been fixed at 25 per cent.

(*iv*) The SEBI ensures through an advertisement code that advertisements do not contain misleading statements. The companies are required to disclose all material facts and specific risk factors associated with their projects. They are also required to specify the basis of calculation of premium on equity issues.

(*v*) The SEBI has laid down the allotment procedure according to which shares are allotted on a pro-rata basis, and mutual funds and Foreign Institutional Investors (FIIs) are allowed firm allotment in public issues.

(*vi*) In the case of over-subscribed public issues, a SEBI representative supervises the allotment process.

(*vii*) Each company is required to complete the allotment process within 30 days of the closure of the issue. In case of delay the company shall pay the interest at the rate of 15 per cent per annum.

(*viii*) The SEBI has prescribed that stock exchanges will collect from the companies making public issues, a deposit of 1 per cent of the issue amount. In the case of companies not complying with the prescribed conditions this amount is liable to be forfeited.

(*ix*) Bonds of Public Sector Undertakings (PSUs) have also been brought within the ambit of the authority of the SEBI.

(*x*) FIIs have been permitted to invest in the capital market after registration with the SEBI and foreign brokers are allowed to assist them on the same conditions.

(*xi*) NRIs and overseas companies can also invest in the Indian capital market without the prior approval of the Reserve Bank of India.

(*xii*) Since November 1996, banks have been allowed to operate in the secondary market.

3. Secondary Market Reforms

The SEBI has also taken a number of steps to regulate and supervise the activities and conduct of intermediaries, like merchant bankers, portfolio managers, underwriters, registrars, brokers, sub-brokers, share transfer agents, etc. Some of these measures are:

(*i*) All brokers have to register themselves with the stock exchange in which they want to operate.

(*ii*) The SEBI has laid down capital adequacy norms according to which individual broker has to deposit 3 per cent and the corporate Member has to deposit 6 per cent.

(*iii*) The SEBI requires that stock exchanges must ensure that contract notes are issued by brokers to their clients within 24 hours of a deal. Time limit has also been fixed for payment of sale proceeds and deliveries by brokers and payment of margins by clients to brokers. In case of default penalties have also been specified.

(*iv*) For the purpose of transparency in their dealings the brokers have to maintain separate accounts for clients and for themselves.

(*v*) Measures have also been taken by the SEBI for controlling rigging of prices and other malpractices rampant in the stock exchanges.

(*vi*) Brokers are required to get their account books audited and the audit report has to be, filed with the SEBI every year.

(*vii*) An institution of share jobbers has been introduced in the stock exchange who simultaneously display the transaction of shares in which they are doing jobbing.

(*viii*) The SEBI undertakes regularly the inspection of the working of stock exchanges.

(*ix*) The SEBI has also made the governing boards of the stock exchanges more broad-based and has also modified the composition of their arbitration, default and disciplinary committees.

(*x*) Screen-based on-line trading has been introduced by NSE, OTCEI and major stock exchanges like Mumbai, Chennai, Delhi, etc.

(*xi*) The trading time in the stock exchanges has been increased to 3 hours from two and a half hours.

(*xii*) In case of non-compliance of the instructions of the SEBI, the stock exchanges have to pay the penalties including fines, and suspension from trading.

(*xiii*) Attempts are also being made to improve the operational efficiency of the stock exchanges. Mumbai Stock Exchange has already introduced important changes to improve its functioning, for example, making BOLT system operational for all the scrips, regrouping of shares and introduction of weekly settlements for A and B group shares, dealing in odd lot shares, etc.

To make the governing bodies of stock exchange broad based the government has decided that they should have five elected members of which not more than four would be nominated by the government or SEBI and three or four members would be nominated as public representatives. The government has also allowed Foreign Institutional Investors (FIIs) to invest in the Indian capital market provided they are registered with SEBI. Till January 1995 as many as 286 FIIs were registered with SEBI, as against only ten in January 1993. The cumulative investments of FIIs had increased from $200 million in January 1993 to $ 3 billion in January 1995. The government has now permitted the joint-venture stock broking companies to have non-Indian citizens on their Board of Directors. From July 2001 the SEBI has introduced rolling settlements to check excessive speculation and volatility in the stock market. But it has not succeeded in achieving the objective.

During 1999-2000 the government promulgated the Insurance Regulation and Development Authority (IRDA) Act in the field of contractual savings.

This Act has put an end to the monopoly of the government in the insurance sector. It gives priority in the utilization of policy holders funds for the development of social and infrastructure sectors. The government has given license to a number of private sector companies to do insurance business.

In January 1995 the government conferred on the SEBI additional powers through an ordinance amending the SEBI Act 1992, for ensuring the orderly development of the capital market and to enhance its ability to protect the interests of the investors. Following are the important features of the ordinance:

(*i*) SEBI has been empowered to file complaints in courts and to notify its regulations without prior approval of the government.

(*ii*) SEBI has been provided with regulatory powers over companies in the issuance of capital, transfer of securities and other related matters.

(*iii*) SEBI has been empowered to impose penalties on capital market intermediaries for listed range of violations.

(*iv*) While investigating irregularities in the capital market, SEBI has been empowered to summon the attendance of and call for documents from all categories of intermediaries. It now also enjoys the power to issue directions to all persons connected with security markets with a view to protect investors or secure the orderly development of the securities market.

Despite all these powers SEBI has not succeeded in preventing a small coterie of brokers in Mumbai to hammer the Mumbai Stock Exchange in March, 2001 and May, 2004. Even today the stock markets continue to be highly volatile.

4. Institutional and Market Development

Following measures have been taken for institutional and market development.

(*i*) *Promotion of the Institution of Market Makers.* It has been observed that not more than 20 per cent of the scrips are actually traded in the stock exchanges. The majority of shares lack liquidity. Consequently, measures have been taken for the promotion of market makers. A market maker is required to make a market for a minimum number of shares which are not included in Group A traded share at a stock exchange. Market makers have to offer two-way quotes for a minimum period of 18 months from the date on which the shares are admitted for trading. The minimum quantity offered have to be three times the market lot. The difference between the two quotes should not exceed 10 per cent. Unlisted companies planning new issues below Rs. 5 crore are required to appoint market maker on all stock exchanges where the proposed share is to be listed. Since market makers, like other traders, require financial support, the Reserve Bank of India has issued guidelines on 5 August 1993, regarding the banks financing their operations. Market makers are approved by the SEBI on the recommendation of the stock exchanges.

(*ii*) *Freedom of Operation to FIIs.* Foreign Institutional Investors like mutual funds, asset management companies, investment trusts, nominee companies and incorporated institutional portfolio managers have been permitted to operate in the Indian capital market. Foreign brokers have also been permitted to assist them in the purchase and sale of scrips in the Indian stock exchanges. They can open bank and custodial accounts, and set up joint ventures in the financial sector. But portfolio investments cannot exceed 24 per cent of the issued share capital in respect of the total holdings of all registered FIIs in one company. For greater participation of such investors, a number of concessions have been allowed, for example: (*a*) repatriation of capital, capital gains, dividends and incomes received by way of interest; (*b*) tax concessions at an average rate of 20 per cent on dividend; and (*c*) tax rate of 10 per cent on capital gains.

(*iii*) *Globalisation of Indian Equities.* Now Indian companies can also sell their scrips in the international capital markets through Global Depository Receipts (GDR) mechanism.

(*iv*) *Over-the-Counter Exchange of India* (*OTCEI*). With effect from 6 October 1992, the ICICI, UTI, IDBI, IFCI, GIC, LIC, SBI Capital Markets and Can-bank Financial Services have jointly setup the OTCEI as a registered stock exchange to provide: (*i*) small and medium companies an access to capital market for raising capital in a cost effective manner; and (*ii*) convenient and efficient avenues to investors in the capital market. The OTCEI is a ringless, electronic stock exchange which deals in selected shares and debt instruments. It is a national stock exchange since all the scrips listed with the OTCEI are traded over its counter throughout the country. No separate listing at different places is required. The OTCEI listed share application form is the same as that of normal public issues of the company, the only difference being that it contains the name of the sponsor who is solely responsible for appraising the company, and for the listing and trading of its shares. In the event of under-subscription the sponsor is responsible for making up the required amount. The OTCEI approves the allotment of applications with the Registrar to the issue and takes it for listing with itself. All refund/allotment letters are issued to subscribers within 28 days of the closing of issue. All share certificates remain with the Registrar. The shareholders are only issued a counter receipt (CR) which is a tradeable document like original share certificate. The OTCEI operates at Mumbai with regional windows at other metropolitan cities and representative offices in a few other major cities. The exact transaction particulars are displayed at the OTC computer. The Infrastructure Leasing and Financial Services (ILFS) is the compulsory market maker for all debt instruments dealt with by the OTCEI. For shares the OTCEI has appointed separate market makers.

5. National Stock Exchange of India (NSEI)

For providing a comprehensive nationwide facility for trading in scrips, debentures and bonds, to investors through electronic screen-based trading, post trade clearance and settlement, the IDBI, ICICI, IFCI, GIC, LIC, SBI Capital Markets, SHCIL have jointly setup the NSEI as a limited company w.e.f. 26 April 1993. The National Exchange deals in: (*i*) Wholesale debt instruments; and (*ii*) Capital market instruments. There are no jobbers or market makers. Since the NSEI is a scrip less trading exchange and is on-line screen-based, the buyers and sellers can operate from anywhere in India. The NSEI has also setup a subsidiary, known as the National Securities Clearing Corporation (NSCC) which guarantees settlement of deals executed through it.

6. National Securities Depository Limited (NSDL)

IDBI, UTI and NSEI have jointly promoted the NSDL which started operations on 8 November 1996, initially to dematerialise the shares often companies, *viz.* ACC, BPCL, CRISIL, LML, HDFC, ICICI, L&T, RSL, TISCO & SIEMENS. The depository participants of the National Securities Depository Limited are: SCHIL, NSCC, IDBI, ILFS, Global Trust Bank, HDFC Bank, IIT Trust Corporate Services, Citibank, Morgan Stanley Custodial, SBI and Standard Chartered Bank. The depository is a bank for share certificates and the investor operates his account in the depository like a bank account. The holders of shares have the choice of depositing their share certificates with the depository through the participants which are *dematerialised* and the names of the holders are registered in the electronically operated registers of the depository or the participants. Thus, the NSDL enables investors to settle "paperless" deals through book entry adjustment. Hence it does away with the risk associated with paperbased settlements like delay in transfers, loss or theft of share certificates, etc. The shares transferred through the depository are exempt from stamp duty. Moreover, it helps the companies, investors, transfer agents and brokers in economising the storage space. The NSDL charges a nominal fee for keeping the share certificates in safe custody. In this way, this system simplifies the settlement problems, reduces the trading costs and improves the volume of trade and returns. It also stimulates FIIs to participate in a big way in the Indian capital market.

8. Shortcomings of the Indian Capital Market

Notwithstanding these reforms, the Indian capital market still suffers from a number of shortcomings. These are as follows:

1. Inadequate Liquidity. According to a recent study, only 20 per cent of the scrips are traded everyday and that too of Group 'A', and another 20 per cent are traded 2 to 3 times a week and only 10 per cent once a fortnight. This proves that the Indian capital market suffers from lack of adequate liquidity.

2. Delayed Delivery. It is a common knowledge that the delivery of scrips and settlement or payments are unusually delayed. Sometimes the delivery of scrips takes 4 to 5 months and the payments are made after 2 to 3 months. There are bad deliveries as well.

3. Insiders Operations. Persons working in a company often deal in shares on the basis of the expected profitability or losses of the company which creates fluctuations in the price of the scrips and adversely affects the interests of the small investors. It has also been seen that big industrial houses also sometimes resort to transactions in the shares of group companies. This sort of insider trading causes fluctuations in the Indian capital market and harms the small investors.

4. Inadequacy of Market Instruments. The Indian capital market deals primarily in shares and debentures which are not at all adequate for its proper and smooth functioning. The newly introduced warrants, zero-coupon bonds, etc. have not yet gained popularity with the general investors.

5. Defective Banking and Postal Services. The defective functioning of the banks and postal services have also added to the problems of the small investors. The refund and dividend warrants sent by the companies to the shareholders by ordinary posts are more often lost in the transit due to the dishonest postal and bank employees.

6. Lack of Availability of Stockinvest. Stockinvest of small denominations are not easily available to small investors. Besides, the bank charges are also high and the use of stockinvest is full of procedural difficulties. Consequently, the small investors keep themselves away from this instrument which is mainly being used by big investors.

7. Grey Market. Sometimes transactions are unofficially conducted in the shares before they are listed. This is called the grey market. This sort of unofficial and unregulated market attracts gullible investors. Such investors are also attracted to invest in new shares by financial analysts whose analysis is neither fair nor objective. The result is that the small investor suffers.

8. Lack of Clarity in Prospectus. The SEBI has no doubt issued guidelines for the preparation of prospectuses issued by individual companies but it has been seen that most of the time the prospectuses issued by the companies do not supply full information to the prospective investors. Consequently they are duped straightaway. A large number of companies have disappeared from the scene after issuing the share certificates and the small investors are unable to find any trace of them.

9. Defective Stock-broking System. The entire system of stock broking is full of defects. The brokers appoint their sub-brokers who in turn appoint their own sub-brokers who cheat the sellers and buyers of shares and debentures in the secondary market by manipulating the prices.

10. Investors Unprotected. In case of default by brokers and sub-brokers the investors have no protection. The present provision regarding the protection given to an individual shareholder under the Consumer Protection Fund created at each Stock Exchange is limited to Rs. 40,000 in case of a defaulting broker which is highly inadequate.

11. Problem of Odd Lot Shares. The SEBI has issued instructions regarding the non-issuing of odd lot shares, bonus shares and rights issue shares by the companies, but they are still continuing to allot odd lot shares. The investors who had purchased shares in odd lots prior to the issue of instructions by the SEBI cannot get any relief. They have to pay a heavy brokerage say, up to 15 per cent for purchasing and selling their odd lots. Fair brokerage for transactions in odd lots is only limited to selective and good scrips.

12. Lack of Transparency. The buyers and sellers of shares are entirely at the mercy of brokers who quote the lowest traded rate of a share to the sellers and the highest to the purchasers. In this way they gain both ways. Moreover, there is no uniformity in the rate of brokerage. The brokers also do not maintain proper accounts. In short, the trading transactions in stock exchanges lack transparency.

13. Defects of Stock Exchanges. Further, the operations of the stock exchanges are also defective. They neither have the proper infrastructure, nor do they have adequate space for enabling the stock brokers to operate efficiently. They also do not have adequate telecommunication and computerisation facilities. Consequently, they are still following the old trade practices.

14. Inadequate Number of Stock Exchanges. There are only 22 stock exchanges functioning in the country. But, during recent years the number of companies listed every month and the number of shareholders have increased by leaps and bounds. Looking to these, the number of stock exchanges is very small and inadequate. That is why in the southern region of the country a number of unauthorised and unregistered private stock exchanges have come into existence which indulge in speculative dealings.

15. Fragmentation of Secondary Market. The secondary capital market is fragmented into the ring-operated stock exchanges, the ringless OTCEI and the on-line screen-based and scripless NSEI. This not only confuses the small investors but also throws them into the lap of the brokers and sub-brokers. Consequently, the small investors stand cheated and the liquidity in the capital market stands reduced.

Suggestions for Improvement of the Indian Capital Market

The following suggestions have been made to improve upon the functioning of the Indian capital market:

1. For improving liquidity the distinction between Group 'A' and Group 'B' shares should be done away with.

2. The working of stock exchanges should be so streamlined that the delay in transactions, delivery of scrips and transfer of shares is minimised. For achieving this goal, the stock exchanges must be computerised. The transfer of scrips and debentures should be scrip less, only through book entry. The shareholders should be issued Counter Receipts instead of share certificates as done by the OTCEI and the share certificates should remain in the custody of the Registrars. Again, the registration of spot transactions should be made compulsory so that illegal trading is eliminated.

3. It is very essential that insider trading is stopped by adopting punitive measures by the SEBI and stock exchanges.

4. New market instruments possessing liquidity, safety and fair return should be introduced to enable the mobilisation of larger capital resources.

5. The grey market operations should be banned and a code of conduct may be prescribed by the SEBI for financial analysts.

6. The prospectuses issued by the new companies should be transparent and should supply all the information truthfully and honestly. Those companies which fail to do this, should be penalised through legal action.

7. It is high time that the interest of investors and brokers is protected. Those companies which do not follow SEBI guidelines and indulge in fraudulent practices should be penalised through legal action. The amount of dividend and interest should be deposited direct by the Registrars into the bank accounts of the investors under intimation to them. This will also discourage bogus transactions. The maximum limit to be paid to an individual shareholder in the case of a defaulting broker out of the Customers' Protection Fund at the stock exchanges should be enhanced at least to Rs. 1,00,000. A similar fund should also be setup to compensate the brokers in case some customers default by not making payments to them.

8. To facilitate investors a separate trust should be set up for disposal of odd lot shares. It would be useful if the SEBI instructs the companies to pay cash instead of allotting odd lots.

9. The number of stock exchanges should be increased to facilitate smooth trading in sharpes and stocks and to enhance liquidity in the capital market and also to stop the multiplication of illegal trading houses.

10. The activities of intermediaries should be regulated by the SEBI so that the secondary capital market may function properly. The SEBI should lay down proper guidelines for the operations of such intermediaries.

11. The activities of the three types of stock exchanges, *viz.*, the traditional stock exchanges, the OTCEI and the NSEI should be coordinated to avoid any overlapping.

12. Finally, more tax concessions should be provided to the investors to give a boost to the capital market. It would be helpful if double tax on dividends is abolished and the minimum tax-free levels of dividends and capital gains are increased.

Exercises

1. Explain the term 'money market'. Distinguish between a developed money market and undeveloped money market.
2. "Smoothly functioning money market is essential for the functioning of a developed modern economy in the world." Discuss the statement.
3. What are the constituents of Indian money market? Do you think that the Indian money market is a perfect market?
4. Discuss the defects of the Indian money market. Suggest suitable measures to remove them.
5. Explain the nature of Indian money market. What are its functions?
6. Explain the main features of the unorganised money market in India.
7. "The most outstanding feature of the Indian money market is its dichotomy." In the light of this statement explain the structure of the Indian money market.
8. Assess the role of non-banking financial institutions and non-banking companies in the Indian money market. What steps have been taken to regulate their activities?
9. Distinguish between money market and capital market. Give the brief account of the institutional set-up in the Indian money market.
10. What are the main causes responsible for an under-developed bill market in India? How is the Bill Market Scheme of the Reserve Bank of India adequate to solve this lacuna of the Indian money market?
11. Discuss the efforts made by the Reserve Bank of India to develop the Indian money market.

Chapter 21

The Indian Banking System

1. Introduction

The Indian banking system consists of the Reserve Bank of India, the State Bank of India, the Indian commercial banks, the exchange banks, the industrial banks, the indigenous bankers, the co-operative banks and the land development banks. The Reserve Bank of India was setup in 1935 and therefore, in the absence of a central bank, organised banking in this country has been a late starter. The three Presidency Banks, in Calcutta, Bombay and Madras were working in the first half of the 19th century and performing the functions of the modern banks. These banks enjoyed the monopoly of banking business in the country and a partial monopoly of note-issue. They were allowed to use government balances free of charge in the presidency towns. They were not allowed to deal in foreign bills and therefore, could not borrow money from abroad. They could not make advances for more than six months and could not issue loans on immovable property. Proposals were made from time to time to amalgamate these banks, but were rejected. So, before the First World War, the banking system in the country was utterly un-co-ordinated and it was only in 1920 that the three Presidency Banks were amalgamated and the Imperial Bank of India was established. Before we proceed further it would be helpful, if a brief history of the development of the modern banking in our country is traced. We may divide this history into two periods: (*i*) pre-Independence, and (*ii*) post-Independence.

2. Development of Banking before Independence

Banking during the pre-British period was generally carried on by the indigenous bankers. Towards the close of the 18th century, the East India Company setup some Agency Houses to carry on the important banking activities which included financing the military requirements of the Company, giving loans for agricultural marketing, issuing paper currency and accepting deposits from the public. These Agency Houses gradually paled into significance after the abolition of the commercial rights of the East India Company by the British Crown in 1813. Consequently, three Presidency Banks, the Bank of Bengal (1806), the Bank of Bombay (1840), and the Bank of Madaras (1843) were established. These were private shareholders' banks and the majority of shares was held by foreigners. Since the Government of India also had some shares, it exercised control on the activities of these banks. In 1860, a law was enacted under which the banks could be organised on the basis of limited liability. Accordingly, establishment of joint-stock banks in India was very much facilitated and a number of banks were established during this period. The main reason for the fast development of banking during this period was the Swadeshi movement, which inspired the people to boycott foreign banks and start transacting business with Indian banks. A large number of banks of different sizes came into existence.

The period from 1913 to 1917 was a very critical period and as many as 87 banks failed. These failures shook the confidence of people in Indian joint-stock banks and checked the growth of banking in the country. The banking crisis continued during the initial years of the First World War; but as time passed, the confidence of the people in the banking system was gradually restored. The three Presidency Banks were amalgamated in 1921 to constitute the Imperial Bank of India. The Reserve Bank of India was established in 1935. The development of Indian banking during the period between 1913-39 was rather lopsided and haphazard. In the former Indian States, banking facilities were completely conspicuous by their absence, while in certain provinces there was a spate of new banking offices, in certain other provinces no new branches were opened.

Indian banking made tremendous progress during the Second World War. The number of banks increased from 59 on 1 September, 1939 to 87 by 7 September, 1945. The volume of commercial bank deposits increased by more than four times during the war. This can be attributed to: (*i*) depositors' overall preference for liquidity; (*ii*) low rates of interest on time deposits; and (*iii*) a heavy decline in the velocity of circulation of money due to wartime controls and rationing, leading to the accumulation of idle funds with people.

But in 1947 a marked departure was noticed from the above trend. Time deposits rose relatively to demand deposits. Total deposits did not decline according to expectation due to the close of the war and reduction in government expenditure due to the falling profits, declining production and increasing taxation, rising prices, increasing cost of living and the transfer of capital to the UK. The time deposits registered a rise not because of the declining liquidity preference, but due to the declining confidence of the people in equities, who preferred to keep their funds in fixed deposits. During the early years of the war discounts and advances had considerably declined, but after 1943, there was a steady recovery continuing up to the first quarter of 1947. This was mainly due to the necessity of making payments for imports, taxes, bonuses and dividends. These advances again declined towards the latter part of 1947, chiefly because of import restrictions and withdrawal of old deposits out of sheer political uncertainties.

We, thus, find that the banks had to incur a greater loss than profits earned by increased holdings of Government securities. Moreover, this reflected a fundamental change in the sphere of commercial banking in India, a change from the financing of trade and industry to the running of specialised investment trusts of government securities. They, thus, instead of providing only short-term capital to industry and trade, provided long-term finance to the government, which was basically against the principles of commercial banking. Not only that, the increase in the balances with the Reserve Bank was chiefly due to the fact that the banks were maintaining a large cash reserve, as a bulk of their funds were payable on demand.

Further, the Indian banks had to maintain a high cash ratio which ranged between 9.98 per cent in 1939-40 to 14.96 per cent in 1944-45. The necessity of such high ratio arose out of a feeling of uncertainty and nervousness prevailing in the country on account of communal disturbances. Although the total investments registered a rise, their ratio deposits fell from 59.3 per cent in 1942 to 50 per cent in 1943 and continued declining till 1947. The number of branches of various banks increased enormously during the war years from 1,471 in 1938 to 5,266 in 1945.

On the whole, the Indian banks faced very well the jerks of the war and the post-war period. However, many non-scheduled banks had to succumb to the shocks of the war and Partition. Moreover, as pointed out by the then Governor of the Reserve Bank, these failures were largely due to "mismanagement, indiscriminate opening of too many small branches, reckless lending operations, speculative operations on the stock exchange and lack of properly trained personnel". The Reserve Bank of India played its role well. The Banking Companies Act of 1946, helped a lot in developing banking on sound lines by checking indiscriminate opening of branches. The Reserve Bank adopted a strict attitude towards the granting of licences for opening new branches.

Indian banking made, thus, tremendous progress only in size and dimensions and not in quality. It suffered from various defects like the opening of banking offices in areas devoid of any banking business, indiscriminate branch expansion, opening of branches in. areas already served by banks, cut-throat competition, lack of trained personnel, interlocking of banks and other concerns, undesirable manipulation of accounts, defective lending policy, speculative activities and so on.

Soon after the close of the war, the structure of assets and liabilities of banks began to return to its pre-war pattern and the process continued up to the middle of 1947. The proportion of fixed deposits to total deposits, which had declined to one-fourth in 1944, rose to one-third mainly because of the return of confidence among the people and consequently the preference for liquidity disappeared. This was definitely a healthy sign. The turnover of the deposits also become quicker. Advances and bills almost resumed their prewar position in the assets of the scheduled banks. In one year, from the end of 1945 to the end of 1946, they increased by Rs. 120 crore. Their percentage to total deposits increased from 34 to 42. The main reasons for this increase were, rise in prices, especially of industrial raw materials and imported goods, revived trade, increased accommodation provided by banks against securities, shares, bullions, immobilisation of funds in goods due to transport bottlenecks, heavy tax payment by businessmen, etc. The percentage of the investments of scheduled banks declined from 53 to 46 during the one year due to a reduction in the investment on government securities. The percentage of cash to liabilities also fell. Thus, this period proved to be more fruitful for the banks than even the war years.

3. Development of Banking Since Independence

During the latter half of 1947 and the early months of 1948, the structure of the assets and liabilities of banks tended to return to the war-time position. The proportion of investments and cash to total assets increased and that of advances and bills decreased. This situation can be attributed chiefly to the communal tension and disturbances all over the country before and after Partition, declining agricultural and industrial production and internal and external trade, destruction of goods and property worth crores of rupees. The banks, therefore, curtailed their investments.

The Banking Ordinance of 1946 helped Reserve Bank to maintain a close watch over the banking system. The opening of branches was restricted by the Banking Companies (Restriction of Branches) Act of 1946. The most prominent developments in the Indian banking system during the post-Independence period are given in the following sections:

Increase in the Effectiveness of the Reserve Bank of India

With a view to equipping the Reserve Bank of India with more powers and making its functioning more purposeful and effective the Government of India nationalised it on 1 January, 1949. The Banking Regulation Act was passed in March 1949, with a view to making its control and regulation of commercial banks in the country more effective. The Act provided extensive powers to the Reserve Bank for carrying out the inspection of scheduled banks. The

Reserve Bank could now check the accounts of the scheduled banks at any time; the scheduled banks could not open new branches without its permission and there were special provisions to safeguard the interests of the depositors. The Reserve Bank also intensified and strengthened the training programmes of the officers and others in the banking industry. It extended the scope of the activities of the Indian Institute of Bankers. It also set-up a training college to impart instruction to the bank employees.

Before we proceed further, it would be worthwhile to highlight the main features of the Banking Regulations Act of 1949. Prior to the passage of this Act, the banks in the country were governed by the Banking Companies Act. The change in the title was necessitated owing to the inclusion of co-operative banks within the fold of the Reserve Bank. The Act contains 56 sections and the last one deals with co-operative banks. Other sections are only concerned with the 'do's' and 'dont's' for commercial banks. As many as 15 sections are concerned with the Reserve Bank's control over the banks. The Act was a sincere effort to remove the shortcomings and improve the working of the joint-stock banks in India. The main provisions are: (*i*) Minimum requirements relating to paid-up capital and reserves of a banking company have been prescribed. The Act states that the paid-up capital and reserves of an Indian bank must not be less than Rs. 50,000 if it has its place of business only in one state and Rs. 5 lakh if it has places of business in more than one state and Rs. 10 lakh if it has an office in Bombay and/or in Calcutta. It is compulsory for every bank to transfer to its reserve fund at least 20 per cent of the profits until the reserve fund becomes equal to the paid-up capital. These provisions were mainly intended to check the indiscriminate establishment of banking companies. (*ii*) To ensure liquidity of assets of banks, the Act requires every banking company to maintain in cash, gold or approved securities an amount not less than 20 per cent of its time and demand deposits. (*iii*) The Act also imposes certain restrictions on the banks on opening subsidiary companies and puts serious limitations on the activities of banks connected with speculative trade or manufacturing business. (*iv*) The provisions of the Act also indicate measures for effective monopoly control over a banking company by a small group of promoters. Thus, according to the provisions the voting rights of anyone shareholder should not exceed 5 per cent of the total voting rights of all the shareholders. (*v*) The Act empowers the Reserve Bank to inspect the books of account of the banks, call for periodic or any ad hoc statements from the banks and to apply qualitative and selective control. (*vi*) The Act prohibits interlocking of directorate among banks and provides an effective safeguard against the use of the resources of the banks by the Directors and Managers for promoting their own companies.

The Act of 1949 was amended in 1950, 1956, 1959, 1960 and 1962. The amendments made in 1956 authorised the Reserve Bank of India to regulate the remuneration and appointment of the Bank executives holding superior positions, to appoint observers to attend Board meetings of the scheduled banks and to obtain information over a wider range than has been possible up to this time. After the amendments made in 1959, the banks can form subsidiary companies for carrying on banking business outside India with the prior permission of the Reserve Bank; the Reserve Bank can inspect the foreign branches and foreign subsidiaries of Indian banks. They further made the provisions relating to payment of dividend and maintenance of the reserve fund more flexible and adaptable to contingencies; enabled the Reserve Bank to issue conditional licences to banking companies; prohibited a banking company from creating a floating charge on its assets without the consent of the Reserve Bank; elaborated the conditions under which the Reserve Bank may initiate proceedings leading to the windingup of a company; and extended to all banking companies the restrictions relating to voluntary windingup. The amendments made in 1960 were in the direction of making a severe effort towards the reorganisation of the banking system of the country, in the sense, that it has extended to banking companies the provisions for compulsory amalgamation as contained in section 396 of the Companies Act of 1956 and makes a provision for an alternative method of compulsory amalgamation and/or restriction of a banking company. According to the amended Act of 1962, the scheduled banks are required to maintain liquid assets amounting to 25 per cent of the demand and time liabilities. The amended Act provides special powers to the Reserve Bank for collecting credit information from various banks and financial institutions. Lastly, the Act raises the limit of minimum paid-up capital in the case of an Indian banking company which commences banking business for the first time after the commencement of the Banking Companies (Amendment) Act, 1962, to Rs. 5 lakh, irrespective of whether it has only one place of business or places of business in only one state, as against the previous lowest minimum capital requirement of Rs. 50,000.

It would, thus, be seen that all these amendments have considerably increased the powers of the Reserve Bank to conduct an effective control on the Indian joint-stock banks and have enabled banking system to grow in healthy directions.

The Banking Laws Act of 1963

In December 1963, the Banking Laws (Miscellaneous Provisions) Act was passed. It simultaneously amended the Banking Companies Act of 1949, the Reserve Bank of India Act of 1934 and the State Bank of India (Subsidiary

Banks) Act of 1959. With the enactment of this Act, the Reserve Bank was further equipped to control the banks and non-banking financial intermediaries. For a moment, let us talk very briefly about the important provisions of this Act. The Act prohibits a bank from sanctioning unsecured advances to: (*i*) any of its directors, (*ii*) firms or private companies in which any of its directors is interested as partner or managing agent or guarantor or any individuals in cases where any of its directors is a guarantor, (*iii*) any public company in which the chairman of the Board of Directors of the bank is interested as chairman or managing director of the public company or as director or partner or the managing agent of such a company. According to the provisions of the Act, a banking company can be forbidden to remit without the prior permission of the Reserve Bank, any debt due to it from the directors of any firm or company in which the bank's directors are interested or if any of the bank's directors is the partner or guarantor. The Reserve Bank has been given the power to nominate up to a maximum of five persons as additional directors of a bank, if, in its opinion, it is essential in the interest of the bank, its depositors and also to issue directives to banks, generally or individually, on: (*a*) the maximum amount of advances in the light of the paid-up capital reserves and deposits of a bank and other relevant considerations that may be made by the bank to any company or individual; (*b*) the maximum amount up to which, keeping in mind the considerations, guarantees may be given by a bank on behalf of any company or individual; and (*c*) the rate of interest and other terms and conditions on which advances may be offered or guarantees given.

The need to bring about these changes in the provisions was to protect the interests of the depositors. This was also evident in the extension of the control of the Reserve Bank to non-banking institutions accepting deposits. It was observed that the volume of deposits accepted by the non-banking institutions had been growing steadily and there was no provision in the existing legislation, relating to banks, to provide any control over these institutions. There was no provision asking them to summit periodical returns on deposits and therefore, was not possible to assess the magnitude of such deposits or to know whether these deposits were safe or the rates offered by them were higher and so on. To cover all these deficiencies and to equip the Reserve Bank with sufficient powers to regulate the activities of these institutions, the 1963 Act also amended the Reserve Bank of India Act. These amendments *inter alia* empowered the Reserve Bank to regulate or prohibit the issue of prospectus or advertisement by non-banking institutions soliciting deposits from the public, to call for returns and information relating to deposits from such institutions and to give them directions in regard to receipt of deposits, including the rates of interest payable on and period of such deposits. The Reserve Bank may prohibit acceptance of deposits by any such institution which fails to comply with its directions, and call for from financial institutions information regarding their paid-up capital, reserve or other liabilities, investments, terms and conditions of their advances, etc. and give directions to them regarding the conduct of their business.

The question of regulating the deposits accepted by non-banking financial institutions will certainly acquire greater significance in future. Both the types of institutions, *i.e.*, banking as well as non-banking, are required to submit to the Reserve Bank of India information related to the receipt of deposits from the public. The data received by the Reserve Bank from the non-banking institutions placed the total deposits of these institutions at Rs. 136 crore as on 31 March, 1964, of which Rs. 158 crore or 85 per cent represented short-term deposits, which meant that these institutions were competing directly with the banking system. Accordingly, in January 1966, regulatory measures were announced for controlling the activities of these institutions. The Reserve Bank of India issued two directives under the Act of 1963, one to non-banking non-financial companies (other than insurance companies receiving deposits only from their members) and the other non-banking financial companies which carry on or finance hire-purchase business. The Reserve Bank of India further issued two more directives in October 1966, because of unduly large commitments by smaller private non-banking companies and the reported failure of some of these companies in and around Delhi. The Reserve Bank of India issued another set of directives known as the miscellaneous Non-Banking Companies Direction, 1973 which was made effective from 1 September, 1973. These directions regulate the acceptance of deposits by companies conducting prize chits, lucky draws, saving schemes, etc. It was made clear that the subscriptions received by such companies were deposits and therefore, they should be regulated like the deposits of other non-banking financial institutions. The Reserve Bank of India Act was further amended in 1974 which vested the Reserve Bank with more powers to exercise control over non-banking institutions receiving deposits and financial institutions.

Nationalisation of the Imperial Bank

The Imperial Bank of India was nationalised on 1 July, 1955, and renamed as the State Bank of India with a view to opening new branches in the rural and backward areas of the country, and to provide special help for the development of co-operative banks in the country. The Imperial Bank was nationalised in accordance with the recommendations of the All-India Rural Credit Survey Committee (1952). The Committee had recommended the creation of a State Bank of India by amalgamating some state-associated banks with the Imperial Bank. Accordingly, the State Bank of India Act was passed in 1955 and the State Bank of India, constituted on 1 July, 1955, took over the assets and liabilities of the Imperial Bank. The Act empowered the State Bank to acquire the business of other banks and to pay compensation to the shareholders of these banks with the sanction of the government. Initially, the State Bank was required to open at least 400 branches by 30th June, 1960. In order to meet the losses that might arise to the State Bank on this account, the Act constituted an Integration and Development Fund into which were to be paid the dividends payable to the Reserve Bank on its shareholding of 55 per cent of the total issued capital in the State Bank and also such contributions as the Reserve or the Central Government were to make from time to time. The branch expansion programme in the rural and semi-urban areas as envisaged in the Act was fulfilled much before the expiry of the prescribed period. The 400th branch was opened in June 1960. The State Bank opened 5000th new branch on the 1 March, 1979. The number of new branches increased considerably and at the end of March 1979 there were more than 5,000 offices of which 75 per cent were in rural and semi-urban areas. The subsidiaries of the State Bank which started participating in the Bank's development activities since October 1959, have opened more than 1,500 new branches. The Bank has undoubtedly led to the provision and expansion of banking facilities in the rural and semi-urban areas of the country.

Social Control of Banks

The Banking Regulations Act, 1949, no doubt, provided homogeneity and coherence to the banking system and gave it a sense of direction in the field of deposit mobilisation and credit dispensation, still it was believed that there was a need for closer dovetailing of credit allocation with the priorities of economic planning. It was felt that since banking sector is a key constituent of the country's economy, it should serve the basic social and economic goals for the attainment of optimum growth rate and prevention of monopolistic tendencies, concentration of power and improper use of resources.

It was, therefore, decided to introduce measures which would impose effective social control over the operations of the commercial banks. Social control of these banks would be—(*a*) to broaden the spectrum of bank advances and to improve the position of agriculture and small industry in the advance portfolio of banks; (*b*) to enable the government to effectively implement the five-year plans; and (*c*) to bring about wider representation in the boards of directors of banks and in the actual decisions regarding advances, etc.

A Bill on social control, called the Banking Laws (Amendment) Bill, 1967, was introduced in the Parliament in the third week of December 1967. It received the assent of the President in the last week of December 1968 and it actually came into effect from 1 February, 1969. The social control legislation envisaged two steps—(*a*) the creation of National Credit Council to formulate credit policy, and (*b*) a change in the composition of board of directors of every bank.

The National Credit Council was set-up by the Government of India at all-India level in January 1968. Under the Act of 1968, banking companies were required to reconstitute their boards of directors, such that, a majority of persons on the boards had the special knowledge of practical experience in agriculture, rural economy, small-scale industries, co-operation, banking, finance, etc. which were considered to be useful to the banking company. Foreign banks were also required to set-up an advisory committee on the lines of Indian banks.

Nationalisation of Major Banks

It was soon realised that social control over banks of the kind visualised by the government under the Banking Laws (Amendment) Act of 1968, was not adequate to fulfil the requirements of a developing economy in conformity with national priorities and objectives. Consequently, the Government through an Ordinance nationalised fourteen major Indian scheduled banks on 19 July, 1969. These banks are: Central Bank of India, Bank of India, Punjab National Bank, Bank of Baroda, United Commercial Bank, Canara Bank, United Bank of India, Dena Bank, Syndicate Bank, Allahabad Bank, Union Bank of India, Indian Bank, Bank of Maharashtra and Indian Overseas Bank. The total deposits of these banks stood at Rs. 3,051 crore on 18 July, 1969. If the deposits of the State Bank of India and its subsidiaries are added to this amount, the total deposits amounted to Rs. 4,650 crore. There was, therefore, an increase in the share of the public sector in the banking industry after the nationalisation of these banks to the extent of 58 per cent.

In 1980, six more banks, whose demand and time liabilities exceeded Rs 200 crore on 14 March, 1980, were nationalised. These banks are: The Andhra Bank, The Corporation Bank, The New Bank of India, The Oriental Bank of Commerce, The Punjab and Sind Bank, and The Vijaya Bank.

Banking Companies Amendment Act, 1994

The Banking Companies (Acquisition and Transfer of Undertakings) Amendment Act, 1944, amended the Banking Companies Act of 1970 and 1980 whereby 14 and 6 scheduled banks were nationalised respectively. This amendment provides for partial privatisation of the public sector banks which are 20 (including the SBI) at present, after the merger of New Bank of India with the Punjab National Bank in 1993. The main features of the amendment are—(*i*) the authorised capital of every nationalised bank has been set at Rs. 1,500 crore divided into 150 crore fully paid-up shares of Rs. 10 each; (*ii*) the Government of India may in consultation with the Reserve Bank of India and by notification in the official gazette increase or reduce the authorised capital subject to the condition that the authorised capital shall not exceed

Rs. 3,000 crore or be less than Rs. 1500 crore; (*iii*) the Central Government shall retain 51 per cent of the shares in these banks and the private individuals and companies shall hold up to 49 per cent of the shares; (*iv*) the holdings of non-resident Indians shall not be more than 20 per cent of the 49 per cent private shares; (*v*) the shares not held by the Government of India shall be freely transferable; (*vi*) no shareholder other than the Government of India shall be entitled to exercise voting rights in respect of any shares held by them in excess of 1 per cent of the total voting rights of all. shareholders of the bank; (*vii*) each bank shall have 15 Directors on its Board, out of whom 9 shall be nominated by the Government of India and the other six shall be non-official nominees. There shall be one Director from among the workmen of the bank and one from other employees; (*viii*) every bank's total capital shall be equal to at least 8 per cent of its risk weighted assets, by 31 March, 1996:

Traditional Banking to Social Banking

During the post-nationalisation period the emphasis has been on the diversification of the banking activities in terms of expansion of branch offices, deposits and advances on the one hand and on social banking on the other, for achieving the twin objective of rapid economic growth and removal of poverty. Various programmes to achieve these objectives have been undertaken during this period. Following is the present status of these programmes:

1. Expansion of Branch Offices. The commercial banks have made phenomenal progress in the field of branch expansion, chiefly to: (*i*) narrow down regional imbalances; and (*ii*) provide on an extensive scale banking facilities in rural and semi-urban areas. In June 1995, there were 62,346 bank branches in the country of which 56.1 per cent were in rural areas as compared to 32.5 per cent in June 1969.

2. The Lead Bank Scheme. The scheme was introduced by the Reserve Bank of India in December 1969, as a supplement to the branch expansion programme of commercial banks to ensure the flow of bank credit to priority sector and to coordinate the activities of the various agencies such as banks and developmental agencies of the government at various levels. Under the Lead Bank Scheme a particular district was allotted to a particular bank which was made responsible to develop banking and credit in that district. The bank so selected was designated as the Lead Bank for that district. It was expected to perform the following functions—(*i*) to conduct a survey of the resources and potential for the development of banking services; (*ii*) to determine the centres of growth for opening branches in a phased manner; (*iii*) to identify commercial units and other establishments which do not have bank accounts and which are dependent on moneylenders; (*iv*) to take stock of the facilities for marketing of agricultural produce, industrial production, storage and warehousing and the linking of credit with marketing in the district; (*v*) to obtain details of facilities for the stocking of fertilisers and other agricultural inputs and for the repair and servicing of equipments; (*vi*) to recruit and train staff for offering advice to small borrowers and farmers and for the supervision and monitoring of end-use loans; (*vii*) to provide assistance to other primary lending agencies; and (*viii*) to maintain liaison with government and semi-government agencies.

The scheme has been a great success in so far as branch expansion and provision of credit facilities in rural areas are concerned. It extended banking facilities to the under-banked and un-banked rural and semi-urban areas by increasing the number of branches from 5,175 in June 1969 to 47,211 branches in June 1995. The share of public sector banks in priority sector advances rose from 14.9 per cent to 36.6 per cent per cent over the period. Up to the end of June 1995, 504 districts had been covered under the scheme.

3. The Service Area Approach (SAA). The Lead Bank Scheme succeeded only quantitatively and failed qualitatively by not extending timely credit to the needy people. To assess the impact of the programme the Reserve Bank of India asked the Chief Executives of the public sector banks to carry out field visits in rural areas of different districts all over the country. They visited 88 districts in 21 States and discussed their findings in a seminar convened by the Reserve Bank in January 1988. They recommended that the time was opportune to adopt a system in which each bank would concentrate in a specified area to develop lending for production purposes. Thereafter, the Reserve Bank of India set-up a Committee under its Dr. Governor Dr. P.D. Ojha to examine the operational aspects involved in implementing this approach. The recommendations of the Ojha Committee were accepted and as a consequence thereof the 1988-89 Budget announced the 'Service Area Approach' which involves the following five stages:

1. *Allocation of Service Area.* Each branch on an average has been allocated 15 to 25 villages under its Service Area. However, at least in five States, *viz.*, Himachal Pradesh, Andhra Pradesh, Manipur, Meghalaya, Orissa and one Union Territory Andaman and Nicobar the average number of villages allocated per branch exceeds 25. Similarly, the average number of kms to be covered by each branch is more than 100 sq. km for at least nine States and one Union Territory.

2. *Survey of Villages.* Each branch has to undertake villagewise surveys of the allotted villages and prepare village profile which is to be updated periodically taking into account the development changes, if any, taken place in the intervening period.

3. *Preparation of Credit Plans.* Each branch has to prepare an annual

credit plan for its service area. First the credit plan is prepared for each village and then on the basis of the village credit plans the service area credit plan is prepared reflecting the potentialities and needs of the people of the area. The regional rural banks' branches are responsible for preparings credit plans for the target group only while the designated bank prepares the credit plans for the non-target group.

4. *Co-ordination of Activities.* A Block Level Bankers' Committee has to coordinate the activity of the banks and Government agencies. The lead bank officer is the convener-Chairman of this Committee. The managers of all the bank branches including cooperative banks located in the block, block development officer and extension officers in the block are its members. This committee finalises the branch credit plans and these plans are thereafter integrated into block credit plans.

5. *Follow up.* The Block Level Bankers' Committee holds periodical meetings, at least once in a quarter, to review the progress of implementation of credit plans and solve operational problems.

Recent Modifications in SAA. The following modifications have been introduced in recent years by the Reserve Bank of India in the Service Area Approach—(*i*) service Area branches may be grouped blockwise without disturbing their identities or their obligation to prepare village level/service area plans so that the borrowers have the flexibility to approach other branches within the block for fulfilling their credit requirements; (*ii*) in Service Areas which are very large and which are located in tribal/hilly and inaccessible areas satellite or mobile offices be set up; (*iii*) to facilitate the use of their infrastructure to the maximum the area of operation of the specialised branches like the agricultural development branch, the agricultural banking division and Gram Vikas Kendras may be enlarged; (*iv*) realigning the sacred service areas; and (*v*) exemption of large projects covering several districts/States from the Service Area Approach.

During 1994-95 the all India sectorwise targets and achievements were as follows—in agriculture and allied activities loans worth Rs. 16,885 crore were disbursed against the target of Rs. 16,469 crore; in small scale industries loans to the tune of Rs. 5,605 crore were given against the target of Rs. 4,914 crore and in services, loans amounting to Rs. 4,081 crore were advanced against the target of Rs. 3,672 crore.

4. Local Area Banks. P. Chidambaram, Finance Minister, Government of India in his Budget Speech for the year 1996-97 announced the Local Area Banks Scheme to redress the complaints of many State Governments that public sector banks were taking away their resources to lend them in other States. Unlike the regional rural banks these banks will be set-up in the private sector and registered and licensed as scheduled banks. The Reserve Bank issued the following guidelines on 24th August, 1996 regarding the establishment of Local Area Banks:

1. *Area of Operation.* The area of operation of a bank shall be a maximum of three geographically contiguous districts.

2. *Capital.* The paid-up capital for starting a bank shall not be less than Rs. 5 crore of which Rs. 2 crore would be the contribution of promoters which may comprise individuals, corporations, trusts or societies.

3. *Objectives.* The objectives of these banks are: (*i*) to cater to the credit needs of the local people and to provide efficient and competitive financial services in their area of operation; (*ii*) to promote rural savings and provide credit for viable economic activities in their area; and (*iii*) to bridge the gaps in credit availability and enhance the institutional credit framework in rural and semi-urban areas.

4. *Functions.* The focus of their activities will be on the local customers. They will promote and mobilise savings, provide finance to agriculture and allied activities, small scale industries, agro-industrial units, trading units and the non-farm sector in their area. They will observe the priority sector lending target of 40 per cent of net bank credit as applicable to other commercial banks. Within this target they will lend at least 25 per cent or 10 per cent of net bank credit to the weaker sections.

5. *Prudential Norms.* Each bank shall follow prudential norms, and policies as prescribed by the Reserve Bank. All norms set by the RBI for income recognition, asset classification and provisioning will be applicable right from the very start. The statutory liquidity ratio, CRR, deposit and lending rates will be the same as that for regional rural banks. Each bank will have to achieve capital adequacy ratio of 8 per cent from the very start.

However, the wisdom of the government and the Reserve Bank in adding yet another institution to the existing large number of financial institutions and agencies for providing credit to the rural areas, has been widely questioned. People ask, what is the guarantee that the local area banks will be a success? We may at this stage simply hope that these banks will be successful where the regional rural banks will fail. This would be possible only if their staff is recruited locally. But would the success of these banks not mean the gradual death of regional rural banks?

5. Financing of Priority Sector. Those sectors of the economy which have not been able so far to avail of the bank finance but which occupy an important position from the economic point of view and deserve help from the banking system have been called as the 'Priority Sectors'. This concept of 'priority sector' was evolved in 1968 with the introduction of social control over banks. Initially the priority sectors included agriculture, small-scale industries and exports. Later on all hitherto neglected sectors were included in the term 'priority sectors' like, small road and water transport operators, retailers including petty shopkeepers and self-employed persons such as artisans, craftsmen, etc. and deserving students desirous of improving upon their educational qualifications. It was the Working Group set-up by the Reserve Bank of India with or. K.S. Krishnaswamy as its Chairman, included 'weaker sections' in this category. So, now the priority sector includes—(*i*) agriculture and allied activities; (*ii*) small-scale industries; (*iii*) road and water transport operators; (*iv*) retail trade and small business; (*v*) setting of industrial establishment; (*vi*) professional and self-employed persons; (*vii*) education; (*viii*) ex-servicemen; (*ix*) Urban Micro Enterprises; and (*x*) weaker sections, comprising of—(*a*) small and marginal farmers with land holdings of up to 5 acres, landless labourers, tenant farmers and share croppers; (*b*) artisans, village and cottage industries enjoying credit limit up to Rs. 25,000; (*c*) beneficiaries under the Integrated Rural Development Programme; (*d*) beneficiaries belonging to Scheduled Castes and Scheduled Tribes; (*e*) beneficiaries under the schemes of DRI and Urban Micro Enterprises and also under the Scheme for Liberation and Rehabilitation of Scavengers; and (*f*) Self-help Groups under NABARD's Pilot Projects.

Progress of Priority Sector Lending. The advances of public sector banks to the priority sector increased from 14.6 per cent as in June 1969 to 36.6 per cent at the end of March 1995. The share of agriculture was 13.9 per cent as compared to 5.4 per cent in June 1969. The share of small scale industries was 15.3 per cent in comparison to 8.5 per cent at the end of June 1969 and advances to others increased from 0.7 per cent to 7.4 per cent during the same period. The advances to the weaker sections constituted 8.2 per cent of the net bank credit of public sector banks as against the target of 10 per cent ending March 1995 Advances of public sector banks under the DRI scheme were 0.5 per cent of their total advances against the target of 1.0 per cent at the end of March 1995.

So far as the foreign banks are concerned their net bank credit was 38.5 per cent which included credit to export 28.5 per cent and to small-scale industries 10 per cent. Only eight foreign banks deposited Rs. 124 crore with the SIDBI for not achieving the overall target of 32 per cent prescribed by the RBI.

The advances by private sector commercial banks to the priority sector were 30 per cent against the target of 40 per cent at the end of March 1995. Advances given under the scheme of Urban Micro Enterprises were of the order of Rs. 110 crore during 1994-95. This scheme was launched on 15 June 1990 with the sole object of providing employment to poor people in urban areas, whose annual family income did not exceed Rs. 11,850.

Innovative Programmes Undertaken by Indian Commercial Banks

Following innovative programmes have been started by the public sector banks in India during the last one decade:

1. Merchant Banking. On the pattern of the foreign banks the public sector banks in India have also started merchant banking services by establishing their subsidiaries. Some of these are SBI Capital Markets Ltd., Bank of Baroda, Merchant Bank Division, Canbank Financial Services Limited, Union Bank of India, Merchant Bank Division, PNB Capital Services Limited, etc. Merchant banking includes services like management of public issues, loan syndication, financial and management consultancy, project counselling, mergers and acquisitions, management of non-resident investments, etc.

2. Leasing. Under leasing industries make a contractual arrangement with a leasing company for the use of assets, like plant, equipment, etc. on payment of rent for a mutually agreed period of time. This activity was being undertaken by the private companies but after the establishment of merchant banking subsidiaries, public sector banks have also started doing leasing business. At the end of June 1991, there were nine equipment leasing-cum-merchant banking subsidiaries set-up by Indian public sector banks. But their business in this regard has been only marginal.

3. Venture Capital. Venture capital is the finance provided to small/ medium business units floated by firms or individuals for implementing projects which involve new technology or products. The banks provide venture capital in the form of equity investment in the beginning. Financial institutions like ICICI, IDBI, UTI and IFCI have been the prominent organisations in promoting venture capital finance in India. Among the banks, SBI Capital Markets Limited is the most prominent.

4. Mutual Funds. The UTI was the first Mutual Fund set-up in India in 1964. In recent years a number of banks like the Indian Bank, Bank of India, State Bank of India, Canara Bank, Bank of Baroda, Punjab National Bank, etc. have set-up their own mutual funds as their subsidiaries. In 1989, the SBI Group also launched the Indian Magnum Fund, a maiden offshore fund which was privately placed with institutional investors and others primarily in the USA. The mutual funds mobilise savings from the public and invest them in different types of securities in the stock market. They earn interest, dividend and capital gains from such investments and distribute them to small investors. They provide stability to share prices by buying them when their prices are falling and selling them when their prices are rising. They, thus, provide safety, liquidity and income to investors and additional resources to entrepreneurs for the growth of industry.

5. Factoring. Factoring is a collection and finance service designed to improve the cash flow of small firms by providing ready cash in lieu of their sales invoices. A 'Factor' is a commission agent who offers funds to its clients and also undertakes—(*i*) management of accounts receivables, collection of debts of the client and safety against risk of default; and (*ii*) providing finances on the basis of accounts receivables. The Factor, in turn, receives the service charge by way of a discount or rebate deducted from the bills. It was after the amendment of the Banking Regulation Act in July 1990 that the Reserve Bank of India allowed the banks to undertake factoring through separate subsidiaries and the State Bank of India was the first to launch its subsidiary called the SBI Factors and Commercial Services Limited on 30 July, 1991.

The procedure involved in factoring is like this. The factor buys sales invoices from its client, prepays up to 80 per cent of its value immediately, undertakes the accounting function of sales ledger maintenance and the collection function of realising the amount mentioned in the invoices purchased. The suppliers invoice their customers in the usual fashion but only add that debt due on the invoice must be paid to the Factor. The suppliers offer the assigned invoices to the Factor with a schedule of offer, along with a copy of the receipted delivery of the challan. The Factor provides pre-payment up to 80 per cent of the value of the invoice. After the Factor collects the debts the supplier receives an official intimation and personalised statement of accounts from the Factor. When the supplier settles the invoice, the Factor pays the supplier the balance 20 per cent of the invoice value. The Factor charges discount on the pre-payment drawn by its client. The discount rate is comparable to bank lending rate and is collected monthly on the actual drawings. In addition, the Factor charges a fee which is normally between 1 and 5 per cent depending on the services utilised and volume of transactions made. Factoring services provide benefits to all the parties, namely, the supplier, his customer and the banker. This service is still in its initial stage and it will take some time before it comes into full swing.

6. Housing. A National Housing Bank was established in 1988 as an apex institution to provide housing finance. It has been providing assistance through a number of schemes. Subsequently, the banking sector also started providing housing finance to low and middle income groups to purchase or construct houses or flats. Interest rates are fixed by the Reserve Bank and the National Housing Bank. Banks have also been allowed to provide housing finance to builders by way of term loans for periods varying between 3 and 5 years under the refinance scheme of the National Housing Bank w.e.f. 5 June, 1991. State Bank of India, Bank of Baroda, Andhra Bank, Central Bank of India, Vijaya Bank Limited are the prominent public sector banks which have promoted housing finance companies.

7. Use of New Technology. A large number of commercial banks have started making use of the new technology in their operations. They have provided Electronic Accounting Machines and Advance Ledger Posting Machines in their branches. They have also taken up the project of total computerisation of their operations. About 260 offices of banks have been hooked through BANKNET, a data communication network for the Reserve Bank and public sector banks at Mumbai, New Delhi, Chennai, Kolkata, Bangalore, Hyderabad and Nagpur. Banks have also been asked by the Reserve Bank of India to introduce Magnetic Ink Character Recognition (MICR) cheques. The RBI is offering facilities for the clearance of these cheques at all the centres mentioned above except Bangalore. Several banks are also using Society for Worldwide Inter-Bank Financial Telecommunications (SWIFT) network. A number of banks have extended satellite disk antennae at their offices in a number of cities. When fully operational, these would form part of the Remote Area-Business Message Network and would be used for transferring messages between bank offices, in India and abroad, safely and speedily. A number of banks have started Electronic Clearing Service which is being used by several corporate bodies for payment of dividend/interest to their shareholders.

8. Customer Service. This is another area in which the banks have started taking positive steps. To elicit customers' reaction about the quality of their service the system of holding Customer Meets at regular intervals has been introduced. Some banks have constituted Customer Service Committees and Customer Councils. Some banks have also introduced courier service to expedite collection, remittances and transfer of accounts of their customers.

9. Banking Ombudsman. For settling the customer complaints against deficiency in banking services expeditiously the Banking Ombudsman has been appointed on a full-time basis each at Mumbai, Delhi, Bhopal, Chandigarh, Hyderabad, Patna, Jaipur, etc. This scheme covers all scheduled commercial banks except regional rural banks and primary cooperative banks.

10. Credit Cards. On the pattern of foreign banks major public sector and private sector banks have introduced their credit cards. Under this scheme the card holders are allowed credit facilities for a specified period. No security is obtained from them. The cardholder can make purchases and avail services without making cash payment. This system has become a profitable area of business for Indian banks.

11. Introduction of ATMs. Large number of banks have also introduced Automated Teller Machines (ATMs) in their licenced branches and extension counters to facilitate their clients to withdraw cash 24 hours a day up to a fixed limit.

12. Hire-purchase Business. On 7 September, 1990, the Government of India recognised the hire-purchase business as a legitimate activity for the banks. Accordingly, Canara Bank, State Bank of India, Punjab National Bank and Indian Bank have started doing this business.

13. Consumer Credit. Consumer credit is another profitable area in which the banks have started taking interest. They provide credit to the middle-class customers for the purchase of consumer durables and earn interest. In this way, the consumer goods industry also gets a fillip in its sales and additional job opportunities are also created.

Protection of Deposits and Bank Loans

The Deposit Insurance and Credit Guarantee Corporation (DICGC) was constituted on 15 July, 1978, after the taking over of the Credit Guarantee Corporation of India (CGCI) by the Deposit Insurance Corporation (DIC). The DIC was established on 1 January, 1962, for protecting the deposits made by savers by insuring them. If the insured bank failed, the Corporation was to pay to depositors up to a specified limit which was originally fixed at Rs. 1,500 per depositor in respect of deposits held by him in an insured bank. This limit was subsequently raised to Rs. 5,000 in 1968, to Rs. 10,000 in 1970, to Rs. 20,000 in 1976 and to Rs. 30,000 in 1980. The DIC was established with an authorised and paid-up capital of Rs. 2 crore. It could also borrow from the Reserve Bank of India up to Rs. 5 crore. To start with only commercial banks were eligible for insurance cover but in 1971 the cooperative banks were also declared eligible for insurance provided the State Government concerned passed the necessary legislation. Till now all the State Governments have not enacted such a legislation.

The CGCI was set up as a government company in January 1971, to administer the scheme of guarantees in respect of advances given by the credit institutions and to indemnify them in respect of such advances.

Obviously, now the DICGC has to perform two functions—(*i*) to insure the deposits of the small depositors in banks; and (*ii*) to provide guarantee support to eligible credit institutions for the priority sector advances to small borrowers and small-scale industries. At present, the limit of insurance cover is Rs. 1 lakh per bank. The insured bank has to pay a premium at the rate of 5 paise per hundred per annum on their accessible deposits. As on 31 March, 1995, the number of insured banks was 2,064 comprising 92 commercial banks, 196 regional rural banks and 1,776 cooperative banks in 21 States and 2 Union Territories. 99.2 per cent of the total number of accounts were fully protected and the insured deposits formed 73.3 per cent of the total accessible deposits.

Improvement of Customer Services

The Reserve Bank appointed a Committee under the Chairmanship of Shri M.N. Goiporia in September 1990 to examine the problem of unsatisfactory customer service in banks and to suggest measures for the improvement of the situation. The main recommendations of the Committee are—(*i*) change in the commencement of working hour for bank staff to facilitate timely opening of bank counters; (*ii*) extension of banking hours for all transactions except cash; (*iii*) enhancement of interest rate on saving account; (*iv*) introduction of tax benefits against bank deposits; (*v*) immediate credit of outstation cheques up to Rs. 5,000 as against Rs. 2,500 at present; (*vi*) extension of teller's duties (*vii*) modernisation of banks; (*viii*) opening of specialised branches far different customer groups; (*ix*) introduction of restricted holidays in banks; (*x*) full use of discretionery powers vested in the bank staff at all levels; (*xii*) expeditious despatch of document far collection and regular follow up with the foreign bank to facilitate timely realisation of export proceeds in the case of export finance.

Some of these recommendations have already been implemented.

4. Shortcomings of the Indian Banking System

There is no doubt that the Indian commercial banks have made commendable progress during recent decades. They are still suffering from a number of shortcomings. These are:

1. Growing Volume of Bad Debts. The volume of bad debts of the commercial banks has been rapidly increasing. These are called as non-performing assets. Bad debts include—(*a*) debts recalled; (*b*) suitfiled accounts, *i.e.*, where recovery proceedings have been initiated; (*c*) debts classified as bad and doubtful; and (*d*) decreed debts, that is, where suits have been filed and decrees obtained. Such debts accounted for 1.5 per cent of outstanding bank credit at the end of March 1995.

2. Inadequate Capital. The capital base of the Indian commercial banks was neither uniform nor adequate. There has been no increase in the capital base of 28 public sector banks since nationalisatian.

3. Non-transparent Balance Sheets. Despite compulsory audit of banks many banks continue to manipulate their balance sheets by artificially increasing their deposits in the last week of the fiscal year.

4. Faulty Loan Procedure. Same commercial banks have been showing favour to certain companies in granting loans which mare often than not turn into bad debts. Often these advances are made an extraneous or political considerations. The extension of letters of credit and guarantee limits without adapting authentic commercial procedure is a routine affair.

5. Speculation in Shares. A large number of banks have also been indulging in share speculation and thus misutilising public deposits. This has resulted in security scams.

6. Low Profitability. Irregularities in maintaining accounts, corruption in lending operations, frauds, increasing operating casts, misappropriation, have all led to considerable decline in profitability of commercial banks.

7. Inadequate Social Banking. In spite of a well-defined policy far helping the weaker sections of society, the commercial banks have been mainly catering to the needs of the corporate sector. This is evident from the fact that while in 1994-95 the bank credit to medium and large scale industries increased by 44.4 per cent aver 1993-94, the bank credit to small-scale industries increased by 6.8 per cent to agriculture by 26.1 per cent and to trade by 6.1 per cent.

8. Dual Administrative Control. The Indian banking system is at present being administered by two authorities, the Ministry of Finance and the Reserve Bank of India. Consequently, all the investing and lending programmes and appointments of Chief Executives and Directors are determined by ardors from above. The internal administration and credit decisions in individual cases are, therefore, subject to excessive administrative and political pressures.

5. Financial and Banking Sector Reforms

The Government of India constituted a Committee under the Chairmanship of Shri M. Narasimham, former Governor, Reserve Bank of India to examine the structure and functioning of the existing financial system of India and suggest suitable reforms. The Committee submitted its report in 1991 which was tabled in the Parliament on December 17. So far as the Indian banking system is concerned the committee made wide ranging recommendations which are summarised as follows:

1. Structure of the banking sector should be revamped so as to have three or four large banks.

2. Eight to ten national banks with a network of branches throughout the country should be engaged in 'Universal' banking. Rural banks should confine their operations only to rural areas mainly to finance agriculture and allied activities but their eye should be on profitability.

3. Local bank should operate only in a specified region.

4. Regional rural banks should be permitted to undertake all types of banking business.

5. One or more rural banking subsidiaries should be set-up by each public sector bank to take over all its rural branches.

6. The policy of branch licensing should be abolished and individual banks should have the freedom to open or close any branch.

7. Foreign banks should be subject to the same requirements as the Indian banks. They should be permitted to open offices in India as branches or as subsidiaries.

8. Indian banks' foreign operations should be rationalised.

9. Computerisation of bank operations should be speeded up.

10. Individual banks should have the freedom to recruit their own officers.

11. Inspection by supervisory staff should be guided by the internal audit and internal inspection reports.

12. The Reserve Bank of India should be the primary agency for regulating the banking system and the dual control over the banking system should end.

13. A separate authority under the aegis of the Reserve Bank of India should be set up to supervise banks and other financial institutions.

14. Depoliticisation of the appointment of Chief Executives and Directors of the banks.

15. Cash reserve ratio should be progressively reduced.

16. Statutory liquidity ratio should be brought down to 25 per cent over the next five years.

17. The priority sector should be redefined.

18. Directed credit programmes should be phased out.

19. Interest rate should be deregulated so as to reflect emerging market trends

20. Uniform accounting practices should be adopted by banks.

21. Balance sheets of banks should be transparent.

22. The commercial banks should achieve a minimum 4 per cent capital adequacy ratio in relation to risk weighted assets by March 1993.

23. Government should constitute special tribunals for the quick recovery of loans.

24. An Assets Reconstruction Fund should be established to take over from banks and financial institutions a portion of their bad and doubtful debts at a discount.

Measures Taken to Improve the Banking System

In pursuance of the recommendations of the Narasimham Committee the following measures have been taken to reform the Indian banking system.

1. Capital Adequacy Norms. In April 1992, the Reserve Bank of India laid down capital adequacy norms for compliance by banks by March 1996. Accordingly all the banks were required to achieve a risk weighted capital adequacy ratio of 4 per cent by 31 March, 1993 and 8 per cent by 31 March, 1996. Foreign banks operating in India and Indian banks operating abroad were to achieve 8 per cent norm by 31 March, 1993 and 31 March, 1994 respectively.

2. Prudential Accounting Norms. The Reserve Bank has also introduced prudential accounting norms for banks since 1992-93. If interest or instalment of principal are in arrears for any two quarters in the accounting year the credit facility will be treated as non-performing asset. Provisioning requirement for such assets with balances of less than Rs. 25,000 was increased to 10 per cent of the aggregate amount outstanding at the end of March 1995 from 7.5 per cent a year ago. For substandard and doubtful advances of Rs. 25,000 and above the banks are required to make 100 per cent provision.

3. Recapitalisation. With a view to enabling the public sector banks to meet the capital adequacy ratio the government of India contributes to the capital of such banks. The Government accordingly provided Rs. 57,000 crore towards recapitalisation of 19 nationalised banks in 1993-94, Rs. 5,293 crore to 13 banks in 1994-95, Rs. 850 crore to 6 banks in 1995-96 and Rs. 909 crore to 4 banks during 1996-97.

4. Recovery of Debts. For the recovery of bad debts The Recovery of Debt due to Banks and Financial Institutions Act, 1993 has been passed to constitute debt recovery tribunals. Such tribunals have been set-up at major centres.

5. Partial Privatisation of Public Sector Banks. In view of the limited resources of the government, recapitalisation is not a permanent solution and, therefore, banks have, been allowed to mobilise equity resources from the public. For this purpose the State Bank of India Act was amended and the Reserve Bank of India share holding has been reduced to 67 per cent. Subsequently, by the Banking Companies (Acquisition and Transfer of Undertakings) Amendment Act, 1994, the Government's share in the paid-up capital of public sector banks was reduced to 51 per cent.

6. Freedom to Open Branches. Banks have been given freedom to open new branches and upgrade extension counters on attaining the prescribed capital adequacy norms. They are also permitted to close down non-viable branches except in rural and semi-urban areas.

7. Entry of Private Sector Banks. To promote competition in banking operations for improving the customer services, private banks have been allowed to be set-up as per Reserve Bank guidelines. Ten new private sector banks have been established since 1994.

8. Department of Supervision. A department of supervision has been set-up in the Reserve Bank of India with effect from 22 December 1993, to supervise the working of commercial banks.

9. Banking Ombudsman Scheme. The scheme has been started with effect from June 1995, for quick and economical settlement of customer complaints about the deficiencies in banking services.

10. Board for Financial Supervision. The Board has been set-up in the Reserve Bank in 1994. It insures implementation of regulations in the field of credit management, asset classification, income recognition, provisioning, capital adequacy, etc.

11. Scheme of Disclosure Regarding Defaulting Borrowers. The scheme for disciosure of information regarding defaulting borrowers of banks with outstandings aggregating to Rs. 1 crore and above as on 31 March and 30 September every year, was introduced in April 1994.

12. Central Board of Bank Frauds. The Finance Ministry, Government of India has set-up this Board in January 1997 for rendering advice on cases being pursued by the CBI against bank officials up to the level of General Manager.

13. Consortium Arrangement. Large borrowers above a specified credit limit have been allowed to operate through consortium of scheduled commercial banks headed by a lead bank. The threshold limit for such consortium arrangement is Rs. 50 crore. The number of borrower accounts subject to this procedure has been fixed at 76. Banks are permitted to leave the consortium after two years of joining it.

14. Liberalisation of Lending Norms. Lending norms for the banks have also been liberalised. They can now decide the levels of holding of individual items of inventory and receivables to be permitted to borrowers and also the quantum and period of ad hoc credit limits without charging additional interest.

15. Measures to Streamline Working of Banks. Measures like management information systems and the internal audit and control mechanisms, computerisation of banking operations, prudential norms for income recognition assets, etc. have been introduced to improve the quality of performance and management of banks.

16. Liberal Credit Control Measures. Statutory liquidity ratio on incremental net demand and time liabilities has been reduced to 25 per cent. The banks have been permitted to fix their deposit and lending rates. They have also been given the freedom to invest in corporate shares, debentures and units of mutual funds not exceeding 5 per cent of their incremental deposits. They can also purchase scrips and debentures of companies from the secondary market.

17. New Private Banks. For allowing greater participation by private sector banks, the RBI issued in 2001, revised guidelines, as under:

(*a*) The bank should have a minimum paid-up capital of Rs. 200 crore to be raised to Rs. 300 crore within three years of the start of business.

(*b*) The promoters' stake should be 40 per cent.

(*c*) NRI contribution in primary equity not to exceed 40 per cent.

(*d*) The new bank cannot be promoted by any large business house, but individual companies can contribute upto 10 per cent equity.

(*e*) NBFCs with AAA rating and 12 per cent capital adequacy can function as a bank.

(*f*) The new bank will have to maintain a capital adequacy ratio of 10 per cent.

(*g*) The total net bank credit 40 per cent will be for priority sector lending.

(*h*) 25 per cent branches of the new bank will be in rural/semi-urban areas.

18. Entry into Insurance Business: Any bank fulfilling the above criteria, and with a minimum network of Rs. 500 crore, can undertake insurance business.

The reforms initeated in the financial sector since 1992, on the recommendations of Narasimham Committee (1991) were directed to transform the highly regulated banking system into an open, competitive and liberally supervised system. The objective was clearly spelt out by the RBI: "Commercial Banks thus need to become conscious that they are entering a challenging environment and will have to redefine their position within the financial industry. New ways and methods will have to be determined in order to successfully respond to the new challenges particularly, the growing demands from customers for high quality service".[1] Consequently, the banks will be required to: (*a*) give better returns on the savings of the depositors; (*b*) generate greater revenues; (*c*) create new services for reducing unforeseen risks; (*d*) improve income-cost ratios; and (*e*) improve profitability and reduce the NPAs.

Banking Sector Reforms (1998)

The Government of India, constituted another Committee under the chairmanship of Shri M. Narasimham specifically to suggest measures for reforming the banking sector. The Committee submitted its report in April 1998. The report covered a wide range of issues like capital adequacy, bank management, bank legislation, bank mergers etc. The principal recommendations are summarized below:

(*i*) *Stronger Banking System:* The Committee laid great emphasis on the need of a stronger banking system particularly in the context of capital account convertibility which will necessarily involve huge flows of capital to and from the country, and would require cautions management of exchange rate and domestic liquidity. For this purpose the Committee has recommended the merger of strong banks. The Committee has cautioned the government on

1. Report on Trend and Progress of Banking in India : 1992-93, Reserve Bank of India.

the merger of strong and weak banks as this may dilute the asset quality of the stronger bank.

(*ii*) *Narrow Banking:* For the rehabilitation of weak banks with high NPAs, the Committee has suggested the concept of narrow banking *i.e.* these banks should lodge their funds in short-term risk free assets. This implies that they should match their demand deposits by safe liquid assets. If this concept is found unworkable then the closure of such banks be seriously considered.

(*iii*) *Small Local Banks:* Along with its recommendation for 2 or 3 banks with global orientation and 8-10 large national banks, the Committee suggested the establishment of small local banks to serve the needs of a State or even a cluster of districts in respect of agriculture, small industry and trade.

(*iv*) *Capital Adequacy:* To improve the strength and risk absorption capacity of banks the Committee suggested the raising of their capital adequacy ratio. It further suggested the establishment of an Asset Reconstruction Fund to take over the NPAs of the banks.

(*v*) *Real Autonomy:* The Committee has strongly pleaded for with-drawing government ownership and control of banks and providing greater autonomy and flexibility in the working of public sector banks. The bank boards should be made autonomous and responsible for enhancing the value of shareholders. The RBI should perform only regulatory functions and not get into the day-to-day management of the banks. The Committee has suggested that the RBI should withdraw its nominee from bank boards and, "should be concerned with laying down procedural and disclosure norms and sound procedures and ensure adherence to these...."

(*vi*) *Review of Banking Laws:* The Committee has stressed on an urgent review of all banking laws and amendment of their provisions to bring in line with the current needs of the banking industry.

The Committee has also made recommendations for the computerisation, professionalisation and depoliticisation of bank boards, review of recruitment procedures, training and remuneration policies etc.

Conclusion : Barring a couple of recommendations *viz.* relating to the total rejection of merger of strong with weak banks and the concept of narrow banking, there is hardly any thing new that the Committee had not recommended in the 1991 report. It is felt that there was no need for appointing the Banking Sector Reform Committee and it was a brainwave of the Banking Division of the Finance Ministry of the Government of India. In fact, this division is totally useless in the presence of RBI and should be disbanded. Two members of the Narsimham Committee (1998) had also made similar recommendation which was not accepted.

Exercises

1. Explain briefly recent trends in the Indian Banking System.
2. Write notes on: (*i*) Lead Bank Scheme, (*ii*) Service Area Approach, (*iii*) Financing of Priority Sector, (*iv*) Factoring, (*v*) Deposit Insurance and Credit Guarantee Corporation.
3. Explain the main features of Innovative Banking in India,
4. What are the principal defects in the Indian Banking System? Give suggestions to remove them.
5. Give the main recommendations of the Narasimham Committee relating to the Indian Banking System.
6. Explain the provisions of the Banking Regulation Act, 1949.

●●●

Chapter 22

Commercial Banks in India

1. Introduction

Since the major component of the Indian banking system comprises commercial banks, whatever the various commissions and committees have suggested from time to time for the improvement of the banking system in the country applies more to commercial banks than to other banking institutions. In this chapter we propose to throw some light, in a general way, on the commercial banks, their types, functions, difficulties and problems, etc. Since the State Bank of India occupies a unique position we shall deal with it in a separate chapter.

2. Classification of Commercial Banks

The commercial banks have been classified into: (*i*) scheduled banks; and (*ii*) non-scheduled banks. The scheduled banks are those which have been included by the Reserve Bank of India in the Second Schedule of the Reserve Bank of India Act, 1934, according to which the following conditions must be fulfilled before a bank is included in the schedule—(*a*) the paid-up capital and reserves of the bank must not be less than Rs. 5 lakh; (*b*) the banks must deposit 3 per cent of their demand and time liabilities with the Reserve Bank in the form of cash reserves; this percentage can be increased by the Reserve Bank up to 15 per cent; and (*c*) the banks must send to the Reserve Bank a statement of their financial affairs every week.

The Reserve Bank provides certain special facilities to the scheduled banks, *e.g.*, they can borrow funds against approved securities, can get their bills rediscounted and can remit their surplus funds with the Reserve Bank. The non-scheduled banks, obviously are those which are not included in the Second Schedule of the Reserve Bank Act, 1934, mentioned above. The Reserve Bank, therefore, does not exercise any special control on these banks, although they are required to send a monthly statement of their financial affairs to the Reserve Bank and they have also to maintain a certain percentage of their deposits with the Reserve Bank in the form of cash reserves.

There were 287 commercial banks in India as on 30 June, 1995. Of these 89 were scheduled banks and 196 were regional rural banks. There were two non-scheduled banks. The scheduled banks had 62,314 branch offices while the non-scheduled banks had 32. The total deposits of scheduled banks on that date were Rs. 3,76,144 crore. They had advanced loans to the tune of Rs. 2,08,688 crore. There were 29 foreign commercial banks in India with 156 branch offices and 33 private banks with 4,089 branches.

The commercial banks have also been classified on the basis of proprietorship into—(*i*) public sector banks; and (*ii*) private sector banks. The public sector bank is a Government of India undertaking while a private sector bank is owned by the shareholders. Both these types of banks perform the same functions, and their interest rate structure and salary and allowance structure are the same except the non-scheduled banks. State Bank of India was the first public sector bank established on 1 July, 1955, after nationalisation of Imperial Bank of India. It had 7 subsidiaries which were nationalised in 1959. These are State Bank of Hyderabad, State Bank of Bikanet and Jaipur, State Bank of Travancore, State Bank of Mysore, State Bank of Patiala, State Bank of Indore and State Bank of Saurashtra. 14 major scheduled banks were nationalised on 19 July, 1969. These were Allahabad Bank, Bank of Baroda, Bank of India, Bank of Maharashtra, Canara Bank, Central Bank of India, Dena Bank, Indian Bank, Indian Overseas Bank, Punjab National Bank, Syndicate Bank, Union Bank of India, United Bank ofIndia and United Commercial Bank. On 15 April, 1980, 6 more scheduled banks were nationalised. They were Andhra Bank, Corporation Bank, New Bank of India, Oriental Bank of Commerce, Punjab and Sind Bank and Vijaya Bank. Later, on 4 September 1993, New Bank of India was merged with Punjab National Bank.

The regional rural banks are also public sector banks and their number is 196. Hence there are in all 223 public sector banks comprising State Bank of India and its 7 subsidiaries, 19 nationalised banks and 196 regional rural banks.

3. Functions of Commercial Banks

Broadly speaking, the functions of the commercial banks in India are the same as elsewhere. These are: (*i*) Accepting deposits such as fixed deposits, current deposits and saving bank deposits; (*ii*) advancing loans; (*iii*) undertaking agency functions under which the banks function as agent of their customers, *e.g.*, they receive money on their behalf, make payments on their behalf, buy and sell stocks and shares, issue traveller's cheques, etc.;

(*iv*) providing locker facility for the safe custody of their clients' valuables; and (*v*) providing remittance facility in which they transfer funds of their clients from one place to another and also issue drafts of their branches or on the branches of other banks.

The Banking Regulation Act, 1949 lays down the functions of these banks as under:

1. Borrowing, raising or taking of deposits of money.
2. Lending or advancing of money.
3. Drawing, making, accepting, discounting, buying, selling, collecting and dealing with bills of exchange, hundis, promissory notes, coupons, drafts, bills of lading, Railway receipts, warrants, debentures, certificates, scrips and other securities whether transferable or negotiable or not.
4. Granting and issuing of letters of credit, traveller's cheques and circular notes.
5. Buying, selling and dealing in bullion and species and foreign exchange including foreign bank notes.
6. Acquiring, holding, issuing on commission, underwriting and dealing in stocks, funds, shares, debentures, bonds, obligations, securities and investments of all kinds.
7. Purchasing and selling of bonds, scrips or other forms of securities on behalf of constituents or others.
8. Negotiating loans and advances.
9. Receiving all kinds of bonds, scrips or valuables on deposit or for safe custody or otherwise.
10. Providing safe deposit vaults for the custody of their clients' valuables.
11. Collecting and transmitting of money and securities.
12. Acting as agents for any government or authority or any other person or persons but not as managing agent or secretary and treasurer of a company.
13. Contracting of private and public loans and negotiating and issuing them.
14. Insuring, guaranteeing, underwriting, and participating in managing and carrying out of any issue of loans or securities made by State, Municipality, company, corporation or any association and also lending for the purpose.
15. Carrying and transacting every kind of guarantee and indemnity business.
16. Managing, selling and realising any property which may come into its possession in satisfaction of its claims.
17. Undertaking and executing of trusts, as also administering estate as executor, trustee or otherwise.
18. Acquiring, holding and dealing with any property or any right, tide or interest therein which forms the security for any loans or advances sanctioned.
19. Establishing and supporting or aiding in the establishment of

associations, institutions, funds, trusts and conveniences for the benefit of its present and past employees and their dependents and granting or guaranteeing moneys for charitable purposes.

20. Acquiring, constructing, maintaining and altering any building or works necessary for its purposes.

21. Selling, improving, managing, developing, exchanging, leasing, mortgaging, disposing of, or otherwise dealing in all its properties and rights.

22. Taking over and undertaking the whole or any part of the business of any person or company when such business is of a nature described above.

23. Doing of all such things as are incidental or conducive to the promotion and advancement of its business, such as giving information about its customer's financial standing as a referee.

24. Engaging in any other form of business which the Central Government specifies to be lawful.

In addition to the above, the commercial banks have also started performing a number of other functions during recent years, such as issuing credit cards, establishing mutual funds, engaging in merchant banking, giving loans to priority sectors, consumption loans, education loans, housing loans, etc.

4. Progress of Commercial Banks

Since the nationalisation of 14 major banks in July 1969, there has been an all-round progress in the field of banking business and services. This can be known from the following:

1. Expansion of Branches. The most notable feature of banking development in the post-nationalisation period has been the increasing number of bank offices. In June 1969, there were 8,262 bank offices which increased to 62,346 by the end of June 1995. Subsequently, it was realised that the expansion of branches at such a rapid pace has adversely affected the viability and so the branch licencing policy for the period from April 1985 to March 1990 was focused on the consolidation and achieving a coverage of 17,000 population per bank office in rural and semi-urban areas and providing banking facilities in those parts of rural areas where wide gaps exist. Accordingly, 5,360 rural/semi-urban centres were allotted to banks in addition to 1,454 rural centres allotted under the service area approach and 635 centres in urban/metropolitan/port town centres. Out of 7,449 centres allotted as above, banks were able to open offices at 6,912 centres up to the end of June 1992. Subsequently all pending licences are cance.lled. The focus of the branch licencing policy for 1990-95 was on providing freedom to banks to rationalise the structure of their branches. Accordingly, the distance stipulation of 400 metres between two branches of banks in towns has been withdrawn. Banks have been allowed to open one specialised branch per centre each in the category of industrial finance, Non-Resident Indians and Treasury branches without the prior approval of the Reserve Bank of India. They were also allowed to convert their non-viable rural branches into Satellite Offices on certain conditions and provide locker facilities in extension counters. Further, these banks were allowed to close, on mutual consultation, one loss making branch at rural centres served by two commercial bank branches excluding regional rural banks.

Regarding expansion of bank offices abroad, the position was that there were 59 banks offices of 7 Indian banks in 14 foreign countries. After nationalisation in 1969, 19 foreign offices had to be closed down between 1969 and 1973 mainly because the laws of certain countries did not allow the functioning of any State owned or foreign bank. However, after 1973, a mass acceleration in the field of overseas branch took place. As a result, in June 1993, there were 115 branches of 9 Indian banks in 25 countries besides 13 representative offices.

2. Dispersal of Bank Offices. The main focus of branch expansion was to provide banking services in unbanked areas and to reduce regional disparities in banking development. Of the 52,986 offices opened between July 1969 and June 1993, about 66 per cent offices were opened in unbanked centres. The proportion of bank offices in rural areas rose from 22.1 per cent to 57.8 per cent during this period. The policy objective of achieving a coverage of one branch for every 17,000 persons in rural and semi-urban areas are largely achieved. The regional disparities in the distribution of bank offices have also declined substantially.

3. Mobilisation of Deposits. The commercial banks have made appreciable efforts at deposit mobilisation through a series of schemes. The deposits increased very rapidly after nationalisation of major banks. Aggregate deposits of scheduled commercial banks at the end of March 1994 stood at Rs. 3,15,132 crore. The annual rate of growth in deposits between 1969 and 1994 was 18 per cent as compared with 9.3 per cent between 1951 and 1969. No doubt, the high rate of inflation during this period would reduce the growth rate in deposits by more than 50 per cent; but a real average annual growth rate of 8 to 9 per cent is still creditable.

4. Expansion of Credit. Bank credit of scheduled commercial banks increased from Rs. 3,590 crore to Rs. 1,64,418 crore between June 1969 and March 1994. On an average basis expansion in bank credit in 1993-94 declined from 21.0 per cent in 1992-93 to 8.2 per cent in 1993-94. This was mainly because of two reasons—(*i*) decline in advances made for food procurements; and (*ii*) the corporate bodies started raising large amount of funds from the capital market because the banks had restricted credit in the context of prudential norms.

Investment in government securities showed a massive growth rate of 33.3 per cent in 1993-94. In the case of scheduled commercial banks it increased from Rs. 1,055 crore in March, 1969 to Rs. 1,01,201 crore in March 1994. This was only in respect of government securities. Investment in other approved securities was in addition to this investment.

Regarding lending to priority sector and weaker sections of the society, commercial banks have extended liberal credit facilities. The areas included are agriculture, small scale industries and other priority sector comprising small borrowers such as road and water transport borrowers, retail traders and small businessmen, professional and self-employed persons and persons desirous of receiving higher education. The government had advised the commercial banks that their priority sector lending should attain a level of not less than one-third of their out- standing credit by March 1979, which was subsequently raised to 40 per cent of their total advances up to the end of 1985. Advances to the priority sector increased from Rs. 505 crore to Rs. 18,407 crore between June 1969 and March 1985. Percentage of advances to priority sectors in total bank credit increased from 14 per cent to 39.9 per cent during the same period as against the target of 40 per cent of total bank credit to be achieved by March 1985. The priority sector advances constituted 44.6 per cent and 42.3 per cent of total net bank credit at the end of June 1989 and June 1990 respectively. Of the total priority sector advances agriculture and small scale industries together accounted for about 80 per cent. The share of small borrowers was, however, not substantial. Advances to weaker sections at the end of June 1993, formed 8.9 per cent of total outstanding advances as against the prescribed target of 10 per cent. Priority sector advances of private commercial banks formed 33.2 per cent of their total advances. Priority sector advances of foreign commercial banks were 9.4 per cent at the end of March 1991, which declined to 7.9 per cent in the following year but increased to 11.4 per cent by June 1993. A scheme of differential interests rates on advances by public sector banks to be made to the weaker sections of the community was initiated by the government in March 1972. The public sector banks' advances under this scheme at the end of March 1993 totalled up to Rs. 705 crore which was only 0.6 per cent of their total outstanding advances. The export sector has received high priority in the provision of bank credit. Consequently the export credit outstanding at the end of March 1994 amounted to Rs. 17,094 crore which was 11.2 per cent of total net bank credit against the stipulated target of 10 per cent to be achieved by end of June 1993.

5. Rural Lending. Rural branches of commercial banks constituted about 58 per cent of total branches. These branches and the regional rural banks provide multipurpose and multi-term credit for agriculture and allied activities. Service Area Approach to rural lending which has been in operation since April 1989, envisaged that each rural and semi-urban branch of commercial banks would be assigned a specific area comprising a cluster of villages within which they will operate. Only one branch was to operate in the allotted cluster of villages so as to prevent multiple financing and scattered lending and to ensure greater credit discipline. The objective of Service Area Approach is to make bank branches effective instruments of rural development. Each Branch Manager is supposed to make a detailed survey of the village included in his service area and formulate his plan for providing banking facilities on the basis of such a study. The annual credit plans are prepared by bank branches.

6. Lead Bank Scheme. This scheme was introduced by the Reserve Bank of India in December 1969, with the sole object of orienting bank development in the country towards an "Area Approach" and thus ensure that the developmental needs of all regions and all sections of the society are served by the banking system in conformity, with national priorities. The administrative unit is 'district'. The lead banks prepare the district credit plans for their district and also annual Action Plans before the beginning of each, year. This scheme has been operating in 483 districts of the country at the end of March 1994.

7. Diversification of Business. Commercial banks have also been encouraged to diversify their business and enter fresh areas like merchant banking, venture capital, mutual funds, equipment leasing, housing finance and other financial services. They have introduced innovative schemes of deposit mobilisation providing consumer credit, issuing credit cards etc. A number of banks have set up separate subsidiaries for the purpose.

5. Failures of Commercial Banks

Despite these achievements, their performance in certain respects has been found lacking. Some of the Principal shortcomings of these banks are as follows:

1. Regional Disparities. Despite the phenomenal growth in the number of bank office, the regional imbalances in respect of banking infrastructure still persist. This can be known from the following—(*i*) the average population served per bank office is still higher than the national average in some of the State like Assam, Bihar, Madhya Pradesh, Manipur, Orissa, Tripura, Uttar Pradesh and West Bengal; (*ii*) north-eastern and eastern regions are still far behind than other regions in the matter provision of banking facilities; (*iii*) in respect of credit deployment also there are large regional variations. The credit-deposit ratio in most of the States is below the all India level which means that the deposits mobilized in these States are not fully utilized for advancing loans in those States; (*iv*) the credit-deposit ratio of scheduled commercial banks both as per sanction and utilization was 61.9 per cent at the end of March 1991. The ratio exceeded the all India level in southern and western regions. The northeastern region had the lowest ratio, *i.e.*, 46.9 per cent. It was 49.2 per cent in the eastern region, 50.3 per cent in the central region and 53.7 per cent in the northern region. The credit-deposit ratio as per utilization was below the all India average in 21 States/Union Territories out of 32 States/Union Territories.

2. Faulty Sectoral Deployment of Credit. Despite the declared policy of giving preference to priority sector and rural development a sizeable portion of bank credit is still deployed for financing industries, facilitating temporary build up of inventories and for helping general investment activity. In the field of agriculture a major part of loans is given to big farmers after neglecting small and marginal farmers. In the field of small scale industries a major part of loans has been cornered by rich-managed small and ancilliary industries. In the category of professionals and self-employed, well to do doctors, architects and chartered accountants with urban background have been included. Hence, the really needy and poor people have been left out. Recovery position in priority lending is also not encouraging. The recovery of public sector banks in respect of their direct agricultural advances as a percentage to demand which was 58.1 per cent in 1990-91 declined to 54.1 per cent in 1991-92, partly due to the write-off under the Agricultural and Rural Debt Relief Scheme, 1990.

3. Unsatisfactory Progress in Deposit Mobilisation. It is true that the aggregate deposits of commercial banks have shown an upward trend. But keeping in view the rapid rise in money supply and money incomes and the large expansion of bank offices, the progress does not appear to be satisfactory, particularly, the performance of rural offices has been most unsatisfactory.

4. Inefficient Management. It has been observed that the management of these banks has not been up to the mark. The Chairman and the Board of Directors constantly oppose each other. This can be because of the fact that the Directors neither owe their selection, nor their appointment or continuance to the Chairman. There is also a conflict among the Directors. Consequently, the banks have not been able to: (*i*) strike a balance between profitability and social service and lending and investment policies; (*ii*) motivate their staff to reduce the costs and increase productivity; and (*iii*) develop a team spirit for planning for growth and development. It has also been remarked that the present structure of public sector banks is wasteful and stimulates all sorts of malpractices in banking operations.

5. Inefficient Customer Service. The quality of banking services provided to the customers is very low. There are delays at the counters, the clients are treated with utter indifference and carelessness by the bank staff, frequent strikes, agitations and go-slow campaigns also dislocate the functioning in branches and clearing houses. The Committee on Customer Services, under the Chairmanship of Shri M.N. Goiporia, made wide ranging recommendations in this regard. On the basis of these recommendations the Reserve Bank of India issued detailed guidelines to the banks but most of the banks have not followed them.

6. Slow Progress of Lead Bank Scheme. This scheme has not made satisfactory progress in all districts. Initially district surveys have taken more than twice the schedule time. The progress of the second phase has been very slow. District credit plans have been prepared but not effectively implemented. The lead banks have constituted district consultative committees but gainful use of these committees has not been made.

7. Declining Profitability of Banks. Owing to rising costs and declining returns the overall profitability of banks has considerably declined. There has been a tremendous increase in their social obligations which has increased the cost without commensurate increase in their earnings. The indiscriminate branch expansion has also increased expenditure but without much return. The imposition of a lending pattern favouring priority sector and the weaker sections has cut short a part of credit on which profit could be earned. Increase in the liquidity requirements of banks has also attributed to the slow growth of earnings. Administered interest rate structure has also been responsible for the slower growth of earnings. Finally, rising staff costs has also contributed towards narrowing the profit margin. Besides lack of supervision over proper utilisation of loans, the recovery of loans has been adversely affected resulting into ever increasing overdues. Consequently, provision for bad and doubtful debts becomes the first charge on the profits of a bank. The Reserve Bank of India appointed in April 1976, a Committee under the Chairmanship of Shri J.C. Luther, which recommended a drastic cut in expenses through cost control and other methods so that the banking system may not become a drag on the economy.

It is disheartening to note that in November 1990, the Reserve Bank of India declared eight nationalised banks as "sick". These banks were Bank of India, New Bank of India, Punjab and Sind Bank, United Commercial Bank, United Bank of India, Vijaya Bank, Syndicate Bank and Bank of Maharashtra. All these banks except Bank of India and United Commercial Bank had shown profits in their balance sheets. Detailed investigations by the Reserve Bank of India showed that these banks had not provided for depreciation on investment which had fallen in value. A large amount of funds was locked up in long-term low yielding securities, the depreciation on which was also not reflected in the balance sheets. They had also not made adequate provision for bad and doubtful debts. Consequently, as on 30 June, 1991, 103 commercial banks were under liquidation.

8. Irregularities and Malpractices. In the wake of the 'securities scam' which was a result of irregularities committed by the banks and financial institutions the Reserve Bank set-up a committee with Shri R. Janakiraman, Deputy Governor of the Reserve Bank of India on 30 April, 1992. The Committee submitted its final report in April 1993. Findings of the Committee reiterate the nexus between brokers and banks and the fact that the banks and their subsidiaries continually circumvented the Reserve Bank's guidelines on Portfolio Management Services. The report has identified four key factors leading to these irregularities: (*i*) improper and indiscriminate use of Bankers Receipts; (*ii*) brokers increasingly dealing on their own accounts and taking possessions; (*iii*) banks failure to periodically reconcile investments; and (*iv*) complete breakdown of internal control system in a number of banks. Consequently, the investment portfolios of banks have become fragile and weak. The committee observed that the irregularities could possibly have been avoided if their had been greater coordination among the different controlling agencies. The committee, therefore, stressed that remedial action should be taken to introduce proper control system, strengthen monitoring and remove lacunae in the existing system and procedures so as to prevent recurrence of similar lapses in future.

The government immediately initiated action to identify and punish those who were responsible for committing these fraudulent transactions and if possible to recover the amount lost to the banks. Accordingly: (*i*) The government appointed a special court to try all cases of securities scam and legislations were enacted for attaching the assets of the persons involved in the scam; (*ii*) A special judge of Bombay High Court was appointed for the purpose; (*iii*) A custodian was also appointed for prompt disposal of the attached assets; (*iv*) The Central Bureau of Investigation was asked to take over the investigation of these cases; (*v*) In view of the seriousness of the matter a Joint Parliamentary Committee (JPC) was set up with Shri Ram Niwas Mirdha as Chairman to enquire into all aspects of the matter, to fix responsibility and to suggest measures for future reforms of the banking system.

The Scam exposed the weaknesses of our banking system. The rules and procedures were deliberately violated with the criminal intention of defrauding the banks. The various parties colluded between themselves; these were brokers, bank officials and officials of stock exchanges. The most potent factors responsible for this scam however, were: (*a*) our banking system did not have any internal control mechanism; (*b*) It also did not have any supervisory mechanism, (*c*) the Finance Ministry of the Government of India pressurized the banks to deploy their resources at low rate of interest and (*d*) the system was highly over-regulated. Rigid control over interest rates which pulled them away from market-determined rates of interest was not workable and only created opportunities for bypassing the rules in search of high rates of interest.

Accepting the recommendation of the Janakiraman Committee, the RBI took remedial measures to improve the internal control mechanisms and to strengthen the supervisory system so as to ensure that these occurrences do not happen in future. Subsequent steps only go to show that the government was not serious to find out the truth and was interested in merely covering up the matter. The Joint Parliamentary Committee did nothing. The officers in the Reserve Bank of India and in the Finance Ministry were not touched at all and it has to be accepted that the scam only affected the small investors and that there was every possibility of such scams occurring in future as well.

Yet, another scam happened almost after a decade, in March 2001. In 1992 it was a collusion between Harshad Mehta, UCO Bank and Standard Chartered Bank; this time it was a collusion between Ketan Parekh, Medhavpura Urban Cooperative Bank and Bank of India. Ketan Parekh jacked up the prices of 10 scrips with the help of the funds obtained from the banks. A group of brokers in Mumbai Stock Exchange came to know of this and hammered down the prices of these scrips. The stock markets crashed through out the country. The crash was so steep and prolonged that thousands of stock brokers and investors were ruined. This time, too the government appointed a Joint Parliamentary Committee to look into the matter and fix responsibility but unfortunately nothing came out.

Exercises

1. Describe the working of scheduled commercial banks in India. Point out their defects.
2. Explain the main provisions of the Banking Regulation Act, 1949, and its management with regard to the regulation of Indian banking system. Discuss its effects on the growth of banking in India.
3. Give an account of the working and progress of commercial banking in India after the nationalisation of 14 major banks in 1969.
4. Assess the achievements of commercial banks in India in respect of branch expansion, deficit mobilisation and extension of credit to priority sectors after 1969.

•••

Chapter 23

Nationalisation of Banks in India

1. Introduction

The year 1949 marked the beginning of a new era in the economic history of India. It was the beginning of a period of remedy and a period of seed time. As soon as India became independent the government embarked upon a programme of removing the ills of the past and sowing the seeds of economic independence, economic growth and economic prosperity. As a first step the government, realising the need for a proper coordination between monetary and fiscal policies, nationalised the Reserve Bank of India on January 1, 1949 and promulgated the Banking Regulation Act in March to equip it with more powers and authority for regulating and supervising the banking system. The history of bank nationalisation, therefore, starts with the nationalisation of Reserve Bank of India, w.e.f. 1 January, 1949.

In the second phase of bank nationalisation the Imperial Bank of India was nationalised and the State Bank of India was set up on 1 July, 1955. In the third phase, 7 State associated banks were nationalised in 1959 and attached with the

State Bank of India as its subsidiaries. These banks were the State Bank of Hyderabad, State Bank of Bikaner and Jaipur, the State Bank of Travancore, the State Bank of Mysore, the State Bank of Patiala, the State Bank of Indore and the State Bank of Saurashtra.

1969 marked the fourth phase when 16 major banks were nationalised. These banks were Allahabad Bank, Bank of Baroda, Bank of India, Bank of Maharashtra, Canara Bank, Central Bank of India, Dena Bank, Indian Bank, Indian Overseas Bank, Punjab National Bank, Syndicate Bank, Union Bank of India, United Bank of India and United Commercial Bank.

The final phase in the history of bank nationalisation in India was the nationalisation of six other commercial banks on 15 April, 1980. They were Andhra Bank, Corporation Bank, New Bank of India, Oriental Bank of commerce, Punjab and Sind Bank and Vijaya Bank.

Subsequently the New Bank of India having been declared a sick bank was merged with the Punjab National Bank in 1993. So, in June 1966, there were 27 nationalised commercial banks, including the State Bank of India and its subsidiaries.

2. Arguments in Support of Nationalisation

The following arguments were advanced in favour of the nationalisation of banks:

1. It was held that the commercial banks have only taken interest in the financing of large scale industries and have totally neglected the priority sectors such as agriculture, small scale industries, etc. After the nationalisation of commercial banks, the priority sectors will receive proper attention. It will be interesting to note that of the total bank credit towards the end of March 1968, the share of agriculture was only 2.2 per cent, of retail trade only 2 per cent and of small industries 6.9 per cent. So, it would be possible after nationalisation to make a proper use of bank credit in the interest of the development of the country.

2. It was argued that although the country has embarked on a programme of planned economic development, the commercial banks have neglected plan priorities and have diverted credit into less important channels. After nationalisation bank credit will be used according to plan priorities.

3. It was generally held that huge profits earned by the banks were being used for serving the interests of big industrial houses and the shareholders earned almost nothing. These profits were disproportionate to the capital invested in the banks. It was estimated that in 1968 the scheduled commercial banks were earning a profit of Rs. 42.5 crore annually while their capital base had declined. The ratio of paid-up capital and reserves to deficits also declined from 9.7 per cent in 1951 to 2.6 per cent in 1968. It was, therefore, felt that these huge profits will be available for financing the plan programmes.

4. Some economists had put forward the argument that the commercial banks through their operations were increasing regional disparities. They pointed out that till December 1967 not even 1 per cent villages were served by commercial banks. In 13 districts of the country there was not a single commercial bank office. More than 6,000 towns did not have commercial banking facilities. The two metropolitan cities of Bombay and Calcutta accounted for one-third of total deposits and one-half of total credit disbursed by banks. It, therefore, means that deposits were mobilised in smaller centres but were diverted to big business centres. The bank nationalisation would remove these disparities and ensure the judicious spread of banking activities in all parts of the country.

5. It was also observed that commercial banks were not cooperating with the Reserve Bank of India and were not following its directives and instructions. Consequently Reserve bank had not succeeded in implementing its monetary policy effectively. Therefore, bank nationalisation would remove this anomaly and would enable the Reserve Bank of India to obtain greater cooperation from the commercial banks.

6. The commercial banks, as a general rule were indulging in anti-national and anti-social activities. They were providing credit facilities for such activities as speculation, blackmarketing, profiteering, etc. Bank nationalisation would be able to stop these activities.

7. It was pointed out that the management in most of the commercial banks had not been up to the mark. Consequently the operational efficiency and the quality of service provided to the customers were at a very low ebb. By bank nationalisation these evils will be removed, banking operations would be standardised, the employees would have greater sense of security and the management would be able to develop and provide adequate training and techniques to the staff. This would certainly improve the efficiency of the banks.

8. The supporters of bank nationalisation argued that nationalisation of banks has been very successful in other countries. 90 per cent of commercial banking is in the public sector in Italy, 80 per cent in France and 70 per cent in Germany. In other developing countries the nationalised banks have been very successful. So there is no need to entertain any, fear on this account.

3. Arguments against Nationalisation

The main arguments given against the nationalisation of commercial banks were:

1. The nationalisation will not be in the best interest of the country and the society as a whole, because after the nationalisation, the personalised services provided by the private sector banks will not be available. The decisions will not be quick, the initiative would be lost and the smooth functioning of the banking system would be greatly impaired.

2. The efficient functioning of the State Bank of India cannot lead to the conclusion that all banks after nationalisation will function efficiently. The State Bank of India has been functioning effectively because it has to face stiff competition from the well organised and well managed private sector banks. Obviously, when all the banks are nationalised the banking services will definitely deteriorate.

3. Since the commercial banks have to follow certain norms and rules regarding the liquidity of their assets, they cannot afford to lock their funds for a long time in dangerous ventures and therefore, it will not be wise for

them to provide finance for agriculture and small industries. Therefore, these activities should necessarily be financed by the Reserve Bank of India, the State Bank of India and the Cooperative Movement.

4. The establishment of the Indian Deposit Insurance Corporation has provided already 100 per cent security to the depositors. This Corporation has been functioning efficiently and therefore, now there is no need to nationalise commercial banks.

5. The malpractices of commercial banks in the private sector can very well be eradicated by an integrated approach in which monetary measures would be hooked up with fiscal tools and physical controls, if effectively implemented. Thorough inspection and strict watch by the Reserve Bank of India can also help to a considerable extent in removing some of the malpractices.

6. Nationalisation will need a huge amount for making payment of compensation to the shareholders which would mean a loss of huge revenue to the public exchequer.

7. Finally, even after nationalisation, sufficient margin of profits would be required to be kept aside for strengthening the reserve fund.

4. Objectives of Nationalisation

The Prime Minister Indira Gandhi listed the following objectives of nationalisation of banks in the statement she made in the Indian Parliament on 21 July, 1969.

1. Mobilisation of savings and their use for productive purposes, in accordance with the priorities indicated in our Five-Year Plans.

2. Meeting all genuine credit needs of private sector industries.

3. Ensuring that banks operate for a larger social purpose and are subject to close public regulation and scrutiny.

4. Meeting the needs in a large measure of priority sectors specially small industries, self-employed groups and farmers.

5. Fostering the growth of new entrepreneurs and neglected and backward areas.

6. Checking the misuse of bank credit.

7. Developing professional management and promoting the use of modern technology and practices in banking operations.

8. Making provision for training and providing reasonable terms of service to the bank staff.

9. Expanding branch network all over the country.

10. Reducing regional and sectoral imbalances.

5. Achievements of Nationalisation

We have already enumerated the achievements of the commercial banks in some detail in an earlier chapter and, therefore, we feel that it is not necessary to repeat the same here. However, by way of recapitulation, we repeat the same points here but in a summarised and brief form.

1. Expansion, disposal and removal of regional disparities. In the realm of credit expansion, there has been a tremendous progress since nationalization of banks. The total advances which stood at Rs. 3,035 crore in June 1969 increased to Rs. 15,07,080 crore in March 2005. The deposits increased from Rs. 3,897 crore in June 1969 to Rs. 21,09,050 crore in 2005. Consequent upon the nationalisation of banks they have followed a deliberate policy of opening their branches in rural and semi urban and the 63.1% of the branches of 19 nationalised banks were operating in rural areas in 2003 as againt 22% in June 1969. The nationalisation of 19 commercial banks has also led to a considerable reduction in regional disparities. The banks have opened new branches in rural areas where they did not exist before. For example, in June 1969, these banks had 74 branches in Assam, 172 branches in Haryana, 42 in Himachal Pradesh and only 2 in Nagaland. But in June 2003 their number increased to 1,212, 1,580, 784 and 70 respectively. As a consequence of the opening of the new branches, the average population per banking office were reduced to 15,000 from 65,000 during the period from June 1969 to June 2005.

2. Diversification of activities. The nationalised banks have also introduced some non-traditional programmes. They have launched number of new savings and other innovative schemes and in addition have taken up merchant bank and leasing, have floated mutual funds and venture capital funds. A number of facilities are being provided to the customers like collection of outstanding cheques, nomination facilities to depositors, new customer service centres in all major cities, personal attention to customers' grievances etc. Some of these banks have also opened offices in foreign countries.

3. Developmental role of banks. The banks after nationalisation have started playing a developmental role in the interest of the country. Under the lead bank scheme each lead bank has been actively involved in the development of banking facilities in the district allotted to it. The lead bank has been coordinating the operations of commercial banks, cooperative banks and other financial institutions for the intensive and overall development of the allotted districts.

4. Investment in government securities. After nationalisation, banks have started investing in government and other approved securities with the result that there is a flow of fund for implementing the economic plans of the country. The investment of these banks in government and other approved securities increased from Rs. 1,727 crore in March 1970 to Rs. 7,072 crore in December 1992.

5. Importance to priority sectors. After nationalisation these banks have started paying less attention to big industries and taking greater care of priority sectors particularly agriculture, small scale industries and small industrial units.

6. Credit to weaker sections. After nationalisation these banks have increased the flow of their credit to the weaker sections of the society which include marginal farmers, landless labourers, tenant farmers and sharecroppers, artisans, village and cottage industries, scheduled castes and scheduled tribes, etc. By December 1991, these sections have been provided bank credit totalling Rs. 10,630 crore. These sections of the society are also being provided credit at concessional rate under the differential rate of interest scheme from April 1972. Under this scheme the banks provide loans at 4 per cent rate of interest to the weaker sections of the society who do not have any tangible security to offer but who can improve their economic condition with the financial support of the bank.

7. Export credit. After nationalisation the commercial banks have started extending finance for promoting exports at concessional rates and terms.

6. Failures of Nationalisation

Despite above achievements the public sector banks have failed in more than one respect. While enumerating the defects of commercial banks in a previous chapter[1] we have already spelt out all those defects from which the commercial banks, which include the nationalised banks, have been suffering. in view of this we only briefly and broadly point out the failures of nationalised commercial banks in the following paras:

1. Regional Disparities. Although, after nationalisation regional disparities have been substantially reduced with the opening of bank branches and their spread over the unbanked areas, still these regional disparities are continuing, particularly in States like Assam, Bihar, Madhya Pradesh, Manipur, Orissa, Tripura, Uttar Pradesh and West Bengal in so far as the coverage of population is concerned. Northeastern and Eastern regions are lagging behind in respect of banking facilities. There are also large variations in respect of credit deployment.

2. Faulty sectoral deployment of credit. Despite the avowed objectives of giving preference to priority sector and rural development, a sizeable part of bank credit is still being deployed for financing industries and helping general investment activity. Even in the field of agriculture major part of

1. Please see Chapter 25.

loans have been cornered by rich-managed small and ancilliary industries. Among the professionals and self-employed, the well-to-do and well-established with urban background have been included.

3. Deposit mobilisation not satisfactory. Certainly the aggregate deposits of commercial banks have substantially increased but taking into account the increase in money supply and money incomes, expansion of branches, the rate of mobilisation of deposit doesn't appear to be satisfactory. More importantly the rural branches of these banks have not produced the desired results.

4. Inefficient management. The working of most of these banks has been marked by a conflict between the Chairman and the Board of Directors and between the Directors themselves. This has led to inefficient management resulting in low profitability, lack of motivation of staff and absence of team spirit.

5. Inefficient customer service. There is no gainsaying the fact that the customer service has reached the lowest point. There is utter indifference and carelessness on part of bank staff and frequent strikes, agitations and go-slow campaigns have been dislocating the functioning in branches and clearing houses.

6. Slow progress of lead bank scheme. The progress of the scheme has been very slow. District plans have no doubt been prepared but not effectively implemented and the Consultative Committees have been constituted but gainful use has not been made.

7. Declining profitability of banks. Rise in costs, increase in social obligations, discriminate branch expansion, preference to priority sectors and weaker sections in lending, increase in the liquidity requirements of banks, administered interest rate structure, rising staff costs, lack of supervision and utilisation of loans and the evermounting bad loans have all been responsible for the declining profitability of these banks. Consequently, a number of banks have been declared sick by the Reserve Bank of India.

8. Irregularities and malpractices. The working of these banks has also been marked by a number of irregularities and malpractices committed by them. They have been found guilty of circumventing the Reserve Bank's guidelines on portfolio management services and also for perpetuating the nexus between brokers and their officers. This situation has arisen only because of lack of coordination among the different controlling agencies.

7. Partial Privatisation of Nationalised Banks

Instead of augmenting the financial resources of the government the nationalisation of banks has increased the financial burden, and the villain of the piece has been their declining profitability. During the period from 1985-

86 to 1992-93 the government contributed Rs. 4,000 crore to their paid-up capital. In the budget for 1994-95 a provision of Rs. 5,700 crore had been made to enable them to meet the capital adequacy norms prescribed by the Reserve Bank. Therefore, the government felt that it would not be in the fitness of things to contribute, at such a large scale, to the paid up capital of these banks for enabling them to meet capital adequacy norms. Accordingly the Banking Companies (Acquisition and Transfer of Undertakings) Amendment Act, 1994 was passed, to enable these banks to raise money from the capital market and meet shortfalls in their capital requirements. Now the government will hold only 51 per cent of the paid-up share capital and 49 per cent would be held by individuals and companies. Consequently this amounts to partial privatisation of public sector banks. Already, the State Bank of India, Oriental Bank of Commerce, Bank of Baroda, Panjab National Bank, Union Bank of India, Bank of India, Syndicate Bank etc. have raised their share capital from public issues.

Exercises

1. What were the objectives of the nationalisation of commercial banks in India? Have these objectives been achieved?
2. "The nationalisation of commercial banks was essential to reform the banking system and ensure the proper functioning of the commanding heights of the economy in consonance with the national policy." Discuss.
3. Why have the foreign banks in India not been nationalised? Discuss their position in regard to the Indian banking system.
4. Discuss the achievements and failures of nationalised banks in India.
5. Give arguments for and against nationalisation of banks in India.
6. Do you consider the nationalisation of banks to have been a success in India?

•••

Chapter 24

The Reserve Bank of India

1. Introduction

The Reserve Bank of India (RBI) was established on 1 April, 1935 under the Reserve Bank of India Act, 1934. After its establishment, it took over the function of issuing paper currency, from the Government of India and of controlling credit from the Imperial Bank of India. It originally started as a shareholders bank with a paid-up capital of Rs. 5 crore. It was nationalised on 1 January, 1956 and since then it has been functioning as a State-owned and State-controlled Central Bank. Under the Reserve Bank's Transfer to Public Ownership Act of 1948, compensation was paid to the shareholders according to the market value which at that time was Rs. 118-10-0 per share of Rs. 100.

2. Management of RBI

The Reserve Bank had a paid-up capital of Rs. 5 crore divided into 5 lakh shares of Rs. 100 each. All shares are owned by the Government of India. The management is vested in the Central Board of Directors which has twenty members as given below: (*i*) one Governor and four Deputy Governors appointed by the Government of India for a period of five years. Their emoluments, etc., are decided by the Central Board of Directors in consultation with the Government of India; (*ii*) four directors nominated from the local boards, located at Bombay (Mumbai), Calcutta (Kolkata), Madras (Chennai) and New Delhi by the Government of India. Their tenure is also five years; (*iii*) ten other directors nominated by the Government of India whose term is four years; and (*iv*) an official of the Government of India to attend the meetings of the Central Board. His tenure is not fixed and he does not enjoy the right to vote in the meetings.

The Central Board is required, under the Act, to meet at least six times a year. The Governor of the Reserve Bank can call the meeting of the Central Board whenever he thinks necessary. Each local board has at least four members, appointed by the Government of India for a period of four years and representing all interests. The local boards render advice to the Central Board and also perform the various jobs assigned to them by the Central Board.

3. Organisational Set-up of RBI

The headquarters of the Reserve Bank is in Bombay. It has established, for its efficient functioning, local head-offices and branches at different places, for example, Banking and Issue Departments at Bangalore, Mumbai, Bycula (Mumbai), Kolkata, Kanpur, Chennai, Nagpur, New Delhi, Hyderabad, Patna, Ahmedabad and Bhubaneswar. It has also opened its sub-offices at Ahmedabad, Bhubaneswar, Guwahati and Jaipur. It has also its office in London which looks after the maintenance of High Commissioner's accounts and controls rupee debt in London besides performing other agency services. At places where there is no sub-office or local office of the Reserve Bank, the State Bank of India with its subsidiaries acts as its agent.

4. Departments of RBI

There are sixteen departments of the Reserve Bank of India. These are:

1. *Issue Department.* This department undertakes the job of issuing paper currency and therefore it also makes arrangement for the distribution of paper currency. It maintains regular accounts of the notes printed at Nasik Press. Its branches are at Bangalore, Mumbai, Kolkata Hyderabad, Kanpur, Chennai, Nagpur, New Delhi and Patna.

2. *Banking Department.* This department performs two primary functions, one of dealing with Government transactions and floating of loans on behalf of the Central and State Governments and arranging remittances of government funds from one place to another; and the other regarding the maintenance of cash reserves of scheduled banks, extending financial assistance to them, whenever required, and functioning as the clearing house for the scheduled banks.

3. *Banking Development.* This department is concerned with the expansion of banking facilities in the rural and semi-urban areas. It also imparts training to the scheduled banks.

4. *Banking Operations.* This department undertakes periodical inspections of the scheduled banks, analyses their balance sheets, issues licences for opening of new banks, considers requests for opening new branches, examines the requests of scheduled banks for increasing the paid-up capital, examines the possibilities for the amalgamation of existing banks and tenders advice to the scheduled banks in their day-to-day functioning.

5. *Agricultural Credit.* This department studies the problems connected

with agricultural credit, conducts research on rural credit problems, formulates rural credit policy of the Reserve Bank, grants rural credit to State Governments and State Cooperative Banks and publishes reports on agricultural credit.

6. *Exchange Control.* This department regulates and controls the sale and purchase of foreign exchange.

7. *Industrial Finance.* This department extends financial assistance to small scale and medium scale industries and also tenders advice to various industrial financial corporations for their d~y-to-day working.

8. *Non-Banking Companies.* The headquarters of this department is at Calcutta and it is chiefly concerned with the supervision of the non-banking companies and financial institutions in the country.

9. *Legal Department.* This department tenders advice to the various departments of the Bank on legal matters, prepares directives and communiques of the Bank and gives advice to the Bank on the proper implementation of legal matters relating to banking in the country.

10. *Research and Statistics.* This department undertakes research on problems in the areas of money, credit, finance, production, etc., collects statistics about the various sectors of the economy and publishes them; and tenders advice to the Government for the solution of various economic problems and in the formulation of its economic and financial policies.

11. *Department of Planning and Reorganisation.* The department formulates new plans and reorganises existing policies so as to make them more effective.

12. *Economic Department.* This department formulates banking policies for better implementation of economic policies of the Government.

13. *Inspection Department.* This department undertakes inspection of various offices of the commercial banks.

14. *Department of Accounts and Expenditure.* This department maintains proper records of all receipts and expenditures of the Reserve Bank of India.

15. *RBI Services Board.* The Board deals with the selection of new employees for different posts in the Reserve Bank of India.

16. *Department of Supervision.* This department was set up on 22 December, 1993, for conducting proper supervision of commercial banks.

5. Objectives of RBI

The main objectives of the Reserve Bank of India have been:

1. Promotion of monetisation and monetary integration of the economy.
2. Amendment of currency and regulation of foreign exchange.
3. Institutionalisation of savings through promotion of banking habit.
4. Building up of a sound and adequate banking and credit structure.

5. Evolving a well-differentiated structure of institutions for providing credit for agriculture and allied activities.

6. Promotion of specialised financial institutions at national and regional levels to augment facilities for term finance to industry.

7. Provide support to planning authorities and governments towards the acceleration of economic development with stability and social justice.

6. Functions of RBI

The Reserve Bank of India has been performing a variety of functions. The primary function of the Reserve Bank is to regulate the monetary system of the country so as to promote economic stability within the framework of the general economic policy of the Government. According to the Preamble to the Reserve Bank of India Act, 1934, the main function of the Bank is, "to regulate the issue of Bank notes and the keeping of reserves with a view to securing monetary stability in India and generally to operate the currency and credit system of the country to its advantage". The regulation of the monetary system involves the control of the volume of currency in circulation, banking and credit system of the country.

The second important function of the Bank is the conduct of the banking and financial operations of the government. It also plays a significant role in the maintenance of the exchange value of the rupee and for this purpose, the Bank has been entrusted with the custody and management of the country's entire foreign exchange reserves. It also controls the payments and receipts involving foreign currencies in conformity with the import and export trade policy of the government. These are the traditional functions of a central bank. With the task of economic development assuming a new urgency and impetus, the range of the functions of the central banks has been considerably widened, particularly in less-developed countries. Similarly, the Reserve Bank of India now performs it variety of developmental and promotional functions which in the past were considered as being outside the purview of central banks. The Bank's responsibilities in this connection, comprise the development of sound banking system and to gear it to the needs of trade and commerce, agriculture and industry. The Bank's functions are thus wide and varied, representing the superimposition of new lines of activity on orthodox central banking principles. The Bank also collects data on the operations of commercial banks and other financial institutions, balance-of-payments, national income, price indices, company and government finances and security markets and publishes them periodically. We now describe the functions of the Bank in detail.

1. Central Banking Functions

1. Monopoly of Note Issue. Since the most important function of a central bank is to maintain the stability of the monetary standard, the Reserve Bank of India has been from the very beginning entrusted with the sole right of note-issue, with the exception of one-rupee notes, coins and small coins which are issued by the Ministry of Finance, Government of India, the entire note-issue function vested with the Reserve Bank of India. This has been done to give the Bank a complete and unified control over the currency and credit system of the country and also maintain the stability of paper currency. The Bank is not governed by the desire of earning profits and is compelled under the law to keep an adequate reserve. For this purpose, the Bank maintains a separate Issue Department the assets and liabilities of which are kept entirely separate from those of the Banking Department.

2. Maintenance of Foreign Exchange Value of Rupee. This is a very important function of the Reserve Bank, and for its success in this regard, the Reserve Bank sells and purchases foreign exchange at fixed rates through its exchange control department. This department was set up in 1939, immediately after the outbreak of the Second World War. Since then all foreign exchange transactions are being handled by this department. After the devaluation of the US dollar in February 1973, the Indian rupee was linked with the pound-sterling at 18.9677 rupees per sterling. This linkage continued until 24 September, 1975 when the rupee was delinked from the pound-sterling and was linked to a basket of a number of selected currencies of the countries which are India's important trading partners. The Reserve Bank, now, sells and purchases the currencies of those countries which are the members of the IMF, at a rate determined from time to time. With the assistance of exchange banks and a few other authorised commercial banks, the Bank has been administering the exchange control system of the country.

3. Banker to the Government. Like all other central banks in the world, the Reserve Bank also fulfils its functions as a banker to the Government. It keeps the banking account of the Government of India, State Governments, accepts moneys in their accounts and makes payments up to the amount standing to the credit of their accounts. The Bank also carries out exchange remittances and other banking operations, including the management of public debt on behalf of the government. It is not entitled to any remuneration excepting for the holding of government cash balances free of interest. The State Governments have to keep with the Bank, such minimum balances, as may be required under the terms of the Agreement. Temporary deficits in this minimum are met either by the issue of their own treasury bills or by obtaining advances from the Bank. These advances must be repaid within three months. The rupee loans of the State and Central Governments are floated by the Bank.

The Bank has to keep currency chests at government treasuries, sub-treasuries and agencies to provide currency for government transactions. It makes arrangements for the supply of foreign exchange to the Central and State Governments. It also raises short-term loans for the governments by selling treasury bills issued by them for a period of ninety days. In case, governments require accommodation for a shorter period, they obtain ways and means advances from the Bank. It gives advice to the governments, regarding the issue of new loans, conversion of old loans, investment of funds, agricultural credit, cooperative banking and legislation, etc. It co-ordinates the borrowing programmes of the Central and State Governments.

4. Bankers' Bank. The most important function of the Bank is that of granting accommodation facilities to the commercial banks, co-operative banks and other eligible financial institutions. In this respect, the Bank is a lender of last resort. The Reserve Bank of India Act of 1934 laid down rigid eligibility conditions which had considerably limited the scope of granting accommodation facilities to the commercial banks. The banks had to fulfil both the eligibility and acceptability criteria. Since the passing of the Indian Banking Companies Act of 1949, these rules have been substantially relaxed and the Reserve Bank has been empowered to rediscount any paper which it considers to be eligible, though the particular banking company, bringing the paper, may be involved in a financial crisis. The Act has given wide powers to the Reserve Bank for selecting eligible papers and granting accommodation facilities to commercial banks. During recent years, the dependence of the banking system on the Reserve Bank for accommodation has increased considerably.

The Bank gives financial assistance to the scheduled banks in the form of rediscount of eligible bills or advances against approved securities. In the interest of sound and healthy banking, the Bank takes into account not only the nature of the security, but also the financial condition of the applicant, the manner of its total business, whether it pays unnecessarily high rates on deposits or asks for financial assistance, even in easy money conditions or has been guilty of unwise lending, etc. It may even refuse to rediscount the paper of any scheduled bank without giving any reason.

The Bank purchases, sells and rediscounts bills of exchange, promissory notes, maturing within ninety days, agricultural bills or promissory-notes payable in India, bearing two good signatures and issued for financing seasonal operations or marketing of crops and maturing within fifteen months from the date of purchase or rediscount by the Bank; bills and promissory-notes drawn in India for trading in government securities, maturing within ninety days and bills of exchange including treasury bills maturing within ninety days, provided the purchase, sale or rediscount is made in India with a scheduled bank. The Reserve Bank also gives remittance facilities to scheduled banks and co-operative banks. The Reserve Bank can also borrow from any scheduled bank in India or from any foreign bank subject to the condition that such borrowings cannot be for a period of more than 30 days and should not exceed the share capital of the Reserve Bank.

5. Clearing House Function. Prior to the setting up of the RBI the clearing house function was performed by the Imperial Bank. There were only four clearing houses in Bombay, Calcutta, Delhi and Madras. Now there are more than two hundred clearing houses of which besides the four metropolitan cities, those at Kanpur, Bangaluru, Nagpur, Hyderabad, Patna, Bhubneshwar and Ahmedabad are managed by the RBI and the remaining are managed by the SBI and its group.

6. Controller of Credit. For the proper performance of its function as a controller of credit, the Bank must have a complete control over currency and banking system in the country. We have already stated that the Bank has the sole right of note-issue, that is, it can determine to a very great extent, the total supply of media of exchange for credit expansion. The purpose of credit control is to arrange for suitable credit avoiding either excess or shortage and bring about stability in the price level. Credit control is related to the monetary policy of the Bank. There are two types of credit, *viz.*, bank credit and capital credit. It has a direct control over the former; so far as the organised part is concerned, while its control over the latter is only indirect.

We have stated that in India the commercial banks are required to keep a minimum balance with the Reserve Bank about which it is very strict. The main object is to exert some control over the credit creating capacity of the banks. It also holds the government balances and carries out the banking transactions of the government, which serve as a useful means to the Bank for exercising control over the credit situation in the country. But the effectiveness of a central bank's credit policy largely depends upon the nature and character of the money market in which it operates. The more organised the money market, the more effective would its credit policy be.

2. Ordinary Banking Functions

The following ordinary banking functions are performed by the Reserve Bank of India:

1. Acceptance of deposits from various governments and individuals without interest.

2. Purchase, sale and rediscounting of the bills of exchange and promissory notes of the scheduled banks without limit.

3. Granting of loans and advances to various Governments, scheduled banks, State cooperative banks for 90 days.

4. Purchase and sale of government securities and foreign securities.

5. Purchase and sale of foreign exchange to scheduled banks for minimum amount of Rs. 1 lakh.

6. Borrowing from scheduled Indian banks or from any foreign bank.

7. Opening an account, if it so desires in the World Bank or in any foreign central bank.

8. Safe custody of valuables, securities, etc.

9. Sale and purchase of gold and silver.

3. Miscellaneous Functions

The Reserve Bank of India performs a number of other functions which do not fall in any of the categories mentioned above. These functions are:

1. With a view to providing better and intensive training to the staff of banks at different levels, the Reserve Bank of India has set up a number of training colleges and centres. These are: (*i*) Banker's Training College located at Mumbai-provides training to senior officers of the Bank in the areas of application of statistical methods, negotiating skills counselling, import-export financing, Service Area Approach etc. (*ii*) Reserve Bank's staff College-located at Chennai, conducts training programmes for officers of the Bank in the areas of investment and fund management, financial services, housing finance, customer service etc. These are also available to the officers of the foreign banks. (*iii*) College of Agricultural Banking—located at Pune, caters to the training needs of personnel of cooperative banks, commercial banks, regional rural banks NABARD, Reserve Bank of India, Deposit Insurance and Credit Guarantee Corporation, government officials and officials from South Asian and African countries, in the fields of agricultural finance, rural banking etc. (*iv*) Zonal Training Centres situated in Mumbai, Kolkata Chennai, New Delhi—provides training to Class IV Staff of the Bank also conducts training programmes in computer and customer service. (*v*) Indira Gandhi Institute of Development Research set-up in 1987, conducts research on projects and arranges workshops, conferences and seminars. (*vi*) Training in Computer Technology. The Reserve Bank of India set-up the Department of computer technology in 1995 for speedy introduction of new technology by the Bank and provides incentive to incentive to the staff to acquire qualifications in computer technology.

2. Collection and publication of statistical information relating to banking, finance, credit, currency, agricultural and industrial production, etc. It also brings out monthly bulletins and periodicals which contain the results of various studies and reviews of the economic situation of the country.

4. Promotional and Developmental Functions

The Reserve Bank also undertakes the following promotional and developmental functions:

1. It encourages the expansion of branches by commercial banks in the semi-urban and rural areas. In this way it helps in the development of banking habits among the people and reduces their dependence on indigenous bankers and money lenders.

2. With the establishment of Deposit Insurance and Credit Corporation the Reserve Bank has been helping in building the confidence of the depositors as well as in avoiding bank failures.

3. By promoting institutions like Unit Trust of India, the Reserve Bank helps the mobilisation of savings in the country.

4. Promotion of institutional agricultural credit and development of cooperative credit institutions.

5. Promotion of the process of industrial is at ion by setting up specialized institutions for providing industrial finance.

6. Development of bill culture in the country.

7. Forbidden Business

The Reserve Bank of India cannot undertake the following functions:

1. Provision of direct financial assistance to any business, trade or industry;
2. Purchase of shares of commercial banks or industrial undertakings or any other bank;
3. Granting of unsecured loans and advances;
4. Granting of loans against mortgage of security;
5. Payment of interest on deposits;
6. Acceptance of bills not payable on demand; and
7. Purchase of immovable property except for its own offices.

8. Reserve Bank and Rural Finance

The Reserve Bank of India has taken the following measures for the fulfilment of its objective of formulating agricultural credit policy, development of infrastructure for its implementation and advising on these matters to the State and Central Governments and providing credit for agricultural and allied activities.

Agricultural Credit Department. Initially the Bank had a special Agricul-tural Credit Department for: (*i*) maintaining an expert staff to study all questions of agricultural credit and making them available for consultation by the Central and State Governments, State Cooperative Banks and other banking organisations; and (*ii*) coordinating the operations of the Bank in connection with agricultural credit and its relations with State Cooperative

Banks and any other banks or organisations engaged in the business of agricultural credit. This department was also engaged in the collection of statistics and research in rural credit. With the introduction of economic planning this department was entrusted with the financing of processing, marketing and other agricultural activities through State Cooperative Banks and other agencies of rural credit. In July 1982, this department was merged with the NABARD.

All-India Rural Credit Survey Committee

In 1951, the Reserve Bank appointed the All India Rural Credit Survey Committee. In pursuance of the recommendations of this Committee the Reserve Bank took the following steps to develop cooperative credit movement and provide agricultural finance:

1. Integrated scheme of rural credit. Under this scheme the Reserve Bank (*a*) promoted State partnership in cooperative credit institutions, marketing and processing societies; and (*b*) strengthened the administration by providing adequately trained and efficient staff to fulfil the needs of the rural population.

The Reserve Bank has also been playing an active role in (*a*) the development of cooperative credit, (*b*) the coordination of credit with marketing, processing and warehousing activities, and (*c*) training of cooperative personnel.

2. State Bank of India. With the nationalisation of the Imperial Bank of India and establishment of the State Bank of India, the Reserve Bank became its major shareholder. The State Bank has been taking an active part in financing agricultural operations.

3. Agricultural Credit Board. In 1956, the Reserve Bank constituted the Standing Advisory Committee on Agricultural Credit which was reconstituted in 1970 as the Agricultural Credit Board. It was entrusted with the formulation of policies relating to agricultural finance and coordination of the activities of cooperative credit institutions, the Reserve Bank and commercial banks in providing refinance facilities. Since July 1982, these activities of the Board have been taken over by the NABARD.

4. Rural Credit Funds. In 1956, the Reserve Bank established two funds, namely: (*i*) National Agricultural Credit (Long-Term Operations) Fund to grant long-term loans to State Governments and land development banks for subscribing to the share capital of cooperative banks and cooperative societies; and (*ii*) National Agricultural Credit (Stabilisation) Fund for converting short-term agricultural loans into medium-term loans by the State Cooperative Banks to enable cooperative societies to repay loans in case of default by borrowers as a result of natural calamities like drought, famines, floods, etc. Both these funds were transferred to NABARD in July 1982 and have been renamed as National Rural Credit (Long-term Operations) Fund and National Rural Credit (Stabilisation) Fund.

Other Organisations

For the enlargement of credit facilities to the rural sector the Reserve Bank has promoted the following organisations:

1. Nationalisation of Banks. Fourteen scheduled banks were nationalised in 1969 and six commercial banks were nationalised in 1980 for spreading a network of branches in rural areas with the purpose of providing larger credit facilities for the development of agriculture and allied activities.

2. Agricultural Refinance and Development Corporation. In July 1963 the Reserve Bank established the Agricultural Refinance Corporation which was subsequently renamed as Agricultural Refinance and Development Corporation. With the establishment of NABARD in July 1982, the corporation was merged with it.

3. Regional Rural Banks. In 1975, the Reserve Bank helped the establishment of regional rural banks. Since July 1982, the work of financing and supervising these banks has been entrusted to NABARD. The chief function of these rural banks is to grant loans and advances to the weaker sections of the rural population and to cooperative societies.

4. National Bank for Agriculture and Rural Development (NABARD). As already stated this bank was established in 1982 as an apex rural development bank. The Reserve Bank gives loans to the NABARD under the general line of credit for short periods and also contributes to the national rural credit funds of the NABARD. The NABARD provides credit, refinance and institutional building facilities for integrated rural development.

5. Service Area Approach. This scheme was introduced in April 1989, for preparing a credit plan relating to agriculture and allied activities for the target groups and for lending to the priority sector categories of borrowers under the service area (covering 15 to 25 villages) of the branch of a commercial bank.

Help to Cooperatives

The Reserve Bank helps the cooperatives in the following ways: (*i*) inspects and audits their accounts; (*ii*) provides cheap remittance facilities to them; (*iii*) renders advice about adjustment of their loans and assets; and (*iv*) conducts training programmes for their personnel in the field of agricultural finance, rural banking and allied subjects in its college of Agricultural Banking at Pune.

Financial Assistance

The Reserve Bank of India has been providing financial assistance to agriculturists, not directly but through the State Cooperative Banks and the NABARD. The position of these advances is as follows:

1. Short-term Advances. These are given to State Cooperative Banks against government and other approved securities. The Reserve Bank also routes short-term financial assistance to the State Cooperative Banks through NABARD for agriculture and other purposes under the general line of credit. The short-term advances of the Reserve Bank of India/NABARD to the State Cooperative Banks amounted to Rs. 7,358 crore in 2002-03.

2. Medium-term Advances. Medium-term advances are made by the Reserve Bank to the State Cooperative Banks against the pledge of government and other approved securities for a period of 15 months to 5 years. The NABARD also provides medium-term advances from its national rural credit funds. Such loans and advances given by Reserve Bank/NABARD to the State Cooperative Banks totalled at Rs. 493 crore in 2002-03.

3. Long-term Advances. Long-term advances are provided by the Reserve Bank for agriculture and allied activities to the State Governments to enable them to contribute to the share capital of cooperatives and the National Rural Credit Funds of the NABARD. The total loans sanctioned by Reserve Bank/NABARD under this head to State Governments amounted to Rs. 61 crore during 2002-03.

9. Reserve Bank and Industrial Finance

For promoting industrialisation, the Reserve Bank has been providing finance, through various institutions, to large, medium and small-scale industries. For this purpose it has helped the establishment of a number of financial institutions at the centre as well as in States and provides credit facilities to them. These institutions are:

1. Industrial Finance Corporation of India. It was set up in 1948 for providing financial assistance (medium and long-term loans) to the industrial sector. The Reserve Bank subscribed 40 per cent of the issued capital and to its debentures. It provides credit limits to the Corporation against the security of eligible usance bills rediscounted by it. In 1964, the Corporation was made a subsidiary of the Industrial Development Bank of India.

2. National Industrial Credit (Long-Term Operations) Funds. The Fund was created in 1964 for providing long-term credit to the leading financial institutions.

3. Industrial Development Bank of India (IDBI). The bank was established in 1964 as the main financial institution for industrial finance in the country. It is a wholly owned subsidiary of the Reserve Bank and provides direct assistance to medium and large industrial concerns by purchasing/underwriting their shares and debentures. It also provides refinance facilities to other term-lending institutions.

4. Industrial Credit and Investment Corporation of India (ICICI). The Corporation was set up in 1955 as a public limited company. It provides assistance for the development of industries and investment in the for of rupee and foreign currency loans, by underwriting and direct participation in shares, debentures and guarantees. The RBI provides medium and short-term credit limits against the security of eligible usance bills rediscounted by it.

5. Industrial Reconstruction Bank of India (IRBI). It was set up in 1985 after reconstituting the erstwhile Industrial Reconstruction Corporation of India mainly to help the rehabilitation of sick and closed industrial units by granting term loans and advances, underwriting of stocks, shares, bonds and debentures and guarantees for loans/deferred payments.

6. State Financial Corporations. These Corporations are the State level organisations set up for the development of medium and small-scale industries in the States. These corporations have been providing financial assistance to industrial units by way of term loans, direct subscription to equity/debentures, discounting of bills of exchange and guarantees. Most of the IDBI schemes for assistance to small and medium industries are operated through these Corporations.

7. Small Industries Development Bank of India (SIDBI). It is a wholly owned 'subsidiary of IDBI and was set up in April 1990 to ensure larger flow of financial and non-financial assistance to small-scale industries. The major activities undertaken by it include: refinancing of loans and advances, discounting and rediscounting of bills, extending seed capital/soft loans, providing services like factoring, leasing, etc. and extending financial support to Small Industries Development Corporations. The Reserve Bank of India provides long-term credit to this bank which was of the order of Rs. 224 crore during 1995-96.

8. Exim Bank. It was set-up in 1982 as a statutory corporation of the Government of India for providing assistance for promoting Indian exports through direct financial assistance, overseas investments, term financing for export production and export development shipment credit, buyers' credit, lines of credit, relending facility, export bills rediscounting, refinance to commercial banks, finance for computer software exports, finance for export marketing and bulk import finance to commercial banks. It also provides non-fund facility in the form of guarantees to India exporters. The focus of its lending programme is on the export of manufactured goods, project exports, exports of technology services, and export of computer software. It had received Rs. 120 crore from the Reserve Bank of India as long term assistance in 1991.

9. National Housing Bank. The National Housing Bank after established in 1988 with a paid-up capital of Rs. 250 crore subscribed by the Reserve Bank of India, provides assistance under Home Loans Account Scheme and through liberalized lending by commercial banks and re-financing facilities for land development and shelter programmes of public private agencies and cooperatives.

10. Reserve Bank and Exchange Control

The Reserve Bank of India is responsible for managing and controlling the foreign exchange reserves of the country and the external value of the rupee. The Reserve Bank controls the inflow and outflow of foreign currencies to overcome the deficit in the balance of payments, under the authority provided by the Foreign Exchange Regulation Act, 1973 and Foreign Exchange Regulation (Amendment) Act, 1993.

Foreign currencies coming into India can be sold to and exchanged by the Reserve Bank or by the dealers authorised by it in rupees or in other foreign currencies. The dealers authorised by the Reserve Bank to deal in foreign currencies include commercial banks, hotels, firms, shops, etc. They are also authorised to lend and borrow up to a limit, foreign currency among themselves. This limit is fixed by the Reserve Bank depending upon the size of its operations and other relative factors. The authorised dealers are allowed to: (*i*) maintain with overseas branches and correspondents, balances in foreign currencies at levels which are commensurate with normal requirements of their business; and (*ii*) transfer foreign currency funds rendered surplus on a day-to-day basis to special interest bearing accounts. Exporters are allowed to receive export proceeds through normal banking channels. The payments for imports are made either under the Direct Payment Method of Reimbursement Method. Since 1991, several changes have been introduced in the exchange rate system by the Reserve Bank. In July 1991, the rupee was devalued by about 20 per cent *vis-a-vis* US dollar. Exim Scrip Scheme was also introduced permitting certain imports only against export entitlement. On 1st March, 1992 partial convertibility of rupee in 60 : 40 ratio was introduced, which was known as the Liberalised Exchange Rate Management System (LERMS). Under this system the entire foreign exchange receipts on current account were to be surrendered in full to the authorised dealers at the rate quoted by them. These dealers surrendered 40 per cent of their foreign currency receipts to the Reserve Bank at the rate announced by it. The authorised dealers were free to sell the balance 60 per cent of foreign currency left with them in the free market, and the importers and persons travelling abroad bought these currencies from the authorised dealers. The authorised dealers were not required to seek prior approval of the Reserve Bank for this purpose. However, leaving exporters, in all other cases the sale of foreign exchange limit had been raised from $ 100 to $ 500.

On 2 March, 1993, the dual exchange rate system was replaced by the Unified Exchange Rate System (UERS) under which the 60:40 ratio was withdrawn and 100 per cent conversion was allowed. Under this system the exchange rates was determined by market forces of demand and supply. The Reserve Bank had been announcing its buying and selling rates at the on-going market rates for transactions with authorised dealers. But the official Reserve Bank exchange rate continued for the conversion of items (more than half a dozen invisible items of current account and all capital account payments) not permitted under the UERS. However, various exchange control norms of the Reserve Bank continued with minor relaxations.

As a consequence of these measures the exchange rate remained stable. With stability in the exchange rate and larger inflow of resources owing to the liberalised foreign investment policy and the withdrawal of industrial and trade restrictions the current account deficit was substantially reduced. This led to the current account convertibility of the rupee w.e.f. 1 March, 1994. The Reserve Bank further relaxed exchange rate regulations in respect of a number of invisible items as part of the current account convertibility of the rupee. The foreign exchange regulations were further liberalised in August 1994. Now there is no officially fixed exchange rate of the rupee. The rate is determined by the demand and supply conditions in the foreign exchange market. The Reserve Bank takes suitable measures to maintain orderly market conditions and to curb excessive speculation in foreign exchange. In July 1995 the Reserve Bank further permitted authorised dealers to provide exchange facilities to their clients without its prior approval on the condition that they should satisfy themselves about the genuineness of the requirement of the applicants. But they have to report all such transactions to the Reserve Bank.

The process of liberalisation towards current account convertibility has been continued by delegating more powers to the authorised dealers. They have been permitted to: (*i*) export their surplus stock of foreign currency for realisation of proceeds to private money changers abroad, in addition to their overseas branches and correspondents; (*ii*) allow Exchange Earners Foreign Currency account holders to utilise funds in such accounts for making remittances in foreign currencies connected with their trade and business transactions which are of current account nature. The Reserve Bank has set up an Inter-Bank Forex Clearing House where foreign exchange transactions by authorised dealers are cleared. The Reserve Bank has also set up Market

Intelligence Cell to study and monitor the developments in the Indian foreign exchange market on a day-to-day basis.

11. Achievements of the Reserve Bank of India

Following are the main achievements of the Reserve Bank of India:

1. It has very successfully regulated credit to meet the requirements of trade, industry and agriculture.

2. As a partner to the government it has been admirably managing the public debt.

3. It has developed and promoted sound banking practices in the country. This has inspired public confidence in the banking system.

4. The Reserve Bank has successfully promoted the institu-tionalisation of savings by: (*i*) promoting banking habits, (*ii*) extending banking facilities all over the country, and (*iii*) establishing specialised financial agencies.

5. It has achieved appreciable success in promoting cooperative credit and rural credit.

6. It has achieved great success in the field of industrial credit by promoting a number of institutions for providing medium and long-term credit.

7. The Reserve Bank has succeeded in providing credit facilities to exporters by extending concessional credit, refinance facilities and guarantee to commercial banks. It has been instrumental in setting up the Export-Import Bank for providing credit and other facilities to exporters.

8. As a guardian of the banking system the Reserve Bank has been providing deposit insurance and credit guarantee facilities to the banks through DICGC.

9. The Reserve Bank has played a crucial role in promoting social banking in the country.

10. The Reserve Bank has also been successful to a large extent in developing bill culture in the country.

11. The Reserve Bank has been rendering a very useful service in providing information and data on the different sectors of the economy through its publications.

12. The Reserve Bank has been successfully providing clearing house facilities through its 15 branches and 2 offices and the State Bank of India.

13. The management and control of foreign exchange by the Reserve Bank has been admirable.

14. The Reserve Bank has set up a number of training centres and colleges to impart training to the staff of cooperative banks, commercial banks, regional rural banks, NABARD, etc., and thus is contributing in a big way to the development of human resources in the sphere of banking.

15. Through its department of information technology the Reserve Bank has modernised its functioning by introducing advanced computer technology for inter-office communication and Internet technology for information collecting and sharing. It has also encouraged computerisation of the branches of commercial banks.

12. Failures of the Reserve Bank of India

The Reserve Bank has not achieved success in the following spheres:

1. It has failed to control the unorganised money market and consequently the indigenous bankers are still functioning. independently.

2. The Reserve Bank has failed in establishing uniformity between the bank rate and other money market rates.

3. The Reserve Bank has failed to contain inflation in the economy.

4. The policy of credit squeeze adopted by the Reserve Bank has led to the decline in the profitability of commercial banks. About 54 per cent of the total deposits of banks are blocked into reserves and only 46 per cent are available for lending. Of this 40 per cent is required to be given to the priority sector. It thus means that the commercial banks are unable to earn enough profits.

5. In spite of its best efforts the Reserve Bank has not been fully successful in developing an organised bill market. It has also not done anything to systematise and recognise hundis as bills of exchange.

6. In spite of expansion of credit facilities in rural areas, sufficient funds are not available to meet the credit needs t the rural population.

7. The Reserve Bank has also not succeeded in developing Indian exchange banks. The State Bank of India and a few public sector banks have not been able to cut much ice in this connection because of the want of clear guidelines from the Reserve Bank.

8. In spite of the measures adopted by the Reserve Bank the customer service in public sector banks continues to be of a very low standard.

9. Finally, the Reserve Bank has also failed to check the multiplication of black money in the country. As a matter of fact its policy of credit squeeze has encouraged the generation of black money.

Exercises

1. Describe the Constitution and organisational structure of the Reserve Bank of India.
2. Explain the main functions of the Reserve Bank of India. How far has it succeeded as the Central Bank of the country?
3. Discuss the achievements and failures of the Reserve Bank of India.
4. How does the Reserve Bank of India regulate currency and credit in India?
5. Explain the working of selective credit control in India.

6. Critically examine the monetary policy of the Reserve Bank of India.
7. What has the Reserve Bank of India done to develop and regulate banking in the country?
8. Examine the role of the Reserve Bank of India in the economic development of the country.
9. Explain the role of Reserve Bank of India in developing the bill market.
10. Explain how the Reserve Bank of India manages the exchange control system.
11. Explain the role of the Reserve Bank of India in the provision of agricultural finance in the country.
12. Evaluate the working of the Reserve Bank of India since 1949.
13. Discuss the role of Reserve Bank of India in promoting industrial finance.
14. "The Reserve Bank of India policy has been one of controlled expansion." Discuss the statement.

•••

Chapter 25

Monetary Policy of Reserve Bank of India

1. Introduction

The general issues related to the monetary policy from the theoretical angle have been discussed already. Now we deal with the various aspects of monetary policy in the Indian context. The monetary policy, as in other countries is formulated and operated by the Reserve Bank of India (RBI) which is the Central Bank of the country.

2. Objectives of Monetary Policy

Right from 1949, the Reserve Bank's monetary policy has been guided by three objectives, *viz.*, stability, growth and social justice; of course the emphasis on one or more of these objectives has changed from time to time according to changing situations. So, the main focus of Reserve Bank's monetary policy has been on controlled expansion of money supply.

Since independence and more particularly, since the beginning of the First Five Year Plan, the principal objectives of the monetary policy as adopted by the RBI have been economic development and price stability; the objective of financial stability was added after the introduction of economic reforms in 1991. 'Caution' has been the watch-word for the RBI in regard to the operation of the monetary policy—both in the matter of supply of money and expansion of credit in the money market. So far as the supply of money is concerned, broadly speaking, it should be adequate to meet the demand for money. Similarly, in respect of expansion of credit; it is imperative to ensure that the legitimate requirements of industry and trade are not stultified.

In a developing country like India, in the context of development planning, it is necessary that the money supply is expanded only to match the growth of real national income with expansion of credit in certain sectors and control in others. It is also necessary that the legitimate credit requirements of production and trade are met. This means that the monetary policy aims at controlled expansion of money supply, but there should be a balance between control and expansion. The Reserve Bank has been treading on a difficult path but it has been fairly successful in handling the situation. So far as the expansion of money supply is concerned, the Reserve Bank of India has adopted various measures to enlarge the institutional supply of rural and industrial credit and has paid attention towards insulating sensitive sectors such as exports and other priority sectors from the impact of general credit squeeze.

In the context of a developing economy, like India, the chief objective of the monetary policy has to be to ensure rapid economic growth with financial adequacy and price stability. Economic growth implies growth of national income and the supply of money for the smooth flow of economic activity has to be higher than the projected growth of real national income; because firstly, money is a component of savings which tend to grow with increase in income and secondly, non-monetised sector goes on contracting and the monetised sector of the economy goes on expanding. In short, the money supply has to be expanded adequately in accordance with the growth of real national income. So far as the control of money supply is concerned the Reserve Bank has been using various instruments of credit control to regulate: (*i*) the cost of credit; (*ii*) the quantity of credit; and (*iii*) the purpose of credit. Since government fiscal deficits have been an important source of monetary expansion the Reserve Bank has hardly any scope for controlling it. However, the Reserve Bank has tried to restrict the secondary expansion of credit by banks through control of their cash reserves. Even here, the Reserve Bank's efforts have not borne fruits to the desired extent because of the priorities indicated by the Government of India. Hence, the implementation of monetary policy has not been an easy task for the Reserve Bank. Further, it is not an easy task to make a choice in the context of factors which are not easily reconcilable, such as: (*a*) the need to control inflationary pressures; (*b*) raising the level of aggregate output and the expansion of credit for the same; and (*c*) restricting the use of credit for non-productive activities.

An underdeveloped economy like India, where there is no certainty about the continuity of aggregate supply, particularly the agricultural output, has to be constantly vigilant since monetary expansion has always been larger than the output supply. The adjustment of the pace of monetary expansion in accordance with the constantly changing situations, is, therefore, a very difficult task. The policy of controlled expansion has also to reconcile the objectives of growth and social justice with price stability. It is mainly for this reason that expansion of credit may have to be allowed in the long run for sustaining and increasing productive activity in the economy, and it may have to be controlled in the short run to create conditions for price stability. The monetary policy of the Reserve Bank has to be judged in the light of these considerations. It may, however, be noted that the chief objective of the Reserve Bank's monetary policy in recent years has been to narrow down the difference between the rate of monetary expansion and that of the growth in national income.

3. Regulation and Control of Money Supply

In a developing country the central bank has to be extremely vigilant towards the expansion of credit in the money market, because unbridled expansion of credit will lead to inflationary rise in prices which will retard the process of economic growth. Financing of investment outlays through budgetary deficits is a common feature of developing economies following the path of planned economic development. These deficits are a potent source of expansion of money supply in the economy *i.e.* the secondary expansion of credit for the public sector as well as for the private sector. Hence, the central bank, has to use, from time to time, various instruments of credit control, according to the requirements of the situation. In India, the RBI has also been using these instruments as per the demands of the situation, as empowered under the RBI Act, either single, or in a combination of two or three instruments. The choice of instruments has to depend on a number of factors like: (*a*) condition of the money market, (*b*) demand for credit, (*c*) rate of inflation, (*d*) impact of black money, (*e*) balance of payments, (*f*) financial activities of banking institutions and non-banking financial intermediaries etc. But, the focus of the monetary policy has been, throughout, on financial adequacy and price stablity.

Methods of Credit Control Adopted by the Reserve Bank

The authority of the Reserve Bank of India for the control of the credit system is embodied in the Reserve Bank of India Act, 1934 and the Banking Regulation Act, 1949. The former Act confers on the Reserve Bank the traditional powers of general credit control while the latter Act provides special powers of direct regulation of the operations of commercial banks and cooperative banks. The Reserve Bank of India has made use of the general or quantitative credit control measures in combination with the selective credit control measures. The general credit control measures include variations in the bank rate, open market operations and changes in the reserve requirements. All these measures operate through their effect on the level of bank reserves because bank's capacity to provide credit largely depends on their cash reserves. Selective credit control measures relate to the distribution or direction of available credit supplies. These measures are meant to curb excesses in selected areas and channelise the credit to the desired areas, without effecting each other. Selective credit control measures are considered as a useful supplement to general credit control measures. They are used to regulate areas which do not respond to measures of general credit control and their effectiveness is considerably increased when they are used in combination with general credit control measures. During the decades of 1950 and 1960, RBI made use of selective credit controls, open market operations and Bank rate; in the decade of 1970, the RBI added CRR and SLR in its armoury; in 1980, the RBI used CRR, SLR and selective credit controls; in the 1990s the RBI mostly used SLR and CRR and occasionally used bank rate and open market operations and in the current decade the RBI has used CRR, open market operations, bank rate and Repos and Reverse Repo auctions under (*i*) Liquidity Adjustment Facility and (*ii*) Market Stabilisation Scheme. We shall now see how the Reserve Bank of India has made use of the different tools of credit control.

1. Open Market Operations

Open Market Operations refer broadly to the purchase and sale by the Reserve Bank of a variety of assets such as foreign exchange, gold, government securities, etc. The Reserve Bank, however, conducts these operations almost entirely in government securities, for obvious reasons. In the context of monetary management, open market operations as a tool of central banking policy, may have any or all these objectives, *viz.*, (*a*) to assist in the management of public debt and government borrowing; (*b*) to provide finance to commercial banks; (*c*) to create and maintain a desired pattern of yield on government securities; (*d*) to control the reserve base of the banking system. In general, open market operations have been employed more to assist the government in its borrowing operations and to maintain orderly conditions in the government securities market than to influence the availability and cost of credit. The sale of securities by the Reserve Bank of India has normally exceeded their purchases.

Open market operations can also be used to provide seasonal finance to banks. Prior to November 1951, the Reserve Bank was following the policy of comparatively free purchase of securities. This policy was changed in November 1951. Since then the Bank's purchases of securities have been mostly 'switch operations', *i.e.*, purchasing one security against the sale of another and vice versa to maintain an orderly pattern of yields and to cater to the changing requirements of investors. The open market operations have been more flexible and purposeful after 1961. The Indian giltedged market is narrow and a sizeable portion of the public debt is held by a few large institutions, *i.e.*, government-owned institutions and the scheduled commercial banks. There are, however, no continuous buying and selling of securities that are so essential for an active market. Moreover, the gilt-edged market in India is mainly a brokers 'market rather than a dealers' market. These operations are only limited to the sale and purchase of government securities to control money supply, rate of interest and the price level. These days the RBI uses them only for monetary control necessitated by the massive inflows of foreign exchange owing to the weakening of the U.S. dollar and opening the Indian economy to foreign direct investments. In view of these limitations the open market operations in India have not performed the role of a full-fledged instrument of credit policy. Since 1992-93 steps have been taken to develop a Government securities market in the country, for example, the introduction of dated securities, Zero-Coupon Bonds, 91-day Treasury bills, 364-day Treasury bills, etc.

2. Bank Rate

The Reserve Bank of India Act defines Bank Rate as "the standard rate on which it is prepared to buy or rediscount bills of exchange or other commercial papers eligible for purchase under this Act". That is why the Bank Rate is also known as the 'Rediscount Rate'. The Reserve Bank has been changing its bank rate as and when required by the prevailing conditions. However, the efficacy of this as a tool of credit control has often been questioned. The Reserve Bank has used bank rate primarily as a pace setter to other market rates of interest it has been fixing the deposit rates for saving as well as time deposits. It has also been prescribing ceiling for advance rates. In India, the application of selectivity has also been an important feature. Certain sectors are given preferential treatment in comparison to others. Hence accommodation at concessional rates is available for making advances to some particular sectors. On the whole the approach of the Reserve Bank has been to restrain the availability of credit rather than to raise the cost of credit. Since 1935 to 14 November, 1951, the bank rate remained stable at 3 per cent. For the first time it was raised to 3.5 per cent in November 1951, followed by further increases: to 4 per cent in May 1957, 4.5 per cent in January 1963, 5 per cent in September 1964, 6 per cent in January 1971, 7 per cent in May 1973, 9 per cent in July 1974, 10 per cent in 1981, 11 per cent in July 1991 and to 12 per cent in October 1991. Whenever the bank rate was increased the main objective was to follow a policy of dear money with a view to checking a rise in prices.

As a measure of reform the structure of interest rates was rationalised. The number of prescribed lending rates of banks were brought down from 6 to 3 in 1991-92. The Reserve Bank's credit policy announced in October 1994, minimum lending rates of scheduled commercial banks for credit limits over Rs. 2 lakh were abolished. A uniform rate of 13.5 per cent for all advances over Rs. 25,000 and up to Rs. 2 lakh was introduced. The term deposit rate was brought under a single ceiling of 10 per cent and within this cap banks were left free to fix the maturities and rates. Thus, the banks were provided more freedom to determine rates that they paid on the funds received and the rates that they charged from their clients, by this partial deregulation of interest rates. With effect from 22 April, 1992, the banks were given freedom to determine the rate and in respect of term deposits 3 maturity slabs of their choice, subject to a ceiling of interest rate not exceeding 13 per cent. When the inflation rate came down, the ceiling rate was reduced to 'not exceeding 10 per cent' by 2 September, 1993. It was increased to 'not exceeding 12 per cent' w.e.f. 18 April, 1995, with a gradual increase according to the term of deposit ranging from 46 days to three years and above, owing to a rise in the rate of inflation. On 1 October 1995, the banks were allowed to fix their own rates on domestic term deposits of over 2 years maturity. This measure was taken chiefly to enable the banks to increase their resources and to impart greater flexibility to term deposit rate structure. The rate of interest up to one year was prescribed at 11 per cent which was reduced to 10 per cent w.e.f. 21 October, 1996, the saving deposit rate was lowered from 5 per cent to 4.5 per cent w.e.f. November 1994.

Since April 15, 1997, the BR has been used as the reference rate for general refinance provided by the RBI and also for foreign currency deposits of similar maturity. Now all interest rates on RBI advances and penal rates on short falls in reserve requirements have been linked to the BR. This development will ultimately make the BR as the refinance or the signal rate as is the practice in other countries. During 1997-2003 the BR was frequently changed. It has not changed since April 2003, because now the RBI uses the reverse repo rate for providing liquidity. Moreover, the demand for money being stable the rate of interest plays a more inportant role and so the BR is now not so effective.

Under the DIR (differential interest rate) scheme term loans are being provided to small and water transport operators, professionals and self-employeds at the concessional rate of 4 per cent. Both the commercial banks and the urban cooperative banks are required to lend 40 per cent of their total advances to the priority sector.

Interest rates on export credit have also been revised from time to time. On pre-shipment export credit, banks have been permitted to charge 13 per cent interest up to 180 days and 15 per cent beyond 180 days to 270 days since 1 March, 1993. On post-shipment export credit up to 90 days the interest rate has been 13 per cent since 1 March, 1993; beyond 90 days to six months the rate has been 15 per cent w.e.f. 21 October, 1996 and beyond six months the banks have the freedom to charge their own interest rates.

3. Variable Reserve Ratios

According to the RBI Act a commercial bank is required to keep with the RBI, a preseribed portion of its deposits in the form of cash reserves. This is known as the cash reserve ratio (CRR). In addition, a commercial bank has also to keep with itself a certain portion of its total deposits in the form of liquid reserves. These are known as the Stautory Liquid Reserves (SLR). These are the two tools available to the RBI for controlling the powers of a bank to create credit. Until 1956 the commercial banks were required to keep 2 per cent of their time deposits and 5 per cent of their demand deposits in the form of reserves. This means that the Reserve Bank has not made use of this tool of monetary policy since its inception till 1956. The amendment made in the Reserve Bank Act in 1956 empowered the Reserve Bank to raise the ratio of reserve on time deposits of commercial banks from 2 to 8 per cent and on demand deposits from 5 to 20 per cent. The Act was again amended in 1962 to the effect that the distinction between time and demand deposits was abolished and the banks were required to keep the CRR between 3 to 15 per cent. Thereafter the Reserve Bank has been making changes in the CRR according to the changing monetary and economic conditions. A uniform CRR of 15 per cent of the entire net demand and time liabilities (NDTL) was introduced w.e.f. 1 July, 1989. It was reduced to 14 per cent on 15 May, 1993, but again raised to 15 per cent on August 1994, to meet monetary pressure caused by large capital inflows. When the conditions settled down and the money growth slowed, the CRR was reduced from 15 per cent to 14 per cent on 9 December, 1995 and to 13 per cent on 11 May, 1996, to 12 per cent on 6 July, 1996 and to 10 per cent in four stages beginning from 21 October, 1996 to mid-January 1997, and was reduced to 6.5% on April 28, 2007. The RBI pays to the banks interest on these reserves. Before September 11, 2004 the RBI used to pay interest at the Bank Rate, but from that date the rate of interest was reduced to 3.5% and now it is 0.5% w.e.f. March 30, 2007. This reduction in the CRR was made to enable banks to release more liquidity into the monetary system. As a policy tool the changes in the CRR have been more successful in controlling credit in comparison to open market operations and bank rate.

4. Statutory Liquidity Ratio (SLR)

It is another instrument of monetary policy. According to the Banking Regulation Act, 1949, the commercial banks have to keep 20 per cent of their Net Demand and Time Liabilities (deposits) with them in the form of liquidity ratio, which include excess reserves, current account balances with the Reserve Bank of India and other gold and unencumbered approved securities. The experience of the Reserve Bank had been that whenever it raised the CRR, the commercial banks defeated the purpose by increasing their liquidity power through the sale of government securities. With a view to check this tendency the SLR was raised to 25 per cent in 1962 (excluding cash reserves with the

RBI), 30 per cent in November 1972 and 38.5 per cent on 22 September, 1990. After that to increase the liquidity power of commercial banks, the SLR on NDTL was gradually reduced and was ultimately brought down by the end of 1996 to 25 per cent. The incremental SLR is 25 per cent. By combining SLR with CRR the Reserve Bank controls the liquidity of banks and thus limits their power to create credit, and contains the inflationary pressures. It also makes more financial resources available to the government for its own use.

5. Selective Credit Controls (SCCs)

The Reserve Bank acquired the powers of Selective Credit Controls under the Banking Regulation Act, 1949. These controls are meant to regulate and control the supply of credit and channelise the flow of bank credit from speculative and other undesirable purposes to socially desirable and economically useful purposes. Such controls are very effective in checking the rise in prices of commodities. The Reserve Bank of India has been operating these controls since 1956, and these have now become a regular feature of its policy of credit control. These controls are operated by fixing: (*i*) minimum margins for lending against specific securi-ties; (*ii*) ceilings on the amounts of credit to traders against the stock of certain commodities; (*iii*) minimum discriminatory rates of interest charged on certain types of advances; and prohibits: (*a*) advances for financing hoarding of certain commodities; and (*b*) prohibits the discounting of bill of exchange relating to the sale of selected commodities.

The Reserve Bank has made use of selective credit controls in respect of such commodities like cotton, wheat, paddy/rice, pulses, oil seeds, vegetable oil, sugar, *gur* and *khandsari*, man-made fibre and cloth. The rate of interest charged on advances against the security of these commodities is higher than on other securities. If the Reserve Bank wants to check speculation on the prices of such other commodities it raises the minimum margins. If it wants to liberalise credit facilities, the margins are lowered. The use of these controls are also made to check the upward rise in the rate of inflation. The Reserve Bank has also put restrictions on loans for purchase of consumer durables and other non-priority sector personal loans. However, the banks have been allowed w.e.f. 22 December, 1996 to advance loans against shares/debentures up to a maximum limit of Rs. 10 lakh.

The selective credit controls have, over the years become complicated and there was the need for rationalising them without deviating from the main objective of preventing speculative hoarding of essential commodities. Consequently, the system has been gradually simplified and controls have been removed wherever considered necessary. These controls have been under continuous review and changes have been made in response to emerging commodity supply situations and trends in prices. The selective credit controls can be effective only when they are operated in the framework of overall credit restrictions. In fact the Reserve Bank has also admitted the fact that these controls have been only marginally effective in checking the rise in prices. The existence of unaccounted sector in the economy, mainly comes in their way.

Credit Authorisation Scheme (CAS)

Under the see, the RBI, in November 1965 introduced the CAS which required the commercial banks to obtain RBI's authorisation before allowing any new credit of Rs. 1 crore or more to any singie party This limit was gradually raised to Rs. 6 crore by April 1986 and covered both public and private sectors. For manufacturing units and exporters the cut-off point was Rs. 7 crore. However, this scheme in October, 1988.

Credit Monitoring Arrangement (CMA)

To enforce fmancial discipline, the RBI introduced the practice of monitoring and scrutiny of all sanctions of bank loans Rs. 5 crore for working capital requirement and Rs. 2 crore as term loans. More than 930 parties are covered under CMA.

6. Liquidity Adjustment Facility (LAF)

It is an indirect instrument of credit control used by the RBI to meet day-to-day liquidity mismatches in the system and check volatility in the short-term money market rates. It comprises: *(i)* Repo Rate and *(ii)* Reverse Repo Rate: the former being the rate at which the banks borrow for short terms from the RBI and the latter is the rate at which the banks park their surplus finds for short-term with the RBI. These rates are fixed by the RBI in accordance with its monetary policy. In January 2001, the repo rate was 8.5% which was reduced in stages to 4.5% in August, 2003, again raised to 4.75% on October 26, 2004 and by March 30, 2007, it reached 7.75% in stages. The globalisation of the economy and the endeavour to introduce full convertibility of the rupee on capital account have necessitated the frequent variations in the repo rate.

7. Direct Action

The Banking Regulation Act, 1949, also empowers the Reserve Bank to caution or prohibit banks generally from entering into particular transaction or class of transactions and also to inspect any bank and its books and accounts. If the Reserve Bank reports to the Government of India, it may prohibit any bank from accepting fresh deposits or direct the Reserve Bank to order its winding up or its merger with some other bank.

8. Moral Suasion

With the help of this method the Reserve Bank makes suggestions and advises the banks, to follow its declared monetary policy, through circular letters or call a meeting of Directors of Bank. The Reserve Bank also pursuades them not to pro-vide loans for speculative activities or to provide credit facilities on soft terms to priority sectors of the economy.

9. Market Stabilisation Scheme (MSS)

A short-tenn objective of the monetary policy has also been the maintenance of the exchange rate of the 'Indian Rupee'. In 1994-96 and again in 1998, the RBI took a number of steps to check the heavy depreciation of the rupee against the U.S. dollar.

Intervention by the RBI in the forex market, for stabilising the exchange rate of the rupee *i.e.* for checking the sharp appreciation of the rupee the RBI injects additional liquidity in the system creating favourable conditions for inflation. To mop up the additional liquidity the RBI launched the MSS in April 2004, under which it uses its stock of short-term Treasury Bills/ securities, Following are the principal features of the MSS.

(*i*) The government will, besides, it normal borrowing issue T-Bills by way of auctions to be conducted by the RBI, upto a fixed annual aggregate ceiling.

(*ii*) The amounts so raised will be held in the MSS Account, to be maintained and operated by the RBI, and will be used only for redemption and/or buyback of T-Bills issued under MSS.

(*iii*) The payments of interest and discount will not be debited, nor the receipts by way of premium or interest will be credited to the MSS account.

(*iv*) The impact of these operations on the revenue and fiscal balances of the government would only be marginal *i.e.* to the extent of interest payment on T-Bills.

Thus, MSS is a very handy tool of monetary management. It facilitates curbing of short-term volatility in the forex market in particular and money market in general. It enables the RBI to stabilise short-term interest rates and facilitates the enalargement of the government bond market.

An Evaluation of Reserve Bank's Monetary Policy

Monetary and fiscal policies are two instruments of economic stabilistation; but monetary policy is found to be more effective as a short to medium term measure, than the fiscal policy chiefly because the time lag between action needed and action taken is much shorter. Monetary policy action can be initiated any time during the year but fiscal policy measures can be initialed only after the approval of the parliament.

In India, the monetary policy has not been effective for a variety of reasons. Firstly, the RBI does not have control on the entire credit structure in the country—it only has control on the banking institutions; whereas the volume of credit provided by the non-banking sector is much large. There are also no effective linkages between the banking and non-banking sectors. Hence, the measures initiated by the RBI do not impact the total transactions of the non-banking agencies to the extent desired or required. Besides, the banks also tap non-deposit resources for funds like the call money market and participation certificates on which the RBI has no control. Hence the credit control measures introduced by the RBI fail to produce the desired result.

Secondly, the policy of globalisation, has led to greater integration of the Indian financial sector with the global financial system. Any change in the global trend impacts our financial system. The RBI, therefore, cannot adopt an independent policy without taking into account the global trends. Further, the RBI's hands are also tightened, in so far as the effective use of monetary instruments is concerned, by the over-riding importance of objective of economic growth and social justice.

Thirdly, during the last fifteen years or so a new dimension has been added to liquidity in the economy which is not included in the official money supply accounts. For example, the mutual funds, finance companies etc. all add a sizable portion of liquidity and the RBI has no authority to regulate their activities; but which certainly influence the level of effective demand.

Fourthly, despite the expansion of banking facilities and spread of education a large proportion of population particularly in rural areas, still prefers to hold money in the form of cash and the RBI has no control over it. This reduces the effectiveness of the monetary policy.

Fifthly, the RBI is also handicapped in the exercise of its authority by the existence of a number of special or preferential windows for offering concessional rediscount facilities to certain sectors, like food, exports, agriculture, small industry etc. The RBI finds it difficult to close these windows when the banks are keen to use them.

Sixthly, India being a developing country credit curbs can not be applied indiscreetly, certain sectors, like small and marginal farmers and rural artisans have to be protected from credit squeeze to the maximum possible extent, and this without doubt leaves holes in the monetary policy.

Seventhly, a weak data base and monitoring system makes the task of the monetary authority very deficient, specially in inplementing the policy of selective credit control which requires fast and timely changes. This also makes the monetary policy rigid. Lack of timely availability of basic data allows the authority to continue in a mechanical fashion—being guided by the previous year's experience—and not by the emerging needs of a growing economy.

Eighthly, the autonomy of the RBI has been marred by a variety of factors: For example, the existence of a number of private investment institutions like the mutual funds and non-banking financial institutions reduces the authority of the RBI to control credit. These institutions mobilise huge funds and disburse them on their own terms making the use of credit control instruments by the RBI quite ineffective. Secondly, there is undue and frequent interference by the Ministry of Finance of the Government of India. Thirdly, while the RBI has been loaded with the responsibility of supervising and controlling the monetary system, it does not enjoy full authority to do so. This fact has also been highlighted by the Sukhmoy Chakravarty Committee. Finally, the RBI does not have complete freedom to control the creation of the reserve money. The monetisation of fiscal deficits at an increasing pace has created enormous difficulty for the RBI to formulate an effective monetary policy.

To sum up, the monetary policy in India has not been able to fulfil the role it should have for the reasons stated above. And there is no hope of its being effective so long as the RBI is not given the sole authority to regulate the monetary system.

Exercises

1. Critically examine the monetary policy of the Reserve Bank of India.
2. How does the Reserve Bank of India regulate currency and credit in the country?
3. Explain the main functions of the Reserve Bank of India. Critically examine its monetary policy.
4. Explain the main functions of Reserve Bank of India. To what extent it has been successful in achieving its objectives?

•••

Appendix-I

Full Convertibility of Rupee

A convertible currency is a free currency *i.e.* it can be used for payment of goods and services including travel without any limitations in any foreign currency. The convertibility of a currency can be for current account transactions with restrictions on capital flows or capital account transactions or for both current and capital account. Each of these has benefits as well as risks. This would however, require an appropriate economic environment. If the countries do not have confidence in macroeconomic stability and the competitiveness of domestic enterprises establishment of capital account convertibility involves the risks of capital flight and greater volatility in exchange rates, external reserves or interest rates. That is why many countries have not established full convertibility of their currency.

India has made the rupee fully convertible on the current account and rupee convertibility on capital account will take some time. The capital account convertibility can be useful in a number of ways.

(*i*) It will increase the allocative efficiency and competitive discipline to the economy through the optimization of savings and investment by setting the prices right.

(*ii*) It will provide an opportunity to the savers and investors to protect the real value of their assets.

(*iii*) It will stimulate efficiency stabilization and innovation by exposing the financial sector to global competition.

(*iv*) It would attract the riches of the world through a free forex regime.

(*v*) It will attract foreign capital as well as encourage foreign investors to invest in domestic enterprises and persuade them to share technologies, management practices and markets by making economy open and free.

(*vi*) It would help in linking the Indian stock, money, foreign exchange bond and commodity markets to the global markets making the Indian market an integral part of the global economy. Interest rates would be aligning with the global rates and ensure availability of adequate credit at reasonable rates, to Indian industry and agriculture.

(*vii*) It shall provide investment opportunities abroad to the resident Indians.

The capital account convertibility will involve the following costs: (*i*) it would stimulate flight of capital; (*ii*) the neutralization of capital outflows will take some time because it would require an equal volume of inflows in the form of foreign investments or increase in export earnings. The former would require confidence in our economy's potential as also in the government; (*iii*) in the present circumstances total capital decontrol appears to be difficult until the trade sector reforms are complete; (*iv*) the fiscal consolidation which is so important can be eradicated by premature capital decontrol. In the event of net inflows the fiscal cost of monetizing them can be heavy and because of the volatility in the exchange rate it can be uncertain too. The RBI will lose control over the money base and the monetary policy will be totally ineffective in curbing inflation. So, capital convertibility cannot be established until fiscal consolidation is complete.

Since full convertibility implies full scale trade liberalization, it would be highly detrimental to the Indian industry and stock markets. The slow down in domestic industrial growth under the impact of greater foreign competition would bring adverse impact on the corporate profitability and send the stock market into a tailspin. But, for attracting foreign capital, we would be sending more positive signals by robust macroeconomic adjustment rather than by premature capital account convertibility.

In any case, apparently full convertibility of rupee may sound interesting in theory but in practice it would be disastrous and the government should not go through it.

Before taking a decision on full convertibility of rupee it would be necessary to make a few adjustments: (*i*) fiscal consolidation should be stable and healthy; (*ii*) the balance of payments adjustment should be strong; (*iii*) inflation should be low and stable; (*iv*) trade and financial sector reforms should be complete; (*v*) interest rates should be globally competitive; (*vi*) infrastructure should be efficient, production procedures should be streamlined, productivity levels should be high and people should be conscious of making good quality products.

Appendix-II

Management of Foreign Exchange Reserves

Foreign exchange reserves are for countries, as bank accounts are for individuals. The country may hold foreign exchange reserves for a variety of purposes, for example for maintaining confidence in monetary and exchange rate policies; for augmenting its capacity to intervene in forex markets; for limiting external vulnerability; for providing confidence to the markets that external obligations can always be met; and for adding to the comfort of the market participants by demonstrating the backing of domestic currency by external assets.

In India forex reserves are held for precautionary and transactions motives, to provide confidence to the markets that foreign obligations can always be met. India's forex reserves comprise (*i*) foreign currency assets of the RBI, (*ii*) Gold held by the RBI, and (*iii*) SDRs held by the government. The process of stockpiling of forex began in 1991 and till about 1994 we had forex reserves worth $20 billion. Since then these have skyrocketed, particularly during the period 2002-07 and presently stand at over $200 billion *i.e.* about Rs. 8.5 lakh crore. The principal factors responsible for this situation are follows:

(*i*) Weakening of the dollars has encouraged exporters to remit export proceeds at home over fears of a stronger rupee.

(*ii*) Several MNCs are converting themselves into 100% subsidiaries of their foreign parent and delisting this from the stock market.

(*iii*) Prolonged recession during 2002-04 resulted in lower non-oil and capital goods imports resulting in a large surplus on current account.

(*iv*) Stronger Euro and Yen against the dollar have also fuelled upward revaluation of reserves.

(*v*) Continuing net inflow of NRI remittances and deposits.

Despite the massive increase in our forex reserves the relative position of India is as under: While the ratio of reserves to GDP in the case of China stands at 25%, in the case of Taiwan and Malaysia more than 30%, in the case of India it is 20% as compared to western developed countries where it is much lower; in UK, US, Germany and France it is less than 5%. These reserves can take care of about 11 months of our imports, as compared to 11 months in China, one month in the US and two months in the UK.

The big question is whether these forex reserves are adequate. To find an answer to this question we shall have to consider a number of factors. In an economy with restrictions on capital account flows the adequacy or otherwise of forex reserves is determined by factors like the level and volatility of current receipts and payments; leads and lags in exports and imports and debt service payments. For an economy were capital account movements are relatively high, level of short term debt liabilities and composition of capital inflows would overshadow the conventional adequacy measures. In a market determined exchange rate system, the reserve management strategy primarily reflects the need for intervention to ensure orderly conditions in the market.

However, maintenance of large forex reserves also involves costs to the government/central bank; for example, cost on account of the difference in the rate of return on holding such foreign assets against holding domestic assets; cost in the form of inflationary pressures on the money supply in the face of incomplete sterilization; cost in the form of distortions in capital markets producing an adverse impact in future, and cost in the form of the eventual appreciation of the domestic currency. It is estimated that the annual cost of holding reserves in India is about 2.95% of GDP. It is therefore, clear that the adequacy of forex reserves depends upon the benefits arising out of such reserves *vis-à-vis* the cost of holding them.

The report of the Committee on Capital Account Convertibility has proposed four indicators for determining the adequacy of forex reserves *viz*; (*i*) cover at least six months of imports; (*ii*) cover at least three months of imports plus half of annual debt service payments plus one month imports and exports to take into account the possibilities of lags and leads; (*iii*) the short term debt and portfolio stock to be no more than 60% of the level of reserves; (*iv*) net foreign exchange assets to currency in circulation to be maintained around 70% with a minimum of 40%. Our forex reserves generally satisfy these criteria.

The Reserve Bank of India consults the Government of India in the management of forex reserves. Since the liquidity and safety are the guiding principles in the management of forex reserves, importance is given to the currency composition and duration of investment to ensure that a significant proportion can be converted into cash at short notice. The RBI Act 1934 requires that investments be made in foreign government securities with maturity not exceeding 10 years and that deposits be placed with other central banks, international commercial banks and the Bank for International

Settlement. A small proportion of reserves is also placed with external asset managers to access their market reserves and help the RBI staff to acquire adequate skills in reserve management.

However, the direct financial return on holdings of foreign currency assets is low because of the low interest rates prevailing in the international markets. But when compared with the costs involved in reviving international confidence and with benefits of retaining confidence of the domestic and international markets, including that of the credit rating agencies, the low returns on foreign investment of forex reserves holdings do not matter at all.

Policy for Reserve Management

While formulating a policy for the management of forex reserves a number of factors are taken into account; for example (*i*) the current account deficit and its size, (*ii*) short term liabilities and their size, (*iii*) the possible variations in capital flows, (*iv*) unexpected pressures on the balance of payments due to the global developments and (*v*) movements in the repatriable foreign currency NRI deposits.

The RBI intervenes in both spot and forward segments of the exchange market but it ensures that the outstanding forward liabilities at any time are maintained at a reasonable proportion of the total stock of foreign currency assets. For the transparency of its operations it publishes its outstanding forward liabilities every month. The reserve assets are invested in highly liquid and safe instruments. The reserve management strategy is guided by the prevailing concerns and is closely linked to the exchange rates policy.

The RBI has initiated several liberal measures for the free flow of capital across the borders. These *inter-alia* include (*a*) expansion of the automatic route of FDI, (*b*) provision of greater flexibility to Indian corporates to prepay their external loans, (*c*) permission to commercial banks to invest abroad in quality instruments (*d*) pre payment of external debt, (*e*) adoption of LIBOR linked interest rates on non-resident rupee deposits. The Reserve Bank of India has till now not used forex reserves for financing infrastructure projects, and expediency also does not warrant the same, because infrastructure projects generally yield low or negative returns and also create difficulties in monetary management. The RBI invests about 75% of forex reserves in US treasury yielding return of 2%. The surplus stock is generally deployed in retiring high-cost debt including high cost commercial loans obtained from Japan and other multilateral agencies. These may take the form of (*i*) pre payment of high cost loans and (*ii*) borrowing against the foreign currency deposits and money so raised be used for retiring high-cost debt. While the former does not involve any additional cost, the latter may involve the balancing of the interest cost, on new loans against the old. However, borrowing against the deposits is more safe. Before finally deciding about use of forex reserves for retiring high cost debt the following points need to be considered: (*i*) pre payment would include a penal interest which would have to be factored into the cost of managing the external debt, (*ii*) forex reserves is a function of the demand for US dollars against its supply. The current demand for US dollars from importers being low, acceleration in growth may augment the demand for dollars from importers, (*iii*) portfolio inflows may slow down and then the government may face with less comfortable reserve position. Drawing down the forex reserves would push up the fiscal deficit.

Forex reserves can also be used for a number of other purposes like purchase of oil and gas, purchase of not-so-well performing companies in aeronautics, computers, thin films etc. which are necessary for our development; give external credit to other countries and reduce high taxes on oil products. All these factors may be built-in an effective policy for management of forex reserves.

●●●

Public Finance

PUBLIC FINANCE

Chapter 26

Nature and Significance of Public Finance

1. Introduction

"Public Finance" is that branch of general economics which deals with the financial activities of the state or government at national, state and local levels. With the broadening of the activity base of governments over the past three centuries or so, the study of "public finance" has assumed lot of importance. Economic theorists, right from the classical times to the modern, have been influenced in determining the subject-matter and scope of "public finance" by their views regarding the role of the state in the life of a nation. Consequently there has been lack of unanimity among them.

Prior to Adam Smith not much thinking was done by economists on the subject of "public finance" and whatever references one comes across, are confined to the area of public revenue or taxation. It was Adam Smith who gave a detailed account of the problems of "public finance" and recognised the close connection between the science of finance and the theory of economics. Following Smith, other classical economists went on writing on one issue or the other in the field of "public finance". The neo-classical economists did not, however, show much concern to the financial problems. It was only during and after World War I that the theory of "public finance" attained maturity and today it is recognised as a science by itself.

2. Definition of Public Finance

Since the classical economists assigned a minimal role to the government and advocated freedom of the individual, they generally defined "public finance" as the subject dealing with the revenue and expenditure of the government. While Adam Smith gave greater importance to expenditure, Ricardo and Mill gave precedence to revenue. However, they had included the study of government debt as well. They, however, failed to provide a scientific, logical and precise definition of public finance. For the first time Bastable produced a systematic treatise on public finance in 1892. According to him, "Public

Finance deals with expenditure and income of public authorities of the State and their mutual relation as also with the financial administration and control."[1] Subsequently in 1922 a more authentic and scientific work, *Principles of Public Finance* was produced by Dalton, who defined public finance as "concerned with income and expenditure of public authorities, and with the adjustment of one to the other".[2] Similarly Plehn said that public finance "has come, by accepted usage, to be confined to a study of funds raised by governments to meet the costs of government".[3] In his book, *Public Finance* published in 1928, Pigou also treated the subject in more or less a similar vein. Prior to the publication of, *General Theory* of Keynes in 1936, almost all the economists considered "public finance" as an enquiry into how the governments raise their income and how do they spend it and how do they administer their finances. These economists did not consider it necessary to study the economic and social effects of their income raising and spending operations in the economy.

It was Keynes who for the first time emphasized that the financial or fiscal operations of the government can be used to remove distortions in the economy by influencing the general level of income and employment and also to mobilise resources for rapid and balanced development of the economy. Since then, the study of economic and social effects of fiscal policy and operations has been considered as an integral part of the theory and practice of "public finance". This change in outlook can very well be noted from the literature published after the appearance of Keynes' book. In the same vein Pigou and Dalton brought out later editions of their books. Subsequently, Rolph and Break defined public finance "as the discovery and the appraisal of the effects of government financial policies".[4] Prof. Shoup has explained it more elaborately. He says: "The discipline of public finance describes and analyses government services, subsidies and welfare payments and the methods by which the expenditures to these ends are covered through taxation, borrowing, foreign aid and the creation of new money." He further says that, "Public finance deals with a resource allocating system that makes little use of the pricing mechanism, through considerable use of money. But not even money is employed in one branch of public finance: the free supply of government sevices.... And money, but no pricing is involved in the distribution of subsidies and welfare payments. On the other hand, both money and pricing are utilised when the government engages labour and other factor services or

1. Bastable, C.F., *Public Finance.*
2. Dalton, Hugh, *Public Finance,* 4th edn., p. 1.
3. Plehn Carl, C., *Introduction to Public Finance,* Macmillan, 1926, p. 1.
4. Rolph, E.R. and Break, G.F., *Public Finance,* 1st edn., p. 1.

purchases goods and services produced by firms."[5] In the words of Brownlee and Allen: "It is with the public economy... with the effects of governmental money-spending and money-raising activities upon the allocation of resources, the distribution of income and general level of economic activity within the economy that the bulk of our analysis is concerned."[6] It is thus clear that the discipline of public finance, nowadays, does not only study the fiscal policy and operations relating to money raising (taxation and borrowing) and money-spending of the governments, but also their socio-economic effects, *i.e.*, allocation of resources, distribution, stabilisation and economic growth.

3. Scope of Public Finance

(1) Economic Activities of the State

From the above discussion, we can say that there has been a sea change in outlook towards the study of public finance after the 'Great Depression'. The classical and neo-classical economists had only included money raising and money spending activities of governments in its scope—thereby limiting its scope and treating it as a positive science. But the modern economists broadened its base and enlarged its scope by including in it the socio-economic effects of all fiscal policies and operations. Public finance is now considered as 'compensatory finance'—a device to remove distortions in the economy, to mobilise resources and to influence the general level of economic activity according to the need of the times.

This change in outlook was caused by the change in attitude towards the role of the state in the life of individuals and its functions. For example, Adam Smith and his followers advocated the policy of *laissez-faire* and assigned minimum functions to the government, *e.g.*, defence, internal justice and erection and maintenance of those public institutions and works which may be of great advantage to the society but which may not return the cost to any individual. It was with the rise of socialism that the role of the state was greatly extended: ownership and use of means of production to save the working class from exploitation. The 'Great Depression' completely exploded the myth of *laissez-faire* and put the reins of the administration of the economy into the hands of the state. Now the extent of the state activity stood vastly enlarged *e.g.*, the promotion and maximisation of the welfare of the community by providing medical facilities, education, poor relief, social security and other community services; the augmentation of productive power of the people by providing infrastructural facilities like means of transport and communications,

5. Shoup, C.S., *Public Finance,* 1st edn., p. 4.
6. Brownlee, O.H. and Allen, R.D., *Economics of Public Finance,* p. 11.

power etc.; the regulation of the general level of economic activity by counteracting inflation and depression; the reduction of inequalities in the distribution of wealth and income; the regulation of the production and distribution of scarce and harmful commodities; the controlling of the prices of essential commodities. In most recent times, particularly after the disintegration of the USSR, there has been a reversal of the process and the number of countries adopting the policy of liberalisation and privatisation is on the increase. Nevertheless, the state continues to hold its sway on economic, social and political policies and programmes.

(2) Functions of a Modern State

Thus, the area of state activity has enlarged over the past few decades and with it the scope of 'public finance' has also widened. The fundamental objective of all state policies and programmes, however, remains maintenance of level of economic activity at the point of 'full employment' in the case of developed economies and rapid economic development in the case of under-developed economies and developing countries. Broadly speaking the state, in varying degrees, undertakes to provide its services in the following spheres.

(*i*) Defence against external aggression.
(*ii*) Maintenance of law and order and administration of justice.
(*iii*) Regulation of economic enterprise including standardisation of weights and measures, business practices etc. and participation in entrepreneurial activities.
(*iv*) Control of anti-social activities.
(*v*) Promotion of social welfare, social security and cultural activities.
(*vi*) Conservation of natural resources and maintenance of ecological balance.
(*vii*) Development of basic infrastructural facilities.
(*viii*) Production and distribution of essential and rare commodities.
(*ix*) Stabilization of levels of income and employment.
(*x*) Maintenance of the rate of growth of the economy.
(*xi*) Maintenance of international relations.
(*xii*) Protection of human rights.

We find that with the change in the concept of state from a 'police state'; to that of a 'welfare state', the state now plays the role of a guardian, a caretaker of the economy and the people. It has not only to determine the sphere of its own activities but also of its people, which it does through a judicious use of fiscal tools at its disposal.

(3) Fiscal[7] Operations

The fiscal operations of the government involve the use of fiscal tools, in varying degrees, according to the need and demand of the situation. The economic and social objectives of governments' economic policy form the nucleus around which the fiscal operations revolve. Their magnitude is determined by the nature and quantum of its economic, social and other programmes. The fiscal operations include: Raising of Public Revenue; Public Spending and Financial Administration.

The fiscal tools, therefore, used by governments are: taxation, expenditure and public debt. These tools are always used in a combination. What shall be the proportion of these shall depend upon the state of the economy and the goal set by the government for itself. Each government has to adopt a firm but cautious approach. For example, the objectives of the fiscal operations will be different for an advanced economy like USA as compared to an underdeveloped country like Brazil or a developing country like India.

Objectives of Fiscal Operations

Following can be the broad objectives of fiscal operations:

(*i*) *Allocation of Resources.* Annual budget is the single instrument through which the governments attempt to achieve the goals of their economic policy. Through its budgetary policy, a government can bring out adjustments in the allocation of resources between different sectors of the economy for the production of various goods and services. In a free market economy the price mechanism alone cannot provide all the goods and services required by a community. The market mechanism cannot produce all the goods required for the satisfaction of what Musgrave calls the 'collective wants', such as defence, justice, social security and welfare, basic infrastructure. The government, therefore, has to bring about proper adjustment in the allocation of resources between the production of goods and services for satisfying collective wants and those satisfying individual wants and also for determining the proportion in which these goods and services should be produced.

(*ii*) *Promotion of Distributional Justice.* In a market economy the distribution of wealth and income is generally unequal and is directly related to the ownership of the factors of production and their pricing in the market. The market mechanism, therefore, not only generates but perpetuates as well, the inequalities in the distribution of income and wealth. The rich goes on becoming richer and the poor, poorer. A modern state does not allow this sort of situation and uses fiscal tools to reduce these disparities and brings about a redistribution of incomes. Such fiscal measures may be: (*a*) progressive taxes

7. The Italian term *fisc* means treasury.

on higher incomes; (*b*) subsidised or free public services such as housing, education, health etc. for the benefit of the poor and low income groups; (*c*) higher taxes on articles of consumption of higher income groups and subsidies on goods consumed by people with low income; and (*d*) schemes exclusively for the benefit of particular class of people, such as, pension for the old and widows, unemployment insurance, homes for the disabled and destitutes, poor relief measures etc.

(*iii*) *Removal of Distortions in the Economy.* Economic fluctuations or distortions are injurious for the health of the economy. A modern state is duty bound to remove all such distortions and bring about economic stability. Since the overall level of employment and prices depends on the level of aggregate demand, the governments can stabilise the level of employment and prices by maintaining aggregate demand at an optimum level. For example, it can increase public expenditure and reduce taxation in times of falling levels of employment and prices, and it can reduce public expenditure and increase taxation in the event of rising price level, or if the employment and price levels are at the optimum, then it can maintain public expenditure and taxation at the existing level.

(*iv*) *Capital Formation and Economic Growth.* In underdeveloped or developing countries the government has a special role to play. Such countries suffer from lack of capital formation and improper use of resources. Consequently, the per capita income is low, level of consumption is high and rate of savings is low and the economy is caught in a "vicious circle of poverty"[8] —low income and high propensity to consume→low rate of savings→low capital investment→under- employment of resources and hence low per capita income. In such countries the government has to make use of the fiscal devices in such a way that besides fulfilling its normal duties it undertakes to plan the use of resources in a well-conceived manner. It can, through the use of taxation, borrowing and deficit spending mobilise resources and accelerate the rate of economic growth to raise capital investment, achieve full-employment of resources and increase in the per capita income. By judiciously using the instrument of taxation, the government can transfer resources from consumption to investment, increase the rate of savings and level of investment, increase public investment in projects of mass benefit and welfare and minimise income and wealth inequalities. Additional resources can be raised through borrowings and deficit financing which can be used for the same purpose. This is what is known as "activating finance"[9] and "functional finance"[10].

---

8. Nurkse, R., *Problem of Capital Formation in Underdeveloped Countries,* p. 4.
9. *Ibid.*
10. Lerner, A.P., *Functional Finance and the Federal Debt,* Soc. Research, February 1943.

4. Subject Matter of Public Finance

Such is the importance of 'public finance'. Fiscal tools are essential for maintaining an economy, running it and developing it. In advanced countries the objective is economic stabilisation and in less developed countries, it is economic development. Thus, the fiscal operations change the direction of economic activities in the economy through a change in the various financial outlays. So, neither the nature of public finance is so simple nor its subject matter so limited as it was supposed to be prior to 'Great Depression'. Public finance now does not only deal with the operations of the public treasury but also with the repercussions that its policies might have on the functioning of the economy as a whole. Since the techniques of raising public revenue have undergone a sea change, the objectives of public expenditure and sources of public borrowing have enlarged and the overall effect of governments' financial operations are so enormous that it is difficult to determine the exact subject matter of public finance. Moreover, in modern democracies, the government for administrative convenience, operates generally at federal, state and local levels and therefore, the study of public finance should also include the financial problems and policies of the governments at different tiers and their financial relations. That's why we find that even modern economists' opinion on the subject varies. For example, Taylor regards that it "deals only with the finances of the government".[11] Musgrave says that the "subject matter of public finance is logically, though not solely, concerned with the financial aspects of business of government".[12] According to him the basic problems are concerning "those aspects of economic policy that arise in the operation of the public budget".[13] Broadly speaking, the subject matter of public finance may comprise:

(1) The Theory of Public Revenue and Public Expenditure

The theory of public revenue includes the study of various sources of government income, their relative merits and demerits, and principles governing the choice between them. In this connection taxation and deficit financing and public investments would require a detailed treatment with reference to the economy concerned. The theory of public expenditure includes a study of the principles, objectives and effects of public spending. Since public expenditure and disbursements add to the financial flows in the economy and determine the demand and supply patterns a deep study of the welfare,

11. Taylor Philip, E., *The Economics of Public Finance.* Macmillan, 1957, p. 3.
12. Musgrave Richard, A., *The Theory of Public Finance: A Study in Public Economy,* McGraw-Hill Book Co., 1959, p. 3.
13. *Ibid.*

stabilisation, growth, planning and other policies of the concerned government would be essential.

(2) Public Borrowing and Public Debt

In modern times public debt forms a major source of government funding both from the point of view of controlling the demand and of raising finances for implementing long-term projects. Modern governments are taking resort to both internal and external debts. Servicing of public debt has much wider repercussions for the economy than what they appear to be. Its study is also essential.

(3) Financial Administration

Since in modern democracies the government operates at different levels, the financial problems and policies of the government at all levels are to be looked into. Inter-governmental financial relations are also to be studied. The preparation of budget, its passing, its implementation, the budgetary policy and its socio-economic effects are other important constituents of financial administration.

5. Positive and Normative Aspects of Public Finance

As stated before, opinions of economists have been divided regarding the true nature of the discipline of public finance. Adam Smith and his followers, who advocated the philosophy of *laissez-faire,* did not favour too much intervention of the government in the activities and decisions of the individuals and therefore wanted it to perform minimum functions. Accordingly the subject of public finance was concerned with pure and simple fiscal problems and consideration of social and economic policy were alien to it. Although Bastable gave it the much deserved treatment and separated its study from the general economics, he and other economists continued to treat the subject as a study of the "funds raised by governments to meet the costs of government"[14] or as "a field of enquiry that treats of income and outgo of governements"[15] or it "deals only with the finances of the government".[16] Thus, according to them public finance is a positive science—it deals with the facts as they are, it enquires into the expenditure-income process (how does a government collect its revenue and how does it spend it?) and does not deal with its good or bad consequences or with the welfare aspect of a certain tax or expenditure or

14. Plehn, Carl C., *op. cit.,* p. 1.
15. Groves, H., *Government Finance,* 5th ed., p. 1.
16. Taylor, P.E., *op. cit.,* p. 3.

with the retarding effects of a certain taxation measure or budgetary provisions or policies.

The normative aspect of fiscal operations or the normative character of the science of public finance received due emphasis from Keynes in his *General Theory.* He stressed that the fiscal operations can be used effectively to influence the general level of economic activity in the economy. The concepts of 'compensatory finance' and 'functional finance' were developed thereafter. Economists like Musgrave, Brownlee, Allen Herber and those following them, therefore, emphasised the inclusion of the "principles of public economy" in the scope of public finance. For example, Musgrave says: "The complex of problems that centre around the revenue-expenditure process of government is referred to traditionally as public finance". While operations of the public household involve money flows of receipt and expenditure, the basic problems are not issues of finance. They are not concerned with money, liquidity or capital markets. Rather, they are problems of resource allocation, distribution of income, full employment and price level stability and growth. Therefore, we must think of our task as an investigation into the principles of public economy: more precisely, into those aspects of economic policy that arise in the operation of the public budget."[17] According to Herber, "In addition to the allocation function, public finance is also concerned with the three major areas of economic activity-distribution, stabilisation and economic growth."[18]

This change in outlook towards the role of the government clearly reflects that public finance is not only a study of the revenue-expenditure process, but also of its effects on the economy as a whole. This emphasises the normative aspect of public finance. It is thus, clear that modern governments are not merely concerned with the fund raising and spending exercise but also with the good and bad effects of every move involved in that process which means that the governments do exercise some value judgements while taking any step in matters related to taxation, borrowing, deficit financing, public investment and public expenditure. That the governments, all over the globe, have been making use of fiscal devices to control cyclical fluctuations, regulate the distribution of income and wealth, promote capital formation, full employment, and economic growth, and to remove regional imbalances, amply prove the normative aspect of the science of public finance.

6. Distinction between Public and Private Finance

While the financial operations of public authorities or governments form the

17. Musgrave, Richard A., *op. cit.,* p. 3.
18. Herber, B.P, *Modern Public Finance,* 1st edn., p. 4.

subject matter of public finance, the financial operations of individuals comprise the subject matter of private finance, and the financial operations of corporate bodies are the subject matter of corporate finance, although corporate finance also falls within the broad category of private finance. Both, the private and public finance, are similar in nature, since: (*i*) both entail activities which involve transactions like sale and purchase, transfer and creation of assets, etc; (*ii*) both are engaged in activities which lead to production, consumption, exchange, savings, investment and capital accumulation; (*iii*) both perform activities whose ultimate aim is to satisfy the wants of the society; (*iv*) both raise funds for financing their activities through borrowing etc; and (*v*) both are guided in making decisions by the fundamental principle: most important wants are given top priority.

But, both types of finances also sharply differ from each other:

(1) First, although in both types of finances, borrowing can be resorted to as a means of raising funds for meeting expenditure, the private economic unit cannot go beyond a certain limit and for a long period whereas the public bodies can borrow limitlessly and for a long period. In the case of the former the limit to borrowing is set by the creditworthiness the unit enjoys; it cannot borrow unless it has repaid its previous loans. This is not the case with public authorities. That's why in many countries public debt is a high proportion of their national income. Not only that, the government can command loans at a much lower rate of interest than the private economic unit because of its high creditworthiness. Since the government enjoys vast authority, it can even resort to coercive methods to borrow at lower rates from the banks and other financial institutions with the help of the central bank. Again, while the government can raise loans internally as well as externally the private economic unit can only borrow externally.

(2) Secondly, the most fundamental difference between the two is that while the private finance is governed by the 'profit motive' or by the prime consideration of 'economic return', the government is chiefly guided by political, administrative and social benefit considerations. Thus, the private economic unit takes decisions purely on the basis of 'economic' considerations, the government is guided chiefly by 'welfare' considerations. The government is not guided by short-term considerations; the interest of the entire economy reigns supreme and even at the risk of running economic losses, it ventures into programmes like pollution control, flood control, maintenance of cultural heritage and so on.

(3) Thirdly, for discharging its debt obligations the government can create currency, but a private economic unit does not have this authority. After the breakdown of the gold standard, the introduction of paper currency has provided unlimited power to the government to increase currency supply at

will. Thus, this enables the government to usurp a share of the produce in the market, reduce the total supply of goods and increase the total money supply in the economy. A private economic unit does not have this facility.

(4) Finally, while a private economic unit adjusts its expenditure to income, the government just does the reverse. Though it is largely true, it is not the sole truth. It is true that the government has full powers of raising revenue through taxation, borrowing, deficit financing etc.; but it has to exercise great caution because excessive use of these measures may prove suicidal for the economy of the country. For example, taxation beyond a limit would be detrimental to savings and investment and would adversely affect production. Similarly, excessive borrowing by the government may dry up resources for private investment and too much use of deficit financing would create inflation and other problems for the economy. Moreover all these measures simply cause transfer of resources from the private sector and do not create additional productive resources which policy the government cannot and will not afford to stick for long.

From the foregoing analysis it is amply clear that there are basic differences between the public and private finance. But, if we take into account the totality of the economy then both these are complementary to each other. They are like two compartments—not water tight—but inter-connected and supplementary—each sustaining the other. Notwithstanding the public authorities—their policy and activities—give direction to the economy as a whole and therefore for a proper understanding of the nature of public finance one has to have a full view of the working of the economy.

6. Significance of Public Finance

As stated already, the study of public finance assumed real importance towards the beginning of the 20th century specially after the great depression of the 1930s. In modern times, public financial operations play an extremely important role in the economy of a nation. A modern state, does not merely act as a police state but performs a variety of political, social and economic functions. The economic activities of the state have, in the last few decades, increased tremendously and consequently, the amount of public expenditure has become so enormous that every modern state is forced to raise revenues at an increasing rate to defray its expenses. Not only the public expenses are increasing every year but the rate of increase is also very rapid. Now a modern state acts as a welfare state and performs many functions for enhancing the social welfare *viz.*, education, public works, control of consumption and production etc. Since the Great Depression, the governments of various countries have started taking more and more interest in business and trade. Now, the government is the largest employer of labour within the country and so influences greatly the wage-rates and conditions of employment of labour. Thus, the government revenues and expenditures influence production, distribution and consumption of wealth enormously. The expenditure of the government has also increased tremendously in performing the age-old functions relating to the defence and the maintenance of law and order. The two world wars in the last century have led to an enormous increase in the national expenditures and to the multiplication of the national and international obligations. Again, the governments have started assuming more and more responsibilities towards planning and development of the economy, construction of social overheads, investment in human capital, etc. Thus, there has been an intensive as well as extensive increase in the public expenditure of a modern state. To meet this expenditure every modern state has to raise large revenues, which has vast repercussions on the economic and political conditions of the community. A major portion of the national income is spent on satisfying public wants. Similarly, individuals receive a large part of national income through public spending which influences the level of employment, production and prices in the economy. And hence the importance of public finance. The significance of public finance has also increased on account of the growing use of money in recent times. With the use of money all the government activities have a financial aspect. Credit now plays a crucial role in bridging the gap between public expenditures and revenues. So during recent decades the scope of public finance has been expanded with the stepping in of the phenomenon of public debt.

Now, fiscal policy, *i.e.*, the tools of taxation, public expenditure and public debt, has become an important instrument for influencing the economic life and to achieve the desired social and economic goals. Fiscal measures have come to stay as an effective means of stabilising business conditions in a highly industrial or advanced economy. Such measures are supposed to be the best tools in achieving and maintaining full employment, controlling inflation, mitigating the corrupt influences of depression and achieving rapid economic growth. They are also considered significant for an equitable distribution of income and wealth. According to Keynes: "The weakness of the inducement to invest has been at all times the key of the economic problem." Keynes, at one stage said that monetary policy was enough to influence the inducement to invest but subsequently, he gave up this idea and advocated fiscal policy for the purpose. He, however, considered public expenditure as the most important factor in stabilising economy. In his opinion, "the chief plank of a stabilising fiscal policy is public outlay and by introducing changes therein the total outlay can be controlled." So Keynes held that instability is caused by an unequal rate of growth of aggregate demand in comparison to out-put in a free market economy. The aggregate demand, therefore, can be controlled and stabilised through budgetary policies, taxes and public debt, all of which are the planks of fiscal policy.

Since there are some fundamental differences between advanced and underdeveloped economies, public finance has to play a somewhat different role in underdeveloped economies. While the main problem of an advanced economy is that of stability, in an underdeveloped economy, the main problem is that of scarcity of resources and paucity of capital formation and investment. In an underdeveloped economy the state has to play an active role in promoting economic development specially through control and regulation of economic life, and fiscal policy can prove to be an effective instrument in this direction. Again, public finance operations, specially taxation can prove really effective in augmenting the rate of capital formation in underdeveloped economies.

7. Modern Trends in Public Finance

(1) Sound Finance vs. Functional Finance

The theory of public finance cannot be segregated from the general economic theory. During recent years there has been a revolutionary departure in the economic theory from the classical theory and the theory of public finance has, therefore, not remained unchanged. The classical economists assumed that supply creates its own demand and, therefore, there cannot be any crisis of overproduction or under-production, of under-employment or over-employment. They also recognised that one man's income was another man's expenditure, and therefore there would not be many ups and downs in the level of economic activity or the economy. Consequently, they thought that since all factors of production are normally used by private individuals, the state can make use of such factors only by depriving the private individuals from using them. This concept can have two implications. Firstly, the state can compete with private individuals for the use of available factors of production by using its authority of creating money and secondly, any expenditure incurred by the state would not enhance the total demand for factors of production. Consequently, the classical economists held that: (*i*) the budgets should be balanced; (*ii*) the state should not undertake any business activity because the factors of production were already under full employment; (*iii*) the best budget is the smallest budget, since taxes, to some extent or the other would certainly discourage private savings, which would mean that capital accumulation would be adversely affected; (*iv*) direct taxes like death duties, super-taxes, business taxes were harmful and undesirable; (*v*) deficit budgets are economical, harmful and socially undesirable because they lead to inflation and impede economic progress, unless the government spends for productive investment. Be it noted that all these propositions of classical economists were essentially based on the assumption that private business automatically maintains full employment. And, therefore, the classical economists advocated the principle of 'sound finance' which implies that the government which spends the least was the best.

On the contrary, the modern economists hold that savings lead to unemployment, a fall in national income, and thus a reduction in capital accumulation. Thus, the modern economists do not believe that the society has any choice between consumption and investment. On the other hand, they believe that consumption leads to investment. Unlike the classical economists they regard the total income and outlay as changeable, and therefore, hold that consumption and investment can rise or fall together. This change in the general economic theory has profoundly affected the theory of public finance in a number of ways. Firstly, the modern economists have completely rejected the principle of a balanced budget; secondly, the state, through public finance measures taxation or deficit financing, can maintain full employment irrespective of the volume of private investment; thirdly, the volume of savings does not only depend upon the size of the national income but also on the distribution of income. A more even distribution of incomes would increase the average propensity to consume and thus, the level of investment. A government, therefore, for ensuring full employment must endeavour to redistribute national income in such a way that the savings never exceed current investment. Re-distributive taxation has been suggested as the best means for achieving this end by the modern economists.

Modern economists have, therefore, developed the concept of functional finance. It was Keynes who advocated fiscal measures for controlling capitalism and for curing economic ills. He laid stress on compensatory actions through fiscal measures for improving and maintaining the level of effective demand and thus the level of economic activity in the country. According to him, fiscal measures were the most effective tools for taking the economy out of depression. This concept is known as functional finance. According to this concept, fiscal policy is the major part of any economic policy. Fiscal measures like taxation, public expenditure and public debt must be adopted according to the needs of the time and the chief objective should be to influence the money supply. The aim of public finance is not to raise revenues but to correct imbalances in the economy. For example, the objective of taxation should be to reduce the purchasing power of the community and that of public expenditure to regulate the level of effective demand. They are the most effective instruments of promoting economic stability and progress. In periods of inflation a policy of surplus budgets must be adopted while during depression a policy of deficit budgets or deficit financing must be followed.

According to the advocates of functional finance the government budgets must act as an instrument of economic change.

The chief author of the concept of functional finance is A.P. Lerner who holds that the value of fiscal measures should be judged only by their effects. According to him, "the way fiscal measures function in society may be called functional finance."[19]

Lerner believes that public finance has to function in the total interest of the society and, therefore, every measure whether it is of taxation or ownership and operation of public utilities, or of borrowing and spending must be judged in accordance with the desirability or undesirability of the effects that it produces or is likely to produce on the society as a whole. It imposes upon the government the onus or responsibility of keeping a close watch over the economy and whenever the state finds that employment is falling, income is dwindling, level of profits is falling and the economy is slackening the government should take immediate steps to counteract these tendencies by unleashing the opposite forces which would provide strength to the economy and bring the situation back to normalcy. The government, as the classical economists advocated, must not act as an idle spectator. The concept of functional finance is, therefore, unorthodox in nature. It advocates that the government should adopt a vigorous policy of intense activity on behalf of the community.

According to Lerner, the objective of taxation should never be the raising of income. The fundamental object of taxation should be the accomplishment of a socially desirable objective. Ilersic holds that, "the purpose of taxation is to maintain full employment of all resources and to achieve a particular distribution of income and wealth, considered most desirable."[20] Lerner says that the government can raise as much revenue as it wants through the printing of notes and, therefore, it should not adopt taxation as a tool for raising revenue. Taxes can be imposed for curbing consumption, for reducing inequalities of income and wealth, etc. Every public expenditure would be justified if done for a right purpose. Spending for providing help to the destitutes and unemployed, pensions to the old, medical care to the sick and handicapped, financing schemes of public works, providing free education, etc. would always be justified. Taxation and public expenditure should always, therefore, follow the objective of equalising marginal social cost and marginal social benefit. So should be the case with lending and borrowing and purchasing and selling of government securities. So long these functions are performed with a social objective, these will be justified. Despite the attacks of the orthodox people

19. A.P. Lerner, *Economics of Control,* p. 302.
20. A.R. Ilersic, *Government Finance and Fiscal Policy in post-war Britain,* p. 59.

the concept of functional finance has come to occupy a prominent place in general economic theory. It has enormously affected the policy of the government in recent decades. A.P. Lerner has explained the concept of functional finance as follows: "Functional Finance rejects completely the traditional doctrine of 'sound finance'...it prescribes: first, the adjustment of total spending (by everybody in the economy, including government) in order to eliminate both unemployment and inflation, using government spending when total spending is too high; second, the adjustment of public holdings of money and of government bonds by government borrowing or debt repayment, in order to achieve the rate of interest which results in the most desirable volume of money as needed for carrying out the first two parts of the programme.

Seligman and others of his clan spoke of the pure theory of public finance, dealing with the problems of public income and expenditure and public debt in an objective manner without relating it to the concept of welfare or socially desirable objective. Subsequently, Wagner, Edgeworth and Pigou considered fiscal policy as a tool for transferring income from the rich to the poor in order to maximise social welfare. Then came Keynes and Hansen who gave us the concept of functional finance. Finally, Dr. Baljit Singh provided us the concept of 'activating finance',[21] The concept of functional finance is different from that of activating finance in the sense that while the former emanates from the assumption that there is a gap in demand and production because of the deficiency in spending and, therefore, the government must come to the rescue of the economy by spending more, the latter is based on the assumption that the government must activise the economy and make such fiscal adjustments which will enhance the flow of investment to bring about an optimal allocation of resources and thus enhance the national income. Thus, spending is the starting point of functional finance while production is the starting point of activating finance. Van Philips considers the latter concept superior to the former.[22]

(2) Redistributive Taxation

The classical economists, as said earlier, considered taxation as a means for raising revenue. But, modern economists consider taxation as a tool for redistributing incomes among the various sections of the society on a more rational basis, especially by transferring income from the rich to the poor. It has been agreed upon by all that inequality of incomes leads to depression and unemployment and, therefore, redistributive measures are not only

---

21. The term has been used for the first time by Baljit Singh, *Federal Finance and Underdeveloped Economy,* p. 85.
22. Van Philips, *Public Finance and Less Developed Economies.*

commended on the grounds of social justice but on economic grounds as well. Redistributive taxation has two functions to perform. first, the reduction of private savings, and second, the equalization of living standards. But, redistributive taxation can be adopted within certain limits. High direct taxation may lead to tax evasion and, therefore, the tax should be imposed in such a way that it does not affect adversely the incentives to investment. A redistributive fiscal policy may not only decrease the income of the rich but may also increase the income of the poor through the provision of old age pensions, family allowances or the provision of free services and amenities or by state subsidies aimed to reduce the cost of living. If redistributive taxation does not prove to be a disincentive to investment, the rate of capital accumulation is bound to increase. Redistributive taxation, employed for the purpose of raising the propensity of the people to consume, may promote private investment in case the taxes are designed in such a way as to allow such investments to yield profits. Excessive consumption may lead to inflation which would certainly disturb the set-up of the economy by destroying the value of money. Thus, the prime object of a rational fiscal policy should be to protect the economy from the dangers of inflation and deflation and, therefore, taxation and public expenditure should go together.

(3) Anti-Inflationary Taxation

Broadly speaking, under normal circumstances private expenditure on consumption and investment does not lead to inflation. Similarly, public expenditure does not lead to an abnormal rise in the price level which may be called inflationary, as it is during the war time. But, in a modern welfare state, collective activities require large expenditures of public funds. Even if the distribution of gross income were so arranged as to meet the public demand for consumption and investment for keeping all available resources under employment, taxation would still be required to make available resources to the state for its use. Taxation, thus, has a double role to play. It prevents the private individuals from utilising resources which the state itself requires for meeting collective needs as well as it modifies the distribution of incomes. Progressive taxation affects a reduction in the propensity to save while anti-inflationary taxation reduces the propensity to consume, Taxes designed to reduce the savings may not always make available resources for the use of the state but taxes designed to cut consumption, would definitely free resources from private use, for the use of the state. This sort of taxation can be justified if the resources which have been released from the private use, are used by the state in increasing welfare of the society. Ethically speaking, the state must make proper use of funds derived after reducing the consumption of the people more rationally and in the best interests of the society than the funds derived from loans or from taxes which affect savings. Funds derived through consumption taxes are the funds which the people would have otherwise used for themselves and the funds derived from taxes which affect savings are those which might have been left unused by the people. This sort of distinction is framed by undertaking the true nature of taxation measures. The classical theory, however, did not recognise the importance although it made a distinction between both these taxes. The conclusions drawn from this distinction were however, very different in character. The classical economists held that since private savings lead to accumulation of capital, all taxes affect private savings. The classical theory did not conceive of any resources lying idle and so all taxes were considered equal so far as anti-inflationary effect was concerned. According to modern theory, the anti-inflationary effect of different taxes is different. Neither all taxes are anti-inflationary nor expenditures are inflationary. Whether a tax is anti-inflationary or expenditure is inflationary should be judged from the stage of economic progress of the country. It is also not necessary that every increase in the state revenue may be a brake on the inflationary spiral. May be that the increase is due to inflation. And, therefore, it will not be safe to prescribe any percentage of expenditure being incurred out of taxation or out of borrowing. Whether any expenditure out of borrowing or out of taxation would have the desired effect, will depend on the sources of these taxes and loans. Under normal conditions, taxes which directly affect consumption or provide investment can prove to be an anti-inflationary weapon. But, in normal conditions like war, even such taxes would fail to control inflation and that is why we find that under such conditions the governments generally resort to direct methods for controlling expenditure.

Exercises

1. Define Public Finance and discuss its scope and subject-matter.

2. Define Public Finance. Distinguish between Public and Private Finance.

3. Discuss the subject-matter of Public Finance and describe the true nature of the discipline of Public Finance.

4. Define Public Finance and explain its nature and significance.

5. Write short notes on:

(*a*) Functional Finance

(*b*) Activating Finance

(*c*) Redistributive Taxation.

•••

Chapter 27

The Theory of Public Finance

1. Development of the Theory—A Historical Perspective

A theoretical study of public finance started only after the dissolution of the middle-ages economy. During those days the financial flows were very limited since the king had limited functions to perform. Most of the income of the kings was derived from the royal property *e.g.*, forests, mines, cultivable lands and from dues, rents, fees etc. It was Bodin who in 1576 in his book *Republic* devoted one chapter to the examination of the various forms of public revenue. He talked about import and export duties and direct taxes, only when necessary, and tax on luxuries. Petty and Locke raised the question of incidence of taxation. The physiocrats dealt with the question of justice in taxation and its effect on the growth of national wealth, sources of revenue and the extent to which each could contribute to the public requirements. They advocated a single tax on the net product of land. Adam Smith in 1776 in his *Wealth of Nations* touched all the important problems of public finance; formulated canons for adjudging the suitability of a tax and introduced the subject of public debt. As a theorist he not only determined the future course of developments in this field (public finance) but also made an original contribution in recognising the close connection between the science of finance and the theory of economics.

Following Smith, Ricardo, McCulloch and J.B. Say sharpened the tools of analysis but their effort was confined only to the field of taxation. Towards the end of the nineteenth century a number of writers in England broadened the scope of analysis and examined a number of problems relating to local taxation, local finance, local rates etc. Among these writers the most prominent were Cannan, Chapman, Edgeworth, Sidgwick, Nicholson and Bastable. In Germany, the economic theorists towed the line of thought of Adam Smith upto the middle of the 19th century, but during the latter half of the century economists like Stein, Wagner, Roscher, Eheberg, Locke and Conard dealt at length, with a number of questions like evolution of financial systems, progressive taxation, incidence of taxation, justice in taxation. In other countries of Europe also appreciable contribution was made by economists in the field of public finance. In the United States, financial problems were studied by Plehn, Daniels, Adams and Seligman.

During the last century, three important events *viz.*, World War I, Great Depression and World War II made irreparable dents on most of the economies of the world. World War I caused an unprecedented increase in government expenditure followed by the problem of repatriation of war debts and adjustment of the economy from war to peace conditions. The depression of the thirties brought entirely new problems in its wake. Despite the fact that in some parts of the world it was recognised that during the boom period expenditure on public works should be kept to the minimum, in the period of depression it should be increased, no theory of fiscal policy was propounded. It was Keynes who made an advance in this direction. He held that in the case of unemployed resources not being put to use by the private sector, the government should put them to use by additional public debt which need not be matched by additional government revenue. This principle was later on developed by Hansen, Lerner and Pigou. Hansen held that public debt also should be determined in relation to the aggregates of national income and its distribution and the expenditure and receipt side of the government budgets should be viewed in relation to the total level of economic activity. Lerner propounded the theory of functional finance and advocated that government revenue, expenditure and debt are instruments of control of aggregate community expenditure. These are the tools and the goal is the maintenance of stable employment at constant prices. The World War II created conditions of unprecedented inflation and it began to be considered that the main object of fiscal policy was the control of inflation. Keynes and Hart advocated higher taxation to check inflation. Subsequently, it has been advocated that the achievement of economic stability is the chief goal of fiscal policy, but by itself it cannot achieve the objective and therefore, it must be supplemented by devices like monetary policy, debt management policy and other types of controls such as those on monopoly, production and prices. And the current view is that the fiscal policy should aim at securing: (1) adjustment in the allocation of resources; (2) adjustments in the distribution of wealth and income; and (3) economic stability and growth.

2. The Theory of Public Goods

Wants being unlimited and productive resources required to produce goods and services needed to satisfy these wants being limited the basic problem, be it an individual or an economy, is one of adjustment between wants and resources. While wants are ever increasing, resources are not. Resources have alternative uses, they can, at best, be taken out from one use and put to another. So the solution of the problem only lies either in keeping the wants limited to the extent of the availability of resources, or in making use of the resources judiciously and to the maximum. At the macro level an economy is constantly engaged in the pursuit of this objective.

In the pre-industrial era, when there were monarchical empires, matters were not so complicated. Political set-up used to be very simple and socio-economic life was mostly governed by the dictates of religion. International as well as inter-regional trade were rather limited. Obviously management of an economy was not difficult. Financial operations of the monarchs were also limited. With the emergence of democracies and after the industrial revolution things started becoming complex. The area of activities of government expanded and expenditure increased. Governments were required to bear more and more responsibilities on the home front as well as internationally. Wars became costlier. Trade expanded. And sectoral division of economy started.

The industrial revolution gave birth to capitalism and capitalist economy. In such an economic system, the ownership and use of factors of production are in the hands of individuals. The production and investment are guided by the profit motive and consumption is guided by the satisfaction of wants and its maximisation. The entire economic activities are guided by "invisible hand" *i.e.*, self interest as Adam Smith called it. Market mechanism is the sole guiding factor. The role of the government is limited to external defence, administration of justice and maintenance of law and order and provision of essential public services. The whole lot of individuals and economic units which act and take decisions independently comprise the private sector while the government and the organisations run by it form the public sector which take decisions and act for the common good and in the interest of the community as a whole. In a *capitalist economy* the size of the public sector is tiny and small and the private sector has a dominant role in administering the economy. The capitalist system has its own defects: inequitable distribution of wealth and income; monopolisation of production and trade, exploitation of labour and consumers; cyclical distortions and fluctuations in the economy; social and industrial insecurity; neglect of civic amenities and infrastructural facilities; deterioration of standards of health, sanitation and housing, environmental pollution, increase in economic and social crimes and so on. Consequently, there has been the emergence of the *Socialist System.* In such a system, the economy is dominated by the public sector. Here the government decisions and activities are guided not by profit motive or by price mechanism but by the objective of common good and general welfare of the people. In such an economy, market mechanism has only a marginal role to play. In between these two extremes is the mixed economic system, commonly known as the *mixed economy*—

a combination of both public and private sectors. Both have their own areas of operation assigned by the law of the country framed from time to time in pursuance of the overall objectives laid down under the constitution. The state acts as a friend, philosopher and guide to the private sector. The national policies are formulated by the government and the economic units are left free to act and take decisions within the framework of these policies. In such a system both the public and private sectors are important. In majority of countries such a system has been adopted.

3. Public Sector *vs.* Private Sector

The subject: 'Public Sector *vs* Private Sector' has been debated for long by the economists. Over the decades, public sector has not only grown in size but also in its influence on the private sector. And the economists have been justifying the increase in state activities in an economy on a number of counts, for example, owing to the failure of market mechanism to strike a balance in the production of goods and services required by the poor and the rich, the state has to step in to ensure that the production of luxuries does not get precedence over the production of necessities. Again, if due to the fall in the private investment the level of employment declines, the state has to raise its level by increasing public investment. Further, the state has to take action to correct cyclical distortions. Modern writers on public finance emphasise the role of the state in increasing the rate of economic growth and in ensuring an equitable distribution of wealth and income. Prof. Musgrave justifies the need of government action (public sector) on the following grounds:

(1) To ensure the availability of those conditions under which market mechanism may lead to the efficient use of resources, for example, free entry and perfect competition between buyers and buyers, sellers and sellers and buyers and sellers of factors, goods and services.

(2) To provide a legal structure, protect it and enforce it for working out the contractual arrangements needed for market operations.

(3) To make available those goods and services which cannot be provided for through the market.

(4) To secure social justice by removing inequalities in the distribution of wealth and income created by the market mechanism and laws of inheritance.

(5) To formulate policy for securing high level of employment, price stability and accelerated economic growth.

Hence, the importance of public sector and public finance is concerned with the study of public sector and its activities. The public sector is engaged in the production and supply of common goods and services (called as public goods) and the private sector undertakes the production and supply of goods which satisfy some particular sections of the people (called as private goods).

With a view to understanding the true nature of the problems and principles of public finance, we shall first bring out the distinction between the nature of public and that of private goods.

4. Public Goods *vs.* Private Goods

Public goods, also known as social or merit goods are those which satisfy public wants, social wants or merit wants and private goods are those which satisfy private or individual wants. Private goods can be provided by the market system, public goods can be provided only by the public sector through budgetary provisions. Private goods satisfy the wants of only that person who consumes or uses them; other persons do not derive any satisfaction automatically. Thus, private goods are rival in consumption. Public goods are non-rival in consumption *i.e.*, their consumption by one person does not reduce the amount available to others. Again, private goods are priced in the market and those who can pay for them are allowed their use, those who cannot are excluded from their use. Thus, the principle of exclusion applies in the case of private goods. This principle does not apply to public goods—the benefits are available to all in the community and none is excluded; for example, the malaria eradication or family welfare programmes introduced by the government, provide benefit to all. Finally, private goods are divisible in so far as their use is concerned. Those who want to use the goods pay for them and have them from the market. This is not the case with some public goods. Take for example, the police service. Once the internal law and order is maintained every person is more or less equally benefited. No particular person or section of the society can be deprived of this benefit. In this respect, police service is indivisible. It cannot be priced in the market. In sum, we can say that a particular good is a private good if it is available freely at a price in the market and people pay for it voluntarily, if it is divisible, and if the exclusion principle is applicable to it. All these go together in the case of a private good, and distinguish private goods from public goods.

5. Social Wants and Merit Wants

Prof. R.A. Musgrave calls public goods as social wants. According to him public wants are of two types: (*i*) Social wants, and (*ii*) Merit wants.

Social wants are those "which are satisfied by services that must be consumed in equal amounts by all". The benefits of such services accrue to all and are not subject to price payments. And so the principle of exclusion does not apply at all to them; for example, free mid-day meal for children in schools, provision of public parks, flood control measures, maintenance of the Judiciary system, defence service and the like. All such measures promote the welfare of the whole society. The benefit that accrues to any individual is independent of his or her contribution. He or she cannot be excluded from enjoying that because he or she is not making any payment. Such goods and services must be provided by the government out of the general budget.

Merit wants are those, which are satisfied through the public budget on merit. The inclusion of such wants in the category of public wants involves interference with consumer preferences it impinges upon the individual's freedom of choice making. This also involves goods which are private. Some goods are good for human use and promote social welfare while some are detrimental to human interests and depreciate social welfare. The use of the former type of goods is to be encouraged and supported while that of the latter category of goods is to be discouraged and penalised. The goods whose consumption and use are to be encouraged are known as "merit goods" and goods whose consumption and use are to be discouraged are known as "non-merit goods"[1] or "demerit" goods[2]. Free education, mid-day meals for school children, supply of essential food articles at subsidised prices, low-cost housing are examples of merit goods; their satisfaction is provided for through public budget in addition to what is provided through the market system and paid for by private buyers.[3] Smoking, liquor drinking, narcotic drugs' consumption fall within the category of "demerit" wants.

To elaborate further, the distinctive features of both these types of wants we may add that firstly, the satisfaction of merit wants interferes with consumer preferences, the satisfaction of social wants provides benefit to all. Secondly, the social wants are not subject to the conditions of exclusion, divisibility and rival nature of consumption goods, whereas the merit wants may or may not be subject to these conditions. Thirdly, certain public goods may appear to be merit goods but may contain a substantial element of social want. For example, free education facility, social security measures or free health schemes provide benefit to particular individuals or sections of the society, but at the same time all others, not directly benefited, will get the satisfaction of living in a more enlightened, healthier and socially secure community. Fourthly, when the consideration behind the satisfaction of a merit or non-merit want is the welfare of an individual or a particular section of society (by restricting the supply of certain commodities like, alcohol, narcotic drugs, etc. or by supplying certain commodities at subsidised rates for example, health aids, education material, essential food articles, etc.) the objective behind the satisfaction of social wants is the welfare of the entire society. In conditions of perfect

1. Pague T.F. and Spontz, L.G., *Government and Economic Choice,* p. 78.
2. Musgrave, R.A. and Musgrave B. Peggy, *op. cit.,* p. 85.
3. Musgrave, R.A., *op. cit.,* p. 13.

competition both merit and non-merit goods are not available in the market and hence government action to supply merit goods becomes necessary not because these goods involve external costs to the consumer of these goods or they confer external benefits to other persons but because their consumption is good (merit) or bad (non-merit) for the consumer concerned. The government may also provide merit goods for administering distributional justice. If the objective is to make available to everyone a minimum level of basic necessities of life (food, clothes, house, education, medical care etc.) then this objective cannot be met by paying cash grants to the needy persons. The payment of cash grants will certainly increase their income, but will not ensure that it will be spent on the consumption of basic necessities of life and not on articles of comforts and luxuries. Hence the payment of grant in kind is always preferred.

6. External Effects of Public Goods

The production and use of pure public goods may generate external effects called externalities. These are economic effects on other persons or economic units and have also been named as *spill-over effects* or *neigbhourhood effects* or *third party effects.* These effects may be good or bad (economic gain or loss) to other parties. For example, education improves the personal skills, makes one enlightened and better informed and knowledgeable. An educated person generally, acts in common interest and produces benefits which are external to him, for other members of the society. These benefits are public goods. Ecological imbalance caused by building of dams, pollution of air caused by the smoke emitting buses and trucks, pollution of water in rivers caused by the chemicals discharged by the toiletries, noise pollution generated by aeroplanes, railways etc. are all health hazards to the general community and for those living in the vicinity of the loco sheds, railway stations, aerodromes etc. These are the examples of public bads. These are the social cost of the good in question as against its private or internal cost. Market price is fixed in terms of the internal cost of the goods and services, *i.e.*, the cost of the inputs required to produce them plus the overheads and the consumers reveal their preferences in the light of the internal cost. But the social cost of certain goods and services are borne by the community in the form of sickness or diseases and physical inconvenience.

According to Herber[4], external effects can be of two types: (*i*) market and (*ii*) non-market. The non-market external effects are those effects which cannot be valued in money or expressed in terms of price in the market as determined by the forces of demand and supply. In other words, the individual economic units cannot either be protected against economic loss or excluded from the

---

4. Herber, B.P., *Modern Public Finance,* Richard D. Irwin, 1967, p. 27.

economic gain generated by the public good. For example, it would not be easy to apportion the economic gains of a flyover built on a highway amongst its beneficiaries because some would be actual users, while others may not use it at all. It, therefore, follows that the production and supply of public goods and services having non-market external effects should be included in the public sector and those public goods which have market external effects may be left to the care of the private sector. Similarly pure private goods may be left to the private sector. But this may not happen in every case, particularly in the case of merit wants as already explained before. Besides, there may be other considerations like cost conditions, social and political ideology, availability of resources etc. which may force the government to undertake their production and supply.

A word may be added here about the cost conditions. It is generally held that the marginal cost of a pure public good is near zero. This means that its use by one more person will neither increase the marginal cost nor will its availability to others be reduced. Furthermore, public goods are subject to the law of increasing returns or decreasing costs because these are always provided on a large scale.

However, in practical life, it is nearly impossible to find either pure public goods or pure private goods. Most goods possess the features of both. And therefore, when the element of publicness is predominant in a good then it may be called a public good and when the element of privateness is predominant then it may be called a private good.[5]

According to Prof. Musgrave, if social wants (public goods) are necessary to be satisfied then these must be satisfied through the budget. In other words, public goods must be provided for by the public sector. Since the satisfaction of social and merit wants by the public sector raises the basic question of the efficiency in the allocation of resources, we shall discuss it in some detail before proceeding further.

7. Public Goods and Allocation of Resources

(1) Allocation of Resources and Distribution of Income

Each society is composed of rich and poor people, each group consumes articles of necessities, comforts and luxuries in different proportions of its income which is unevenly distributed. The goods of different categories are produced according to their demand and resources of the nation are used accordingly. If in a society the number of rich is more, then the quantity of luxuries and comforts demanded and produced would be larger than the

5. Musgrave, Richard A., *op. cit.*, p. 8.

necessities and greater proportion of community's resources will be used to produce them. Similarly if the number of poor people is larger than the rich, then the quantity of articles of necessities demanded and produced would be larger and greater proportion of community's resources would be used for their production. Any change in the income of these groups would affect the total production of the various goods and services as also the quantum of resources used in their production. Thus, the distribution of income amongst various groups of people affects the allocation of resources for the production of various goods and services. In a free enterprise economy this allocation of resources is done by the market which is hardly efficient or judicious. Since resources are scarce their efficient use is necessary. For this reason the government steps in, makes budgetary allocation for the supply of articles of necessities and other essential services. Hence, the importance of public sector for the efficient allocation of resources through the supply of public goods.

(2) Allocation of Resources and Market Imperfections

(*a*) The market mechanism can successfully lead to an efficient allocation of resources if the consumer is able to base his decisions on a complete knowledge of the market conditions, and the quality of goods and their substitutes available in the market. But in the modern economy the consumer is generally led away by advertising, which does not provide complete knowledge of various products. His choice making and preference structure are distorted and efficient allocation of resources is not achieved. Hence the need of government intervention.

(*b*) Further, the market mechanism gets vitiated because the producers' decisions are based on the principle of maximisation of profits in the short run. The private entrepreneurs will rarely be interested in projects which will bear profits in the long run or where the element of risk is high and the margin of profit is low, *e.g.*, flood control, erosion control, pollution control etc. In such areas government action becomes imperative.

(*c*) Again, the objective of maximisation of profit is sought to be achieved at the cost of economic stability which should not be sacrificed at any cost. It has been seen that under conditions of falling demand individual entrepreneurs reduce production and investment in plant and inventory, and in a period of rising demand they expand their operations. Such actions cause instability in the economy which from the social point of view is harmful and has to be checked by the government through guarantees and subsidies. This would ensure proper use and allocation of resources between the private and public sectors.

3. Allocation of Resources and Pure Public Goods

(*a*) Since certain public goods by their very nature cannot be priced, the principle of exclusion does not apply in their case, as already explained before. In the case of these goods, the market principle cannot ensure efficient allocation of resources and hence should be abandoned in favour of others.

(*b*) As already explained, there are third party effects involved in the case of pure public goods and therefore, the market mechanism may not achieve efficient allocation of resources and hence government interference will be justified.

(*c*) It has also been stated earlier that public goods are non-rival in their consumption and therefore, such goods cannot be supplied through the market. Moreover, the marginal cost of these goods is near zero. A resource is supposed to have been used efficiently when the price is equal to the marginal cost of the product. So such goods must be supplied by the market at zero price. This can never be possible. Therefore such goods must be supplied by the government through budgetary provisions, for efficient allocation of resources.

(*d*) Since in the case of public goods, overhead costs are very high, they are subject to the law of increasing returns or decreasing costs. If these goods are produced in small quantities, their average cost would be high. If the supply of such goods is left to the private sector then there would be under-production and these will be sold in the market at a higher price. This may not be desirable from the social welfare point of view particularly in such areas as communications, transportation, health and sanitation, etc. Thus, such social goods must be produced in the public sector.

(*e*) In the case of public goods the failure of market mechanism is caused also by their non-exclusivability. The number of users is so huge (take for example the case of a busy vegetable market where the total level of provision will not be reduced appreciably by the addition of one more person) that each participant feels inclined to use the provision as a "free rider", since their participation is not made contingent on payment. Thus, all the people are not compelled to indicate their preference in bidding for social goods. The market system breaks down and thus a different method of provision is required.

According to Prof. Musgrave[6] in a democracy, the decision to satisfy one or the other social want cannot be thrust upon the people in a dictatorial fashion. A political process of budget determination, therefore, becomes necessary. This political process would help in identifying the social goods to be provided by the government and also in equipping it with the necessary fiscal measures for the same. This can be achieved through the public budget-the budgetary provisions can reflect the public preferences for various public wants.

6. Musgrave, R.A. and Musgrave. P.B., *op. cit.,* pp. 56-61.

Prof. Taylor also holds the same view.[7] We may, therefore, sum up by saying that in view of the incapability and inefficiency of the market mechanism to reflect consumer preferences for social goods, such goods must be entrusted to the public sector to ensure efficient allocation of resources.

Principle of Allocation of Resources

As already explained earlier, the productive resources available to a nation are scarce and wants to be satisfied are unlimited. Decisions about the use of resources and satisfaction of wants at individual, group and state levels are to be taken very cautiously. These decisions at the level of an individual are mostly taken on the basis of his or her income which is solely determined by the allocative and distributive decisions of the state.

The second noteworthy feature of productive resources is that they can be put to alternative uses. It means that for the production of a particular commodity or service, some other commodity or service that could be produced with the help of those resources will have to be foregone. For example, while deciding to release more resources for increasing the production of cars, the community sacrifices the opportunity of using these resources for the production of some other commodity, may be cloth, houses, medicines or any other thing. In other words the loss of one thing is compensated by the production of some other thing. This is what is called the opportunity cost. Thus, the production of every commodity entails an opportunity cost, which is the value of those goods and services which those resources would have otherwise produced.

This is the general principle of opportunity cost. Now coming to its application to the field of public finance, we find that it is of great use in taking decisions about investment spending; for example in times of recession *i.e.*, falling demand declining production and increasing unemployment the government has to make a choice whether to induce private investment spending or to increase public investment spending. In the former case the government may give grant, interest free loans or subsidies and in the latter case it may undertake public works projects. So the government has to judge the opportunity cost of each policy decision before allocating resources. Economic growth means minimisation of economic scarcity *i.e.*, improvement in the available supply of goods and services. Economic scarcity exists because during a particular period of time the existing state of technology and productive resources in an economy determine the limit beyond which production of goods and services cannot be increased. Economic scarcity

---

7. Taylor, P.E., *op. cit.*, p. 166.

determines decisions regarding allocation of resources and distribution of income. These decisions can be of several types:

Firstly, a choice is to be made between the production of consumer goods and capital goods. Consumer goods are exhausted within a short time. Their economic value gets depleted as soon as they are brought into use. On the other hand, capital goods are more durable, they have long-term economic value and they help in the production of further goods and services. If more resources are allocated for the production of consumer goods then the productive capacity of the economy will be reduced and the process of economic growth will be reversed. If more resources are allocated for the production of capital goods, then there will be shortage of consumer goods, the general level of consumption will fall and people's efficiency will decline. So a balance is to be maintained between the two. These decisions pertain to the choice between consumption spending and investment spending. Increase in consumption spending beyond the required level would result in a reduction in the productive capacity and lower consumption in future, since investment spending or production of capital goods in the present means higher consumption in future. A certain level of investment spending is, therefore, necessary for the maintenance of the productive capacity of the nation, which means investment on: (*i*) the replacement of worn out capital goods, (*ii*) repair and maintenance of the capital goods, (*iii*) quality of the labour force *i.e.*, education and training, (*iv*) maintenance of ecological balance and natural resources.

Secondly, a choice is to be made between the production of goods and services by the government (public sector) and that by the individual entrepreneurs (private sector). Too much production in the public sector (*i.e.*, higher allocation of resources to the public sector) implies less production in the private sector (*i.e.*, lower allocation of resources to the private sector). The decision regarding optimal allocation of resources between the two sectors depends upon the political ideology, economic philosophy and the economic system adopted by the country.

Thirdly, a choice is to be made between labour and leisure. In other words, the labour force may be made to work for long hours and given less *leisure* or *vice versa*. The traditional and conservative view is that by working for longer hours the labour will produce more goods and services and will increase the economic welfare. But more work and less *leisure* may also adversely affect the efficiency of the individual worker in the long run. So, the choice for the producer is between more goods (output) in the present and less in future or maintenance of an optimum level of efficiency throughout the life of the worker. From the individual's point of view the choice will have to be made on the basis of individual welfare: whether more work and more money income or more *leisure* and less money income would add to or reduce his or her welfare.

Finally, a choice is to be made between various fiscal measures to be taken by the government to affect the distribution of income such as taxing the rich and transferring the income to the poor, affecting the intergeneration distribution of income etc. Intergeneration distribution of income can be influenced in a number of ways: financing the capital projects by imposing taxes on the present generation and thus subsidise future generations or to tax the younger workers for making social security payments to old people.

So, the scarcity and alternative usage of productive resources demand that the available resources must be used so effectively as to promote maximum welfare of the community. With this end in view the resources must be allocated between different uses most efficiently, economically or optimally as Pareto calls it. Optimal allocation is that which cannot be changed to increase the economic welfare of some persons without a fall in the economic welfare of some others. Optimality also requires that only those goods and services are produced in the economy which are most valuable to the consumers. But the significance of economic evaluation of goods by the consumer will depend on his share in the income. People with high incomes are certainly more important than people with low incomes. In a community where distribution of income is very unequal, people with low incomes have hardly any role. So efficiency of the resource allocation can also raise the income of the poor and make the distribution of income in the community fair and equitable. From the foregoing analysis it is clear that the process of decision-making is a tedious one for the policy makers since they have a large number of objectives to achieve. And since it is well nigh impossible to achieve all the objectives they shall have to forego some depending on their opportunity cost.

Exercises

1. Trace the development of the theory of Public Finance.
2. Explain the Theory of 'public goods'. What is the significance of 'public sector'?
3. Distinguish between 'public goods' and 'private goods', explaining the chief characteristics of 'public goods'.
4. Distinguish between 'merit wants' and 'social wants', explaining in detail their distinctive features.
5. 'Explain the 'externalities' of public goods'.
6. What is a 'public good'? Discuss its importance in a welfare state.

•••

Chapter 28

The Principle of Maximum Social Advantage

1. Aim of Public Finance—Maximum Social Advantage

The financial activities of governments at various levels affect the allocation of resources, transfer of resources from one channel to another, and hence, the level of income, output and employment. With a view to judging the appropriateness of any particular operation of public authorities in the field of finance it is desirable that some sort of standard is laid down. In modern times, when the concept of welfare state has come to stay as the ultimate objective of all state activities, such a standard can only be the economic welfare of the people. It, thus, follows that any activity which augments the economic welfare of the people would be considered as desirable and an activity that does not increase the economic welfare of the people would be considered undesirable.

According to Dalton, the chief objective of public finance is the maximisation of social advantage and the guiding principle of state policy technically described by him is the principle of maximum social advantage. He regards this principle as the most fundamental and extols that system of public finance which secures the maximum social advantage from its fiscal operations. He has also exploded the misconceived notions of some of the earlier writers that "every tax is an evil" and "all public expenditure is unproductive". This principle states that incomes and expenditures of the government should be so managed that after comparing the social burden of taxation and social benefit of public expenditure, the net advantage accruing to the society is the greatest. It is obvious that, like the individual, the state must balance its revenues and expenditures. Taxation results in a loss of utility to the people while expenditure adds to the utilities accruing to the community. When the government levies some taxes, certain amount of disutility or disadvantage is faced by the society. This disutility is expressed by payment of taxes or by parting with the purchasing power. Similarly, when the government incurs any expenditure, some satisfaction is gained by people on whom or for whom that expenditure has been incurred. As such, the advantage accruing to the society as a result of all these operations would be maximum when the surplus of social gain or utility (accruing from public expenditure) over the social sacrifices or disutility (resulting from payment of taxes) is maximized. Thus, the government has to prepare a balance-sheet of the sacrifices and benefits accruing to the society through its fiscal operations. If the aggregate of social benefits is more than that of the social sacrifices, the increase in the financial activity of the state would be justified. But, if more and more public revenues are raised through taxation or other sources, the sacrifices of the people go on increasing at a faster rate. The law of increasing marginal disutility comes into operation as people pay more and more taxes because the marginal utility of money for the people goes on increasing with the reduction of their incomes. Consequently, every additional dose of taxation involves greater sacrifice than the preceding ones. Similarly, for the same reason, the benefits resulting from public expenditure will go on diminishing with increase in expenditure. People will, thus, experience diminishing marginal social benefit with increasing public expenditure. Any rational state, would thus, seek to maximize the net social advantage of its fiscal operations. The net social advantage would be at the maximum when the aggregate of social benefits is maximum and the aggregate of social sacrifice is the minimum. The execution of the principle of aggregate maximum social advantage or least aggregate sacrifice in practice, entails comparison of the sacrifice made by people in divergent economic and social circumstances. Applying the law of diminishing marginal utility it may be said that the payment of a certain tax by a wealthy person means less of sacrifice than the payment of the same amount of money by a poorer person. Technically speaking, the net social advantage would be maximum when the marginal disutility of taxation is equal to the marginal utility of public expenditure. The point at which the marginal social sacrifice would be equal to the marginal benefit is the point of aggregate maximum social advantage or of least aggregate social sacrifice. If expressed with the help of a diagram, the point of equilibrium would be as shown in Fig. 28.1.

In Fig. 28.1 the vertical axis *OA* indicates the sacrifice/benefits and the horizontal axis *OC* indicates the units of money paid in the form of taxes or spent by the state. The *MSS* curve is an upward sloping curve which implies that the social sacrifice per unit of taxation goes on increasing with every additional unit of taxation. The *MSB* curve is a downward sloping curve which implies that with every increase in public expenditure the social benefit per unit diminishes. These two curves intersect at *P*. This is the point of equilibrium and this point indicates the optimum limit of the financial activity of the state. Beyond this point any increase in the financial activity of the state would mean that the marginal social sacrifice would exceed the marginal social benefit resulting in a net loss to the society. The shaded area *APB,* thus, represents the quantum of maximum social advantage, which would result only when the financial activities of the state are at the optimum level of *OQ.*

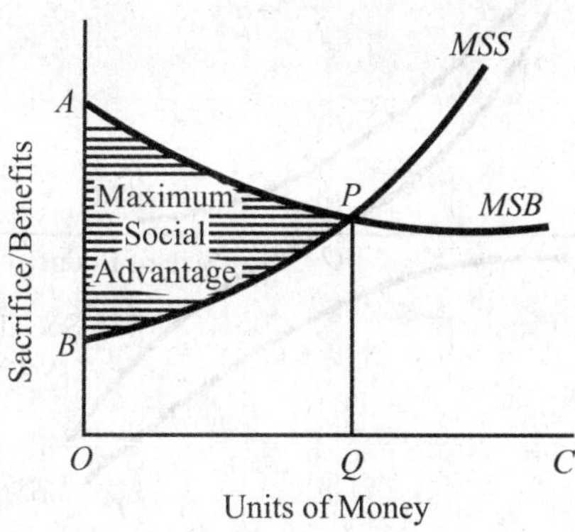

Fig. 28.1

According to Professors Pigou and Dalton, the size of the budget of government should be determined according to this principle. Professor Musgrave is of the view that the optimum size of the budget should be determined at a point where the marginal net benefits are zero. There is fundamentally no difference between the thinking of Musgrave and that of Dalton. As a matter of fact, Professor Musgrave has used the term "the maximum welfare" instead of "maximum social advantage".

This has been illustrated by Professor Musgrave as shown in Fig. 28.2.

In Fig. 28.2 the line *nb* represents the net social benefits curve, which is obtained by deducting *MSS* from *MSB.* It intersects the horizontal axis at point *Q* where the marginal net benefits are zero. Point *Q* indicates the optimum size of the budget because it is at this point that the total net social benefit or advantage is maximum, and also that at this point marginal social benefit is equal to marginal social sacrifice.

The principle of maximum social advantage or the principle of maximum social welfare as illustrated above is based on the law of substitution. Technically speaking, public expenditure should be incurred or distributed among public uses in such a way that the marginal return in each type of use is equal. So long as the marginal satisfaction resulting from each type of outlay is equalised, the state will have to go on substituting the dispersal of expenditure from one use to other. Similarly, to keep the total social sacrifice at the minimum, burden of taxation should be divided among different sources or individuals in such a way that the marginal sacrifice undergone by each

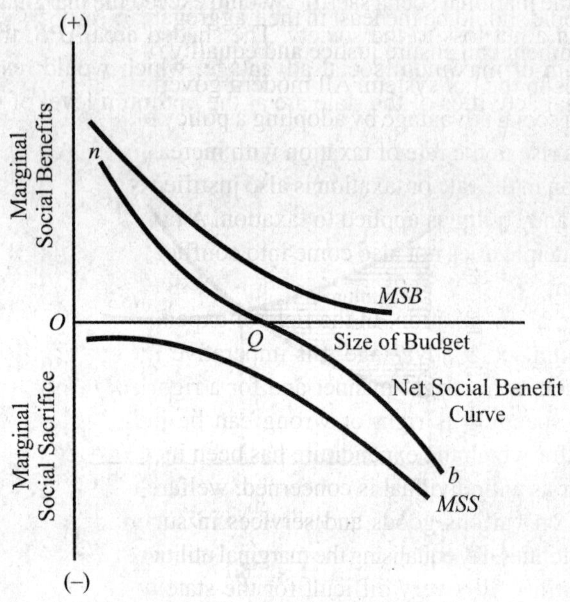

Fig. 28.2.

individual or source is equal. Theoretically speaking, therefore, the following three conditions are necessary for obtaining the maximum social advantage.

(1) The marginal utility of public expenditure should be equal to the marginal disutility/sacrifice resulting from taxation.

(2) The marginal utility from public expenditure in each use should be equal.

(3) The marginal disutility resulting from taxation from each source or individual should be equal.

2. Least Aggregate Sacrifice and Principle of Maximum Social Benefit

The principle of least aggregate sacrifice is the focal point of principle of maximum social advantage. The principle of least aggregate sacrifice describes that the deprivation of the people by the imposition of taxes should be the minimum possible. The execution of this principle in practice, involves comparison of the sacrifice made by the people in divergent economic and social circumstances. On the basis of the law of diminishing marginal utility, we conclude that the payment of a certain tax by a rich man means less of sacrifice to him than the payment of the same amount made by a person who is poorer than him. This principle lays down that the sacrifices made in general by the people should be the least in their aggregate. By following this principle the government can ensure justice and equality of sacrifices on the part of the individuals in the tax system. All modern governments apply the principle of maximum social advantage by adopting a policy of progressive taxation which involves a rise in the rate of taxation with increasing incomes. The element of progression in the rate or taxation is also justified on the basis of the principles of ability and equity as applied to taxation. A tax system evolved on the basis of this principle does not also come into conflict with the canons or principles of taxation.

So far, about taxation. In the field of expenditure, from the point of view of maximum social advantage it is imperative for the governments to spend public incomes in a right manner and for a right cause. Whether the purpose of public spending is right or wrong can be judged from the fact that the objective for which the expenditure has been incurred, is socially desirable or not. So far as an individual is concerned, welfare is maximum by distributing resources on various goods and services in such a way as to equalise their marginal utilities. By equalising the marginal utilities, the individual can maximise his total utility. It is very difficult for the state to choose sets of schemes of expenditure which may confer the maximum benefit on the society. The state cannot act like an individual. Nevertheless, the state must ensure that there is no wastage and no malallocation of resources. For example, in our country, public funds are allotted to the construction of luxury buildings, which, if allotted to the construction of a large number of small residential quarters would confer greater benefit on the society. In short, a rationalisation of public expenditure, on the basis of principle of maximum social advantage, would go a long way in conferring a greater benefit on the society. In practice, however, we find a tug of war between various government departments and there is always a scope for controversy about the manner and purpose of public spending. Broadly speaking, public expenditure with a view to maximising social benefit can be incurred with three broad objectives *viz*., (*a*) defence of the country and maintenance of law and order; (*b*) maximisation of production so as to meet the basic requirements of the society; and (*c*) equitable distribution of income and resources among the members of the society.

Prior to industrial revolution it was generally held that the state should keep its activities to the minimum and, consequently, the sphere of state activity was limited to defence and administration of justice. Other activities were best left to the individuals. The economists as well as the policy-makers during those days were of the view that social advantage could be maximised only when individuals were granted the maximum freedom in the choice of occupation, the pattern of consumption and the modes of production. The industrial revolution gave a big jolt to this concept and glaring inequalities of incomes, the rise of monopolies, the miserable plight of the workers, the growing urbanisaton with all its concomitant evils and other socio-economic problems compelled people to assign a more active role to state. Subsequently, the great depression of the thirties further created a revolution in economic thinking, more especially about the role that the state should play in the economic life of the individual and the country. Consequently, taxation and public expenditure were supposed to be the most effective tools for stabilising the economy at a high level of employment and production and for equalising the distribution of wealth and income in the country. Thus, the principle of maximum social advantage is now applied through the introduction of an element of progression in taxation for reducing the incomes, of the rich and through a progressive system of grants and subsidies for improving the wage earning capacities of the poor.

3. Criticism of Principle of Maximum Social Advantage

Despite all these practical advantages and applications, the principle of maximum social advantage has been severely criticised on some fundamental grounds. Firstly, it has been pointed out that the utility being a subjective phenomenon cannot be measured precisely. Hence, it is difficult to measure marginal benefit accruing to each individual from each and every unit of public expenditure. Similarly, it is difficult to measure the marginal dissatisfaction caused to each individual. Thus, inter-personal comparison of utilities and dissatisfactions is difficult. This problem is further aggravated by two factors, *viz.*, (*i*) in the process of spending and taxing, a large number of people and government departments are involved; and (*ii*) certain public expenditures are incurred for future benefits. The measurement of utility arising from these expenditures cannot be determined in the present. Moreover, some of the governmental activities are influenced by non-economic factors and political considerations and are not always in the best interest of the society.

It has been further pointed out that the balancing of the marginal social sacrifice of taxation with the marginal social benefit from public expenditure is intractable because the disutility arising from taxation to the individual taxpayer is a micro problem for him, whereas the benefit of public expenditure is a macro problem, since it is a matter of concern for all the individuals in the society. Further, the sacrifice is made by the individual in the form of payment of taxes and therefore, there is an element of disutility involved in it. In public borrowings no such disutility is involved and consequently, public expenditure can be financed through public borrowings to any extent. Thus, this sort of public spending cannot, be governed by the principle of maximum social advantage.

Lastly, in modem times, the fiscal operations are adopted to reduce the imbalances in the economy and so the consideration of equalising marginal disutility and utility cannot be applicable. The fiscal measures are adopted more as a contra-cyclical measure than merely for maintaining internal and external security of the country. Taxes, therefore, cannot be reduced or increased beyond a certain limit. Public expenditure is incurred for reducing unemployment and improving the level of effective demand and, therefore, the consideration of measuring its marginal social benefit can hardly be kept in view. Again, in the development-oriented financial operations this principle can hardly govern public expenditure and taxation.

We can, therefore, conclude that the principle of maximum social advantage can be applied only under static conditions and under those conditions which were visualised by the classical economists but under dynamic conditions like those of ours, where the chief objective of public financial operations is to control the cycles and to promote rapid economic growth, this principle has no practical value.

4. Dalton's Objective Tests of Social Advantage

Social advantage being a subjective phenomenon and its measurement being fraught with difficulties, Dalton has suggested certain objective tests of social advantage or economic welfare. These tests are: (*i*) to protect the society against external attacks and internal disorders; (*ii*) to increase the general economic welfare of the community by increasing production and by improving the distribution of wealth; (*iii*) to maintain economic stability; (*iv*) to pursue the goals of economic growth and full employment; and (*v*) to safeguard the interest of future generations.

Some explanation of these objective tests appears to be necessary. So far as the first objective is concerned, it should be the prime requisite of social advantage, and should be the first item in any list of public expenditure. Security of persons and property of citizens is the first condition of civilised living. This requires expenditure on the maintenance of armed forces, police and judiciary. While any expenditure on these items may be justifiable, it is necessary that the government should not follow an unsound public policy in other spheres which may lead to discontentment within the country or provoke its neighbours to acts of aggression. Similarly, any inexpedient and unwise foreign policy may result in unfriendly relations with the bordering countries and may require the maintenance of a big army on the borders specially for a country like India. Thus, for maximising the economic welfare of the people in the country the maintenance of internal law and order and provision for defence against external aggression are necessary. It is equally necessary that the government adopts a public policy which may be in the best interest of the country and which may result in minimising the expenditure on these items.

The second objective can be achieved by increasing production and equalising the distribution of wealth. The fiscal operations can bring about desired improvements in the field of production through: (*a*) improvement in the productive efficiency of the workers by: (*i*) exempting the low income group people from direct taxes so that they spend their income on the improvement of their standard of living. Similarly, public expenditure should be incurred on providing various social services like free education, free medical services, better housing facilities, etc. which may provide more benefits to the people belonging to this category; (*ii*) the system of production should be better organised, which means, that the tax system should not in any way prove to be a disincentive to the producers and workers. It should not affect adversely their willingness to work hard. This can be achieved only when there are provisions for granting development rebate, tax exemptions and concessions for innovations and reduction in the production cost. Not only that, public income and expenditure should be integrated in such a way as to lead to the maximum utilisation of productive resources; and (*iii*) the production should be organised in such a way that the various goods and services are produced to meet the requirements of the people and this can be achieved only through well thought-out fiscal operations. To achieve this objective steps may be required to be taken to restrict certain types of consumption and production. It may also mean the taking over by the state of the production of certain commodities in the interest of the society. For example, it may be generally necessary, as has been in almost all the countries, that public utilities like electricity, gas and water supply, the operation of railways, etc. are owned by the state. The production and consumption of narcotic drugs like L.S.D., opium, etc. may also be controlled through the creation of state monopoly, as has been done in a number of countries in Europe as well as in Asia. (*b*) The distribution of wealth can be rationalised with the help of fiscal measures. This involves reduction in inequalities of income and wealth and improvement in the standard of living of the masses. By reducing inequalities in the distribution of incomes social advantage can be maximised, and for meeting this objective, progressive taxation is quite justifiable. For improving the standard of living of the masses, the government can introduce welfare programmes which may involve a huge public expenditure but which are essential from the point of view of maximising the social advantage. Such programmes can be of the type as introduced in India like the community development projects, the Harijan welfare programmes, the family planning programme, the *Antodaya* programme, the rural drinking water programme, etc.

Economic stability is as essential as political stability from the point of view of social advantage. Economic instability, in fact, can have a devastating effect on the life of the people, and therefore, the fiscal policy must be designed with the objective of maintaining economic stability in the country. Fiscal measures, therefore, adopted as a counter-cyclical policy are quite justifiable. This would involve large scale borrowings, heavy taxation during the period of inflation and huge public expenditure during the period of depression.

In a welfare state, the government is responsible for maintaining the level of full employment and rate of economic growth in the country. Public finance operations should, therefore, be designed keeping these aims in view.

According to Dalton, the government is the trustee for the welfare of the future generations, equally as it is for the present generations. All the decisions of the government should, therefore, be taken from a long-term point of view. Fiscal operations of the government should prefer a larger social advantage in the future to a smaller one in the present. This is necessary for safeguarding the interest of the future generations. In economic terms this would mean that any fiscal measure which leads to a reduction in the national savings, will not be conducive to the maximisation of social advantage or economic welfare because it would adversely affect the productive capacity of the future generations. On the other hand, a huge public expenditure on constructing social overhead capital would be justifiable since it would increase the productive capacity of the future generations.

5. U. Hick's Optima

Mrs. Hicks has suggested the productive optimum and utility optimum as the objective criteria for all fiscal operations. Under the productive optimum she suggests that production must be increased to increase the economic welfare of the people since the objective of all economic activity is to satisfy human wants. In other words, production optimum means the maximisation of production and this is realised "when it becomes impossible by re-allocating factors, to increase the output of one product without diminishing that of another."[1] The production optimum is realised by equalising the marginal returns of all the factors of production. All fiscal operations should, therefore, aim at maximising production in the country. But this is not easy to achieve. A number of factors create difficulties in the way, e.g., market imperfections, immobilities and imperfect substitutes of labour and capital, control of resources by monopolists, etc. According to Mrs. Hicks, while maximising

1. U. Hicks, *Public Finance*. p. 106.

production we must choose that set-up which may yield maximum satisfaction and thus the optimum utility. This can be achieved by redistributing income, to increase the satisfaction of one individual without diminishing the satisfaction of another, after full allowance has been made for compensation.

The fiscal operations can achieve optimum utility only when the gap between the rich and the poor is removed. Mrs. Hicks considers these optima as practical directives of a public policy since these can be treated with statistical and econometric enquiries.

These objective criteria can no doubt, help in judging the desirability of a particular fiscal operation. But a comparison of the balance of probable social gain and loss of any proposed fiscal operation is not an easy task because it involves lot of conjecturing and is influenced by many subjective and non-economic factors. Public opinion also plays a vital role in such an assessment. Thus, the measurement of social advantage in absolute terms is impossible. We can, therefore, conclude that no measure of public finance can be judged in isolation but a comprehensive view should be taken of the entire operations of public finance and their overall effect. From an objective point of view it may be more helpful if public financial operations are considered as an integral part of the general economic policy of the state.

Exercises

1. Explain the Principle of Maximum Social Advantage. Suggest Criteria for public policy designed to secure maximum social advantage.
2. "The best system of Public Finance is that which secures the maximum social advantage from the operations which it conducts".—(Dalton). Explain the statement and discuss the role of public finance in a modern state.
3. Explain the principle of Maximum Social Advantage with the help of a diagram. What objective criteria are required to achieve this principle in practice?

•••

Chapter 29

Public Expenditure—General Issues

1. Introduction

A study of public expenditure involves a probe into the nature of expenses and objectives for which, the various expenses are incurred by public authorities—Central, State and local in a federation—in the discharge of their obligations, *viz.*, the preservation of the nation and the promotion of economic development of the country. Some general principles undoubtedly can be formulated to judge the merits of such expenditures but it is difficult to lay down any definite rules for its administration.

2. Growth of Public Expenditure: Wagner's Law of Increasing State Activities

In the *laissez-faire* era the state was assigned a very limited role to play. The functions assigned to the state were based on the principle of least interference or "that state is the best which governs the least." Accordingly the state was supposed to undertake activities relating to the administration of justice and maintenance of internal law and order and to look after the defence of the country against external aggression. This concept held sway over the minds of the people for quite a long time. But, it started receding after the success of industrial revolution in Great Britain. And since then the sphere of state activity has been persistently increasing all over the world. This tendency, in economic parlance, is known as "Wagner's Law of Increasing State Activity." Adolf Wagner (1835-1917) was a celebrated German fiscal theorist of the 19th century. He observed: "Comprehensive comparisons of different countries and different times show that, among the progressive peoples with which alone we are concerned, an increase regularly takes place in the activity of both the central and the local governments. This increase is both extensive and intensive. The central and local governments constantly undertake new functions, while they perform both old and new functions more efficiently and completely. In this way, the economic needs of the people, to an increasing extent and in a more satisfactory fashion, are satisfied by the central and local governments."

F.S. Nitti supported Wagner and on the basis of empirical evidence said that this law was not only applicable to Germany but to various governments which differed widely from each other. So, the emphasis was on the fact that the expenditure of the government was increasing because of the following reasons:

(1) There was an extension of traditional functions of the state. Defence, administration of justice, formation of laws due to democratic political set-up, were becoming more and more expensive day by day. Besides, various complexities of social and economic nature were also developing due to which the administration and governance had become more complex and expensive.

(2) The sphere of state activity was also expanding. Originally the state activities were only confined to defence, justice, maintenance of law and order and some social overheads but, with growing consciousness among the people and also on the part of the government towards its responsibilities to the society, many activities in the field of social welfare have been added. Among these are the enrichment of the cultural life of the society and provision of social security to the people. Besides, subsidies for a direct supply of various merit goods and public goods were also increasing.

(3) The government also felt the need of expanding the sphere of public goods. Consequently, there has been a shift in the composition of national produce in favour of public goods and this requires the expansion of the public sector in industry, trade and commerce.

Thus, Wagner's law, since it was based on historical facts, was applicable to modern progressive governments only, which were interested in enlarging the sphere of state activity *i.e.*, public sector; and also the services for the general benefit and welfare. This tendency definitely had a long-term trend. And Wagner emphasised this long-term trend rather than short-term changes in public expenditure. He, however, did not analyse the quantitative relationship between the increase in public expenditure and the time taken in it. Besides, the factors enumerated by Wagner, there are some other factors as well which have contributed to the increase in public expenditure. Among these the most prominent are:

1. Growth of Population. Population explosion has been a major contributor to the growth of public expenditure and with the growth in population, if not proportionately, then at least to a greater extent the public services have also to be increased. For example, more schools, hospitals etc. have to be provided to meet additional needs of the growing population.

2. Industrial Development. The industrial revolution has been responsible for the rapid industrialisation of certain economies and also for political and social transformation in those countries. It has created new problems in the areas of labour relations, regulation of industry, protection of consumers, distribution of income and wealth and economic security. These problems have arisen because of the new forces released by the industrial development. Consequently, the governments have to spend more on solving these problems, which has led to an enormous increase in public expenditure.

3. Social Security Measures. With the growth of the concept of welfare state, modern governments have taken upon themselves the responsibility of promoting social welfare and of protecting interests of socially and economically weaker sections of the society. Consequently, most of the governments are spending large amounts on providing benefits to people belonging to the economically and socially under-privileged sections of the society like, sickness benefits, accident benefits, old age pensions, maternity benefits, outright grants, free medical and educational services for industrial workers, subsidised housing and unemployment benefits, medical and health facilities etc. The governments have been spending large amounts on these items and therefore the public expenditure has grown substantially in the 20th century.

4. Nationalisation of Industries and Trade. With the spread of socialist philosophy and emergence of socialist states more and more governments have started undertaking commercial activities to provide consumers with goods and services at low costs. This also includes the regulation of monopolies, improvement of the conditions of labour and equitable distribution of income and wealth. Besides, the governments have also taken over some business and trade in order to provide goods at reasonable prices.

5. Development of Agriculture. In under-developed countries, the governments have to take upon themselves the responsibility for sustained and rapid economic and social development of the country. The governments of most of these countries have realised that development of agriculture holds the key to economic prosperity of the country. In fact agricultural and non-agricultural activities are inter-dependent. Increased agricultural incomes create demand for industrial goods, which leads to rapid industrialisation. Agriculture supplies raw material and other inputs to industry which supplies various inputs to agriculture. Agriculture supplies wage goods to the industrial sector, whereas industrial sector supplies tools and implements to the agricultural sector. Hence, it is imperative that agriculture is developed on a sound footing so that rapid development of a country like ours is ensured. It is to meet this objective that the governments of developing countries have been spending large amounts on the development of agriculture. Almost all governments have been providing funds to the cultivators at low rates of interest, giving export subsidies, ensuring minimum guarantee prices and also tariff protection.

The governments have also to spend large sums of money on research, soil conservation etc.

6. Cost of Administration. Since the second world war, the entire world has witnessed a rising trend of prices. Consequently, the governments have to pay more for the commodities and services and increase the salaries, dearness allowance of their employees. This has also led to an increase in public expenditure. It may be noted that it is not necessary that the public expenditure has gone up only due to an increase in public activity; the expenditure has also substantially increased due to rise in prices.

7. Problems of Defence. During past decades maintenance of defence forces has become very costly. Moreover, due to arms race and nuclear arms proliferation almost all the countries have to spend huge amounts on defence preparedness. The modern governments have therefore, to spend a lot on the manufacture of war weapons and maintenance of armed forces. Over the years there has been a tremendous change in the techniques of war and now new weapons of war are required for the army. So, in almost all countries of the world the defence expenditure has been on the increase. This also includes expenditure on the training and maintenance of army, air and naval forces and purchase of conventional and nuclear weapons for both offensive and deterrent purposes.

8. Urbanisation. An increasing shift of population to the urban areas has taken place. New cities have come up and old cities are growing. Growing urbanisation means huge expenditure on the provision of civic amenities and infrastructure like power, transport, communication, roads and so on. The per capita cost of water supply, health facilities, traffic service and control, public protection, has been rising without any limit. The governments have also to make provision for additional hospitals, roads, streetlights, community halls, parks, play grounds etc. and also for the distribution and control of essential commodities. All these have been responsible for increase in public expenditure.

9. Dependence of People on Government. There has been a sea change in the attitude of the people towards government. The common man has become more dependent on the government for safety, security, decent living etc. The common man now believes that without government assistance social and economic life cannot be made comfortable. This change in attitude has been caused by a number of factors like: (*a*) technical changes which have created a feeling of inter- dependence among people and the government, and the inability of majority of people to work out their own solutions due to forces which are totally beyond their control, (*b*) the free market system has so many imperfections that people now look to the government for combating business depression and for the maintenance of economic stability, for reducing exploitation and for maintaining the level of economic activity, (*c*) the elimination of poverty requires collective action and therefore the government is required to step in which has also increased the outlays for public welfare and public works, and (*d*) over the years the political and economic problems have become so complex and complicated that they require a large expenditure on social services like education, health and hygiene, medical aid, housing and home administration.

10. Economic Development. Modern governments have accepted the ideas of planning and economic growth particularly in under-developed countries. The development programmes include provision for infrastructure facilities like means of transport and communication, power etc. The government is required to make provision on an increasing scale for economic and social overheads so that rapid indusrialisation of the country may be possible. Besides, the government also undertakes various programmes to provide help to the private economic units in increasing their productivity through bounties, loans and grants-aid. Government also provides assistance in acquiring technical know-how and raw materials. All these have led to an increase in public expenditure.

11. Growth and Social Justice. The chief objective of economic planning and development is to establish a prosperous society. Till recently the emphasis has been on the growth of national product but it has been experienced that growth by itself has not been able to eliminate poverty. Studies have shown that while the satisfactory rates of growth of the economy have been achieved, appreciable difference has not been made in unemployment and poverty. On the other hand, unemployment and inequality in the distribution of income and wealth have increased as a result of economic development and planning. Further it has led to regional imbalances. This is particularly true of almost all developing countries including ours. It may, however, be noted that the objectives of growth and social justice are not conflicting, if a policy is designed to achieve distributive justice. Therefore, the governments of developing countries have been spending large sums of money on providing various facilities and amenities to economically weaker sections of the society so as to achieve distributive justice.

3. Wiseman and Peacock Hypothesis

Wiseman and Peacock undertook a study of public expenditure in U.K. for the period from 1880-1955, according to which public expenditure does not increase in a smooth and continuous fashion but in jerks or steps like fashion. This is because of the fact that the need for public expenditure increases due to some social or other disturbance, which cannot be met by the existing public revenue. Consequently, the expenditure as well as taxation move to a new higher level which according to the authors is the *displacement effect.* Since the existing revenue falls short of the required public expenditure it creates an *inspection effect.* The position is reviewed by the government and the people and with a view to finding out a solution of some of the important problems, they agree to finance the increased expenditure. As a result, the people attain a new level of 'tax tolerance', which means that people are willing to bear a higher burden of taxation. This means that the general level of expenditure and revenue goes up and so both public expenditure as well as revenue get settled at a new level until another disturbance occurs leading to a *displacement effect* with each major disturbance. The government's sphere of economic activity goes on extending and the consequence is the *concentration effect* which implies that the economic activity of the central government tends to grow faster than the governments at the state and local levels.

Undoubtedly the Wiseman and Peacock hypothesis appears to be quite relevant but as a matter of fact they are laying emphasis on unusual and abnormal situations which lead to a sizeable increase in the public expenditure and revenue. As a matter of fact, due to certain variable factors like growth of population, urbanization and the growing consciousness among the people as well as the government of the civic rights and duties, lead to an upward increase in public expenditure. It implies that constant and regular changes take place in the economy because of these variable factors, which lead to an expansion of public expenditure as well as revenue. In under-developed economies, like ours, the state is deliberately undertaking a number of activities of regulatory nature, particularly to protect the economy against instability and to minimise the inequalities of income and wealth, its activities are increasing and also the efforts of the government to raise funds for these activities through various tax efforts are increasing. In this way the Wiseman-Peacock hypothesis only describes a particular tendency and does not take into account all the relevant factors.

4. The Critical Limit Hypothesis

According to the Critical Limit Hypothesis, when the share of the government sector exceeds 25 per cent of the total economic activity of the country, inflation occurs even under balanced budgets. Colin Clark has put forth this thesis in his "Public Finance and changes in the value of money" published in *Economic Journal,* December, 1945. This hypothesis is based on the study of inter-war data of several western countries. According to Colin Clark when the share of the government in the aggregate economic activity reaches the critical limit of 25 per cent, the income earners are so affected by reduced incentives due to high taxes that their productivity goes down. The production falls and the supply is curtailed. On the other hand, the government financing increases which leads to inflation due to lack of adjustment between demand and supply. The main defect of this hypothesis is that Clark has relied fully on the institutional frame work of the economy and the choice of a definite figure *i.e.*, 25 per cent as the critical limit. It has been seen that even after the government in certain countries has reached a limit higher than 25 per cent significant inflation has not been caused. Whether a government's budget activities would result in inflationary pressures or not will depend upon the manner in which public expenditure is organised.

5. Wagner's Views on Public Expenditure

We have given a general explanation of Wagner's law of increasing state activities earlier in this chapter. Now we spell out his views on public expenditure in some detail. According to Wagner as a nation experiences economic development and growth there is an increase in the activities of the public sector. In other words, in terms of expenditure the ratio of public consumption expenditure to GNP, both in totality and by functions rises as GNP rises. Wagner, therefore, divided public expenditure into: (*i*) expenditures for internal and external security, and (*ii*) expenditures for cultural and welfare activities which include education, health, recreation, transportation, banking etc. So far as external security is concerned expenditures would increase as the nature of the use of force by the state changes from simple aggression to prevention of attack. For internal security, greater expenditure is required because of greater friction between economic units and people as urbanisation progresses. Public sector would, therefore, encroach upon the private sector, as it could produce goods and services more efficiently because: (*i*) the public sector goods would be of better quality; (*ii*) public sector would have better and easier access to capital; and (*iii*) public sector is in a position to avoid market crises created by the private economic units. Therefore, Wagner held that the income elasticity for government services is greater than unity *i.e.*, public expenditure will increase faster than the increase in the income of the people. He, therefore, spells out the various items as follows:

(1) Factors that affect both the demand and supply of public expenditure: (*i*) Per capita income and wealth which affects the demand as well as the cost of government services; and (*ii*) density and the rate of growth of population which affect the demand for infrastructural facilities such as roads, hospitals etc. in addition to the cost of supply of services.

(2) Factors affecting the demand side of public expenditure: (*i*) Urbanisation and industrialisation; (*ii*) distribution of income; (*iii*) literacy level of population; (*iv*) age-composition of the population that determines the demand for schools, pensions, old age homes, etc.; (*v*) alternative private

services supplied determine the demand for socialised medical and health services.

(3) Factors affecting the supply side of public expenditure: (*i*) Scale of production of government services; (*ii*) quality of production; (*iii*) inter-government grants.

6. Professor Musgrave's Views on Public Expenditure

Professor Musgrave has listed the following reasons for the growth of public expenditure in matured economies: (*i*) maximisation of economic welfare through allocation of resources; (*ii*) achievement of full employment and economic stability; (*iii*) equitable distribution of income; and (*iv*) acceleration of economic growth. Professor Musgrave, therefore assigns four functions to the state in matured economies for the purpose of public expenditure: (*i*) activities relating to the re-allocation of resources; (*ii*) activities aiming at the re-distribution of income and wealth; (*iii*) activities relating to economic stability; and (*iv*) activities in the field of commerce and trade. According to Musgrave the need for public expenditure on these activities arises because of the imperfections in the market economies, growing unemployment and economic instability, inequitable distribution of income and operation of certain enterprises by private sector, which are socially undesirable.

7. Comparison between Private and Public Expenditure

Most authors of textbooks on Public Finance have highlighted the distinction between public and private expenditure. In the same tradition we also very briefly mention some of the basic similarities and dissimilarities between the two.

Similarities between Private and Public Expenditure

1. Avoidance of Wastage. Both private economic units and public authorities try to avoid wastage in public expenditure. Both of them try to obtain maximum advantage or return from minimum of expenditure. If somehow there is a gap between expenditure and the attaining of the target on the wrong side then it may be due to inefficiency, uncertainty or lack of farsightedness.

2. Flexibility. Both private and public expenditures have a common element of flexibility. Both private economic units and public bodies take an overall view of the income, expenditure and possibilities of adjustment in each. While an individual may make a choice between an effort to earn and leisure, a firm may compare between the cost of earning more and spending more, the public bodies will compare the effects of additional revenue raising efforts with the results of additional expenditure.

3. More than One way of Raising Additional Income. Both the private economic units and the public bodies can raise additional income in more than one way. The public bodies can raise additional revenue by imposing additional taxes or by raising the tax rates or by increasing non-tax revenue or by borrowing, a private economic unit also resorts to more than one way. The main problem in both the cases is related to an efficient and integrated management of finances. The problem basically pertains to the choice of alternative ways in which finances can be raised, the effort required in that regard, effects of such efforts and the corresponding benefit of the expenditures involved.

4. Problem of Equilibriating Solution. Both the private economic units and the corporate bodies face the common problem of finding out an equilibriating solution. Such a solution will differ from one circumstance to the other. In some cases a larger tax and higher expenditure level might be indicated, in others a lower tax and smaller expenditure level might be required. The same position exists in regard to the private finance.

Dissimilarities between Private and Public Expenditure

Following dissimilarities between private and public expenditures have been pointed out.

1. Difference in Objective. This dissimilarity is quite prominent. An individual economic unit generally takes into account the utility derived from the expenditure incurred and attempts to equate marginal utility of the good or service purchased against the disutility of expenditure. For example, a commercial economic unit will compare the marginal returns from an expenditure with the amount spent. Public bodies cannot adopt this attitude which is purely commercial. They have to keep in mind the social benefits which are quite vague and beyond measurement. The government has to impute social valuation to these benefits and decide whether it is worth anything to undertake these expenditures. Moreover there are certain expenditures whose benefits cannot be evaluated directly. For example, expenditure incurred in connection with the promotion of social and economic justice in matters of distribution of income and wealth.

2. Planning for Future. Since state has to undertake activities for augmenting social welfare and promote economic and social health of the society, certain items of expenditure are such which cannot be related to the cost of providing those services like, social security. These services provide long-term benefit to the society. On the one hand an individual does not bother for the long term, he plans only for a foreseeable future. So, while the state can plan to incur public expenditure from long-term point of view a private economic unit cannot.

3. Income Plan. According to Professor Hicks, "Private Finance, whether of firms or individuals, starts with a given income plan as the framework within which expenditure must be planned; public finance on the contrary starts with a given expenditure plan, and the authorities adjust their incomes (revenue) by means of taxes and resources, to match the expenditure."[1] It implies that the public bodies try to adjust their income to their expenditure whereas a private economic unit tries to adjust its expenditure according to its income.

4. Compulsory Character. State has to incur expenditure compulsorily whereas it is not necessary for an individual to incur an expenditure which he or she does not want. Hence certain expenditure, like expenditure on the maintenance of law and order, defence preparedness against foreign aggression etc. is to be incurred by the government. So far as private economic units are concerned one does not come across with any such expenditure which may be of a compulsory nature.

5. Profit Motive. According to Professor Shirras public expenditure is incurred not with a view to earning profit as is the case with the expenditure incurred by a private economic unit. Since state is the guardian of social welfare, economic and social health of the community, it cannot afford to keep an eye on the profit earned from these services. Therefore, certain items of public expenditure cannot be related to the cost of providing services like social security, health and education etc.

8. Classification of Public Expenditure

A classification of public expenditure is significant for having a clear understanding of the nature and effects of various kinds of public expenditure. Obviously, while classifying public expenditure we also classify the functions of the state. It is, therefore, necessary that the classification of public expenditure should be done on some logical and rational economic basis, so that one is able to know the true effects and nature of each kind of expenditure and compare the effect of one expenditure with the effect of another expenditure. According to Professor Shirras the test of public expenditure is not the aggregate expenditure, but it is the relative amounts which are assigned to different heads from time to time. According to him, the classification of public expenditure is important from the point of view of relative importance of each head of expenditure at different periods of time. A classification of public expenditure is important for other reasons as well. In a democratic set-up, public expenditure, if properly classified, will provide useful information about the way in which the revenue is being collected and is being spent.

1. Ursula K. Hicks, *Public Finance.* p. 17.

People, then, would be 'able to know whether the revenue collected from them has been spent properly, whether the expenditure incurred is beneficial to them or not, whether the resources have been allocated in the interest of the entire community or for the benefit of a particular section of people.

There is hardly any unanimity among the economists regarding the methods of and bases for classifying expenditure of public bodies. John Stuart Mill distinguishes various types of public expenditure on the basis of the functions performed by the state *i.e.*, necessary and optional functions. Roscher divided public expenditure into necessary, useful and superfluous or ornamental expenditure. This classification is analogous to that of private expenditure *viz.*, necessaries, comforts and luxuries. Such classifications, however, do not appear to be very useful in the sense that they are unable to solve the fundamental problems. Moreover, they are quite conservative in their outlook and are based on a pre-conceived notion of the merits and demerits of a particular type of expenditure.

Nineteenth Century Economists' Classification

The 19th century economists specially, Cohn and Plehn classified public expenditure on the criterion of 'benefit' conferred. According to this principle public expenditure has been classified into four broad heads as follows:

(1) Productive expenditure *i.e.*, expenditure which confers, common benefits on all citizens like expenditure on defence, education, building of roads, community halls, parks etc.

(2) In the second category fall all those expenditures which are incurred for the benefit of particular sections of the community, *e.g.*, expenditure on poor relief, social security, unemployment insurance etc.

(3) Expenditures which confer a special benefit on certain people and at the same time confer benefit on others are included in the third category, *e.g.*, administration of justice.

(4) Lastly, those expenditures which confer special benefits on a particular group are included in the fourth category, *e.g.*, subsidies to a particular industry or funding of small irrigation schemes in a particular state or providing funds for famine relief in a particular state etc. This sort of classification, no doubt, analyses the nature of benefit conferred on the people, but it is defective and imperfect because one cannot easily demarcate whether a particular expenditure is conferring a special benefit on a particular section of society or on the society as a whole.

Fredrick Nicholson's Classification

Nicholson has based his classification of public expenditure on the amount of revenue received by the state in return of the services which it renders. He has, therefore, classified public expenditure as under.

(1) Expenditure without direct return of revenue, for example, poor relief or in some cases even with direct loss, for example, war expenditure.

(2) Expenditure without direct return but with indirect benefit to revenue, for example, expenditure on education.

(3) Expenditure with partially direct return for example, education for which fees are charged.

(4) Expenditure with full return or even with profit, for example, gas service, water supply etc.

The above classification has, however, not been accepted by economists because it is overlapping and not clear cut. There may be considerable doubt regarding a group in which a particular item is to be placed.

Adam Smith's Classification

Adam Smith's classification is based on the functions of the government. He classifies public expenditure as follows:

(1) *Productive Functions:* These include expenditure on items like defence, police, courts etc.

(2) *Commercial Functions:* These include expenditure on items which help commerce like bounties, subsidies, expenditure on industrial exhibition etc.

(3) *Development Functions:* Expenditure which helps in the increase of the national income and general welfare of the country is included in this group, for example, expenditure on infrastructure, education, public recreation etc.

It has been pointed out that this classification is also not satisfactory because it is difficult to fit in various kinds of expenditure under these heads. For example, expenditure that helps commerce will also help development. Similarly expenditure on production also promotes development. Like the previous classification, this classification also suffers from the defect of overlapping.

Mill's Classification

According to J.S. Mill public expenditure is of two types: optional and obligatory. Mill holds that optional expenditure is one which is incurred on performing those functions which are not necessary and which is a subject of difference of opinion, while obligatory expenditure is one "in respect of which owing to past contracts and other legal commitments" the state has no option but to incur the expenditure.

But this classification is also not satisfactory because over the years the expenditure which once was considered as optional has now become necessary for the state; for example, expenditure on education, public health, social security etc. Moreover, it is not correct to assume that state can also incur superfluous expenditure.

Roscher's Classification

According to Roscher public expenditure can be classified as necessary, useful and superfluous. Necessary expenditure is one which in any case state has to incur and it cannot afford to postpone it. Useful expenditure is desirable and can be postponed. Superfluous expenditure is one which the state may or may not incur.

This classification also does not solve the fundamental problem. It is based on a pre-conceived notion of the merits and demerits of particular expenditure but the merits and demerits of any public expenditure change with the change in the circumstances and economic conditions. Moreover the state cannot afford to incur superfluous expenditure. Obviously, this classification also suffers from the defects from which earlier classifications suffer.

Findlay Shirras' Classification

Shirras has classified public expenditure into: (*a*) primary expenditure and (*b*) secondary expenditure[2]. According to him primary expenditure covers all those expenditures which governments are obliged to undertake. It is obligatory on the part of the government to incur such expenditure as on defence, law and order etc. Secondary expenditure includes social expenditure, like education, public health, poor relief, unemployment insurance and expenditure on other similar social services. It also includes expenditure on public undertakings like commercial and industrial enterprises such as railways, irrigation, public works, post and telegraphs and subsidies for industrial and agricultural research. Miscellaneous expenditure like pension charges has also been included under this head.

This classification appears to be rather vague since the terms primary and secondary have no fixed meaning and can change with change in circumstances. What Shirras considered as primary *i.e.*, defence expenditure, according to many economists, is now considered as secondary. Nowadays expenditure on education, public health and infrastructure are considered as primary.

2. F. Shirras, *The Science of Public Finance.* p. 50.

Dalton's Classification

According to Dalton public expenditure is of two types: grants and purchase price. To quote Dalton, "Payments by a public authority to any of its employees by way of salaries and wages, or to contractors whom it employs, are purchase prices. On the other hand, payment of old age social insurance, are grants."[3] If the government by incurring an expenditure gets in return some services or goods then it is a purchase price and when it does not get anything in return it is called grant. Dalton was of the view that these two types of public expenditure may go simultaneously. In the case of a price which is more than what a non-monopolist private buyer would offer, an element of grant is also included alongwith the purchase price. For example, if the salaries or wages paid to public sector employees are higher than the private sector employees then it is a case of a purchase price inclusive of grant.

In practice, however, it is not easy to distinguish between a grant and a purchase price. For example, according to Dalton payment of interest on public debt and pensions are grants, if looked at from the point of view of the present, but it is a purchase price when looked at from the point of view of the past. Dalton does not accept that interest is the price for the use of loan, but prefers to consider it as grant. If we look at from this angle, then most of the public expenditure can be considered as a grant. There is always a time gap between the receipt of commodities or services by the government and the payment of their price. However, when both the activities take place simultaneously then there would be no time lag, but this hardly happens. Similarly, there is a gap between the services rendered by the employees and the payment made by the state for those services. Dalton considers this payment as purchase price and that of interest as grant when there is time lag in both. Since the state goes on getting returns from the loan continuously, it would be more correct to treat interest as purchase price.

Dalton has also distinguished between direct and indirect grant. According to him a grant is direct when the entire benefit goes to the person whom the grant is made and it is indirect when the benefit is passed on in whole or in part from the person to whom the grant is made to some other person. In this sense old age pension is a direct grant whereas a subsidy to a private enterprise is an indirect grant.[4] Here again there is difficulty in knowing precisely how much benefit has accrued to a person, whom the grant is made and how much benefit he has passed on to others. For example, when the old age pension money is spent on the purchase of commodities, the benefit is also passed on to the sellers of the commodities. Similarly the benefit of the subsidy is passed on to the purchasers of the commodities in the form of lower prices.

---

3. H. Dalton, *Public Finance*, p. 146.
4. *Ibid*.

Pigou's Classification

According to Pigou, "Expenditure of money by government authorities may conveniently be separated under two heads, expenditure that purchases current services or productive resources for the use of these authorities and expenditures on existing property rights to private persons."[5] The former type of expenditure includes expenditure on defence forces, civil services, judicial services, educational services etc. whereas the latter includes expenditure on the payment of interest on government loans, pensions, social security payments, subsidies on the production of commodities etc. Pigou has also been changing the nomenclature of the two types of expenditure. In the first edition of his book he calls first type of expenditure as exhausted, in the second as real and in the third as non-transfer expenditure. Likewise, in the third edition of his book he calls the latter type of expenditure as transfer expenditurc. In the social accounting sense transfer expenditure does not generate any income or output while non-transfer expenditure generates output and equivalent money income. Non-transfer expenditure implies the actual consumption of commodities and services which would have otherwise been used for some other purpose. Transfer expenditure, on the other hand, implies a mere transfer from the state to others—who get a command over commodities and services. This classification has been considered more or less satisfactory in so far as it is associated with essential characteristics of public expenditure.

Mehta's Classification

According to Professor J.K. Mehta, public expenditure can be divided into two categories *viz*., (*i*) constant expenditure, and (*ii*) variable expenditure. He says, "constant expenditure is that, the amount of which does not depend upon the extent of the use by the people, in whose interest it is incurred, made of the services that are financed by it." And "variable expenditure likewise, is that which increases with every increase in the use of public services by the people for whose benefit it is incurred."[6] Expenditure on defence is the example of the constant expenditure which expenditure is incurred by the state without taking into account the number of people using the services. Constant expenditure cannot be influenced by the people. The variable expenditure varies with the number of people using the services provided by the state. With the growth of population the number of post offices will have to be multiplied, the number of postal clerks and postmen will have to be increased by the government. And, therefore, variable expenditure is influenced by increase in the number of people and volume of the load on the services concerned.

5. A.C. Pigou, *Public Finance*. p. 19.
6. Mehta, J.K., *Public Finance*. p. 51.

However, it is not easy to clearly demarcate between these two types of expenditures in actual practice. Professor Mehta himself recognised this fact. The novelty of Professor Mehta's classification is that it is based on 'cost' and not on 'benefit' approach. In his opinion public expenditure from the angle of the government is the cost just as the public revenue is income and therefore like all costs it must lend itself to the division between prime and supplementary cost. Constant expenditure is like prime cost.

Productive and Unproductive Expenditure

Productive expenditure is that expenditure which leads to the creation of income yielding tangible assets of the government. The more the government is able to create tangible assets the more it would be helping the economy to produce more income in future. Public expenditure incurred on setting up enterprises of commercial type is included in this category. It would be a source of profit to the public bodies depending of course on the pricing policies and other factors. Such public expenditure may be self-liquidating either partly or fully. It implies that the government might be able to recover the public expenditure from the beneficiaries of the projects. Unproductive expenditure is one which is consumed in the process of rendering the service. For example, expenditure on administration, defence, justice, law and order are unproductive because these expenditures do not directly add to the productive capacity of the economy.

The above views are, no doubt, deficient in their realistic contents. The productivity of the economy does not only depend upon the addition of tangible assets by the government. It is also increased by the productiveness of the private sector. And since the government sector is an integral part of the economy, the position has to be viewed in totality. Besides, there would be many assets which are not income yielding but which are necessary for maintaining productive efficiency of the economy like maintenance of parks, water works etc. These assets according to the income yielding concept cannot be viewed as productive. But they are necessary for maintaining and even increasing the productivity of the economy and therefore expenditure on the creation of such assets should be viewed as productive expenditure. These expenditures are self-liquidating in an indirect manner because they definitely augment the national product and the authorities will be able to collect more revenue even without raising the tax rates.

Again, it is not necessary that the productive assets may be only in some tangible form such as building, machinery etc. The productive power of the society can also be in the form of human wealth. If education, training, health, better living conditions etc. make the people of a country capable to produce more or increase their productive power, the expenditure on such items should be considered as productive, although they do not make any direct addition to the productive effort and national income. It is a different thing that some of these expenditures may be useless. For example, expenditure on education and training of some people may not help in raising the productive power of the economy if those people leave the country and serve in another country. But this can also happen with some of the tangible assets.

Certain public expenditures are such that no economy can maintain its productivity without them. Such expenditures indirectly help the economy in raising the level of productivity. Defence expenditure, expenditure on research are examples of such expenditures. Likewise, certain expenditures indirectly add to the health and efficiency of the economy like efficient administration, postal and telecommunication services. Hence an exact distinction between productive and unproductive public expenditures is not easy to makc, and therefore each case is to be judged on merits.

Factual Position—Economic Classification

Classification of public expenditure given by various economic writers and thinkers, as discussed above, are only important from the theoretical point of view. In practice, we find altogether a different classification of public expenditure. Most countries of the world have adopted economic classification, according to which income and expenditure of public bodies is divided into two classes *i.e.*, (*i*) Revenue Account, and (*ii*) Capital Account. Economic classification is the scheme in which "classification of government expenditure and receipts by economic categories that are of significance for analysing the short-run effects of government transactions in the working of the economy"[7] are classified. The Government of India also adopted this classification in its budget for the year 1957-58. The budget is divided now into: (*i*) Revenue Budget, and (*ii*) Capital Budget. It means that the income and expenditure of the Government of India are divided into two groups: (*i*) income and expenditure on revenue account and (*ii*) income and expenditure on capital account.

Revenue expenditure of the Government of India includes all current expenditure on administration including defence and public undertaking such as railways, posts and telegraph and grant-in-aid to the States. It simply means that this expenditure does not lead to the creation of assets. Capital expenditure includes all capital transactions including the defence, capital transactions of public undertakings these transactions consist of capital expenditure on the acquisition of assets like land, building, machinery, equipment etc., investment

7. *A Manual for Economic and Functional Classification of Government Transactions*, 1958 UN, p.3.

in shares, and loans and advances granted by the Government of India to the State governments and union territory governments, government undertakings, corporations and other parties. Capital expenditure also incorporates transactions in Public Account.

Functional Classification

Functional classification provides a description of revenue and capital disbursements under different heads of expenditure. It is a more detailed break down of revenue and capital expenditure. In other words, it is a more detailed analysis of economic classification. Functional classification is a scheme "for classifying the purposes for which expenditure is incurred from the point of view of those concerned with showing that public money is spent to the best advantage." It provides purpose-wise information about government expenditure irrespective of the organization incurring that expenditure. This is achieved by clubbing programmes and activities of organizations according to the basic services provided, each of which is important from the point of view of the duties and responsibilities of the government as a whole. Hence, a functional classification aggregates budget data to indicate the share of public expenditure on each public service. Thus, a functional classification is very useful from the point of view of formulation, evaluation and implementation of broad policies. Many developing countries of the world have introduced this system.

Plan and Non-plan Expenditure

The Government of India has adopted this classification. Plan expenditure refers to the current development outlays as well as investment outlays while non-plan expenditure refers to the expenditure which the government is bound to do and cannot do without it. It includes all those expenditures of the government, which are not included in the plan. It includes both developmental and non-developmental expenditure. Part of this expenditure is obligatory in nature and part of it is essential in nature. For example interest payment, pensionary charges and statutory transfers to the States are expenditures of obligatory nature, while expenditure on defence and internal security are expenditures of an essential nature. Expenditure incurred on the maintenance of the assets created during previous plans is included under non-plan expenditure in the next plan. For example, plan expenditure on educational and health facilities incurred from the First Five-year Plan to the Tenth Five-year Plan would be a non-plan expenditure in the Eleventh Five-year Plan. And, therefore, as more plans are completed a large amount of expenditure on the operation and maintenance of facilities and services created in earlier plan periods will be added to the non-plan expenditure of the future plans.

Exercises

1. State and explain the Wagner's Law of increasing State Activities with suitable examples.
2. Discuss the causes for the increase in government expenditure during the last century.
3. Distinguish between public and private expenditure.
4. Discuss the various classifications of public expenditure. Which one of these is important from the practical point of view?

●●●

Chapter 30

Objectives and Principles of Public Expenditure

1. Objectives of Public Expenditure

Traditional economists considered public expenditure as subsidiary and complementary to private expenditure. The private expenditure either on consumption or on investment was considered to be defined by the price mechanism. This concept of complementarity of public expenditure to the market-determined allocation has been the most significant constituent of the writings of the economists right from the times of Adam Smith down to Keynes. It was only after the Second World War that economists assigned an independent role to public expenditure for shaping the national economy. During the war years most of the Governments in the world had developed the habit of spending and, therefore, public spending had to come to stay as a normal feature. There also developed a growing realisation of the importance of public investment for the development of less developed countries through a well thought out plan of public expenditure. The success achieved by Soviet Russia in the field of planned economic development and the hardships experienced during the Great Depression, also made people to realise the importance of public investment expenditures. Finally, the 'Keynesian Revolution' revolutionised the entire thinking on the subject.

Broadly speaking, there are four objectives of public expenditure, *viz.*, (*i*) allocation of resources; (*ii*) distribution of income; (*iii*) stabilisation of the price level, income and employment and the balance of payments; and (*iv*) economic growth and development. We briefly describe these objectives in the following paragraphs.

(1) Allocation of Resources

(*a*) **Current Consumption *vs.* Current Investment.** The resource allocation can be undertaken either for the distribution of current consumption or for the distribution of investment or for the fulfilment of collective wants. It has universally been recognised that a high level of current consumption is always better than a low level especially when we consider current consumption independent of other goals of public expenditure. This is particularly true of advanced and mature economies. For less developed countries it may be useful to keep the level of current consumption down to obtain savings for stepping up investment, at least in the initial stages of economic development. In so far as public investment is concerned it affects other fields of public policy such as employment, stability and growth. Public investment may be undertaken either to secure or to maintain full employment or for securing the highest rate of economic growth. Investment, if undertaken for the purposes of growth, might come into conflict with the objective of maximising current consumption. So, should not the question of balancing current consumption and future consumption be left to individuals independently, with the help of market mechanism? But, an optimum solution may not be possible because the market mechanism has so far failed to induce the individuals to save to the extent desired in terms of the welfare of society.

(*b*) **Fulfilment of Collective Wants.** The supply of goods and services for satisfying collective wants is another area in which the allocation through public expenditure is necessary. These goods and services are such that they cannot be provided through the market. They are indivisible and cannot be supplied on the basis of "exclusion principle". These goods are consumed equally by every member of the community. According to Professor Musgrave there is still another category of collective wants, *viz.*, *merit wants* which fall in between collective wants and private wants, "where the exclusion principle can be applied to part of the benefits gained but not all." Public expenditure on free education, free health services, navigation aids and public parks, free distribution of milk in schools, etc. fall in this category. Such services not only benefit the individual recipients but the community as a whole; in some cases the benefit to an individual is much more than what one actually realises. These are often relatively of greater importance to those having low incomes than those with larger incomes. The external effects of these services are so complex that no individual on his own initiative can do anything about them and, therefore, it is the government which has to provide the general framework within which the decisions and actions of individual members of the community are made to produce the desired results.

The government has also to take recourse to spending when in a particular area productive efficiency cannot be ensured; in other words when the market is handicapped of private goods and services at competitive rates and in optimum quantity. This is particularly true of industries with high fixed cost and technical over-capacity and where the tendency to cut throat competition and hence to monopoly is exceptionally strong. It is not in the interest of the individual producer to expand its output to the point of social optimum, *i.e.*, to expand its production to the level where marginal cost will be equal to the price. This theory has been developed over the years by a number of economists including Marshall, Pigou and Samuelson.

But, the entire issue of allocation of resources cannot be considered in isolation without relating it to income distribution, *i.e.*, the considerations of efficiency cannot be separated from those of distributional equity. Professor Musgrave believes that such a separation is a better approach and more useful to public finance theory; on the other hand Samuelson believes that both these problems are intermingled and should be treated simultaneously.

(2) Distribution of Income

Distribution of national income and welfare is considered as the most fundamental function of the state these days. Since a democratic government and society is considered to be the best it is the responsibility of the state to preserve individual liberty and promote social welfare through a sufficiently equitable distribution of income and welfare. The maximisation of social welfare is thus necessarily related to an equitable distribution of income and wealth. The traditional theory of welfare economics which was based on the Benthamite principle of utilitarianism regarded social welfare as the sum total of the utilities of all the members of the society. Since utility could not be measured, the Pareto School dispensed with this concept and replaced it with the concept of maximisation of welfare.

The question of maximising social welfare through an equitable distribution of income has been thoroughly investigated among others by Lange and Lerner and Amartya Sen, who have demonstrated that the social welfare can be maximized through equal distribution of income only under certain assumptions.

Despite these writings, the science of economics has not been able to offer an acceptable or operational solution to the problem of optimal distribution of welfare. Probably, because the "social issues continue to be discussed in serene indifference to the categories of time and place."

Taxes and Subsidies. Progressive income-taxes and the inheritance taxes, coupled with the corporation taxes are considered to be powerful instruments for redistribution of income. But, even after such high taxes the rich people are left with sufficient income to maintain their accustomed high standards of consumption and, therefore, there is no redistribution of income from this taxation in the sense of it permitting the poor to live better. However, since the rich people would not be able to save and invest to the extent they were doing earlier the government will have to spend and invest more to make up the deficiency. In case the objective is to achieve a just distribution of welfare between individuals without adversely affecting the balance between work and leisure and the time pattern of consumption, then, this can be achieved through the system of lumpsum taxes and subsidies. A lumpsum tax is preferred to a progressive income-tax because it does not upset the optimum balance between work and leisure and the optimum time pattern for consumption. Similarly, subsidies help to redistribute income in a more equitable manner (some lines for production might be subsidised by the state to raise the income of a particular section of the community, or the state might itself undertake the construction and operation of certain industries to get the same objective.)

According to Buchanan, a fiscal system is redistributive if the individuals in the higher income brackets are made to bear a 'net tax' and those in the lower income brackets are provided with a 'net benefit'. The 'net tax' or the 'net benefit' is arrived at by estimating for the individual, in cost values, his share of total taxes and total benefits from government, expenditure. After subtracting the cost value of expenditure benefits for the individual, from the cost value of his share of taxes, if the balance is positive, the individual bears a 'net tax'; if it is negative then he enjoys a 'net benefit'; if it is zero the system is neutral in regard to its distributional effects. Both the measures of fiscal policy, *viz.*, taxation policy and public expenditure policy are to be used simultaneously for bringing about an effective redistribution of income in a more equitable manner. Such an integration of the two policies is all the more necessary for a developing economy, since it has a built-in tendency to totally unbalance the existing state of income distribution, particularly, in the initial stages when money incomes rise faster than the output. In such a situation the government will have to exercise its taxing and expenditure powers more effectively. Tax rate on increment of income will have to be higher than the average rate. The most appropriate tax would be one which would mop up the increment in income, *i.e.*, a progressive personal income-tax. This may have to be supplemented with appropriate types of public expenditure to increase the income of the lower groups.

(3) Stabilisation

The third objective of public expenditure policy can be stabilisation. The object of a policy of stabilisation can be to stabilize the level of employ-ment or income or price level or balance of payments or all of these. A government can influence economic stability either through its monetary policy or fiscal policy or by both. As stated already monetary policy directly affects the supply of money whereas fiscal policy affects the volume of total public expenditure and total tax collections. We shall concern ourselves here with public expenditure only. In a closed mature economy with a constant price level, it is easy to ensure suitable level of income with a view to achieving a desired level of employment through investment. If the level of investment is sufficiently responsive to changes in the rate of interest and if the demand curve for money does not become horizontal at any range of its length, monetary policy could be relied upon to bring about the desired changes in the level of income and employment through 'multiplier effects'. In case the monetary policy somehow does not prove to be effective the government can make use of its fiscal policy. It is in such a situation that the theory of functional finance becomes important. The aggregate expenditure in a closed economy is the total of consumption expenditure, investment expenditure and government expenditure. The aggregate production to match this total demand should exactly utilise the available productive capacity. In such a situation the aggregate demand would be equal to aggregate supply; there will neither be inflation nor deflation; and the aggregate money income will be at optimum level. But, this equilibrium situation does not arise owing to the automaticity of the economic system. It has to be consciously achieved, and it is here that the government steps in. The government uses the tools of taxation and expenditure and manipulates them in such a way that the aggregate expenditure reaches the optimum level. This manipulation falls in the domain of functional finance.

Stabilisation of the price level is another important objective of public expenditure. A rising price level is not in itself in any way detrimental provided that it does not: (*i*) create balance of payments problem; (*ii*) disturb calculations for the future adversely affecting the programme of economic growth; and (*iii*) does not transfer wealth from persons with net monetary claims to those with net debts. It is to avoid these problems that public expenditure policies aim at stabilising the price level.

In developing economies, any policy of economic growth, it is generally believed, leads to inflation because the savings are inadequate and the government in order to push up the level of investment, has to resort to inflationary credit. The low savings are firstly due to the defective social structure and secondly due to the typical structure of production and imports. These defects of the structure of the economy tend to generate further imbalances which help the prices to rise further. In addition to these, a policy of increasing taxes and duties in order to divert surplus import demand into domestic market and to affect mass consumption commodities also contributes to inflation. In short, inflation is caused chiefly by a credit expansion policy in a structurally defective economy in the process of economic growth. The object of public expenditure policy should, therefore, be to prevent increase in the price level and hence to keep the rate of inflation consistent with the rate of development. While economists like H.G. Johnson hold that inflation promotes growth and those like Dorrance believe that it is a positive hindrance to growth. Dudley Seers holds that price level stability is neither helpful nor detrimental to the process of growth of an economy and this dynamic process will release many de-stabilisation forces in an economy, one of which is the de-stabilisation of prices. When public expenditure aims chiefly at development, its power to stabilise prices may have to give way to its ability to promote development if they come into clash.

A situation of disequilibrium in the balance of payments can be corrected by the mature economies through an appropriate combination of both the monetary and fiscal policies. In the case of balance of payments deficits, an expansionary programme financed through public expenditure but not accompanied by money supply increases would tend to increase interest rates. This will attract an inflow of foreign capital. If the programme of expansion is undertaken through public expenditure, it will adversely affect the balance of payments position on current accounts owing to the increased demands for imports resulting from increased income but this adverse effect may be mitigated through a policy of monetary contraction. So, a combination of monetary contraction and an expansionary programme financed through public expenditure or other fiscal measures would be helpful in improving the balance of payments position on capital accounts, and would, at the same time, prevent its deterioration on current account by adversely affecting the propensity to import. In the less developed countries an adverse balance of payments has become a normal feature chiefly because of the existence of a persistent excess demand and that of an over-valued exchange rate of the domestic currency. This problem could be solved by reducing the level of domestic prices in relation to world prices. This would induce the necessary shift of resources from the production of commodities for the domestic market to those for export market. But, owing to certain inherent socio-political factors in such economies such a drastic income redistribution and relative price adjustments would not be possible. Therefore, alternative solutions have been found in measures like import quotas, import substitutes, exchange control, etc. The fiscal policy may resort to subsidisation of exports and penalisation of imports. Production of import substitutes can also be encouraged. Since these fiscal measures would impose costs on the economy, it is essential to ensure that the results achieved are in consistence with the objectives proposed to be achieved.

(4) Economic Development

Economic development is another important objective for the fulfilment of which public spending is considered very necessary. The prevalent theories of economic growth, however, are not of much help in explaining the relationship between the two. Most of these theories developed from the Keynesian theory treat public expenditure as something external to their system of logic. However, all these theories emphasise that savings are crucial for furthering the process of economic development in its early stages. The neo-classical growth models, which are relevant for advanced economies, which seem to under-rate the significance of the role of saving and investment emphasise the role of technical innovations, improved quality of labour, changes in the organisational and managerial techniques, etc. It can, however, be inferred that in the ultimate analysis they do recognise the contribution made by saving and investment in determining the rate of development. Although the term investment does not generally include expenditure on education, training, health services, etc. which directly lead to the improvement of the human capital, such expenditures are no doubt significant, since they mean the sacrifice of present consumption. From this point of view expenditure on education and health is an act of investment in human capital and is meant for increasing the growth of the economy. The contribution that education makes to the annual output of an economy is reflected in the fact that the per capita income tends to increase with the level of education. True, that differences in money income distribution in any society cannot be entirely attributed to education and differences in inherent abilities and inherited economic and social advantages are also responsible for the difference in the money incomes earned. But, the role of education cannot be minimized. Similarly, improved health of the population through an increase in life expectancy and a corresponding decrease in death rate, has facilitated an increase in the size of the labour force as well as an improvement in the efficiency of the labour force which ultimately lead to increased national output. Investment in knowledge, *i.e.*, in research and development necessary for technological improvements is considered to be a major factor responsible for the growth of mature economies. Thus, whatever the theoretical model of growth may be it is on saving and investment that the development of an economy depends. This is more true of the less developed and over-populated countries. Earlier, we have described the factors that hinder the realisation of an optimal level and rate of saving and investment if the choice is left to be determined by the market mechanism. And we had concluded that if the desired rate of economic development was to be achieved, it is imperative for the government to intervene. Besides these technical considerations there are other factors also which necessitate the state to undertake investment through public expenditure. For example, Nurkse recommends that Schumpeter's theory of economic development may be used as a mould for the purpose of intensifying the process of more balanced growth of less developed countries. Thus, in the context of development of the less developed countries it is necessary for the state to assume the major responsibility for investment designed for development.

Before we conclude this section a word may be added about the role of export earnings in the process of economic development. The rate of economic development is to a large extent determined by the rate of growth of a country's exports in relation to its imports. The higher the value of exports of the country, the faster would be its rate of development. Fiscal policy should, therefore, aim at promoting exports and discouraging imports. The fiscal policy will have to aim at stability as well as growth. Special fiscal measures will have to be adopted for promoting exports and producing commodities that are likely to influence significantly development efforts. Excise duties may be levied on domestic consumption of exportable commodities, and expenditure measures will have to be taken such as direct subsidies on export sales, to promote exports. Rebates on income-tax linked to export performance is another measure which would help in promoting exports.

All said and done, it is necessary far accelerating the rate of economic development that the volume of savings available for investment must be increased. Domestic savings can be increased by curtailing consumption. It may be necessary, therefore, to control consumption through budgetary and other measures. Consumption can also be restricted by regulating prices, wages and profits, through taxes and export subsidies.

2. Principles of Public Expenditure

The principle of public finance, which we have discussed earlier, actually governs all aspects of fiscal activity, in a country. The principle of maximisation of social benefit is central to public finance but, it is more relevant to public expenditure because expenditure incurred by public bodies is of greater consequence than taxation. In the wards of Dalton, "Public expenditure in every direction must be carried just so far that the advantage to the community of a further small increase in any direction is just balanced by the disadvantage of a corresponding small increase in taxation and in receipts from any other source of public income. This gives the ideal of both of public expenditure and of public income." Similarly Pigou states this principle like this: "Expenditure should be pushed in all directions up to the point, at which satisfaction obtained from the last shilling expended is equal to the satisfaction lost in respect of the last shilling called up on government service."

According to this principle therefore, all benefits accruing to all or certain sections of the community and of sacrifices involved in financing the public expenditure must be equal or the former should be more than the latter so that the satisfaction received by the community should be the highest. This principle implies that the government should spend its limited income in such a way that the marginal social benefit is the same at all times. It is similar to and based on the principle of equi-marginal utility which is the guiding principle in the case of individual expenditure. The only difference between the two principles is that the sources of income in the case of individuals and the government are different. Since the government draws its income from the people which entails some sacrifice for the community as a whole, it should be more careful in spending that income.

This principle further implies that the entire community should derive benefit from the expenditure incurred by the government and the benefit should not accrue to any particular section or group of the community. Far ensuring this Dalton and Mrs. Hicks have suggested certain tests, which we have described earlier. Generally speaking, this is the best principle and has no substitute. But it has its awn limitations which we have already talked about. But, despite these limitations, it is necessary that the public authorities should be prudent about their expenditure.

According to Professor Pigou, the second principle of public expenditure is that: "expenditure should be distributed between battleship and poor relief in such-wise that the last shilling divided to each yields the same return of satisfaction." It means that the public bodies should distribute their resources on different heads in a manner which obtains the same marginal utility from each head. It is not easy to measure the marginal utilities or marginal social benefits obtained from each head as we have already explained earlier. Moreover it is well nigh impossible far any government to equalize marginal social benefit of the last penny to that of marginal sacrifice imposed by the last penny on the tax payer. There are different departments in the government for administering taxes and public expenditure and therefore a comparison between them is very difficult. Moreover, marginal benefits and marginal sacrifice are also influenced by various political and social factors and therefore a comparison is not possible. We may, therefore, conclude that the two principles enunciated by Professor Pigou are only ideals, in practice it is very difficult to follow them.

3. Canons of Public Expenditure

Besides the fundamental principle of maximum social benefit, Findlay Shirras has formulated other canons of public expenditure. These canons are:

1. Canon of Economy. This implies that the public expenditure should be governed by the principle of economy, *i.e.*, it should not be wasteful; it should be productive and efficient. In other words public expenditure must be incurred prudently, only on very essential items of common benefit. In most of the developing countries, lack of adequate planning or sense of responsibility among bureaucrats and inadequate financial control lead to wasteful and extravagant expenditure of many government departments. That is why a number of countries have now introduced a system of financial administration. In India, for example, there are the Public Accounts Committee and the Estimates Committee at the Centre and the Ministry of Finance maintains persistent control over departmental expenditure. In addition, Economy Committees are also appointed from time to time to suggest measures for exercising economy in government expenditure. A word may, however, be added here regarding the concept of economy. Gladstone and many of his generation did not appreciate the advantages of public expenditure on such items as old age pensions, sickness benefits, unemployment benefits, etc. So, economy does not mean parsimony; but every expenditure incurred by the government is not necessarily praiseworthy. The government should not pay for commodities more than private individuals. In fact, it should pay less for it buys in bulk, and its payments are certain. But, we find that in a number of cases the government pays more for buying commodities than what is paid by private individuals.

2. Canon of Sanction. According to this canon, no expenditure should be incurred without the prior approval of the appropriate authority. This aims at preventing the misuse of public funds. As a rule, money must be spent for the purpose for which it is sanctioned by the superior authority. This principle also aims at preventing the possibility of reckless spending. That is why, in almost all countries there is a system of auditing of accounts at the end of the financial year. In democratic governments, there is an elaborate system of sanction, checks and controls and auditing. In India, for example, the government first obtains the sanction of the Parliament before it can secure and spend any money; within the government, each department has to obtain the sanction of the Ministry of Finance for any expenditure; within each department each section has to obtain the sanction of the head of the department, and so on. Although all this procedure involves waste of time, and red-tape, this is the price that the government has to pay for preventing misuse of public funds.

3. Canon of Surplus. This principle refers to the avoidance of deficits in government finance. In other words, the government should live within its means and should not spend more than its income. Literally, this principle implies that the public bodies should aim at surplus budgets, like every prudent individual. It also implies that the routine expenditure of the state should invariably be met from current revenues and not from borrowings. It also implies that the government should avoid continuous deficit budgets in order to maintain its own creditworthiness. Modern economists are particularly against this principle, *i.e.*, they are against balanced budgets. They hold that to meet the rigours of depression deficit budgets are essential and to mitigate the pressure of inflation budget surpluses are indispensable. Balanced budgets may be adopted only when there is full employment and the price level is stable. It may also be mentioned that for developing countries deficit budgets are a common phenomenon since deficit financing is considered as an important means of capital formation and of expanding the public sector.

4. Canon of Benefit. This principle is based on the ideal of maximum social advantage, *i.e.*, public expenditure should be planned in such a way that it may yield maximum social advantage and social welfare of the entire community and not of any particular group or section of society. Therefore, public expenditure should result in increased production, preservation of the community against external aggression and internal disorders and minimization of inequalities in the distribution of incomes. It is only then that public expenditure would be most conducive to the public interest and it can be possible only when the public bodies equalize the marginal utility of each use. To summarize, we can say that the public bodies should allocate resources with a view to: (*i*) increasing the total production in the economy, (*ii*) maintaining sufficient army and police forces for serving the community against external aggression and internal disorders, (*iii*) reducing inequalities in the incomes of its subject, and (*iv*) maximising the welfare of the community. In short, it implies the greatest good of the greatest number.

5. Canon of Elasticity. According to this canon the policy relating to public expenditure should contain an element of flexibility so that it may be moulded according to circumstances. In other words, the govern-ment should be able to extend or contract its policy in the domain of public expenditure according to the requirements of the situation. In emergencies like war, floods, earthquakes etc. the state should be able to switch on its expenditure to meet the exigencies arising out of these abnormal situations *i.e.*, the state should be in a position to divert its resources from one head to another without dislocating the economic life of the country.

6. Canon of Productivity. This canon implies that public spending should aim at improving the productive capacity of the economy. In other words public spending must be undertaken more and more for develop-mental purposes. It means that public expenditure should be directed to raise the levels of employment, output and income. This is very much true for underdeveloped countries but unfortunately in developing countries the state, on the other hand, is required to spend a major portion of its revenue on increasing the output of social and public services and on providing general amenities to the general public.

7. Canon of Neutrality. The canon of neutrality implies that public expenditure should be neutral in so far as the bad effects are concerned. It should aim at increasing production, improving the distribution of income, raising the level of aggregate consumption and not at producing adverse effects on these economic parameters.

8. Canon of Equitable Distribution. According to this canon public expenditure should be incurred in such a way that the inequalities in the distribution of incomes are minimized. In other words, public expenditure should be incurred in the direction of securing, as far as possible, equitable distribution of income among different sections of the society. This may be achieved by conferring more benefits on the poorer sections of the society by way of medical facilities, educational facilities, housing facilities, old age pensions etc. This is more important for developing countries like ours. That is why in these countries education and employment benefits are being provided to economically and socially backward sections of the society on a priority basis. Likewise several institutions have been established for the benefit of some particular sections of the community. Take the case of India. We have so many organisations for the benefit of scheduled castes, scheduled tribes and other weaker sections of the society. This sort of expenditure certainly leads to reduce inequalities in the distribution of incomes.

These canons are good in their place but the fact remains that the principle of maximum social benefit is fundamental to all public finance activities; other canons are simply administrative rules and guidelines.

Buehler's Guidelines for Public Expenditure

Professor Buehler has laid down certain guidelines to be followed by public bodies while incurring public expenditure. According to him, the theory of expenditure is not so highly advanced as the theory of taxation, "but there are certain obvious, yet fundamental principles which may serve as a guide to legislators and the public until more adequate standards have been "'devised." Therefore, Buehler has suggested the following guidelines:

(1) The primary aim of public expenditure should be to promote social welfare. He adds that even if the public expenditure is incurred in such a fashion" that it primarily promotes the welfare of a particular section of society, it will be good because ultimately it will help in adding to the total welfare of the society. But for the welfare of a particular section or group the total welfare of the society should not be jeopardized. The social welfare is infinite and above all individual or group interest.

(2) The benefits accruing from public expenditure on each public service or good should be more than the cost of providing that good or service. It implies that the government should be able to utilise funds in such a way that the expenditure is more conducive to social welfare than the funds, when utilised by private economic units.

(3) High priority should be given to those items of expenditure which result in the promotion of maximum social welfare while low priority should be given to those heads of expenditure which lead to the promotion of least

social welfare. It is necessary for making a comparison between the gains and cost of public services.

Exercises

1. Enumerate the various objectives of public expenditure and discuss their relative importance.
2. Discuss the canons of public expenditure as given by Findlay Shirras.

●●●

Chapter 31

Effects of Public Expenditure

In the previous chapter, we have analysed the causes responsible for the phenomenal growth of public expenditure in the last two centuries all over the world. We have seen that a number of developments on the economic, social and political fronts have led to the present situation. However, the most important factor has been the total change in the thinking of the political administrators and academicians regarding the role of the state in a nation's life. The *laissez-faire* philosophers believed in the policy of least interference by the state in the free operation of market forces. Since private economic units always work in their own interest the government would not do better and therefore the only sphere of activity for the government was the preservation of the society and undertaking those activities which do not generate any profit. That is why the state's legitimate sphere of activities was limited to defence, law and order, justice, administration and social overheads.

However, the failure of market mechanism to achieve the desired results led to the increasing intervention of the state in an individual's life. Consequently, the government sector rapidly grew and public expenditure increased by leaps and bounds. Not only that, it also gave rise to a number of analytical hypotheses concerning the utility or otherwise of public expenditure. The approaches adopted by various economists were so fundamentally different from each other that it is difficult to find a general agreement regarding the way in which public expenditure should be used and the way in which it would affect the working of an economy. Some authors were of the view that public expenditure is a powerful tool for bringing about stability in the economy; others were sceptical about the utility of public expenditure; they considered it as redundant and superfluous and a burden on the economy. Some others regarded public expenditure as an instrument for establishing an egalitarian society.

However, the fact to be accepted is that the public sector is the major player in the game of bringing about changes in the economy. Like other sectors it is also connected with the rest of the economy, with one usual difference, of course, and that is that while the private sector is guided by the market forces, the government sector is not. It can be used by the public bodies for bringing about desired changes in the economy. It can also work as a means of giving directions for the functioning of the economy. It is this position of the government sector that makes one to analyse the possible effects of public expenditure on the economy.

We now study the effects of public expenditure.

1. Public Expenditure and Level of Employment and Production

According to Professor Dalton the level of production and employment in any country depends on: (*i*) ability of the people to work, save and invest; (*ii*) willingness to work, save and invest; (*iii*) the diversion of economic resources between different employments and regions. In his words: "Just as taxation, other things being equal, should reduce production as little as possible so the public expenditure should increase it as much as possible." To have a correct view of the effects of public expenditure on production, Dalton has analysed the effects of public expenditure on the factors as enumerated above. We now explain Dalton's analysis in some detail.

(1) Ability to Work, Save and Invest

Public expenditure can influence all these factors either adversely or favourably. If public expenditure increases the efficiency of a person to work, it will certainly promote production and national income. As already stated, expenditure on education, health services, cheap housing facilities, etc. increases the efficiency of persons to work. When a person's efficiency to work increases, his or her earnings increase and consequently his or her ability to save also improves. Public expenditure can also increase the domestic savings by providing additional income to the people. As a matter of fact, salaries and wages paid out to the government servants, pensions and allowances, unemployment and sickness benefits, all tend to raise the purchasing power of the recipients, their consumption increases, their standard of living goes up, their efficiency improves and consequently their ability to work increases. People with larger incomes can be normally expected to save larger amounts. Lastly, public expenditure in the form of repayment of public debts, places additional funds at the disposal of those who can invest. Thus, public expenditure can promote ability to work, save and invest.

On the contrary, if a public expenditure is largely incurred on social functions or on the production of harmful drugs and intoxicants which impair the health and efficiency of the people and their production is subsidized then it will be a sheer waste. It will produce an adverse effect on the ability of the people to work, save and invest. Likewise if the government spends a lot on the construction of Film Studios, Cinema Houses, Hotels etc. and neglects the maintenance of roads and other means of communications or does not invest on education particularly technical education and production of useful and life saving drugs, then the ability of the people to work, save and invest will be adversely affected. In sum, public expenditure should be judiciously incurred so as to bestow the maximum benefits to the community as a whole.

(2) Willingness to Work, Save and Invest

Public expenditure also affects the willingness of the people to work, save and invest. Pensions, interests on loans, provident fund and other governments payments provide security to the people which ultimately reduce their willingness to work and save. Similarly, the likelihood of unconditional fixed grants in the future like war pensions and interest on war loans may also adversely affect the people's will to work and save. However, if these benefits are conditional and judiciously administered, the adverse effects can be minimized. For example, transfer expenditure like unemployment and sickness benefits related to past earnings may not diminish the willingness to work and save because these benefits are conditional. Moreover, such benefits may also encourage them to work harder. Similarly, the expenditure policy of the government also influences people's decisions regarding their future savings and investment. If the people do not expect their incomes to rise in future, their desire to work is adversely affected. If they are sure that their present savings and investment will not bring in substantial income, they are likely to be discouraged to save more. The inflationary trend generated by unproductive and wasteful public expenditure certainly kills people's incentive to save more while a prudent public expenditure which promotes capital formation encourages people to save and invest more.

Sometimes it is argued that public expenditure on social security schemes reduces willingness of people to work, save and invest. But this is not correct. In fact these are measures which are socially desirable and the truth is that social security methods would lead to good results. Even then such public expenditures should be incurred to the extent they do not produce an adverse effect on savings and investment. Besides, public expenditure should also extend opportunities for the promotion of further savings and investment.

(3) Diversion of Economic Resources

Diversion of resources between different uses can also be influenced by public expenditure. Expenditure incurred on armaments and maintenance of armed forces has been considered by many economists as wasteful use of resources and, therefore, the diversion of economic resources from the use of general public to government use does not add to economic welfare. But, is the safety and security of people not necessary? If the people are not safe and secure the country cannot flourish economically. And, therefore, defence expenditure, these days is considered to be very essential. Public expenditure generally has a beneficial effect on produc-tion through diversification of resources between different employments and regions. By diversion of resources productive power of the community increases. Expenditure on items like roads, railways, irrigation projects, etc. helps in promoting economic development, by expanding the size of markets and by increasing industrialisation. In the long run, it helps to stimulate private investment. Public expenditure can also lead to the utilisation of unutilized resources of the economy, especially in areas where the private sector does not come forward to invest. Public expenditure on items like education, research, inventions, public health services, social security measures, productive projects like irrigation, afforestation, land reclamation, etc. and debt redemption has far reaching effects on the efficiency, productivity and optimal use of the economic resources of the country. Public expenditure can also bring about a better allocation of resources between the present and the future. In a free enterprise economy, investors are always motivated by immediate gain. The state has to safeguard the interest of the people by making adequate provision for the future. Thus, certain expenditures, *e.g.*, expenditure on multi-purpose projects, urbanization programmes, etc. do not yield immediate benefits certainly confer lot of social and economic benefits in future.

Diversion of resources is also important from the point of view of economic stability. It is possible that the volume of new investment may not always be in proportion to the increase in the volume of savings, this lack of co-incidence can be one of the causes of economic instability. To achieve a balance between saving and investment, government interference is considered necessary. In a situation where savings exceed investment, recession in the economy takes place. In such a situation the government should increase its expenditure even to the extent of keeping it higher than its revenue. So, during a period of depression the government should take recourse to deficit budgeting and undertake several public works programmes which would increase the disposable income of the people leading to an increase in the aggregate effective demand.

The gap in saving and investment in the private sector should be covered up by public spending and investment in the public sector. Thus, public expenditure must aim at overcoming cyclical fluctuations in mature economies.

Special expenditure made by the government in backward areas helps in a balanced regional growth in the country. This sort of diversification of resources between different regions is generally undertaken in a federal state by measures like grants-in-aid so that resources are transferred from more developed to the less developed areas.

Diversion of economic resources through public expenditure between different localities not only increases productive power but also reduces regional imbalance. The government by making special expenditure in backward areas may secure a balanced economic development of the country as a whole. For the development of backward areas, the government can introduce schemes for special loans, subsidies and other facilities to the industries, which are established in these areas.

Moreover, under the programme of planned economic development the government can pay more attention to the backward regions and provide special concessions or facilities for the development of new industries in such regions. For example, the Government of India has promoted the establishment of Industrial Estates in backward areas in order to have balanced growth of all the regions in the country.

Public expenditure in the form of bounties and subsidies helps in the diversion of resources of the people to the establishment of new industries as well as augmenting the protection of existing industries. Similarly public expenditure on social overheads like education and training, public health, social security schemes etc. increases social welfare along with an increase in the efficiency and skill of human beings and therefore makes a direct contribution to the economic growth and development of the economy, more so in developing countries. Hence such diversion of resources from private use to public use should not be regarded as unproductive. As a matter of fact such expenditure is essential to provide external economies to enterprises and to promote and accelerate the rate of private investment in productive activities. In fact Dalton has observed that these forms of expenditure are socially desirable because it will increase more productive power than it would have increased if the funds required were left in private hands.

Diversion of economic resources takes place differently in different economic systems. According to Dalton the role of public expenditure in the diversion of economic resources from private use to government use and as between different regions is important only when the area of economic activities of public bodies is limited *i.e.*, in a capitalistic economy. The importance of such diversion of resources and role of public expenditure goes on depleting as the sphere of state activity enlarges *i.e.*, in a socialistic economy. In such an economy because of the overall control of the government on the means of production, the question of diversion of resources from private use to public use, does not arise. The entire economy is under the direction of a central planning authority to achieve the already determined objectives. In a mixed economy both the private and public sector have equal role to play and public expenditure influencing the diversion of resources is therefore very crucial for the development of the economy as a whole. We may, therefore, conclude with Dalton that "whereas taxation taken alone, may check production, public expenditure, taken alone should almost readily increase it."

2. Public Expenditure and Distribution

Reduction of inequalities in the distribution of income and wealth has been one of the major objectives of modern state policy, especially in socialistic countries and developing countries like India which are developing a socialistic pattern of society, and public expenditure has been used as an important tool for achieving this objective. The effects of public expenditure on distribution of income would depend on the principles on the basis of which such expenditure is undertaken. The government spends its funds either on the purchase of goods and services or for giving grants and subsidies. The purchase of goods and services does not bring about any material change in the existing distribution pattern of the economy since the government has to purchase these goods and services almost at their 'opportunity' costs in the free market. At the most it can bring about a slight alteration in the sense that government spending would increase the level of total spending in the economy and would cause the price level to rise upwards which may cause some changes in the pattern of distribution.

Public expenditure in the form of grants, aids and subsidies, supply of goods and services free or below cost, however, produces a direct effect on the pattern of distribution. How much and in what way the public expenditure would affect the distribution pattern would depend on the nature of the expenditure incurred by the government. There are certain types of public spending which would benefit certain individuals or certain groups of people while there may be expenditures which may benefit the entire society. Any expenditure incurred particularly to benefit the people in the low income strata of society like expenditure on free medical aid, free education, unemployment benefit, etc. will without doubt benefit the poor people more than the rich. Obviously, this expenditure will have to be met from the funds raised by taxing the rich people, and in this way the distribution pattern would be considerably affected. Grants and subsidies are, normally made to benefit the less well-to-do members of the society and, therefore, they reduce the gap between the poor and the rich. The principle governing the distribution of grants is: greater the income of a person, smaller is the marginal utility of gains. The poorer people, therefore, receive a major part of government grants and to that extent the inequalities are reduced. In a capitalist society the distribution of incomes is mainly determined by the ownership of resources. Those who own capital or land or possess specialised skills, obtain a significant rental income on which the pattern of public expenditure does not produce any effect. To have a full view of government's fiscal policy one would have to take into account the effects of taxation in conjunction with the expenditure policy of the government. Where the government adopts the ideal of a welfare state and undertakes social security schemes on a large scale, public expenditure does produce a direct effect on the pattern of distribution. Expenditures incurred with a view to benefiting the society as a whole do not bring about a considerable change in the distribution pattern since all are equally benefited and sometimes the rich are benefited more than the poor. Such expenditures can be on projects like construction of roads, highways, railways, electrification, water supply, defence, police, etc. It cannot be denied that police and courts are more beneficial to the rich who own large property than to the poor.

According to its effects, Dalton[1] classifies public expenditure into: (*i*) regressive; (*ii*) proportional; (*iii*) progressive. Any grant or public expenditure would be regressive in character if the addition it makes to the income of a beneficiary is smaller in the case of people with small income and higher in the case of people with high incomes; for example, interest on public debt or subsidy on private savings are regressive in their effect. In such a situation the income inequalities would increase. The public expenditure would be proportional when the proportion of additional benefit provided by the grant is the same in all cases. In such a case there is no change in the existing inequalities in the distribution of income. Any public expenditure would be progressive when the additional benefit provided by the grant is larger in the case of low income people and lower in the case of high income people; for example, free medical aid, free education, subsidised housing, etc. provided for the poor people is a progressive expenditure. Such an expenditure reduces inequality of incomes and sharper the progression, the stronger will be the tendency to minimise the inequalities in the distribution of income and wealth. Progressive expenditure can be either in the form of cash grants or in the form of free or cheap goods and services. Cash grants can be in the form of old age pensions, unemployment benefits, sickness

1. Dalton, H., *Principles of Public Finance.* pp. 164-167.

benefits, etc. Cash payments made under the Employees State Insurance Act in India is an example of progressive public expenditure. Free or cheap goods and services can take the form of free primary education, freeships to the economically and socially disadvantaged sections of the society in the field of higher education, distribution of free milk and meals to the children of poor sections in schools, etc. Such expenditures benefit the poorer sections of the community and thus reduce the gap between the rich and the poor. They also improve the standard of the masses. Similarly, the provision of public parks, libraries, etc. also benefits the low income people. Public expenditure in the form of food subsidies, subsidised clothing, etc. would also have a greater and socially desirable effect on the pattern of distribution of incomes. Dalton is also of this view but he holds that if the public expenditure could be adjusted to each individual's or family's requirements from time to time, the distribution can be much improved. That is why in most of the countries which have introduced social security schemes, the legislation has been framed after keeping this aim in view. This certainly means that the distribution through benefits of public expenditure will be on the principle of 'ability to receive'.[2]

A wise policy of public expenditure has, therefore, to be designed with a view to maximising the social welfare. In practice, however, it may be difficult to achieve this ideal and there are many instances in which public would not be interested if judged by this principle. The huge expenditure incurred on palatial buildings, hotels, etc. will not be justified when we consider it from the point of view of returns from that investment. Similarly, expenditure on avoidable wars would also be placed in the same category. In fact, public expenditure should be primarily employed to build up the productive capacity of the economy and on keeping the level of employment and production stable, and inequalities in the distribution of income and wealth to the minimum. In planned economies, public expenditure has to sustain the growth of the economy. The truth of the entire discussion lies in the fact that the objective of public expenditure should be to reconcile the twin objectives of better production and better distribution. Which of the two should be given priority would depend upon the circumstances prevailing at the time when the decision is taken. In a situation of gross inequalities of income and wealth the reduction in the inequalities would obviously claim a higher priority and would demand public expenditure to be progressive.

3. Effects of Public Expenditure on Economic Stability

Economic stability means, fairly stable level of income, employment, saving and investment in the economy. An economy may face cyclical fluctuations

2. *Ibid.*, p. 167.

due to the imperfections of free market mechanism. Such imperfections may cause prices, savings, and investment to fall and aggravate inequalities in the distribution of income and wealth. Falling prices bring losses to businessmen and manufacturers and reduce their confidence for further investment. This leads to a curtailment in production and fall in employment. With a large number of workers thrown out of job, the level of current consumption and effective demand declines and production and employment also decline. In such periods of depression the governments should undertake public works projects and engage more people to execute these projects. This will increase the demand for various commodities and services, the production of these commodities and services will increase and further employment will take place. The ball will be set rolling and the level of aggregate effective demand will rise causing a further increase in production and employment. So, in times of depression the role of public expenditure is to increase the level of aggregate demand and thus maintain economic stability. In periods of inflation *i.e.*, rising prices the public expenditure has entirely a different role to play. In such a situation investment is more than savings and so the government should aim at surplus budgets. In other words the government should spend less than its revenue. The surplus funds may be used by the government to provide capital to those sectors of the economy where there is shortage so that the total production capacity of the economy is increased. The production of goods and services in the country will increase which will check a rise in prices. Such projects may include, minor irrigation projects, distribution of better quality seeds, manure etc. in the field of agriculture and provision of greater facilities for the establishment of new industries and expansion of existing industries. This sort of expenditure will produce the desired results only where the allocation of resources has not reached the optimum level *i.e.*, only in under-developed countries. But in those countries where the factors of production are already working at the optimum level, public expenditure would add to inflationary pressure because it would increase the volume of disbursable income of people without a corresponding increase in production. So, in such economies the government should spend less than its revenue and follow a policy of surplus budgets.

4. Effects of Public Expenditure on Economic Development and Growth

Following Mrs. Ursula Hicks, economic development is different from economic growth in the sense that while the term economic development is used in the context of under-developed economies, the term economic growth is used in the context of advanced economies. According to Mrs. Hicks the problem of under-developed countries is primarily that of the utilization of unused resources, whereas the problem of advanced countries is related to the growth of their resources. So, the problem of under-developed countries is that of economic development *i.e.*, increase in the levels of output, income and employment while the problem of developed economies is to maintain economic stability *i.e.*, a gradual and steady increase of income and output.

The major problem of most of the countries today is the problem of growing unemployment and falling incomes. Public expenditure programmes may provide direct help to solve this problem by increasing people's demand for goods and services and by increasing employment opportunities because it is only then the demand for goods and services will increase and production will rise. But this can happen only when the productive resources of the country are not operating at the optimum level. In case the productive capacity of the country is being utilised at the optimum level, the possibilities of increasing production and employment would be less. It is, therefore, necessary that the public expenditure programmes should be designed in such a way that production and demand for products increase simultaneously. It means that the growth and stability should go side by side. In short, public expenditure on the one hand should increase the level of aggregate demand and on the other stimulate and supplement private enterprise.

The private sector may be encouraged to make additional investment and increase production. This can be possible only when public expenditure is incurred in a larger measure on the provision of social and economic overheads like education, medical facilities, development of infrastructural facilities and so on. Public expenditure should focus on the extension of external economies and provision of internal economies of production. Another important area in which public expenditure can play a useful role is to undertake those enterprises which are either not attractive or remunerative to the private sector. This may be because of the long gestation period or low profit margin or huge capital investment, which the private sector may not undertake. The government in such a situation should enter into these enterprises so that the productive capacity of the economy is increased. The objective of such public expenditure is not to compete with the private sector but to act as a friend, philosopher and guide to the private sector. In democratic countries the objective of public expenditure should be to stimulate and supplement private initiative by making available loans on easy terms, grants and subsidies, tax concessions and exemptions and any other information and research facilities. The government can focus its attention on the provision of adequate banking and financial facilities to the private sector. Besides, the government can also undertake other measures which may indirectly stimulate the private initiative. This can be done by incurring expenditure on social and economic overheads, which are so vital and crucial for the economic growth and development. These economic and social overheads include infrastructural facilities, transport and communications, water and power facilities, education and public health etc. For a steady and balanced growth of an economy it is the duty of the government to determine priorities between various development projects. There may be difference of opinion about these priorities but the best course would be as Lewis has said: "In the development programmes, all sectors of the economy should grow simultaneously so as to keep a proper balance between industry and agriculture, and between production for home consumption and production for export."[3]

Exercises

1. Discuss the effects of public expenditure on (*a*) employment, (*b*) production, and (*c*) distribution.
2. Critically examine the role of public expenditure in economic stabilisation.
3. Explain the significance of public expenditure in promoting economic development and growth.

●●●

3. Lewis W.A., *The Theory of Economic Growth,* p. 27.

Chapter 32

Public Expenditure in India

1. Introduction

In an earlier chapter we have discussed in detail the general issues connected with the theory of public expenditure. In this chapter we propose to discuss the various aspects of public expenditure in India. We have already spelt out the causes of the growth of public expenditure all over the world. The same factors with varying degrees have been responsible for an upward increase of public expenditure in our country. The increase has been extraordinary particularly in the post-independence period owing to the expansion of social and economic services, strengthening of administrative services, increased participation of the Government in capital formation, saving and investment and increase in the cost at all levels due to rising prices. In 1950-51 the total expenditure of the Government of India was of the order of Rs. 530 crore comprising Rs. 350 crore as revenue expenditure and Rs. 180 crore as capital expenditure. In 2007-2008 the estimated expenditure of the Government of India was of the order of Rs. 6,80,520.00 crore comprising of Rs. 5,57,900 crore as revenue expenditure and Rs. 1,22,620 crore as capital expenditure.

Before 1987-88 the revenue expenditure comprised of civil expenditure, defence expenditure and grants-in-aid to States and Union Territories. The civil expenditure included general services, social and community services and economic services. Simultaneously the Government of India had also adopted another classification of expenditure *viz.*, development expenditure, defence expenditure and other expenditure. Defence and other expenditures were actually known as non-development expenditure. Under development expenditure were included the expenditure on social and community services, economic services and grants-in-aid to the States and Union Territories for development purposes. As already stated, defence expenditure was non-development expenditure and it included pensions given to the retired armed personnel and expenditure on the maintenance of armed forces. In other expenditure, were included the expenditure on collection of taxes and duties, administrative services, interest payments, pension and other retirement benefits and other grants to the States.

In the Budget 1987-88 the Government of India adopted a new classification under which public expenditure was classified into: Plan expenditure and Non-Plan expenditure. Plan expenditure includes expenditure on: (*a*) Central plans, such as development of agriculture, rural development, irrigation and flood control, energy, industry and minerals, transport, communications, science and technology and environment, social services and others, and (*b*) Central Assistance for the Plans of the States and Union Territories.

Non-Plan expenditure comprises of: (*i*) Expenditure on Revenue Account, and (*ii*) Expenditure on Capital Account. We now explain these in the following paragraphs:

(1) Expenditure on Revenue Account

All expenditures incurred out of the proceeds of taxes and other revenue receipts are included in this category. It means that expenditure incurred out of money balances created or owned by the Government (like tax collection. receipts and payments of interest, dividends, profits, rents, fees and fines, grants, contribution of railways, posts and telegraphs, civil works etc.) is revenue expenditure, for example, expenditure on the maintenance of physical assets, general administration, police and judiciary and grants given to States and other parties. Revenue expenditure thus, does not result in the creation of physical assets.

(2) Expenditure on Capital Account

Capital account includes all those moneys which are neither owned or created by the Government like loans, deposits, collections etc., which cause changes in physical assets owned by the Government (their creation, acquisition, disposal or addition/alteration thereof) and which lead to changes in financial claims upon third parties. All expenditures financed out of these moneys are known as capital expenditure, for example expenditure on the acquisition of lands, buildings, equipments, machineries, investments in stocks and shares, loans and advances by government to other governments, government companies and corporations etc. for development purposes, capital expenditure on economic services, social and community services, defence and general services. Capital expenditure thus, leads to the creation of physical assets.

2. Components of Revenue Expenditure

Revenue expenditure is composed of the following:

(1) General Services and Defence Services, (2) Social Services,

(3) Economic Services, (4) Grants-in-Aid to States. We now throw light on each of these.

(1) General Services

Expenditure under this head includes expenditure on the following:

(*a*) Organs of the State—Parliament, President, Vice-President, Council of Ministers, Administration of Justice, Elections, Comptroller and Auditor General and his office.

(*b*) Fiscal services like Collection of Taxes, Customs Duties and Currency, Coinage and Mint.

(*c*) Debt service *i.e.*, Interest charges on internal and external loans.

(*d*) Administrative services like Public Service Commission, Secretariat, Supplies and Disposals, Public Works, Printing and Stationery.

(*e*) Salaries, allowances, pension and other retirement benefits to the government employees including defence forces.

(2) Social Services

Expenditure on the following items is included under this head;

(*a*) Education, (*b*) Sports and Youth Services, (*c*) Art and Culture, (*d*) Medical and Public Health and Family Welfare, (*e*) Water Supply and Sanitation, (*f*) Housing and Urban Development, (*g*) Information, Publicity and Broadcasting, (*h*) Labour and Employment, (*i*) Nutrition, (*j*) Relief on account of natural calamities, (*k*) Social Security and Welfare, (*l*) Welfare of Scheduled Castes and Scheduled Tribes and Other Backward Classes, and Secretarial Social Services.

(3) Economic Services

Expenditure in respect of Secretariat and attached offices of the following ministries and departments is included under this head: (*a*) Agriculture and Allied Activities; (*b*) Rural Development; (*c*) Special Areas Programmes; (*d*) Irrigation and Flood Control; (*e*) Energy; (*f*) Industry and Minerals; (*g*) Transport; (*h*) Communications; (*i*) Science, Technology and Environment, and (*j*) General Economic Services.

(4) Grants-in-Aid and Contributions

Grants-in-aid given to the State Governments and Union Territories for filling the revenue gap and for other specific purposes.

3. Components of Capital Expenditure

Capital expenditure of the Government of India is composed of the following expenditure: (1) General Services including defence services, (2) Social Services, (3) Economic Services, (4) Public Debt, and (5) Loans and Advances.

We now give some details about these expenditures in the following:

(1) General Services

Expenditure on general services of capital nature is included under this head, for example, expenditure on Currency Note Press, Bank Note Press, Security Paper Mill and Mints at Kolkata, Mumbai and Hyderabad. It also includes capital expenditure on other fiscal services such as collection of taxes on income and expenditure, collection of taxes on wealth and gift tax, Union excise duties and commodity taxes, stationery and printing, public works and other administrative services and miscellaneous general services. Besides, defence expenditure is also included under this head. The capital expenditure on general services is chiefly on the office and administrative buildings. So far as the defence expenditure is concerned it refers to the non-residential buildings, ordnance factories, machineries, tools and equipment etc.

(2) Social Services

Capital expenditure on education, sports, arts and culture, medical and public health, family welfare, water supply and sanitation, housing and urban development, information publicity and broadcasting, welfare of scheduled castes, scheduled tribes and other backward classes, social security and welfare and other social services, is included under this head. The expenditure increases the standard of living of people and thus leads to an increase in the efficiency and productivity of human resources of the country.

(3) Economic Services

Under this head, capital expenditure on agriculture and allied services (namely, crop husbandry, soil and water conservation, animal husbandry, dairy development, fisheries, forestry and wildlife, food, storage and warehousing; investment in agricultural financial institutions, cooperation) rural development programmes; special areas development programmes; irrigation and flood control, (major, medium and minor irrigation works); capital expenditure on power and energy projects, (petroleum, coal, lignite, non-conventional sources of energy); capital outlay on industry and minerals (small and village industries, iron and steel industries, non-ferrous mining and metallurgical industries, cement, fertilisers, petro-chemical, chemicals, and pharmaceutical engineering, telecommunications and electronics, consumer industries, atomic energy and other industries); capital expenditure on transport (railways, ports, and light houses, shipping, civil aviation, roads and bridges, inland water transport and other transport services); capital expenditure on technology and environment (atomic energy research, space, occeanographic and other scientific and environmental research; capital expenditure on general economic services (tourism, foreign trade and export promotion, financial and training institutions, investment in international financial institutions etc) is included. We have already explained that capital expenditure is one which leads to the creation of tangible assets of durable nature.

(4) Public Debt

This head includes internal and external debts of the Government of India.

(5) Loans and Advances

The Government of India advances loans to States and Union Territories for executing developmental projects in their jurisdiction. These loans and advances are given for the following purposes:

(*a*) Social Services such as education, sports, art and culture, family welfare, housing, information and publicity, medical and public health, water supply and sanitation.

(*b*) Economic Services, such as agriculture and allied activities, special areas programmes, energy, industry and minerals, transport, communications, science, technology and environment and general economic services.

(*c*) Other pruposes: The Government of India also gives loans and makes advances for other purposes to States, Union Territories, foreign governments, government servants etc.

4. Comparative Position of Revenue and Capital Expenditure

We have already stated that revenue expenditure is incurred on the normal running of government departments and services, interest charges on debts and grants given to State Governments and others. It does not lead to the creation of assets. On the other hand capital expenditure leads to the creation of assets. From this point of view the importance of capital expenditure for a developing country like ours is very great. A developing country needs capital expenditure on a large scale for raising the level of production, income and employment and living standards. Moreover, it is also required for executing projects which involve huge investment. Table 32.1 gives a comparative idea of the growth of public expenditure on both accounts in selected years.

It is clear from the above Table that there has been a greater increase in the revenue expenditure of the Government of India. In the First Five-Year Plan, the volume of revenue expenditure was higher than capital expenditure but the situation was reversed from 1956-1957 onwards. Further since 1977-1978, the revenue expenditure again started rising at a faster rate than the capital expenditure which means that the tax revenue had not been adequate to meet the revenue expenditure and the rate of capital formation and economic development of the country had not increased with the increase in tax burden.

Table 32.1
Growth of Public Expenditure

(In Crore Rupees)

Year	*Expenditure on Revenue Account*	*Expenditure on Capital Account*	*Total*
1950-51	350.00	180.00	530.00
1980-81	14,540.00	9,630.00	24,170.00
2001-02	3,01,610.00	60,840.00	3,62,450.00
2007-08 (Budget)	5,57,900.00	1,22,620.00	6,80,520.00

w.e.f. 1.4.99 a new system of transferring 95% of net small savings collections to States and UTs from the Public Account had been introduced.

This means that the revenue deficit has increased over the years. Another implication of the increase in revenue deficit was that the government had not been able to make adequate tax efforts to raise the revenue commensurate with its expenditure or the government had been extravagant in its expenditure.

Development and Non-development Expenditure

Simultaneously, the government also adopted another classification, *viz.*, development and non-development expenditure.

Since capital expenditure is considered to be developmental in nature and revenue expenditure is regarded as non-developmental, an increase in the latter at a faster rate than the increase in the former goes to show that the rate of capital formation in the country is not adequate.

Expenditure on social services, economic services, grants-in-aid to the States and Union Territories for financing development projects is included under development expenditure on revenue account as already explained.

We have already listed the components of each of these before. This expenditure is considered developmental in the sense that all these services help in raising the efficiency and productivity of human resources and thus in raising the level of output, income and employment in the country.

Development expenditure on capital account includes expenditure of capital nature on social services, economic services and loans and advances to States and Union Territories and for financing public enterprises. We have already spelt out the various items of expenditure under each of these earlier.

Development expenditure has increased since 1950-51 manifold only because of the government's launching of the programme of economic and social development through its Five-Year Plans.

The non-development expenditure on revenue account includes expenditure on items, such as audit, collection of taxes and duties, currency, coinage, mint, interest payments, expenditure on administrative services such as police, public works, external affairs and other administrative services, pensions and other retirement benefits to the government employees, grants to States and Union Territories, defence expenditure on salaries, pension etc. All these services are put under the head of general services and therefore we can say that the expenditure on general services on revenue account is non-development expenditure.

Defence expenditure is the major head of non-development expenditure on capital account. It also includes expenditure on trading, currency, mint, security and printing press. Since this expenditure does not lead to promote development it is considered as non-developmental.

The increase in non-development expenditure has been caused chiefly because of increase in the state activities particularly after independence, increasing problems of defence and law and order etc.

However, a comparative study of both of these expenditures leads to the conclusion that the increase in development expenditure has been higher than the increase in the non-developmental expenditure. Developmental expenditure on revenue account is met out of the revenue collected from taxes whereas the developmental expenditure on capital account is financed from the funds raised through loans, internal as well as external. However, in certain years, the increase in non-development expenditure has been faster than development expenditure, but somehow the non-development expenditure on revenue account has always exceeded the development expenditure on revenue account. This was the trend even before independence and there does not seem to be any end to this although there is enough scope for exercising economy in general administration. But the present policy of the government and the vulnerable position of the political party forming the coalition government will never allow this to happen.

Plan and Non-Plan Expenditure

We have already stated earlier that the classification of public expenditure into Plan and Non-Plan expenditure was adopted for the first time in the budget of 1987-88. We have also spelt out the details of such expenditure before. We now discuss some of the general trends of these two types of expenditure. But before doing this we shall make some general observations.

Plan and non-Plan expenditure does not necessarily mean developmental expenditure and non-developmental expenditure respectively. The reason is that both these types of expenditures contain the element of development as well as non-development expenditure. As soon as plan project becomes operative, expenditure on its maintenance and operation are transferred to the non-Plan budget. That is why the non-Plan expenditure has been on the increase. Plan expenditure has also increased overtime, but has not grown as fast as non-Plan expenditure. Consequently, the share of Plan expenditure in the total expenditure of Government of India declined from 40.4 per cent in 1979-80 to 39.80 per cent on an average during the Sixth Plan and 33.9 per cent during the Seventh Plan and had reached 28.0 per cent in 2005-06. On the other hand, the non-Plan expenditure has increased over the years from 59 per cent in 1979-80 to 72 per cent of the total expenditure in 2005-06. Table 32.2 gives details of Plan and non-Plan expenditure of the Government of India. It would be observed that currently about 77 per cent of the Plan expenditure is used for financing the Central Plan while the balance is given as central assistance for Plans of States and Union Territories.

In the total non-Plan expenditure, capital expenditure comprises a little more than 1.2 per cent and therefore about 99 per cent of the non-Plan expenditure is incurred on revenue account which includes debt-servicing charges, defence expenditure, subsidies, grants and other non-Plan expenditure. The first three components were expected to account for more than 71 per cent of the expenditure in 2005-06.

Let us now look in some detail at the position of individual items under non-Plan expenditure.

Debt Servicing Charges

We have already stated that debt servicing charges or interest payments are a committed charge on government revenue. It has grown over the years by leaps and bounds. The rate has increased significantly with the new market-oriented policy, and the increase has reached to such an extent that now it is being talked about that the government is on the verge of falling into a debt trap. From the Table 32.2, it is clear that these charges are increasing at the rate of about 20% per year. The situation is really disturbing and it is high time that this expenditure is reduced. This can be possible only when government makes an all out effort to economise this expenditure and to, mobilise more resources on revenue account to cut down on its borrowings.

As shown in Table 32.2 the defence expenditure increased from Rs. 3,164 crore to about Rs. 83,000 crore during 1979 and 2006. This increase may appear to be highly satisfying, but in real terms the situation is far from satisfactory. The real worth of funds made available for country's defence needs has been declining fast, owing to the fall in the rupee's purchasing power on the one hand and increase in the prices of defence equipment on the other. India is surrounded by neighbours who are passing through severe political crisis be it Nepal, Pakistan, Sri Lanka, Bangladesh or Mayanmar. Our allocation for defence, in fact, has declined from 29% to 17.8% as proportion of non-Plan expenditure and from 17.8% to 16.1% as a proportion

Table 32.2

GOI Expenditure—Plan and Non-Plan

	1979-80	6th Plan*	7th Plan*	1990-92	1992-97	1997-2000	2002-03	2003-04	2004-05	2005-06
Total Expenditure	17,787	31,058	71,172	2,16,712	8,04,492	14,97,349	4,13,248	4,71,368	5,05,791	5,14,344
A. Plan Expenditure	7,189	12,360	24,146	59,326	2,27,608	3,85,940	1,11,470	1,22,280	1,37,387	1,43,497
I. Central Plan	4,196	8,110	15,826	34,592	1,25,879	2,19,099	67,126	71,842	82,529	1,10,385
II. Assistance for State and UT Plans	2,993	4,250	8,819	24,734	1,01,730	1,66,840	84,344	50,438	54,858	33,111
B. Non-Plan Expenditure	10,598	18,698	47,026	1,57,386	5,76,884	11,11,408	3,01,778	3,49,088	3,68,404	3,70,847
1. Interest Payments	2,210	4,101	12,009	48,096	2,21,399	4,40,542	1,17,804	1,24,088	1,25,905	1,33,945
2. Defence Expenditure	3,164	5,169	11,638	31,773	1,19,033	2,26,174	55,662	60,066	77,000	83,000
3. Subsidies	1,543	2,604	6,887	24,411	62,448	1,24,668	43,533	44,256	46,514	47,432
4. Grants to States and UTs	624	790	1,924	7,903	19,581	45,625	13,305	13,721	14,828	33,953
5. Other grants	58	76	116	286	927	1,853	605	688	936	1,094
6. Other Non-Plan Exp.	2,215	3,550	9,756	23,002	96,124	2,05,186	49,786	55,977	63,000	63,160
7. Other Non-Plan Capital Exp.	107	427	662	1,729	5,481	8,383	13,328	46,745	36,019	4,460
8. Loans & Advances to States & UTs+	132	1,109	5,751	13,138	41,889	41,886	2,481	178	715	100
9. Other Loans	545	708	1,207	7,050	1,00,021	9,509	3,385	1,587	1,560	1,219

*Annual Average.

+Change in figures due to the creation of National Small Savings Fund.

Source: GOI Budgets and Expenditure Budgets.

of total expenditure. This neglect of defence preparedness may prove very costly to us some day. The earlier it is realised by the government, the better would it be for maintaining congenial investment climate so essential for our economic growth.

Subsidies

Subsidies are another major item of government expenditure. Subsidies can be open as well as hidden. Open subsidies can be given in the form of cash assistance, tax concessions, purchase preference prices and interest rate differentials, subsidised inputs etc. A subsidy implies that a section of the community is being protected at the cost of other. Subsidies are being used in many countries particularly for counteracting the failure of market mechanism, in bringing about optimum allocation of resources and distribution of income and wealth. Advanced countries are using subsidies for helping selective economic sectors but in backward countries subsidies are being used for a number of objectives like increasing employment, developing village and small industries and agriculture, promoting exports, reducing regional imbalances, executing anti-poverty programmes etc.

Table 32.3 (Page 98) shows that the amount of subsidies has been increasing continuously. Subsidies are good only upto a limited extent but their indiscriminate use may create enormous problems for the Government as well as for the society. In our country the major portion of subsidies is consumed by food, fertilisers and export promotion. Fertilisers claim the largest share followed by food and export promotion. Other items include interest subsidies, debt relief to farmers etc. These subsidies can be justified on a number of grounds. Subsidies to individual industries promote employment and remove regional disparities. Subsidies on food prevent starvation and malnutrition. Subsidies for health care, education, drinking water etc. are necessary for maintaining the health of the society.

But it need not be forgotten that subsidies entail a cost to the economy and limit the scope of budgetary manoeuverability. It is a sort of secret help to the beneficiary. It leads to the creation of vested interests. It also encourages other sections of the society to ask for subsidies. Sometimes it also happens that the benefit of subsidy does not reach the people for whom it is meant. Vested interests snatch this benefit at the cost of the poor people, backward areas and backward industries. In this respect subsidies do not promote distributive justice. Subsidies may also lead to waste of resources if these are given to sick and inefficient units indulging in under-utilisation of capacity, over-staffing etc. That is why it has been said that instead of checking market failures subsidies generate ‘government failures and create distortions in the economy'. It has, therefore, been suggested that subsidies should not be given on a permanent basis.

It may be interesting to note that open subsidies generally constitute a very small portion of the total subsidies. Hidden subsidies constitute a major portion like tax concessions, purchase preferences, losses of public sector undertakings, low administered prices, social welfare services like medical and health care, education etc.

Grants

Most of the non-Plan grants given by the Government of India to the States and Union Territories are statutory and are given on the recommendations of the Finance Commission. Their proportion is about 9.5% in the total non-Plan expenditure. The Government of India also has been providing assistance in the form of grants, although to very limited extent, to other under-developed friendly countries.

Other non-Plan expenditure constituted only about 17 per cent of the total non-Plan expenditure in 2005-06.

General Trend of Government of India Expenditure

On the basis of what has been stated in the preceding paragraphs, we can now briefly state the main trends of the expenditure of the Government of India:

(1) The revenue expenditure of the Government of India has increased at a very fast pace, *i.e.*, from Rs. 350 crore in 1950-51 to Rs. 6,55,625 crore (BE) in 2007-2008.

(2) Non-development expenditure constitutes a large proportion of the total expenditure.

(3) Non-Plan revenue expenditure has been rising very fast in recent years mainly because of: (*a*) increase in the amount of interest payments due to the increase in public debt and other liabilities from Rs. 165 crore in 1979-80 to Rs. 1,59,000 crore in 2007-08, (*b*) increase in defence expenditure chiefly because of the growing tension in the Indian Ocean Region. Defence expenditure has increased from Rs. 10,870 crore to Rs. 54,100 crore during 1991 and 2008, (*c*) The amount of subsidies has increased very fast from Rs. 1,543 crore in 1979-80 to Rs. 54,330 crore in 2007-08, (*d*) Expenditure on general services of the Central Government has also increased very fast from Rs. 2,060 crore in 1985-86 to Rs. 30,420 crore in 2007-08, (*e*) Consequently the total expenditure on these four items alone accounts for more than 92 per cent of the current non-Plan revenue expenditure.

(4) Despite our objectives of economic development and establishment of a welfare state, the expenditure on defence constitutes a major item; but it is on decline.

Table 32.3
GOI Subsidies

	1979-80	6th Plan*	7th Plan*	1990-92	1992-97	1997-2002	2002-03	2003-04	2004-05	2005-06
Total Subsidies	1,543	2,604	6,887	12,158	62,448	1,24,688	43,533	44,256	46,514	47,432
A. Major Subsidies	1,487	2,158	5,961	4,581	55,320	1,17,499	40,716	43,455	45,187	46,358
1. Food	600	799	2,105	2,450	24,888	2,13,013	24,176	25,160	25,800	26,200
2. Indigenous fertilizers	243	620	2,224	3,730	21,712	40,627	7,790	8,521	10,143	10,110
3. Imported fertilizers	283	272	322	659	6,022	1,177	—	—	473	944
4. Decontrolled Fertilizers					2,700	19,708	3,225	3,326	5,046	5,200
5. Petroleum Subsidy	—	—	—	—	—	—	5,225	6,292	3,553	3,644
6. Grants to NAFED	—	—	—	—	—	353	300	158	172	260
B. Other Subsidies	56	446	926	2,577	7,128	7,169	2,817	801	1,324	1,074

* Annual averages

(5) Interest payment is now the single largest item of expenditure.

(6) Prior to the start of the Sixth Plan the Government of India used to have surpluses under revenue account. From the beginning of the Sixth Plan it started having deficits and now it has become a permanent feature.

(7) It was from the beginning of the Seventh Plan that the deficit on capital account of the Government of India turned into surplus which is still continuing.

(8) This reversal of trend clearly indicates that funds which are being diverted to meet conventional expenditure could have been used for creating tangible assets.

(9) Not only this, the Government of India is meeting its revenue deficit by borrowings and printing new currency. As a proportion of total debt, the capital expenditure of the Centre had decreased from 83.25 per cent in 1987-88 to 57.30 per cent in 2001-02.

Fiscal Deficits and Corrections

This only reflects gross mismanagement of finances by the Central Government, which is in utter neglect of the fundamental principle of sound finance, *i.e.* consumption should not exceed current income. In any case this is the most disturbing aspect of the fiscal scene. Although the fiscal deficits of the Centre have come down from 8.33% of the GDP in 1990-91 to 3.30% in 2007-08 (BE), the present level is still high. High fiscal deficits may expose the economy to a number of risks:

(*i*) Fiscal deficits may cause a slow-down in the pace of economic growth owing to a decline in the level of aggregate investment caused by a fall in the rate of national savings. The whole economy, thus, can go off the track.

(*ii*) Large fiscal deficits, if financed through printing of new currency, may jeopardise macroeconomic stability.

(*iii*) Persisting fiscal deficits, in the long run, will certainly increase the tax burden of the people since higher taxes would be required to repay internal debt.

(*iv*) Continued large fiscal deficits may also affect the balance of payments if the current account deficit is financed through external loans.

Economic Reforms and Fiscal Adjustments

As a part of economic reforms introduced in 1990-91 steps were also taken by the Government of India to contain fiscal deficit. During the first seven years *i.e.* upto 1996-97 positive results were achieved and there was a marked reduction on all fronts. The gross fiscal deficit fell from 8.33% to 4.90% of the GDP, the revenue deficit fell from 3.47% to 2.40% of the GDP and the gross primary deficit came down from 4.32% to 0.53% of the GDP. This change took place because of a number of factors: (*i*) In the total tax receipts, the contribution of direct taxes went up while that of indirect taxes came down; (*ii*) there was an appreciable increase in the central assistance for State and union territory plans; (*iii*) the budgetary support for the Central Plan was very much reduced; (*iv*) there was overall increase in budgetary expenditure in areas like rural development and social sectors; (*v*) the staff strength of the Central Government had been reduced by about 10%.

But the situation again went out of control in the following two years, when the gross fiscal deficit, revenue deficit and gross primary deficit increased to 6.43% 3.85% and 8.05% of the GDP respectively. These percentages again came down in 2001-02 to 4.70 and 3.20 and 0.20 respectively, yet the situation cannot be considered by any means as satisfactory. The gross fiscal deficit is still high. The revenue deficit is almost the same as it was when economic reforms started. While the proportions of non-Plan expenditure, budgetary support for Central Plan, and expenditure on social and economic services in the total expenditure have remained stationary, the staff strength of the Central Government has increased. In the non-Plan expenditure the share of interest payments, defence and pensions has progressively increased.

The measures adopted by the Central Government to reduce fiscal deficit, in the wake of economic reforms have produced certain disconcerting effects; (*i*) increase in revenue expenditure → increase in market borrowings → increase in interest payments → increase in revenue expenditure and so on, (*ii*) reduced capital expenditure has led to a reduction in the rate of capital formation, (*iii*) States have to suffer owing to the reduction in net transfer from the Centre. Consequently, the States have to face lot of problems in putting their fiscal house in order specially in respect of those sectors which are their primary responsibility, *viz.* agriculture, education, health etc.

In the last three budgets, the Government of India has taken steps, the result of which will be available after three or four years. On the revenue side, besides broadening the tax base by introducing one of the six scheme and service tax, and rationalising the excise and customs duties, has taken steps to make tax administration simple and transparent and to plug evasion and leakages.

On the expenditure side the government has continuously cut down the rate of interest on small savings and market borrowings reducing thereby the burden of interest payments, has reduced subsidies on petrol, diesel, fertilizers etc., has withdrawn the administered price system for a number of commodities, has undertaken the privatisation of PSUs and has cut down the staff strength in a number of departments.

For increasing the pace of economic development and for sustaining higher rate of economic growth, the government has taken some positive steps, like opening of the banking, insurance, energy, information technology sectors to foreign investors, dereservation of items from the reservation list of the small sector, demonopolisation of infrastructure sector like generation and distribution of power, building of roads and highways, decentralisation of economic policy making etc.

Fiscal Responsibility and Budget Management Act, 2003

The Fiscal Responsibility and Budget Management Act was passed in 2003. The key features are:

(*i*) To lay before the Parliament with the annual budget: (*a*) Medium-term Fiscal Policy Statement, (*b*) Fiscal Policy Strategy Statement, and (*c*) Macro-economic Framework Statement.

(*ii*) The Medium-term Fiscal Policy Statement shall set-forth a three year rolling target for prescribed fiscal indicators specifying all underlying assumptions and also include an assessment of sustainability relating to: (*a*) the balance between revenue receipts and revenue expenditures, and (*b*) the use of capital receipts including market borrowings for generating productive assets.

(*iii*) The Fiscal Policy Strategy Statement shall, among other things contain: (*a*) the policy of the Central Government for the next financial year relating to taxation, expenditure, liabilities, lending and investments, pricing of administered goods and services, securities and other activities which have significant budgetary implications; (*b*) the strategic priorities of the government in the fiscal area for the next year; (*c*) the prominent fiscal measures and rationale for any major deviation in fiscal measures, and (*d*) an evaluation of how the current policies of the government are in conformity with the fiscal management principles set out in the Strategy Statement and the objectives set out in the Medium-term Policy Statement.

(*iv*) The Central Government shall: (*a*) reduce revenue deficit as well as fiscal deficit by an amount equivalent to one half per cent or more of the estimated GDP at the end of each financial year starting from April 1,2001; (*b*) reduce revenue deficit to nil by March 31, 2006; (*c*) build up surplus revenue and use it for discharging liabilities; (*d*) reduce fiscal deficit for a year at the rate of not more than 2% of the estimated GDP for that year, upto March 31, 2006, starting from April 1, 2001; (*e*) not give guarantee for any amount beyond one-half per cent of the estimated GDP in any financial year, (*f*) ensure that, upto March 31, 2011, the total liabilities (including debt at current exchange rate) at the end of a financial year, do not exceed fifty per cent of the estimated GDP for that year.

(*v*) The Central Government shall not undertake any direct borrowings from the RBI after three years except by way of advances to meet temporary cash needs.

(*vi*) The Central Government shall take appropriate steps to ensure greater transparency in fiscal operations and minimum secrecy in the preparation of annual budget.

(*vii*) The Finance Minister shall undertake quarterly review of the trends in receipts and expenditures in relation to the budget and place its outcome before both Houses of Parliament.

(*viii*) While protecting the 'charged' expenditure the Central Government, in the event of a shortfall in revenue or excess of expenditure over specified targets, shall cut expenditure authorisations proportionately.

(*ix*) The Finance Minister shall make a statement in both Houses of Parliament explaining any deviation in meeting the obligations cast on the Central Government under this Act and the corrective measures the Government proposes to take.

(*x*) Relaxation from deficit reduction targets, to deal with unforeseen demands on the finances of the Government on account of national security or natural calamities of national dimension.

Some Comments on the Act

Fiscal experts[1] have made certain valuable comments on fiscal policy legislation in India.

1. It has been pointed out that the fundamental requirement of fiscal responsibility legislation is transparency in institutional arrangements and fiscal reporting. This would happen only when: (*a*) there is greater clarity in the delineation of the public sector and its components *i.e.* an open relationship between government, public utilities and public accounts; (*b*) the inter-governmental fiscal relations are clear and transparent; and (*c*) accrual-based approach is adopted in accounting practices and the measurement of public sector liabilities is timely and consistent.

2. A clear cut distinction between current and capital expenditures is also essential.

3. The Act does not address to the issue relating to the fiscal responsibility at sub-national levels.

4. Provisions relating to balanced budget requirements and debt in the Act are weak and inadequate.

5. The targets fixed for reducing fiscal deficits and for using revenue surpluses for retiring public debt will perpetuate the declining trend of government investment, at least for the next ten years.

1. George Kopits: "Fiscal Policy Rules for India", *EPW*, Vol. XXXVI, No.5, March 9, 2001 and Mihir Rikshit: "Restoring Fiscal Balance through Legislative Fiat", *EPW*, Vol. XXXVI. No. 23, June 15,2001.

5. Expenditure of State Governments

Like the Government of India, the expenditure of the State Governments is also divided into revenue and capital accounts. Revenue account covers the current receipts and expenditures while the capital account deals with the acquisition and disposal of physical assets and liabilities such as loans, investments etc.

Expenditure on revenue account has three components *viz.*, (*i*) developmental expenditure, (*ii*) non-developmental expenditure, (*iii*) contribution to local bodies. Developmental expenditure constitutes about 51.5 per cent of the total expenditure whereas non-developmental expenditure is about 46.7 per cent and the balance *i.e.*, 2 per cent goes to local bodies. Developmental expenditure, like that of the Government of India, is incurred on social services *viz.*, education, art and culture, medical and public health etc. and economic services which include forests, agriculture, soil conservation, dairy development, roads, bridges, irrigation, multi-purpose river valley projects. The non-developmental expenditure includes debt servicing charges, expenditure on administrative services, maintenance of state organs, cost of collection of taxes and duties etc.

Expenditure on capital account consists of capital outlay, repayment of internal debt, repayment of loans of the Government of India, loans and advances by other State governments and appropriation to contingency fund.

The main features of expenditure on revenue account can be briefly stated as follows:

(1) It has grown faster than the revenue receipts but the growth has been only marginal and therefore the State budgets are generally in deficit.

(2) The developmental expenditure has increased at a fast pace. It is now around 62 per cent of the total expenditure of the State Governments. Developmental expenditure includes expenditure on education, medical and public health, civil works, rural and community development projects, agriculture, cooperation, water supply and family planning etc. Non-developmental expenditure includes the cost of collection of taxes and duties, civil administration and debt servicing. Over the years, debt servicing charges have increased rapidly. A major portion of this expenditure is accounted by the indebtedness of the States to the Government of India.

Capital expenditure of the States has also grown over the years. The most satisfying feature of the expenditure on capital account is that almost the entire capital outlay goes into development schemes. Since market borrowings of States are rather small the servicing charges of internal debt constitutes a very small percentage of the total capital outlay. State Governments mostly borrow from the Central Government. The volume of State indebtedness to the Centre would have been much more had the Central Government, on the recommendations of the Finance Commissions not granted them debt relief.

Key Features of State Finances

'The fiscal deficit of State Governments increased from 3.3% of GDP in 1990-91 to 4.2% in 2001-02 (RE). Higher growth of revenue expenditure has largely contributed to this situation. The revenue deficit has nearly trebled from 0.9% of GDP in 1990-91 to 2.6% in 2001-02 (RE). Revenue from States' own taxes witnessed a marginal improvement from 5.3% of GDP in 1990-91 to 5.8% in 2001-02 (RE). In the State Budget for 2006-07 the fiscal deficit is budgeted to come down to 2.6% of GDP and the revenue deficit to come down to 20% of GDP as shown in the Table 32.4.

State Level Fiscal Reforms

The States have also taken a number of steps for fiscal adjustment *viz.*; enactment of FRBMA and introduction of monthly cash flow system for improving their financial position. The Twelfth Finance Commission (TFC) also recommended a two stage benefit scheme, named as Debt consolidation and Waiver Facility (DCRF) for enabling the States to improve their fiscal performance. The first stage related to the consolidation of Central loans from Ministry of Finance contracted by States till March 31, 2004 and outstanding as on March 31, 2005 for a fresh term of 20 years at 7.5% rate of interest, prospectively from the year they enact FRBMA. The second stage was the debt write off scheme after debt consolidation linked to fiscal performance subject to: (*i*) reduction of revenue deficit every year starting from 2004-05, when compared to the average of the preceding three years in the process, if revenue deficit is eliminated completely by 2008-09, the State gets full benefit of waiver; (*ii*) reduction in revenue deficit should be equal to at least the interest rate relief on account of consolidation; and (*iii*) Containing fiscal deficit/GSDP ratio at the 2004-05 level in all subsequent years.

According to TFC estimates, the debt award during 2005-10 for all States would be Rs. 21,275 crore in interest payments and Rs. 11,929 crore in repayment of consolidated central loans. If all States eliminate revenue deficit by 2008-09, the amount of debt waiver available to them would be around Rs. 33,205 crore. For eliminating revenue deficit and to bring down the fiscal deficit to 3% of GSDP and to achieve other targets of TFC, they are required to draw up their own 'Fiscal Correction Paths' (FCP). Till 2006-07 , 23 States had enacted FRBMAs and 21 States had drawn up their FCPs. Debt consolidation had been done for 19 States, *viz.*, Andhra, Assam, Bihar,

Table 32.4

Receipts and Disbursements of State Governments

(*Rs. Crore*)

		1990-91	2001-02	2002-03	2003-04	2004-05	2005-06 (RE)	2006-07 (RE)
I.	Total receipts (A + B)	91,160	3,73,886	4,25,073	5,27,097	5,82,910	6,16,397	6,65,260
	A. Revenue receipts (1 + 2)	66,467	2,55,675	2,80,339	3,16,535	3,72,075	4,54,152	5,13,166
	1. Tax receipts	44,586	1,80,312	1,98,798	2,26,999	2,67,683	3,17,502	3,60,898
	of which:							
	State's own tax revenue	30,344	1,28,097	1,42,143	1,59,921	1,89,132	2,24,780	2,52,573
	2. Non-tax receipts	21,881	75,363	81,541	89,536	1,04,392	1,36,650	1,52,268
	of which:							
	Interest receipts	2,403	9,205	9,502	8,617	9,470	9,666	9,648
	B. Capital receipts	24,693	1,18,211	1,44,734	2,10,562	2,10,835	1,62,245	1,52,094
	of which							
	Recovery of loans & advances	1,501	7,766	3,905	16,414	8,568	7,456	4,813
II.	Total disbursements (a + b + c)	91,088	3,77,311	4,20,461	5,26,023	5,72,354	6,10,751	6,59,530
	(a) Revenue	71,776	3,14,863	3,35,450	3,77,681	4,08,497	4,71,437	5,14,952
	(b) Capital	13,556	50,145	70,664	1,22,429	1,44,014	1,20,495	1,29,848
	(c) Loans and advances	5,756	12,303	14,347	25,913	19,843	18,819	14,730
III.	Revenue deficit	5,309	59,188	55,111	61,145	36,423	17,284	1,786
IV.	Gross fiscal deficit	18,797	95,994	1,02,123	1,23,070	1,09,256	1,13,978	1,05,895
			(As per cent of GDP)					
I.	Total receipts (A + B)	16.0	16.4	17.3	19.1	18.6	17.3	16.2
	A. Revenue receipts (1 + 2)	11.7	11.2	11.4	11.4	11.9	12.7	12.5
	1. Tax receipts	7.8	7.9	8.1	8.2	8.6	8.9	8.8
	of which:							
	State's own tax revenue	5.3	5.6	5.8	5.8	6.0	6.3	6.2

Contd...

	2. Non-tax receipts	3.8	3.3	3.3	3.2	3.3	3.8	3.7
	of which:							
	Interest receipts	0.4	0.4	0.4	0.3	0.3	0.3	0.2
	B. Capital receipts	4.3	5.2	5.9	7.6	6.7	4.5	3.7
	of which:							
	Recovery of loans & advances	0.3	0.3	0.2	0.6	0.3	0.2	0.1
II.	Total disbursements (a + b + c)	16.0	16.5	17.1	19.0	18.3	17.1	16.1
	(a) Revenue	12.6	13.8	13.6	13.7	13.1	13.2	12.6
	(b) Capital	2.4	2.2	2.9	4.4	4.6	3.4	3.2
	(c) Loans and advances	1.0	0.5	0.6	0.9	0.6	0.5	0.4
III.	Revenue deficit	0.9	2.6	2.2	2.2	1.2	0.5	0.0
IV.	Gross fiscal deficit	3.3	4.2	4.2	4.5	3.5	3.2	2.6

Note: 1. The ratios to GDP for 2006-07 (BE) are based on CSO's advance Estimates. GDP at current market prices prior to 1999-2000 based on 1993-94 series and from 1999-2000 based on new 1999-2000 series.

2. Capital receipts include accounts on a net basis.

3. Capital disbursements are exclusive of public accounts.

Source: Reserve Bank of India.

Chattisgarh, Gujarat, Haryana, H.P., Karnataka, Kerala, M.P., Maharashtra, Manipur, Orissa, Punjab, Rajasthan, T.N., Tripura, Uttarakhand and U.P., Six States *viz.* Assam, Bihar, Kerala, Maharashtra, Tripura and Uttarakhand were not found eligible for debt waiver in 2005-06. In case of 13 States the debt waiver amount was estimated at Rs. 3,856 crore.

Conclusion

The situation, really, is so alarming that it needs immediate correction. While, increase in the rate of growth of revenues, no doubt, can be a solution but if the rate of growth of expenditure continues to be higher than that of revenues, then the only reasonable step would be to curtail expenditure. We have already discussed the various measures which the governments should take and no useful purpose would be served to repeat them. The governments should select such measures which may not only produce immediate result but also have a long run effect of regulating the growth of total expenditure in such a way that the debt/GDP ratio will stabilise at a reasonable level.

Exercises

1. Explain the classification of public expenditure adopted in the budgets of governments in India. What is the importance of non-plan expenditure?
2. Distinguish between 'Revenue Expenditure' and 'Capital Expenditure'. What is their relative importance, in the budget of the Government of India?
3. Explain the main trends of the expenditure of the Government of India since 1990-91.
4. Explain the main trends of the expenditure of the State Governments in India, since 2000-01.

•••

Chapter 33

Public Revenue—General Issues

1. Introduction

Public bodies raise funds to finance their activities from various sources; the most important being taxes and non-tax sources like currency and mint, fees, fines, sale of public assets, income from public undertakings etc. Dalton prefers to distinguish between public receipts and public revenue. While the former comprises of all sorts of income from each and every source, the latter does not include public borrowings, income from the sale of public assets or from the printing of currency notes.[1] We briefly deal with the fundamental issues related with public revenue in this chapter.

2. Classifications of Public Revenue

Some writers on public finance have attempted to classify public revenue in various categories just to explain the nature of different sources and their relative importance in the total structure of public revenue. We give below a brief account of some of these classifications:

(1) Adam Smith's Classification

Smith divided public revenue into: (*i*) revenue from the people, and (*ii*) revenue from state property. Tax revenue falls in the first category while income from public undertakings and assets falls in the second category.

It is a very simple classification and seems alright in the context of the limited role assigned to the state by Smith and other writers of his clan. But this classification is very narrow from the modem point of view.

(2) Bastable's Classification

According to Bastable the state derived its income in two capacities: (*i*) as an individual, and (*ii*) as state. Income derived from sources other than taxes and levies is included in the first category, while that derived from taxes and levies is included in the second category.

This classification is also narrow like Smith's.

(3) Adams' Classification

According to Adams, there are three categories of public revenue, *viz.*, (*i*) direct, (*ii*) derivative, and (*iii*) anticipatory. Income derived from the ownership of productive enterprises, like land, railways, roads, post and telegraph, satellites etc. belongs to the first category, for example, profits from public undertakings, gratuities, confiscations, royalties etc. In the second category falls the income which is derived from the people *e.g.*, fines, fees, charges, taxes, etc. And the income derived from the public credit like sale of bonds, treasury note etc. falls in the last category.

This clubbing of different sources of revenue by Adams into the three categories does not appear to be logical and scientific.

(4) Seligman's Classification

Seligman has divided public revenue as: (*i*) gratuitous, (*ii*) contractual, and (*iii*) compulsory. The first consists of that income which is derived without incurring any cost, *e.g.*, gifts, donations, etc.; the second comprises of income received as price for the goods and services offered for sale by the state; and the last category consists of income derived from taxes, fees, fines etc.

This classification also does not conform to real life conditions and hence is not satisfactory, for example, price, fees, taxes are in one sense optional payments. Price is paid by those who avail of the services and goods and not by each and everyone. Similarly, fees is paid for the services of the court; those who avail of these pay it, others do not and likewise taxes are paid by those who engage in activities which involve their payment and not by everyone.

(5) Dalton's Classification

Dalton has classified public revenue as: (*i*) compulsory payments, and (*ii*) voluntary payments. Compulsory payments include taxes, tributes and indemnities, compulsory loans, pecuniary penalties imposed under law. Voluntary payments include receipts from public property and enterprises, fees for services and voluntary loans.

Besides the two main sources of public revenue, *viz.*, taxes and prices, Dalton has also added four more sources which are neither covered under taxes nor under prices. These are: (*i*) receipts from enterprises which are of the sort of monopolies, (*ii*) receipts from special assessment, (*iii*) printing of new paper currency, and (*iv*) voluntary gifts.

Technically speaking, this is not a classification, it is merely an enumeration of the sources of public revenue. And it does not help either in economic interpretations or in comparative analysis of the different sources.

(6) Findlay Shirras' Classification

Professor Shirras has divided public revenue into two broad categories: (*a*) tax, and (*b*) non-tax. Professor Shirras has included, besides income from taxation, income from special assessment and fees in this category of public revenue. In the category of non-tax revenue he has included revenue from: (*i*) public enterprises like forests, mints, security printing, public works, railways, stationery, post and telegraph, telephones etc. (*ii*) social services like education, legal aid, health and sanitation etc., (*iii*) loans and debt services, and (*iv*) miscellaneous.

In this classification also the division of sources, in the two categories, is not clear cut and is overlapping, and does not help in making a comparative study of income and expenditure of a state.

(7) Taylor's Classification

Taylor has divided public revenue into four classes, *viz*., (*i*) grants and gifts, (*ii*) administrative revenue, (*iii*) commercial revenue, and (*iv*) taxes.

Grants are voluntary payments made by one government to another, for specified purposes *e.g.*, grants-in-aid given by the Union Government to the State governments in India, while gifts are voluntary payments made by individuals and institutions to the governments for particular purposes like earthquakes, famines, floods, wars etc.

Payments received by any government due to its administrative control, like fees, fines and penalties, forfeitures and confiscations, special levies and assessments etc. have been included by Taylor in the second category.

Payments received by a government by way of price for the goods and services produced by it have been grouped together in the category of commercial revenue, like electricity and water charges, telephone charges, postal charges, toll charges etc.

Payments received as tax by the government have been included by Taylor in the last category. These are compulsory payments and their non-payment is considered as crime.

This classification is by far the most logical, scientific and practical.

(8) Mehta's Classification

Prof. J.K. Mehta has classified public revenue into: Taxes, Fees and Duties. He has used the term tax with a wider connotation. According to him, "When the object is to obtain money for the finance of services, the levy should be regarded as Tax. The word tax should, therefore, possess a wide denotation. It should include all those charges which are meant to bring finance to the government."[2] If the object of the levy is to discourage the use of goods and services produced by the government then it should be called as Fee and if the object is to discourage the consumption of goods and services produced by the private sector then the levy is a Duty.

Prof. Mehta's classification is based on the motive with which the government imposes a levy and the effect which the levy has on the production and consumption of the various goods and services. This classification also suffers from the same defects with which others suffer. Nevertheless it is more satisfactory than others.

(9) Pragmatic Classification

We have seen that none of the classifications mentioned above is satisfactory, for making comparative study of income and expenditure of a government or for making economic interpretations or for analysing the suitability or otherwise of each source of revenue or from the point of view of accountability and control. Hence, most of the modern governments have adopted an economic classification of government receipts and disbursements on revenue and capital account. Such a classification facilitates the study of the impact of the government fiscal operations on the economy and make the necessary changes.

The Government of India first adopted this classification in 1957-58. The budget of the Government of India is divided into two portions: revenue and capital. The former includes the current receipts and disbursements while the latter includes the creation and disposal of assets and liabilities. Interest, dividends and profits form a part of the revenue budget.

Revenue receipts include income from: (*i*) taxes on income, expenditure, property and capital transactions, taxes on common services; and (*ii*) from non-tax sources *e.g.*, (*a*) currency, coinage and mint; (*b*) interest receipts, dividends and profits; and (*c*) government activities and services. Capital receipts include market loans, external loans, provident funds and receipts from other transactions like special loans from Reserve Bank of India, deposits, Railway Funds, P&T Reserve Resources Fund etc.

3. Sources of Public Revenue

We shall now throw some light on the various sources from which the state derives its income. Each of these sources is important, because each contributes

2. Mehta, J.K., *Public Finance.* pp. 71-80.

to the kitty, each serves some purpose, each has an impact on the production and distribution of wealth and each affects the level of economic activity and employment in the economy. A brief reference to them is, therefore, necessary.

These sources can be very broadly divided into two: (1) Tax, and (2) Non-tax. We take them up one by one.

(1) Taxes

Every tax is a compulsory payment, without any direct and proportionate benefit to the tax-payer.[3] According to Bastable it is a compulsory contribution for the service of public power. Seligman considers it as a compulsory contribution without reference to special benefits conferred[4] and according to Taussig the distinction between a tax and other charges is noted by the absence of a direct *quid pro quo* between the tax payer and the government.[5]

So, there are three essential features of a tax:

(1) It is a compulsory payment; each one, without any distinction of caste, colour or creed, of age or sex, has to pay it and the refusal to pay it entails punishment and even a delay in payment invokes penalty. This makes a tax different from other sources.

(2) It imposes a personal obligation on the tax payer, that of making payment of the tax amount, according to law. Tax evasion and tax avoidance, both are punishable under law.

(3) Tax paid by the person is utilised for meeting common needs and not for providing any direct service or benefit to the tax payer. At the same time the tax payer is not debarred from enjoying his or her share of the common benefit or general public services.

(2) Non-Tax Sources

(1) The first and the most important source under this head is the income earned from public enterprises and undertakings or the prices of goods and services produced and supplied by the government like postal stamps, electricity, gas, potable water, railway transport, telephone facility, etc. Unlike taxes, prices are a voluntary payment, made by those who consume the goods and services and confer direct benefit to the payer of the price. But the prices charged for public goods and services do not contain any element of profit and are generally below cost. They contain high element of social welfare. Revenues so received by governments have been called by economists as commercial revenues.

---

3. Taylor, P.E., *The Economics of Public Finance,* p. 259.
4. Seligman, E.A.R., *Essays in Taxation,* p. 432.
5. Taussig, E.W., *Principles of Economics,* Vol. II, p. 414.

(2) The second most important source under this category is the fee in various forms charged by the government for rendering service and for granting permission to perform a service. Some fees are charged for meeting the cost of administrative service rendered to confer special benefit to the fee payer, for example, fee paid by a student for getting the benefit of education. Some fees are paid for regulating and controlling individual activities in the interest of maintenance of law and order, like licence fee for the use of firearms, for the sale of liquor or for driving an automobile and for administration of justice like court fees.

Fees are different from prices in the sense that whereas fees are paid for intangible goods, prices are paid for tangible goods; prices confer direct and immediate benefit, fees confer indirect and distant benefit; prices contain a high element of social welfare whereas fees do not.

(3) The third most important source under this head is special assessment or levies to recover the cost of the project undertaken to improve civic amenities like construction of roads and parks, provision of sewerage system, road lighting etc. Such projects also confer special benefit on those property owners whose properties are situated nearby.

A special assessment, like a tax is a compulsory payment and the income derived is spent for the benefit of the whole community. Unlike a tax, the income derived from a special levy is spent for special local project and it is levied on the basis of the benefit conferred. Unlike fees, it is a compulsory contribution.

(4) Fines and forfeitures are an insignificant source of public revenue but are to be mentioned only for academic interest. *Fines* are imposed for infringement of law as a punishment. *Forfeiture* of surety or bonds by law is also a penalty imposed on an individual for breaking the contract or for failing to comply with the commitment made to the court. The government may also sometimes earn an income under the rights of *escheat i.e.*, acquisition of unclaimed property of individuals or trusts.

(5) Gifts and grants or donations from individuals or charitable organisations during natural calamities like earthquakes, famine, floods, etc. or during war also add to government coffers. However, gifts are not a significant source of public revenue.

Grants are also given by one country to another. In modern times, particularly after the second World War, grants have become an important source of public revenue for developing countries. These have been termed as "foreign-aid", and are in various forms like, economic aid, technical aid, military aid etc.

In a federal form of government, grants from the Centre to the States and from the States to the local governments are a common feature.

(6) Currency and mintage are yet another source of income to the governments. Since the face value of coins and paper notes is much more than the actual cost, the profits arising there from are an important source of revenue in modem times. These are a form of compulsory levy on the people as they have no alternative but to accept them.

(7) Finally, deficit budgeting (excess of public expenditure over public revenue) is an important source of public revenue. Budget deficits can be met either by internal loans (market borrowings), foreign loans or by printing new currency notes. Market loans and printing of paper currency are indirect taxation on the people because market loans are obtained by the government at much lower rates of interest than what the lenders would otherwise get by investing their funds elsewhere. By printing additional currency notes the government acquires purchasing power and by using it takes away some of the resources from the market, which otherwise would have been used by the people for meeting their own needs. This kind of deprivation of the people is a sort of tax on them. Thus, like a tax, deficit budgeting also possesses a high degree of compulsion.

4. Canons of Taxation

Taxes are the most important source of public revenue in modern times. In ancient times imposition of taxes was resorted to only in emergencies. The practice of adopting taxation as a source of regular income started with the feudalistic system and developed step by step into a full fledged system during the last two centuries. With every critical change in the economic, political and social scenario, the theory and practice of taxation have undergone sea change with regard to its objective, nature, coverage, administration etc., so as to make the tax system look better and judicious, effective and remunerative than before. The goodness or badness of every tax measure is to be judged in two ways: (*a*) in its individual capacity, and (*b*) in totality as an integral part of the entire system.

For adjudging the merits of a tax, Adam Smith was the first to give us a set of basic principles, called by him as the canons of taxation.[6] We first take up these in the following paragraphs:

Adam Smith's Canons of Taxation

1. Canon of Equality. "The subjects of every state ought to contribute towards the support of the government, as nearly as possible, in proportion to their

6. Smith, Adam, *The Wealth of Nations* (Ed. Edwin Cannan), New York, The Modern Library, pp. 777-79.

respective abilities; that is, in proportion to the revenue which they respectively enjoy under the protection of the state. In the observation or neglect of the maxim consists what is called the equality or inequality of taxation." According to this canon the tax should establish economic justice, that is, the rich should pay proportionally more than the poor. In other words, the higher the income the higher should be the rate of tax. He, therefore, advocated that taxes should be progressive.

2. Canon of Certainty. According to Adam Smith, the tax which each individual is bound to pay ought to be certain, and not arbitrary. The time of payment, the manner of payment, the quantity to be paid, ought all to be clear and plain to the contributor, and to every other person." This canon is to ensure that the tax machinery does not become corrupt and the tax payer is not harassed. The greater the element of uncertainty the greater will be the scope for tax payer's harassment and greater will be the chances for the tax officials to become corrupt Adam Smith considered uncertainty more dangerous than inequality. To use his words, "a very considerable degree of inequality is not near so great an evil as a very small degree of uncertainty."

3. Canon of Convenience. Adam Smith said that "every tax ought to be so levied that the time or the manner in which it is to be paid is most likely to be convenient for the contributor to pay it." This canon is meant to protect the tax payer from the hardship that the inconvenient time and manner of payment may cause. According to Smith, taxes on articles of luxuries were the best as they were the most convenient to collect and most convenient to pay. The consumer has the freedom to pay or not to pay. He may buy the article if he wants to pay the tax otherwise he may go without the commodity.

4. Canon of Economy. In the words of Adam Smith, "Every tax ought to be so contrived as both to take out and keep out of the pockets of the people as little as possible over and above what it brings into the public treasury of the state." What Smith meant by economy was that the cost of collection of a tax should be the minimum. The administrative procedure should be simple and intelligible to all without any ambiguity and requiring the least paper work. The number of staff administering a tax should also be the minimum so that the wage bill is not so heavy as to eat the major portion of the revenues collected from the people. Smith further said that besides keeping the administrative cost low, the tax should not impair the productive efficiency of the people, otherwise the industrial production will suffer and tax collection will fall. Finally, according to Smith, the penalties and forfeitures should not be so heavy as to tempt people to take recourse to tax evasion, affecting adversely the total tax revenue.

Other Canons

After Adam Smith the following canons have also been suggested by writers on public finance:

1. Canon of Productivity. It was Bastable who suggested this canon. By productivity he meant the yield of a tax which should be a satisfactory amount to maintain the state.

Besides the yield, the tax should not adversely affect industrial production. Hence, it means that every tax levied by the state must be so productive as to yield adequate revenue for the treasury, otherwise the government will be compelled to resort to deficit budgeting. This is similar to the canon of economy advocated by Adam Smith.

2. Canon of Elasticity. This was the second canon laid down by Bastable. Elasticity means that the tax revenue may increase automatically whenever needed by an upward revision of rates or by extension of its coverage.

3. Canon of Diversity. With a view to ensuring that the tax burden is well spread over all the citizens and that the element of inequality is the minimum the tax system must be diversified. This implies that different type of taxes must be introduced so as to cover each and every citizen. Opinion is, however, divided on this issue: whether a multiple tax system is better than a single tax system? We shall discuss both the viewpoints in some detail later.

4. Canon of Flexibility. The tax system should have adequate flexibility so that a change in the tax structure, when needed, may be introduced, without undue delay to meet the changing needs of the economy and the treasury.

5. Canon of Simplicity. The tax system should be so simple as to be understood even by a layman. It should be free from all ambiguities and provisos to avoid differences in interpretation and legal disputes. Simplicity in respect of language regarding the bases, conditions and calculation of the tax amount is important to secure administrative efficiency, to save the tax payer from harassment and to obtain maximum collections.

5. Characteristics of a Good Tax System

Some authors have mixed up canons of taxation with the characteristics of a good tax system. Canons are broad criteria for adjudging the appropriateness or otherwise of a tax. Sir Josiah Stamp also did not consider Smith's canons as basic principles of taxation. He preferred to analyse a tax from three angles, *viz.*, (*i*) tax payer, (*ii*) government, and (*iii*) community. Whatever may be the thinking of Stamp, one cannot overlook the contribution of Adam Smith to the development of the science of public finance and ignore these canons. Professor Findlay Shirras is right in saying that, "No genius, however, has succeeded in condensing the principles into such clear and simple canons as has Adam Smith. His acute and capacious mind gave an entirely new turn to former enquiries, and his successors have not, to any material degree, improved on these principles or succeeded in displacing them from the position they hold in the science of public finance." According to Shirras that tax is good, which brings in a large net revenue without protest from the tax payers and without any political influence. He, therefore, considers indirect taxes as the best.

It does not, however, mean that in an economy, if all taxes are individually good, together they shall form a good tax system. In fact, every tax should be looked at as an integral part of the whole system. As a part of the system, even a good tax may be bad, as it may neutralise the good effects of another tax or may exaggerate the bad effects of other taxes. So, in a tax system all the taxes should be effectively linked with each other so that the system may be a unified and well balanced one. The system in order to be good must possess at least three merits *i.e.*, equity, efficiency and convenience. Both direct and indirect taxes must be used with skill and dexterity, taxing the rich and sparing the poor (taking out from their pockets as little as possible and spending as much as possible on the services beneficial for them), ensuring the growth of the economy with reference to the overall social objectives.

Secondly, besides being a balanced and co-ordinated system, it should be designed in such a way that the overall burden of taxation is equitably distributed among all sections of the community. It should adopt the principle of progression—heavier tax on the rich than the poor. Each tax should be universally and uniformly applied to all the individuals falling within a particular category (not like India where agricultural income is not taxed to the extent as non-agricultural income is taxed.) The system should also be automatic in increasing the tax collection with an increase in the per capita income, consumption and wealth and gross domestic product.

Thirdly, a taxation system can be considered as good if it causes the economy to grow through development of trade and industry by augmenting people's ability and willingness to work, save and invest, and also if it makes the distribution of income and wealth as equitable as possible, maximising the welfare of the society.

Musgrave's Views

According to Prof. Musgrave, following should be the characteristics of a good tax system:

(1) The distribution of the tax burden should be equitable; every one should be made to pay his or her *fair share.*

(2) Taxes should be so selected as to minimise interference with economic decisions in otherwise efficient markets. Such interference imposes "excess burdens".

(3) When tax policy is used to achieve other objectives, such as for giving investment incentives, this should be done with minimum interference with the equity of the system.

(4) The tax structure should facilitate the use of fiscal policy for stabilization and growth objectives.

(5) The tax system should allow fair and non-arbitrary administration and should be understandable to the tax-payer.

(6) Administrative and compliance cost should be as low as is compatible with other objectives.

6. A Sound Tax System

However, over the years, change has taken place in the ideas of the people about the role and activities of the state. Consequently, ideas regarding what should form a good tax system have undergone a sea change. The soundness or otherwise of the tax structure must be viewed in the context of a number of points.

First, while considering the effects of taxation, the tax system should not be viewed in isolation, since the effects of taxation are always intermixed with those of non-tax and expenditure parts of the budget.

Second, no tax system can be the "best" in an absolute sense. Every tax system has many dimensions. One will have to look into its volume, tax rates, coverage, time and mode of collection to study the effects in their totality. Hence the slant and focus of enquiry may vary from person to person and time to time and so the choice between different objectives may be determined by our preferences for a particular tax system.

Third, since theoretical considerations are entirely different from real life situations, it is not necessary that a tax system which is the best in the context of theoretical concepts may be the best in practice as well or may be worthy of implementation (the conditions conceived in theory may be ideal hardly to be found in real life.) And hence one will have to keep in view all the practical difficulties and problems before passing a judgement on the tax system.

Lastly, the attitude of the tax payers is also very important—some may be judicious, objective and impartial, while others may not be. It may be difficult for any state to evolve a tax system to suit the entire lot.

To conclude, we may say that a tax system is good, if it is in conformity with the national objectives; if it accommodates, as far as possible, attitudes and problems of tax payers; if it is administratively practical; if it is productive and if it is dynamic to change with the changing circumstances.

Exercises

1. Critically examine the different classifications of 'public revenue' which of these; according to you, is the most satisfactory?
2. State and explain Adam Smith's canons of taxation.
3. How would you characterise a tax system as good? Give your answer in the light of Musgrave's views.

●●●

Chapter 34

The Distribution of Tax Burden

1. Introduction

In this chapter we discuss the various issues related to the burden of a tax and its distribution among the members of the society. The study of this subject assumes importance because of the need of making the tax system fair, equitable and justice based. Modern writers on public finance, unlike their predecessors, lay great emphasis on this aspect of taxation. They do not consider taxation merely as an instrument of raising revenue for the government, but also as a tool for administering social justice. That's why they advocate the principle of equity in the distribution of tax burden.

2. Equity in Taxation

In the context of taxation, equity means fairness in the distribution of burden of taxation. Equity can be horizontal as well as vertical. *Horizontal equity* means that equally rich people should pay equal amount of taxes, while *vertical equity* means that the differently placed persons should pay different amount of tax *i.e.*, more rich persons should pay more than the less rich. This looks to be pretty good in theory but in practice it is difficult to apply.

What is the Tax Burden?

The burden of taxation can be direct as well as indirect. *Direct burden* can be direct money burden and direct real burden. Money burden of a tax refers to the amount of money paid by a tax payer to the government, whereas the real burden of a tax means the sacrifice made by the tax payer in foregoing the use of goods and services by parting with the purchasing power in the form of payment of taxes. *Indirect burden* of a tax refers to the effects of that tax on the price level, income, output, consumption and employment. When we use the term 'burden of taxation' we simply mean the money burden of taxes and do not include in it the effects and the real burden of taxation.

Three Approaches to Tax Burden

The issue relating to the distribution of the tax burden has been approached by the theorists in three ways. We now briefly explain them in the following paras:

Some theorists hold that there is no need to relate the payment of taxes with the benefits provided by the authorities to the tax payers. One comes across two approaches in this connection, *viz.*, (1) Socio-political, and (2) Expediency.

The Socio-political Approach

According to this approach ultimate social and political objectives set by an authority should be the determinants of a taxation policy. It was Wagner, the German economist, who advocated this approach. In those days most of the German thinkers deplored the individualistic approach of the classical economists and considered society above the individual. Hence, according to them the tax system should be designed to meet the overall needs of the society and not of its individual members. Wagner, therefore, held that all taxes should aim at curing the ills of the society like reduction of income inequalities. To meet this objective, small incomes should be exempted from tax and unearned incomes and inherited properties should be heavily taxed. To extend Wagner's approach to modern times, all economic malpractices like hoarding, production of harmful drugs and other goods, monopolistic and restrictive trade practices etc. should be curbed and social ills should be cured with the help of taxation.

The Expediency Approach

According to this approach, the only consideration that should weigh, while considering a tax proposal, with the authorities is that of practicability. It implies that the government before introducing a tax must examine the practicability aspect of that tax from the angles of administrative feasibility, cost of collection, its compatibility with other taxes of the system, its acceptability by the people who are intended to be affected, its revenue earning capacity, etc. In the context of the economy as a whole and the overall tax system the practicability aspect should also include, besides other things, the overall effects of the tax system on the economy *i.e.*, its role in boosting the economic growth, and in reducing economic disparities and regional imbalances.

Theories of Distribution of Tax Burden

Both these approaches have their own merits, but they cannot provide the base for a fair taxation policy. The fairness of the tax system is determined by the element of equity *i.e.*, how equitable is the distribution of the tax burden among different individuals? The consideration of the question of equity leads us to the Ability-to-Pay approach which we shall take up later. We now take up those theories which establish a link between the tax burden and the benefits received by the members of the society or the cost of the services provided by the government.

1. The Cost of Service Theory

This theory is based on the balanced budget approach *i.e.*, the government should not provide any service to any individual free, but should realise the cost of the service from the citizens who take advantage of that service. Hence the basis of taxation should be the cost of the different services rendered by the government to the tax payers.

Difficulties of This Theory

But, the application of this theory is rather difficult. Firstly, its acceptance would imply that the state should not undertake welfare and relief activities like free education, medical aid etc. which are primarily meant for very poor people. Then, the state will also not be concerned with the problems of income distribution or cyclical fluctuations or social security. When the cost of service will be the determinant of taxation, the question of imposing taxes on capital gains, windfall gains, inheritance, gifts, expenditure etc. cannot arise.

Secondly, since the principle of exclusion does not apply to most of the state services and goods, the apportionment of the cost of the service between different beneficiaries is not possible. Besides, the computation of the cost of a service for a particular individual is also not easy since most of the services rendered by the government, for example, provision of roads, highways, parks, dams, defence, justice etc. are for the people as a whole and not for any particular individual or a group of individuals. Moreover, the identification of proper beneficiaries of any service is also a problem.

Thirdly, if cost forms the basis of taxation, how to ensure that the cost charged is just and not high and that the cost of inefficiency is not being passed on to the consumers?

Finally, since some of the state services have externalities, the question arises whether the state should determine the tax liability on the basis of commercial costs or on the basis of net social costs? It would be detrimental if the state behaves like a private entrepreneur and bases its decisions on commercial considerations.

2. The Benefit Theory

Like the cost of service theory, the benefit theory also assumes that there is a contractual relationship between the state and its citizens. The government is an entrepreneur and whatever services it renders to the people, provide some benefit to them. The people should share the burden of taxation in proportion to the benefits received by them. This provides justification to the state for imposing taxes on its people.

This approach is very old and it originated from the social contract theory of the state, *i.e.*, taxation is the price paid to the state for the protection of life and property of its citizens in the form of goods and services. This view was very much prevalent in Germany and France in the seventeenth and eighteenth centuries and was mainly advocated by writers like, Grotius, Hobbes, Hume, Locke and Rousseau. In England Adam Smith held almost the same view, when he talked about the ability to pay.

Since benefit is a subjective thing and is difficult to measure, the benefits accruing to different persons cannot be determined, nor a comparison is possible to determine the tax liability of different persons. That's why Adam Smith adopted income as the criterion for determining the benefits and the relative tax liability of different individuals. So, according to the benefit approach, tax is a payment made by an individual in lieu of the protection it receives from the state. But all the economic thinkers were not agreeable to this view. For example, Rousseau thought that the rich people were benefited more than the poor from the protection of the state. John Stuart Mill was of the view that the poor needed more protection specially against the exploitation by the rich. According to him it would lead to regressive taxation.

This approach was also used in the 19th century and early 20th century to show the optimum state activity and optimum division of tax burden. In this exercise taxes were taken as the price for the goods and services supplied by the state. So, the tax level at which the demand for and supply of state services equated with each other was worked out. In this connection the views of certain economists expressed in the last quarter of the nineteenth century are worth mentioning.[1]

Italian economist U. Mazolla in 1880 pointed out the fundamental difference between private and public goods *i.e.*, public goods are shared by all consumers and so, the principle of exclusion does not apply to them. Therefore, each individual instead of paying the same price for public goods (*i.e.* tax) should pay according to the marginal utility of that good to him or her. And hence each tax payer would equate the marginal utility of his expenditure on public and private goods. On the other hand, Emil Sax, an Austrian economist distinguishing between 'personal collective wants' and 'collective wants proper' asserted that since the principle of exclusion does

1. R.A. Musgrave and A.T. Peacock (Eds.), *Classics in the Theory of Public Finance,* International Economic Association, Macmillan and Co., 1958.

not apply to the latter and each individual derives benefit from them, each has to pay according to the relative benefit derived from the consumption of public services. A proportional income tax according to Sax would be a good measure of this relative benefit.

On a similar assumption as that of Sax, that the members of the community use public services in proportion to their incomes, in 1888, Antonio de Viti de Marco an Italian economist asserted that the richer members of the community should pay more tax than the poorer members because with increase in incomes the marginal utility of money goes on decreasing and they have to make lesser sacrifice than the poorer people. De Marco did not advocate proportional taxation because it hurt the poorer people more than the rich. He emphasised on equitable distribution of sacrifice, and therefore, the basis of equal distribution of burden of taxation was thus not the benefit received, but the extent of sacrifice made by the rich people relative to poorer people.

In 1896, Knut Wicksell in Sweden put forward a theory for the equal distribution of burden of taxation on ethical grounds. According to Wicksell, taxation should be based upon voluntary and unanimous action. Individual members of the community are free not to avail of any state services and thus not to pay taxes. But, if this sort of approach is followed then the taxation will have nothing to do with the equitable distribution of income and wealth. Wicksell admits that his theory would be applicable only when the distribution of income was equitable.

In 1919 another Swedish economist, Erik Lindahl, explained the benefit approach within the framework of voluntary exchange theory of public finance. To simplify things he tried to find a solution of the problem by taking only two tax-payers who are free to express their preferences for state services *vis-a-vis* corresponding tax liability. According to Lindahl a kind of voluntary exchange takes place between the taxes paid and state services availed by the tax payers, which is to be determined by the demand schedules of the tax payers for those services. Lindahl, in this connection did not bother about the problem of equitable distribution of income. He has tried to seek the solution of three problems, *viz.*, (*i*) the extent of expenditure to be incurred by the state on various goods and services and the level of taxation; (*ii*) allocating the total expenditure of the state amongst various goods and services produced by it; and (*iii*) allocating the tax burden amongst the tax payers. Lindahl for solving these problems, first assumes that the two individuals form the community and then proceeds to discuss the solution of these problems. These two individuals are *A* and *B*. *A* and *B* both have a given demand schedule for public services and goods. These goods and services are consumed jointly by both of them. *A* agrees to contribute different proportions of the cost of these services and goods depending upon his elasticity of demand for them.

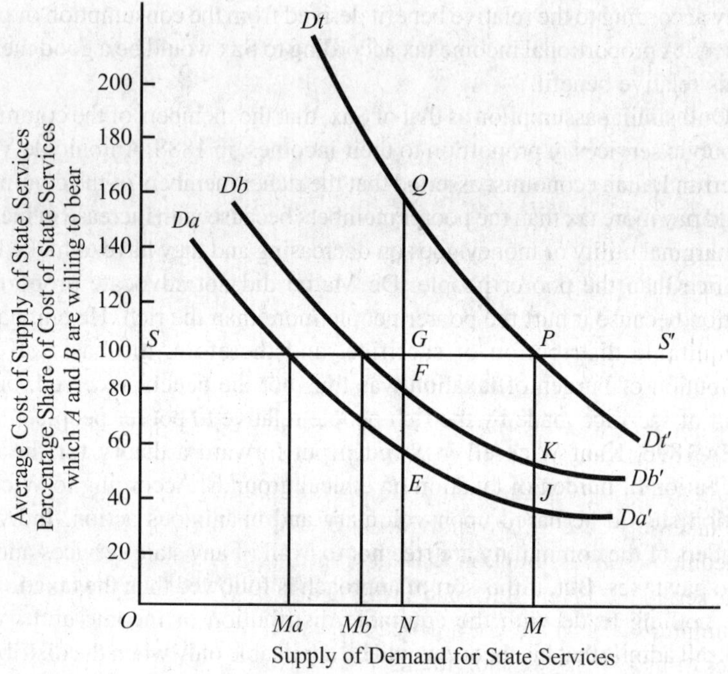

Fig. 34.1.

Lindahl's theory has been explained by H.R. Bowen with the help of Fig. 34.1 as shown before.

In Fig. 34.1, the supply and demand for state services have been shown on the horizontal axis while the average cost of these services and the percentage share of costs which *A* and *B* are ready to bear have been shown on the vertical axis.

SS′ is the supply schedule of the state services. *Da Da′* is the demand schedule of *A* while *Db Db′* is the demand schedule of *B*. For any supply upto *OMa, A* is willing to bear more than the full cost of the services. When the supplies are larger than *OMa, A* is willing to bear a smaller proportion of the cost. For example, out of the total cost of *NG* per unit, *A's* contribution is only *NE* per unit against the supply of state services equal to *ON*. Since the supply of *ON* of state services is to be jointly consumed by both *A* and *B, B* will bear *NF* and as such the state can collect a tax equal to *NQ* per unit of state services. *Q,* therefore, lies on the combined demand schedule of state services represented by *Dt Dt′*. Since the object of the state is not to earn profit on the supply of its services, it increases the supply. But for increased supply, *A* and *B* are willing to bear a lesser proportion of the cost. That is why for the supply of OM of state services the combined contribution of A and B is $MJ + MK = MP$ which is equal to the cost of supply. P is the point of equilibrium where the combined demand curve $Dt\ Dt'$ intersects the supply curve SS'. In Fig. 34.1 it has been assumed that the production of services takes place under the law of constant returns. That is why the supply curve is horizontal. However, even if the supply is subject to law of diminishing or increasing returns it won't make any difference because in that case too, different proportions of taxes will be borne by A and B.

Lindahl's solution provides answer to only two out of the three problems indicated above. It shows the optimum level of state activity and also the allocation of tax burden amongst the tax payers. It, however, suffers from certain weaknesses. First, it is not possible to know the actual preferences of individual tax payers, since those public goods and services to which the principle of exclusion does not apply, will be produced by the public sector, the use of which cannot be denied to any individual. Therefore, the tax payers would tend to understate their preferences for such services. Second, Lindahl has taken the case of two individuals in which each formulates his demand schedule on the assumption that the contribution of the other to the cost of state services is given. But, such a state of affairs would require highly rigorous assumptions which are not practicable. Third, to generalise the discussion to cases of more than two individuals and for more than two goods and services, complex mathematical techniques will have to be applied which could make the entire process extremely cumbersome. For example, we will have to obtain data about the cost function of each goods and services supplied by the state and the demand function of each tax payer for each goods and services. Then the constraints covering the inter-dependence of these functions have also to be taken into account along with specification of each individual function. Again, the stability of all these functions has to be ensured. Since all these conditions cannot be easily fulfilled, Lindahl's explanation is difficult to apply and this makes it impracticable. Fourth, in actual life individual tax payers hardly get an opportunity to reveal their preferences for state services. The preferences of the tax payers are expressed by the legislative or the executive authority which can hardly be a perfect system. Fifth, Lindahl's theory is based on the assumption that distribution of income is optimal, which is not valid. Finally, Lindahl's explanation assumes that the state services are funded only through taxation which is not the real position because we know that state obtains large amount of funds for running its activities through public loans and deficit financing.

Limitations of the Benefit Theory

The benefit theory suffers from a number of weaknesses which are as follows:

(1) The foremost difficulty relates to the measurement of the benefits to the individual members of the community, since benefit is a subjective thing and cannot be measured directly. Any index used for representing the benefit received by the tax payers will be subject to debate. Although some thinkers have taken income as the representative of the benefits received by the tax payers it itself is a questionable index, particularly if we do not know the expenditure pattern of the state, will the benefit of the state services be the same for the two individuals if one gets essential food items on subsidised rates under the public distribution system and the other buys from the open market?

(2) The benefit theory is based on the assumption that the individual benefits are independent of each other. In other words, the benefit received by an individual is independent of what other people are getting. But this is not correct. We are aware of the fact that the satisfaction that an individual derives from his income depends not only upon his own absolute income but also on the incomes that other individuals residing in his neighbourhood get. Similarly, the benefits derived from the state expenditure do not depend upon the absolute amount received by an individual but also upon the share that others are getting.

(3) Another major difficulty in this theory is that taxes are not the only source from which the state collects its funds. There are also other forms of contributions made by the members of the community to the state coffers. And these are in the nature of prices voluntarily paid by the citizens for availing of services provided by the state. It is true that the decisions pertaining to the supply of services by the state and contributions made by the members of the community are not taken on an individual basis but on a collective basis by bodies like parliament and legislature. From this angle prices can only partially be considered as taxation since these are compulsory payments without any *quid pro quo.*

(4) The assumption of the benefit theory that the income earned by members of the community is connected directly with the benefits received from the state, is debatable. It is not always possible to quantify the relationship between income and benefits. For example, some people may assert that since income is subject to the law of diminishing marginal utility, the richer people derive lesser benefit as compared to poorer people from the state services. Others may argue that since poorer people need protection from the state against exploitation by the rich, all the legislation and connected activities of the state are undertaken to achieve this object and therefore, the poorer people receive more benefits from state services than the richer people. Still others

may contend that the enactment of various legislations provide great opportunities to the rich people to acquire additional income and enjoy their wealth and income under state protection. The richer people get larger protection from the state, since the opportunities available to the poor are always very limited.

(5) The benefit principle negates all the welfare activities, particularly those aimed at changing the pattern of the distribution of income and wealth. It, therefore, implies that all those receiving benefits under social security schemes, like maternity and sickness benefits, old age pensions etc. being specific and certain will have to return the same to the state by way of taxes. In fact, the basic assumption of the benefit approach is that the distribution of income is already just which is quite wrong. If the taxes are imposed by the state in accordance with the benefits received the end result would be an inequitable distribution of income. Hence to assume that the income distribution is already proper is wrong and reduces the entire relationship between the state and its citizens to a commercial level only.

(6) Basically it is not always possible to assign the net benefits of the state activities and the tax burden since majority of these cannot be quantified at all. There are a larger number of benefits and costs which cannot be ascribed to a particular group or section of the community, particularly in the case of those goods and services which have "externalities".

(7) Since most of the governments have to tackle the problem of economic growth in developing countries and of stabilisation in developed countries, the benefit theory is unable to provide adequate guidance to the government in this regard because the benefits resulting therefrom cannot be distributed proportionately among the individual members of the community.

(8) Further, it is not necessary that all the individuals may have a complete knowledge of the programmes and activities undertaken by the government. It is also possible that some activities undertaken by the government are more beneficial to the society as a whole or even to certain sections of the community. So, to presume that all the citizens are free to voluntarily opt for the services and pay for the same will not be correct. For example, in most of the underdeveloped countries a large number of people are unable to take advantage of the health programmes like polio vaccination or hepatitis-B injections because of lack of knowledge.

(9) Another lacuna in the benefit approach is that it does not recognise the objective of equity in taxation.

(10) Still another weakness of this approach is that the relationship between the government and the people is treated purely as commercial, neglecting the basic utility of various programmes undertaken by several governments for the welfare of the under-privileged sections of the society.

(11) Benefit approach has also been questioned on the basis that the decisions regarding raising of funds and their spending are not governed by the market mechanism of demand and supply but by a political process. Most of these decisions are contained in the state budgets which are accepted and approved by elected representative of the people in the legislature and parliament. The individuals also change their outlook towards taxes not on the basis of individual interests but on the basis of political factors.[2]

(12) The benefit theory does not also suggest any solution for the problem when the revenue collected through taxes falls short of the government's requirements. In such a situation should the government raise the required funds through market loans or through deficit financing?

(13) It has been seen that the measures taken by the government at times, lead to the benefits or losses to those economic units or sections of the community as well which are not covered by the introductory impact of these measures. The impact of these measures is felt by those economic units which fall in the second or third round of the benefits or losses, because the economic units in an economy through economic transactions are inter-dependent. The benefit theory does not advocate the imposition of taxes on the secondary or later beneficiaries.

From the foregoing it is clear that it is extremely difficult to use the benefit principle as a basis for the distribution of tax burden in practice.

3. Ability to Pay Theory

Like the benefits received theory the ability to pay approach does not treat the relationship between the state and its citizens as commercial or semi-commercial. According to this approach taxes are a compulsory payment without any equal or proportionate return. An individual has to pay taxes because he or she is in a position to pay and his relative share in the total tax burden is determined by his relative paying capacity. This approach has received support from both socialist as well as non-socialist thinkers and forms an important part of welfare economics. The basic tenet is that taxation should be based on the principle of justice and equity. This approach is much older than the benefit approach. The suggestion regarding progressive taxation based on ability, was contained initially in an essay by Guicciardini which was published in the first half of the sixteenth century. Thereafter a number of writers restated and amended this principle on various grounds. Among them the chief are Rousseau, Sismondi, Mill, Wagner and Roosevelt.

---

2. Gerhard Colm, *Essays in Public Finance and Fiscal Policy,* Oxford University Press, New York, 1955, pp. 32-33.

Some Generalities of the Concept

Before proceeding further let us note down a few things about the concept of ability to pay. These are as follows:

(1) The concept does not refer to any absolute quantity. It is related to many things particularly to the expenditure incurred by the state.

(2) Different criteria can be adopted for determining the relative ability to pay of the individuals. These can be income, property, size of the family, consumption expenditure etc.

(3) When the concept is related to the welfare of the society, the ability to pay is interpreted in terms of sacrifice which is a subjective phenomenon.

(4) In case income is used as index of ability with the twin objective of equity and welfare then progressive taxation is considered as the end result. But in practice the conditions may also warrant a proportional or even regressive taxation.

(5) In a broad discussion on the ability to pay, generally the repercussive effects of fiscal policy are not taken into account. For example, the fiscal policy of the government will generally affect the entire economy *i.e.*, level of savings, investment, production, employment and growth, which will in turn affect the ability to pay of the citizens, both absolutely and relatively.

(6) It may also be noted that in any discussion on ability to pay of tax payers, taxation alone is not to be considered because it is the overall budgetary policy of the government which is important. And budget has both the sides, revenue as well as expenditure. Besides, on the revenue side taxation is only one of the sources. So, a serious discussion on the ability to pay should refer to all these aspects of budgetary policy but for the sake of simplification, the focus of our discussion will be on taxation alone.

Justification for the Criterion of Ability to Pay

The protagonists of the concept of ability to pay justify it on the following grounds:

(1) It gives psychological satisfaction to the tax payer, that he is making a contribution in the running of the government. And the tax payer also feels that by paying taxes he is also making a sacrifice.

(2) Since increase in incomes results in decreasing marginal utility of income, the burden of the tax is more on the rich people than on the poor and this brings about an equality in sacrifice.

(3) According to Hobson taxes are paid by an individual out of the "economic surplus". In this connection he has distinguished between that part of income which has the ability to bear taxes and the part which does not have any ability to bear the taxes. The part of income which may bear taxes has been called by Hobson as economic surplus. Hence on a higher level of

income and property the level of taxation should increase more than proportionately.

Criteria for Ability to Pay: Two Approaches

The fundamental question is how to determine the ability of an individual to pay taxes? In this connection two approaches have been suggested: (*i*) Objective approach, and (*ii*) Subjective approach.

I. Objective Approach

This approach includes objective indices like wealth or property, income, consumption expenditure etc. as the basis for determining the ability to pay taxes. The subjective approach relates ability to pay to the extent of sacrifice that an individual tax payer undergoes in meeting the tax liability. We now explain these approaches in some detail in the following paragraphs:

Objective Criteria of Ability to Pay

According to the objective approach there are various criteria for determining the ability to pay of an individual tax payer. These objective indices have been pointed out as:

(1) property or wealth, (2) income, (3) size of the family, and (4) consumption expenditure. We now deal with them one by one.

1. Property or Wealth as an Index of Ability to Pay. In a market economy the institutions of private property and inheritance occupy an important place. The economy grows with the increase in private property through the process of savings and investment. And it is not therefore, wrong to think that people should be taxed according to the property or wealth that they hold. Moreover, the private individuals amass property and wealth only because of the protection provided by the government in the form of rules and laws. It is, therefore, natural that private individuals should contribute towards the expense involved in the administration of the economy. But there are a number of conceptual and other difficulties in adopting property or wealth as an index. Firstly, if taxes are imposed on an individual's property or wealth, people would be discouraged to save and invest. Their enthusiasm for work and for putting in hard labour would be dampened. It will, therefore, affect the growth and capital accumulation in the economy adversely.

Secondly, the setback to saving and investment would be even greater if the property and wealth are taxed at high rates. This is particularly true in an underdeveloped country where the inequalities of wealth are great and the taxable property is already very low.

Thirdly, property as an objective index suffers from a number of anomalies. For example, income from property may not be the same in all cases. Some properties may yield more income than others and some may not yield any income at all. Moreover, the income from property may not be continuous and may vary according to the location, use, etc.

Finally, a tax on property is levied on its capital value. But if it does not yield any income, the tax may be unjust. But, it does not mean that property and wealth should not be taken into account while estimating the ability to pay. They certainly indicate the tax paying capacity of the individual. Moreover, from the point of view of general welfare, accumulation of property and wealth leads to concentration of economic power which in turn creates possibilities of economic exploitation and therefore it is necessary that property and wealth should be taxed. No one can deny that the property and wealth enhance the paying capacity of their owners as compared to those individuals who earn the same income from other sources. It is also said that in a market economy the owners of property and wealth may wield undue influence on the economic policies of the government to serve their own interest. However, property and wealth cannot be relied upon as the sole source of taxation. But, it can certainly be considered as an important source of public revenue, only as a supplementary index of ability to pay.

2. Income. Income of an individual has been widely accepted as an objective index of ability to pay. But, it is not considered as the sole source of taxation and a number of the tax indices have been adopted to supplement it. Adam Smith was the first economist who accepted income as a proper measure of ability to pay. He maintained that such ability is in proportion to respective incomes of the tax paying individuals. But income as an index of ability to pay can have more than one interpretation. It would, therefore, be advantageous if we look at the various conceptual and practical difficulties before finally arriving at any conclusion. Firstly, income has two parts, earned and un-earned; the former is in the form of wages, salaries etc. while the latter is in the form of capital gains, windfall income etc. The latter, therefore, should be subjected to heavier taxation. Some expenses are incurred to earn income which cannot be expressed in money terms. Further, the individual also foregoes some leisure in earning the income. So it is not the gross income but the net income which is to be taken into account for the purpose of taxation. It means that out of the gross income the expenses and cost of leisure should be deducted. But even when net income is measured in a rigorous way it cannot be a good index of ability to pay. We will have to take into account both income and needs of the tax payer.

We shall also have to consider whether the form of taxation should be direct (income tax) or indirect (excise duties or sales tax) because in the case of corporate bodies, income can hardly be a relevant index of ability to pay. Similarly, we cannot use indirect taxes because they are levied on commodities and services. If we levy indirect taxes it will have to be assumed that consumers can be classified into homogeneous groups according to the types and quantities of goods and services purchased by them. This sort of assumption will be highly unrealistic.

Further, in developed countries it may be true that wealthier people spend more on luxury goods. But in underdeveloped countries this may not be true in every part of the country, particularly in the rural areas where such luxury goods cannot be put into use. However, it will have to be accepted that income as an index of ability to pay has come to stay as the more acceptable index.

3. Size of the Family. For the proper distribution of tax burden another index of ability to pay suggested by certain authors is the size of the family. A small family has a higher tax paying ability as compared to a large sized family. On the same analogy a bachelor has a large tax paying ability than a married couple having a family of four or five members, when the circumstances, income etc. in both these cases are the same. Apparently, it appears to be logical but this index cannot be accepted as the primary measure of the tax paying ability.

4. Consumption Expenditure. It was Prof. Fischer who had suggested consumption expenditure as a measure of tax paying ability of an individual. In the recent past Prof. Kaldor also advocated a tax on expenditure. The idea was that an expenditure tax or a consumption tax would bring about greater equity in the tax system and would also check tax evasion. Hobbes has actually given the idea of a tax on that part of income which an individual uses and not a tax on that income which is saved and is left to be used by the next generation. Thus, on ethical grounds a tax on consumption and not on savings is considered as a proper kind of tax. In this respect also it has been argued that consumption expenditure is not a satisfactory index of an individual's tax paying ability. It is not easy to construct this index and then the administration of tax determined on the basis of consumption expenditure is all the more difficult. It has also been argued that people's wants are not only limited to consumption alone and in every economy saving and investment are equally important. Hence it is not judicious to tax that part of income which is consumed and leave that part of income which is saved and invested untaxed. So, a tax on consumption expenditure cannot be regarded as the sole source of revenue from taxation and can be adopted alongwith other forms of taxes.

According to Prof. Seligman the ability to pay approach has the following defects:

(1) A general property tax is regressive in nature as it falls heavily on smaller property than on larger property.

(2) It lacks uniformity in assessment.

(3) It cannot reach each personal property.

(4) It may promote dishonesty.

So, the question of a stable index for measuring the tax paying ability of individual tax payer is still unresolved. For a long time property remained as a basis of taxation and now for quite some time income has been continuing as an index of ability to pay. Income has an advantage in that taxation can be made progressive without much difficulty. Moreover, while computing the total income of an individual the taxation authorities have scope to include income from all sources whether from property or from personal services. In short, income has come to stay as an appropriate index for estimating the tax paying ability of an individual.

II. Subjective Approach

This approach involves the consideration of the burden of a tax felt or the sacrifice undergone by a tax payer. It is based on the assumption that the payment of tax involves hardship or suffering. It is also assumed that the sacrifice or hardship of a tax payer depends only on his own tax liability and not on the tax liability of others. Since payment of tax implies hardship to an individual the question of determining tax liability can be considered either with reference to the principle of equity or with reference to the objective of general welfare. With regard to equity, it can be said that each tax payer should be made to suffer or sacrifice to the same extent. From the point of view of welfare, the aggregate sacrifice of all the tax payers should be the minimum so that the consequential loss of welfare to the community is the minimum. The equity criterion was first suggested by J.S. Mill. John Stuart Mill advocated the equality in taxation as equality in sacrifice, which means "the apportioning of the contribution of each person towards the expenses of government so that he shall feel neither more nor less inconvenience from his share of the payment than everybody experiences from his" and therefore he stated that "tax payers are be treated equally if their tax payments involve an equal sacrifice or loss of welfare"[3].

III. Principle of Equal Sacrifice

It thus implies that to bring about equality in taxation all persons in similar position should be treated similarly and all persons in dissimilar position should be treated dissimilarly. The former is known as horizontal equity while the latter is known as vertical equity. This is known as the principle of equal sacrifice. This principle simply means that if the marginal utility of income is same for all tax payers then people with equal income should contribute equal amount of tax and those with different incomes should pay different amounts

3. J.S. Mill, *Principles of Political Economy* (1921), p. 804.

of tax. But the basic question is how to determine these amounts. Three interpretations have been given in this regard. These are: (*i*) Equal absolute sacrifice, (*ii*) Equal proportional sacrifice, and (*iii*) Equal marginal sacrifice. Prof. Dalton has added a fourth interpretation, *viz*., constant inequality of incomes.[4] He has also expressed his predicament about preference for anyone of the above. He said, "*prima facie,* it is not clear, on grounds of equity, which of these four is to be preferred.'[5]

For applying the utility criterion we shall have to know the way in which the marginal utility of income changes according to the change in the income of the tax payer. But this is not an easy task. Since equity is a subjective thing, it cannot be measured in absolute terms. One can at the most have an inter-personal comparison which is also not easy. But without any measurement or inter-personal comparison of utility, it is not possible to derive any definite conclusion regarding the apportioning of tax burden. At the same time, the assumption of similarity of income utility schedules has been accepted even by those who do not believe in its scientific validity. The fact, however, remains that it is not easy to have an objective measure of utility. We may now throw some light on the different interpretations of "equal sacrifice" in the following paragraphs:

(a) Equal Absolute Sacrifice

According to this interpretation loss of utility through payment of tax should be equal to all tax payers. This means that people with higher income should pay more than those who have lower income, in such a way that the sacrifice undergone by each tax payer is the same. In other words, the difference between the aggregate utility from income before tax and after tax should be the same for every tax payer. Algebraically it can be expressed as $U(Y)–U(Y–T)$ should be the same for all tax payers, where U is the total utility, Y is the income before tax and $Y–T$ is the income after tax. Thus, every member of the community will have to pay some tax and no one will be exempted. But what would be the nature of the tax? Whether it would be progressive, proportional or regressive? If the marginal utility of income is identical in all cases and if the marginal utility of income is constant then each individual should pay the same absolute amount of tax. It implies that higher incomes will be taxed at a lower rate and lower income will be taxed at a higher rate. In other words the tax will be regressive in nature. If the marginal utility of income is declining at the same rate as the rate of rise in incomes, then higher incomes will be taxed at a higher rate and lower incomes will be taxed at a lower rate.

4. H. Dalton, *Principles of Public Finance,* London, Routledge and Kegan Paul Limited, 1949. p. 41.
5. *Ibid.*

For bringing about equal absolute sacrifice a proportional tax will be levied. If the marginal utility of income declines at a rate faster than the rate of increase in income then a progressive tax will result in equal absolute sacrifice. It may be mentioned in this connection that the above conclusions can be drawn only when the slope of marginal utility curve is known.

(b) Equal Proportional Sacrifice

According to this interpretation also, no one will be exempted from paying tax. This means that the tax should be proportional to the total income and the ratio of sacrifice to income will be the same for all tax payers although people with higher incomes will pay more tax. In other words, the direct real burden of the tax payer would be proportionate to the economic welfare which he derives from his income. It, therefore, implies that the satisfaction which the tax payer parts with in the payment of tax bears the same proportion to the satisfaction from the pre-tax income in the case of every individual tax payers. In the case of equal proportional sacrifice, however, it is not easy to draw a general conclusion about progressive, proportional or regressive tax rates. Here the relative rate of change in marginal and average utility of income will have to be taken into account. If the marginal utility of income remains unaltered then a proportional tax would result in equal proportional sacrifice. If the marginal utility of income declines then the relative percentage changes in the marginal and average utilities will have to be taken into account. If the fall in the marginal utility of income is the same as the decline in average utility then a proportional tax will lead to equal proportional sacrifice. If the marginal utility of income falls at a rate faster than the fall in the average utility, a progressive tax will satisfy the objective of equal proportional sacrifice. If the marginal utility of income declines at a rate lower than the average utility, then a regressive tax will enable us to achieve the objective of equal proportional sacrifice.

(c) Equal Marginal Sacrifice or the Least Aggregate Sacrifice

After having a clue from Bentham's utilitarian dictum of "greatest good of the greatest number", Edgeworth interpreted the principle of equal sacrifice as equal marginal sacrifice. According to him, in a competitive economy, the determination of rate of exchange at which marginal utilities can be equated, is not easy and therefore another basis for equating marginal utilities has to be discovered. He therefore, advocated the application of the principle of least aggregate sacrifice in the domain of distribution of tax burden. He asserted that various individuals, guided by self-interest, in the absence of competition, must find out an arrangement which leads to the greatest amount of welfare to all concerned provided no individual suffers loss in this arrangement.

It is in that situation only that the welfare of all the individuals taken together would be the maximum. In his view no individual would be unwilling to accept this arrangement because everybody would expect to get a share of total welfare which would not be less than what would be provided by the maximum welfare principle. Each individual, therefore, realises that the arrangement which maximises aggregate utility will be to each person's advantage. Thus, Edgeworth took a more realistic view and considered the least aggregate sacrifice principle as the rule to be applied by the government and to be left to be established by the market forces. It, therefore, follows that marginal sacrifice imposed by the last unit of money upon the tax payer and not the total sacrifice for the different tax payers should be the same so that the aggregate sacrifice for the community as a whole will be the minimum.

According to this interpretation of equity the burden of tax would be distributed among different tax payers in such a way that the marginal utility of income left after the payment of tax by an individual, would be the same for all individual tax payers. So, this principle emphasises the welfare of the community as well. According to Pigou, "in the special field of taxation this general principle is identical with the principle of least sacrifice."[6]

He further elaborates, "Thus the distribution of taxation required to conform to the principle of least aggregate sacrifice is that which makes the marginal—not the total—sacrifice borne by all the members of the community equal.[7]

To sum up, according to this philosophy the aggregate sacrifice imposed by taxation on the community should be the minimum. To bring about equality, rich may be taxed and the relatively less rich or poorer people can be given bounties from the revenue of the tax till equality is obtained. So long as it does not happen, the richest people should be taxed and the poorer people should not be taxed until the higher income level is brought down to the lower income level. It, therefore, implies that the tax should first be levied on people with highest income. When their income is reduced by tax to the level of the second highest income the tax should be levied on people with second highest income and when the second highest income level is brought down to the level of the third highest income, then people with third highest income should be taxed, and so on.

This process should continue till the desired revenue is obtained. According to Pigou, it is the "ultimate principle of taxation."[8] The application of this principle, therefore, requires maximum progression, since utility cannot be measured objectively and any other personal comparisons are also not feasible. It has been held by certain writers that the above conclusions have

6. A.C. Pigou, *A Study in Public Finance,* 3rd edn., Macmillan & Co., 1951, p. 43.
7. *Ibid,* p. 57.
8. *Ibid.*

not been drawn on a scientific basis. According to these writers, in the absence of relevant data it is not possible to prove that the best way of distributing tax burden would be to enforce equal incomes after the payment of tax. But Lerner believes that even in the absence of relevant data it is possible to conclude that the equality in income distribution would maximise the aggregate satisfaction of the community. He bases his argument on probability of a loss or a gain and maximisation of probable aggregate satisfaction.[9] But the conclusions drawn on the basis of probabilities cannot be objective.

Which of the Different Principles of Sacrifice is Superior?

Beginning with Adam Smith the principle of sacrifice gained currency and received the support from all important writers. Adam Smith said that people should "contribute in proportion to their respective abilities." It may mean either equal absolute sacrifice or equal proportional sacrifice. John Stuart Mill also advocated equal sacrifice principle but did not define the concept of equality. Even when the equality in sacrifice was interpreted in three different ways, there was no unanimity regarding the suitability or practicability of anyone of these. Likewise, there has been no agreement on the determination of the tax rate schedule under the interpretation considered to be the best. Even those writers who lend support to these three interpretations, did not agree regarding their merits. Cohen-Stuart upheld the principle of equal proportional sacrifice. Sidgwick and Marshall advocated equal absolute sacrifice. Carver treated equality as equal marginal sacrifice. Edgeworth and Pigou believed that there was no logical choice between the two. On welfare ground, however, they considered equal marginal sacrifice as the most suitable principle. According to Edgeworth the equal marginal sacrifice principle is the most superior because it is based on the utilitarian principle of greatest happiness. He also asserted that the implementation of this principle would be most feasible than other principles of sacrifice since we only need to know that the common marginal utility curve is downward sloping and not the exact rate at which it declines. But, as already realised by Edgeworth as well as Pigou, a progression in taxation and extreme measures of equalisation may adversely affect the total output of the economy and therefore the principle of least aggregate sacrifice has to be implemented with great care.

Limitations of Subjective Approach

The application of the subjective approach to the measurement of ability to pay has only a very limited application. Since sacrifice is subjective in nature the entire concept does not appear to be very practical due to the following reasons:

9. A.P. Lerner, *Economics of Control,* Macmillan & Co., New York, 1944, p. 30.

(1) As stated already sacrifice is subjective in nature and cannot be measured objectively. Sacrifice can only be felt by the person who makes it. It is also not possible to ensure that the total sacrifice of all individuals in an economy would be minimum. Hence, it is not possible to adopt it as an index of ability to pay and for the distribution of tax burden.

(2) Since exact measurement of the declining rate of marginal utility with increase in income is not possible, any attempt to bring about progression in the rate of taxation may not lead to the equalisation of marginal sacrifice because it will be only arbitrary and not based on any data.

(3) The subjective approach also does not differentiate between the sources of income and their nature. A tax on the income earned through the inherited property will involve less sacrifice than a tax on an income earned by an individual through frugal living and hard labour. Accordingly it is very difficult to exactly know and, quantify the sacrifice made by an individual in the payment of taxes.

(4) Equalisation of the marginal sacrifice of all tax payers is full of difficulties because even when different persons have the same income and tax liability, they may not undergo the same amount of sacrifice because of differences in their tastes, outlook, psychology, size of the family etc.

Exercises

1. Explain the meaning of the term: 'burden of taxation'. Among the different theories on the distribution of tax burden, which one according to you, is the most acceptable?
2. What do you understand by the 'doctrine of justice', in a system of taxation? Which, in your opinion, is the best principle to achieve the objectives of justice in taxation?
3. Discuss the 'Ability to Pay' principle of taxation. How can one's ability to pay be measured?
4. 'The ability to pay approach collapses completely if one accepts the hypothesis that inter-personal utility comparisons are inadmissible'. Examine various interpretation of the ability to pay concept.
5. Examine the relative merits of minimum and equal sacrificed principles of taxation.

•••

Chapter 35

Taxable Capacity

1. Introduction

Quite analogous to the concept of ability to pay is the concept of taxable capacity. By taxable capacity we generally mean the maximum limit of taxation which a country can bear in any circumstances and beyond which productive efforts and efficiency begin to suffer. Under the concept of ability to pay we refer to the tax paying capacity of an individual, whereas under the concept of taxable capacity we refer to the tax paying capacity of a group of individuals, a region, a country and the economy as a whole. While the ability to pay refers to a method of distributing tax burden amongst the tax payers, taxable capacity refers to the maximum amount of tax which can be collected at a particular time from a group of tax payers. In the ability to pay approach the apportioning of the tax burden may not determine the share of the tax payer according to his capacity to pay. Moreover, the ability to pay is judged with reference to the existing circumstances and the repercussive changes are not taken into account. So, it is not easy to define taxable capacity or even to measure it. That is why Dalton regarded the concept of taxable capacity as "dim and confused".[1] According to Professor Musgrave, the term taxable capacity invites bias, it refers to the sacrifice, the community is able to sustain. He, actually, uses this concept in an entirely different context *i.e.*, in determining regional contribution to federal finances or the "fair" contribution of various countries to an international organisation. He is of the opinion that the concept of taxable-capacity only takes into consideration the tax side of the budget while overlooking the expenditure side. Similarly by focusing the attention on capacity it suggests the maximum size of public household which the private sector can support without taking into account the need for a lower limit without which the private sector cannot exist.

The taxable capacity is therefore not an absolute figure. One can only indicate pointers to show that the limit of taxable capacity is reached. It is not

1. H. Dalton, *op.cit.*. p. 163.

easy to measure with accuracy the precise limits. According to Sir Josiah Stamp, the taxable capacity is "the maximum amount, the citizens of a country could give towards public expenditure without having a really unhappy and down-trodden existence and without dislocating the economic organisation too much".[2] To quote Prof. Shirras, "Taxable capacity is the limit of squeezability. It is the total surplus of production over the minimum of consumption required to produce that volume of production, the standard of living remaining intact.[3] So, according to Shirras, taxable capacity is the maximum amount which the community can contribute by way of taxes without dislocating production. By minimum consumption Shirras meant the maximum of subsistence for the people, and also an amount for the replacement or an addition to capital for the purpose of industrial and commercial progress. But, it is not easy to estimate these amounts because they are never static. Therefore, the term 'minimum consumption' is not clear.

2. Absolute and Relative Taxable Capacity

When we refer to the taxable capacity of a whole economy, a region, an industry or a group of individuals, we refer to the absolute taxable capacity. While dubbing the concept as dim and confused, Dalton refers to absolute taxable capacity. Dalton has also referred to only absolute or relative taxable capacities of the entire communities and not of individual members of a community. The concept of absolute taxable capacity, as already stated above, refers to the maximum amount of tax which can be collected from the tax payers. If the state has a total control over the resources of a country the limit to taxable capacity would be the total resources of the community.

Relative taxable capacity refers to comparison between one community and the other in so far as the capacity to pay taxes of the community as a whole is concerned. It also refers to the proportion in which two or more regions or states should contribute to the common expenditure of a federation, through taxation. According to Professor Colin Clark, the maximum taxable capacity of most of the countries is 25 per cent of the national income. It means that the safe limit of tax is 25 per cent of national production. If taxation exceeds this limit it may adversely affect the people's desire to work and save. But, this may not be true for advanced industrialist countries. In any case, we can conclude that the limit of taxable capacity is not absolute or fixed, it can change from country to country and for the same country from time to time.

2. Sir Josiah Stamp, *Wealth and Taxable Capacity.* p. 134.
3. Findlay Shirras, *The Science of Public Finance.* p. 132.

According to Amotoz Morag taxable capacity is related to deficit financing and the limit of taxable capacity will be reached when the marginal social cost of additional taxation exceeds the cost of borrowing from banks. In whatever way we define the concept it must be remembered that it is not a constant entity. It is bound to change with changes in the level of savings, investment, employment, economic growth etc. And so, it cannot be quantitatively measured, but can be expressed only in qualitative terms in a general way. But such qualitative statements will be of hardly any use. We can simply express the factors which determine or affect the taxable capacity of a country.

3. Factors Determining Taxable Capacity

If we assume the maximum limit of taxable capacity as the maximum tax which can be levied upon people regardless of the harmful effects or sufferings resulting therefrom, then it is equal to the absolute resources of the community. The minimum limit would be the amount of tax which does not inflict any hardship to the tax payers, then it will be zero. In between these two limits a number of determining factors will have to be taken into consideration. These factors are discussed in the following paragraphs:

(1) Size of the National Income

The size of the national income of a country determines its taxable capacity. The size of the national income is determined by its natural and human resources and their proper utilisation, the quality and skill of the working force and so on. The larger the size of national income of a country the greater will be its taxable capacity.

(2) Distribution of Income and Wealth

The distribution of income and wealth within the country also determines the taxable capacity of the country concerned. If the distribution of income and wealth is unequal, the taxable capacity of the country would be high because the government can easily raise most of the required revenue from the rich sections of the community. If the national income and wealth is equitably distributed, the taxable capacity of the country would be low. But in the event of distribution of income and wealth being equitable, the government need not raise huge funds because it will not have to spend much on removing inequalities in the distribution of income and wealth.

(3) Stability

The taxable capacity of a country whose income is stable will be higher. The stability or instability of income of a country also affects its taxable capacity than those countries whose income is unstable. In industrially advanced countries the national income is more stable than the agriculture dominated countries. It is true that both agriculture and industry are inter-dependent but agriculture is more susceptible to the vagaries of nature like floods, lack of rains etc. In agriculture dominated countries the failure of crops brings debacle to the economy and erodes the income of the government.

(4) Size and Growth of Population

National income remaining the same if the population is growing at a faster pace, the taxable capacity of the country will go on declining with every increase of population. If the growth of population takes place at a rate lower than the growth of income the taxable capacity of the country would go on increasing.

(5) The System of Taxation

The taxable capacity of a country is also determined by the tax system prevailing in that country. In a single tax system the taxable capacity of the country will be low but if the system of taxation is broad based and contains all sorts of taxes then the taxable capacity of the country would be high. The pattern and rate of structure of taxation and the mode of tax collection are also very important. Indirect taxes are generally preferred to direct taxes because psychologically they are supposed to inflict less hardship. Taxes on unearned incomes and capital gains do not worry the tax payer much. The timings and methods of tax payment are, also worrisome to the tax payers if they are not properly determined by the government. So if the tax system takes care of all these things then the taxable capacity of the country would definitely be higher than those countries where the tax system is either lop-sided or ill-planned.

(6) Psychology of the Tax Payers

The psychology of the tax payers also influences the taxable capacity of a country. Psychologically people do not mind paying indirect taxes since they are distributed over the year and not paid in lump sum like a direct tax. During war or natural calamities people readily agree to contribute to the government expenditure. People generally are willing to bear heavier tax burden if the tax is collected on nationalistic or patriotic ground. Heavy taxation may lead to the impoverishment of the people by dampening the enthusiasm of the industrious, enterprising and hard working people.

(7) The Nature of Public Expenditure

The manner in which public expenditure is incurred, also affects the taxable capacity of a country. If the government spends its income on social and economic programmes or on the economic development of the people or country as a whole then the production of the country will increase and the national income will go up. It will also increase the taxable capacity. If the government spends most of its revenues on unproductive projects, the national income will not increase and the taxable capacity will also not increase. If the government pays external debt out of the tax revenue then the taxable capacity will be reduced. If the tax revenue is spent on the redemption of internal debt the taxable capacity of the country will increase because taxes collected from the people are returned to them, their income increases and so the tax paying capacity of the people also increases.

(8) Administrative Efficiency

Efficiency or inefficiency in the administration of taxes also affects the taxable capacity of the country. If the administration of taxes is efficient and the rules and tax laws are enforced without any bias or favour, the tax evasion would be reduced, and revenue from taxes would increase. Inefficient tax administration will reduce the taxable capacity because people will not get any incentive to pay taxes, and they would indulge in tax evasion.

(9) Economic and Political Stability

Economic and political stability also influences the taxable capacity of a country. During boom or prosperity the taxable capacity of the country will be high, because the manufacturers, traders etc. would be making huge profits. During period of depression because of losses, the taxable capacity of the country will be low. Similarly political stability is also important. It is under stable political conditions that the country's economic development can be successfully planned and implemented. In such a situation the tax payers do not mind to pay taxes on time but during conditions of political instability, the development programmes get blocked, the rate of growth is slackened, the industrial progress suffers, the trade of the country is adversely affected and the faith of the tax payer is totally shattered. Consequently, there are huge tax arrears, tax evasion is high and the taxable capacity of the community as a whole is at the lowest ebb.

(10) Standard of Living of the People

People with higher income have a higher standard of living as compared to those whose income is low. The higher income group people willingly pay taxes. Their standard of living is high because their consumption expenditure is high. That is why Professor Kaldor had suggested a tax on consumption expenditure because in his opinion it is the best index of a person's tax paying ability. Hence, the taxable capacity of a country is also influenced by the standard of living of its people.

In the light of the foregoing account we may conclude, that the taxable capacity of a country is not an absolute amount or a constant entity. It depends on a number of factors which we have explained above.

4. Measurement of Taxable Capacity

We have already seen that an objective measurement of taxable capacity of a country is its national income. The national income of a country depends upon its natural resources and the quality of its human resources. According to Prof. Alfred Marshall, "The labour and capital of a country, acting on its natural resources produce annually a certain net aggregate of commodities, material and immaterial, including services of all kinds. This is the Net Annual Income or Revenue of the Country or the National Dividend." Earlier Professor Fisher defined National Income as consisting "solely of services as received by ultimate consumers whether from their material, or from their human environments." According to Prof. Pigou national dividend "is that part of objective income of a community including, of course, income derived from abroad, which can be measured in terms of money." If the national income is computed in terms of the definitions of Prof. Fisher or Prof. Pigou, the computation will not be easy. It will create a number of anomalies which cannot be removed. So, generally Prof. Marshall's definition of national income has been accepted. According to Marshall, national income is the main source of income of every individual within the country and it can be arrived at by adding the income of every individual, free from duplication. Thus, for estimating the taxable capacity the national income of a country should be calculated without any duplication.

5. Methods of Estimating Taxable Capacity

Prof. Findlay Shirras has suggested the following methods for estimating the taxable capacity of a people.

(1) The Aggregate Income Method

The incomes of the individuals as given in their income tax returns should be analysed and supplemented by data regarding death duties and other property taxes and added to find out the total national income of the country. It, therefore, implies that the income of all the citizens of a country from various sources *i.e.*, income from employment, land and buildings, farm profits, profits from trade and profession, all should be estimated and added to obtain the national income. This is the aggregate income method of calculating the national income and hence the taxable capacity of a country.

(2) The Production Method

Under this method the net produce from agriculture, industry, trade etc. is estimated and added to get the national income. Taxable capacity is directly dependent on net production and varies with the changes in the net production.

Since each of the above methods has its own difficulties it would be advisable to use both the methods according to the demand of the situation. If we use income method alone then estimating an agricultural income would be difficult because production and consumption go simultaneously in agriculture. If we follow production method alone it will be difficult to estimate the production of an advocate or a doctor. Hence, both the methods should be used according to the need of the situation.

6. Limits of Taxable Capacity

The limit of taxable capacity is supposed to reach when the taxation is so heavy that it lowers the level of national consumption and cripples the industry. It means that if the taxation reaches such a limit that it adversely affects the level of consumption and production in a country, then it should be supposed that the taxable capacity has reached its upper limit. In such a situation the cost of collecting revenue would be high and additional tax will not bring additional income. It is also believed that in such a situation the tax payers are forced to sell their securities or take loans from the banks for paying their taxes. Like production, consumption of the people also declines or does not rise in the same proportion as the national income. If, on the other hand the national income declines but the level of consumption does not decline accordingly, smaller surplus would be available for the payment of tax and so the limit of taxable capacity would be supposed to have reached.

Significance of the Concept of Taxable Capacity

The concept of taxable capacity is important because of the following reasons:

(1) It helps us in knowing how much revenue can be raised from the people by way of taxes to finance extraordinary expenditure, like war.

(2) It also helps in the mobilisation of resources for the economic development of the country.

(3) It may discourage a government from levying further tax which may adversely affect the production and consumption of the country.

(4) The concept also helps in providing a useful basis for comparing the tax burden of different regions of a federation.

(5) Finally, the concept also helps in formulating a national policy for the balanced economic development of the country.

Exercises

1. Explain the concept of taxable capacity. Discuss the factors that determine it.
2. Define taxable capacity. How can it be measured? Explain its significance.

●●●

Chapter 36

Impact and Incidence of Taxes

1. Introduction

In the system of taxation and functioning of modern economy, where production and marketing of goods are carried on a large scale, where consumers have no role to play, where production determines the demand and where different economic units are interdependent, it is a reality that the person who may be legally required to pay the tax does not actually pay it. Therefore, the burden of tax does not fall on the person who initially pays it and the actual burden is borne by someone else. It is, therefore, necessary to know on whom the initial burden of a tax falls and on whom the ultimate burden of a tax falls. For understanding these problems three terms are used: (*i*) Impact, (*ii*) Incidence, and (*iii*) Effects of taxes.

The impact of a tax is on the person on whom the tax is imposed in the first instance and who deposits the tax in the government treasury. The incidence of a tax is on the person who ultimately bears the money burden of it. So, the person who deposits the initial amount of a tax in the government treasury bears the impact of the tax while the incidence of this tax is on the person on whom the money burden of this tax has been passed on and who ultimately bears it. The process in between is known as the shifting of a tax. The effects of a tax are the reactions of the tax payers and the economy to the imposition of the tax. Now, we explain these three concepts in the following paragraphs in some detail.

2. Impact of a Tax

The impact of a tax is the first point of contact. Impact of a tax is on the person who is responsible for the payment of the tax. The person immediately on the imposition of a tax is affected and hence bears its impact. The incidence of a tax is its final resting place; it is the ultimate burden of the tax. Some people have wrongly called the impact of a tax as, 'original incidence' or the 'primary incidence'.

3. Incidence of a Tax

As stated already, incidence is the ultimate burden of a tax. It is the money burden of the tax which is borne by the last person. We can also say that when the money burden of a tax comes to rest on the final tax payer, it is called the incidence of tax. The ultimate tax payer cannot shift the burden to any other person. Thus, the impact of a tax is the imposition of the tax, the shifting of a tax is the transfer of a tax and the incidence of a tax is the final resting of a tax. While the impact of a tax is the initial stage in the process of taxation, the shifting is the intermediate stage and the incidence is its final stage. According to Dalton[1] the burden of a tax can be direct as well as indirect. The incidence of a tax is its direct money burden. If a tax payer pays an amount larger than the tax then it is the indirect money burden of the tax. The sacrifice of economic welfare imposed on a person because of the payment of a tax is the direct real burden of a tax, while the reduction in the consumption of a commodity caused by the imposition of a tax is the indirect real burden of a tax.

Mrs. Ursula Hicks has distinguished between 'formal' and 'effective' incidence'.[2] The direct money burden of a tax is the formal incidence of the tax according to Mrs. Hicks. The overall economic effects of a tax on the economy as a whole are the effective incidence. The above definition had been adapted by the Taxation Enquiry Commission in India, while examining the problem of incidence of taxation. According to the Commission "formal incidence is the money burden of taxes resting with the subject on whom the burden is intended by the taxing authority to fall and effective incidence is the real or final distribution of tax burden after its shifting in consequence of changing demand and supply conditions of tax on commodity or services."[3]

It is therefore clear that the formal incidence is an integral part of the theory of incidence of taxation while effective incidence is an important constituent of the general effects of taxation. The incidence of a tax is according to Musgrave[4] "the resulting change in the distribution of income available for private uses," and is known as specific tax incidence. If a choice is to be made between two taxes as a better means for raising real resources, then "distributional changes that result as one such tax is substituted for another are referred to as the differential tax incidence."[5] We shall examine the views of Musgrave on this subject in another chapter.

It would be of advantage to note, in this connection, that the formal incidence of a tax is equal to the amount of that tax collected by the government.

1. Hugh Dalton, *op. cit.*, p. 30.
2. U. Hicks, *Public Finance,* pp. 158-59.
3. Report of Taxation Enquiry Commission, 1953-54, Government of India, p. 45.
4. Musgrave, *op. cit.*, pp. 211-12.
5. *Ibid.*

It is thus, equal to the total tax revenue of the authorities if we consider the formal incidence of the tax system as a whole. It also implies the transfer of final resources of the community to the government through tax system. The effective incidence on the other hand, as stated already, is the effect of taxation which includes all the advantages and disadvantages that the economy derives from a tax system.

4. Effects of Taxation

The imposition and collection of a tax produce effects on an individual as well as on the whole economy, which can at times be very serious. In the case of an individual the minimum effect of a tax can be reduction in income, decline in consumption and savings and thus overall fall in the standard of living. Such effects can be of different kinds. Taxation can also influence in a big way the working of the economy in the sphere of production, growth, regional imbalances, inequalities in the distribution of income and wealth, saving, investment etc. These are collectively known as the effects of the tax.

The effects of a tax can be beneficial as well as harmful. The harmful effects are referred to as the burden of the tax. Such a burden has two aspects: (*i*) money burden, and (*ii*) real burden. The former refers to the cut in the disposable income of the tax payers. Money burden can be direct as well as indirect. The former refers to the amount of tax paid by an individual economic unit to the government and is therefore equal to the amount of tax collected. Besides the payment of money in the form of tax to the government, a tax payer also incurs some expenditure in this connection. For example, the tax payer may incur some expenses on commuting from his residence to the treasury; he may be required to fill up certain forms for which he may be required to pay the cost etc. These expenses are in addition to the amount of the tax and therefore known as the indirect money burden of the tax.

The harmful effects of a tax are actually the real burden of a tax. It is the loss of welfare to the tax payers and community as a whole. It may occur in the form of decline in production, fall in the overall standard of living and level of consumption, increase in unemployment and so on. The real burden can be direct as well as indirect. In the former aspect a tax may involve some sacrifice of welfare by the tax payer. It is net of the benefits, if any, resulting from the imposition of the tax. Indirect loss of welfare due to the imposition of a tax would be its indirect real burden which would also not be net of the possible benefits of the tax.

Difference between Impact and Incidence

Following are the main points of difference between impact and incidence of a tax.

(1) Impact of a tax is felt by the tax payer at the point of imposition, whereas incidence is felt by the tax payer at the point of resting of the tax.

(2) The impact is the initial burden of a tax while incidence is the ultimate burden of the tax.

(3) The impact of a tax is on the person who deposits the amount of the tax in the treasury while the incidence is felt by the person who ultimately bears the burden of the tax.

Distinction between Incidence and Effects of Taxation

Incidence of a tax is directly on the individual in terms of a fall in consumption and investment, savings etc. because of a reduction in the income of the person on whom the incidence rests. It can also be viewed as effect of taxation or the pressure of incidence. In fact it is not easy to distinguish between impact and effect of a tax. To simplify things we may say that effects of taxation result in a greater loss than the loss inflicted by the incidence of the tax. When the producer of a commodity, after the imposition of a tax, raises the price of a commodity not only by the amount of the tax but something more than that amount, it means that the producer is getting an amount which is more than the amount of the tax and the consumer is paying not only the amount of the tax but something in addition to it. So the tax payer's loss is greater than the gain to the government. So, the effect of taxation includes this extra loss to the tax-payer while the incidence of a tax includes only the amount of tax which is paid to the government. Particularly, the effects of a tax have to be viewed in terms of the resultant changes in the market demand and production, loss of incentive and efficiency of the producers, flight of capital, social and political unrest and so on.

Professor Findlay Shirras, however, does not make any distinction between the incidence and effects of a tax. In his words, "Every tax, no matter who pays, has its impact, beyond the direct money burden on individuals in particular and society in general, and it is unnatural to talk about incidence and effects of taxation differently.

5. Importance of Incidence

From the foregoing it is clear that the study of incidence of a tax is of importance particularly when the question of the distribution of burden of taxation in an equitable manner arises. If we are able to locate the person or persons who bear the ultimate money burden of a tax, then the equitable distribution of tax burdens can be undertaken. In short, this will provide the knowledge of circumstances under which a tax can be shifted and also the persons who will ultimately have to bear the burden of tax. However, Professor Cannon has a different view altogether. He says that "the mere fact that the incidence of tax is on a particular individual or class does not necessarily imply that he or that particular class is bearing a heavier burden (in real sense) than others. In fact, the burden of a tax may be felt by those who do not pay as well as by those who do. Hence, the persons, who pay a tax, are often less injured by its imposition than those who pay no portion of it. The man, who goes two miles out of his way daily to avoid a bridge toll; would be more benefited by the freeing of the bridge than many of those who pay the toll." So a study of the theory of incidence would include a study of the theories of shifting of tax. The real problem is not how the tax is shifted or is not at all shifted and if it is shifted, then the shifting is forward or backward. There are some economists who do not approve of the idea of undertaking an analysis of tax shifting because of the difficulties involved in it. They find it totally impracticable. However, from our point of view, we now discuss the various theories of shifting in the following paragraphs.

6. Theories of Shifting of Tax

Broadly speaking, three approaches have been adopted for analysing the problem of shifting of incidence of a tax. We discuss these approaches one by one.

(1) The Concentration Theory

This approach was adopted by the economists of the sixteenth and seventeenth centuries. The Physiocrats (a school of economic thinkers in France in sixteenth and seventeenth centuries) believed that agriculture being the only productive occupation yielding surplus, the landlords should pay the tax. Hence the rent of land was the only source from which the tax revenue could come. Any tax imposed on any other sector of the economy would be finally got shifted to land rent through the inter-dependence of the different sectors and the land rent would be the final resting place. It would, therefore, be better if a single tax on land is imposed and realised from the landlord.

However, subsequently Adam Smith repudiated the contention of the Physiocrats and held that all economic activities were productive and a single tax on land was not conducive to welfare. The burden of taxation should be distributed equitably on all the tax payers in the community and should not fall only on a particular section of the society. The classical economists, therefore, held that there were two sources of surplus in the economy *viz.*, rent and profit. So, all tax incidence would be absorbed by these two. To elaborate this point further, Ricardo held that rent arises because agricultural production is governed by the law of diminishing returns and therefore with every increase in production the marginal cost goes up. The classical economists also upheld the subsistence theory of wages and the theory of population enunciated by Malthus. According to these theories the wage rates need to settle at subsistence level. If the wages fall below this level, the labour supply would be reduced because labour would die of starvation. In the long run if the wages go beyond the level of subsistence, the labour supply would increase. In the short period the labour supply can be taken as fixed. So, if a tax is imposed on agricultural produce the marginal cost of cultivation would increase and since in the short run the demand for agricultural produce does not fall, its price would go up. This would enhance the cost of subsistence of the workers. If wages are increased, the profits would be reduced. Rent is not likely to decline because the landlords pay tax on agricultural produce out of higher sale proceeds obtained through higher agricultural prices. So, the incidence of the tax finally stays on the profits. If the tax is imposed on the land rent, the landlords will not be able to shift the tax on others because rent is not a part of cost of production. If the tax is imposed upon wages, the workers will have to be given additional wages to maintain their level of subsistence. Higher wages would lead to an increase in the marginal cost of cultivation, the agricultural prices would move upward and so the tax incidence will be shifted to profits. If a tax is imposed on profits, it cannot be shifted and it rests over there because the wages which are already at the level of subsistence cannot be reduced any further.

However, the merit of the theory cannot be questioned because it is a fact that all taxes are ultimately paid out of the surplus. When there is no surplus, efforts will be made to shift the burden of the tax to others. Hobson also supported the theory because, according to him, if the taxes were not imposed directly upon the economic surplus, it would result in adversely affecting production and consumption owing to the exercise undertaken to shift the taxes in the form of higher prices.

(2) The Diffusion Theory

The theory states that the taxes do not concentrate on any particular class as held by earlier writers but get diffused throughout society because of the inter-dependence of various economic units and constant interaction between them through sale/purchase transactions. It, therefore, does not matter on whom the tax is originally imposed and how just or unjust it is. After repeated transactions the burden of the tax stands equally distributed and the injustice is remedied. Since diffusion takes time and the society is able to adjust itself to the tax, the burden of an old tax is not felt and that is why, it is said that 'old tax is no tax'.

This theory was put forward by French economists among whom the prominent are Mansfield[6] and Canard.[7] According to Mansfield "a tax is like a stone falling into a lake and making a circle, till one circle produces and gives motion to another, and the whole circumference is agitated from the centre." According to Canard, the imposition of a tax is like extracting blood from one of the veins of a human being. Although the blood is extracted from only one vein, the loss is spread over the whole body and the body remains in equilibrium. He, therefore, believed that through buying and selling transactions all taxes are diffused among the members of the community and finally rest upon the surplus. He also believed that this diffusion takes some time and therefore old taxes were better to the new taxes because new taxes disturb the existing harmonious distribution of the tax burden.

The theory is based upon the implicit assumptions that the market is sufficiently competitive and that there is perfect mobility of factors of production between different employments. Consequently, factors can move from one job to another without difficulty and without involving much cost. But these assumptions are illusory and unrealistic. Even if these assumptions were correct, one cannot afford to remain indifferent to the effects that the tax produces on the economy. Walker also was of the same view. Firstly he held that perfect competition cannot exist so long as there is ignorance, inertia and poverty in the society. The wealth of the society from which taxes are paid is not like a fluid but like a tree or the body and no part of which can be cut without being disfigured.[8] Dalton, also, does not support the theory. According to him, this sort of approach only pushes the basic problem of ascertaining the incidence and the effects of a tax to the background because of the enormous difficulties involved in the exercise. He agrees that the effects of certain taxes get widely diffused but with a proper analytical approach it should be possible to have an estimation of the incidence and 'wider' effects of the tax. It has been held, therefore, that this theory is not based on proper interpretation of facts. Firstly, knowledge of the incidence of a tax, is not the only matter of prime importance as Musgrave points out that there is no sense in distinguishing between the incidence and the effects of taxation. According to him the incidence of a tax is important and so are its effects and therefore, the authorities should not be indifferent about the effects of taxation. Secondly, the assumptions of the theory are unrealistic. The markets are hardly competitive. There are various types of imperfections in the market. Factors of production are not mobile. Therefore the tax incidence is not likely to get diffused in an economy. Moreover, as we shall see later, shifting of a tax and

---

6. C.f. Seligman, E.R.A., *The Shifting and Incidence of Taxation,* p. 153.
7. *Ibid.,* p. 161.
8. Findlay Shirras, *The Science of Public Finance,* p. 187.

the diffusion of the tax burden amongst the different tax payers depend upon the elasticities of demand and supply and the day-to-day sales transactions.

All said and done, the theory has been found of certain advantage because of its emphasis that taxes do not rest where they are imposed. But all in all the theory is misleading and does not solve the problem of injustice in taxation. Moreover, even if we accept that certain taxes get diffused, we should not ignore the fact that this diffusion is not automatic and the government has to take certain measures in the direction of the just and equitable distribution of the tax burden.

(3) Demand and Supply Theory

This theory has been widely accepted for explaining the incidence of a tax. It has been agreed that tax incidence can be shifted only through business transactions and a revision of the price is determined by the relative strength of the elasticities of demand and supply. This theory is based upon the marginal analysis of value and price as done by the neo-classical economists, especially Marshall in the nineteenth century. Subsequently, it was applied to tax-shifting by Seligman and Edgeworth. Several versions of this theory have been put forward, and the emphasis of each version is on different points.

While retaining all the virtues of the earlier theories, this theory upholds that all taxes should be imposed directly upon the taxable economic surplus.[9] So long as the tax payer enjoys an economic surplus he will not mind paying the tax but as soon as the economic surplus disappears he will try to shift it. According to the theory, tax constitutes a part of cost of production and therefore enters into the price.[10] So, a tax is shifted through a change in the price. Hobson also held that to avoid wastage and damage to production and consumption arising from the struggle to shift taxes in the form of higher prices, all taxes should be imposed directly upon the taxable economic surplus. Since shifting of taxes takes place through prices which are determined by the forces of demand and supply, tax shifting therefore, depends upon the behaviour of sellers and buyers. The behaviour of buyers and sellers is governed by the elasticity of demand and supply of various products and services and the laws of returns.

Elasticity of Demand and Supply

In this connection Dalton has laid down two general propositions; firstly, other things being equal, the more elastic the demand for the object of taxation, the higher will be the incidence of the tax upon the seller. It, thus, follows that

9. Buehler, *Public Finance,* p. 343.
10. Findlay Shirras, *The Science of Public Finance,* p. 187.

in the situation of a perfectly elastic demand of a commodity, the entire burden of the tax will be borne by the seller. Any increase in the price due to tax will reduce the demand of the commodity to zero. If the demand for the commodity is perfectly inelastic the entire burden of the tax will be borne by the buyers because any increase in price due to tax will not lead to any reduction in the demand. If the demand is relatively elastic, a major portion of the burden of the tax will be borne by the sellers.

Secondly, if the supply of the commodity is more elastic the incidence of the tax will be higher on the buyers, if the supply is less elastic the incidence of the tax will be higher on the sellers and if the supply is perfectly elastic the entire burden of the tax will be borne by the buyers.

When the tax is imposed, the cost of production of the commodity goes up, its price rises, the demand falls and this results in a loss to the seller. But the seller would curtail the supply of the commodity, increase its price by absorbing the entire amount of tax and will shift the burden of tax to the buyers. If the supply of the commodity is perfectly inelastic the entire burden of the tax will be borne by the seller. If the supply of the commodity is more elastic then the major portion of the tax burden will be borne by the buyers.[11]

So, there is a constant tussle between the buyers and the sellers for shifting the tax burden. Their relative ability to achieve their objective with the minimum loss to themselves, ultimately determines the result.

From the above propositions Dalton has given a general proposition of the theory of incidence of taxation which is as follows.

The direct money burden of a tax levied on any commodity is shared by the buyers and sellers in proportion of the elasticity of supply of the commodity to the elasticity of demand for it. The direct money burden on the buyers would be to the extent of the rise in the price of the commodity due to the taxation. This general principle of incidence of taxation can be explained with the help of the Fig. 36.1.

In Fig. 36.1 *DD* is the demand curve and *SS* is the supply curve of the commodity on which the tax is imposed. *PM* is the price of one unit of the commodity before the tax is imposed and *OM* is the amount of the commodity sold per unit of time. A tax equivalent to *PR* is imposed. Consequently the supply curve moves to the left to *S′S′*. Accordingly, the new price is *P′M′* and the amount sold per unit of time is *P′N′*. The price rises by *P′Q* and the sale of the commodity falls by *PQ* after the imposition of the tax. The incidence of the tax *i.e.*, *P′R* is shared by the buyers and sellers. The buyers bear *P′Q* and the sellers bear *QR*. We shall now see how the incidence of the tax is divided

11. Dalton, H., *op. cit.*, p. 39.

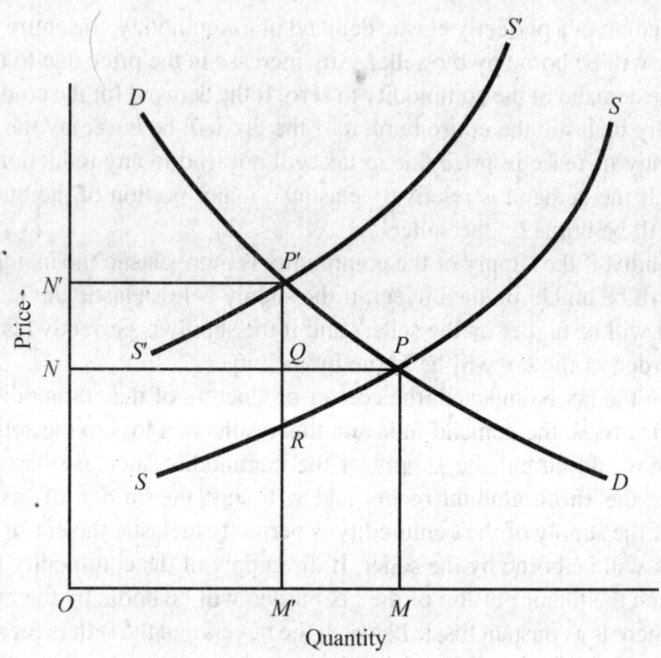

Fig. 36.1.

between buyers and sellers in the ratio of the elasticity of supply to the elasticity of demand.

Let e^d be the elasticity of demand

So $$e^d = \frac{\text{Proportionate change in demand}}{\text{Proportionate change in price}}$$

Mathematically it can be expressed as under

$$= \frac{\frac{\Delta Q}{Q}}{\frac{\Delta P}{P}} = \frac{\Delta Q}{Q} \times \frac{P}{\Delta P}$$

Where Q represents the quantity demanded or supplied and P represents' the price

Now $$e^d = \frac{MM'}{OM} \Big/ \frac{P'Q}{OM} = \frac{MM'}{PM} \times \frac{PM}{P'Q}$$

Similarly e^s which represents the elasticity of supply will be:

$$= \frac{MM'}{OM} \bigg/ \frac{QR}{PM} = \frac{MM'}{OM} \times \frac{PM}{QR}$$

$$\therefore \quad \frac{e^s}{e^d} = \left(\frac{MM'}{OM} \times \frac{PM}{QR}\right) \bigg/ \left(\frac{MM'}{OM} \times \frac{PM}{PQ}\right)$$

$$= \left(\frac{MM'}{OM} \times \frac{PM}{QR}\right) \bigg/ \left(\frac{OM}{MM'} \times \frac{P'Q}{PM}\right)$$

$$\frac{e^s}{e^d} = \frac{P'Q}{QR}$$

$$\therefore \quad \frac{\text{Elasticity of supply}}{\text{Elasticity of demand}} = \frac{\text{Burden of the tax upon the buyer}}{\text{Burden of the tax upon the seller}}$$

Conclusions

From the above the following conclusions can be drawn:

(1) If the $e^s = e^d$, the burden of the tax will be equally divided between the buyers and sellers and price of the commodity will increase by half the amount of tax.

(2) When the e^s is $> e^d$, the burden of tax will be borne by the buyers in higher proportion than the sellers and the increase in price will be more than 50 per cent of the amount of tax, as shown in Fig. 36.2.

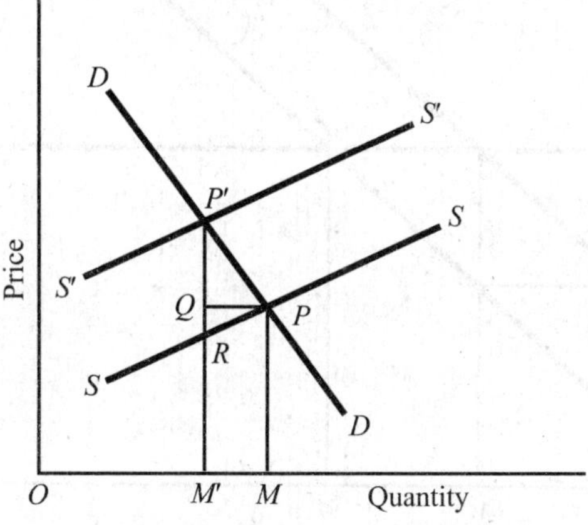

Fig. 36.2.

(3) When the e^s is $< e^d$, the burden of the tax will be borne by the sellers in higher proportion than the buyers and the increase in price will be less than

50 per cent of the tax, as shown in Fig. 36.3.

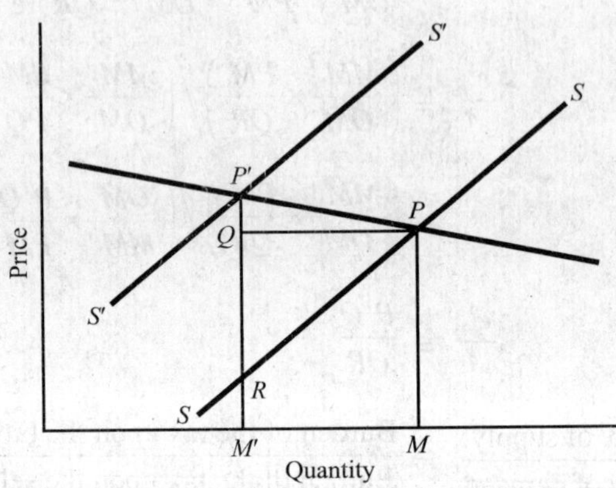

Fig. 36.3.

(4) If the demand for a commodity is perfectly elastic and its supply is perfectly inelastic, the entire burden of the tax will be borne by the sellers, as shown in Fig. 36.4.

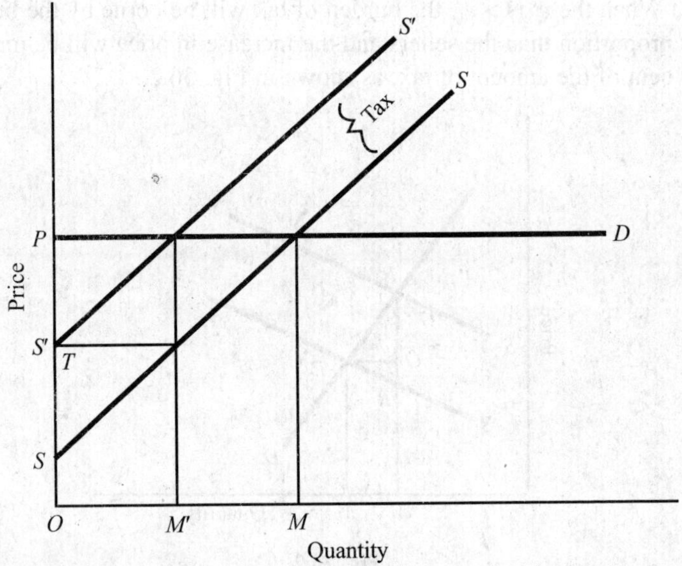

Fig. 36.4.

(5) If the demand for a commodity is perfectly inelastic and its supply is

elastic the entire burden of the tax will be borne by the buyers as shown in Fig. 36.5.

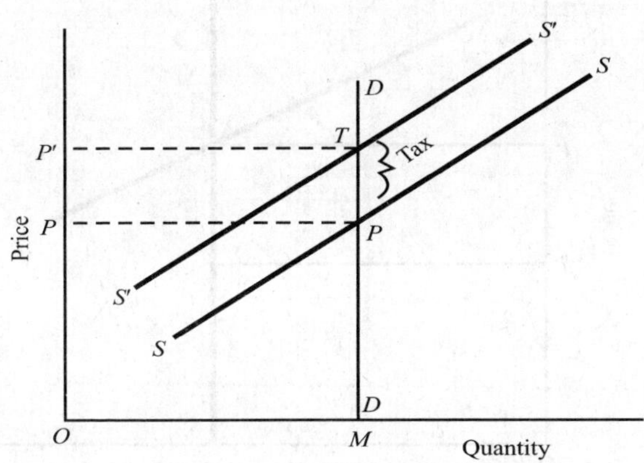

Fig. 36.5.

(6) If the supply of a commodity is perfectly elastic and its demand is relatively inelastic the entire burden of the tax will be borne by the buyers as shown in Fig. 36.6.

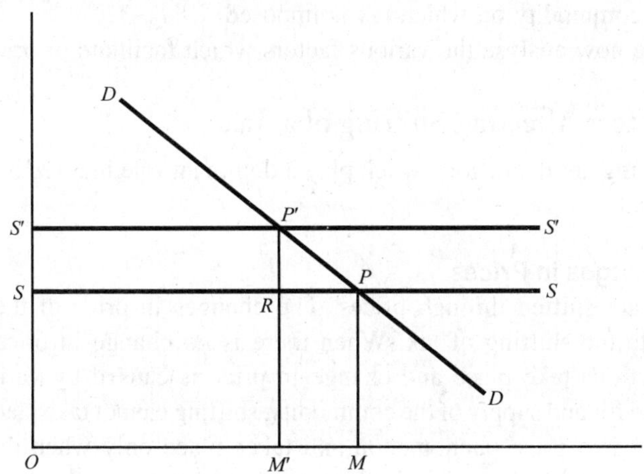

Fig. 36.6.

(7) If the supply of a commodity is perfectly inelastic and its demand is elastic the entire burden will be borne by the sellers as shown in Fig. 36.7.

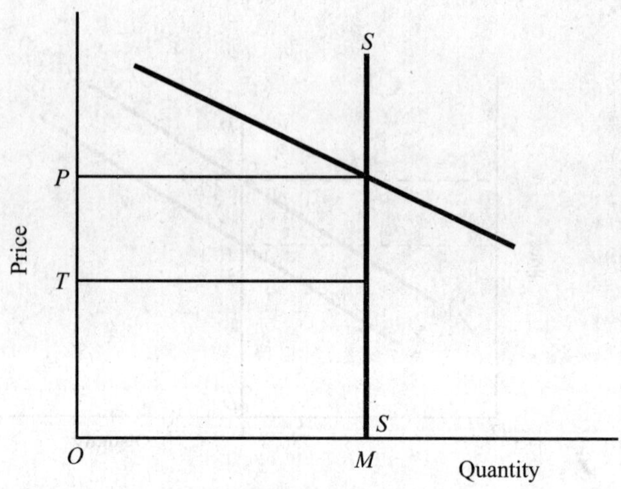

Fig. 36.7.

In this connection it may be noted that the cases of perfectly elastic demand are rare and those relating to absolutely inelastic supply are only imaginary. Therefore, the incidence of a tax will be divided between the buyers and sellers according to the relative strength of their demand for and supply of the commodity on which tax is imposed.

We now analyse the various factors which facilitate or prevent shifting.

7. Factors Affecting Shifting of a Tax

Following are the factors which play a dominant role in affecting the shifting of a tax:

(1) Changes in Prices

Taxes are shifted through prices. The changes in price of the commodity indicate the shifting of tax. When there is no change in price or no price transactions take place and change in price is caused by variations in the demand for and supply of the commodity, shifting cannot take place. Therefore, shifting is a price phenomenon and takes place only when the changes in demand and supply are caused by the imposition of tax. The shifting of a tax may be forward or backward. The forward shifting of a tax takes place when prices rise which will be determined by the elasticity of demand. The greater the inelasticity of demand, the greater will be the proportion of the tax shifted to the buyers.

(2) Elasticity of Demand and Supply

We have already explained above how a tax is shifted and how the process of shifting is determined by change in price and how the prices are affected by demand and supply of the taxed commodities. So, the relative forces of demand and supply influence the shifting of a tax. The sellers and buyers constantly endeavour to avoid any monetary loss to them owing to the imposition of a tax. In this exercise the buyers try to reduce their demand to put pressure on the sellers and on the other hand the sellers try to reduce the supply of the commodity to put the pressure on the buyers. It is the relative ability of the two groups that determines the final result. Other things remaining the same, the greater the elasticity of demand, the higher will be the incidence of the tax on the sellers and the greater the inelasticity of demand for the taxed commodity the higher will be the incidence of the tax on the buyers. Likewise the greater the elasticity of supply of the taxed commodity, the higher will be the incidence of the tax on the buyer and the greater the inelasticity of supply of the taxed commodity, the higher will be the incidence of the tax on the seller.

(3) Nature of Demand for Commodity

We are quite familiar with the fact that the demand for different commodities differs in nature. The demand for necessities is inelastic and the demand for luxuries is elastic. So the relative incidence of a tax on different commodities would be different. In the case of necessities, the total burden of a tax would be higher on the buyers than on the sellers. And therefore, the taxation of commodities of necessities has a regressive effect. In the case of comforts, the demand being more elastic, the incidence of a tax is divided almost on 50:50 basis between the buyers and the sellers. In the case of luxuries the demand being elastic the burden of the tax will be more on the sellers because it cannot be easily shifted to the consumers.

(4) Nature of Supply of Commodities

The nature of supply of commodities is governed by various conditions. Those industries which have large fixed capital and which involve huge investment, their commodities have a very inelastic supply because the producers cannot afford to stop manufacturing of the commodity even in the short period. Therefore, in the case of these commodities the supply being inelastic, the burden of the tax cannot be shifted to the buyers easily. However, in the long period, the manufacturers of such commodities can be in a position to reduce their supply because of their wear and tear of machinery and equipment. So, in the short period the supply of such commodities cannot be re-adjusted to the changes in demand. There may be some commodities whose supply may be elastic. So to summarise we can say that in the case of commodities having inelastic supply the tax imposed on them cannot be easily shifted to the buyers and in the case of commodities having elastic supply, the shifting of the tax may be comparatively easier. From the supply side a tax can be shifted either forward or backward. In the case of commodities with perfectly elastic supply the entire burden of the tax will be shifted to the buyers and that will be forward shifting. But when the supplier does not find forward shifting easy, he may shift it backward on the factors or services which he employs in the production of the commodity. In backward shifting the price of the factors of production is reduced by the amount of tax whereas in forward shifting the price of the commodity is raised by the amount of the tax.

(5) Tax Area

The area to which a tax is applicable also plays an important role in the process of shifting of a tax. It has been seen that it is not easy to shift a purely local tax, if it is relatively heavy; but if it is light then it may be shifted without much difficulty. Shifting of a local tax becomes difficult because the people living in the locality may purchase the commodity from outside to avoid the tax.

(6) Effect of Time on Shifting

It is not easy to shift a tax in the short period because the supply of the commodity remains more or less inelastic in the short period. In the long period the supply would be relatively elastic because the manufacturers would be able to reduce the output. That is why, in the short period the shifting of a tax is difficult while in the long period it is easy.

(7) General Business Conditions

During periods of rising prices and prosperity it is easy for most of the producers to sell their goods at prices equal to or more than the cost than it is during a period of depression or falling prices. It is easy to shift the tax alongwith other costs in the former situation than in the latter. That is why, new taxes, generally, are not imposed during business crisis or depression.

Shifting of a tax is also determined by seasonal changes. In certain seasons certain goods are in greater demand and can be sold at a profit but in other seasons the same commodities may be sold at a loss. Shifting of a tax is easier in the former situation than in the latter. Similarly, shifting is also influenced by secular trends because they sometimes cause fundamental changes in the supply and demand of a commodity. But secular changes take place rather slowly and therefore, it is easier to discount them in anticipation. In any case, sellers must cover their costs and therefore they should charge prices accordingly and costs of course are inclusive of taxes. If they are not able to do that they will prefer to close down their shops.

8. Shifting of Taxes under Different Market Conditions

We now take up the shifting of taxes under different market conditions *i.e.*, different time periods and cost conditions. We first discuss the shifting of tax under perfect competition and then under monopoly and monopolistic competition.

(1) Shifting of a Tax under Perfect Competition

Perfect competition means the presence of numerous buyers and sellers having perfect knowledge of the market, production of identical products, each firm producing a very small amount of the total supply of the commodity and therefore the market price is not influenced by any of the above factors. The demand curve of each firm is perfectly elastic and hence the tax cannot be shifted forward. Similarly the demand of each firm for factors of production is a small part of the total supply in the market and therefore an individual firm cannot influence the supply of the factors of production and so, the supply curve of each factor of production to firm is perfectly elastic. Therefore, producers cannot shift the tax backward by paying less to the factors of production. Taxes can be shifted only when the supply is cut down and the price of the commodity is increased. Since the factors of production and the producers are free to enter into and leave an industry at their will, the supply of a commodity can be curtailed only in the long period and not in the short period. So, taxes can only be shifted in the long period. Again, in the short period the stock of commodity is fixed. If the commodity is perishable the entire stock will be for sale regardless of the price. So, the supply of this commodity will be perfectly inelastic and therefore the entire tax burden will be borne by the sellers. In the case of non-perishable commodities the entire tax burden will be shifted to the buyers. In the short period the plant capacity of the firm being fixed, the supply of the commodity cannot be curtailed and therefore it is only in the long period that the supply can be curtailed. Since some of the producers always produce goods on the margin of production, a rise in the cost of production due to the imposition of the tax will make it unprofitable for them to continue with the production of that commodity. Such marginal producers will stop the production of that commodity. Others will also curtail their production to some extent. This reduction in supply will cause the price to move up and hence the buyers will share the tax. The larger the increase in the price the greater will be the shift in the tax incidence from the sellers to the buyers. Thus, shifting power of the sellers is determined by the elasticity of supply of the commodity concerned. We have already illustrated this with the help of Figs. 36.2 to. 36.7.

Shifting of Taxes and the Laws of Returns

The production of a commodity is governed by three laws of returns, namely, the law of increasing returns *i.e.*, the law of decreasing costs; the law of decreasing returns or the law of increasing costs and the law of constant returns or the law of constant costs. We now discuss the position regarding shifting of tax in the case of commodities produced at different costs in the following paragraphs.

(*a*) **Commodities Produced under Decreasing Cost Conditions.** If the production of a commodity is taking place under decreasing cost conditions, a tax on the commodity will raise its price by an amount greater than the amount of the tax. This happens because by the imposition of the tax the price goes up, demand decreases and the supply is to be reduced accordingly. Consequently, the average cost will rise and the price will rise by an amount greater than the amount of the tax. This can be explained with the help of Fig. 36.8.

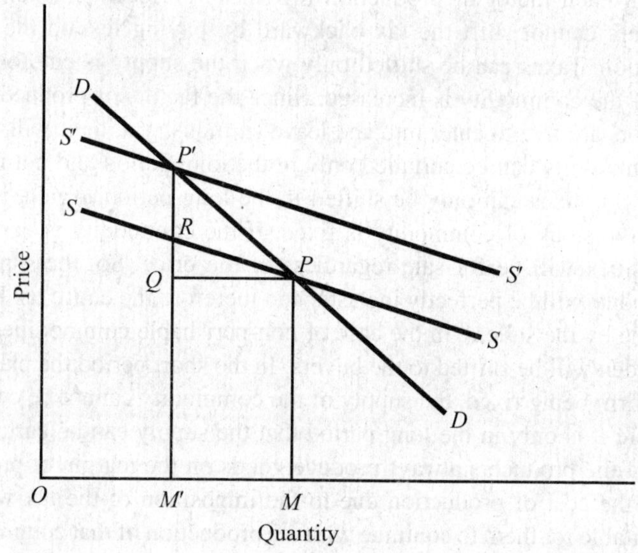

Fig. 36.8.

DD is the demand curve and *SS* is the supply curve before the imposition of the tax. When the tax is imposed the SS curve moves to the right and becomes *S′S′*. *PM* is the price before the imposition of the tax and *P′M′* is the price after the tax has been imposed. *P′R* is the amount of the tax which is equal to the rise in the price *i.e.*, *P′Q*. *P′Q* is greater than *P′R* and hence the rise in price is greater than the amount of the tax.

(*b*) **Commodities Produced under Increasing Cost Conditions.** If the production of a commodity is taking place under the increasing cost conditions or under the law of diminishing returns, a tax on that commodity will increase its price by an amount smaller than the amount of the tax and therefore only a part of the tax will be shifted to the buyers. This happens because the imposition of the tax will not only increase the price of the commodity but also reduce the demand. Consequently supply will have to be reduced. The reduction in supply will reduce the average cost and therefore the imposition of the tax does not lead to a rise in the price by the full amount of the tax. This is explained in Fig. 36.9.

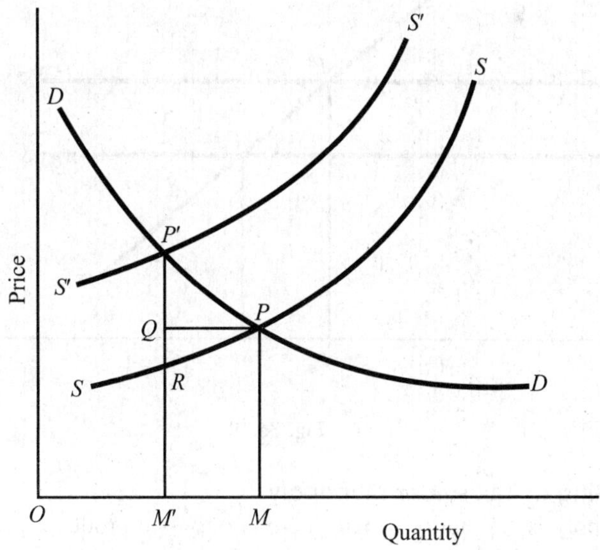

Fig. 36.9.

Before the imposition of the tax *DD* is the demand curve and *SS* is the supply curve. After the imposition of the tax the supply curve moves to the left and becomes *S′S′*. Consequently the price *PM* before the imposition of the tax becomes *P′M′* after the imposition of the tax. The amount of the tax is *P'R* which is equal to *P′Q* + *QR*. So the rise in price is equal to *P′Q* and therefore the burden of the tax on the buyers is *P′Q* which is less than *P′R*.

(*c*) **Commodities Produced under Constant Cost Conditions.** If the commodity on which the tax has been imposed is being produced under the conditions of conditions of constant costs, its supply will be perfectly elastic and therefore price can be raised by the amount of the tax as shown in Fig. 36.10.

In Fig. 36.10 *DD* is the demand curve and *SS* is the supply curve before the imposition of the tax. Supply curve becomes *S′S′* after the imposition of the tax. *PM* is the price before the tax was imposed, and *P′M′* is the price after the imposition of the tax. The amount of tax is equal to *P′R* which is equal to the increase in the price after the imposition of the tax.

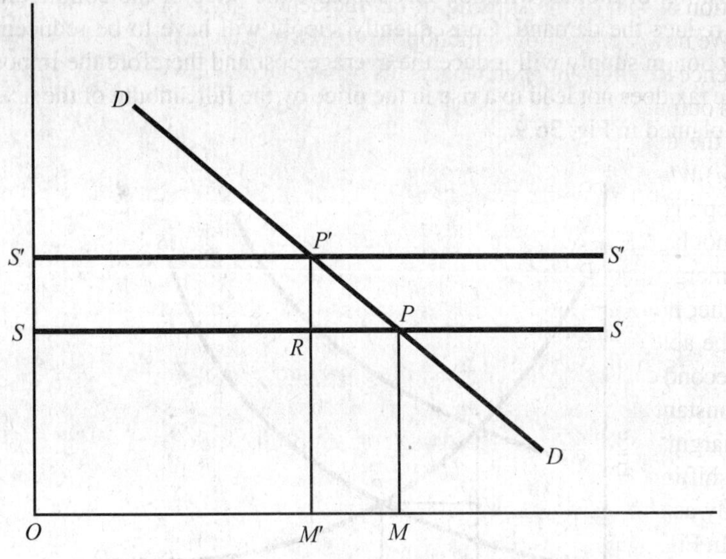

Fig. 36.10.

(2) Shifting of Tax under Monopoly

A monopoly is a situation where there is only one producer producing only one product and there are no substitutes for this product. A monopolist firm represents the whole industry. The main interest of a monopolist is in the maximisation of profit and therefore he fixes his output and prices accordingly. He fixes his production at a point where the marginal revenue is equal to the marginal cost, which means that the monopolist fixes the price of his commodity at the point where the total net profit is the highest. So a monopolist has full control over the supply of the commodity very much unlike perfect competition. The imposition of the tax will certainly increase the cost of production but how much of the tax would be borne by the monopolist and how much by the consumers will depend upon the elasticity of demand and elasticity of supply of the commodity produced by the monopolist. Since the monopolist has complete control over the supply of his commodity, he will regulate it in such a way that he secures the maximum monopoly revenue. So, if a tax is levied upon profits or sales, the monopolist cannot shift it because he has already fixed his output and price at a point where his profits are at maximum. Yes, if the monopolist is not exercising fully his monopolistic power, which is generally the case he may charge the full monopoly price after the imposition of the tax *i.e.*, he may raise the price of his product. But here the cause for the higher price is not the tax and therefore one cannot view the situation as that of the shifting of tax incidence.

We now analyse how a monopolist behaves when the tax is imposed with reference to his output, *i.e.*, what is his behaviour when the tax is proportionate to his output or when it is in the form of a fixed sum or when the tax decreases with the decrease in output.

(*i*) *When the tax is proportionate to output.* When a tax is imposed on the monopolist in proportion to his output, his marginal cost will increase and it will not be profitable for him to sell his product at the old price. Therefore, he will merge the tax into the cos1 of production of the commodity and sell it at a higher price so as to keep his total revenue at the maximum. In this way, he will be able to shift the tax to the consumers. According to Taylor, "Taxes of the second degree are generally shifted forward. For marginal cost is increased by constant amount throughout the whole schedule, creating a new intersection of marginal revenue and marginal cost and thus a new price and quantity." But shifting of the tax will depend upon the relative strength of demand and supply as shown in Fig. 36.11, on the following page.

In Fig. 36.11 *AR* is the average revenue curve or the demand curve for the product. The average cost and marginal cost before the imposition of the tax has been shown by *AC* and *MC* curves respectively. After the imposition of the tax the average cost and marginal cost curves are AC_1 and MC_1. *MR* is the marginal revenue curve. *MR* intersects *MC* at point *I′* which means that *MR* is equal to *MC* before the imposition of the tax. *I″* is the point where *MR* intersects MC_1 and hence $MR = MC$ after the imposition of the tax. *PM* is the price before the tax and *P′M′* is the price after the imposition of the tax. The burden of the tax is equal to *P′Q* which is equal to the rise in price *i.e.*, *BA*. Hence the burden of the tax on the consumers is equal to *P′Q*. Amount of the tax is *ST* which is greater than *BA*. It therefore follows that the burden of the tax upon the consumers is less than the amount of the tax. Similarly the monopolist's profit before the tax is *APCC* and after the tax is *BPC′C′*. But it is less than the revenue which the monopolist got before the imposition of the tax; because a part of the tax is also absorbed by him.

(*ii*) *When the tax is independent of output.* If a fixed amount of tax is imposed on the monopolist, it becomes a part of fixed cost. Such a tax has no relation with his output. It does not influence his marginal cost of production. It only raises the average cost of production. If the monopolist reduces his supply after the tax and raises the price, his total profit will fall as his marginal

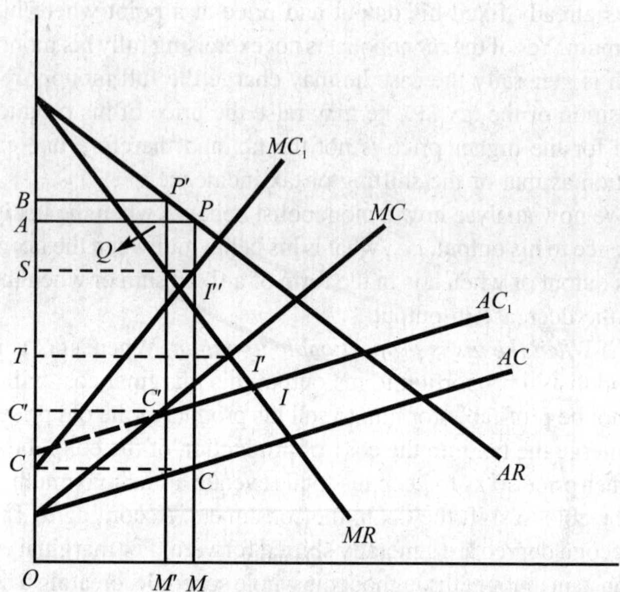

Fig. 36.11.

cost will not remain equal to his marginal revenue. So a monopolist cannot shift the tax to the buyers. It is no doubt true that the imposition of the tax will reduce the profit of the monopolist but his net profit after deducting the tax will be the highest if he continues to keep his production at the same level as before and sells it at the same price as before. And if he tries to push the incidence of the tax on the buyers, his monopoly revenue will be reduced more than the amount of the tax. Therefore, he will himself bear the burden of the tax. This is explained in Fig. 36.12.

In Fig. 36.12 total revenue and total cost have been shown on vertical-axis and the total quantity produced has been shown on horizontal-axis. *TR* is the total revenue and *TC* is the total cost before the tax. *OF* is the total fixed cost. TC_1 is the total cost curve after the tax. Before the imposition of the tax, *RC* is the maximum monopoly revenue at *OM* output. *FF′* represents the tax which is imposed on the commodity. Even after the imposition of the tax the best output will be *OM* because *RC′* will be the highest monopoly net revenue after the payment of the tax. So, in the case of a fixed amount of tax on the profits of a monopolist there does not take place any change in the price or the quantity of the commodity and the entire burden of the tax is borne by the monopolist.

(iii) When the tax diminishes with increase in output. When the tax diminishes with the increase in output the monopolist will increase his output

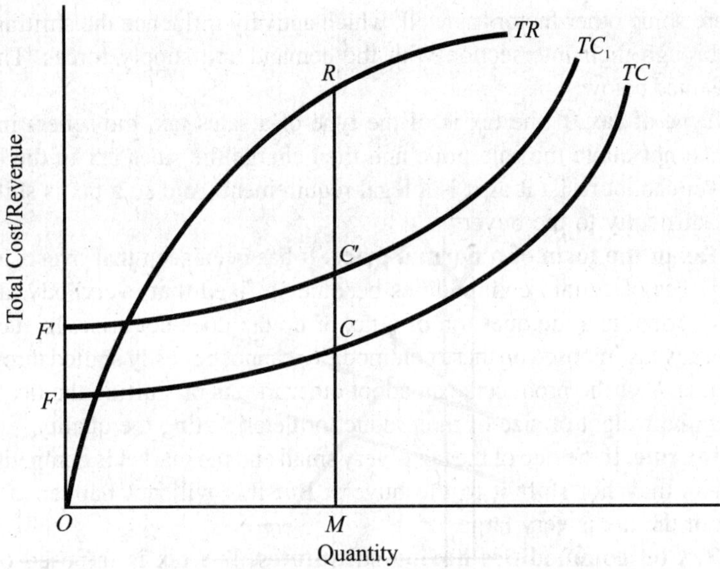

Fig. 36.12.

and reduce the price of the commodity produced by him. The monopolist will bear the entire burden of the tax and shift some of his monopoly profits to the buyers through a reduction in the price of the commodity. Such a situation will never arise in practical life.

(3) Incidence of Tax under Monopolistic Competition

In this situation there are a few firms which produce the same commodity and compete with each other. The policy of each firm regarding output and price affects the policies of other firms and gets affected by the policies of other firms. Price is determined by the price leader. Despite the existence of a number of firms only one or two act as the price leaders. If a tax on the commodity affects the cost of production of the price leaders, its burden may be shifted to the buyers if their demand is not elastic. On the other hand if a tax affects the cost of production only of small firms then it may not be easy to shift the tax to the buyers, because they cannot influence the price; they simply follow the price determined by the leaders. In that case the smaller firms will bear the burden of the tax themselves. If the amount of the tax is very small and it takes away only a small portion of the normal profits then these firms will have no difficulty in bearing it. But if the amount of the tax is very large then the burden will have to be shifted to the buyers in the long run, because these smaller firms will withdraw from the market.

Additional Factors which Influence Tax Shifting

There are some other factors as well, which actively influence the shifting of a tax, through their intersection with the demand and supply forces. These are explained below:

1. Type of tax. If the tax is of the type of a sales tax, the sellers more often than not quote the sale price and then charge the sales tax in the bill. The buyer cannot resist it as it is a legal requirement. And so a tax is shifted without difficulty to the buyers.

2. Tax in the form of a normal price. It has been seen that over a long period prices of certain commodities become so fixed that everybody takes them as normal and the question of a tax or no tax does not arise. In such a situation any tax imposed on these commodities cannot be easily shifted through a price rise. Yes, the producers can adopt other means of shifting the tax like reducing the weight or size of the product or deteriorating the quality.

3. Tax rate. If the rate of the tax is very small and the market is competitive the sellers may not shift it to the buyers. But this will not happen if the amount of the tax is very large.

4. Tax on commodities having substitutes. If a tax is imposed on a commodity which has substitutes it will not be easy to shift it to the consumers. If the sellers increase the price to the extent of the amount of the tax the consumers can switch over to the substitutes of that commodity, the demand will fall and the sellers would be forced to bear the tax themselves. In case a tax is also imposed to the same extent on the substitutes then the shifting of tax will be determined by the general pattern of the demand elasticities for this group of commodities as a whole and also by the pattern of their supply elasticities.

5. Geographical area of a tax. The geographical coverage of a tax also influences its shifting. If a tax is imposed on a commodity, in a particular area, which is available in the neighbouring areas without tax, the buyers will resist to bear the tax and therefore the sellers would not be able to raise the price of the commodity to the extent of the amount of the tax. In such a situation the authorities generally impose a "trade tax or 'use tax' on commodities which are brought from the neighbouring areas".

Incidence of Some Particular Taxes

We now very briefly analyse the incidence of certain taxes for the sake of clarification and understanding of the problem of shifting of tax incidence.

1. Customs duties. These are export and import duties and like other commodity taxes. As we have seen already, tax on a commodity is shared between the buyers and sellers in the ratio of elasticities of supply and demand of the taxed commodity. If the demand of the commodity in question is sufficiently inelastic and the supply is sufficiently elastic then the producers can restrict supplies if the price offered is reduced. They can either raise the export price of the commodity directly or by imposing export duties which the foreigners have to pay. If the importing countries impose import duties on that commodity then that will also have to be borne by the importing countries and not by the exporting countries for the reasons stated above. The case of primary products is rather different. It is a common knowledge that over the years the developed countries have found out very close substitutes for primary products like agricultural and mineral raw materials for which they were depending on the developing countries. They have also developed their agriculture and industry to the extent that now they have surplus in the production of certain commodities and are exporting them to those very countries from where they were importing before. Consequently, the import duties on these products imposed by the developed countries or export duties imposed by the underdeveloped countries are being borne by the exporters of these products. This is so, because the demand for these products is more elastic than supply. In the case of manufactures the situation is again different because the developed countries have already enough demand for these products in their own countries and underdeveloped countries are depending for these commodities on the developed countries. So, duties on such products are being borne by the under-developed countries.

In this connection it may be noted that if the demand for a particular commodity of a certain country to import is very small then the incidence of the import duty will be borne by the importing country and if the importing country's demand for the import is huge and forms a major share in the world imports, then the incidence of the import duties will be partially borne by the exporting country. The same is true for the export duties. This analysis is based on the assumption that there is free trade among the countries. If the trade is not free and trade restrictions can be imposed by various countries then the operation of the demand and supply forces will be restricted only to particular segments of the world market and so the problem of the shifting of tax incidence will have to be considered in the context of these markets.

2. Taxes on property. In the head property are included: (*a*) durable consumption goods, and (*b*) capital goods. If a tax is imposed on durable consumption goods, it will be paid by current owners of the property. If they bear the tax themselves then they will suffer a loss in satisfaction from the use of these goods. The tax can be shifted only if these goods are sold and purchased. The current owners of the property can only shift the tax incidence forward and the purchasers of the property can only shift the tax incidence backward since the purchasers are likely to estimate the net satisfaction which they can get from the purchase of the property. They would be willing to pay reduced prices. Even otherwise too the prices of these durable goods can hardly rise under normal circumstances unless there is an expectation of inflationary rise in prices. Even in that situation the prices of these goods after including the tax would not be higher than what they would have been without tax. So, the tax will be borne by the current owners of the durable goods and not by the new purchasers because the purchasers would capitalise the tax. It is a different thing that the new purchasers are ignorant or their expectation of full capitalisation of the tax is not correct, then the tax incidence may be shifted to the new purchasers.

In the case of capital goods say, financial assets like bonds, securities etc. both the sellers as well as the purchasers are fully aware of the tax rates. And, so the incidence of tax will depend upon the relative elasticities of demand and supply of investment fund. In the case of machinery, equipment etc. the possibility of backward shifting of tax incidence is very prominent, through capitalisation which will also depend upon the elasticities of demand and supply of the taxed commodity.

To understand the problem of forward shifting of such a tax we shall have to see whether the tax is added to the fixed cost or the variable cost of production. In the short period the costs of such item like machinery, equipment etc. are fixed costs and a tax on them will be added to the fixed cost. Since marginal cost depends on the variable costs, it will not change. It implies that in the short period the supply conditions won't change. In the long period the factors of production are all variable which means that any tax imposed on the commodity will be added to the marginal cost of output which will raise the price of the product and the tax incidence will be shifted forward. It is also worth noting that a tax on capital goods may be shifted in more than one stage. For example, a tax on building will be first borne by the manufacturing firm housed in that building and then it will be shifted to the purchasers of the commodity produced by that firm. If the purchasers happen to be the wholesalers then the tax will be shifted to the retailers and the retailers will shift the tax incidence to the final consumer.

3. Tax on profits. Generally all profits are taxed at the same rates and therefore the profit earner cannot avoid the tax. He cannot move from one line of production to another. However, in some industries if the elasticity of demand for the product is very low then the tax incidence is likely to be shifted to the buyers. If this takes place, the net profits (net of tax) in these lines will be higher than any other competing lines and therefore, the resources in the long run will move from other lines into these lines raising the profit rate in the former. In this way some part of the tax incidence may be considered to have been shifted to the buyers in certain industries. But in practice, broadly speaking, it is not possible to identify all the sources of profits, to have a fairly good estimate of such profits and then to impose a tax on them at uniform rates. In practice, therefore, tax on profits are imposed in a discriminatory manner. Consequently, some profit incomes are taxed, others are not. The shifting of the tax incidence by the tax payers to others will again depend upon the respective elasticities of demand and supply of those commodities through which the profit incomes are being obtained and also the elasticities of demand and supply of those inputs which are being used in the production of those commodities.

4. Tax on house property. A tax on house properties will be subject to the forces of tax capitalisation. The purchasers of the houses will endeavour to shift the tax backward at the time of purchase through reduction in the price. In the short-run, if the supply and demand of the houses are inelastic the rents are likely to go up and the sharing of the tax incidence will be determined by the relative strength of the short-run elasticities of demand and supply. In the long run, if the investment in houses is found less profitable their construction will be discouraged and the tax incidence will be borne by the tenants. If a tax is imposed on the house rent then the incidence of tax will be shared between the landlord and the tenant according to the relative elasticities of demand and supply. Broadly speaking, unless all investment incomes are taxed simultaneously the incidence of a tax on house rent will be borne by the tenants.

5. Tax on net income. Net income means the income of an individual or a family after excluding the expenses incurred on earning that income. A tax on income may be specific or general, implying that only income from some particular sources may be taxed or all incomes derived from any source may be taxed. Income taxation may also differentiate between 'earned' and 'unearned' incomes and the rates of taxes may be different for both. If only the income from specific sources is taxed then people will shift from one line of employment to those lines of employment where the income is not taxed. Those persons who continue to stick to the existing jobs whose income has been taxed, will try to shift the tax incidence by raising the supply prices of their products. They will succeed in their effort only if they do not belong to 'non competing groups'. If a general tax is imposed on all incomes then people will not be able to avoid the tax by changing the line of employment. The tax incidence will be borne by the assessees themselves even if the rate of tax is progressive.

6. Inheritance and gift taxes. Some people hold that the incidence of inheritance taxes or estate duties is borne by the testator who is leaving behind the property to be taxed. In this case the tax is paid by the testator only after his death. It is also said that testator may have saved additional property to ensure that the successors get the estate of a certain value which he wants them to inherit and therefore the incidence will fall on the testator: But these arguments are not convincing because—

(*i*) the dead person does not pay the tax. (*ii*) the tax will not distinguish between the testator who saved additionally to leave after-tax estate of a given value and the other where the testator did not save additional property. (*iii*) the inheritance tax is imposed not on the value of the estate but on the portion of the estate inherited by a successor. The same situation exists in the case of gift taxes also.

Shifting of Tax Through Capitalisation

Taxes on durable items like land, houses, long-term bonds etc. may be capitalised in advance by their buyers who pay a reduced price to the seller because of the tax. This is known as tax capitalisation. It implies that a buyer by purchasing an asset tries to shift the whole series of future taxes to the seller by deducting a lumpsum from the price of the asset so that incidence of the tax may remain with the seller. Tax capitalisation is calculated by dividing the net annual income by the percentage rate of income that the buyer of the asset wants from his investment or that which is prevailing in the market.

Conditions for Capitalisation

It may be noted that capitalisation is possible under the following conditions: (*i*) when there are adequate opportunities for alternative investment, (*ii*) when the tax is imposed on only one form of property, (*iii*) when the asset is of a durable nature, (*iv*) when the taxed commodity has a capital value, and (*v*) when the ownership of the taxed asset changes hands quickly.

9. Deficit Financing as a Tax

When budget deficits are financed by the government through sources other than revenue receipts, it is known as deficit financing. These sources can be loans or borrowings, creation of new money or drawing upon cash balances. Loans can be incurred by the government either within the country or outside the country. Loans raised within the country merely transfer the purchasing power from the private sector to the government sector and they may come out of genuine savings of the people. Hence, such loans do not increase the total supply of money in the market. But, if the funds are raised through the sale of treasury bills or drawing down of cash balances, the total money supply in circulation would increase and release inflationary forces. In deficit financing the government creates purchasing power through which it acquires the goods and services. Consequently, the total demand in the market increases; price goes up and the people are not able to purchase the same amount of goods and services as before with the same money balances. Therefore deficit financing is indirectly a tax in so far as the government takes away a portion of the purchasing power of the people. Since it is a hidden-tax, the question arises, on whom the incidence rests. Since deficit financing, in most of the cases, causes inflation, income inequalities are widened and therefore people, particularly salaried and wage earning classes lose in terms of 'real income'. So far as profit earners are concerned their income increases and they are benefited because for them both money and real incomes increase.

Exercises

1. Distinguish between impact and incidences of a tax. Explain the difference between incidence and effects of taxation.
2. State and explain the various theories of shifting of incidence of a tax.
3. Discuss the problem of incidence of taxation under a competitive economy.
4. What is the importance of the study of incidence of a tax? Point out the incidence of (*a*) Income Tax, (*b*) Property Tax, and (*c*) Excise Duty.
5. What do you understand by formal and effective incidence of taxation ? Analyse the incidence of outlay taxes under competitive and monopoly conditions.

●●●

Chapter 37

Prof. Musgrave on Shifting of Incidence

1. Introduction

As already stated Musgrave's interpretation of incidence is quite different from that of the traditional or neo-classical economists. According to him incidence refers to distributional changes in income owing to a change in the budget policy. Budget policy includes both taxation and expenditure. In other words, whenever a change is introduced in the tax system or in the pattern of public expenditure it will cause certain effects which will in totality be known as incidence. These can be of three types: (*i*) transfer of resources from private to public use, (*ii*) effect on total national output, and (*iii*) changes in the distribution of income.

Musgrave uses the term incidence to include the third type of effect. Since resources can be transferred even without taxes and output can be affected by a number of factors, and therefore the changes in the distribution of income are referred to by Musgrave as incidence. It is to be noted that Musgrave gives importance to the role of both public revenue and public expenditure, quite unlike the traditional economists. He says that distributional changes may be caused by three different policies namely: (*i*) introducing changes in the tax policy without disturbing the pattern of public expenditure in real term, (*ii*) changes in public expenditure without disturbing the tax structure, and (*iii*) changes in both tax structure and pattern of public expenditure to obtain the required yield. The first change has been called as 'tax incidence', the second as 'expenditure incidence' and the third as 'balanced buduget incidence'.

According to Musgrave an analysis of incidence can be done in two ways: (*i*) specific, and (*ii*) differential, both in relation to taxation and public expenditure. Let us look at the views of Professor Musgrave on these aspects in some detail.

(1) Specific Tax Incidence

Specific tax incidence is the incidence arising due to the changes in the taxation policy without any change in public expenditure in real terms. Let us take an example. If the economy is operating at the full employment level then any decrease in income tax rates would lead to more income with the people, increase in their aggregate demand for goods and services, increase in price and costs and ultimately an increase in public expenditure in money terms, to maintain the same level of purchases. To meet the increased expenditure the government will have to create money *i.e.*, print new notes. This will create inflation. On the contrary, if the rates of income tax are increased, the money income with the people will decline, aggregate demand for goods and services will fall and ultimately deflationary conditions would be created. In this way both inflationary and deflationary conditions affect the distribution of income and wealth. In inflationary conditions, the income and wealth will be transferred from the poor to the rich and in deflationary conditions the reverse will happen. So in this case the incidence is of two types: (*i*) due to the changes in a particular tax, and (*ii*) due to inflation and deflation. This is how Musgrave has explained the concept of 'Specific Incidence'.

(2) Differential Tax Incidence

It refers to the distributional effects caused by the substitution of one tax for another, presuming that the money income from both the taxes remains the same. It implies that the substitution of one tax for the other, in the event of money income of the government remaining the same, the public expenditure will also remain the same. It also implies that there will be no change in the transfer of real resources from private to public use. But, it may certainly affect the aggregate demand and the price level, because different taxes have different effects on the people. With the change in the price level the government will also have to change the pattern of public expenditure in money terms to maintain the transfer of real resources at the same level. Therefore, according to Musgrave differential incidence is the change in the distributional pattern resulting from the two tax policies which provide for equal yield.

(3) Specific Expenditure Incidence

When changes are introduced in the public expenditure without disturbing the tax rate structure and the assessment formula, any effect resulting therefrom in the distribution of income and wealth will be called specific expenditure incidence. A change in public expenditure in money terms may not cause any change in the transfer of resources from private to public use. But, if it changes the income of the people then it will be known as the specific expenditure incidence. For example, an increase in public expenditure would increase the income of the people, prices of goods and services would rise and inflationary conditions would develop. Similarly, a reduction in public expenditure will reduce the income of the people, resulting in a reduction of the aggregate demand for goods and services and creation of deflationary conditions. The distribution of income is affected by changes in public expenditure in two ways: (*i*) due to the changes in public expenditure, and (*ii*) due to inflation and deflation.

(4) Differential Expenditure Incidence

Differential expenditure incidence refers to the changes in the distribution of income for private use owing to the changes in public expenditure on different items under the balanced budget policy without changing the tax structure. A balanced budget policy implies that an increase in public expenditure on some items should be offset by a decrease in expenditure on some other items. Whatever effects such changes in public expenditure produce on the distribution of income and wealth are known as differential expenditure incidence. According to Musgrave the concept of expenditure incidence whether specific or differential is not so useful as the concept of differential tax incidence for analysing the problems of incidence of taxation and transfer of resources.

(5) Balanced Budget Incidence

Changes in the distribution of income and wealth caused by changes in the expenditure policy and taxation policy under the overall policy of a balanced budget have been referred as balanced budget incidence. For example, to meet the requirement of increased real expenditure of the government if changes are introduced in the tax structure to obtain additional income, the resultant changes in the distribution are referred to as the balanced budget incidence. This implies that there would be no inflation or deflation and hence the changes in the distribution of income and wealth will not be due to these forces.

2. Measurement of Incidence

Musgrave has suggested a measure of incidence in terms of Lorenz curve as shown in Fig. 37.1.

The percentage of income recipients has been shown on the horizontal axis and percentage of income has been shown on vertical axis. *OB* is the curve showing perfect equality. *OLB* is the Lorenz curve corresponding to the initial distribution. The coefficient of equality now is given by *OLBA/OBA* as a result of changes in the tax structure or expenditure or both. The Lorenz curve becomes *OMB* which indicates the changed pattern of distribution after

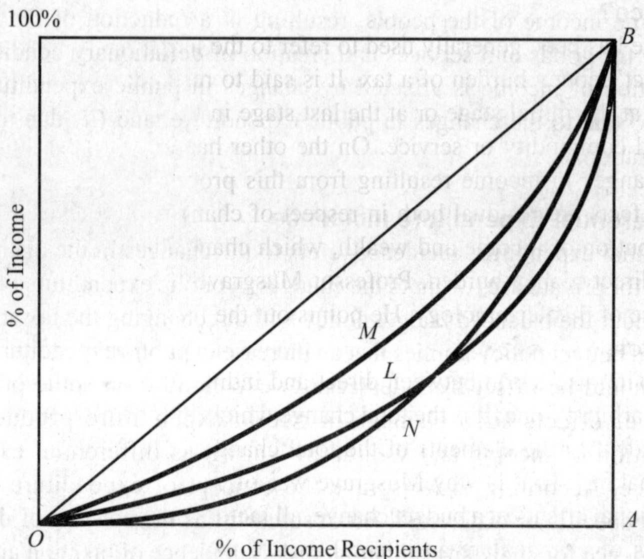

Fig. 37.1

the implementation of the budget policy. Accordingly the coefficient of equality will be *OMBA/OBA*. Incidence is then measured by the ratio as follows:

$$R = \frac{OMBA / OBA}{OLBA / OBA} = \frac{OMBA}{OLBA}$$

= If $R > 1$ the incidence is progressive;
= If $R = 1$ the incidence is proportional; and
= If $R < 1$ the incidence is regressive.

Since it is difficult to distinguish, most of the times, between incidence and effects, the ultimate decision on these issues according to Musgrave, 'is a matter of taste'. To quote him, "Whether the element of distributional change should be given the label of incidence is a matter of taste. Some readers may prefer to call it merely the distributional effect of budget policy."

It has also been pointed out that the definition of incidence would also depend on the objectives set by one, the government, while analysing the incidence. Different tax authorities may have different objectives. If the welfare is an objective then both distributional and output effects should be included under incidence.[1]

---

1. Please see Krupp Hans Juergen, "Econometric analysis of Tax Incidence" in A.T. Peacock, (Ed.), *Quantitative Analysis in Public Finance.*

Is Musgrave's Analysis Superior to the Traditional Theory of Incidence?

Incidence has been generally used to refer to the location of the 'ultimate' or the 'direct' money burden of a tax. It is said to rest with the final tax payer, whether at the initial stage or at the last stage in the series of transactions in the taxed commodity or service. On the other hand effects of a tax refer to other changes in income resulting from this process of adjustment. In this sense, effects are residual both in respect of changes in output and changes in distribution of income and wealth, which changes are not considered as a part of direct money burden. Professor Musgrave, however, is not in favour of the use of this terminology. He points out the following difficulties in this connection.

(1) The distinction between direct and indirect effects of incidence of a tax is an arbitrary one. It is the total change which is important and it is neither easy to identify the elements of the total change nor is it of importance for policy making. That is why Musgrave was of the view that while analysing distributional effects of a budget change, all factors must be taken into account. All kinds of changes are an integral part of the process of adjustment and constitute in totality the system of general equilibrium. In Musgrave's view it is not difficult to make a distinction between resource transfer, distributional change and output effects. These are measurable and can be identified. Now the element of distributional change, if one likes, can be given a label of tax incidence but some others would like to label it as the distributional effect of the budgetary changes.

(2) The concept of incidence is based on the false notion that a tax has an element of burden. Taxes may be levied or withdrawn or substituted for each other without resulting in the transfer of resources for public use. It is, however, necessary that a clear line is drawn between the combined result of increased resource transfer to public use due to a tax and the effects of a change in methods of financing alone without any change in the resource transfer to public use. The distributional effects of the former type of change are referred to as budget incidence while those of the latter as tax incidence. According to Musgrave in the context of tax incidence the problem ‹ f differential incidence is of special interest.

(3) It would be useful if, while examining the consequential changes in the real income of individuals, all changes are allowed such as those resulting from the income source side, those generated by changes in the net prices (after tax) of the services they have to sell, also those changes which result from the income use side caused by the changes in the gross prices (after tax) of the products they have to buy. Therefore, Musgrave has observed that while looking at the problem of incidence either from the point of view of particular

individual or of public policy it is not of much importance to know how the distributional changes have taken place. These changes must be allowed for without bothering into how and why of these changes.

(4) In tracing the distributional changes occurring due to an adjustment in budgetary policy both losses and gains must be looked into. It will not be correct to say that the imposition of a tax only causes a loss to the tax payer. In fact imposition of a tax does not only lead to transfer of resources from private use to public use, it is also accompanied by gains to some others. Even while estimating budget incidence, the net result of the adjustment will be to reduce the total income available for private use, but this does not imply that all individuals income would be reduced. Some people may find their position improved.

To conclude, we may say that Professor Musgrave's contention is right when he says that without any bias or prejudice we must consider distributional changes owing to tax incidence in totality. That is all individual gains and losses must be taken into account simultaneously.

1. Explain the interpretation of tax incidence as given by Musgrave. Also explain, how he measures it.

2. Give the analysis of tax incidence according to Musgrave. Is it superior to the Traditional Theory?

●●●

Chapter 38

Classification and Choice of Taxes

1. Introduction

While discussing the characteristics of a good tax system, and the question of distribution of tax burden, we have already talked about the objectives of a good tax system as efficiency, economy, equity, resource allocation etc. If each tax in its individual capacity was able to fulfil some or all of these objectives, the task of the tax authorities in selecting a combination of taxes which would yield the maximum revenue would have been much easier. But this does not happen. Each tax, while fulfiling some of the objectives unleashes forces which to a great extent mitigate its beneficial effects. So the crucial question is: How to make a choice between different taxes and their rate schedule? We now discuss this question in this chapter.

It must be clearly understood that when we discuss the question of choice of taxes we do not mean to replace the old tax structure by a new one. Neither do we mean that a choice between different taxes can be absolute. What we mean is that we can merely introduce some changes in the rates of taxes. Withdrawal of some old taxes and introduction of some new taxes, can also always be undertaken, depending upon the exigencies of the situation. A discussion regarding merits and demerits of different taxes is only theoretical in nature and can at best provide some general guidelines to the authorities for tax reforms. Moreover, what is found to be correct and logical in theory may not be so in practice. This is more true in the case of taxation. Again, in a democracy every proposal for tax reform must be approved by the people through their representatives *viz.*, the parliament and the legislature. It is also not easy for the government to carry out all sorts of changes in the tax system because some of them may not be acceptable to strong and powerful sections of the society. Besides, some tax variations may certainly be warranted by the needs of the economy, but the government may not be able to introduce them either because of the inability of the existing administrative machinery to implement them or because of the high cost involved in introducing those changes. In any case whatever changes the authorities wish to introduce, they must ensure that the policy and structure of taxation are to the best advantage of the economy and the people. We now very briefly discuss the relative merits and demerits of some broad classes of taxes.

2. Single vs. Multiple Tax System

Earlier economists, particularly from 17th to 19th century, advocated a single tax system. A single tax means only one kind of tax. Such a tax is collected at regular intervals, may be monthly or annually or any other shorter or longer duration. It can be a tax on all classes of things or on all expenditures or on all incomes. A single tax may be proportional, progressive or regressive. It may also be a lumpsum tax. The 17th and 18th century economists were in favour of a single tax on expenses. Towards the latter part of the 18th century some people in England advocated a single tax on houses. In the 19th century many people in Europe advocated a single tax on income. French economists advocated a single stamp tax besides some economists who favoured a single tax on capital. Earlier physiocrats advocated a single tax on land, since according to them agriculture was the only productive industry and capable of paying the taxes. Issac Sherman proposed a single tax on all real estates—on land—because it was convenient in administration and payment. Henry George also advocated a single tax on land chiefly because he thought that it was not possible to shift the tax.

The advocacy of a single tax was primarily because the functioning of the economy in those days was very simple and the main function of the state was to protect its people from external and internal dangers. The activities of the government were confined to defence and maintenance of law and order in the country. With the change in the concept of the state from a Police State to a Welfare State, the nature and scope of public finance stand completely changed. Now the main concern of the state is economic growth, equitable distribution of wealth and income, economic stability, full employment and so on. No single tax can raise funds for all these objectives and hence a multiple tax system has become essential, comprising of taxes of different kinds, some falling on the rich, others falling on the common man; some restricting consumption, others encouraging production and so on blended in such a way as to minimise their ill-effects and maximise their beneficial effects.

We now discuss the merits and demerits of a single tax system.

Merits of Single Tax System

It has been pointed that the greatest merit of a single tax is its simplicity. Since there is only one tax the work of the government becomes very simple as compared to the multiple tax system. There is also no complication in the collection of tax and its influence on production and distribution is rather insignificant. Consequently the cost of collection of revenue and administration of the tax is not high.

Demerits of Single Tax System

It has been remarked that from the point of view of yield a single tax may not provide the necessary revenue to the government. These days, the government generally needs huge funds to perform the various functions. Sometimes the need of the government increases suddenly. And, so a single tax will not be adequate to provide the necessary revenue. Moreover, the yield of a single tax cannot be made to increase as faster as that of the multiple tax system.

A single tax system cannot be made equitable because it cannot be levied according to the ability to pay of the tax payer. For example, if a tax is levied on property it is very difficult to impose it on everybody in proportion to the ability to pay. In this connection it has been pointed out that a tax on income can be made equitable. But an income tax is also evaded by rich and well to do people and therefore the objective of equitable distribution of income is difficult to achieve.

It has also been observed that a single tax cannot be helpful in achieving the social and economic objectives such as those relating to economic growth.

Merits of Multiple Tax System

In view of the above it has been asserted that it is a multiple tax system which can help the economy to grow and enable the government to achieve all the socio-economic goals. We find that a modern economy has to fulfil many objectives like those of growth, equitable distribution of income and wealth, economic stability, full employment and so on. Since no single tax can help the economy to achieve all these objectives simultaneously, a choice obviously falls on the multiple tax system in which different taxes will contribute to the achievement of different objectives. Some taxes will make the distribution of income and wealth more equitable; some would help the economy to achieve the objective of regional balanced growth; some others may be used to raise adequate revenue and so on.

Secondly, in a modern economy income is generated by many sources. It would therefore not be wise and just to tax only one source. In the interest of justice and equity, all sources must be tapped.

Thirdly, it may not be of advantage to depend on a single tax, because if it helps fulfilment of certain objectives, it can also work against others. To cite an example a tax on income which helps in the redistribution of income and wealth, might dissuade people from saving and investment. This would certainly adversely affect capital accumulation and economic growth. Multiple tax system, therefore is just and equitable because it is a mixture of progressive, proportional, direct and indirect taxes.

Fourthly, tax evasion is not easy under a multiple tax system. If a person evades a tax on one account he is made to pay the tax on another account because of the existence of multiple taxes.

Fifthly, in a multiple tax system the tax structure becomes broad-based covering all the persons in the country.

Sixthly, multiple tax system conforms to the criteria of equity, elasticity, diversity, flexibility etc.

We may therefore conclude that a multiple tax system is by all means preferable to a single tax system. But too much multiplicity is also not desirable. If the number of taxes is very large most of them would yield only a small amount of revenue and the cost of collection would become very high. So, instead of being a boon the multiple tax system would become a curse. Therefore, a multiple tax system does not mean too many taxes. Excess multiplicity than what is desirable may prove hazardous and may sacrifice economy, productivity and finance. That is why Dalton has stated that "it is better to rely on substantial taxes for the bulk of revenue." Finally, care will have to be taken to ensure that this system does not become regressive in its effects. The burden of taxation will have to be dispersed so that the base is widened and no one is harmed excessively.

3. Progressive, Proportional and Regressive Taxes

We have made a passing reference to these taxes earlier and have also explained these terms. Without repeating what we have already stated we carry our discussion further by using the terms "tax base" and "tax rate". Tax base is the object to which the tax applies such as the income or the value of a property. Tax rate is the amount of tax per unit of the tax base. The tax will be called proportional when the tax rate remains the same for each unit of the tax base; it will be progressive when the tax rate rises with every increase in the tax base; and it is regressive when the tax rate increases with an increase in the tax base. Let us explain in this connection another relationship corresponding to the relationship between proportionality and progressiveness. This is the relationship between average and marginal tax rates. The former can be derived by dividing the total tax liability by the total tax base and the latter can be calculated by dividing the change in the total tax liability by the change in the total tax base. If for example, for a tax base of Rs. 20,000.00 the tax liability is Rs. 3,000.00 and for a tax base of Rs. 30,000.00 the tax liability is Rs. 7,500.00 then average tax rate for the two tax bases would be 15 per cent and 25 per cent respectively. The marginal tax rate would be: additional tax liability (*viz.*, Rs. 4,500.00) for an additional tax base (Rs. 10,000.00) *i.e.*,

45 per cent. In a proportional tax the marginal rate is always equal to the average rate, in progressive taxation the marginal rate is. always higher than the average rate and in regressive taxation both the rates decline with the increase in the tax base and so the marginal rate is always lower than the average rate.

Progression can also be degressive. It can be in two ways: in the first case a certain amount of the tax base is accepted totally and on the rest tax is charged at a single rate. In the second case tax rate does not rise faster with increase in the tax base; rather the degree of progression declines as the tax base increases. In other words, taxes which are mildly progressive and in which the high income groups do not make due sacrifice, such taxes from the point of view of equity are called degressive. This can be illustrated with the help of Table 38.1.

Table 38.1

Tax Base	*Tax Rate*	*Amount of Tax*
Rs. 10,000.00	5%	Rs. 500.00
Rs. 20,000.00	6%	Rs. 1,200.00
Rs. 30,000.00	7%	Rs. 2,100.00
Rs. 40,000.00	8%	Rs. 3,200.00
Rs. 50,000.00	8%	Rs. 4,000.00

Figure 38.1 explains a degressive tax.

The concept of progression, it must be added here, refers only to the money burden of the tax and not to its real burden or the sacrifice which a tax payer suffers. In the context of sacrifice a proportional income tax will be regressive because tax payers with lower incomes will part with greater utility in terms of money than those with higher incomes. Taylor defines the proportional, progressive and regressive taxes as below:

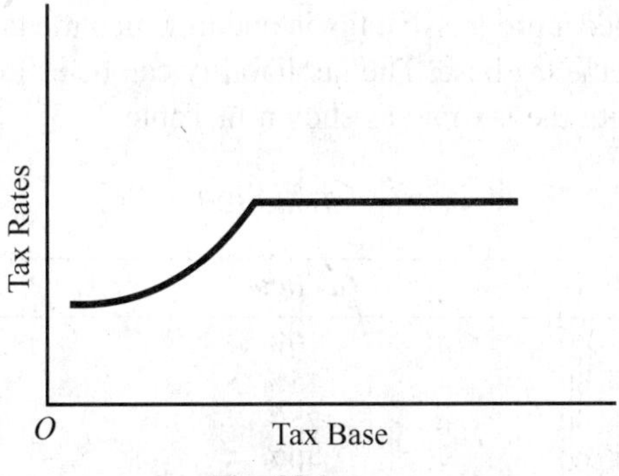

Fig. 38.1.

(1) Proportional Tax

In a proportional tax the rate schedule is one in which the rate of tax remains constant with the change in the tax base. The amount of tax payable can be estimated by multiplying the tax base with the tax rate. This is explained in Table 38.2.

Table 38.2

Tax Base	*Tax Rate*	*Amount of Tax*
Rs. 40,000.00	10%	Rs. 4,000.00
Rs. 60,000.00	10%	Rs. 6,000.00
Rs. 80,000.00	10%	Rs. 8,000.00
Rs. 1,00,000.00	10%	Rs. 10,000.00

Figure 38.2. illustrates proportional tax rates.

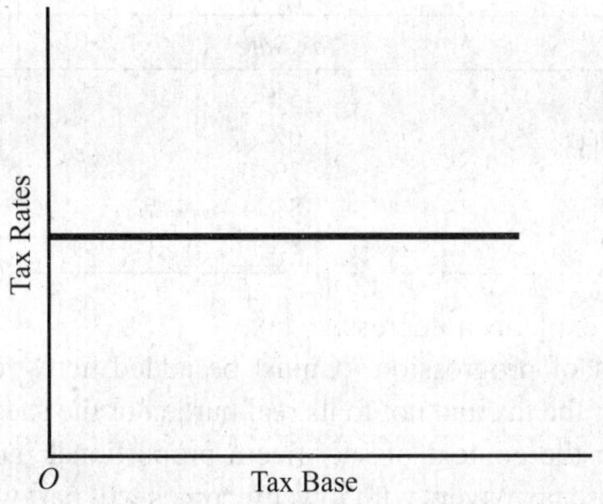

Fig. 38.2.

(2) Progressive Tax

As already stated a progressive tax is one in which the tax rate increases with the increase in the tax base. The tax liability can be estimated by multiplying the tax base with the tax rate as shown in Table 38.3.

Table 38.3

Tax Base	*Tax Rate*	*Amount of Tax*
Rs. 40,000.00	10%	Rs. 4,000.00
Rs. 60,000.00	15%	Rs. 9,000.00
Rs. 80,000.00	25%	Rs. 20,000.00
Rs. 1,00,000.00	40%	Rs. 40,000.00

This is illustrated in the Fig. 38.3.

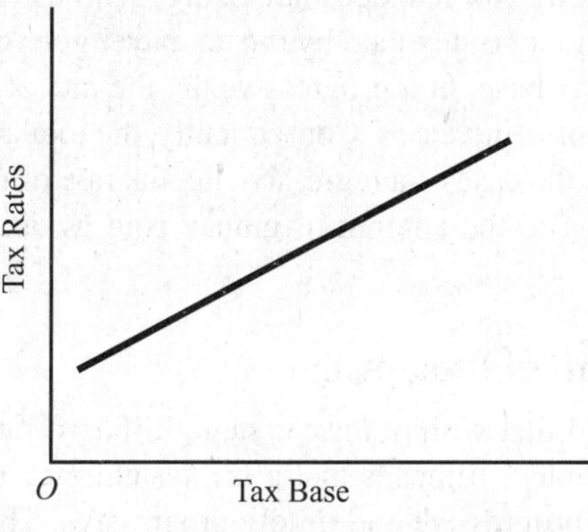

Fig. 38.3.

(3) Regressive Tax

In a regressive tax, the tax rate decreases with the increase in the tax base as illustrated in Table 38.4.

Table 38.4

Tax Base	*Tax Rate*	*Amount of Tax*
Rs. 40,000.00	10%	Rs. 4,000.00
Rs. 60,000.00	8%	Rs. 4,800.00
Rs. 80,000.00	7%	Rs. 5,600.00
Rs. 1,00,000.00	6%	Rs. 6,000.00

This can be illustrated with the help of the Fig. 38.4.

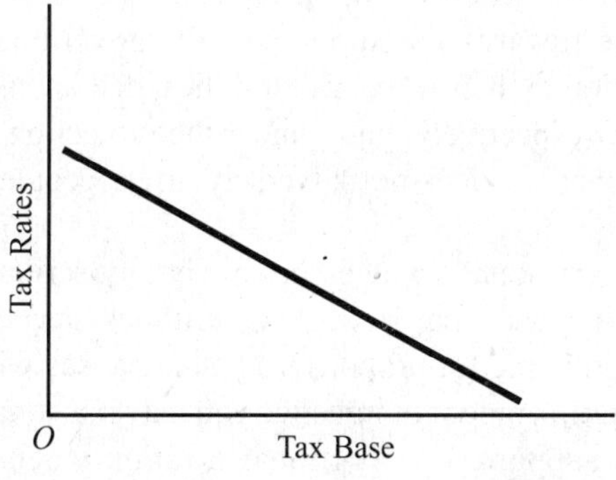

Fig. 38.4.

On the basis of the above we can now summarise the position as under. In a proportional tax the tax rate does not change with the increase in the tax base but the total amount of tax paid by the tax payer goes on increasing with the increase in the tax base. In a progressive tax the rate of tax increases at a faster rate as the income increases. Consequently, the total amount of tax also increases rapidly. In the case of a regressive tax the rate of tax decreases with increase in income. But the amount of money paid as tax, increases with a rise in income.

4. Different Forms of Progression

It may be mentioned that within a tax system, different rates of progression in taxes may be adopted. It means that a tax system may be simultaneously progressive, highly progressive and mildly progressive. The same is true for regression, if the rate decreases with the increase in the tax base.

We may now enumerate the merits and demerits of proportional and progressive taxes.

Merits of Proportional Taxation

Following arguments are given in favour of proportional taxation:

(1) The proportional taxation is simple and uniform. Its rate is uniform for all the tax payers and therefore no one objects against this tax. Because of its simplicity the estimation or calculation of the tax liability is easy both for the government and the tax payer and therefore it is in conformity with the canon of certainty. That is why the proportional tax system has been considered better than arbitrarily graded progressive tax system.

(2) The tax is also in consonance with the principle of equity, because the money burden increases in the same proportion as the increase in income. That is what Adam Smith meant when he said "the subject of every state ought to contribute towards the support of the government, as nearly as possible, in proportion to their respective abilities, that is, in proportion to the revenue which they respectively enjoy under the protection of the state".

(3) A proportional tax does not adversely affect people's willingness to work and save.

(4) Again a proportional tax does not affect any serious changes in the position of the tax payers. That is what Mc Culloch said that: "Where you abandon the plain principle (of proportion) you are at sea without rudder and compass and there is no amount of injustice you may not commit." John Stuart Mill also strongly supported proportional taxation when he said that, "a graduated income tax was an entirely unjust mode of taxation and in fact a graduated robbery."

(5) Proportional taxation has been favoured primarily because it is not easy to decide upon an exact and appropriate degree of progression, since the extent by which marginal utility of money decreases for an individual cannot be measured.

(6) Finally, it is said that proportional taxation does not disturb the existing allocation of resources of the economy and therefore the developmental course of an economy is not affected. This argument is based upon the point that under proportional taxation the same proportion of purchasing power is taken out of the pockets of all the tax payers and hence the gap in the disposable income of the tax payers remains the same and therefore the relative demand and supply position in the economy does not change. But this sort of argument is rather misleading; chiefly because when the tax payer's income is reduced by the payment of a tax, he adjusts his demand for various goods and services accordingly. A well to do person would endeavour to maintain his consumption by reducing his savings and therefore the supply of investment funds and demand for capital goods would decline. This certainly would lead to a fall in the rate of economic growth. It is a different thing that the state may take steps to make up the deficiency in this regard. The less well to do people or the poorer sections of the society will reduce their consumption which may not be desirable from the point of view of their health and efficiency. In fact a progressive tax would be more acceptable in the light of the above. The potential savings of the rich can be easily diverted through a progressive tax to the state and the state can use them for the development of the economy. It will also not adversely affect the consumption standards of the poorer people.

Demerits of Proportional Taxation

Proportional taxation has been opposed on the following grounds:

(1) It would not help in achieving the objective of equitable and just distribution of burden of taxation because it falls more heavily on smaller income groups than on the higher income groups, Since the marginal utility of money declines with an increase in income the poor have to make greater sacrifice in paying a tax in proportion to their income than the sacrifice made by rich in proportion to their income. To achieve equity in the distribution of tax burden it is necessary that the rich should be taxed at a higher rate than the poor.

(2) In the system of proportional taxation the tax rates for all people, rich as well as poor, are the same. It means that the rich do not contribute to the state according to their capacity. These days when the financial requirements of the governments are increasing at a fast pace the system of proportional taxation would not be able to raise adequate revenue for the government.

(3) The system of proportional taxation also lacks elasticity and therefore

it cannot meet the growing needs of the government. Since the rich and the poor are, taxed at the same rate and if the rate is already heavy on the poor, the government has no scope of raising the rate of taxation in the case of the rich classes. Therefore, the government may not succeed in increasing its revenue in times of need.

Merits of Progressive Taxation

The following arguments have been given in favour of progressive taxation:

(1) Progressive taxation has been generally favoured on the plea that the marginal utility of money to the rich declines with rise in income, as is manifested by the way these people indulge in extravagance and outward pomp and show. This also leads to the argument of "taxing people according to their ability to pay". If the rich are not taxed heavily, they would go on indulging in extravagant and superfluous expenditure and uneconomical use of the productive resources of the society. Again, if the rich are not made to contribute according to their ability, they would go on becoming richer and the inequalities in the distribution of income and wealth will go on increasing resulting ultimately in the mal-allocation of resources of the society in favour of luxuries. Professor Kaldor has also emphasised the role of progressive taxation in reducing the inequalities of distribution of income and wealth.

(2) In a modern free enterprise economy progressive taxation acts as a stabiliser and helps in the maintenance of economic stability. Higher incomes are taxed at a higher rate during the period of rising prices and during depression the higher income earning people get larger tax relief. It is in this way that the economy continues to get a stable demand base even during periods of depression and its extra purchasing power is taxed during period of boom. This is how the upward and downward movement of income and prices are stabilised.

(3) In an underdeveloped economy progressive taxation helps in raising the required revenue. It is well known that a poor country does not have an adequate economic surplus which may serve as a source of savings and therefore, such savings have to be forced upon the society to a very great extent. Therefore, the state has to take recourse to indirect taxes in order to raise adequate revenue. These indirect taxes touch even articles of mass consumption and are not limited only to items of luxury generally used by the rich.

(4) Further, it is argued that progressive taxation is quite convenient from the point of view of administration. In the case of proportional taxation or regressive taxation the tax authority has to cover a large number of items and so the administration of the tax is not very convenient. Moreover, it also leads

to the harassment of the small tax payers and increases the cost of tax collection as well. In progressive taxation such costs are very low.

(5) Progression in the tax rates secures equity in sacrifice and leads to justice in the distribution of tax burden. Progressive taxes are also elastic. They can be used with ease for raising public revenue by increasing the rate of taxes any time according to need.

(6) Progressive taxation also helps in combating inflation. Higher rates of taxes reduce consumption, demand and the resources so saved are directed towards productive investment and thus supply of commodities can be increased.

(7) Finally, under a system of progressive taxation the loss of satisfaction to the community as a whole is the minimum, because the rich people are taxed at high rates and the poor people are either exempted or are taxed at very low rates. Even otherwise too, if the income of the rich and wealthy people is reduced through progressive taxation, their relative position continues to remain the same and the loss of satisfaction to all of them is not felt by them.

Prof. Taylor has justified progressive taxation on these grounds:

(*i*) Revenue productivity, (*ii*) optimum individual allocation of tax burden, (*iii*) promotion of stability and growth, and (*iv*) optimum social allocation of resources.

Demerits of Progressive Taxation

Progressive taxation has been opposed on the following grounds:

(1) Under progressive taxation rates are fixed arbitrarily. There is no guiding principle.

(2) Progressive taxation assumes that the marginal utility of money declines with increase in income and wealth. This means that the marginal utility of money is less to a rich person in comparison to a poor person. But, satisfaction or utility is a psychological phenomenon and inter-personal comparison is not possible. Moreover, while applying the law of diminishing utility to public finance it has been assumed that human behaviour remains the same under similar circumstances but in practice there can be exceptions. Thus, progressive taxation is valid only under the assumption that the marginal utility of money declines with increase in income.

(3) According to some, progressive taxation may affect production adversely and discourage capital formation. Mill was particularly of this view. He says that "to tax the higher incomes at higher percentage than smaller is to lay a tax on industry and economy." But this apprehension appears to be far fetched because a progressive tax is always on surplus and therefore it does not adversely affect the desire to save and work more. Moreover, the tax

authority can always exercise the caution of ensuring that progression in taxation does not reach a point where it may hamper capital formation and growth of industry.

(4) According to some people progressive taxation is a sort of punishment to prudent and virtuous people. It rewards extravagance and idleness. According to J.S. Mill beyond a certain limit a graduated tax appears to be an entirely unjust mode of taxation, and in fact a 'graduated robbery'. Similarly William Newmarch observed that progression is "confiscation, punishing prudence and virtue, taxing a man for being good to himself and doing good to others." In this connection it has been pointed out that this sort of observation appears to be out of tune. It is an established fact that people have been able to amass wealth and property not always through hard work and thrift. Sometimes economic changes due to defective government policies also bring unexpected incomes to the people. Moreover, the existence of large income and large property has been possible only because of the existing social, legal and public institutions and therefore there is no harm in taxing such income and properties at progressive rates.

(5) Lastly, some people oppose progressive taxation because it provides ample scope for tax evasion. According to these people the tax payers are always busy in finding ways and means for tax evasion which does not happen in the case of a proportional tax. People are always ready to find loopholes in the existing laws and rules.

5. Direct and Indirect Taxes

A number of economists have expressed their opinion on direct and indirect taxation. They have, in their own way, identified the points of distinction between these two types of taxes. Most of the writers have agreed that direct taxes are those which are paid by the persons on whom these are imposed and the real burden is also borne by them, such as taxes on income, property, consumption, inheritance, expenditure etc. Taxes which reach the income and property of persons through their acts and enjoyment and also through their consumption of commodities are known as indirect taxes such as excise duties, sales tax, entertainment tax etc. We very briefly reproduce the ideas of some of the prominent economists in this regard.

According to Dalton, "A direct tax is really paid by a person on whom it is legally imposed, while an indirect tax is imposed on one person, but paid partly or wholly by another, owing to a consequential change in the terms of some contract or bargaining between them.'[1] Thus according to him in direct

1. Dalton Hugh, *op. cit.,* p. 33.

taxes the impact and incidence are on the same person whereas in indirect taxes the impact is on one person and the incidence is on some other person.

J.S. Mill opined that while imposing the tax if the government wants that a person who legally pays the tax must bear it, it is a direct tax. But when the government wants that a tax collected from one should be passed on to others, it should be called an indirect tax.[2]

According to Mill, therefore, it is the intention of the government on the basis of which these two types of taxes can be distinguished. But it is not always easy to know the exact intention of the government nor is its realisation always possible. The intention of the government may be that the tax may be shifted but it is not always easy to shift the tax. Bastable holds that taxes levied on permanent and recurring occasions are direct, but those levied on occasional and particular events are indirect.[3]

Prof. De Marco says that if the income of an individual is appraised directly, it is a direct tax and if it is appraised indirectly when it is spent, it is an indirect tax. He also holds that both these taxes are complementary.

Prof. Findlay Shirras is of the view that those taxes which are levied immediately on the property and the income of the persons and those that are paid by the consumers to the state direct are called direct taxes and those which affect the income and property of persons through their consumption may be called as indirect taxes.

6. Merits and Demerits of Direct and Indirect Taxes

Merits of Direct Taxes

Direct taxes have the following merits:

1. Economy. The cost of collecting direct taxes is low as compared to indirect taxes, because the same staff who assess small incomes and properties can also assess large incomes and property. The payment of these taxes is made direct by the tax payer to the state and therefore every single paisa is deposited in the state treasury.

2. Certainty. These taxes are certain for the tax payer as well as for the government. The tax payer knows fully how much he has to pay and the state also knows how much it has to receive.

3. Equity. Direct taxes are equitable because they are based on the principle of progression and fall more heavily on the rich than the poor.

4. Reduce Inequalities. Since direct taxes are progressive and tax rich

2. J.S. Mill, *Principles,* Book V. Chapter III.
3. C.F. Bastablc, *Public Finance,* p. 291.

people at higher rates, and poor people are exempted or taxed at low rates, they help in reducing inequalities in income and distribution of wealth.

5. Elasticity. Direct taxes are also elastic and the government can increase its revenue simply by raising the rate of taxation. Even otherwise too, the income from direct taxes automatically increases with the increase in income of the people.

6. Civic Consciousness. It is believed that direct taxes create consciousness among the tax payers regarding their duty towards running of the government. In a democratic system this is very important because every citizen should be aware of its responsibilities towards the government and should pay taxes willingly and ungrudgingly.

The argument relating to civic consciousness runs counter to the argument which says that direct taxes leave the tax payers better off than the indirect taxes. If that was so then people will not be conscious when the taxes are paid directly. Again because of their consciousness about the payment of the tax, the tax payers would try to evade it. That is why we find that the possibility of tax evasion is greater in the case of direct taxes than indirect taxes.

Demerits of Direct Taxes

Following are the demerits of the direct taxes:

1. Unpopularity. Direct taxes are not as popular as the indirect taxes because they cannot be shifted and they inflict pain and burden on the tax payer. That is why there is a general opposition to the direct taxes.

2. Possibility of evasion. Direct taxes have been believed to be a tax on honesty but generally it has been observed that the tax payers are not cent per cent honest and they strive to evade the tax through various undesirable methods.

3. Inconvenience. A great demerit of direct taxes is that they are not in conformity with the canon of convenience. Indirect taxes are convenient because they are paid in bits and for each transaction. Direct taxes are, however, not convenient because they are paid in lump sum and even in advance. Again, the tax payers are required to maintain the accounts of their income meticulously and submit the same to the tax authority, which is a cause of irritation to them.

4. No tax on low income group. If the tax system comprises of only direct taxes, the low income group people cannot be taxed because their ability to pay is less and a tax on poor people will not be just.

5. Possibility of injustice. From the practical point of view it is difficult to make an accurate assessment of the income of all classes of people and therefore, the direct taxes may not put equal burden on all classes. Besides, the rates in the case of direct taxes are fixed arbitrarily and not strictly according to the ability of the tax payers to pay.

6. Effect on the will to work and save. Since direct taxes reduce income a tax payer will be dissuaded from working more and therefore he will substitute leisure for work. Therefore, direct taxes adversely affect the will to work, which ultimately slows down the overall rate of economic growth. Similarly, if the tax is levied on property and inheritance, people will be reluctant to save. Consequently capital accumulation in the economy will decline and again the economic growth of the economy will be retarded. The reason for this is that the tax payer generally compares the utility from current consumption with the utility from future income. Since the taxation causes a decline in the utility going to the heirs, the tax payers themselves start consuming more and save less for their heirs.

Merits of Indirect Taxes

1. Convenience. Indirect taxes have the merit of being less inconvenient and therefore less burdensome. Since the tax is paid in instalments and at the time when the business transactions take place, their payment does not cause any inconvenience to the tax payers. Moreover these taxes are included in the price of goods and services and therefore most of the tax payers are not even aware of their payment. These taxes are also convenient to the government because they are collected generally from the manufacturers or the importers.

2. Tax evasion difficult. Indirect taxes are difficult to be evaded. If these taxes are administered properly then the chances of tax evasion are minimum. Take the case of excise duties which are very difficult to evade if the tax collectors are vigilant and there is a proper system of checks at the point of collection. Again, in the case of sales tax also the evasion is difficult but because of large number of exemptions their administration is not easy and therefore sometimes the tax is easily evaded. Moreover, the points of collection of sales tax are quite large in number and spread over widely. That is why sometimes, additional excise duties are levied in place of sa1es taxe. We also have such indirect taxes where the collection is not very difficult because in the case of these taxes the points of collection are limited and accounts of transactions are properly maintained. The case in view relates to the taxes on railway and bus fares. In sum, we can say that evasion of the tax is not as easy as in the case of direct taxes.

3. Guide the resource allocation in the economy. It is argued that indirect taxes act a powerful medium of directing the production and investment activities of the economy. Experience has shown that market mechanism 'if left free' is not able to make the resource allocation optimum. It suffers from many imperfections. Consequently, not only the distribution of income and wealth is inequitable, the pattern of consumption, production and employment also gets distorted. If the indirect taxes are properly structured, they can enable the authorities to influence the forces of demand and supply in such a way as to yield satisfactory results. For example, the government through the use of the tool of indirect taxes can encourage high priority industries and discourage low priority industries—by imposing a high rate of excise duty or sales tax on low priority industries—which will discourage their demand, profitability will be reduced and investment will be diverted to high priority industries where profitability will be comparatively higher. In a similar way indirect taxes can also be used for increasing employment and encouraging the use of new technology. For instance, an extra duty on commodities will make them expensive and reduce their demand while exemption of certain commodities from the tax will reduce their cost of production and price and boost their demand, and also employment in those industries. Similarly, if the government wants to encourage capital-intensive techniques then it can lower the duties in the industries where such techniques are used and impose a heavy tax on the labour-intensive outputs. The same reasoning can be applied to customs duties. The sum and substance of the whole argument is that indirect taxes can be highly selective both rate-wise as well as commodity-wise and can be used as a powerful instrument for guiding the economy in resource allocation.

4. Flexibility. Another merit of indirect taxes is that they are quite flexible because of their selectivity. The rates of indirect taxes and their coverage can be quite selective and changes can be introduced without much difficulty whenever required. This is specially the case with the customs duties.

5. Special importance for underdeveloped countries. Indirect taxes have a very important role to play in an underdeveloped economy. In such economies the rate of capital accumulation and savings is very low. Secondly, the national income is low and the tax revenue is rather limited. The government is required to provide certain basic facilities and welfare activities for which it requires funds. But scope for direct taxes being limited, only indirect taxes can serve the need.

6. Productivity. Indirect taxes are also highly productive. The government, by merely imposing a few taxes can have a high yield of revenue. The objective can easily be attained only by imposing tax on few commodities, whose demand is inelastic. But too much use of these taxes may also have adverse effects on the distribution of income and wealth.

7. Elasticity. Elasticity is a great merit of indirect taxes. It is because of their elasticity that these taxes are productive. However, elasticity and the ability to pay are contradictory to each other because the elasticity of indirect taxes demands that those commodities should be taxed whose demand is inelastic but such taxes will fall more heavily on the poor than the rich.

Demerits of Indirect Taxes

1. Unjust to poor. Since these taxes are not imposed according to the principle of ability to pay they are unjust to the poor and less well to do people. Indirect taxes generally cover those commodities, which are consumed by the poor. Therefore they are regressive in their effects. It is because of this reason that indirect taxes are against the principle of least aggregate sacrifice. This demerit of indirect taxes can be neutralised by imposing heavy taxes on luxuries. But only partial success can be achieved because a tax on luxuries alone will not yield adequate revenue for the government.

2. Inflationary in nature. Another demerit of the indirect taxes is that they help in augmenting the inflationary pressure. Since direct taxes reduce the purchasing power of the tax payer, the automatic result is that the demand and prices also stand reduced. On the contrary, indirect taxes lead to a rise in prices without reducing the purchasing power of the tax payer. Consequently, the inflationary forces are strengthened by higher prices, higher costs and wages.

3. High administrative costs. Administrative cost of collecting indirect taxes is generally high because they are to be collected at large number of points in small amounts. They are therefore uneconomical.

4. Uncertainty. It is argued that indirect taxes are uncertain because it is not possible for the tax authority to have an accurate estimate of the total yield from different taxes chiefly because it is not easy to know exactly the demand for different goods which is influenced by a number of factors.

5. No civic consciousness. Indirect taxes do not create vigilance in the tax payer as the direct taxes do. Therefore, they are unable to make them conscious about the payment of the tax and the proper use of the tax revenue by the government. Since indirect taxes are included in the price of the commodities their presence is not felt by the tax payers and therefore they do not create civic consciousness.

Which of the Two is Better?

With a view to judging the superiority of either of these taxes sometimes a comparison is made between them on the basis of their effects. We can broadly divide these effects into three, as: (1) Allocative Effects, (2) Administrative Effects, (3) Distributional Effects.

We now deal with these in the following paragraphs:

1. Allocative effects. Generally direct taxes are supposed to be superior to indirect taxes in terms of their allocative effects. It means that if a certain amount is to be collected through taxes, then the indirect taxes will entail greater sacrifice for the tax payer than direct taxes. Indirect taxes are expected to affect the relative prices of goods and services and therefore result in an allocation of resources different from the one achieved by the free operation of the market forces. A direct tax on the other hand, say, for example, income tax, is expected to allow the relative prices to remain unaltered and, therefore, is considered to be neutral in the matter of allocation of resources. If the resource allocation in a situation where no tax is imposed, is already optimum, then an indirect tax would create distortions in it and would be burdensome to the economy. If the resource allocation is not optimum, then indirect taxes are expected to bring about the allocation of resources nearer optimum. Economists like Hicks maintain that direct taxes are superior to indirect taxes because the tax payers suffer lesser amount of sacrifice in satisfaction in the case of direct taxes. From the point of view of welfare also direct taxes are superior to indirect taxes. But this sort of analysis about superiority of direct taxes over indirect taxes is not without faults. According to D. Walker the first defect relates to the assumption that the tax payer's indifference map does not undergo any change owing to changes in the rates and form of taxes. But this is not the real situation as we know that tax payers are very sensitive to the changes in the rates and form of taxes. Generally, the tax payers do not like direct taxes because they are more open. Even if we speak theoretically that direct taxes enable the consumers to obtain a higher indifference curve, they would never like to be taxed directly. In fact this assumption that the indifference curve of the tax payers does not change according to the changes in the rates and form of taxes leads to the conclusion that the elasticity of demand for goods and services is zero in each case, but that is not true.

Another weakness of this analysis is that assuming a no tax situation, it tries to analyse the best manner in which a given amount of revenue would be raised. But the assumption of a no tax situation is wrong because every economy has some taxes and a decision is only to be taken regarding a change in their form and rates. So the net effects of a tax will depend upon the position from where one starts. In the words of Walker, "Broadly speaking, then, the Joseph-Hicks theoretical demonstration of the superiority on welfare grounds of direct and indirect taxation is only a satisfactory proof on the twin assumption of a completely inelastic supply of labour with respect to income and outlay taxes and "ideal initial conditions."[4]

Milton Friedman has also questioned this approach. According to him the analysis related to a single tax payer. It did not apply to the whole community of tax payers because this approach did not take into account the expenditure side of the budget and the production possibilities in the economy.[5]

---

4. D. Walker, "The Direct-Indirect Tax Problem. Fifteen Years of Controversy," *Public Finance,* Volume X, 1995, pp. 153-77.
5. Milton Friedman, "The Welfare Effects of an Income Tax and an Excise Tax," *Journal of Political Economy,* February 1952, pp. 25-33.

The comparison between these two types of taxes as given above is based on the assumption that the resource allocation brought about by the operation of the market forces of demand and supply is an ideal one. But this can be questioned. The most important reason for government interference in the market is that its working is highly defective and full of imperfections. To assume that a perfectly competitive market exists, is merely a figment of imagination. A large number of market imperfections are found which are the main cause for defective allocation and uneconomic utilisation of productive resources. Free operation of market forces has never been able to correct regional imbalances and therefore most of the times the economy has not been able to generate the required savings and capital accumulation. Secondly, the income distribution in a pure market economy is not determined by the relative needs of the members of the society, but is governed by the pricing and ownership of the factors of production. Consequently, these conditions perpetuate income inequalities which are further widened by the existence of the institutions of private property and inheritance. It is therefore necessary that the allocation of resources is brought to optimum level through the imposition of various taxes and in this respect indirect taxes of specific type may be more relevant than the direct taxes.

2. Administrative effects. Direct and indirect taxes can also be compared on the basis of administrative cost and efficiency. In under-developed countries direct taxes are not levied on people belonging to the low income group merely to keep the administrative cost low. It is not easy to approach each and every individual through direct taxes firstly, because they are not liked by people and secondly, the administrative cost would be very high. It is on the ground of low administrative cost that Professor A.R. Prest has supported indirect taxes. He has analysed the reasons due to which indirect taxes would be more suitable than the direct taxes. According to him these are: (*i*) existence of a large number of small, independent producers; (*ii*) existence of a large number of illiterate people incapable of maintaining accounts; (*iii*) existence of barter system; and (*iv*) existence of a large number of people living at subsistence level. But this does not imply that direct taxes are inferior to indirect taxes in all respects and at all times.

3. Distributional effects. Another basis of comparison between direct and indirect taxes is their distributional effects. Since direct taxes are progressive in their nature they, are considered as the most important tool for removing inequalities in the distribution of income and wealth. Direct taxes fall more heavily on the rich than the poor. On the contrary, indirect taxes fall on all incomes and are generally regressive in nature. They are therefore not suited from the point of view of removing the inequalities of income and wealth.

Prof. De Marco's Views

Professor De Marco is of the opinion, and rightly so, that both direct and indirect taxes are complementary. According to him a direct tax is directly appraised or ascertained and an indirect tax is indirectly assessed and appraised. In the case of income tax, if an individual's income is directly appraised, it is a direct tax. Since it is not possible to appraise each and every person's taxable income directly and exactly, because many people try to evade and conceal their income, the income which escapes from direct appraisal may be ascertained indirectly at the time when it is spent and therefore it will be an indirect tax. In this way both taxes are complementary to each other. Elaborating this point further, De Marco says that direct appraisal of income generally leads to a figure which is less than the real income. If it was less than the true figure by the same amount in the case of all incomes the problem could be solved by raising the rate appropriately according to the need and then there was no need of indirect taxation. But in real life the errors of underestimation are not equal for all tax payers falling within the same category and more unequal for the tax payers belonging to different categories. Therefore, for removing these errors and for distributing the burden of taxation equally it is very much necessary to appraise the income both directly and indirectly. De Marco further says that the changes in an individual's income take place from time to time and it is not possible to take account of each and every change in the appraisal and therefore correct appraisal of an individual's income is rather difficult. But since an individual's level of consumption varies according to his income, indirect taxes can ascertain a person's changing income and therefore they are complementary to the direct taxes.

According to De Marco there are other conditions also which prove that both these taxes are complementary. For example, indirect taxes do not take into account that portion of the produce which the producers retain for self-consumption as in the case of agriculture. Further, indirect taxes cannot be levied on all commodities and services. Income of individuals can also not be appraised correctly and taxed through indirect taxes and hence in all these cases, direct taxes have to be used as a supplement.

According to De Marco indirect taxes reduce frictional forces, generally found in the appraisal of income and collection of direct taxes. The tax payer is very much alive to the payments he makes in the form of direct taxes because this leads him to cut down his private needs. He feels disturbed because of the periodic appraisal of income and payment of tax. Consequently, frictions are caused in the direct ascertainment of income and payment of taxes which can be minimised if the taxes are calculated at the source. In indirect taxes these frictional forces are reduced to the minimum because the tax is generally included in the price and is paid when the tax payer purchases a commodity.

He makes the payment of the tax while satisfying his wants and therefore instead of conflicting the tax payment coincides with the satisfaction of tax payer's wants. Hence, De Marco holds that both direct and indirect taxes are complementary to each other.

7. Ad Valorem and Specific Duties

Ad Valorem tax is levied according to the value of the commodity or property while specific duties are levied according to the weight of the commodity or according to some external measures. The former is generally expressed as a percentage of the value of the commodity whereas the latter is expressed as a definite sum. Broadly speaking, these duties are levied on commodities entering import and export trade, as customs duties.

Arguments for and against Specific and Ad Valorem Duties

Arguments for and against these duties have been advanced by a number of writers as follows:

(1) Specific duties lead to higher revenues only when the physical volume of output increases. They do not yield additional revenue when there is improvement in the quality of a good or when the value of output goes up for any reason. Secondly, whenever the price rises, the proportion of price rise which accrues to the government treasury declines and the elasticity of revenue tends to be less than unity.

(2) Ad Valorem duties lead to a rise in price and therefore cause inflation. But this argument has not been bought by many quarters. In 1976, the Indirect Taxation Enquiry Committee (India) pointed out that when due to shortage of the supply of commodities or due to inflationary conditions prices rise and windfall profits are earned by the producers and traders, ad valorem duties augment revenues and play an anti-inflationary role. But, when the rise in prices is due to a rise in costs, then ad valorem duty leads to a further rise in prices. When inflationary conditions prevail due to an imbalance between demand and supply caused either by the shortage of basic commodities or by a general increase in money supply, ad valorem duties under such conditions restrict and do not augment inflationary conditions. It is also said that ad valorem duties are not easy to administer as disputes over valuation are wide spread. While accepting these arguments the Indirect Taxation Enquiry Committee (India) in 1976 had opined that the administrative difficulties could be reduced by proper legal and procedural reforms.

(3) It is also argued that specific duties tend to be regressive. They fall more heavily on the lower income groups since they heavily strike the cheaper commodities.

(4) It is also said that specific duties encourage the production of expensive varieties of goods because the producers are more interested in producing them. It is no doubt true that ad valorem duties are difficult to administer, they are more equitable in incidence since they are levied on the value of the article. They satisfy the canon of ability to pay. Since they are levied in proportion to the price, they fall more heavily on the rich people. Specific duties are regressive in character, the burden is relatively heavier on cheaper goods and those goods which are of general consumption. The burden of duty, therefore, is more on the poor. So from the point of view of equity they are less preferable to ad valorem duties.

Exercises

1. Would you advocate a single tax system or a multiple tax system? Give reasons for your answer.
2. Distinguish between a progressive and regressive taxes. Which one would you prefer and why ?
3. Distinguish between progressive and proportional taxes. Which of the two is better from the point of view of equity?
4. "Both direct and indirect taxes are complementary". Discuss.
5. "The proportional tax is a real tax, the progressive is a personal tax". Discuss.

●●●

Chapter 39

Effects of Taxation

1. Introduction

The term 'effects of taxation' refers to the changes in the economy generated by the tax system and its variations. Tax being the main source of state funding, is the most potent fiscal tool to influence the various economic parameters and to achieve the various socio-economic objectives set by the state for itself. It is now firmly believed that the state by following a policy of tax neutrality based upon the concept of "general fiscal rationality"[1] can't make optimum use of national resources for maximising the welfare of its subject. In a market economy the taxation by influencing forces of demand and supply regulates the working of the market mechanism and in this process produces tremendous impact on all sectors of the economy. We now discuss the effects of taxation in some detail. Our discussion will be confined to the effects of taxation on "aggregative level" —taking the economy as a whole and that too pertaining only to the private sector—without referring to any of the counter balancing effect produced in the government or the private sector through changes in the pattern of expenditure. Our analysis will be focused only to effects of taxation on the following four areas: (*i*) Production and growth, (*ii*) Distribution of wealth and incomes, (*iii*) Economic stabilisation, and (*iv*) Inflationary pressure.

2. Effects on Production and Growth

We shall follow Dalton while analysing the effects of taxation on production and growth. Dalton has analysed the effects of taxation with reference to: (*i*) capacity to work, save and invest; (*ii*) desire to work, save and invest; and (*iii*) composition or pattern of production, which means: (*a*) a shift in the allocation of existing productive resources and (*b*) a change in the supply of these productive resources. It is only for making the entire discussion simple

1. B.P. Herber, *Modern Public Finance,* Richard D. Irwin, Inc., 1967, p. 213.

that the study is split in such a manner, otherwise the problem is highly complicated because these effects are intermingled and multi-dimensional in nature. We now throw light on Dalton's analysis in some detail.

(1) Effects on the Ability to Work, Save and Invest

Taxation results in the transfer of purchasing power from the private sector to the government sector. Consequently the purchasing power in the hands of the individual tax payer is reduced and so his ability to purchase articles of necessaries, comforts and luxuries is also reduced. The effect is more pronounced on the poorer sections of the society. Poor people have to reduce their consumption of necessaries and comforts and consequently their standard of living declines. This adversely affects their efficiency and ability to work. On the other hand, the tax does not affect so much the efficiency and ability to work of relatively rich classes because at the most the rich people are forced to reduce their expenditure on luxury goods which does not affect their efficiency and ability to work. It is, therefore, necessary that the burden of tax should be minimal on the poorer sections of the society so that their health, efficiency and ability to work are not adversely affected. Therefore, tax on low incomes and articles of consumption of the poor people should either be avoided or should be the minimum. This would not affect production. It may be understood that all taxes are not similar in their effects. Some taxes adversely affect the ability of the people to work to a great extent, others do not. For example, taxes on liquor, harmful drugs do not affect the ability to work of the people. The consumption of these articles adversely affects the ability of the people to work. Therefore a tax on these articles of consumption would positively be beneficial to the poorer people.

Looking at the effect of taxation from another angle we find that a tax on income will reduce disposable income of the people and since savings depend on income, these will automatically decline. Particularly, a tax on income reduces the ability of the people to save. So far as the poorer people are concerned the tax which fully falls on them, does not lead to a reduction in savings because the poor people live from hand to mouth and there is no scope for them to have any savings. So, obviously a heavy tax on the rich people would certainly lead to a decline in their ability to save.

In so far as the ability to invest is concerned, it entirely depends on savings. Since savings are reduced by taxation, ability to invest is obviously reduced. In short, taxation certainly affects the ability of the people to work, save and invest.

(2) Effects on the Desire to Work, Save and Invest

For keeping the economy in good health it is necessary that people's desire to work, save and invest must be very strong. If the desire is strong then the people will work hard to save more and invest more and consequently the production will automatically increase. However, people's desire to work, save and invest is determined by: (*i*) the nature of taxes, and (*ii*) psychological reaction of the tax payers. We shall presently see how these two factors affect the desire of the people to work, save and invest.

(*i*) Nature of taxes. Although the effects of individual taxes very much differ from each other the overall effect, it is believed, is positive on the tax payers. The taxes, it is believed, induce people to work hard and save more. Some taxes have bad effects and some have good effects on the tax payers desire to work and save. Take for example a tax on abnormal profits in short period, an inheritance tax, a special assessment on the rise in the value of land etc. All these taxes are on incomes, which were unexpected, or in other words which were windfalls and therefore these taxes will not affect the people's desire to work and save. In the case of a tax on monopoly profits, the effect will be neutral because the monopolist adjusts his production at a point where his marginal profit is equal to his marginal cost so that his profits are maximised. If he reduces his production merely because of the taxes, his profits would decline. Therefore the monopolist would prefer to pay taxes and maximise his profits. If, however, the monopolist is taxed moderately or at a low rate then he will be happy to reduce the price of his products, produce more, sell more and earn more profits. So a moderate tax on monopolist would increase his desire to work and save.

Similarly, a moderate tax on commodities like excise duties and sales taxes will not adversely affect the producers' desire to work and save. In case the taxes on commodities are very heavy then a large chunk of people's income would be taken away by the taxes and savings are likely to decline. On the other hand, the demand for these commodities would also decrease due to a rise in prices because of the tax. Consequently, output of these commodities would fall and the whole economy would be affected. That is why import duties are more preferred to protect domestic industries against foreign competition. Likewise, low export duties are favoured to boost exports and to capture foreign market. So, low export duties increase the desire of the people to work, save and invest.

Let us also look at the effects of taxes on people's desire to work and save. Taxes on income, wealth, inheritance and expenditure also differ in nature. Income and wealth tax generally lower the desire of the people to work and save. A highly progressive income tax discourages most of the people from working hard and saving more. Although the effect of the wealth tax would also be the same, it would be less than the income tax in so far as the desire to work hard is concerned. But wealth tax certainly affects people's desire to save to a greater extent than the income tax. In comparison to income tax, the inheritance tax is favoured because in the former case the present income is taxed while in the latter case the future income is taxed. In the latter case the income or wealth is unearned for heirs and therefore they do not mind paying the taxes. In this way, the income tax affects the desire to work and save more than the inheritance tax and therefore tax on income adversely affects the production of a country as compared to an inheritance tax.

In comparison to the above three taxes, an expenditure tax may be the most preferable because it does not produce any bad effects on people's desire to work and save. A progressive tax on expenditure will lead people to reduce consumption on luxuries and encourage them to save more. The government can use this tax to change the composition of consumption. However, a tax on expenditure may create deflationary conditions in a developed economy because a fall in consumption expenditure will lead to a reduction in the effective demand and hence profits which will ultimately adversely affect savings, investment and income. In sum, we can say that a progressive income tax produces greater adverse effects on people's desire to work, save and invest in comparison to a tax on wealth and property. In this way different taxes affect people's desire to work and save in different ways because of their different nature. It is, however, certain that if a proportional tax reduces work effort, a progressive tax reduces it in a greater degree and if a proportional tax increases the work effort, a progressive tax increases the work effort in a lesser degree. A regressive tax will lead to a greater increase in the level of work effort as compared to a proportional tax of an equal yield. A tax on articles of necessities will not kill the incentive to work and save to the same extent as a tax on luxuries because luxuries are generally associated with the enjoyment of leisure while necessities are essential means of subsistence.

(*ii*) Psychological reaction of the tax payers. By psychological reaction we mean the immediate effect on the mind of the tax payer of the announcement of a new measure of taxation. It implies a change in the mental state of a tax payer by the imposition of a new tax or by the withdrawal of an old tax or by variations in the rate of the existing taxes. Pigou calls it as "announcement effect of taxation". When a new tax is imposed or the rate of existing taxes is increased the tax payer's psychological feelings that this measure will adversely affect his income and therefore his desire to work hard and save more are adversely affected. The reaction may, however, be different on different persons. It depends upon the elasticity of demand for income for each tax payer.

Elasticity of Demand for Income

The demand for income is considered as elastic when a person is not willing to work hard to maintain the same amount of income, after the imposition of tax. For example, if a person is earning an annual income of Rs. 20,000 and he pays a tax of Rs. 2,000/-. If the rate of tax is increased and he has to pay a tax of Rs. 3,000, his income stands reduced from Rs. 18,000 to Rs. 17,000. But he is satisfied with his position and does not want to work more to earn extra so that he may make up the deficiency in income caused by the levy of tax. His demand for income will be called elastic. Tax payer's demand for income would be inelastic if his desire to maintain a given income is high and he is willing to work more to maintain his level of income. So, in the case of an elastic demand for income, tax payer's desire to work and save is dampened by the imposition of a tax and therefore aggregate production in the economy suffers. If on the other hand tax payer's demand for income is inelastic, he will be encouraged to work harder and save more and therefore his desire to work and save will increase. The elasticity of demand for income can be unity if the desire to work and save remains the same after the imposition of the tax. This may happen when there are chances for the people to work more and earn more *i.e.*, by working overtime or by taking up additional jobs in extra time. In another situation where people are accustomed to work hard and save whatever may be the position of taxes, the elasticity of demand for income in the case of such people would be unity and their desire to work and save will not be affected by the imposition of taxes.

Reasons for Inelastic Demand for Income

Although it is very difficult to measure the elasticity of demand for income because it varies from person to person, it is generally believed that people's demand for income is generally inelastic because of the following reasons:

(1) Some people are ambitious and wish to have a definite minimum income from their savings either for themselves or for their children. Therefore, after the imposition of the tax such people may like to work harder and save more.

(2) Some people firmly believe in maintaining a certain standard of living for themselves and their families in all situations. In the case of such persons the desire to work and save more would be strong even after the imposition of the tax.

(3) There are some people, who believe in accumulating wealth, acquire power and distinction in society through the accumulated wealth. Such people also would continue to work and save more after the imposition of the tax.

(4) Some people who are fond of action and enterprise, will continue to work hard and save more after the imposition of the tax.

(5) Finally, some people always like to enjoy relatively higher position in comparison to others and therefore work more and save more. In other words,

some people want to have relatively more satisfaction from their income and wealth than others. In this connection Pigou says that, "a large portion of the satisfaction yielded by the incomes of rich people comes from their relative rather than from their absolute amount. This part of it will not be destroyed if the incomes of all rich people are diminished together."[2]

Other Conditions

In addition to the conditions listed above there are some other situations as well, in which the taxation casts its influence on the psychology of the tax payers. We very briefly discuss these conditions as follows:

(*i*) **Effects of taxation in economic fluctuations.** During a period of prosperity and rising prices the traders and producers do not mind paying heavy taxes because they are optimistic about earning huge profits. So, progressive and heavy taxation in a period of rising prices will not adversely affect people's desire to work and save and therefore production in the economy will not be adversely affected. However, on the other hand, in a period of depression and falling prices taxation would discourage people's desire to work, save and invest and hence production will suffer.

(*ii*) **Effects of taxation in times of war.** During a war prices also rise because of extensive increases in public expenditure and abnormal demand for goods and services. The businessmen and producers hope to earn more profits and therefore taxation will not adversely affect their desire to work, save and invest. On the contrary, the citizens out of sheer national feelings will not mind paying more taxes during a war.

(*iii*) **Effects of taxation and types of industries.** Well established industries earning sufficient profits will be in a position to bear heavy burden of taxation than new industries. So, heavy taxes adversely affect the production in new industries. That's why in most of the cases infant industries are exempted from taxation.

(3) Effects of Taxation on Corporate Enterprises

We have so far discussed the effects of taxation on individual's desire to work and save but since a major portion of the savings and investment are in the corporate sector, it would be in the fitness of things to analyse the effects of taxation on corporate enterprises. We are all aware that taxation does not affect corporate enterprises in a similar fashion as it does in the case of individuals. But, it certainly affects their policies relating to investment, production and extension. For example, if the profits are heavily taxed then production will certainly be adversely affected because profits are generally

2. Pigou, A.C., *Economics of Welfare,* p. 90.

ploughed back in the industry and therefore heavy taxation will discourage investment. If on the other hand dividends distributed to the shareholders are heavily taxed and that part of the dividend, which is re-invested is exempted, then the production will certainly increase.

We may therefore conclude that taxes do not always produce bad effects on people's desire to work and save. They may also produce encouraging effects. It is however certain that a highly progressive taxation certainly affects the incentive to work and save badly, particularly, among the higher income groups.

3. Effects of Taxation on Diversion of Resources

So far, we have discussed the effects of taxation on production and national income of a country from the point of view of the ability and the desire to work and save. However, production is also affected, and sometimes very seriously, by the changes in the allocation of resources between different industries and localities. Taxation is considered as an effective fiscal tool for changing the allocation of resources and hence for influencing the composition and pattern of production.

Income taxation reduces the purchasing capacity of the tax payers whereas commodity taxation raises the cost of commodities. If the burden of these taxes falls on particular types of productive activities the producers may be compelled to curtail their production. The demand for the taxed commodities will also fall. Consequently, economic resources will be diverted to the increased production of those commodities which are not subject to taxation or are subjected to a lower rate of taxation. A tax on harmful commodities of consumption or on luxuries will cause the production and consumption of these commodities to decline and stimulate the diversion of capital and labour to the production of articles of necessities. Concessional taxation of high priority industries and heavy taxation of non-priority industries may encourage diversion of resources from the latter to the former. Similarly heavy taxation of articles of necessities may encourage the flow of resources to the production of less necessary articles or luxuries. Likewise, as explained earlier, a tax on monopolist's profits or on windfall gains will be neutral in its effects and therefore there will be no change in the allocation of resources.

Diversion of resources from taxed industries to non-taxed or low taxed industries will, however, depend upon the relative elasticities of demand and supply of products of various industries. If the demand for the taxed commodity is inelastic and its supply is elastic this diversion of resources will not take place since the incidence of the tax will be more on the buyer. On the contrary, if the supply of the product is inelastic and the demand is elastic then the incidence of the tax will be on the producer and diversion of resources may take place from the taxed industries to the non-taxed industries.

Beneficial and Harmful Diversion

The diversion of resources or the change in the pattern of allocation of resources due to taxation may be harmful as well as beneficial. A tax on injurious articles of consumption may discourage their production and lead to the shifting of labour and capital engaged in these industries to some other industries. This happens because the imposition of tax will raise the price of these articles and their consumption will be reduced. Consequently, the demand for such commodities will fall and the profits of the producers will also decline. Consequently the resources will be diverted to the consumption of other articles, their demand will increase and hence the production will also increase. Moreover a decline in the consumption of these harmful products will increase the health and efficiency of the consumers. So taxation of such articles is socially warranted and the diversion of resources from the production of these harmful commodities to the production of other useful articles will be useful. This is particularly beneficial for the underdeveloped countries. If a tax is imposed on articles of necessities or articles of mass consumption then the consumption of these articles will decline owing to the increase in their prices. This will certainly produce a bad effect on the health and efficiency of the people. Moreover, this will lead to the diversion of resources from the production of useful commodities to less useful commodities, which will not be in the interest of the society.

Diversion from Present to Future Use

Taxes may also lead to the diversion of resources from the present to the future use. If taxes are levied to discourage consumption and to encourage savings particularly in times of emergency, the resources will be diverted from the present to the future uses. On the other hand, if taxes discourage savings, and consumption is increased, the resources will be diverted from the future to the present use. This will produce harmful effects on production. This will be more applicable to cases where the revenue collected from taxes is spent to meet the day-to-day requirements of administration or is spent on unproductive activities which otherwise would have been saved and used for productive activities.

Geographical Diversion

If we look from the point of view of geographical diversion of resources, we find that taxes may also lead to such diversion. In a federal type of political set-up, if different States follow different patterns of taxation or adopt different rates for the same taxes, the resources may be diverted from one State to the other particularly, from that State where the tax burden is heavy to those States where the tax burden is not so heavy. Similarly, resources may also be diverted owing to tax imposition from one country to another. If the tax burden in a country is very heavy and unbearable, the enterprises will find it more profitable to invest their capital in countries where the burden of the tax is relatively light.

The industrial policy of the country may also cause diversion of resources. If a government follows a policy of protection under which bounties, grants and exemption from taxes to certain industries, are granted to enable them to face foreign competition or to enable them to become self-sufficient, the diversion of resources may take place from other industries to the protected industries.

Taxes which do not Lead to Diversion of Resources

There are certain taxes which do not lead to any diversion of resources from one industry to another or from one place to another. These taxes are:

(*i*) Taxes on windfalls. A tax on unexpected income and profits, in the nature of windfalls does not lead to any diversion of resources because the income is totally unexpected and so the tax payer will not mind the payment of taxes imposed on such incomes. Consequently there will be no shift in the use of resources.

(*ii*) Taxes on land values. A tax on the value of land irrespective of its use will be borne by the landlord. Such a tax will not cause any diversion of resources because even if the landowner wants to change the use of the land and shift the incidence of tax, it will not be possible because the landowner will not earn any benefit out of it.

(*iii*) Taxes on monopoly. A tax on a monopolist may not result in diversion of resources because a monopolist fixes his output and price at a point where the marginal revenue and marginal cost are equal. If he reduces his production to escape from the tax, his profits will decline. Hence, instead of reducing his production he would prefer to bear the burden of the tax. In this way a monopolist will not be benefited by diverting resources from the present production to the production of other commodities.

(*iv*) A uniform tax. If the burden of the tax is falling uniformly upon all the uses of economic resources then. diversion of resources will not be caused either from the present use to future use or to some other uses in the present, because the diversion of resources will not in any way lessen the burden of the tax.

4. Effects of Taxation on Distribution

In modern times taxes have been used to remove inequalities in the distribution of income and wealth. While public expenditure achieves the objective through the levelling up of the wealth and incomes of the poor, taxation achieves this objective through levelling down the wealth and income of the rich. In this respect both are complementary. Taxation diverts the wealth of the rich for funding the programmes of public expenditure beneficial to the entire community particularly to the under-privileged sections of the society. The first economist who stressed that taxation should be used for reducing inequalities of incomes was German economist Wagner. The effects of tax on distribution of income and wealth can be analysed with reference to the following two factors: (*i*) nature of taxes and tax rates, (*ii*) kinds of taxes.

(1) Nature of Taxes and Tax Rates

From the point of view of their nature, taxes have been classified into three categories: Proportional, Progressive and Regressive. We have already explained the nature and effects of these taxes before.

We know that regressive taxes tend to increase the inequalities in the distribution of wealth as they fall more heavily on the poor; the progressive taxes tend to decrease the inequalities in the wealth distribution as they fall more heavily on the rich. Proportional taxation also increases inequalities in the distribution of wealth. Broadly speaking, taxes on income, property, inheritance, articles of luxury are progressive in nature and taxes on articles of general consumption are regressive in their effect.

From the point of view of equitable distribution of income and wealth, a tax system should be sharply progressive but it may tend to reduce production and ultimately adversely affect distribution also. According to Simons, "the case for drastic progression in taxation must be rested on the case against inequality on the ethical or aesthetic judgement that the prevailing distribution of wealth and income reveals a degree (and or kind) of inequality which is distinctly an evil or unlovely."[3] Equal distribution implies that all incomes above a certain level should be brought down to that level through taxation and as Dalton remarked "cutting heads of all the tallest poppies." But as stated already this will adversely affect production. So a happy balance have to be struck between the two objectives and the tax system is to be devised in such a way that it may encourage production as well as reduce inequalities in the distribution of wealth. In underdeveloped countries since large resources are to be mobilised for economic development, taxes on rich alone cannot attain

3. Simons, H.C., *Personal Income Taxation,* p. 26.

the objective. So alongwith progressive taxes, indirect taxes may also be used and welfare schemes for the benefit of the poor may also be introduced simultaneously.

(2) Kinds of Taxes

Now we may very briefly analyse the effects of particular taxes on distribution. We know that all taxes can be broadly divided into two classes: indirect taxes and direct taxes. We shall analyse the effects of these two broad categories of taxes in the following:

(*i*) **Indirect taxes and distribution.** Since indirect taxes are imposed on commodities of mass consumption, their effect is regressive, because the taxes fall heavily on the poor. But all indirect taxes cannot be put into this category. For example, taxes on harmful products are beneficial from the point of view of the poor people but taxes on foodstuffs will be socially undesirable because they fall more heavily on the poor who spend larger proportion of their income on the consumption of foodstuffs. However, generally speaking, if the indirect taxes are made progressive, by taxing articles of necessities and subjecting luxuries to heavy taxation then the inequalities in the distribution of wealth may be reduced. Some economists have pointed out, that import duties do not produce any bad effects on the distribution of income. If such duties are imposed to give protection to home industries, particularly to those industries where the wage rates are higher than other industries, then with the growth of the protected industries, the workers will move to these industries from industries where wages are low. This would lead to the removal of inequalities of income. Import duties may also prove beneficial in another respect. If these duties are imposed on such commodities which are being consumed by the rich people, then their consumption would be reduced and their imports will fall, which will be in national interest.

(*ii*) **Direct taxes and distribution.** Direct taxes can be suitably used as a tool to reduce inequalities in the distribution of income and wealth. Direct taxes are progressive in nature and fall heavily or exclusively on the rich. Take the case of income tax. It can be made progressive by the use of graduated scale of rates. It will be in accordance with the canon of equity and will also reduce inequalities of income. This may have a desirable effect if a super tax is charged alongwith the progressive income tax. Besides, income below a certain level can be exempted from the tax, taking into account the size of the family etc. Unearned income and other windfall profits may be taxed at higher rates than the income earned by honest means. A property tax can also be made progressive. It will, therefore, reduce the property in the hands of property owners and also have beneficial distribution effects. If the income from an inherited property is subjected to higher tax than income earned from property acquired by hard work, it will have more desirable effects. Likewise, a progressive tax on the value of land and a progressive capital levy may also reduce inequalities of income and wealth. The same will be true of inheritance taxes. However, it may be noted that direct taxes can be helpful in reducing all equalities of income and wealth only when they are progressive otherwise, they may increase inequalities instead of removing them.

5. Other Effects of Taxation

Taxation and Economic Stabilisation

A common feature of a free market economy is the recurrence of trade cycles. Economists have given different explanations for this phenomenon. But, it is generally agreed that the general availability of purchasing power and the speed of its use are the two important variables in the occurrence of recurring phase of rising and falling incomes, output, employment and prices. These changing phases produce innumerable difficulties for all the sections of the society. During the rising phase of a cycle the purchasing power of the people will increase and so the effective demand in the country will also increase. In the downward phase of a cycle it is just the opposite that happens. Another aspect of variations in the effective demand is that it is not uniformly spread over all the sectors of the economy, with the result that some sectors face greater inflationary pressures than others.

Earlier economists believed that a free market economy possesses inherent corrective forces and therefore the government need not take any action to correct the rising or falling phases of the trade cycle. According to these economists the tax system of the country acts as a stabilising force. In an upward phase of a cycle there is an all round increase in prices and economic activities. This will bring greater tax revenue and if the system is progressive then even more revenue would be collected. If the public expenditure remains unchanged the government will have surplus budgets which will produce a contractionary effect on the overall level of economic activity. Likewise, in a downward phase of a cycle the system of taxation would stimulate economic activity and therefore a system of taxation, according to earlier economists, was a sort of built-in stabiliser.

However, the Great Depression of the 1930s brought about a sea change in the outlook of the governments and the economists. Keynes put forth the thesis that a developed market economy does not have the capability to meet the situation of persistent deflationary trend owing to lack of effective demand created by a declining marginal propensity to consume and marginal efficiency of capital. He made a number of suggestions to meet the situation by increasing public expenditure. On the other hand Professor A.P. Lerner made suggestions by putting forth the concept of functional finance to meet the situation of inflationary pressures. According to these economists the government should not bother about deficit or surplus budgets but should aim to balance the demand and supply in the market through its policies of taxation and expenditure. According to Lerner the primary function of public finance should be the maintenance of economic stability. Taxation, through its effects on consumption and investment, affects the level of economic activity. Taxes which discourage consumption and investment and encourage savings reduce business activity and lower down the general level of employment. Thus, modern governments should use taxation as a tool to stabilise the level of economic activity in the economy. During inflation, taxation should be employed to mop up the excess spending power (by increasing rates of existing taxes, by introducing new taxes, by trading surplus budgets and withdrawing taxes which tend to raise production costs etc.) and to relax taxes to encourage production of goods and services. During depression, taxation should be used for increasing the spending power of the people. The rate of existing taxes should be lowered or some of the taxes may be dropped, especially those which fall on the poor people. Taxes falling on rich people should not be reduced. In fact taxes on savings and hoarding during depression will encourage people to spend more.

Simultaneously government should supplement these measures by making suitable changes in its policies of expenditure. It should increase its expenditure during depression and reduce it during a period of prosperity. So, while Keynes emphasised remedial measures against depression, Lerner suggested measures for curbing inflationary trend.

It may be noted that both Keynesian analysis and Lerner's approach were for a competitive market. Their analysis was in terms of the aggregates. They stressed that balanced budgets have no merit and therefore the government should go in for raising public debts. It is also a fact that government budgets cannot be neutral even in their aggregate effects and therefore the tax system should be viewed in its disaggregative form. It is true that increased taxation can combat inflationary tendencies but a policy of taxation should be looked into by analysing the roles of direct as well as indirect taxes. Indirect taxes raise the cost of production. If the commodities on which a tax has been imposed have a low elasticity of supply and high elasticity of demand, then a greater portion of the incidence will fall on the producers and therefore help in checking inflation. If indirect taxes are levied on goods, which have a low elasticity of demand and high elasticity of supply, then the incidence will be greater on the buyers and this will strengthen the forces of inflation. If the taxed commodities are of general consumption, then the cost of living of the workers would increase and they will make demand for higher wages. This will complete the circle. Taxes raise the cost of living which in turn increases the demand for higher wages, which again raises the cost of production and so on. The effect will spill over even to those commodities, which have not been taxed, because some of the inputs from the high cost industries would be used in those industries whose products are pot taxed. And so the prices of these commodities will also rise due to the rise in the cost of production. So the process of inflation would gain momentum with the passage of time. It is therefore necessary that a judicious combination of both direct and indirect taxes should be made use of by the government. Besides, a rational choice will have to be made between the commodities to be taxed and the rates of taxation. The argument, therefore, boils down to the fact that necessities should be exempted from taxes and luxuries may be taxed at a higher rate. Inflationary or deflationary pressures may also be transmitted from one country to another through foreign trade. Therefore customs duties will have to be used as a potential tool for insulating the domestic economy from these pressures. The rates of customs duties will have to be revised in such a way that they are in consonance with the elasticities of demand and supply of the commodities being traded.

Regulatory Effects of Taxation

The level of consumption and production in an economy can also be regulated with the help of taxation. To increase the production of certain commodities and to reduce the production of some other commodities the government can impose light taxation on the former and heavy taxation on the latter. Some of the products can also be exempted if they are of general consumption of the poor people. Commodities whose consumption is harmful to the poor may be taxed heavily, while commodities which augment the health and welfare of the poor may be taxed at a very low rate or may even be exempted from the tax. Likewise import and export duties may be used to regulate the volume of international trade, to protect the home industry from foreign competition, to check the consumption of harmful products etc. It may, however, be mentioned that taxation can be only a supplementary tool alongwith other measures of control of production and consumption of various commodities entering into foreign trade as well as those being produced within the country.

Exercises

1. Discuss the effects of taxation on (*a*) production and growth and (*b*) distribution.
2. Analyse the effects of taxation on economic stabilisation.
3. "Taxation is considered as an effective fiscal tool for changing the allocation of resources." Discuss.

●●●

Chapter 40

Sources of Revenue of Central Government in India (Tax and Non-Tax Revenue)

I. Tax Revenue of Government of India

During the period from 1950-51 to 2007-08 the tax revenue of the Government of India after taking out the share of the States and Union Territories has increased by leaps and bounds. Table 40.1 shows that it has increased from Rs. 357 crore in 1950-51 to Rs. 5,48,122 crore in 2007-08 (Budget). The revenue receipts have also been increasing as a proportion of Gross National Product.

Table: 40.1: Gross Tax Revenue of the Government of India

(Rs. in crore)

	1950-51 (Accounts)	1980-81 (Accounts)	1990-91 (Accounts)	2007-08 (Budget)
Tax Revenue (Net of States Share)	357	9,390	42,980	5,48,122

Source: Budget at a Glance, Government of India, various issues.

This revenue is mainly collected through (*a*) taxes on income and expenditure, (*b*) taxes on property and capital transactions; and (*c*) taxes on commodity and services, and (*d*) Taxes of Union Territories without legislature.

1. Taxes on Income and Expenditure

Taxes on income and expenditure are a major source of government revenue which comprise of : (*i*) personal income tax and (*ii*) corporation income tax. Income tax is realised by taxing personal incomes while the corporation tax is realised from the companies or corporate bodies on their profits. In the personal income tax, rates are fixed at a progressive slab system while in the case of corporations the rates differ from one category of companies to the other. We now discuss these two components in detail.

(a) Income Tax

The income tax was first introduced in India in 1860. During the last 100 years there had been numberless changes and amendments in the income tax structure and accordingly a number of Acts replaced the Act of 1860. The first replacement took place in 1886. The Act of 1886 was replaced in 1916 in which a graduated income tax and the various categories of incomes were subjected to different rates. This Act was replaced in 1918 which again was replaced in 1922. The Act of 1922 spelt out the mechanism of administering the taxes. It also laid down that the rates of tax would be determined in the Annual Finance Acts. These provisions introduced an element of flexibility in the income tax system and made it more elastic. The Act of 1922 was replaced by the Act of 1961 which is in operation even today.

During the course of these 100 years and thereafter the structure, the pattern, the rates and mechanism of administration of income tax, all have undergone tremendous changes. These changes have been necessitated by the requirements of additional revenues, by changing economic and social conditions, by the decisions of the Supreme Court and the High Courts and by the recommendations made by different Committees and Commissions from time to time. Income tax, today, is a very important source of revenue both for the Central Government as well as for the State Governments.

According to the Act the tax-payers are broadly divided into six categories as follows: (*i*) Individuals; and Hindu Undivided Families or Joint Hindu Families; (*ii*) Companies: public or private; (*iii*) Local Authorities; (*iv*) Firms of Partnerships; and (*v*) Association of Persons.

Accordingly the incomes have also been classified under six categories as under: (*a*) salaries; (*b*) interests on securities; (*c*) income from property; (*d*) profits and gains of business, profession or vocation; (*e*) income from other sources like dividends; and (*f*) capital gains. The tax is imposed on the net income and not on the gross income. This categorisation of income has been done mainly to facilitate the applicability of the prescribed rules for computing taxable income of each category of taxpayers. Taxable income from all sources is to be computed on a single return (form) and only one assessment is made of income from all sources for each unit of taxpayer under all categories. But, the income from capital gains is shown separately and is also taxed at a different but uniform rate.

As already explained the personal income tax in our country is imposed on the total income of an individual, Hindu undivided family, unregistered family, association of persons etc. for the whole year. It is limited to non-agricultural incomes only. However, agricultural income is integrated with the non-agricultural income for assessing the tax liability on non-agricultural income, in pursuance of the recommendations of the Committee of taxation on agricultural income and wealth. Currently the tax base consists of net income or net profits, which remains with the individual or the firm after paying business expenses, depreciation charges and meeting business losses. Thus after deducting all these from the gross income, the net income is arrived at. Besides, other statutory deductions are also made before finally arriving at the taxable income. These deductions may include incentives or development rebate, deduction from profits allowed to certain priority industries etc.

Similarly in the case of an individual, various types of deductions and exemptions are allowed in computing the taxable income. These exemptions and deductions are all decided by the Parliament. The chief objective of these concessions is to bring the tax structure in conformity with the principle of ability to pay. During recent years deduction has also been allowed in respect of the expenditure incurred on medical treatment of physically/permanently handicapped dependent.

The minimum limit of exemption of income tax has been revised from time to time. Similarly, the income tax rates have also been revised from time to time and this revision has been towards the lowering of the rates.

The surcharge on income tax, if any, levied by the Government is not shareable with the State Governments. It is levied on income tax assessed on the income of the tax payers.

Under the Income Tax Act provision also exists for allowing rebate to the tax payers in the total tax for long-term savings just to promote savings. It has also undergone changes during the course of two decades.

Senior citizens who have attained the age of 65 are also provided special relief. According to the budget of 2007-08 upto a taxable income of Rs. 1,95,000 a senior citizen will not be required to pay any income tax.

(b) Corporation Income Tax

The Corporation Income Tax is a tax on the net income of the companies. This tax has been in vogue for a long time. In most of the countries it is on the net income of corporations. It is paid out of a taxable profit (net profit) after meeting all costs *i.e.*, interest charges, wages, salaries, depreciation costs etc., during a particular year by a company and the balance is distributed in such proportion as decided by corporations. The tax base for corporation tax is company's profit minus the deductions allowed under the Act and also the tax concessions and incentives provided under the Act.

In the beginning, the yield of corporation income tax was quite small as compared to that of personal income tax. However, during this period the corporation income tax has outpaced the personal income tax. While the personal income tax has increased from Rs. 133 crore in 1950-51 to Rs. 86,829 crore in 2007-08 (Budget Estimates), the corporation income tax has increased from Rs. 41 crore to Rs. 1,68,401 crore (B.E.) in 2007-08.

(c) Interest Tax

Another from of tax on income and expenditure, which the Government of India started imposing, is interest tax under the Interest Tax Act, 1974. This Act provided for the imposition of a special tax on the gross amount of interest accruing to the commercial banks on loans and advances paid by them in the country. This tax was withdrawn in 1985. It was reintroduced later as an anti-inflationary measure. This tax is levied on the gross interest income of credit institutions *viz.*, banks, financial institutions and companies. The yield of this tax in BE 1999-2000 was expected to be of the order of Rs. 1,000 crore. It has been discontinued after 2005-06.

(d) Expenditure Tax

An expenditure tax on personal consumption was imposed for the first time in 1958 in accordance with the recommendations of Professor Kaldor. Professor Kaldor had suggested the imposition of this tax to prevent the possibility of tax evasion and to discourage superfluous consumption. Since the yield of this tax was quite small and administratively it was expensive, it was abolished in 1962. It was again introduced in 1964 and again abolished in 1966. Again from November 1987, the Government of India introduced it under the Expenditure Tax Act, 1987. The Act provides for a tax on expenditure incurred in hotels where the room charges for any unit of residential accommodation were Rs. 400 or more per day per individual. The rate of expenditure tax was later revised from 10 to 20 per cent and the tax was extended to expenditure incurred in restaurants providing superior facilities of air-conditioning etc. In the budget proposals for 1997-98, it was proposed that expenditure tax will not be charged for a period of 10 assessment years commencing from April 1, 1998 on any expenditure incurred in a new hotel in hilly area, rural area or a place of pilgrimage or such other places that the Central Government may specify in accordance with the provision of the Act. According to the proposal the concessions will be available to eligible hotels established during the period from April 1, 1998 to March 31, 2002. However, hotels located in metropolitan cities like Kolkata, Chennai, Delhi and Mumbai are not eligible for these expemptions.

(e) Fringe Benefit Tax (FBT)

This tax was levied for the first time by the Central Government in 2005-06. Fringe benefit is defined as any privilege, service, or amenity, directly or indirectly provided by an employer whether by way of reimbursement or otherwise to his employees. The FBT does not cover: (*a*) the government sector, (*b*) Charitable institutions, trusts and funds, already enjoying tax exemption, (*c*) individuals and HUF, engaged in business or profession, and (*d*) expenses on statutory obligations work hazards minimisation and first aid cover in company owned medical facilities. The FBT, also covers benefits like free or concessional ticket given by the employer for private travel of the employees and their family members, employer's contribution to an approved superannuation fund. The tax is charged at a uniform rate of 30% on a certain percentage (as listed in the budget) of the expense on an item considered as a fringe benefit.

During 2005-06, Rs. 4,772.28 crore (actual) and during 2006-07, Rs. 5,500 crore (revised) were collected from this tax and it was expected that during 2007-08, Rs. 680 crore will be collected.

The FBT has not been received well. It has been criticized on a number of grounds: (*i*) it is discriminatory as it has left out the government sector; (*ii*) most of the expenses, considered as fringe benefits, are legitimate business expenses and have to be incurred as an essential part of the corporate culture enforced by the global free market economy, and therefore are in no way to provide benefit to the employees, (*iii*) some expenses are clearly for sales promotion which if determined as fringe benefits may give rise to litigation.

2. Taxes on Property and Capital Transactions

The Government of India has imposed from time to time certain taxes on property and capital transactions. The important taxes in this group are: (*i*) Estate Duty; (*ii*) Wealth Tax; (*iii*) Gift Tax; and (*iv*) Capital Gains Tax. We now explain these taxes in turn:

(a) Estate Duty

Article 269 of the Indian Constitution provides for the imposition and collection of the estate duty in respect of property other than agricultural land, by the Centre. The whole proceeds of this duty except those which are attributable to the Union Territories, are assigned to the States within which this duty is leviable and distributed among them in accordance with the law made by the Parliament, on the recommendations of the Finance Commission. The distribution of the net proceeds of estate duty is governed by the Estate Duty (Distribution) Act, 1962, as amended in 1984. Estate duty and succession duty on agricultural land fall within the legal jurisdiction of State legislatures.

But, under Article 252 of the Constitution, the Parliament can legislate on the subject if the States pass a resolution to this effect. Most of the States have passed such a resolution and therefore the Central Government has been empowered to levy estate duty and succession duty on agricultural land. The net proceeds of the estate duty on agricultural land so collected by the Central Government are distributed among the States and the Union Territories.

The estate duty came into force with effect from October 15, 1953. Formerly, estate duty was imposed on the estate of a person, as inherited by his or her heirs. The term 'estate' includes cash, bullion, jewellery, household assets, securities, business assets, debts due, house property, agricultural land, cars etc.

The rate of estate duty ranged between 4 to 40 per cent of the value of estate left behind. The tax was, thus, highly progressive and the burden of large properties was very heavy. It was meant to reduce the evasion of tax through inheritance. Unfortunately, the amount of revenue collected was very low considering the cost of its administration, indicating that there was widespread tax evasion. Consequently, the estate duty was abolished from the middle of March, 1985.

(b) Wealth Tax

Wealth tax is imposed on the total value of a person's property or accumulated wealth of an individual, Hindu Undivided Family and closely held companies. This tax was imposed on the recommendation of Professor Kaldor. It was first introduced in 1957. The tax was considered justified on the grounds of equity, economic effects and administrative efficiency. In addition, a tax on wealth also reduces inequalities in income and wealth.

Not all wealth holders were taxed. Wealth below Rs. 2.5 lakh was exempted. Initially the tax rate was very high. It was 15 per cent. Consequently it led to wide scale evasion and avoidance. Subsequently, the rate was reduced to a very moderate level ranging from 0.5 per cent to 2 per cent. In 1992-93 the Finance Minister withdrew the wealth tax on productive assets such as guest houses, residential houses, jewellery etc. With effect from April, 1993, wealth tax is chargeable in respect of the net wealth exceeding Rs. 15 lakh at 1 per cent only. As a consequence of these changes, the revenue from this tax has gone down considerably. It was budgeted as Rs. 315 crore in 2007-08.

(c) Gift Tax

The gift tax was imposed in our country for the first time in 1958. It covered the gifts made by individuals, Hindu Undivided Families, companies, firms and association of persons. Initially, it was levied on the donor and not on the donee. All gifts made by a donor during a particular year were liable for gift tax. Now the gift tax is imposed on the donee. Initially a gift made to the spouse upto Rs. 5,000, gift made to a female dependent on the occasion of marriage upto a limit of Rs. 10,000.00 and gifts made to Central and State Governments, Local Authorities, Charitable and Religious Institutions were exempted from gift tax. In 1993-94, the exemption limit of gifts made to a female dependent on the occasion of marriage, was raised from Rs. 10,000.00 to Rs. 30,000.00. This limit was further raised to Rs. 1,00,000.00 in 1994-95 subject to the condition that the gifts upto this limit could be made only once in life.

Under the gift tax, if the tax cannot be recovered from the donor, it can be recovered from the donee. It may be mentioned that the gift tax was introduced on the recommendation of Professor Kaldor, but it is not in the form in which Professor Kaldor wanted it to be levied. His suggestion was for the imposition of a general gift tax at progressive rates on the recipient in place of present estate duty because he thought that there was no difference between the gift made by a person during his life time or in the shape of legacies, bequests or inheritance.

Gift tax has a number of advantages. Firstly, it checks the avoidance of estate duty and evasion of income tax on unaccounted money. It helps in reducing the inequalities of income and wealth and brings revenue to the government. But it is a very small tax and its contribution to the tax revenue of the Government of India was not substantial. During 1960-61, it was only Rs. 0.89 crore. In 1999, it was only Rs. 9 crore. It has been discontinued since October 1, 1998.

(d) Capital Gains Tax

Capital gains implies a financial gain arising from the sale of a capital asset. The gain arises because of the increase in the value of property or the asset. The tax is imposed on the net gains and not on the gross gains. The sale of an asset may result in two types of gains. If the gain arises out of the sale of mercantile goods as a regular business activity, then it is a business income like other incomes. If the gain arises from the sale of houses, lands, bonds and other types of assets by a person whose regular business is not to deal or trade in these types of assets, then it is a capital gain and is liable to capital gains tax. In short, capital gain is an irregular gain accruing outside a person's normal business. Profits from the 'stock in trade' held primarily in sale to customers in the normal course of business by a person are not called capital gains. In the budget proposals of 1992-93 an initial deduction of Rs. 15,000.00 was allowed on the capital gains arising from the transfer of a long-term capital asset. Prior to 1992-93, the exemption limit was Rs. 10,000.00. The 1992-93 budget proposals also provided total exemption from tax on capital gains arising out of transfer of a residential property upto a value of Rs. 2 lakh and proportionate exemption if the value of sold out property exceeded Rs. 2 lakh.

(e) Securities Transactions Tax (STT)

This tax was introduced in 2004-05. The current tax structure is as given below:

Transaction	Purchase/Sale of equities, units of equity Oriented Mutual Fund (delivery based)	Sale of equities units of equity Oriented Mutual Fund (non-delivery based)	Sale of derivatives	Sale of units of an equtiy Oriented Fund to the Mutual Fund
Rates Paid by	0.125% Purchaser/Seller	0.025% Seller	0.17% Seller	0.25% Seller

STT is levied on the sale and purchase of securities at the dealing/strike price in addition to service tax and stamp duties collected for registration and transfer of securities.

The total collection from this tax during 2005-06 and 2006-07 was respectively Rs. 2,559.38 crore and Rs. 3,750 crore. It was expected that Rs. 4,500 crore would be collected from this tax in 2007-08.

(f) Banking Cash Transaction Tax

This tax was imposed for the first time in 2005-06 on withdrawals of cash from a current account in a bank in excess of a specified amount on any single day. The objective is to track the black money transactions: Following is the current status of this tax.

(Rs. in crore)

	2005-06 (Actual)	2006-07 (Revised)	2007-08 (Budget)
Amount of tax collected	321.33	550	645

3. Taxes on Commodities and Services

Taxes on commodities and services are called indirect taxes. From the welfare point of view, these taxes are considered undesirable because they raise prices and change the expenditure pattern of the tax payers. Such taxes are also considered useful because they influence the pattern of resource allocation by introducing changes in the relative prices of different commodities and services. Through the medium of these taxes it becomes possible to bring even those people within the tax net who are left out from the ambit of direct taxes particularly in under-developed countries where the level of income is low and productive activity is highly dispersed. Moreover, since these taxes are included in the price of the commodity, tax payer does not feel the pinch of their payment. Further, any increase in commodity taxation, because of the reduction in consumption owing to the enhanced price, encourages savings. Tax on commodities, further, puts a check on the consumption of items of non-essential nature.

When India achieved independence it got in inheritance a system of indirect taxation in which the main sources of revenue were customs duties and excise duties. Import and export duties were imposed at very low rates on selected items like jute, tea etc. Excise duties were imposed on about a dozen articles including motor spirit, tobacco, salt and matches. Since the beginning of the First Five-Year Plan, the list of articles under both these types of duties has extended vastly and steadily. We now discuss these commodity taxes of the Government of India in the following paragraphs.

(a) Customs Duties in India

Under the Indian Constitution duties on customs, as import and export duties, are levied and collected by the Government of India and wholly owned by it. There is no provision for their distribution among the States. These duties act as a powerful instrument for protecting home industries and trade as well as serve as a popular source of revenue. It may be mentioned, however, that the yield of customs duties is not always certain. It depends very much on international situations and domestic economic changes. In times of war and depression the revenue from customs duties diminishes. It may also fluctuate from year to year because of a number of factors like the fluctuations in the availability of foreign exchange, changes in the export and import policies, changes in the overseas demand for the country's primary exports, availability of supply, changes in the shipping policy and changes in the world prices of main items of export and import.

The items which are imported and on which import duties are levied are quite large in number. Some of the important items are: (*i*) petroleum products; (*ii*) mineral, fuels, oil, wax and bituminous substances; (*iii*) inorganic chemicals; (*iv*) organic chemicals; (*v*) animal or vegetable fats and oils; (*vi*).photographic and cinematographic goods; (*vii*) plastic and articles thereof; (*viii*) rubber and articles thereof; (*ix*) wool and other animal hair; (*x*) pulp paper board and articles thereof; (*xi*) nickel; (*xii*) machinery; (*xiii*) machine tools; (*xiv*) electrical machinery; (*xv*) railway locomotives and materials;

(*xvi*) essential life saving drugs and raw material for such drugs; (*xvii*) motor vehicles; (*xviii*) project imports; (*xix*) baggage etc.

The L.K. Jha Committee, known as the Enquiry Committee on Indirect Taxation, had strongly recommended for the rationalisation of import duties. According to the Committee, since these fall mainly on raw material, intermediate products and machinery, they bring about a general increase in the cost and price which tends to make Indian industries less competitive in international markets. The Committee emphasised that the long-term objective of reform of import duties should be to lower the rates of taxation to a level which would be necessary to give adequate protection to domestic industries and discourage imports. The Committee was, however, of the view that the reform of import duties should be undertaken gradually. The Committee also observed that as soon as the import duties are rationalised they could be harmonised with the operation of the excise tax system because then the countervailing duty on imported products would be given the same treatment as excise duties on these products.

Export duties occupy an important place in the Indian fiscal system. They have been imposed on various commodities from time to time. During the early part of the British rule, such duties were imposed at ad valorem rates on many articles of exports. After 1867, most of the export duties were withdrawn. In 1914, export duty was only Jevied on rice and in 1916 on jute. In 1919, a duty on the export of raw hides and skins was introduced which was abolished in 1955. During the Second World War ad valorem duty was imposed on cotton cloth and yarn. Since 1946 export duties have been imposed on a number of new articles.

Export duties are primarily used for earning revenue. But, such duties may also be imposed on raw materials to give advantage to industries using these raw materials. After the Second World War export duties have been mainly imposed for preventing the impact of foreign inflationary conditions on the domestic market. The devaluation of the rupee in September 1949 and the impact of the Korean War increased considerably the demand for India's exports. With a view to check the rise in prices of export commodities and also to keep the domestic prices under check, export duties were used increasingly. In the final analysis export duties tend to make domestic goods costlier for the foreigners and it is useful to levy them in times of rising prices for achieving fiscal and monetary objectives.

Customs duties are, as already stated above, a major source of revenue to the Government of India. In 1950-51 these duties brought a revenue of only Rs. 157.15 crore which increased to Rs. 20,644 crore in 1991 and were expected to yield Rs. 98,770 crore in 2007-08.

During the last few years, particular emphasis has been given to rationalize customs duties.[1]

(b) Excise Duties

Union excise duties are also a major source of tax revenue of the Government of India. These duties are levied by the government on commodities which are produced within the country. But commodities on which State Governments impose excise duties like liquor and drugs, are exempted from the Central Excise Duties. Initially sugar, cotton, mill cloth, tobacco, motor spirit, matches, cement etc. were the goods which yielded the maximum revenue by way of excise duties. In recent years excise duties have covered a large number of goods.

There are three types of excise duties which are imposed by the Government. These are: (*i*) basic excise duties; (*ii*) earmarked cesses; and (*iii*) additional excise duties in lieu of sales tax. Basic excise duties are levied and collected under the Central Excise and Salt Act, 1944 by the Government of India. At present Central Excise Tariff covers 139 commodities. Of these seven commodities *viz.*, *Maida*, Greases, Coal, Readymade Garments, Mosaic Tiles and Silver are completely exempted. The revenue receipts of basic excise duties, as explained above, are shared with State Governments under Article 272 of the Indian Constitution. It may also be noted that the entire net proceeds of the Union duties of excise on electricity, other than attributable to Union Territories were collected to be paid to the States on the recommendations of the Finance Commission. This duty has been abolished with effect from 1st October, 1984. Earmarked cesses are levied under Special Act and are earmarked for specific purposes. The entire proceeds of earmarked cesses are assigned to the Government of India.

Additional Duties of Excise Act, 1975 provides for the levy and collection of additional duties on sugar, tobacco, cotton fabrics, woollen fabrics and man-made fabrics. These are in addition to the basic duties. The entire proceeds of these duties, excluding those attributable to Union Territories, are distributed among the States on the basis of recommendations of the Finance Commission. These duties are levied in lieu of sales tax.

L.K. Jha Committee's Recommendations

The L.K. Jha Committee stressed the need for rationalising the structure of the excise duties. According to the Committee the structure should be rationalised in such a manner that progression is achieved more easily and our economic priorities are also fulfilled. The Committee also recommended

1. *See* Chapter 40.

that the rationalisation of the rates of duties on raw materials and such materials that are close substitutes will be treated similarly unless special economic reasons demand otherwise. High rates of duties on particular materials imposed for some special reasons in the past should be curtailed in the interest of lowering the cost of production. Finally, the Committee recommended that a time-bound schedule of action towards the solution of the problem of cascading should be undertaken. In this connection the Committee suggested the application of existing procedures of taxation for the relief of input taxation and finally moving over to a system of value added taxation at the manufacturing stage. This was the beginning of the introduction of the Modified Value Added Tax (MODVAT) scheme with effect from 1st April, 1986. Under this scheme the manufacturers were allowed to obtain complete reimbursement of the excise duty paid on the inputs of final products. We have already explained in detail the scheme in an earlier chapter.

In recent years lot of efforts have been made to rationalise the structure of excise duties in India.[2]

The revenue from Union excise duties increased from Rs. 67.54 crore in 1950-51 to Rs. 6,500 crore in 1980-81, Rs. 24,541 crore in 1990-91 and to Rs. 1,30,220 crore in 2007-08 (budget).

(c) Service Tax

Taxation of services was introduced in 1994-95 initially by levying the tax on stock brokers, general insurance and telephone services. In the budget for 2002-03, it was extended to ten new services, *viz.*, life insurance and related auxiliary services, inland cargo handling, storage and warehousing, light agricultural products and cold storage, event management, rail travel agents, health clubs and fitness centres, beauty parlours, fashion designers, cable operators and dry cleaning services. Subsequently, life insurance was exempted from the tax. Hotels were exempted upto March 31, 2003.

Over the years the area of coverage as well as the rate of tax has gradually increased. The current rate is 12% and the member of services has increased to more then 100. The revenue from this tax forms 12.8% of the total tax revenue (Budget estimates 2007-08). It has increased from Rs. 5,000 crore in 2002-03 to Rs. 38,169 crore in 2006-07 and was budgetted at Rs. 50,200 crore for 2007-08.

II. Non-Tax Revenue of Government of India

There has been substantial increase in the non-tax revenue of the governments all over the world, after the First World War. The inconsistencies in the

2. See Chapter 40.

operations of the free enterprise economy have forced the governments to participate increasingly in the economic activities of the people and assume the responsibility of running public utility services for the welfare of the nation. The Government of India also decided to undertake the responsibility of running public utilities like railways, posts and telegraphs and coinage and currency to start with. Gradually the government went on expanding its area of activity to various fiscal services, general services, social services, economic services and commercial and business activities. These are grouped under non-tax revenue sources. We now discuss the various non-tax sources of revenue of the Government of India.

(a) Fiscal Services

Fiscal services include currency, coinage and mint, receipts from penalties realised from the Enforcement Directorate from various companies, firms and individuals for violation of Foreign Exchange Regulation Act and receipts from forfeiture of property. The revenue from currency and coinage includes:

(*i*) The profits of the Reserve Bank of India from: (*a*) the Currency Note Press, Nasik, (*b*) Bank Note Press, Dewas, and (*c*) Security Paper Mill, Hoshangabad. These organisations earn profits through the printing of notes and rendering services to the government. We also include under this head profits from circulation of coins which is the difference between the face value of the coins and the manufacturing costs, mints and silver refinery whose profits relate mainly to refining and assaying charges levied by the mints and the receipts from the silver refinery mainly due to the sale of silver. Other fiscal services include penalties which are realised by the enforcement directorate as stated above, receipts from the forfeiture of property under the Smugglers and Foreign Exchange Manipulators Forfeiture of Property Act, 1976, shares of profits from the sale of gold by the International Monetary Fund and revenue from Indian Security Press, Nasik, and Security Printing Press, Hyderabad and other receipts.

(*ii*) The total revenue collected under this head was estimated at Rs. 306 crore in 1990-91 and was estimated at Rs. 522.12 crore for 2007-08 (Budget).

(b) We include under this head receipt of interest on loans given by the Government of India to various States and Union Territories' Governments, capital invested in railways, posts and telegraphs and others.

(i) Interest Receipts

As recommended by the Ninth Finance Commission and accepted by the Government of India, the State Plan loans advanced to State Governments during the period 1984 to 1989 and outstanding at the end of 1989-90 have been consolidated for 15 years with 9 per cent rate of interest. Since no recommendation was made for change in respect of the pre-1979 consolidated loans, they continue carrying on a rate of interest of 4.75 per cent and loans advanced during 1979-84 and consolidated for terms ranging from 15 years to 30 years carry interest at rates varying from 6 to 6.75 per cent. The rates of interest on other Plan and non-Plan loans from June 1, 1984 to various States and Union Territories vary between 7.5 to 13 per cent. In short, the Government of India earns interest on all such loans.

The Government of India also received interest on the capital invested in the railways. This is a fixed ratio which is determined by the Parliament on the basis of the recommendation of the Railways Convention Committee. It is also treated as dividend on the capital invested. Similarly the Government earns interest on the capital invested out of the general revenues in the post and telecommunication services. It is also treated as dividend on the capital invested. Other interest rates include interest on capital invested in departmental commercial undertakings other than railways and posts and telegraphs, loans and advances to financial institutions and industrial enterprises in the public sector, loans to local bodies, loans to co-operatives and other statutory bodies, government servants etc. Loans advanced to commercial undertakings earn interest at the rate ranging between 12.5 and 17 per cent per annum. But the loans to financial institutions, other bodies and government servants carry a much lower rate of interest.

Total revenue collected under the head of interest receipts from all sources by the Government of India amounted to Rs. 8,730 crore in 1991 and was estimated to reach the figure of 24,307.99 crore in 2007-08 (Budget).

(ii) Dividends and Profits

We include under this head income of the Government of India from dividends and profits from railways, posts and telegraphs, Reserve Bank of India, nationalized banks and others. We now discuss each of these in some detail.

Railways. The Indian railways are the largest national enterprise owned by the Government of India. While discussing the issues related to railway finance, we have already stated that the railway budget was separated from the general budget in 1924. Since then the Government of India has been receiving a fixed proportion of the dividend from the railways under an agreement which was entered between the government and the railway authorities in 1924 and renewed in later years. These agreements have been known as conventions. Since 1950, the Government of India appointed Railways Convention Committee of Parliament to investigate into the problems of Railway finance and suggest measures to solve financial problems of the railways. Since then a number of conventions have been held and according to their recommendations the railways are paying a fixed amount of dividend to the general revenues on the capital invested in the railways in place of interest charges. Currently the amount of dividend paid by the railways to the Government was determined under the railway convention of 1991. Subsequently the arrangement was readopted in 1995 and 1996-97 and the estimates for the year 1997-98 were based on the same. Railways made a net dividend payment of Rs. 3005 crore in 2005-06 and also paid Rs. 663 crore towards outstanding deferred dividend liability.

Posts. This is the second important commercial undertaking of the Government of India. The department of posts and telegraph renders useful services to poor and rich alike. These are important for the development of the country. In India post cards are the cheapest means of communication for the poor people. Inland letters and envelopes are being used by the middle class while the rich people generally use the services of private couriers. Therefore, the incidence of increase in the rates of postal stationery chiefly falls on the poor and the middle class people and in this sense they are regressive in nature. The surplus or the losses arising out of the Department go to the general revenues.

The department of posts and telegraph has not been paying dividend to the general revenues on the capital invested by the government. During 2006-07, the Department of posts was expected to have a deficit of Rs. 1,379 crore.

Other Dividends and Profits. Other dividends and profits include receipts like: (*i*) profits from Reserve Bank of India; (*ii*) profits from nationalised banks; (*iii*) profits from Life Insurance Corporation; and (*iv*) dividends from public undertakings and other investments. The receipts under this head. Dividends and Profits were estimated at Rs. 33,924.85 crore for the year 2007-08 (budget).

(c) Other Non-Tax Revenue Sources

(i) General Services

Under this head we include the revenue received from: (*i*) administrative services, Union Public Service Commission, Police etc.; (*ii*) contributions and recoveries towards pension and retirement benefits; and (*iii*) miscellaneous general services.

In the administrative services are included Union Public Service Commission, police, jails, supplies and disposals, stationery and printing, public works and others. The government provides pension as retirement benefits to its employees for which they are required to make a nominal contribution.

Under the head of miscellaneous general services, the revenue receipts relate to gain by exchange and unclaimed receipts of postal service and marked loans written off to revenue.

The total revenue receipts under the head general services were estimated at Rs. 13,686.79 crore in 2007-08 (budget).

(ii) Social and Community Services

Income received by the government under this head includes income from services like education, art and culture, medical and public health, family welfare, sanitation, water supply, housing, urban development, information and publicity, broadcasting, labour and employment, social security and welfare and other services. Revenue receipts under this head were estimated at Rs. 499.69 crore for the year 2007-08 (budget).

(iii) Economic Services

Economic services include: (*i*) agriculture and allied services; (*ii*) irrigation and flood control; (*iii*) energy; (*iv*) industry and minerals; (*v*) transport; (*vi*) communication; (*vii*) science, technology and environment; and (*viii*) general economic services such as foreign trade and export promotion; civil supplies and others. These broad heads include several minor heads. For example, agriculture and allied services include agriculture, minor irrigation, soil conservation and area development, food, animal husbandry, dairy development, fisheries, forests, community development etc. Similarly, other heads include various minor heads. Receipts from economic services for the year 2007-08 were estimated at Rs. 1,02,188.55 crore (budget).

(iv) Grants-in-aid and Contributions

The Government of India receives assistance from friendly countries in the form of loans, cash grants and commodity grants. India has received in the past cash grants and commodity grants from a number of countries like Canada, Czechoslovakia, Denmark, Japan, USA, USSR and UK. It has received loans and cash grants from financial institutions like IBRD, IMF, IDA, International Fund for Agricultural Development and UN Development Programme. It was estimated that the foreign assistance likely to be received during 2007-08 would be of the order of Rs. 2135.17 crore (budget).

III. Main Trends of the Revenue of the Government of India

Given below are the main trends of the revenue of the Government of India:

(*i*) During 1950-51 and 2008-09 (budget) the total revenue receipts after deducting the share of State Governments and Union Territories, have increased from Rs. 405.86 crore to Rs. 6,02,935 crore.

(*ii*) The net tax revenue increased from Rs. 357 crore to Rs. 4,03,872 crore in 2007-08 (budget).

(*iii*) In order of importance corporation income tax Central excise duties personal income tax and customs duties, are the important sources of revenue of the Central Government.

(*iv*) Taxes on commodities have continued to occupy a frontal position in the revenues of the Government. They have been contributing, around 52 per cent whereas taxes on income and property contributed about 48 per cent. This is a clear indication of the fact that the burden of taxes of the Government of India is largely being borne by the lower and middle classes which is clearly against the declared objective of the government that the rich would be taxed more heavily. However, the trend has shown signs of rapid change in recent years.

(*v*) The share of direct taxes in the total tax revenue has been declining, and the share of indirect taxes has been increasing. The importance of commodity taxes in the tax structure of the Government of India indicates that it has been easier for the government to impose indirect taxes than direct taxes. But, all in all, the burden of the taxation falls more heavily on the lower and middle income groups.

(*vi*) The non-tax revenue is increasing year after year. It was estimated to increase from Rs. 50 crore in 1950-51 to Rs. 82,550 crore in 2007-08 (Budget). However, the contribution of the public enterprises has not been in any way reasonable and satisfactory. It is now expected that under the new policy more and more public undertakings would contribute to the revenues of the Government of India. However, the following significant features of the non-tax revenue are to be noted: (*i*) administrative receipts form a very small proportion of the total non-tax revenue of the Government of India; (*ii*) the contribution of the public enterprises in the form of dividend has been increasing; (*iii*) interest receipts are losing in prominence year by year. Currently they constitute a little than 41% per cent of the non-tax revenue receipts.

Exercises

1. Discuss the importance of 'Service Tax' as a source of revenue for Government of India.
2. Explain Security Transaction Tax, Banking Cash Transaction Tax and Fringe Benefit Tax in India.
3. Give the main trends of Revenues of Government of India.
4. Write note on the Non-tax sources of revenue of the Government of India.
5. Point out the main features of the present tax structure in India. Is the tax system in India regressive?
6. Discuss the role of direct and indirect taxes in Indian tax structure. How do you account for the growing importance of indirect taxes in recent years?

●●●

Chapter 41

Sources of Revenue of State Governments in India

1. Introduction

The functions and resources of the State Governments have been clearly demarcated in the Indian Constitution. We have already, in an earlier chapter, given an exhaustive list of the functions and resources allotted to the Central and State Governments in the Indian Constitution. Like the Central Government, the budget of a State Government also has two components: revenue and capital accounts. The revenue account covers the current receipts and expenditures while the capital account covers the acquisition and disposal of physical assets, cash and financial assets and liabilities.

2. Sources of State Revenues

The receipts under the revenue account are obtained from: (*i*) taxes; and (*ii*) non-tax sources. Revenue receipts from taxes come from two sources, namely, States' own taxes and share of taxes received from the Central Government. The proportion between the two is 69:31. The States levy a number of taxes which like the Central Government can be grouped in three heads: (*i*) taxes on agricultural income and profession; (*ii*) taxes on property and capital transactions; and (*iii*) taxes on commodities and services. In the first group, agricultural income tax contributes about 0.8 per cent and the remaining 99 per cent is contributed by tax on professions. In the second group sales and registration fees contribute more than 90 per cent, land revenue contributes about 9 per cent and tax on urban immovable property contributes marginally at 0.5 per cent. In the third group sales tax occupies the top position contributing a little more than 48.5 per cent; excise duties come next contributing 39.3 per cent, whereas other taxes contribute around 11.2 per cent.

The States receive from the Central Government share of income tax under Article 270 of the Constitution and share of Union excise duties under

Article 272 of the Constitution. Non-tax revenue of the States comprises: (*i*) grants from the Central Government; and (*ii*) own non-tax sources.

Broadly speaking, States' receipts have increased rapidly since 1951-52. On revenue account the total receipts of the States in 1951-52 were of the order of Rs. 396 crore, which increased to Rs. 16,290 crore in 1980-81 and was expected to reach Rs. 5,20,150 crore in 2006-07 (budget, This increase has been caused by the imposition of new taxes, increase in the rates of taxes, increase in the share in Central Government taxes and increase in Central Government grants. During the First Plan the total revenue receipts of the State governments were Rs. 2,335.40 crore and the Seventh Plan recorded a figure of Rs. 2,22,686.00 crore. This increase has been mainly caused by factors like inflationary rise in the prices, expansion in the economic activities of the government, conversion of some Union Territories into States, increase in the size of transfers from the Centre to States and increase in the States' own revenue.

As already stated, the tax revenue of the States comprises revenue from States own taxes and share of the Central taxes. In the budget for 2006-07, the total tax revenue of the States was placed at Rs. 3,66,620.00 crore of which revenue from States own taxes stood at Rs. 2,57,200 crore and the share of the States in Central taxes was put at Rs. 1,09,420 crore.

So far as non-tax revenue is concerned the 2006-07 budget expected to collect Rs. 1,53,530.00 crore. The States anticipated a revenue of Rs. 1,09,420 crore in 2006-07 by way of their share of income tax and excise duties. The States also expected to receive grants from the Centre to the tune of Rs. 1,00,190.00 crore in the same year. Thus, the States expected to receive Rs. 2,09,610 crore from the Government of India in 2006-07 out of the total revenue recipts of Rs. 5,20,150.00 crore *i.e.*, 40 per cent of the total revenue receipts. This clearly points out to the fact that the State governments depend heavily upon the Centre for their current revenues.

Of the three sources of tax revenue the most important was the taxes on commodities and services. The State governments expected to collect a revenue from these taxes to the tune of Rs. 2,22,800 crore in 2006-07. The remaining revenue was to be collected from taxes on income and property which is a mainifestation of the fact that the State governments depend more on commodity taxation. This implies that the tax system of the States is becoming regressive. Now we discuss the specific taxes of the State governments.

3. Taxes on Income

The State governments have been collecting revenue from taxes on income in three forms: (*a*) share of the income tax levied and collected by the Government of India; (*b*) the agricultural income tax; and (*c*) profession tax. The position of these three taxes was as given in Table 41.1.

Table: 41.1: Revenue from Taxes on Income Received by the States

(Rupees in crore)

Items	*1950-51 Accounts*	*1980-81 Accounts*	*1996-97 Budget*	*2006-07*
States' Share of Income Tax	53	1,000	12,350	*
Agriculture Income Tax	4	50	140	22
Profession Tax	—	60	830	2,700
Total	57	1,110	13,320	

*Since 2000, collections from all taxes are lumped together and 30.5% is passed on to the States as recommended by the Twelfth Finance Commission for the period 2005-10.

Agricultural income tax and profession tax are States' own taxes. The proceeds of these two taxes are relatively less important as is evident from Table 41.1.

Bihar was the first State to levy a tax on agricultural incomes. Now almost all States except Andhra Pradesh, Gujarat, Madhya Pradesh and Punjab have introduced a tax on agricultural incomes. However, very little success has been achieved in so far as the quantum of revenue is concerned. The rates of tax are low and the facilities for the determination of the tax have been rather liberal. The base of this tax has been eroded by the introduction of land reform measures particularly by the imposition of land ceilings. The imposition of cesses and surcharge on land revenue has made the land tax quite regressive and therefore a liberal agricultural income tax introduces an element of equity in the system of agricultural taxation. But, the imposition of surcharge on the agricultural income tax would be highly beneficial although the States are not likely to take this seriously because of political reasons and opposition from the landed peasantry which has a powerful lobby. It would, therefore, not be wrong to conclude that as a source of revenue agricultural income tax has not been able to meet the expectations. Further, it has not been able to reduce the inequalities in the distribution of income and wealth and has also not succeeded in making the distribution of tax 'burden equitable between agricultural and non-agricultural sectors.

The States impose tax on profession, callings and occupations. According to the Constitution it appears at No.1 of the State List. The maximum amount that can be levied on anyone person by any State or local authority is Rs. 250 per annum. It is a tax on professions, employments and trades. This tax is not levied on the poor people which is a good feature of the Act. But if there are discriminations in favour of men with unearned income such as pensioners, persons having income from investments or house property or agricultural income of business, such an exemption can hardly be justified. The tax is charged at a flat rate from all people falling within a particular class and therefore the burden of the tax falls more heavily on the poor. Another unfair element of this tax is that it is imposed on lower and middle class and it favours unduly rich people with unearned income. This tax has been in vogue for more than twenty years or so but it has not been a very successful source of revenue to the State governments. That is why the Taxation Enquiry Commission (1953-54) recommended that this tax be reserved for the local bodies. The revenue from this tax has increased gradually from Rs. 0.1 crore in 1950-51 to 0.40 crore in 1960-61, Rs. 3.1 crore in 1970-71, Rs. 62.02 crore in 1980-81 and to Rs. 2,700 crore in 2006-07 (budget).

4. Taxes on Property and Capital Transactions

The State governments receive income under this head from land revenue, stamps and registration tax on urban immovable property. The position of revenue collected from these sources in selected years is given in Table 41.2.

Table: 41.2: Taxes on Property and Capital Transactions

(Rupees in crore)

Items	*1950-51 Accounts*	*1980-81 Accounts*	*2006-07 Budget*
Land Revenue	48	150	3,330
Stamps and Registration	26	430	31,680
Urban Immovable Property Tax	2	20	100
Total	76	600[1]	8,100

[1]Includes Rs. 8 crore as share in Estate Duty imposed and collected by the Centre. The Estate Duty was later abolished.

Land Revenue

From Table 41.2 it is clear that land revenue was the most important source of income of the States in 1951-52. In subsequent years its importance has gone down because the receipts of land revenue vary considerably from State-to-State and so also the basis of land revenue. Since the introduction of land reforms these variations stand very much reduced. However, the tax base still varies from State to State. The rate of tax ranges between 25 to 50 per cent of the net produce or net assets and where the gross produce is the basis it is generally one-sixth of the gross produce. In case of continuous failure of crops the realisation of land revenue is either suspended or remitted. The receipts of land revenue have also been comparatively inelastic because the settlements of land revenue takes place once in 30 or 40 years. The land revenue is also not equitable because its incidence is more heavy on the poor farmers. It is assessed on the value of net assets without taking note of the farmer's capacity to pay. There is no minimum limit as the rate of tax is proportional.

Land revenue system in our country has proved to be unproductive. While on the one hand the functions of the States are expanding and their needs for revenue are increasing, on the other the contribution of agricultural sector by way of land revenue has not increased proportionately. It has remained stable at 1 per cent of the value of the total product. In 1951-52, the total collection from land revenue stood at Rs. 48 crore when the total value of agricultural production was Rs. 4,800 crore. In 1971-72, the total collection from land revenue went up to Rs. 110 crore but the income of the agricultural sector had gone up to Rs. 15,000 crore. This way the yield from land revenue was even less than 1 per cent. Over the years the government has invested large sums in the agricultural sector for providing irrigation facilities, chemical fertilisers, seeds, new implements, tractors etc. As a result the fertility of land has increased manifold. In addition, the Central and State governments have also provided to the farmers a number of services either free or at concessional rates for facilitating them to increase agricultural production. Despite all these measures the agricultural sector has not contributed satisfactorily to meet the growing need of funds for the development of the State. It is argued that most of these facilities and benefits, services and funds provided by the Central and State governments have been availed of by rich farmers. Consequently, the gap between small and big fanners has all the more widened. Therefore, it is necessary that big fanners are taxed according to their capacity to pay. This is necessary not only for mobilising additional resources but also to reduce inequalities in the distribution of income and wealth in the rural sector.

Stamp Duties and Registration Fees

Stamp duties include duties levied on various deeds and documents executed as proof of record of certain legal transactions. Stamp duties are in general use in many countries. These are convenient to collect and there is no relation with the ability to pay of the person concerned. In the case of stamp duties, court fees and registration fees, it is very difficult to generalise the incidence.

In India stamp duties are divided as judicial and non-judicial. Judicial stamp duties are levied under the Court Fees Act, 1970. They represent fees payable by persons having business in law courts and public offices. Non-judicial stamp duties are levied under the Indian Stamp Duty Act, 1899. In regard to Stamp Duty of Bills of Exchange, Cheques, Letters of Credit, Promissory Notes, Receipts etc. the Central Government formulates the law but the proceeds are collected and appropriated by the State governments. Stamp duties on items like transactions of immovable property are levied by the States. Some stamp duties are fixed while others are on ad valorem basis. Some States like Tamil Nadu also levy a surcharge on the stamp duty on transfer of immovable property which is handed over to the local bodies.

It was in 1922 that the subject 'stamp duties' was transferred with certain reservations to the provincial list. Since then several States have increased the duties on almost all of the instruments in the schedule to the Indian Stamp Duty Act except those reserved for the Central Government. During the Second World War the rates of stamp duties were further hiked. In some States like Bihar, Bombay, Madhya Pradesh, Orissa and Uttar Pradesh, the increase was in the form of a general surcharge which was later on absorbed in the rates of stamp duties.

The existing system of levying court fees started from the Bengal Regulation No. 38 of 1795. This was necessitated on account of increase in the quantum of work of the courts because of numberless superfluous litigations and suits. Immediately after the Regulation was passed the fees under it were leviable in the form of stamp duties and that practice still continues. The rates of court fees differ from State to State. They have been revised many a times since administration of justice is a special service rendered by the State. Those people who want to seek justice must pay for it. It is on this principle that the court fees are charged. From another angle it is a sort of penalty on the losing party for unnecessarily creating trouble for the State.

However, the revenue from stamp duties and fees have shown buoyancy during recent years because of the increase in the economic activity, general level of prices, transaction in land etc. As is evident from Table 41.2 the amount expected to be collected in 2006-07 was above Rs. 31,680 crore. As a matter of fact this amount could have been 3 to 4 times more if there had not been extensive evasion of this tax. Most property transactions are heavily undervalued to escape payment of high stamp duty.

Urban Immovable Property

Urban properties generally have more value than rural properties. In rural areas the yield of the land is fixed under the land revenue settlements but in urban areas when land is used for providing residence or for erecting an industrial plant, the owner of the land gets an unearned increment because of the phenomenal rise in the value of land particularly if the towns and cities are growing faster. The growing urbanisation can be attributed mostly to the expenditure incurred by the Government or local bodies. That is why the ground rent of urban land is much higher than the land revenue.

The assessment of urban land varies from State to State. In some States there is a statutory provision for the assessment of non-agricultural land. The tax base as well as the rates of assessment also differ from State to State. The rates in many States are rather nominal. However, this source of revenue has not proved very strong in so far as the contribution to meet the growing needs of the States is concerned. It is because of this reason that many a times it has been suggested that this source may be handed over to the local bodies.

5. Taxes on Commodities and Services

The State governments also levy commodity taxes like excise duties, general sales tax, motor vehicles tax, electricity duties etc. Besides, the States also receive share in Union excise duties which are levied and collected by the Central government. We now give some details of these in the following:

State Excise Duties

The Constitution of India empowers the State Governments to levy excise duties on alcoholic liquors, opium, Indian hemp and other narcotics. These duties are imposed where these articles enter the State's boundaries or are produced in the State concerned. The rates vary from State to State. The rate of excise duty on alcoholic liquors is the highest in all the States where prohibition has not been adopted. It may be noted that the Indian Constitution empowers the States to levy duties of excise on the following goods manufactured or produced in the State and countervailing duties at the same or lower rates on similar goods manufactured or produced elsewhere in India.

(*a*) alcoholic liquors for human consumption;

(*b*) opium, Indian hemp and other narcotic drugs and narcotics; but not including medicinal and toilet preparations containing alcohol or any substance included in sub-paragraph (*b*) of this entry.

It would thus be seen that the States are empowered to levy excise duties the purpose of which is to restrict the consumption of commodities which are harmful. That is why the Taxation Enquiry Committee (1924-25) described these duties as 'restricted excises'.

Excise duties also include revenue from licence fees for sale of imported liquor, licences for bottling it or other similar operations and the duty on Indian made foreign liquor, country made spirits and permitted liquors, denatured spirits and medicated wines etc. and intoxicating drugs *viz.*, *bhang*, *ganja* and *opium*. These commodities are produced in Government distilleries and if an individual wants to produce in the private sector then he has to obtain a licence from the State government.

Till 1921, the policy of the government was to regulate and discourage the excessive use of alcoholic drugs. The movement towards prohibition gained strength thereafter and during the next 15-16 years several State governments adopted measures to minimise the consumption of alcoholic drugs through stricter controls over their manufacture and distribution imposing high excise duties, raising auction bids and increasing licence fees etc. and also by imposing heavy fines on illicit distillation.

In 1937, with provincial autonomy in a number of provinces, the Congress ministries adopted prohibition as their policy. The Congress ministries resigned soon after the breakout of the Second World War and so the policy of prohibition in the provinces was relegated to the background. When India achieved independence, the question of prohibition again came to the forefront. Prohibition was included in the directive principles of State policy. The Constitution lays down: "The States shall endeavour to bring about prohibition of consumption, except for medicinal purposes, of intoxicating drinks and of drugs which are injurious to health."

By 1961, Maharashtra, Gujarat, Madras (Tamil Nadu) and Andhra Pradesh were the States where complete prohibition was adopted. In Kerala, Madhya Pradesh, Mysore, Orissa and Uttar Pradesh, partial prohibition was applied and Assam, Bihar, Himachal Pradesh, Jammu and Kashmir, Punjab, Rajasthan and West Bengal were declared as dry areas. More recently the question of prohibition has again become a topic of heated discussion and review. Several States later decided to abandon it or amend the relevant legislation. Recently Haryana and Andhra Pradesh, which had adopted prohibition, have abandoned it.

The yield of revenue from State excise duties increased from Rs. 49.40 crore in 1951-52 to Rs. 53.10 crore in 1960-61, Rs. 824.28 crore in 1980-81 and Rs. 1,29,530 crore in 2006-07 (budget).

The controversy over the desirability of prohibition has become active during recent years. The main reason for this is that the States' financial position due to prohibition has become very vulnerable. There are people who believe that the surrender of excise revenue is not at all warranted. Even among the members of the Taxation Enquiry Commission (1952-54) there was difference of opinion on this issue. The Commission therefore concluded that, "in view of this equal division of opinion among the members in regard to the future excise policy in terms of the whole of India the Commission is not in a position to make any recommendation on such policy".

This question was also examined by the Tek Chand Committee, which estimated the annual loss due to prohibition of about Rs. 50 crore for all the States taken together. Thus, prohibition leads to substantial loss of revenue to the State governments. In addition, the State governments have also to incur expenditure on the enforcement of prohibition *i.e.*, expenditure on the prevention of illicit distillation for production of liquor and expenditure on publicity and propaganda. In some quarters it is believed that this loss of revenue can be made up by increasing estate duties, rationalising the rate structure and tightening the machinery of tax collection.

The protagonists of prohibition also argue that since most of the revenue is collected from taxation of country spirits, opium and other drugs which are generally consumed by the poor, excise duties are regressive in nature because their burden falls heavily on the lower income groups. Their argument is that no other consumer tax is as high as the excise duties. But this argument can be counteracted on the ground that excise duties are also meant for restricting the consumption of harmful goods and not merely for collecting revenue. In other words, the excise duties are just a deterrent. Besides, drinking is not a good thing. It creates a number of social evils. It leads to broken families, quarrels and crimes of all kinds as Gandhiji said "drinking destroys the body as well as soul". However on ethical and moral grounds it is easy to make out the case for the enforcement of the policy of total prohibition, on economic grounds it is difficult to support it, particularly, when the States are facing resource crunch for the implementation of their development programmes. The policy of complete prohibition has not succeeded even in other countries mainly because of large scale illicit manufacture of liquor and smuggling or bottling. In India also it has been found that the prohibition has led to illegal production, sale and consumption of liquor on a wide scale. There was rampant corruption all around and even the administrative officials were prey to corrupt practices. It is not easy to enforce prohibition successfully. It is because of these reasons that many State governments are not in favour of prohibition and those which adopted the policy of prohibition have already scrapped it.

Sales Tax

General sales tax is the most important source of revenue to the States. Its position as a source of revenue to the States is also not going to diminish in future as well. The Indian Constitution allows the States to impose and collect taxes on the sale or purchase of goods other than newspapers. Article 286 of the Constitution, however, restricts the State governments from taxing: (*a*) sales and purchases in the course of trade outside the territories of India; (*b*) sales of goods delivered for consumption in other States; and (*c*) sales in the course of inter-State trade and commerce. The States are also required to seek the prior approval of the President before imposing taxes on commodities declared 'essential' by Parliament under the Essential Goods Act, 1952.

In pursuance of the recommendation of the Taxation Enquiry Commission, the Constitution was amended in 1955 which allowed the imposition of tax on goods of inter-State sale and purchase by the Union Government and therefore restrictions began to be imposed on the power of the States to tax the sale or purchase, within the States, of those goods which are considered by the Parliament as of importance in inter-State trade or commerce.

Sales tax can be: (*i*) general and selective; (*ii*) multi-point and single-point; and (*iii*) a turnover tax or gross receipt tax.

When the tax is imposed on the aggregate sale of all commodities barring those goods which are exempted under the law, it is called a general sales tax. When the tax is imposed on the sale of selected commodities it is called a selective sales tax. Such a tax is imposed on high priced and luxury goods. The general sales tax can be single-point as well as multi-point. Under single-point a specific amount is added to the price at the time of its sale to the consumer. It is collected at any point of sale *i.e.*, either at the point of production or wholesale distribution or retail distribution. Under the single-point tax system the tax rate is relatively high and therefore commodities which are of mass consumption or essential in nature are generally exempted from the tax. Under the multi-point system the sales tax is imposed at all stages of the sale of a commodity. The rate is relatively low and exemptions are very few.

A selective sales tax was for the first time introduced by Madhya Pradesh in 1983 in the form of petrol tax. The Madras Government introduced for the first time the general sales tax in 1939 on multi-point basis. In 1941, Bengal Government introduced a single-point sales tax system. After that more and more States switched over from single-point to multi-point system and certain other States switched over from multi-point to single-point system. Uttar Pradesh introduced sales tax in 1948 on multi-point basis. Now almost all States have sales tax in one form or other.

Sales tax is certainly advantageous from the point of view of certainty of revenue, cost of collection, effects etc. It is argued that revenues from sales tax are generally more stable than those from income tax. This is because of the fact that the consumption of articles is more or less stable over a period of time than the level of income. It is also to be pointed out that stability of revenue means the rise in the burden of the tax with 'fall in income and fall in the burden with rise in income. This is against the basic principles of taxation and therefore sales tax is not desirable from this point of view. Secondly, it is held that the cost of collection of revenues from sales tax is comparatively less because it gets automatically collected when a commodity is sold. But on the other hand we find that the cost of collection and compliance met by the sellers is considerably higher than the cost of administration of the tax to the government. Thirdly, sales tax is favoured because it is regressive in its effects. It is based on the assumption that in a tax system which is already too steeply progressive, sales tax counter balances by putting heavy burden upon the lower income groups and it is in this way the whole tax system becomes more equitable. There are some who argue that sales tax has the capacity to produce revenue in a very short time. The tax payers also generally do not feel the burden of its payment because it is made in small amounts throughout the year. Some people are of the opinion that like income and property taxes a retail sales tax also creates tax consciousness among the tax payers. The Indirect Taxation Enquiry Committee (1976) recommended that since sales tax is an important source of revenue to the State governments, it is necessary that its structure is rationalised. According to the Committee, the rationalisation of the structure should be based on the following principles:

(*i*) It should essentially be imposed by the State government on its residents without affecting the residents of other States; (*ii*) the principle of a unified market within the country should be preserved; (*iii*) if the tax is to play a distinctive role it should also cover value added at the post-manufacturing stages; (*iv*) as far as possible the procedures and structure of taxation in different States should be uniform. In view of this the Committee recommended that the State governments should gradually move to a single-point tax system.

Secondly, the Committee suggested that the sale of inputs to registered manufacturers should be free of taxation. Finally, the Committee recommended that the inter-State sales tax now subject to a ceiling of 4 per cent should gradually be brought down to 1 per cent. The Committee also recommended that the octroi should be totally abolished.

Points for Abolition of Sales Tax

The fact that sales tax falls heavily on those articles which are generally consumed by the poorer sections of the society, it adversely affects the efficiency and ability to work of the people. It is, therefore, necessary that the item of common consumption are totally exempted and luxury goods taxed at heavy rates.

Sales tax may also adversely affect the ability of the people to save, particularly of those sections of the community which are living from hand to mouth and which have no margin for saving. If the tax is levied on the luxury goods then it may not affect the ability of the poor sections of the community to save and therefore it will not have any adverse effect on production.

Sales tax is regressive in character since it is imposed on commodities which are consumed by poorer sections of the community. And, therefore, it widens the inequalities in the distribution of income and wealth. If sales tax is only imposed on luxury goods it will not be as productive a source of revenue as it is now. The fundamental defect of the sales tax is that it is not linked with the tax paying capacity of the tax payer. Further, sales tax does not take into account the domestic circumstances of the tax payer. Its burden is more heavy on those tax payers who have a large number of dependents. It is, therefore, necessary that the rates of sales tax be structured in such a fashion that it may not adversely affect the productive capacity of the country. The Indirect Taxation Enquiry Committee had acknowledged that the sales tax system as it is evolved and as it exists today is a burden to the producer, because it raises the costs and ex-factory prices. The extensive sales tax on inputs has its own cascading effects. That is why it is now being widely argued that the sales tax should be abolished. Following arguments are advanced in support of the abolition of sales tax:

(*i*) In the present system a commodity is taxed twice, once at the point of origin and the other when it is finally sold out to the consumer. In other words, the State in which the commodity is produced levies the tax and again the State in which the commodity is being sold a tax is levied on its sale.

(*ii*) Inter-State sales tax as imposed by the Government of India has certainly regulated the sales taxation but it is against the principle of unified market. It is an obstacle in the free flow of trade between various States and it facilitates the more industrially advanced State to export a part of the tax to the consumers of other States. It means that if the cost input is taxed at an average rate of 8 per cent in the State producing the commodity it forms about 50 per cent of the ex-factory price of a commo-dity which is exported to other States.

(*iii*) A high rate of inter-State sales tax has encouraged large producers to establish their ware houses in those States where the commodities are sold out and thus evade the payment of tax merely by transferring the goods from the production centres to the warehouses situated outside the State. In this connection it may be noted that this is possible only for the large manufacturers. Small manufacturers are not in a position to do that and in this respect they are placed in a disadvantageous position.

(*iv*) Since the tax is imposed on inputs it has cascading effects and leads to the increase in the price of finished commodities more than the amount of tax.

(*v*) Manufacturers producing a commodity and paying tax at the first point have also to pay the Central excise duty and thus have to deal with Central excise department in relation to the same commodity and the same transaction.

(*vi*) A multi-point sales tax system leads to harassment of the small dealers in so far as they are required to maintain accounts according to the requirements of the sales tax department. More often than not the small dealers are unable to fulfil that requirement and they are prone to harassment by the officials and clerks of the department.

(*vii*) It has been observed that the sales tax officers are generally not well paid; they are not properly equipped for the job and they are not trained adequately for undertaking the job correctly. The dealers find it difficult to deal with such people. Besides, the dealers have to fill in so many forms that it is impossible for them to have a smooth running. Besides involving huge work in filling these forms they have also to face a situation in which these forms are always in short supply. Further, the check post officers on the border of the State have to verify the contents of the trucks against details given in the permit. If there is any discrepancy the truck would be delayed and the penalty would be imposed. If by chance the producer forgets to carry the permit with him, the commodities will not be allowed to be transported beyond the check post until the tax and penalty have been paid. Sometimes, a threat is given by the checking officers for unloading the entire truck for the purpose of verification. Such threats certainly force the transporters to bend their knees and ultimately agree to grease the palms of dozens of officers.

(*viii*) Lastly, the rates of tax vary so much that in the States where it is a single-point tax system the rates of tax vary between 10 and 12 per cent and in most cases it is 1 to 12 per cent which is highly undesirable and which leads to tax evasion. It has been seen that the consumers generally purchase their requirements from those dealers who do not charge sales tax. This leads to a vicious circle and thus sales and purchase take place without entering into the books of accounts. Consequently, a parallel economy in the form of black money is in existence.

It is because of these reasons that the business and trade people are vehemently opposing the imposition of sales tax and are anxious to get it abolished. The business class prefers to get the excise levies enhanced rather than to pay a separate sales tax. In support of this argument it is said that when the same commodities are taxed by different authorities the rationalisation of the tax structure is not possible. When a single authority levies all the taxes on a particular commodity it can take note of all considerations *viz.*, the burden of tax on the consumer, its impact on production and investment in the industry etc. In a Central levy it is also convenient to give rebate when export takes place. In addition, the cost of collection is also less. It also leads to the elimination of problems arising out of differential rates of sales tax and lastly, the dealers and businessmen are also not put to harassment.

Points against Abolition of Sales Tax

The antagonists of the abolition of sales tax hold a different view altogether. They vehemently oppose such a proposal. The State governments are afraid that if excise duties are levied in lieu of sales tax, they will definitely suffer loss in revenue. The bitter memories of the loss of revenue due to the imposition of excise duty in lieu of sales tax on textiles, tobacco and sugar are still fresh in their mind. Secondly, the State governments feel that whatever resources are mobilised for them by the government of India by way of share in the

Central taxes they do not get any credit and, therefore, they do not want this situation to perpetuate. The State governments also feel that this would lead to the curtailment of their powers to tax their own people and will increase their dependence on the Centre. Their autonomy will also be reduced by an increase in their dependence on the Centre.

Case for Rationalisation of Sales Taxation

Taking both the views, for and against abolition of sales tax, into account it appears that the total abolition of sales tax and a combining of commodity taxation to the point of production does not seem to be very easy. It is not correct to believe that the excise duties and sales tax have the same tax base. These two taxes are definitely separate and do not belong to the same category. They also do not serve the same purpose. As a matter of fact there are certain goods like agricultural products or commodities produced by small manufacturers or handicrafts or articles of jewellery which for administrative and other reasons remain outside the preview of the Central excise but are within the ambit of sales tax. It is also true that the area of both kinds of taxes do not overlap fully. The increase in the value which takes place after the product is out of the factory and till it reaches the final consumer cannot be taxed through excise duties. This part of value added is governed by the sales tax. Lastly, confining taxation to the point of production has the disadvantage of preventing the cascading effects of taxation because the tax is levied at a very early stage of the stream of transactions from the manufacturer to the consumer. That is why the Indirect Taxation Enquiry Committee did not uphold the abolition of sales tax. The Committee was of the view that both Central excise duties and sales tax have distinct role to play. Excise duties are more relevant to the process of production while sales taxes are more relevant to the consumption of those commodities.

In view of what has been stated above the only feasible proposition is to rationalise the tax structure of the sales taxation and reform the existing system in such a way that the existing weaknesses of the system are minimised. In this case the Indirect Taxation Enquiry Committee has given the following suggestions:

(*i*) Sales tax should be levied only on finished products.

(*ii*) Sales tax should be a single-point tax *i.e.*, it should either be levied at the first stage or at the last stage. The Committee was, however, in favour of the imposition of sales tax at the last point.

(*iii*) The sales tax system should be rationalised. The rates of Central sales tax be reduced from 4 to 1 per cent.

(*iv*) As far as possible there should be uniformity in sales tax legislation and procedures operating in different States.

(*v*) Since the economy of each State has its own peculiarities and levels and sources of income differ from State to State an Expert Committee in each State should undertake studies of all connected problems so that the reform of sales tax system would be faciliatated.

R.J. Chelliah Committee also was of the same view when it said that the States should not impose a tax on inputs. The rates of sales tax should not be multiple and there should only be four or five rates. The chief object of the sales tax should be to restrict consumption and collect revenue for the State and the administration of sales tax should be simplified.

Value Added Tax (VAT)

The introduction of VAT as lieu of sales tax all over the country has been engaging the attention of governments both at the Centre and the States. A modified system of VAT (MODVAT) was introduced by the Centre on March 1, 1986. It did not have a smooth sailing. Consequently CENVAT (Central VAT) was introduced in the budget for 2000-01.

The VAT was finally introduced w.e.f. April 1, 2005. 31 States have already implemented VAT. Uttar Pradesh has decided to introduce VAT on April 1, 2008.

The experience of implementing VAT has been very satisfying. During 2005-06 the tax revenue of 25 VAT implementing States/UTs registered Year-on-Year increase in VAT revenues of 13.8%. In the first seven months of 2006-07, the 30 VAT States/UTs collectively registered revenue growth rate of 26.1% over the corresponding period of the previous year. According to the compensation package agreed to, a provision of Rs. 5,000 crore was made in the budget of 2005-06 which was revised to Rs. 2,500 crore at the R.E. stage. For 2006-07 a provision of Rs. 2,990 crore was made and an additional provision of Rs. 1000 crore was made through first supplementary. During 2005-06, 8 States in all had asked for compensation for an amount of Rs. 6,765.6 crore and during the first seven months of 2006-07 claims for a total of Rs. 514.3 crore from 5 States were received.

C.S.T. and Steps to introduce G.S.T.

The Union Finance Minister in his speech introducing the Budget for 2008-09 announced that as per agreement reached between the Central Government and State Governments, the rate of Central Sales Tax (C.S.T.) has been reduced from 4% to 3% during the current year and will be reduced to 2% w.e.f. 1st April, 2008. Consultations were going on with the State Governments on the compensation for losses, if any, and the new rate will be notified as soon as an agreement was reached. There was also considerable progress in preparing a road map for introducing the Goods and Services Tax (G.S.T.) w.e.f. April 1, 2010.

Motor Vehicles Tax

Other important sources of non-tax revenue include motor vehicles tax, electricity duties, entertainment tax and taxes on passengers and goods. While taxes on passengers and goods and motar vehicles tax belong to the same group the electricity duties and entertainment tax are certainly different. Regarding the motor vehicles tax the Parliament has been empowered to legislate about mechanically driven vehicles and also to lay down the principles on which taxes are to be levied on such vehicles. But the quantum of such taxes has been left to individual States.

The motor vehicles tax was first imposed on an all India basis in the form of fees under the Indian Motor Vehicles Act of 1940. The chief concern of this Act was to regulate and control motor traffic. Different fees were charged for registration of the vehicles, permits, driving licences, etc,. The motor vehicles tax is now levied by all States and on all carriages. Like other taxes there is lot of variation in the basis of this tax as well as its rates from State to State. Some States levy vehicles tax on the basis of unladen weight, some States levy a tax on laden weight and in some other States the tax is imposed on authorised loads. Private motor vehicles are taxed either on unladen weight or according to seating capacity. Passenger buses are generally taxed on this basis. Some States also impose a tax on passenger fares and goods freights. This tax is supposed to be quite heavy and burden some in a number of States. It has been calculated that more than 50 per cent of the cost of operations of the buses is accounted for by one tax or the other. According to the estimate of the Indian Road Transport Development Association each truck on the road pays on an average taxes amounting to Rs. 11,000 per annum which also include taxes and duties on diesel oil. This is a very favourable source of income of the State governments. Since 1951-52, the revenue from motor vehicle tax had increased from Rs. 10.1 crore to Rs. 10,913 crore in 2004-05.

Entertainment Tax

It was introduced in Bengal in 1922. The Indian Constitution has authorised the State governments to levy this tax. This tax is very simple and is charged at prescribed rates on the value of the tickets at the place of entertainment. All public shows like horse races, theatres, cinema shows, circus, sports etc. meant for entertainment of the people and where admission is by tickets, are required to pay tax. Cinemas contribute bulk of the revenue collected under this head. Tax is collected either in cash or through special adhesive stamps. However, entertainments offered for charitable or religious purposes or for educational or propaganda purposes or for the development of agriculture, industry or public health, are exempted from this tax. In a number of States the entertainment tax collected by the State governments is passed on to the local bodies. The revenue from this tax had increased from Rs. 6.4 crore in 1951-52 to Rs. 969 crore in 2004-05.

Electricity Duty

An electricity duty is either charged on the consumption of electricity or in the form of a surcharge on electricity tariff. According to the Indian Constitution electricity consumed by Indian Railways and the Government of India is exempted from electricity duty. Simirarly, a duty is not levied upon the electricity generated, consumed, distributed or sold by any authority established for regulating, developing any inter-State river or river valley project with the consent of the President and a law by the State legislature. It is expected that with additional generation and consumption of electricity the yield from this source would increase. The revenue from this duty had increased from Rs. 22.6 crore in 1956 to Rs. 6,676 crore in 2004-05.

6. Non-Tax Sources of Revenue

The non-tax sources of revenue of the States, as already stated earlier, are: (*i*) grants-in-aid from the Central Government; and (*ii*) other non-tax sources. State governments receive two types of grants from the Government of India: (*i*) statutory grants on the recommendation of the Finance Commission; (*ii*) discretionary grants sanctioned by the Planning Commission to finance Plan outlays. These grants were expected to be of the order of Rs. 61,176 crore in 2004-05.

State governments also receive revenue from other non-tax sources like inter-state dividends, income from general services, social and economic services. It was expected that the total non-tax revenue from other sources would be of the order of Rs. 53,340 crore in 2006-07.

7. Main Trends of State Revenues

From the foregoing account we can now summarise the main trends of State revenues as follows:

(*i*) State revenues have increased considerably like the Central revenues. With the growing responsibilities of the State governments, new taxes have come into existence and the rates of old taxes have increased. Consequently, the tax revenues have increased from Rs. 280.00 crore to Rs. 3,66,620 crore between 1952 and 2007.

(*ii*) In 1951-52 about 19% of the total tax revenue of the State governments was received from the Government of India as share of the taxes collected by the Central Government and it was expected that in 2006-07 it would account for nearly 30 per cent of the total tax revenue. This means that about 30% of the tax revenue of the States comes from the Central Government.

(*iii*) Commodity and service taxation constitutes a very important source of revenue of the State governments. During 1951-52 it accounted for 62 per cent but in 2006-07 the commodity taxation was expected to go up to 87 per cent of the total tax revenue. It is, therefore, clear that the States also depend upon the general public for their finance and their tax revenue is also regressive in character because it falls heavily upon the middle and lower income groups.

(*iv*) In 1951-52 sales tax occupied the top position as a source of revenue to the States and excise duties and land revenue stood at No.2 and No.3. Sales tax still continues to be the largest source of income to the State governments.

(*v*) Like the tax revenue the non-tax revenue of the State governments has also shown remarkable buoyancy. The increase has been both in the grants from the Central Government and also in the revenue receipts from state enterprises and administrative services. While the State's own non-tax revenue increased from Rs. 90 crore in 1952 to Rs. 55,340 crore in 2006-07, grants from the Central Government have increased from Rs. 30 crore to Rs. 100,190 crore during the same period which clearly shows the growing dependence of the States on the Centre.

Exercises

1. It is a common notion that state revenues in India are elastic, but they have considerably expanded in recent years. How are they inelastic and how do you account for their expansion?
2. Discuss the main trends in state finances in India since 1990.
3. Examine the arguments for and against the taxation of agricultural incomes in the context of state finances in India.
4. Analyse critically the recent trends in the finances of the states in India. Examine the case for and against the abolition of land revenue.
5. 'No amount of central taxation can make good the inadequacy of State taxes'. Discuss the sources of revenue of State Governments in India in the light of this statement.

●●●

Chapter 42

Public Debt—General Issues

1. Introduction

Different writers have defined public debt differently. Broadly speaking, the term 'public debt' refers to the borrowings undertaken by public bodies. In its broad sense it includes all sorts of obligations of a government and in its narrow sense it includes only the loans raised by the government externally. So, there are broad definitions as well as narrow definitions. The former includes all the obligations of a government including the currency obligations while the narrow definitions include only the debt raised by a government from outside the country. The government of a country may obtain loans from banks, business organizations, business institutions and individuals. Public debt is generally in the form of bonds or treasury bills if the loan has been acquired for a short period. These bonds carry the promise of the government to pay interest to their holders at the specified rate of interest at regular intervals or in lumpsum at the end of the stipulated period, in addition to the principal amount. According to Taylor, "The debt is in the form of promises by the Treasury to pay to the holders of these promises a principal sum and in most instances interest on that principal."[1]

Government obligations can be of various types. In the first place in its authority, the government issues a part of total currency in circulation and the remaining currency is issued by the central bank of the country. So far as government obligation is concerned the currency issued by it is its obligation while the currency issued by the central bank is not its obligation. But, if we consider the central bank as a part of the government sector then even the currency issued by the central bank, is a part of overall currency obligations of the government. The government is not obliged to 'payoff' its currency obligations, at the most it replaces one set of currency by another, otherwise the currency obligations of the government remain inactive.

1. Taylor P.E., *The Economics of Public Finance,* p. 178.

Government also incurs some obligations in the form of short-term debt—whose maturity is normally of less than one year at the time of issue and consists of Treasury Bills, Treasury Deposit Receipts and borrowings from the banking sector. These obligations are short-term obligations. Some obligations of the government are called as floating debt which do not have any specific maturity but some part of it may be repayable according to pre-determined terms and conditions. These include provident funds, small savings, reserve funds and deposits and so on. In India, the Central Government issues certain special securities to meet its obligations towards international financial institutions like the IBRD and the IMF. These are known as special floating debt. Then there is permanent or funded debt whose maturity is of more than one year at the time of issue. Some parts of these debts are non-terminable which means that the government only pays the interest and not the principal amount. The above mentioned obligations may be to some extent to the foreigners-individuals, institutions, firms and governments and are called external loans.

It would thus be clear that people may define public debt differently, keeping in mind the purpose and context and institutional arrangements. And therefore, all obligations of the government, including the demand debt, are included in the definition of public debt and in other cases only the above mentioned obligations are included in the definition. Generally, the demand debt of the government is excluded from the definition of public debt and only other items and other obligations are included in it.

2. Causes of Public Debt

The government of a country incurs loans because of a number of reasons. We explain these in the following:

(1) The government has to engage itself in collecting revenue and spending it. It is not always possible that the receipts may exactly match the expenses. Sometimes, the government overspends and sometimes it under-spends. In the former case the government runs into deficit and in the latter case it runs into surplus. In the short period the balancing of inflows and outflows is not possible but in the long run the government budget tends to be in balance. So, to meet temporary deficit the government raises debts.

(2) At times the government due to unforeseen and sudden developments, is forced to borrow if the tax revenue is not adequate for meeting the need of enormous expenditure required for abnormal situations like war, floods or earthquakes and other natural calamities.

(3) There has also been a sea change in the thinking about the role of the government in national affairs. The government now is not only required to worry about the surplus or deficit of the budget but it is also responsible for

correcting the imperfections of free market mechanism and bring about economic stability. The traditional philosophy of *laissez-faire* has given place to the new philosophy of functional finance. And therefore to fulfil this responsibility the government runs into debt which is now not considered as bad.

(4) Now the government in an under-developed country is also required to take care of the development of the economy. Now the budgetary policy is used as an important and potent tool for accelerating the process of capital formation and economic growth. For this purpose the government has to borrow and invest funds in various development projects.

(5) In recent times there has been a phenomenal rise in the functions of the government and more so in the overall cost of performance of these functions due to increase in the price level. Modern wars and defence expenditure as also the maintenance of executive, legislature and judiciary has become very expensive. Consequently, taxes alone cannot enable a government to fulfil its obligations and therefore in all countries the governments have to incur debts.

3. Public vs. Private Debt

Government borrowings resemble private borrowings in certain respects. But the differences between the two are more prominent. First we take up the similarities between the two and then we shall spell out the dissimilarities.

Similarities between Public and Private Debt

(1) Private economic units borrow funds to acquire certain resources which implies the diversion of funds from one use to another. Public debt also leads to the same and in this respect both appear to be similar.

(2) Both government as well as individual economic units borrow to meet their immediate requirements. Both pay interest on loans. The capacity of both is determined more or less by their capacity to repay loans. The classical economists considered both public and private debt as the same. In their opinion just as excess debt leads the individual borrower to a state of insolvency, excess debt by public bodies may also lead to the same situation. But this sort of analogy is not correct.

Dissimilarities between Public and Private Debt

Public and private debts are not similar in the following respects:

(1) A private economic unit cannot borrow internally *i.e.*, from itself or from its own resources. But the government can borrow internally *i.e.*, it can borrow from within the economy.

(2) A private economic unit can repay its loans either out of its income or out of its accumulated assets or by borrowing from other sources. But the

government need not do this. It can create currency and can repay the debt by printing notes. The government of a country does not normally do this because it adversely affects the welfare and stability of the economy. The government on the other hand can raise loans from outside the country. But the repayment of these loans will have to be done in foreign currency or in gold. In that case foreign currency will have to be procured through export earnings or gold will have to be given. This means that external loans are a drain on the resources of the country whereas internal loans are not.

(3) Another important distinction between public and private debt is that the former affects the various dimensions of the economy in a big way, whereas this does not happen in the case of private debt. Public debt affects distribution, economic growth, levels of production, income and employment and so on. In this respect it is both a boon as well as a curse. It has been pointed out that while the private debt increases the purchasing power of the individual economic unit, public debt does not increase the spending power of the government because the government has a number of other fiscal measures at its disposal for mobilizing additional resources.

(4) The servicing and the payment of public debt do not bring about any reduction in the government's income whereas in the case of a private economic unit or an individual the consumption is to be curtailed for the payment of the debt.

(5) Excess debt may lead an individual borrower to state of insolvency but in the case of the government this cannot happen because: (*i*) the government can force the people to pay additional taxes; (*ii*) the government can raise fresh loans for paying old debts; (*iii*) it can print new currency for the repayment of the loans; (*iv*) it can raise the prices of goods and services produced by public enterprises to meet the cost of servicing of debt; (*v*) it can impose a capital levy for the redemption of the debt and (*vi*) the government possesses ample internal and external resources which the individuals do not. The government can compel people to lend whereas an individual cannot do so.

(6) The loans raised by the government are used for the benefit of the entire community while the loans taken by an individual are used by him for his personal benefits.

(7) Another difference is that the rate of interest on public loans is lower than on private loans.

(8) Still another difference is while the individual borrows even for consumption purposes the government borrows only for productive purposes.

(9) Lastly, the government at times borrows, as a matter of fiscal policy, even if it has no requirement for additional funds. For example, the government may borrow to maintain economic stability. During a period of inflation

government borrowing reduces purchasing power in the hands of the people which helps in bringing down the price level. During a period of depression, the government borrows to incur certain types of expenditure, which help to raise the level of economic activity. On the contrary an individual may not borrow when he does not need funds.

4. Objects of Public Debt

A government can raise loans for various purposes. These can be:

1. To Meet Budget Deficits or Current Expenditure. The government of a country, in the event of a shortfall of revenue from taxation may resort to borrowing. The expenditure of the government, as explained before, may increase owing to a variety of factors in which prominent are unforeseen contingencies like wars, famines, floods, epidemics and other natural calamities etc. In such situations the government being caught unawares has no alternative but to raise loans. The government can borrow from within the country as well as from outside the country, depending upon its needs and the availability of ready funds.

Again, the government of a country may not be in a position to increase its tax revenue by imposing new taxes or by raising the rates of old taxes for a variety of reasons. It then has to borrow funds for meeting its current requirements. In developing countries, the government may raise debt to complete the development projects already taken in hand and for that purpose it can approach various institutions, organizations and governments of other countries.

2. To Maintain Economic Stability. If the stability of the economy is jeopardized by cyclical fluctuations, the government may resort to borrowing to correct the situation. During periods of depression when the level of effective demand in the economy is low, the government may use borrowed funds for taking up public works projects or for the expansion of infrastructural facilities. Obviously it cannot use the tool of taxation for raising funds for the purpose because of the market conditions. If government uses taxation in a period of depression for raising funds it may adversely affect the incentive to work and invest and reduce effective demand. During depression, therefore, the government has to borrow particularly from banks. Similarly during period of inflation when the prices are rising, the government by raising loans can withdraw the surplus purchasing power from the people and put a check on the rising prices. For subscribing to public debt people may withdraw their deposits in the bank or use their idle savings. This will reduce their purchasing power and consequently the level of effective demand will come down and so the prices will fall. Some economists are, however, of the view that for combating inflation, taxation would be a better device because public debt increases the liability of the government for its repayment. So far as taxation is considered additional revenue collected can very well be left idle and may not be used. But, as we have explained earlier, taxation may have adverse effects and therefore public debt would be a better proposition if it is utilized for productive purposes making the debt self-liquidating. So government can use public borrowings for maintaining economic stability in the country.

3. Financing of Development Plans. In under-developed countries the government requires additional funds to undertake development projects. An under-developed country is always short of funds. It is not possible for the government to take recourse to heavy taxation because of the poverty of the people. As a matter of fact, it is for breaking the vicious circle of poverty that development of the economy is undertaken. Under these circumstances public borrowing is the best way out. Generally the governments borrow funds from individuals, institutions and governments of foreign countries for making structural changes in the institutional set-up, creating social and economic overheads, and undertaking projects directly related to the improvement of agricultural and industrial production.

4. Financing of Wars. We have already stated before that governments require to borrow funds for meeting emergencies like wars and natural calamities. Since defence of the country against foreign aggression has always been a priority with the governments, since earliest times, it is necessary that a government for meeting the exigency should raise loans because the demand for funds is generally very large which cannot be met from normal tax revenue. Moreover, in modern times wars have become highly expensive. Even otherwise too the army and other defence services need large funds for their maintenance and for acquiring modern sophisticated equipment for which the governments have to raise loans.

5. Optimum Allocation of Resources. The allocation of resources in an economy is hardly at the optimum level and therefore the government is required to act for correcting the imbalance in the allocation of resources. The misallocation of resources occurs because of the imperfections of the market mechanism. For example, monopoly or monopolistic competition is the general outcome of the free market mechanism and therefore the government may take action in the direction of either taking over the monopolistic firms or by increasing or by imposing control. In a democratic society the best way to combat monopolistic tendencies is to encourage the setting up of new firms in competition against the monopoly firm for which the government will have to give subsidies and other facilities and therefore the government has to raise these funds from borrowing.

6. Creation of Social Overheads. With a view to providing facilities to the industries and also external economies to them, the government takes action towards creating overhead capital benefits. Social overhead capital is essential for a systematic development of a country. These, however, are not attractive to private investment and therefore have to be started in the public sector. For this purpose the government requires resources which it musters through debts.

7. To Finance Public Enterprises. Modern governments have also entered into commercial field and have set up public enterprises. These require huge investment and therefore the governments generally borrow funds for setting up these commercial enterprises and also for running them efficiently. These enterprises may be in the field of collective and moderate wants such as production of defence material, setting up of educational institutions and research and training centres, hospitals and dispensaries, production of life saving drugs, generation of power etc. The funds required for these enterprises cannot be raised by increasing taxation beyond limit. Hence the government have to borrow.

5. Classification of Public Debt

Public debt can be of various types. The differences in the various types of loans arise because of a number of factors like the purpose of the loan, the period of the loan, rate of interest offered, the terms and conditions of the loan etc. The public debts have been classified as follows:

(*i*) Internal and External,
(*ii*) Productive and Unproductive,
(*iii*) Redeemable and Irredeemable,
(*iv*) Funded and Unfunded,
(*v*) Voluntary and Compulsory.

We now explain these briefly in the following paragraphs:

1. Internal and External Debt. Internal debt refers to the loans raised within the country while external debt refers to loans raised in a foreign country either from government or foreign nationals or institutions. An internally held debt does not affect the economy of a country because resources of the country are only transferred from the people to the government. The level of national income is also not disturbed. It does not matter at all whether the interest on internal debt is left with the tax payers or is taken from them as taxes and paid out as interest on internal loan. So the repayment of such loan does not affect the productive capacity of the country. However, there may be some indirect effects. But the foreign loans definitely affect the economy of a country, because their repayment requires the transfer of a part of national income abroad. This certainly reduces net income of the debtor country. But foreign loans are not always bad if they are used for productive purposes and if they are made self-liquidating. In other words, if the repayment of the loan and interest is made out of the income of the projects in which it has been invested, then foreign loans should be welcome.

2. Productive and Unproductive Debt. If public debt is used for creating income yielding tangible assets so that it is made self-liquidating, then it is productive and if it is used for purposes which do not yield any income then it is unproductive debt. For example, funds raised through public borrowings, if used for construction of railways and expansion of means of transport and communication, generation of power, irrigation projects, establishment and expansion of heavy and basic industries like iron and steel, cement and fertilizers etc. Then they are productive because they yield an income which can be used for paying interest on the loans acquired for these projects. The loans when used for productive purposes also help in increasing the overall level of production in the economy and therefore such loans are not a burden upon the economy. Unproductive loans like those taken for financing a war and giving relief in times of epidemics, floods and draughts are unproductive, because they do not yield an income and are consumed in the process and therefore such loans are a burden on the economy.

3. Redeemable and Irredeemable Debt. Redeemable debts are those for which the government is committed to repay at an appointed date, whereas loans for which there is no such commitment from the government, are irredeemable loans. The government has to make some arrangement for the payment of interest and principal amount in the case of the former which the government generally does through taxation. In the case of irredeemable loans the government pays the interest and there is no commitment for the repayment of the principal amount. These debts are also known as terminable debts. Redeemable loans can be short-term say for a period of 3 to 9 months like, treasury bills; long-term say for a period of 10 years or more and medium-term debts ranging between a period of 5 to 10 years. The rate of interest is the lowest in the case of short-term debts, highest in the case of long-term debts and it is moderate in the case of medium-term debts.

4. Funded and Unfunded Debt. Funded debts are those debts which are redeemable after a year or so or are not redeemable at all, whereas unfunded debts are those that are repaid within a year. Treasury bonds are an example of unfunded debts because they have a maturity period of 3 to 6 months. In the case of funded debts the government only pays a fixed sum of interest to the creditor, whereas it is the government's option whether it repays the principal or not.

5. Voluntary and Compulsory Debt. Broadly speaking, all public debts are voluntary in nature. Individuals and institutions are invited to purchase government securities and bonds. Generally the government does not put pressure on the people for the purchase of its bonds but during an emergency like war or during a period of rising prices the government may even force the people to buy government securities. Generally because of its high credibility, government loans are over-subscribed and that is why the rate of interest on government securities is low as compared to loans funded by a private company.

6. The Effects of Public Debt

How does public debt affect the economy depends on a variety of factors like the sources from which loans have been acquired, the purpose for which loans have been obtained, the terms and conditions of the loan, the value of the existing loans, and the way the loans are utilized etc.

1. Public Debt and Sources of Borrowing. So far as the sources of public debt are concerned a government can borrow from individuals, institutions, central bank and banking sector, of the country as well as of other countries. Effects of external debts are entirely different from the effects of internal debts. An internally held debt does not add to the total quantity of resources available for use in the economy. It is just a simple transfer of resources from private use to government use. So, it does not create any upheaval in the economy. If, a government activates the idle savings of the people, or if the loans are subscribed to by the central bank or the commercial banks then it will have expansionary effects because all such loans would put additional purchasing power in the hands of the people.

2. Public Debt and Purposes of Borrowing. The purposes for which loans are obtained are also very important. If the loans are used for unproductive purposes it will be a sheer waste and will not create any social or economic overheads and assets and will not lead to any increase either in production or in the welfare of the people. If the same funds are used for productive purposes then it will add to the prosperity of the people and the economy will move towards a higher path of production.

3. Public Debt and Rates of Interest. Again, the rates of interest also play an important role. Higher the rate of interest, higher will be the cost of borrowing. There would be a tough competition in the sphere of investment and a diversion of funds from marginal enterprises would lead to their closure which in turn would affect the level of production and other economic processes, market prices and overall interest rates adversely. If the government allows tax exemptions in the case of its loans, then people would be encouraged to buy government securities and bonds. Government's policy of obtaining debts in this manner may affect private enterprises to some extent, but not always.[2]

4. Public Debt and Amount of Loans. The terms and conditions of the loans as well as the amount also play an important part in producing effects on the economy. According to Beuhler, "The larger the loan is, the more palpable will be its effects on the economic system tend to be. If governments employ borrowed funds more productively, then social income is increased, but if they use this fund less productively the social incomes suffer."[3] If the terms and conditions of the loan are soft and if the loan is available for a longer period then the entire society will be benefited. It may be mentioned that the volume of the existing debt or the creation of the new debts are not solely responsible for these effects. The ownership, the composition and maturity are also important. If the government of a country incurs heavy debts during period of prosperity and boom, it may lead to an increase in the propensity by its inflationary effects. And borrowing in a period of depression or in the beginning of recovery may help the economy to recover fast. Finally, unlike taxation borrowing does not adversely affect private consumption and therefore leads to an expansionary effect.

Borrowing operations involve a two-way transfer of money-first from the subscribers to the government and then from the government to those on whom that money is spent. Again, at the time of payment of interest, the money is collected from the tax payers and transferred to the security holders and finally the money is transferred when the debt is repatriated. All these transfers affect production, distribution and the level of economic activity. How does a public debt affect these, we shall now analyse.

7. Effects of Public Debt upon the Economy

As already stated, the process of public debt and its utilization is a two-way transfer of money. In the first phase it is an income and therefore has revenue effects. In the second phase it is an expenditure and therefore has expenditure effects. In the first phase when loans are acquired by the government, people make necessary changes in their budgets. The consumption pattern of people is not affected directly because generally government securities are purchased out of past or present savings. But if people just increase their savings and cut down their expenditure to purchase securities, the consumption expenditure of these people will certainly be affected. And so, this is the first effect of public debt.

When the loans taken by government are spent, then certain benefits are conferred upon the people and this is the second effect of public debt. It is a

2. A.G. Beuhler, *op. cit.*, p, 707.
3. *Ibid.*, p, 709.

different matter that these benefits are almost the same as those conferred by spending the tax revenue. But mostly government spends its borrowings in ways different from tax revenue. This difference may not be very fundamental. The government may spend the tax revenue on making payment to the salaries and wages while the funds obtained by way of loans may be utilized by the government for the creation of social and economic overheads or income yielding tangible assets. So difference between the two is amply clear. The public debt is used to finance expenditure of a capital nature whereas the tax revenue is used to finance current or revenue expenditure.

1. Effect on Allocation of Resources. Unlike tax revenue, public debt does not substantially affect the allocation of resources. When the government spends its borrowings on the purchase of capital goods, the production of these capital goods increases, the national income rises which produces a multiplier effect on the investment and level of employment.

2. Effect on Overall Liquidity. Unlike taxation public debt increases the liquidity in the economy. The purchasers of government bonds are in possession of highly liquidated assets which can be converted for another purposes, at any time. During a period of boom and inflation the central bank of the country follows the policy of contraction of credit but this can be neutralized if the commercial banks are in possession of government securities and if they dispose of these securities and increase their reserve.

3. Effect on Level of Investment. It is generally argued that public debt adversely affects the level of investment. In case the government obtains loans from the commercial banks or the central banks, extra purchasing power is transferred to the community and therefore there will be no reduction in the quantum of funds available for investment. But if the banks or individuals purchase government securities out of the funds meant for business expansion then certainly the level of investment would be curtailed. In this connection it is to be noted that so long as the rate of interest remains static and the government offers special privileges to the holders of its securities, the possibility of a decline in private investment is very remote.

4. Effect on Money Market. Public debt may also affect the money market of the country. In order to obtain loans, the government will have to compete with the private investors. It will have to offer a higher rate of interest to attract the people to purchase its securities. So the government has to follow the general pattern of demand, supply and prices like other borrowers in the market because all borrowers in the market have to draw on the total supply of investment funds available in the market. If the government borrows from the banking sector more than the available investment funds at an existing rate of interest, it will have expansionary effect (increase in the total currency in circulation.)

5. Effect on the Private Sector. Public bodies incur loans for meeting the needs of their expenditure. All public expenditure increases the demand for goods and services because it increases the purchasing power of the people. When the public expenditure is financed through public borrowings the current consumption is not reduced because people generally purchase securities out of their idle savings. If the government utilizes the borrowed funds for purchasing goods and materials produced in the private sector, the demand for these goods and services will increase accordingly. If the government uses borrowed funds for paying salaries and wages, then again the demand for goods and services will increase because the salary and wage earners will spend the increased income on the purchase of these goods and services. So the spending of the borrowed funds will increase the general level of demand for the products produced in the private sector, without in any way affecting their supply. In sum, the effects of public debt are favourable to the private sector.

Effects of Public Debt on Production

Public borrowing can affect production in two ways. If funds raised through loans are invested in income yielding projects, the overall productivity of the community will increase; if these funds are spent on raising the income earning capacity of poorer sections, their efficiency, ability to work and save will automatically increase and if these funds are invested in projects which would increase the productive and investment capacity of individual entrepreneurs, like railways, power projects, telecommunications etc. the overall production in the economy would increase. But, if these funds are used to meet current deficits or war expenditure, then it will certainly affect production adversely. If the government utilizes the borrowed funds for establishing public commercial undertakings, the total investment funds available for production may not be adversely affected. But, if the government utilizes these funds for non-productive works then certainly the total investment will be adversely affected. This happens because the funds used for unproductive purposes can only be repatriated through additional taxation, which will ultimately affect future consumption. It is to be noted that unproductive loans do not affect consumption. Loans utilised for welfare schemes certainly increase efficiency of the workers and hence production. If the loans are used for productive purposes then they are considered as self-liquidating. They do not affect consumption and both the principal as well as interest can be paid out of the income yielded by the assets created out of these loans.

If people purchase government securities by withdrawing funds from their industrial establishment or by disposing of their shares and debentures, then certainly private investment will be adversely affected.

All said and done the government borrowings do not reduce investment and production in the economy.

Effects of Public Debt on Distribution

As already stated public borrowing causes transfer of purchasing power from one set of persons to another. If these transfers are from well-to-do sections of the community to the not so well off sections, the distribution of wealth will improve. In the first phase of borrowing operations, no doubt, money is transferred from the rich to the government because poor people cannot purchase government securities and subscribe to loans. In the second phase, when taxes are levied for the repayment of loans and interest, the burden falls on the poor. If the major portion of public debt comprises of small savings like post office savings or national saving certificates, then interest will be paid to the poorer sections, since these have been purchased by small savers. But, in reality savings constitute a very small portion of public debt all over the world. If public debt is spent on projects relating to the welfare of the poor people, then the inequalities of income will decrease and a more equal distribution of income between different classes of the society would take place. If the public borrowings create inflation, then some of the beneficial effects upon the distribution of income will be neutralized by rise in prices.

Effects of Foreign Loans on the Economy

Externally held debt of public bodies facilitates the imports of capital goods required for creating and for increasing the productive capacity of the community which leads to the acceleration of the economic growth. It produces favourable effects both on consumption and investment. It is also argued that imports from foreign countries increase the total supply of commodities in the domestic market; they also increase the national income and thus help in the improvement of the standard of living of the people. Besides, the import of these goods will reduce the demand for similar goods in the present and will lead to augment the level of future investment and will thus increase the national output. In this way the import will check the rise in prices and inflationary conditions. In another situation if the goods and services imported by the government are sold to the people then it would lead to the reduction of the total currency in circulation in the economy. It would also help the state to increase the volume of deficit financing which would further enhance the rate of economic growth.

Foreign borrowings do supplement the national resources and help the increase in the level of investment. If increased investment promotes the growth of the economy then the external liabilities can easily be liquidated and increase in external debt will therefore not be a cause for worry. So, the foreign loans should be used for increasing production in the economy and then not only will the growth of the economy be assured but the liability of external debt will also be easily met.

8. Public Debt and Economic Growth

The effects of public debt on economic growth can be studied under two heads: (*a*) Effect on the financial structure of the economy, and (*b*) Effect on the saving effort of the economy. We now analyse the effects of public debt on economic growth under these heads.

(1) Effects of Public Debt on the Financial Structure of the Economy

An important characteristic of economic growth is that economic activities of production, consumption, distribution etc. create financial requirements which go on increasing both absolutely and in relation to national income. This also leads to two important developments in the structure of the financial system. Since the receipts and expenditure of private economic units do not necessarily match, the need for credit goes on increasing and a number of credit instruments come into currency. The total credit structure in an economy is based on "inside money" and "outside money", former represents the loans and financial claims against the private sector of the economy while the latter comprises of the financial claims against the government sector. The entire private credit structure is built on the base provided by the government bonds and securities. Thus government instruments provide abundant opportunity for the development of financial institutions and financial markets of the economy. Since the physical economic growth of a country depends on a strong financial structure, it is necessary that the financial structure must have a wide, varied and acceptable base and this base can only be provided by the public debt. People have very strong faith in government securities. There is no risk involved and these securities possess easy marketability. These qualities are not found in private debt instruments. Sound and acceptable private debt instruments are always short in supply and therefore these cannot provide a strong base for the credit structure of the economy. The banking and non-banking financial intermediaries form important constituents of the credit superstructure of the economy. These institutions collect the savings of the people and put them to various uses. In this way they also help the development of the credit structure of the economy. Banks, as is well-known, can create credit and give rise to a series of claims and counter-claims which is often backed by public debt holdings.

(2) Effects of Public Debt on the Saving Effort of the Economy

Public borrowings can be divided into two classes: (1) Borrowings from the market (2) Borrowings from the Central Bank. So far as the market borrowings are concerned, their effect on savings and capital accumulation will depend upon the sources from which these borrowings emanate. If people reduce their consumption and subscribe to public loans then the rate of savings and capital accumulation will certainly rise. But people generally do not save on their own, particularly the temptation of increased interest income will not be adequate for the purpose. More so, because in an underdeveloped country there is general poverty and people reduce their consumption which is already very low. So, most of the savings are effected by the well-to-do people. There is therefore, another risk and that is, that the savings which would have augmented private investment further would be diverted to public loans. If that happens then the level of saving and investment activity will not be raised. But public debt will have re-allocative effects. Private investment is generally in consumption goods because the aim is to earn more profits. On the other hand the possibility of public investment in the production of capital goods is very great. Hence, public debt helps the economy in raising the rate of growth by diverting the resources to more productive uses.

Now coming to the question of the government borrowing from the central bank of the country, the obvious effect would be like that of the deficit financing or increasing the money supply by printing of notes. Increase in money supply will increase the aggregate demand in the market and a rise in price. Some supply of goods and services will be purchased by the government out of the newly created money and so the market will be left with smaller supplies. Consequently, people will be forced to save. But this is not a desirable practice because it will lead to inflationary rise in prices which will be harmful for all sections of the community.

9. Limits of Public Debt

It is generally argued that a continuously rising public debt is not conducive to the health of the economy. This is a fact that during the last century the volume of public debt in almost all countries of the world has shown an upward trend and various factors have been responsible for the situation. However, the big question is whether any limit can be set forth for the government for raising public debt. The answer is very simple. No government raises loans only for the purpose of raising loans. Each government, particularly after the development of the concept of the welfare state, is burdened with numerous responsibilities for which funds cannot be raised by taxes alone. We have enumerated already the factors that give rise to the growth of public debt. We know it fully well that no government takes pride in borrowing and squandering away borrowed funds. It may use the same funds for consumption purposes, but only that much which is absolutely essential for the strength of the economy: The government cannot be an idle spectator to the sufferings of the people due to war or natural calamities. Similarly government initiates only those welfare programmes which are absolutely essential for the welfare of the society as a whole. Modern governments have also to take necessary steps to protect the economy against cyclical fluctuations. Similarly in under-developed countries the government has to borrow funds for accelerating the growth of the economy. So, the governments do not raise loans for pleasure sake. It should be noted that in these days the government cannot keep the borrowings of fund a closely guarded secret. People have become quite vigilant and therefore the government cannot afford to use borrowed funds for purposes other than public. In certain countries even legal restrictions have been imposed on the government in the form of prescribing certain standards and limits beyond which it cannot borrow.

We have already stated before that the government has to compete for funds with the private sector in the market. If the government wants to raise short-term loans it has to pay higher rate of interest. Government borrowings will reduce the supply of funds in the market and therefore the general rate of interest in the market will rise. The government will have to raise the rate of interest further to attract subscriptions from the public and conversion of the old loans. Consequently, a higher rate of interest will check the government from raising further loans. For meeting emergency like war, the government instead of raising loans will like to increase volume of currency by resorting to printing of notes. This will increase the availability of overall credit in the economy. On the other hand the government to check a rise in the demand for non-essential commodities would impose certain controls and so more funds would be available in the market for investment and the government can borrow them.

In the long term the situation will be different. The volume of public debt can grow with the growth of national income and credit structure and therefore no limit can be fixed for public debt in the long period. It may also be noted that the powers of the government for raising loans are unlimited. It may not pay the older debt at all and may go on renewing and even converting some portion of it into perpetuation.

The most recent development in this regard is the belief that the economy cannot grow without financial growth, which necessitates compulsorily the growth of public debt. Public debt provides a strong base for the structure of the credit system in the country. The Radcliffe Committee of U.K. has emphasized the role of public debt as a powerful tool in the credit and monetary regulation of the economy.[4]

---

4. Radcliffe committee (Committee on the working of the monetary system), *Report:* Cmnd 827. Her Majesty's Stationery Office, Great Britain, August 1959.

This view of the Radcliffe Committee has received support from a number of economists.

Exercises

1. Discuss the importance of public debt in a developing economy. Examine critically the economic effects of public debt.

2. Discuss the role of public debt in developing underdeveloped economies. Point out the importance of small savings in Public Debt.

3. What is the crucial difference between internal and external loans? When is borrowing sounder than an all-tax programme?

●●●

Chapter 43

Management of Public Debt

1. Introduction

Management of public debt refers to the formation of the debt policy by the government to achieve certain objectives and the implementation of that policy. In olden times it meant the raising of loans at cheapest rates for shortest duration. Since the development of the concept of a welfare state the nature and priorities of objectives stand entirely changed, though the objective of keeping the cost of the loan operations as low as possible, still remains intact. In its totality the public debt policy would refer to the determination of the objectives, forms of debt, terms of debt, maturity period of debt instruments, repatriation of debt etc. In short, public debt management is concerned with all issues relating to the public debt structure in an economy. Debt management policy is to be subservient to the overall economic policy of the government. For example, it should help in raising the level of economic activity during the period of depression and in reducing it during the period of boom. In other words it should run in conformity with the monetary management of the country. Secondly, public borrowing must be undertaken at a time when it is most advantageous and economical to the government. Finally, it should not adversely affect the money market of the country. In a big country and particularly one having federal form of government, there should be proper co-ordination between the federation and the federating units in this respect. Not only the units should not raise loans at one and the same time, nor should the terms and conditions of the loans work at cross-purposes. So, public debt management is of great economic, social and political significance because it can produce profound effects on the economy, polity and social structure of a country. In brief, following are the chief objectives of public debt management: (*a*) loans at low cost, (*b*) repayment of the loan in shortest possible time, (*c*) stabilization of the level of economic activity in the country, and (*d*) economic growth of the country.

2. Principles of Debt Management

Some broad principles for the management of public debt have been enunciated. These are briefly stated below:

1. Low Interest Cost on Servicing Debt. This principle lays down that the interest cost of servicing a debt should be as minimum as possible. Let us view the objective laid down by the traditional economists. They believed that the low interest cost of a debt will not have adverse effects. If a debt is not self-liquidating, for the payment of interest the government will have to impose new taxes or increase the rate of old taxes which will be a burden on the poor sections of the society and will adversely affect the people's willingness to work and save. This thinking was alright so long as the volume of loan was small. But with the emergence of welfare state the government's sphere of activity extended, the need for more and more funds grew and the objectives of government expenditure multiplied. The governments have to weigh between various objectives and so long as other objectives like economic growth, economic stability are more important, the objective of low interest cost will have to be sacrificed. Further, a low interest cost loan implies that the general rate of interest in the market should be low, otherwise the government would not be able to raise loans at low rates. The central bank of the country will have to carry out its operations with this objective in view. But such a policy may lead to inflation and may create instability in the economy which will run counter to the basic objective of the debt *i.e.*, maintenance of economic stability.

2. Satisfying the Need of Investors. According to this principle the public debt should be structured in such a way that it fulfils the needs of various types of investors. It means that the types of government securities, the liability schedule, the terms and conditions etc. should be satisfying to the largest number of people in the economy. If this is not done, then there would be disturbances in the security market. If the rate of interest on the new issue is higher, then the people will sell old securities and invest in new securities. That is why it is argued that the public debt should be reduced as it matures. If the public debt servicing is done through the issue of new currency, inflation would be created and if the servicing is done through additional taxation then deflation would be created and, therefore, a judicious balance between the various methods of debt redemption will have to be struck through a skilful management of public debt.

3. Co-ordination between Public Debt, Fiscal and Monetary Policies. Since a common objective of all the three policies is the stabilization of the level of economic activity and it is of great significance for the health of the economy, it is essential that all the policies should work in unison. For example, if the government asks the central bank to maintain a low interest rate in the market so that the cost of interest payment on public debt may be low, it may lead to inflationary pressure and may cause economic stability. The public debt policy in combination with fiscal and monetary policies should be operated in such a way that all together contribute to the maintenance of economic stability and the rate of growth. This means that the repayment of public debt, the conversion of existing debts and the terms and conditions of new securities, all should aim towards this objective.

4. Funding of Short-term Debt into Long-term Debt. According to this principle the public debt management should assist in the funding of short-term debt into long-term debt as much as possible. But the funding operations should be undertaken in such a manner that the economic stability is not disturbed. The funding of short-term loans into long-term loans would lead to a rise in the long- term rate of interest, otherwise the demand for long-term funds will not increase. Consequently, the budget expenditure in future would rise. On the other hand it will lead to a reduction in the short-term interest rates because the demand for short-term funds will decline. But the rise in the long-term interest rates will cause the rate and volume of private investment to fall, leading to a situation of depression. It is, therefore, necessary that funding operations must be undertaken in such a manner that they do not lead to undue rise in the long-term rates of interest. If, the economy needs that the level of private investment should be reduced then the government of course may fund the short-term debt into long-term.

3. Redemption of Public Debt

Redemption means repayment of loans. We have already explained the traditional thinking on this subject. According to that thinking the government should pay off the public debt as early as possible. However, modern thinking is entirely different. It considers debt retirement in the overall context of debt and fiscal policies of the government and would prefer that the debt repayment policy should be shaped in accordance with the requirements of circumstances. All government loans barring permanent investment in self-supporting industries should, as far as possible, be repaid quickly. It is, therefore, necessary that the provision of repayment should be inherent in the scheme itself. There are some economists who believe that the debt should not be redeemed, it should be repudiated. But following are the obvious advantages of debt redemption:

(*i*) It saves the government from going into bankruptcy. (*ii*) It checks extravagance on the part of the government. (*iii*) It preserves the confidence of the lenders. (*iv*) It makes easy for the government to float loan in future. (*v*) It reduces the cost of management of public debt. (*vi*) It saves the future generations from the pressure of public debt. (*vii*) The resources obtained after redemption of the debt would be diverted towards private investment and therefore a favourable climate for investment could be created. (*viii*) Redemption of debt may act as a useful tool to curb deflation.

Now we take up the various methods for repayment of debts.

4. Methods of Repayment of Debt

1. Repudiation. One simple way of liquidating a debt is to repudiate it. But it is highly undesirable from a number of angles. It is unethical on the part of the government to do so and it will certainly lower its credibility and it will face a lot of difficulty in floating loans in future. So far as debt holders are concerned it will be a great loss to them especially in the case of those who had invested their life savings and who were sustaining themselves on the interest income.

Repudiation is inequitable and discriminating because it affects only one class of investors *i.e.*, the class which invests in government securities. Other sections of the society remain untouched. If an external debt is repudiated it may lead to serious difficulties for the country repudiating the debt. The creditor country may resort to economic blockade or military action etc. It is, therefore, not a wise thing to do.

2. Refunding. Refunding is the process of replacing the maturing bonds by the issue of new bonds. Sometimes the government may also redeem its bonds before the maturity date, if the general rate of interest in the market is low or if the government intends to re-arrange the maturity of outstanding debts. The process of refunding is something like this. The government offers new issue to the market and the holders of the old debt are given an option to subscribe to the new debt by surrendering the old one. Some creditors may like to have payment in cash and some refunding is others would like to pay cash for purchasing the new bonds. But refunding is undertaken chiefly for maturity requirements. Usually the short-term loans are cleared off by obtaining and by raising fresh funds through the sale of long-term securities to the public so that the short-term loans are replaced by long-term loans. A major defect of refunding is that the government would be tempted to postpone its obligation of debt redemption and the total burden of public debt would continue to mount in future. In any case refunding is a better alternative to retiring the debt when the government is not able to do so either for budgetary or for other policy reasons.

3. Conversion. Conversion implies the change of new debt for old ones. In this system the loan is not repaid but the form of debt is changed by altering a public debt from a higher rate of interest to a lower rate of interest. The government may be tempted to do so because the rate of interest in the market might have fallen and become lower than what it was at the time when the loan was floated. It would certainly reduce the burden of the debt to the government but it would also lead to less unequal distribution of income. Conversion of loans can be easily carried out if the credit of the government is good which necessarily depends upon the efficient management of the public debt. According to Professor Dalton, the conversion does not really reduce the burden of public debt on the state; because a reduction in interest rates reduces the ability of the creditors to pay taxes which may mean a loss of income to the government thereby reducing its capacity to redeem loans.

It may be interesting to note that most of the times the terms refunding and conversion are used interchangeably. Refunding is the process of postponing the debt payment while conversion is the re-arrangement of interest rates or details. Both the processes could also be confined in a single operation and may be termed either as refunding or as conversion.

4. Redemption. The government can also repay the debt. The speed of redemption can be slow as well as quick. It will depend upon the economic conditions of the borrowing country. Following methods can be adopted by a government to repay the debt:

(*i*) **Sinking Fund.** Sinking Fund is a device through which a debt is made to retire regularly. It is a fund into which a certain amount of revenue is deposited every year towards the redemption of the outstanding debt. The fund is used for the purchase of outstanding debt *i.e.*, securities and bonds. Sinking fund approach has been adopted by a number of governments. The government sets apart a certain amount out of its budget every year for this fund. The balance in the fund is also invested and the interest earned on that is also credited to the fund. It is believed that due to compounding of interest such a fund should be able to absorb a major portion of the retirement cost when the time for debt redemption comes. Sinking fund technique has been considered very sound. But during recent years this technique has been diluted considerably. Compared to the total outstanding debt, very small amounts are credited to this fund. Sometimes it remains on paper only. There are cases where the sinking fund has been misused. There is no doubt that a properly managed sinking fund definitely proves to be a faithful means of orderly debt retirement; although it is a slow process of redemption of debt and there are chances of its misuse by the government during financial crisis.

(*ii*) **Surplus Revenues.** The government may also follow a policy of surplus budgets for clearing off public debt, instead of creating a sinking fund. But during recent years surplus budget is a rare phenomenon.

(*iii*) **Terminal Annuities.** The government of a country may also issue terminal annuities, a portion of which matures every year according to the serial order or as decided by the lottery system. The advantage of this system is that the total volume of debt gets reduced every year and the cost of servicing the debt also stands reduced every year, and by the time of maturity the debt stands fully paid off.

***(iv)* Capital Levy.** Capital levy is a sort of tax on property and wealth. It is a one time tax imposed on the capital assets above certain value. Capital levy has been advocated particularly to repay the debt raised during a war. This levy is imposed on the net property or wealth on progressive scale. It is justified on the following grounds:

(1) Since war loans are unproductive, it is better to relinquish them as early as possible by a capital levy instead of imposing additional taxes for years for repaying them.

(2) Such a levy is justified because it is paid by those who earn huge profits during the war.

(3) It is also justified on the principle of equity because it is the poor who suffer during the war and therefore the responsibility of the repayment of the debt should be borne by the rich.

(4) It is counter inflationary in its effects because it removes the surplus purchasing power from the richer sections of the society.

(5) If after the war depression follows, the burden of public debt in real terms will increase and therefore the bond-holders will gain. Hence it is necessary to impose capital levy on them for the repayment of the debt. It helps to make the distribution of income equitable.

(6) It provides psychological relief to the people because they know that there will be no more taxation in future for the purpose of repaying public debt.

Dalton also suggests that capital levy should be used even for repaying peace time public debt.

However, some people do not favour a capital levy for the following reasons:

(1) It is not easy to work out a fair value of property accumulated during the war and therefore it is difficult to tax that property or wealth.

(2) It checks the inflow of capital from abroad and thus produces a bad effect on commerce and industry.

(3) It appears to be a penalty for thrift because those who save and accumulate wealth are taxed and those who squander away their incomes are saved.

(4) It may lead to evasion.

(5) It may adversely affect people's willingness to work, save and invest.

Capital levy, however, has not received a favourable consideration at the hands of many a economists. According to Mrs. Hicks, "A levy thus, amounts to a major surgical operation on the body politic; it will either kill or cure, and be very different in its effects from regular dosage or massage applied by the normal tax structure."

Exercises

1. Discuss the various methods of debt redemption.
2. What do you mean by debt management? State and explain the principles of debt management.

•••

Chapter 44

Public Debt in India

We have already dealt with the general issues related to public debt in an earlier chapter. In this chapter we propose to discuss the broad issues connected with Indian public debt, debts of the Central and State Governments. We confine ourselves to the analysis of the position of public debt since 1951. Borrowing powers of the Central and State Governments have been prescribed in Articles 292 and 293 of the Indian Constitution. Article 292 lays down that the Union Government may borrow and give guarantees upon the security of Consolidated Fund of India within the limits fixed by the Parliament. Article 293 lays down that the State Governments may borrow within India and give guarantees upon the security of the Consolidated Fund of State within the limits fixed by the State Legislatures. This article also prohibits the State Governments to raise loans from outside India. Even within India a State government having outstanding loan from the Government of India or having a loan for which the Government of India has given guarantee, can't borrow without the consent of the Government of India. Reserve Bank of India which manages the public debt operations of the Central and State Governments does not allow any competition for raising loans in the open market either between the States or the Centre. The Reserve Bank of India fixes an order of priority in respect of State borrowings and also the timing of loans. Ever since India achieved independence its public debt has been on the rise, owing to: (*a*) the implementation of the Five-Year Plans, (*b*) the withdrawal of excess liquidity to reduce inflationary pressure, and (*c*) to meet expenditure. However; the mounting wasteful non-developmental public expenditure, which the governments have failed to avoid, has also led to an increase in public expenditure. Now we take up first the issues related to the public debt of the Government of India.

1. Public Debt of Government of India

The public debt of Government of India has been officially classified as: (*a*) Public Debt and (*b*) Other Liabilities, although "other liabilities" are also the obligations of the Government of India and should not be separated from the public debt of Government of India. But, this classification is justified on the ground that while public debt obligations are to be met out of the Consolidated Fund of India, other liabilities are to be met out of the Public Account Fund of India.

Public debt comprises: (1) Internal debt, and (2) External debt.

1. Internal Debt

It comprises of loans raised within the country. These loans are repayable from the Consolidated Fund of India. Internal debt has been classified further as given below:

(*i*) **Market Borrowings or Loans.** These are known by various names like term loans, funded loans, dated loans and permanent loans. These are generally term loans and dated loans and form a major portion of the internal debt. The government issues market loans every year by the sale of securities or otherwise. For example, the Government of India introduced in 1992-93 a scheme of sale of dated securities by auction, thereby carrying interest rates as determined by the market forces in marked departure from the practice generally followed in raising loans at specific interest rates. The sole purpose was to broaden the market for gilt-edged securities. In 1993-94, two more varieties of dated securities *viz.*, 'Deep-Discounted Bonds' and "Zero Coupon Bonds"—the former of longer maturity and the latter of 5 year maturity—were introduced. Another variety *viz.*, Capital Indexed Bonds (providing for inflation indexing of the principal amount) was also introduced later. Since 2002-03, the government has also been announcing half-yearly indicative market borrowing programme based on its core borrowing needs. On March 25, 2004 the government introduced the Market Stabilisation Scheme under which it issues dated securities/treasury bills upto a specified limit, in favour of RBI to check addition to "hot money" supply for checking inflationary pressures emerging from our mounting foreign exchange reserves. Such securities are in addition to the normal borrowing of the Government of India. The volume of market loans has grown from Rs. 1,438.46 crore in 1950-51 to Rs. 70,528.38 crore in 1990-91 and Rs. 2,396,846 crore in 2006-07 (BE).

(*ii*) Market Loans in Course of Repayment. The loans raised by the Government in the past are repaid by the issue of new securities and are called as market loans in course of repayment.

(*iii*) Treasury Bills. Treasury bills are the most important source of short-term funds for the Government to fill the gap between revenue and expenditure.

They provide an attractive form of investment to the banks. To meet the increasing demand for funds for investment in Five-Year Plans, the Government of India has taken recourse to heavy borrowing through the issue of these bills. The Reserve Bank of India holds the major portion of the treasury bills issued by the Government of India while State Governments, Commercial Banks and other parties stand comparatively lower in order. These bills can be converted into cash without the holder suffering much loss. These are of two kinds: (*a*) Ad-hoc treasury bills issued by the Central Government to the Reserve Bank of India, (*b*) Bills sold to the public.

(*iv*) Treasury Bills Funded into Special Securities. These bills are a source of medium-term loans and are funded into special securities. It implies that these bills are converted into special securities whose payment is made in instalments. Since there is no interest admissible on these securities they are sold at a discount. These treasury bills were introduced in 1992-93.

(*v*) Special Securities Issued to Reserve Bank of India. The Government of India also takes loan as a temporary measure from Reserve Bank of India by issuing special securities, which are non-negotiable and non-interest bearing. The Government has to repay the amount of this debt at the call of the Reserve Bank of India. Hence, these are short term in nature and their maturity period is at the most 12 months or one financial year.

(*vi*) 364 Days Treasury Bills. These bills were introduced in 1992-93 to enable the development of market for government securities. These are not re-discountable with the Reserve Bank of India and are periodically offered for sale on auction basis by the Reserve Bank of India at Mumbai. These bills are of short term and are offered to financial institutions and other parties.

(*vii*) Compensation Bonds. The Government of India has issued from time to time various kinds of bonds in the open market which are of long-term nature. For example, the Government introduced Capital Investment Bonds on 28th June, 1982 carrying a rate of interest of 7% and having a maturity period of 10 years. National Rural Development Bonds of 7 years maturity were issued on 9th July, 1979 and carried an interest rate of 7.5%. These were exempted from Capital Gains Tax. National Rural Development Bonds (second issue) with a maturity period of 3 years were issued on 7 July, 1983 carrying interest at the rate of 7.5%. Besides, the Government of India has also raised loans in the form of Compensation Bonds particularly at the time of the nationalisation of commercial banks. These were issued in 1980 and were of two kinds: (*a*) 6% Bonds 1990 to be issued at 100% and redeemable at par on 15th April, 1990, (*b*) 7% Bonds 2010 to be issued at 100% and redeemable at par on 15 April, 2010.

(*viii*) Securities Issued to International Financial Institutions. By way of its contribution to the share capital of international financial institutions the Government of India issued non-negotiable and non-interest bearing securities to the various institutions like International Monetary Fund, International Bank for Reconstruction and Development, International Development Association, International Fund for Agricultural Development, African Development Bank and Asian Development Bank. These securities were issued in lieu of cash. The Government of India has to pay the amount of these securities at the call of these institutions and in this sense it is a kind of short-term loan upon the Government of India.

The total internal public debt of the Government of India had increased from Rs. 2,022.30 crore in 1950-51 to Rs. 3,34,914.15 crore in 1996-97 and was estimated to be of the order of Rs. 17,33,532.90 crore for the year 2007-08 (B.E.). The total internal debt at the end of 2007-08 for selected years is given in Table 46.1.

Table 46.1: Internal Public Debt of Government of India

(In crore of Rupees)

Year (*End of March*)	*Total Debt* (*Cumulative*)
1950-51	2,022.30
1960-61	3,978.00
1980-81	29,008.49
1990-91	1,54,003.77
2000-01 (RE)	8,04,527.58
2001-02 (BE)	8,92,984.92
2007-08 (BE)	17,33,532.90

It may be noted that the net increase in the burden of internal public debt in a particular year is estimated after making allowance for the repayment of loans in that year out of the gross market borrowings for that year.

Causes for the Growth of Internal Debt

The most fundamental cause for the growth of internal debt has been the continuously rising fiscal deficit of the Government of India. This implies that the expenditure of the Government of India has always been in excess of its total revenue receipts. This situation has been caused by a number of factors: (*a*) Open ended subsidies and other commitments, (*b*) losses incurred by the public sector undertakings, (*c*) all round wasteful public expenditure, (*d*) unending expansion of administrative machinery. The root cause has been an utter lack of financial discipline. Besides, deficit spending is itself a self-sustaining process. It creates a vicious circle. It gives rise to inflationary forces, resulting in increase of government expenditure, necessitating further loans and so on. Over the years, the debt servicing charges have become the most important item of government expenditure and lead to further debt. For instance, the interest payment of the Government of India in 1995-96 was of the order of Rs. 52,000.00 crore which was 30.2 per cent of total budgeted expenditure of Rs. 1,72,151.00 crore. In the Budget for 2007-08, interest payments were budgeted at Rs. 1,63,994.93 crore constituting 32.7% of net revenue receipts of the Centre. Again, most of the loans are not invested in income generating assets. And so the Government of India has to borrow more and more just to service the existing debt.

Ownership pattern is also of importance. The ownership of public debt indicates the capacity of the government in pursuing proper debt management and monetary policies. In the case of internal debt the RBI happens to be official public debt agent. It also underwrites loan flotations and therefore it buys a major chunk of the so-called market or permanent (dated or funded) loans. Such a large holding enables the Reserve Bank of India to conduct open market operations. These holdings also add to the money supply in circulation. Commercial banks are other major holders of permanent loans and the remaining portion is held by provident funds etc. So, the general public holds only a nominal amount of the securities. In addition, the treasury bills are almost totally held by the Reserve Bank of India, State Bank of India and other banks hold only a nominal amount of these bills. Again special securities are also with the Reserve Bank of India. Besides, other special securities are also issued for the Reserve Bank of India, which are normally in the nature of additional instalments of existing loans. Securities issued to international financial institutions are also retained with the Reserve Bank of India. Thus, the Reserve Bank of India holds the major portion of Government of India's internal debt.

2. External Debt

This represents the loans raised by the Government of India in other countries. According to our Constitution only the Government of India can raise external loans. If a foreign loan is meant for the use of a State then the Government of India re-lends it to the State. So, India's external debt is not the same thing as the external debt of Government of India, because the former includes loans to non-government borrowers as well. The Government of India raises loans from different sources which include international agencies, governments and other aid giving organisations. Most of this loan is on concessional terms and of long maturities. Medium-term loans come mostly from the IMF.

The external assistance has been received in various forms, for example outright grants, loans repayable in rupees and loans repayable in foreign currencies. Surplus agriculture commodities have been supplied mostly against payment of rupees and loans and grants have been from the accumulation from such counterpart funds. Foreign suppliers also provide deferred credit.

A number of countries have also made available technical assistance whose terms are different. International Monetary Fund has also provided short-term assistance for correcting the imbalance in the balance of payments. The Government of India has also made borrowings in the form of loans, cash grant, commodity grants and special credits from the friendly countries like Canada, Denmark, France, Japan, Sweden, UK, USA, USSR. Total external debt of India was Rs. 32.03 crore in 1950-51 Rs. 31,524.97 crore in 1990-91, Rs. 53,619.58 crore in 1996-97 and Rs. 8,340.97 crore (BE) 2007-08. Table 46.2 gives an idea of the external public debt of India in selected years.

Table 46.2: External Public Debt of GOI

(In crore of Rupees)

Year	*Total External Debt (Cumulative)*
1950-51	32.03
1960-61	760.96
1980-81	10,782.39
1990-91	31,524.97
2000-01	65,945
2002-03	68,520
2005-06	6,997.84
2006-07 (Revised)	7,921.33
2007-08 (BE)	8,340.97

The rapid increase in the external debt of the Government of India can be due to the following reasons:

(1) Since the Constitution does not allow the States to borrow from abroad, all external loans on their behalf are raised by the Government of India.

(2) The Government of India has to make huge imports covering defence items, essential consumption goods and industrial inputs. In some cases the government collects rupee resources from within the country by selling these goods but then, its debt to foreigners increases.

(3) The Government of India has been following the policy of not encouraging direct foreign investment and instead has been obtaining loans from abroad. These loans have to be repaid with interest, irrespective of the fact whether these have been put to productive use or whether they have been used to generate export earnings or not.

(4) Finally, generally, these loans have not been used to generate adequate earnings. There has been an increase in the debt servicing charges despite the concessional terms on which these loans have been raised.

Other Outstanding Liabilities

Under the category of other outstanding liabilities of the Government of India are included the following deposits:

(1) Small Savings Scheme and Five-Year Time Deposits.

(2) Public Provident Fund and State Provident Fund Contributions.

(3) Deposits in other accounts *i.e.*, special deposits of Non-government Provident Funds and other items.

(4) Reserve Funds and Deposits of various departments.

We now briefly explain each of the above in the following paragraphs:

1. Small Savings Scheme. Small Savings Scheme is the safest source of government borrowing as it takes away the genuine savings of the people and also provides the government with the required capital without creating inflationary pressure in the economy. The greater the volume of small savings to the Government's borrowing, the better it is for the monetary stability of the country. But, the contribution of small savings is rather limited even in developed countries. In under-developed countries it is not an unusual situation because the people are poor and they are unable to save. However, the Government of India has always made efforts to promote small savings. The Government of India has a number of schemes to collect small savings like the Post Office Savings Bank Deposits, Cumulative Time Deposits, National Saving Certificates. Small Savings amounted to Rs. 336.87 crore in 1950-51. Since then there has been a tremendous increase in their amount. In 1990-91 these were of the order of Rs. 50,100.18 crore, in 1995-96 these were Rs. 91,786.03 crore. in 1996-97 these stood at Rs. 1,04,056.03 crore and in 2007-08 these savings were estimated at Rs. 2,59,246.80 crore (B.E.).

2. Provident Fund Contributions. Provident Fund contributions are collected under: (*i*) State Provident Fund, and (*ii*) Public Provident Fund. These outstandings were of the order of Rs. 95.05 crore in 1950-51, which increased to Rs. 11,670.34 crore in 1990-91, Rs. 29,638.50 crore in 1995-96, Rs. 34,788.50 crore in 1996-97 and were estimated to be Rs. 40,338.50 (B.E.) crore in 2001-02. (*iii*) Special Deposits of non-government Provident Funds have also been quite useful. The outstanding liabilities of the Government of India under this head were only Rs. 16.10 crore in 1950-51 but they increased to Rs. 45,336.43 crore in 1990-91, Rs. 1,02,420.95 crore in 1996-97 and Rs. 1,56,451.88 crore (B.E.) in 2001-02. During recent years these have declined from Rs. 40,850.13 crore in 2005-06 to Rs. 19,571.90 crore in 2007-08 (B.E.).

3. Reserve Funds and Deposits. Deposits under the Income Tax Annuity Deposits Schemes and the Special Deposits Schemes, depreciation and other interest bearing reserve funds of departments like railways and post and telegraphs and deposits of local funds and civil deposits and unclaimed balance of old loans (which do not bear any interest from the date of discharge) are included under this head. The total outstanding liabilities of Government of

India on this account were Rs. 363.05 in 1950-51, Rs. 21,922.17 crore in 1990-91, Rs. 33,680.05 crore in 1995-96, Rs. 39,019.78 crore (RE) in 1996-97 and Rs. 41,739.60 crore (B.E.) in 2007-08.

The main reason for the phenomenal rise in other liabilities of Government of India is that the Government in order to fulfil its financial needs has tried to explore all possible means for raising additional resources. Consequently, the Government also exploited this source of funds to the maximum. The Government adopted various means like tax incentives to divert the savings of the economy to the government treasury in the form of various schemes described above. So far as the ownership pattern is concerned this represents genuine savings of the household and corporate sectors. Reserve funds are created from various public concerns while deposits are acquired from the business sector and the general public.

2. Burden of Public Debt

The mounting public debt of India has led to fierce controversy in the Parliament and the State Legislature during recent years. The various parliamentary committees have gone to the extent of emphasising the need for fixing a statutory limit to the government borrowing since in their view the government has been making excessive use of its borrowing power. Article 292 of the Indian Constitution empowers the Parliament to fix a statutory limit on government borrowing. But so far, the Parliament has not fixed any limit within which the Government of India may raise internal and external loans. The question of fixing the statutory limit was raised by the Estimates Committee in their Twentieth Report. The Public Accounts Committee in their Ninth Report had also recommended that the Finance Ministry should undertake a study of the procedure followed in various democratic countries for obtaining parliamentary approval for government borrowing. Accordingly the Finance Ministry studied the practice of fixing a statutory limit in UK, USA, Canada and Ceylon (Sri Lanka) and concluded that even in these countries no real purpose has been served by fixing such limits. In this connection the Finance Ministry stated that "the government is satisfied that no real advantage would be secured by prescribing statutory limits on government borrowing because of the following:[1]

(1) The extent of government's borrowings is indicated both in the Five-Year Plans and annual budgets of the Government. The Parliament exercises its control over government borrowing while discussing Five-Year Plans as well as annual budgets.

(2) Rigid statutory limits would hardly be practicable.

1. Ninth Report of Public Accounts Committee (3rd Lok Sabha 1956) Appendix. pp. 10-11.

(3) Fixation of limit on borrowing from the Reserve Bank of India and external borrowing is not possible. The borrowings from the Reserve Bank of India implies deficit financing and it is resorted to when Government's requirements are not fulfilled from any of the sources including market and external borrowings."

Burden of Internal Public Debt

With a view to examining, whether the present volume of internal public debt is burdensome or not, we have to take into account all relevant factors and study the entire question in relation to the effect of public debt on national income, government revenue and expenditure, asset creation etc. We now take up this in the following:

1. Public Debt and National Income. The relative magnitude of the public debt and the national income is an important indicator of manageability or retirement of public debt and therefore must be taken into account for assessing the burden of public debt.

Looking into the debt position of other countries, the concern expressed in various quarters regarding the burden of internal public debt of Government of India appears to be rather baseless. The debt-income ratio is very much small as compared to other countries. For example, in 1993-94 when this ratio in the case of India was 34 per cent, in Ireland it was 68.70 per cent, in USA it was 41.2 per cent and in Australia it was 40 per cent. However, according to certain economists if the public debt grows at a faster rate than the growth of national income, the magnitude of the burden of the debt servicing will be considered as high. No doubt, in India the magnitude is comparatively small but the rate of growth of public debt is higher than that of national income. Hence, the burden of public debt can be considered as high and it is increasing at a faster pace. The fact, however, remains that it is the low rate of growth of national income which is the villain of the piece and not the high rate of growth of public debt. It is, therefore, necessary that we should make all out effort to increase the rate of growth of our economy.

2. Interest on Internal Debt and National Income. The financial burden of the internal debt can also be measured by the annual interest payment or by the payment of the debt servicing charges. It is also known as debt servicing burden. If the ratio of interest payments to national income is taken into account it will be more meaningful. This ratio had increased from 0.35 per cent in 1950-51 to an estimated 5.1 per cent in 1993-94. This clearly goes to show that the tax burden has been on the increase. Interest cost of this magnitude does not appear to be very burdensome. It is because the rate of interest is very low. Even then it is increasing every year.

3. Tax Revenue and Debt Services. The tax burden ultimately refers to the increase in taxation necessary to finance the debt servicing charges. The portion of tax revenue absorbed by the debt services is therefore an important indicator of the burden of public debt. The position can be known from Table 46.3.

Table 46.3: Ratio of Interest Payment to Tax Revenue

(Rs in crore)

Year	*Interest Payment*	*Tax Revenue to Tax Revenue*	*Interest Payment* as *% age*
1950-51	32.40	314.6	9.50
1960-61	118.80	703.60	16.90
1980-81	2,684.00	9,358.00	27.00
1990-91	21,471.00	42,978.00	49.90
2000-01	1,00,667.00	2,06,166.00	48.8
2001-02	1,12,300.00	2,38,272.00	48.4
2007-08 (B.E.)	1,59,000.00	403,870.00	39.3

This ratio increased from 9.5 per cent to 48.4 per cent during the last 51 years. In recent years it has shown a declining trend owing to the applicable increase in tax revenue. Even then the current ratio is quite high.

4. Ratio of Interest Payments to Public Expenditure. The ratio of net interest payments to public expenditure is another indicator of the debt servicing burden. Table 46.4 indicates the ratio of interest payments to public expenditure on revenue account.

Table 46.4: Interest Payments and Public Expenditure

(In crore of Rupees)

Year	*Interest Payment*	*Total Public Expenditure (Revenue Account)*	*Interest Payment as % age of Revenue Account*
1950-51	32.40	346.00	9.00
1960-61	118.80	926.00	9.84
1980-81	2,604.00	14,410.00	18.00
1990-91	21,471.00	73,516.00	29.20
1995-96	50,031.00	1,39,860.00	35.50
1996-97	1,00,667.00	1,58,988.00 (R.E.)	36.80
2001-02	1,12,300.00	1,83,713.00 (B.E.)	36.90
2007-08	1,59,000.00	6,55,625.27 (B.E.)	24.04

From the above table it is clear that the portion of public expenditure absorbed by the interest payments had been increasing continuously but in recent years it has started declining. Even then it is high. Since this is a sort of non-development expenditure, the position does not seem to be very happy.

5. Public Debt and Asset Creation. The burden of public debt is also determined by the manner in which these funds are used. For example, if the borrowed funds are used in asset creation, the burden of public debt would be less, because this will lead to increase in the income of the nation and the cost or burden of the debt would be offset by the benefits that the debt confers. In India most of the borrowed funds have been utilised for the purpose of asset creation in public sector. From Table 46.5 it would be clear that burden of public debt upon Indian economy has not been unbearable or heavy. Even then the situation is not very satisfactory. It is also a fact that the borrowed resources are not fully being utilised for productive purposes. A very important indication of the unproductive use of public debt is the growing deficit on revenue account. It implies that the Government of India is meeting its current expenditure out of its borrowings. This is true of both the Government of India and the State Governments. And one reason is that the public sector undertakings have not given reasonable returns which has led to increasing budgetary deficits.

Table 46.5: Public Debt and Capital Outlays

(In crore of Rupees)

Year	*Total Liabilities (Net)*	*Capital Outlays and Loans Advanced to States* and *U.Ts*	*Excess Liabilities over Outlays and Loans Advanced to States and U.T.*	*Total of columns* 3 and 4
1	2	3	4	5
1950-51	2,565.40	1,709.69	856.10	2,565.79
1960-61	6,224.24	6,124.69	119.55	6,244.24
1980-81	58,998.36	58,998.81	N.A.	58,998.81
1990-91	3,14,257.81	2,36,740.30	77,517.56	3,14,257.86
1996-97	6,68,518.99	4,32,868.20	2,35,656.79	6,68,524.99
1997-98	7,33,921.19	4,68,651.23	2,65,269.96	7,33,921.19
2007-08	16,11,645.92	17,35,836.40	(–) 1,24,190.48	16,11,645.92

Burden of External Debt

External debt whether in the form of grant or loan or assistance generates resource inflow. Whether external debt is burdensome or not depends upon how it is being used. If it is being used for importing items of food or drugs or capital goods or technical know-how, then it will not be considered as burdensome as when it is used for the imports of avoidable consumer goods. The burdensomeness of foreign debt thus depends upon: (*i*) the terms and conditions of its servicing; (*ii*) addition to productive capacity of the country; and (*iii*) creation of export capability. We may now analyse the issue with reference to the external debt of the Government of India.

As we know, almost the entire amount of foreign loans of the Government of India have been obtained on the most favourable terms, either interest free or at a very low rate of interest with long repayment periods. On that account the burden of foreign debt has been just nominal. Also, because rate of exchange having moved against the rupee, a continuous rise in the international prices the real burden of debt servicing has relatively diminished. So, the burden of external debt arises from its huge size, unproductive and indiscriminate use and other factors. It has been observed that the Government of India even obtained loans for projects and programmes which did not involve any imports. We kept in hanging, a number of high priority social and economic projects merely because the foreign aid was not readily available. We also did not ensure that the foreign loans were used to enhance our export capability. Consequently, our debt service ratio has reached to a very high level and it is believed that we are now on the verge of falling into an external debt trap.

The servicing of external debt creates serious problems of resources because their repayment is complicated. It is not merely a transfer of resources from one group to another. The borrowing country has to surrender a certain amount of purchasing power which could otherwise be used for useful purposes. In addition, it has its own effect on budgetary operations and plans of payment because in the budget the amount equal to the foreign exchange required for debt servicing is to be allocated. The conversion of the rupee into foreign exchange imposes heavy strain on the balance of payments. Again, when a large proportion of Government's revenue is used for external debt servicing, the government has to cut down its investment expenditure. Our total interest payments on account of external borrowings increased from Rs. 13.5 crore at the end of the First Plan to Rs. 237.00 crore by the end of the Third Plan.

3. Public Debt of State Governments

A State Government can also obtain loans from the Government of India. But under the Constitution if a State is already indebted to the Government of India or if the Central Government has given a guarantee to the loan raised by the State and if that loan has not been fully repaid, then the Central Government can impose any condition it considers necessary for fresh loans to the State. Since practically every State Government is indebted to the Central Government, the latter can always exercise that constitutional authority. State Loans are divided into:

(*i*) Internal Debt consisting of: (*a*) Market Loans and Bonds, (*b*) Ways and Means Advances from Reserve Bank of India, (*c*) Loans from Banks and other institutions, (*ii*) Loans advances from the Centre, (*iii*) Provident Fund etc.

Table 46.6 indicates the position of total liabilities of the State Governments in selected years:

Table 46.3: Total liabilities of the state governments

(Rs. in crore)

Items	*As on March 31*		
	1961	1971	2007
(*i*) Internal Debt	590	1850	7,18,190
(*ii*) Loans and Advances from the Central Government	2,020	6,360	2,63,300
(*iii*) Provident Funds etc.	130	540	2,77,180
Total	2,740	8,750	12,58,670

The following characteristics of States liabilities are worth noting:

(*a*) These have increased at the rate of 1% of the GDP per year and now stand around 30% of the GDP. This increase has been more significant during 1997-2007.

(*b*) Internal debt of States as a percentage of total liabilities has increased from 22 to 57.

(*c*) The proportion of central loans and advances in the total liabilities has declined from 74% to 21%.

(*d*) The interest burden (ratio of interest payments to revenue receipts) has more than doubled *i.e.*, it has risen from about 14% to about 29%.

The States do not depend heavily on market loans, because: (*i*) they do not enjoy the advantage of having a 'captive' market like the Government of India; (*ii*) The Central Government collects household savings under various schemes and passes on a portion of these collections to the States as loans; (*iii*) Plan assistance from the Central Government to States is also in the form of debt.

The burdensomeness of the public debt of State Governments originates from the fact that most of these loans are used for consumption purposes, meeting revenue expenditure and debt relief etc. The investments made in State Electricity Boards, irrigation projects, road transportation etc., are not backed by income generating assets. So far as their impact on the economy is concerned they do not add to the inflationary pressure or to inequalities in the distribution of income. States received loans from the Government of India both for Plan and non-Plan purposes. In the past there were a number of interest rates and the terms of repayments also varied. The share of small savings that the States received from the Centre was also in the form of loans.

Successive Finance Commissions have expressed concern over the increasing indebtedness of the States without any increase in their repaying capacity. While the Third Finance Commission advocated a thorough review of the situation, the Fourth Commission desired that the Centre should fix the terms and conditions of loans for each State on a case to case basis. The Fifth Commission recommended that the non-productive category of loans to States should be reduced to the maximum possible extent. According to the Sixth Commission the problem of State indebtedness was not its absolute size but the repaying capacity of the State concerned. It was not in favour of writing off any debt. Therefore, it recommended categorisation of State loans with different degree of relief in terms and conditions of repayment amounting to Rs. 1,969.92 crore. Similarly the Seventh Commission also did not favour the idea of writing off State debts and recommended relief to the extent of Rs. 2,155.80 crore in debt servicing and repayment schedules.

One of the terms of reference of the Eighth Finance Commission was to suggest suitable measures regarding the entire non-Plan capital gap. Therefore, the Commission covered all outstanding Central loans including small savings and overdraft loans. According to the Commission the most serious problem in the Union-State financial relations was of overdrafts. The Commission was not in favour of changing the terms of repayment of overdraft loans. The Commission was also not in favour of converting these small savings loans into perpetuity. They were also not in favour of liberalisation of the terms of these loans. At the same time the Commission provided relief to the States on the remaining loans on a progressive basis. It took the percentage of Central loans (excluding small savings and overdraft loans) as on 31st March, 1984 of the State Domestic Product (average 1976-79) and divided the States into four categories. This classification was modified with reference to their overall non-Plan capital gap. Taking the maximum period of repayment of loans as 30 years, the relief was not to exceed 35 per cent of non-Plan capital gap in the States of Group 1. For categories 2, 3, and 4 these limits were fixed at 55 per cent, 75 per cent and 85 per cent respectively. Pre-1979 loans outstanding on 31st March, 1984 were consolidated into 25 annual instalments for U.P. and into 30 annual instalments for some other States and no change was made in the case of some States. Similarly, the post-1979 loans outstanding on 31st March, 1984 were consolidated into one loan for each State and made repayable from 1984-85 onwards in 15, 20 and 25 equal annual instalments for specified States respectively. Twelve States were given a relief by writing off a debt of Rs. 405.20 crore falling due for repayment during 1984-89. Total relief recommended was equal to Rs. 2,285.00 crore.

The Ninth Finance Commission was asked to review the entire debt position of States as at the end of March, 1989 and suggest measures for dealing with their non-Plan capital gap. The Commission found that the States on that date had a debt of Rs. 79,643.00 crore excluding short-term loans and ways and means advances (Rs. 9,778.00 crore) with a grand total of Rs. 89,461.00 crore. Out of these the Central loans amounted to Rs. 56,052.00 crore against which repayments during 1995 stood at Rs. 15,529.00 crore.

The State indebtedness has suffered from many weaknesses. The States did not maintain any amortisation funds. Two-thirds of loans given by them to State Electricity Boards were in the form of perpetuity. Accordingly, the recoveries were small and inadequate to meet their repayment obligations. The Ninth Finance Commission did not favour the idea of writing off and rescheduling of the payment of loans because they thought that this step would encourage financial indiscipline and violate inter-State equity. Further, the Commission recommended the following debt relief:

(1) to erstwhile Union Territories, Rs. 191.00 crore; (2) against drought loans, Rs. 198.88 crore; (3) against Bhopal Gas Tragedy, Rs. 91.62 crore; (4) against State Plan Schemes, Rs. 494.14 crore; (5) Total relief Rs. 975.62 crore.

While noting the causes responsible for State indebtedness the Tenth Finance Commission concluded that any debt relief to States should satisfy three conditions: (1) Its amount should be limited. (2) States under severe fiscal difficulties should be given preferential treatment. (3) Debt relief should be linked with incentives for better fiscal management.

Accordingly, the Commission provided a scheme of debt relief having two components: (*i*) All States were extended debt relief linked to their fiscal performance. It amounted to a write off of 5 per cent of the amounts becoming repayable during 1995-2000 on loans outstanding on 31st March, 1995. This part of relief worked out at Rs. 5.92 crore. (*ii*) The Commission provided an additional relief exclusively to Special Category States as also to Orissa, Bihar and U.P. This relief was also 5 per cent of loans outstanding as on 31st March, 1995 and repayable during 1995-2000. This relief amounted to Rs. 201.51 crore. In addition, Punjab was given a relief of Rs. 490.63 crore by way of write-offs. The relief under the second component totalled Rs. 701.14 crore and the total debt relief stood at Rs. 1,266.07 crore.

In the context of its terms of reference the Eleventh Finance Commission (E.F.C.) examined in depth the conceptual and practiical issues pertaining to the "long term sustainability of debt" and suggested the basic conditions necessary for achieving it.

With regard to debt relief the E.F.C. increased the limit of incentive-based relief from 10% to 25% and recommended its non-inclusion in grants under article 275, because these were not based on fiscal improvement and these were to decrease over time. The amount of such grants was estimated as Rs. 600-700 crore over the five year period.

The E.F.C. recommended discontinuance of: (*a*) special relief to 13 States facing fiscal problems, and (*b*) incentive scheme for encouraging retirement of debt from the proceeds of disinvestment, recommend earlier by the Tenth F.C.

Another debt relief measure, a major one, was the *debt swap* introduced in June 2002 by the Centre under which the States would swap their loans from the Centre with additional market borrowings and a small part of small savings transfers. It would be useful to note that the practice of treating, the transfers from the small savings collections to the States by the Centre as loans was discontinued from 1999-2000, when the Centre delinked the collections of small savings from its fiscal deficit and created the National Small Savings Fund (NSSF). Since then all small savings collections are credited to this fund and from January 15,2000, the States and U.Ts, share was raised from 75% to 80% and are invested in Central/State government securities. From 2002-03, the entire net collections of NSSF in each State/ U.T. are being advanced to the State/U.T. concerned as investment in its special securities and form a part of its internal debt. And so, the introduction of the *debt swap* scheme has been a major measure of debt relief to the States.

Regarding assistance for externally aided projects, the EFC recommended the continuance of the existing arrangement. The EFC also recommended for (*i*) statutory checks on public borrowings, (*ii*) containment of the growing contingent liabilities, and (*iii*) the setting up of a sinking fund in each State for the amortisation of debt.

The Twelfth Finance Commission (T.F.C.) after thoroughly examining all the aspects of the issue relating to the sustainability of State indebtedness, measures adopted so far on the recommendations of the FCs and the suggestions received from various quarters inter-alia recommended as follows:

(*a*) the enactment of FRBMA by each State—as a basic condition for debt relief.

(*b*) consolidation of all loans outstanding on 31 March, 2005 and rescheduling of their repayment in 20 equal annual instalments, bearing 7.5% rate of interest.

(*c*) A debt write off scheme based on the reduction of revenue deficit of States—implying that if a State brings down its revenue deficit to nil, the entire repayments during the award period would be written off.

(*d*) Except some fiscally weak States (which could be aided by the Centre in raising loans from the market—but the interest rate charged should be aligned to the marginal cost of borrowing for the Centre) other States should be allowed to raise loans direct from the market.

(*e*) External aid related loans should be given to the States on the same terms and conditions as are attached to such assistance by the funding agencies and should be managed through a separate fund in the public account.

(*f*) Each State should set up a sinking fund only for redemption of loans.

(*g*) Each State should set up a guarantee redemption fund through earmarked guarantee fees determined in relation to the risk weighting of guarantees.

It should be noted that these relief measures are not the solution of the problem of State indebtedness. The real solution lies in removing the causes that generate the problem and this requires a concerted effort both by the Centre and the States.

4. Public Debt and Development Finance in India

There has been a phenomenal increase in the public debt of India since the beginning of the Five-Year Plans. Broadly speaking, the Governments in the under-developed countries fully realise that the economic development of the country cannot be undertaken with normal resources. The scope for mobilising additional resources through taxation is very limited and so is the case with deficit financing because it leads to inflation. So the best course is to mobilise resources through public borrowings. Towards the end of 2002-03 the Government of India's total liabilities comprising internal debt of Rs. 17,33,532.90 crore, external borrowings of Rs. 8,340.97 crore and other liabilities amounting to Rs. 9,48,930 crore totalled to Rs. 26,90,803.87 crore which clearly indicates that public borrowings have been of great help in mobilising resources for the execution of our development plans.

Financing of development programmes by raising loans is also considered a better proposition because neither it leads to extra burden for the present generation nor does it affect the standard of living of the people. On the other hand, financing of the development plans through borrowing confers lot of benefits on the people without much sacrifice and therefore the growing public debt should not be a matter of great concern as long as the national income rises at a satisfactory rate. This also leads to the enhancement of the taxable capacity of the people.

In India the national income has increased with the mounting public debt because the loans raised have been invested firstly, in departmental undertakings like Railways, Post and Telegraphs, Telecommunications, Road and Transport Services and Atomic Energy Department. The Government has invested huge amounts in autonomous corporations and companies like Shipping Corporation, Heavy Electricals, Hindustan Steels, Damodar Valley Corporation etc. Secondly, the Government has contributed to the share capital of the industrial and agricultural lending institutions which are contributing to the development of agricultural and industrial development of the country. Thirdly, the Government is giving a part of these loans to State Governments and Union Territories which utilise the borrowed funds for financing industrial, agricultural and other development projects.

Fourthly, the Government has been investing substantial amounts in the development and creation of assets in the field of various services like: (*a*) General services including administrative services such as Public Service Commissions, Police, Supplies and Disposals, Stationery and Printing, Public Works, and Defence Services etc.; (*b*) Social and Community Services which include education, sports, arts and culture, medical and public health, family welfare, housing, urban development, labour and employment, social security and welfare etc.; (*c*) Economic services like agriculture and allied activities (such as animal husbandry, dairy development, fisheries, forestry and wild life, food research, and warehousing etc.), investment expenditure, capital expenditure on financial institutions, rural development and other programmes such as co-operation and on major, medium and minor irrigation projects. Economic services also include power projects, industry and minerals, small scale and village industries, railways, ports and light houses, atomic energy, electronic, metallurgical industries, cement and fertiliser industries etc.; (*d*) Loans to State Governments and Union Territories, Foreign Governments, Public Sector Enterprises, Government servants, etc. Table 46.8 gives the position of capital investments and loans of the Government of India as on 31 March, 2006.

Table 46.8: Capital Investments and Loans by the Central Government

(In crore of Rupees)

	1950-51	1990-91	2000-01	2005-06
A. Capital outlay				
1. General Services	496.74	31,023	1,17,811	2,44,452
2. Social Services	26.50	4,881	10,211	10,652
3. Economic Services	965.02	87,244	2,09,908	2,93,648
Total	1,488.26	1,23,148	3,37,930	5,48,752
B. Loans Advanced by the Central Government	220.68	1,14,726	3,38,651	6,12,701
Total capital outlay and Loans Advanced by Central Government (A + B)	1,708.94	2,37,874	6,76,581	11,61,453
C. Cash Balance under MSS	—	—	—	80,500
D. Total Liabilities	2,565.40	3,14,558	11,68,241	22,31,588
E. Excess of Liabilities over Capital outlays and Loans	856.71	77,817	4,91,660	10,69,492
F. E as % of D	33.4	24.7	42.1	47.9

5. Is India in Debt Trap?

It is a fact that the public debt of India has grown by leaps and bounds during the last fifty years particularly since India adopted development planning. Most of the economists are of the view that the mounting costs of debt servicing is pushing India towards a situation of debt trap because without borrowing afresh or without re-scheduling its payment obligations the Government is not in a position to meet the cost of debt servicing. This is exactly what is known as 'debt trap'. It means that the total indebtedness of the country keeps on mounting and there is no possibility of its down turn. Before arriving at any conclusion we have to analyse and see whether India is in the situation of external debt trap or internal debt trap and whether the State Governments are being pushed in debt trap or the Government of India is being pushed in debt trap or the country as a whole is being pushed in debt trap.

Let us first analyse the position of the State Governments. We have earlier said that the question of the State Governments falling into an external debt trap does not arise. The major part of their debt comes from the Central Government and therefore, if at all a State Government falls into a debt trap it can only relate to the loans from the Central Government. We have already seen that the indebtedness of the States to the Centre has grown quite fast. Therefore, the cost of servicing these debts has increased continuously despite repeated debt reliefs provided on the recommendations of successive Finance Commissions. Even increasing debt obligations resulting into mounting debt servicing charges have become a problem for the States because they have not been able to build their repaying capacity. For meeting their debt servicing obligations they have to use a large portion of fresh borrowings from the Centre. Secondly, the State Governments have not been able to make uptodate recoveries of loans and advances given by them to their debtors. This situation is nothing less than a debt trap and can be remedied only if the States follow strictly some financial discipline and also use the loans in such projects which may give them ample returns so that they may meet their debt obligations.

Now let us look to the position of the Government of India's internal and external debts. Mostly economists are of the view that the Government of India is on the threshold of the internal and external debt traps. We have already seen how the internal and external debts of the Government of India have increased since 1951. But, any absolute increase in the debt liabilities cannot be a conclusive proof of a debt trap. The problem, however, is that the position of the Government of India really appears to be a little vulnerable. Firstly, the Centre has been facing large revenue deficits and the Government has to raise loans to meet it. Secondly, there has been a rapid increase in the short-term liabilities of the Central Government which has ultimately, due to the conversion of treasury bills into long-term securities and their sale to the Reserve Bank of India, led to increase the money supply and thus generate inflationary forces. Thirdly, the growing need for funds by the Centre has led to an increase in the general interest level, which has resulted in raising the prices and costs in the country. Consequently our capabilities and incentives to export have deteriorated. Fourthly, the debt servicing charges of the Government of India have also increased very fast. They are being met out of the Government revenue. Fifthly, the Government has failed to reduce and eliminate its revenue deficit and instead it is reducing its expenditure on capital account which has adversely affected the growth of the economy. So the crux of the problem is that the Government of India has not utilised its debt for increasing its repaying capacity and therefore it has to borrow more and more to service its increasing debt. Sixthly, the Government has utilised its borrowings for unproductive purposes *i.e.*, for consumption and not for investment purposes.

From the above it is clear that the Government itself has been responsible for this difficult situation which is very close to an internal debt trap. Its debt obligations are almost three-fifths of the GDP and its interest payments are more than 280 per cent of its interest receipts.

Regarding external debt obligations of the Government of India we know that they form only a very small portion of the total liabilities. External debt also becomes a total liability if it does not lead to generation of corresponding export earning assets. Since exact data is not available, it is not possible for us to arrive at any firm conclusion, but, certainly there are indications that the Government of India has used a substantial portion of its foreign loans for purposes other than they were raised for. Consequently, the entire external loans have not been used productively and so they have not been able to generate export earning assets and their servicing has become burdensome and there is a possibility that the country may be pushed into an external debt trap.

India is, according to the World Bank Report, the third country, after Brazil and Mexico, which is the largest debtor. By the end of March, 1994 our external debt servicing to our current receipts, was around 30 per cent as against 20 per cent considered 'critical' by the World Bank and the IMF and there is no hope that in the near future the position will improve. On the other hand, we hope that our external debt will go on increasing. Again, compared with the contribution of external sector to our GNP, our foreign debt is very large and so is the debt service ratio. Further, we are also facing adverse balance of payments and we have not been able to wipe out the trade deficit. We are very much short of minerals like petroleum, nickel, gold and silver which can bring adequate export earnings. In future our dependence on imports will continue to remain at the present level or may even increase. Besides, our short-term liabilities are increasing at a much faster rate than what we can afford. So, all said and done, we are heading towards an internal as well as external debt trap and unless an urgent programme for the development of infrastructure and complete liberalisation of the economy is undertaken, any improvement in the situation seems impossible in the foreseeable future.

Debt Management Policy

In the context of planned economic development, the debt management policy of the governments should be guided by two basic objectives: (*a*) to mobilise savings and provide funds for raising investment in public sector without any harm to the private sector; and (*b*) loan operations should not effect price stability. The first objective requires that the government's debt policy should be such as to tap maximum funds from all possible sources in the economy. The policy should be flexible in regard to the instruments of debt—periodicity and offer terms. The second objective requires that the debt spending and retiring operations should have minimal effect on the price level *i.e.*, minimum rise in the price level.

If we look at the debt management policy of the Government of India; we find that it has been very successful in so far as the first objective is concerned. It is gratifying to note that along with dated loans, small savings, provident funds etc. have made notable contribution. Consequently, the size of debt has grown to alarming limits.

So far as the second objective is concerned we find certain dark spots, for example, the government has failed to develop a market for its securities and treasury bills. Consequently, investment in government securities is confined to institutional investors, the commercial banks, the LIC, the P.Fs. and borrowing through treasury bills is limited to the RBI. Genuine savings are not being invested in debt instruments.

Post-Economic Reforms Changes: In the wake of economic reforms introduced in July 1991, changes of far reaching consequences have taken place in the government policy on internal debt management. Firstly, the government has conceded the concept of market determined interest rates on its securities and has taken a number of steps in this direction, *e.g.*,

(*i*) reduction of pre-emption under the SLR to 25%;

(*ii*) shifting to an auction procedure for its dated securities borrowing, since 1992-93;

(*iii*) introducing in April 1992 the 364-Day Treasury Bill on an auction basis without the RBI's support and without a predetermined amount;

(*iv*) introducing the 91-Day Treasury Bill in January, 1993 with RBI support and with a pre-determined amount;

(*v*) conversion of treasury bills, on a voluntary basis, into dated securities of varying maturities;

(*vi*) using of innovations like zero-coupon bonds and tap stocks;

(*vii*) striving to develop a strong secondary market in its securities-with the following steps: (*a*) shift to market determined rates of interest, (*b*) entry of the NSE into operations and the publication of the transactions recorded by the RBI under the Subsidiary General Ledger, have brought in greater transparency, (*c*) development of "delivery vs. payment" system would reduce counter-party risks and also minimise diversion of funds, (*d*) the setting up of Securities and Trading Corporation of India, holding of government securities would become attractive, (*e*) introduction of a system of Primary Dealers would go a long way in developing an organised market; (*f*) liquidity support from the RBI to mutual funds exclusively investing in government securities to the extent of 20% of the holdings would facilitate the development of the retail market of government securities, (*g*) replacement of the Public Debt Act, 1949 by the Government Securities Act would not only make the management of government securities by the RBI better, but would also improve the customer services by treasuries.

Exercises

1. Examine the salient features of Public Debt Policy in India. Is it being used for accelerating development?
2. Account for the mounting external public debt in India after Independence. Do you justify it?
3. Do you think that the burden-of public debt in India is very high ? Suggest measures to reduce the burden.
4. Describe the salient features of public debt in India. Describe its size also. Do you regard the debt position as sound?

●●●

Chapter 45

The Public Budget

1. Introduction

The Public Budget is a financial plan of a government containing details of its programmes and policies, and estimated receipts and proposed expenditure under different heads, for a specific period, usually, one year. A budget is prepared in the form of a statement followed by explanatory notes on each item pertaining to the government's proposals for taxation, borrowings and expenditures. The presentation of budget is made in a cohesive and systematic manner indicating the way in which these would affect the economy. So, broadly speaking, a public budget is an annual statement of the fiscal policies with corresponding financial plans prepared by the government of a country. It is an essential exercise done annually by a government. Generally there are three sections of a government budget: first, containing the final accounts of the previous year, second, giving the budget and the revised estimates of the current year, and the third comprising the budget estimates for the following year.

Although the preparation and passage of the public budget are an annual exercise, sometimes this exercise may have to be done more than once in a year. This may be necessitated as a constitutional requirement. In the final year of the term of a democratic government when elections are due, a 'lame duck' budget is presented for the period until elections are held and a regular budget is presented by the new executive after elections. In the event of the elected government falling during the middle of the year due to loss of majority, the newly elected executive may, if it so desires, present new budget proposals for the remaining part of the year particularly in respect of allocation of outlays for various departments and projects. The requirement for a supplementary budget may also arise due to economic compulsions like the emergent need for an extra expenditure owing to a war or a natural calamity or a shortfall in the revenue receipts.

Sometimes the government may present, as a regular practice, its budget in parts; as in India the railway budget is presented separately from the regular budget of the Government of India, although railway finances are a part of the Government of India finances. In a federal set-up the governments at different layers present their own budget as in India.

Whatever may be the budgetary practice followed by a government it is essential that a budget should be transparent in its performance and clear in its proposals. Transparency implies that an account of the results of the fiscal policies and programmes of the government during the previous year, of the current economic situation of the country and of the position of the treasury should be appended to the budget. This account would serve as a basis for making decisions regarding the programmes and projects which need to be completed or newly started, and the directions in which action is to be taken in future, and for making proposals for the same in the budget. Such an account would not only highlight the relevance of the budget proposals but also make them more meaningful and clear and enable the legislature to take a more positive and objective approach. Clarity of the budget proposals also requires that details of the proposals under major heads of receipts and expenditure accompanied with statistical statements highlighting the achievements (past performance) and future projections must be provided.

As a matter of fact, since a budget is an instrument through which a government regulates and controls an economy, it should like a mirror, reflect the true character of the fiscal policy of the government, and should provide a clear picture of the government's role in the working of the economy without any padding or covering and therefore the estimates and proposals for each department should be as close to the actuals as humanly possible.

2. The Indian Situation

Article 112 of the Indian constitution lays down that an annual financial statement will be placed before both the Houses of the parliament, while Article 202 states that a similar financial statement will be placed before the legislature by the State governments. The government accounts are maintained in three parts, namely: (*a*) Consolidated Fund, (*b*) Contingency Fund, and (*c*) Public Account. All the moneys that the government receives are deposited in the Consolidated Fund. These receipts may be by way of revenues or by way of loans raised by a government or by way of realization of loans given to the institutions etc. Similarly, all expenditures incurred are debited to this fund. For each expenditure the government has to obtain sanction of the Parliament excepting those payments which are specified in the constitution. These expenses (like the salaries of the Supreme Court Judges, Auditor and Comptroller General of India) are included in the budget but are not put to vote in the parliament. In the case of a State Consolidated Fund the sanction for payments and expenditures is to be obtained from the State legislature.

The Contingency Fund comprises of those moneys which are used for meeting those expenditures which cannot be postponed. Although prior sanction of the parliament or State legislature for incurring such expenditures is not required, these have to be approved later by the parliament or the legislature and the Contingency Fund is to be replenished. Funds collected by way of provident fund, small savings, deposits and advances etc. are public funds and are deposited in the public account. These funds do not belong to the government and therefore any payments out of the Public Account does not require the sanction of the parliament or the State legislature.

3. Essentials of Efficient Budgeting

Budget is an art of fiscal or financial management. It is an art of achieving the maximum output with minimum inputs or maximization of output with the use of minimum inputs through elimination of wastage and avoidance of duplication of resources. It implies tightening of all loose ends in the matter of the use of fiscal resources and obtaining the maximum results in terms of achieving the set objectives. Cost effectiveness should be the guiding principle of all economic operations and hence the budget should aim at making people cost conscious at all levels of administration. Finally, budgeting should also involve monitoring and evaluation of the continuing programmes and projects and elimination of redundant and uneconomic and unproductive activities. Thus, objective budgeting can be possible only when the executive is equipped with adequate authority and facilities and is allowed to use discretion in all matters related to budgeting.

Following are the essentials of efficient budgeting:

1. Responsibility. The constitution of the country should hold some specific authority responsible for the preparation of the country's budget. In most of the countries including India the budget is prepared and presented by the finance minister and is a collective responsibility of the cabinet as a whole. However, in USA the budget is prepared by the Bureau of Budget under the overall direction of the president who is responsible for the preparation of the budget. In short, the budget should be prepared by the authority specified in the constitution.

2. Programming. The legislative unit of a government passes the budget presented by the executive on the basis of the programmes contained therein. It is, therefore, essential that the chief executive should first be fully satisfied with the programmes proposed by various departments and then the budgetary provisions may be finalized under its direct supervision. Further, it is also the responsibility of the chief executive to ensure that the departmental programmes are prepared and executed in accordance with the will of the legislature, and that maximum economy is exercised in their execution.

3. Reporting. A budget is prepared on the basis of the financial data and reports presented by the various departments. Legislature's intention is also expressed during the course of discussion in the legislature on various political, economic and social issues in the light of the reports supplied by the various administrative units of the government. It is therefore, imperative for each unit to furnish truthfully latest information and data in its report on every aspect of its working, more particularly, about the progress achieved in the projects under execution both in respect of accomplishment and expenditure incurred and also about the failure points, if any, with full reasons.

4. Authority. For the proper preparation and execution of the budget the chief executive should be provided with full authority and adequate facilities required. For example, it should be provided with adequate and trained staff and proper office and space where all the records can be properly kept and the information and data received from different departments can be safely stored. It should be equipped with full authority to monitor and evaluate the progress of the various projects being executed by the different administrative units and make necessary changes in the allotment of appropriations. This is very necessary for ensuring the execution of the legislative intent and economy in expenditure.

5. Unity in Diversity. A government has to perform a variety of functions in the present times—some are purely administrative, some are quasi-commercial and some are purely commercial—each differing in nature and requiring an altogether different technique of management. Even within the same administrative unit different projects require different management procedures. For example, management of a project involving a long run construction activity would be entirely different from the one involving the sale and purchase of goods. Obviously, the programming and budgeting of different projects/activities will require the use of different methods and procedures but in the government budget this will be reflected in a unified form or manner.

6. Executive Guidance. A budget is a useful tool of public administration. To make it effective it is necessary that all possible details of each project should be spelt out in the budget document and the functions for which allocations have been made should be defined with as much clarity and as in greater detail as possible. While the fund allocation will be made according to broad functions in conformity with the objectives set by the legislature, the details contained in the budget should leave little room for doubt or apprehension for the legislature and should serve as a useful guide to the executive and enable it to use its discretion in selecting the proper means of operation for achieving the main objectives.

7. Flexibility in Timings. A public budget should provide flexibility to the executive regarding the timings and period of completion of a programme or project. Provisions which may allow freedom of operation and adjustment to changing economic conditions and requirements may be included in the budget. This may be particularly useful in the case of construction projects. For example, the legislature may allocate funds for a specific period and the executive may be left free to make adjustment in the timings according to the economic necessities and to increase or decrease the period of completion of project.

8. Active Co-operation of all Departments. Since the budget document is based upon the financial and administrative reports and data furnished by all the administrative units and departments it is necessary that the flow of information should be continuous from the departments and the sub-divisions to the central budget office of the chief executive and at the same time there should be a regular feedback from the central budget office to the departments. This two-way traffic would be possible when each department and administrative unit is provided the facility of a mini-budget office which functions on the same lines as the central budget office. This would stimulate the different departments to extend active cooperation to the central office, so very essential for efficient budgeting.

4. Requisites of a Good Budget

Following are the requisites of a good budget:

1. Comprehensiveness. A good budget needs to be essentially comprehensive. To fulfil this objective the budget document should invariably be accompanied by statements containing the performance of different departments/divisions in regard to the fiscal policies and programmes of the government during the previous year, an account of the fiscal accomplishments and expenditures incurred and also a statement indicating the failure points. Such statements will provide a clear picture to the legislature as well as to the public of the progress achieved in comparison to what was to be achieved and what more remains to be achieved.

2. Clarity. The budget proposals should be as clear as possible, so that it may be easy for the public as well as the members of the legislature to comprehend them. It is only when the legislature can understand the implications of the proposals that it can take correct decisions and also know how the budget would affect the economy in the coming year. This means that the budget proposals must be accompanied by the estimates under major heads, of receipts and expenditures.

3. Objectivity. The budget proposals should be as objective as humanly possible. Although it is not possible to make the financial estimates completely accurate, it is also not proper that the financial estimates are far away from reality or from actuals. They should be as close to the actuals as possible. So, objectivity of the budget proposals and financial estimates is extremely essential. This would enable the legislature to take meaningful decisions in the interest of the society as a whole.

4. Flexibility. A good budget should contain built-in flexibility. It should not be too rigid regarding detailed allocations. It should provide scope for the use of discretion by the authorities.

5. Integrity. Another essential of a good budget is that it should provide an assurance that the fiscal programmes contained therein will be executed to the maximum possible extent and as intended by the legislature.

5. Kinds of Budget

In modern times public budget occupies a very significant place in the economic and financial system of a country. In olden times public budget did not play any role in influencing the working of an economy. But now it is the most important tool for directing and moulding the economic activities of the society. With the growth in the volume of governmental financial activities, size of the budget and bulk of budget document have also grown. There has been a tremendous change in the form of public budget and in the manner of its presentation. The process of budget preparation, its presentation and execution is now not a simple affair. Public budgets have been of different types, varying in form, manner of presentation of information and data, objectives, in their impact on the economy and so on. We now explain these different types of budgets in the following:

1. Multiple and Unified Budget. In USA the government budget used to be divided into parts in such a way that each part would enable to highlight the specialized functions of the government. Subsequently it was felt that a unified budget would be more useful for knowing the total effect on the economy which is more important. And so the need for a unified budget arose. In the case of multiple budgets lot of exercises have to be done for knowing the true results of the fiscal operations of the government through a number of documents etc. In fact, an amalgam of both types of budgets is the best course.

2. Functional and Cash Budgets. In USA again, distinction is made between the functional and cash budgets. The main difference between them being the mentioning of revenue and expenditure figures on accrual basis and excluding those receipts and expenditure which do not belong to the government. Hence, the functional budget suffers mainly from two weaknesses: firstly, it is based on actual accruals. Such budgets present a distorted picture of the flow of funds resulting from governmental activities because the receipts and payments falling due in a period generally differ from those which actually accrue. Secondly, the functional budget invariably presents an inadequate picture of governmental activities. As a matter of fact various receipt and payments, though not falling within the domain of government transactions, also produce important effects on the economy in so far as they add to the total of funds. On the other hand in the cash budget all types of flows of funds are shown and therefore its size is generally larger than the functional budget. Consequently, it presents a better picture of the real situation.

3. Legislative and Executive Budgets. A legislative budget is one which is prepared by the legislature directly or with the help of committees. An executive budget is also passed by the legislature but it is prepared by the executive wing of the government. It is, however, believed that executive budget is better than the legislative budget, because the executive wing being the actual player in the field is in a better position to make a more correct estimate of expected receipts and required expenditures than the legislative wing. Secondly, since the budget is ultimately implemented by the executive it is not fair to force the executive to accept certain estimates and figures and then ask it to achieve the targets particularly if the estimates are not realistic. Finally, if the budget is prepared by the executive, then it is more easy to fix the responsibility for any lapses.

4. Revenue and Capital Budgets. The general practice adopted by many countries is to divide the public budget into revenue and capital accounts; the former covering those items which are of recurring nature while the latter includes items which are of non-recurring nature *i.e.*, which are concerned with the acquisition and sale of capital assets. It is generally held that such a division is useful because every economic unit must be able to separate current expenses from those relating to the acquisition of capital assets. This is necessary because current expenses are in the nature of consumption. It is only depreciation of capital assets which amounts to real expenditure in the sense of consumption. This is based on the theory that private commercial units do not take into account the money spent on the acquisition of capital assets as current expenses of the year. Depreciation of the capital assets is only counted as current expenses. Like commercial units, the government should also adopt the same practice.

Indian Situation. According to the constitution of India the budget must distinguish between expenditure on Revenue Account from other expenditures. Hence the budgets of the central and State governments are divided into two parts, namely, revenue budget and capital budget; the former comprising revenue receipts (tax as well as non-tax) and the expenditure met out of these receipts. The non-tax revenue is collected from currency, coinage and mint, interest payments, dividends, profits, revenue from general services, revenue from social and community services and revenue from economic services.

On the other hand, capital receipts include market loans, borrowing from the Reserve Bank of India, receipts of the sale of treasury bills and loans from foreign governments and others to the central government. Disbursements of capital accounts include expenditure on acquisition of physical assets like lands, buildings, machinery and equipment, shares and debentures and loans to State Governments and other organizations. Till mid-1980s the Plan Budget was also prepared alongwith the main budget. The Plan Budget showed the budgetary provisions for important projects and schemes included in the Central Plan. It contained details of budgetary support for the Central Plan by sectors of development, including the Central Plan assistance to States and Union Territories. Besides, extra budgetary resources for the Central Plan were also mentioned. The breakdown of the proposed outlays between different services was provided alongwith various physical targets. Now this practice has been changed. The budget of the Govern-ment of India is now first divided into two parts: Plan and Non-plan and then each part is further divided into Revenue and Capital Accounts.

5. Economic and Functional Classification. Economic classification of the budget implies the classification of expenditure and the manner of its financing in terms of economic categories. By doing so, one is able to gather a valuable information about the generation of savings, investment, consumption, financial assets and liabilities etc. On the other hand, functional classification refers to the types of functions, which the government undertakes, or the services which it provides. Such a classification cuts across the departments and ministries and presents a picture of what the government's achievements are in various areas. Such a classification can be helpful in making decisions for the achievement of set objectives. This approach is better than the traditional approach because the traditional approach does not co-relate the purposes with the account heads. It, no doubt, enables the legislature to have an effective control over the executive and is useful for government auditors to keep an effective check on the misappropriation of funds and other unfair practices. But, it does not provide information for the formulation of fiscal policies. It does not help in making an assessment of the effects of alternative policies and operations and for making any improvements in the existing policies.

It may, however, be pointed out that no single classification can be ideal for every country and for all times because the budgetary classification is full of practical implications. It helps in assessing the magnitude of various budgetary categories and their relative importance. Its ultimate shape would be determined by the way each category is defined. Sweden and some other countries adopted such a classification in consonance with the recommendations of a committee of experts on financial statistics set up in

1940. Subsequently, in the beginning years of the decade of 1950s regional workshops on the problems of budgetary classification were organized under the auspices of the United Nations. Even then, the budgetary classification, as found in India, was far superior to that prevailing in many countries. During 1956 economic classification of the Government of India budget was undertaken by the Economic Division of the Ministry of Finance. This classification covered central government and departmental commercial undertakings. Functional classification of the budget was adopted in 1967-68 alongwith an economic-cum-functional classification. So the economic classification of the Government of India budget started from 1957-58 and the functional classification was added to it in 1967-68. However, we do not yet have a combined economic-cum-functional classification of both State and Central Government budgets.

(*a*) **Economic Classification.** This classification has six accounts which are as follows:

Account 1—Transactions in commodities and services, and transfers; Current Account of Government Administration.

Account 2—Transactions in commodities and services, and transfers; Current Account of Departmental Commercial Undertakings.

Account 3—Transactions in commodities and services, and transfers; Capital Account of Government Administration and Departmental Commercial Undertakings (combined).

Account 4—Changes in financial assets, Capital Account of Government Administration and Departmental Commercial Undertakings.

Account 5—Changes in financial liabilities; Capital Account of Government Administration and Departmental Commercial Undertakings.

Account 6—Cash and Reconciliation Account of Government Administration and Departmental Commercial Undertakings.

This classification has been designed in such a way that it is easy to link it with a system of national income and expenditure accounts depicting the activities associated with the generation of national income and capital formation. It, therefore provides a breakdown of government expenditure into consumption and capital formation and also shows the impact which such expenditure has upon the rest of the economy. It also provides information regarding financial assets and liabilities which is very useful in assessing the changes occurring in the composition and ownership of financial assets as also borrowing and lending transactions of the government. It also helps us in making an assessment of the indirect contribution of budgetary operations to capital formation by other agencies. These accounts also distinguish between transactions in goods and services on the one hand and financial transactions on the other.

(*b*) **Functional Classification.** Function means a purpose. Functional classification only covers expenditure side. The current expenditure of departmental commercial undertakings is however excluded and the capital expenditure is included in this classification. The functional classification of the Government of India Budget has four main categories: (*a*) General Services, (*b*) Social Services, (*c*) Economic Services and (*d*) Unallocable.

Limitations of Economic and Functional Classification of Budget

This classification suffers from the following weaknesses:

(1) It does not provide any idea of the effect of the budgetary activities of the government.

(2) It does not provide the relevant information regarding various regulatory devices, which have an important role to play, because the fiscal figures are given only as broad aggregates.

(3) It also does not reflect the impact of fiscal operations on income and wealth inequalities or on many growth variables like regional disparities, institutional framework etc.

(4) It excludes the budgets of all public authorities.

(5) The accounts are highly aggregative.

(6) It uses some arbitrary and unrealistic ratios which should be replaced by factual data.

6. Significance of Public Budget

These days public budget occupies an important place in the socio-economic life of the society. In olden days, public budget was considered only as a simple statement of receipts and expenditures of the government. Then it had only two objectives: firstly, how little money a government can take out of the pockets of the tax-payers, which is just adequate to maintain its essential activities at a proper level of efficiency; and secondly, since parliament had to vote funds it was necessary for it to know the plan of expenditure of the government. That was the position of public budget in a *laissez-faire* economy but, since the development of the concept of the welfare state the activities of the government have expanded at a very rapid rate and now they encompass almost every aspect of the socio-economic life of the community. Modern governments are now held responsible for promoting the general welfare of the citizens and therefore they plan the use of public resources to achieve pre-determined objectives through the instrument of budget. So, now budget is a significant instrument of government policy and in that respect it has wide ramifications. It affects the economy of a country on all fronts.

As compared to olden days the size of the budget has swollen enormously. Its capacity to affect the national economy has greatly increased. The government activities are reflected through public budgets and they affect the production and distribution of national income and the utilization of the resources of the country. Thus, the government with the help of the budget can produce a powerful impact on the level of economic activity through its policies on taxation, expenditure and borrowing. That is why Van Philips remarked "The superiority of the budget is due to its more firm and direct hold on the economy, the results of the budgetary policy are more direct."[1]

To sum up, budget is a powerful instrument used by the government to influence the levels of national income, employment and output. The taxation and expenditure policies may minimize the inequalities in the distribution of income and wealth. Similarly the policies of public expenditure and production may help in eradicating poverty, unemployment and unequal distribution of wealth and rapidiate the rate of economic growth. The borrowing policy of the government may lead to an increase in the rate of savings and mobilization of resources for economic development of the economy.

Exercises

1. What is a public budget ? Explain the essentials of efficient budgeting.
2. Define a public budget. What are the requisites of a good budget?
3. Describe the importance of public budget in the working of an economy. Among its various types which one do you consider as the best?

●●●

1. Philip Van Philips, *Public Finance and Less Developed Economy,* p. 81.

Chapter 46

Techniques of Budgeting

1. Introduction

In the previous chapter we have highlighted some of the general issues relating to public budget. In the present chapter we propose to throw light on the techniques of budgeting. By technique of budgeting we mean the method of preparing public budget and its presentation keeping in view the set objectives. A number of economists during the previous century evolved new concepts of public budgeting and propounded theories in that regard. Until the beginning of the 19th century the controversy only waged round the concept of balanced and unbalanced budgets. But later on the debate centred round a number of new concepts. The classical economists believed that a balanced budget was neutral in its effect on the working of the economy and therefore it was the best. On the other hand they held that deficit budget implies transfer of resources from the private sector to the public sector which was unproductive. This concept was based on the premise that the government had no role to play in the economic life of an individual and therefore, it should undertake minimum activities. Consequently public expenditure beyond a certain point was regarded as harmful.

2. Techniques of Budgeting and Economic Stability

Modern economists, on the other hand consider budget as an instrument of curing irregularities and correcting the imperfections of the free market economy. According to modern economists, depression and boom, both are harmful because they create uncertainty in the functioning of the economy. During depression economic activities are at a low level causing unemployment, business losses and generating a wave of pessimism among the entrepreneurs. During the period of boom or inflation the prices rise due to which the fixed income people suffer and give rise to a tendency to promote speculation. Government can intervene in both the situations and stabilize the economy. During depression the government can borrow money and spend it on public works. This will increase employment, raise the level of effective demand for goods and services and encourage investment. It means that the government will employ deficit budgets during a period of depression. Similarly during a period of boom the government can check the tendency of rising price by imposing heavy taxes and withdrawing money from the market so that the purchasing power of the people will diminish and prices will fall. It means that government will have to take recourse to surplus budgets during a period of prosperity or boom. It is, therefore, clear that the concept of balanced budget advocated by classical economists is not always helpful in maintaining economic stability. It is through the techniques of budgeting that this objective can be achieved. In this sense the techniques of budgeting are inseparable to the fiscal policy.

3. Balanced and Unbalanced Budgets

According to Dalton, "A balanced budget is that, over a period of time, revenue does not fall short of expenditure. If expenditure exceeds revenue the budget is said to be imbalanced." So, a government budget is balanced when the tax revenue and expenditure are equal and when these two are not equal then the budget is unbalanced. The imbalance in the budget may be caused either by an excess of income over expenditure or by an excess of expenditure over income. The former is called a surplus budget while the latter is called a deficit budget. When we talk of government expenditure we must bear in mind that only those outgoings are included therein which are spent on the purchase of goods and services required for the performance of government functions. But those outgoings which are meant to cancel public debts are not included in the government expenditure. Just as the borrowed money is not government income similarly the payment of debt or interest is not government expenditure.

In the case of deficit budget the amount of deficit is covered either by public borrowing or by drawing cash from the central bank or by printing new currency. In any case a deficit budget results in increasing the liability of the government or decreasing its reserves. A surplus budget decreases public debt or increases reserves of the government. In other words a surplus budget decreases the liabilities of the government and increases its accumulated surplus. For a clear understanding of the implication of a deficit budget it is necessary to note how the deficits are covered. We have already said that budget deficit can be covered by borrowing money from the public or from the central bank. When a loan is raised it has to be redeemed in stages in future. It would require the levy of taxes for a number of years which implies that government while incurring debt pawns its future. It does not matter if it is expected to benefit from current expenditure. Hence a sacrifice in future can be made out of additional benefits *i.e.*, the government may make the people to sacrifice a part of their current consumption in lieu of greater additional consumption in future.

Now take the case of a surplus budget. We have already said that it means a reduction in public debt or liabilities. Public debt can be remitted only by drawing on the present or past excess of income over expenditure. A surplus of revenue over expenditure is to be deliberately created. It will not be a bad proposition if the government utilizes the surplus for paying off its loans. If the government has used loans for productive purposes then national income must have increased and taxes can be paid out of it without much inconvenience.

Budgeting Techniques for Redistributing Incomes

Public budgeting techniques can also be used for the distribution of incomes. During a period of inflation, owing to brisk economic activity and rising prices, income shifts from wage earners to rentier class. It happens because profits rise faster than wages. Again, due to rise in prices, the value of money declines, lenders of money suffer a loss from capital depreciation and real value of their capital declines. Hence, real income shifts from lenders to the borrowers. During depression when prices are falling the real income shifts from the producers to the wage earners and the lenders benefit at the expense of borrower. Fiscal devices are therefore needed to be adopted to correct the situation. For example a deficit budget will create conditions of boom while a surplus budget will create conditions of depression. Both will cause the shift of income from one class to the other and correct the distribution of income.

Budgeting Techniques and Economic Development

The techniques of budgeting have also to be different according to the stage of country's progress and development. In under-developed or developing countries the budgeting is necessarily to be in the direction of promoting economic development of the country or for the welfare of the people as a whole. In such countries the objective of the government is to raise the level of employment, income and output, to increase the growth and development of the economy, to check the growth of population and to ensure an equitable distribution of income and wealth. Professor Musgrave has grouped these objectives as allocative functions, distributive functions and stabilisation functions of the budgetary policy in developing countries. Fiscal policy should be moulded in such a fashion that it leads to the fulfilment of these objectives and all fiscal matters should be taken towards this goal. The budgetary policy should also aim at the maximum utilisation of the existing economic resources and economic infrastructure and also simultaneously strive for their development so that the basic foundation of the whole economy is strengthened. Hence for under-developed countries the budgetary policy should include three kinds of public expenditures namely: (1) the normal expenditure required for maintaining the regular services at a reasonable level of efficiency; (2) capital expenditure for asset building or investment expenditure and (3) development expenditure *i.e.*, expenditure towards development of infrastructure. This can also be called as growth promoting expenditure. For meeting this expenditure the funds could be obtained either through taxation or through public debt. Loans should be obtained for strengthening infrastructure and tax revenue should be used for meeting recurring expenditure. Another objective of the budgetary policy should be to promote savings so that productive activities could be strengthened. In short, for promoting economic development, the techniques of budgeting have to be entirely different from those required for stabilising the economy.

4. Performance and Programme Budgeting

The Performance and Programme Budgeting is the most recent technique of the formation and execution of government budgets. In this system the government budget is first divided into the major functions of the government, then each major function is further divided into specific programmes, activities and projects and then funds are allocated according to the achievement expected from a department or ministry over a specific period from the proposed expenditure. The emphasis, is, therefore, on the size of the programme, its implementation and the costs involved. It is a new approach to budget formation which makes it easier to allocate funds since the cost of each programme and benefits expected therefrom are given side by side. The focus is on the efficient and economic use of the government resources which are scarce in relation to the ever increasing development and welfare activities of the government. The various expenditure proposals made in the budget are rated in terms of their costs and benefits and then chosen for implementation and put to tests of actual performance *vis-a-vis* their expected results.

The concept of performance budgeting is therefore based on the idea that since the successful implementation of a proposal is entirely dependent on its soundness, the efficiency and integrity of the implementing authority and other relevant circumstances and since the actual performance does not conform to the expected results, a system of continuous assessment is a must. The performance budgeting, therefore, involves the spelling out of the sequence of steps to be taken for executing a programme alongwith the expenditure required at each stage and results expected to be achieved. This part of budgeting is known as programme budgeting. Tests are also necessary for assessing the performance efficiency of the programme by comparing the actual and expected results. This part of budgeting is known as the performance budgeting. When budgeting covers both these activities, it is called as Performance and Programme Budgeting (PPB). So, it is a system of presenting government expenditure in relation to functions, programmes, activities, projects etc. reflecting government output and its cost. While the programme budgeting emphasises the need for an efficient programme management in the light of long-term objectives, the emphasis of performance budgeting is on efficient internal management in the light of results to be achieved and their costs. To quote James Cutt, "The fundamental premises of programme budgeting are that policy and budgets are inseparable, and that the relationship between the structure and implementation of budgets and the determination and achievement of policy objective should be made explicit. Programme budgeting is then a set of procedures designed to improve the basis for policy decisions and to secure a more effective and efficient allocation of scarce resources in the public sector, the output of which does not generally command any market price."[1]

The Fundamental Premises of the Concept

The concept of PPB is based on the following fundamental premises:

(1) Fundamental scarcity of resources is at the root of all economic problems.

(2) Efficient implementation of the programme is as important as their allocation for which certain norms have to be laid and methods have to be found for achieving it. (3) The conventional budgetary system does not possess any built-in devices through which it may be possible to know when the usefulness of a given project has ceased or changed immensely. PPB system can provide for such a device in the form of assessment which helps in obtaining the necessary feedback on the efficacy of various decisions and their results. (4) The conventional budgetary system provides ad-hoc solutions, which at times are very useful but ad-hocism as a policy can be dangerous as the present policy affects future as well. (5) In the conventional system the government budget covers only a period of one year whereas a large number of programmes extend over long periods. Proper assessment of and effective co-ordination between budgetary provisions and policies over a period of time is therefore extremely essential. The PPB lays special emphasis on "forward programming".

The point about PPB to be noted is that while continuing to rely on sound human judgement and recognising the importance of human factors, the PPB

1. James Cutt, *A Planning, Programming and Budgetary Manual—Resource Allocation in Public Sector Economics,* Praeger publications, 1974, p. 2.

system aims at improving the decision-making process by eliminating all redundant and superfluous issues. This sort of analysis requires a detailed description of all the assumptions on which decisions are based and the modification of the programmes, if necessary, in the light of the changes occurring in those assumptions.

Programme Budgeting and Performance Budgeting: A Comparison

The two budgets are inter-linked and supplementary. They are similar and not identical. Programme budgeting has three components. The first relates to the defining of objectives of the fiscal policy and methods to be adopted. Since the concern is with the output or results it involves the drawing up of various programmes for achieving the objectives. The second component involves a cost-benefit analysis of the various alternative courses for achieving the said objectives and the selection of the most economical alternative. The third component concerns with the linking of the current programmes and policies with future problems, costs and benefits and other developments. In the words of Burkhead programme budgeting is "essentially a long-term 'rolling planning' under which budget is an allocative process between the competing claims, and the budget itself a statement of policy for the appropriate planning period."[2]

A performance budget is to assess the achievements and failures of a programme budget. Thus a programme budget is more comprehensive (includes several performance units) whereas a performance budget centres on the efficiency of input-output relationships for attaining a specific budgetary goal.

Secondly, programme budget relates to broad programmes and helps policy making decisions at top levels whereas the performance budget is useful for efficiency control within a particular government department or ministry. Thirdly, programme budgeting is forward looking and is concerned with *ex-ante* programmes and projections, whereas the performance budgeting is backward looking and is related to *ex-post* analysis of the efficiency of the action already taken.

Conceptual Difficulties of PPB

From the above it is clear that PPB approach is all inclusive—all costs and contributions are taken into account and then an evaluation is done for individual projects. It is superior to the traditional budgetary system. Since the overall objective of PPB is to increase efficiency in decision making and economy in the use of public resources, it may follow either the maximisation

2. Burkhead, *Government Budgeting,* New York, 1956, p. 139.

of output approach or the minimisation of input approach. In short, the emphasis is on the application of scientific budgetary methodology to public sector decision making but it also suffers from certain conceptual difficulties which are briefly stated as follows:

(*a*) Multiplicity of programmes and objectives is the first difficulty. For one programme there may be more than one objective. (*b*) Quantitative measurement of the achievement of a number of programmes like those falling in the category of social services or social security may not be possible. (*c*) The institutional framework of an economy may affect the efficacy of the PPB system. So each economy shall have to devise its own system. (*d*) People responsible for preparing and executing a PPB may not possess the analytical skills required for its success. That is why even in an advanced country like USA it is not being used at all levels of public budgeting even after more than three decades of its adoption. (*e*) PPB requires an efficient functional classification of the budget and the accounting system. It cannot be applied to aggregative categories at the national level, like agriculture, industry, public health, because specific programmes and their relative costs cannot be identified. (*f*) According to Schultz, from the political point of view less flexibility is available in those areas of economic activity where it is easier to apply analytical techniques and where there is less political rigidity, the data usually do not permit the use of analytical technique.[3]

Conditions for the Success of Performance Budgeting

We can now take up the conditions on which the success of performance budgeting depends. These are as follows:

1. Workmanship and Performance Standards. The success of performance budgeting depends on the existence of some yardstick for measuring work and performance. Each administrative unit, should, therefore lay down some criterion for measuring activity and for assessing performance. Anyone standard cannot be used to measure all activities and assess performance of each activity. Each department and division or unit shall have to devise methods suitable for its programmes, according to the nature of each programme and past records, allowing flexibility *i.e.*, scope for corrective action in the case of variance between the actual and expected performance. This will certainly increase the importance of budget control.

2. Reporting the Progress of Each Activity. Another factor important for the success of performance budgeting is the establishment of a system of reporting on the progress of each activity or programme. Such a system should be established in each government department. The reporting should cover all

3. C.L. Schultz, *The Politics and Economics of Public Spending,* The Brookings Institution, 1968, pp. 88-89.

aspects of each activity, such as the volume of work done, the quality of the work, the time duration, the expenditure etc. Even the weakest units should provide data on the work allowed for each programme and variance between the budgetary provision and the actual expenditure. This would enable the management to check the performance of each of the operational factors and take suitable remedial measures to correct the situation.

3. Proper Accounting System. The success of performance budgeting also depends on a proper accounting system. This means that accounting should be according to the functional classification. The system of accrual accounting would be the most appropriate. But it cannot be used everywhere because it is not easy to determine costs and expenses related to changes in assets and liabilities. In the case of trading, commercial and manufacturing activities, accounting should be done on a double entry basis and a balance sheet should be prepared at the end of the year.

4. Improved Organisation for Programme Management. A successful performance budgeting system requires that the higher levels of the executive wing of the government should be always on the look out to improve its programme management. It means that senior level executives should constantly endeavour to improve upon the existing methods, procedures, techniques of operation, system of internal audit etc. on the basis of available data. This will certainly improve operational efficiency and bring about economy in expenditure.

5. Proper Classification of Expenditure. For the success of performance budgeting it is necessary that for each major activity, programme and project, the total expenditure should be classified and shown in the budget separately according to the nature of the expenditure. For example, expenditure on capital items such as the acquisition, construction or improvement of property or equipment such as land, building, plant and machinery is different from expenditure on recurring items like salaries and wages and should be presented separately in the budget.

Conclusion. Performance budgeting is useful in a number of ways. It is an effective handy instrument of management of government resources. It is a useful medium for judging the efficiency of current operations and for planning future programmes and activities. It helps the improvement of public sector decision-making process. It allows the utilisation of public resources to the maximum advantage of the society. It makes the legislative review and control of budget more meaningful. It makes the budgeting more informative and understandable to the common tax-payer. Despite these advantages the technique of performance budgeting cannot be used in all areas of governmental activity, particularly those which are not capable of measurement, where allocation of costs is not easy and where the benefits cannot be quantified, for example, diplomacy, defence, fire protection, epidemic control, health, education etc. In the initial stages success is also bound to be limited and as suggested by Schultz "at least a beginning be made with important areas."[4]

5. Indian Situation

In India the suggestion for adopting the PPB System was made by the Twentieth Estimates Committee. It considered this technique ideal for a proper appreciation of the schemes and outlays included in the budget. But, it preferred its use for "large development activities". Subsequently, the Study Team of the Administrative Reforms Commission on financial administration recommended the use of performance budgeting for linking the financial and fiscal aspects of economic development. The Study Team observed that the prevailing budgetary system was good from the point of view of financial and legal accountability but from the view-point of effectiveness of expenditures it did not give adequate information and did not help the people and the parliament to have a complete knowledge of the operations and activities of the government. According to the Study Team the use of performance budgeting in India will confer the following advantages:

(1) The presentation of the purpose and objectives of seeking funds would be more clear and the progress and accomplishments would be expressed in financial terms.

(2) It would help the legislature to have a better understanding of the budget and to review it more effectively.

(3) It will improve budget formation and the decision making process at all levels in the government.

(4) It will increase the accountability of the executive for the control of financial operations.

(5) It will make performance audit more effective and meaningful.

According to the Study Team neither current budgeting structure nor the accounting system was appropriate for the introduction of the PPB System. The budget heads did not correlate with the development heads under the Five-year Plans. The budget heads were determined by the CGA, while the plan heads were decided by the Planning Commission. That is why, these were different from each other. Again the Plan outlays are determined by the Planning Commission while the expenditure under different heads is determined by the Finance Commission and the demands of the different ministries. Consequently, it is difficult to know the exact provisions made in

4. C.L. Schultz in J.W. Davis, Jr. (ed.), *Politics, Programmes and Budgets,* Prentice Hall, 1969, p. 189.

the budget for the Plan Schemes and to make assessment, accounting and audit of the central assistance for State Plan Schemes. For a proper PPB System an efficient functional classification of the budget and accounting system is necessary. Classification into aggregative categories such as agriculture, industry etc. is not suitable for the implementation of the PPB system. To quote from the report, "One of the prime requisites of the introduction of performance budgeting is a complete interaction of budgetary and accounting classification and the progress in its application will hinge substantially on the degree to which a parallel and well-co-ordinated accounting structure can be developed to provide timely and current data for the appraisal of performance and various programwes and activities."[5]

However, the Study Team also realised that the regrouping of budget heads corresponding to the Plan heads was not practicable and therefore suggested that in order to seek a greater measure of uniformity between the two, some of the minor heads and sub-heads and detailed heads in the budget may be modified to correlate with Plan Heads.[6]

In the words of the Study Team, "The best way of bringing the accounting heads and development heads in line with each other, under the existing structure of account heads, is to provide a link between Plan Schemes and the budget provisions by way of supplementary exercise through the publication of a separate Plan Budget linking document by each State Government. This document would contain a statement of schemes included in the Annual Plan arranged under heads of development including the provisions made for each of the schemes under the various budget heads of accounts."[7]

Accordingly, the Study Team recommended the introduction of PPB System in India in a phased manner with priority assigned to those departments and organisations, which handle programmes which involve large expenditure. In India, all the ministries and developments had started preparing performance budget from the year 1975-76. These budgets contain main projects, programmes and activities with reference to the specific objectives, an assessment of the previous year's budget and achievements. But these are not yet perfect.

6. Zero-Base Budgeting

It is a technique of budgeting to augment the productivity of public expenditure and eliminate unproductive expenditure. It is a form of rationalistic budgeting

5. Administrative Reforms Commission, *Report of the Study Team—Accounts and Audit,* September 1987, para 5.6.
6. *Ibid.,* p. 31.
7. *Ibid.,* p. 29.

aimed at minimising wastage in government expenditure, not through auditing but by examining the rationale of each item of expenditure under consideration. According to Peter A. Phyrr, it is an "Operating, planning and budgeting process that requires each manager to justify a budget request in detail, from scratch." To this end each administrative unit has to start with the assumption that it does not exist (and hence no budget provision for it) and compare it with alternative levels of its operation with corresponding budgetary provisions. If it fails to justify its own existence it would be closed down. If it succeeds in justifying its existence then it will have to defend the optimum level of its operations and the corresponding budget provisions. To put it differently, no activity or programme is essential or indispensable. It has to justify its existence and also why the demanded provision may be made for it. This exercise is to be repeated every time without any consideration for its past performance or present existence. According to Musgrave, "The idea is to consider the budget as a whole, rather than to examine incremental change only."[8] According to the concept of Zero-base Budgeting all financial requirement included in the budget of an administrative unit are analysed, evaluated and justified annually and not just the increased or additional requirements.

Procedure for Introducing ZBB

For the introduction of ZBB, following steps will have to be taken:

(1) Spell out the organisational goals and objectives as clearly as possible so as to leave no room for ambiguity or dilution.

(2) A thorough examination of the existing organisational structure, functions, programmes and activities, whether they are adequate for the. achievement of the said goals and objectives.

(3) Identification of the decision units *i.e.*, sub-divisions of the organisation which will be responsible for spending the allocated funds.

(4) Development of decision packages comprising objectives, current operations, alternatives and possible levels of funding for each decision unit. Each package will contain detailed financial requirements to support a particular level of operation.

(5) Review and ranking of decision packages.

(6) Finalisation of budget proposals.

(7) Preparation of the budget.

---

8. R.A. Musgrave and P. Musgrave, *Public Finance in Theory and Practice,* p. 42.

Benefits from ZBB

It is clear that the introduction of ZBB will benefit the organisation in a number of ways. These are briefly stated as under:

(1) The budgetary process will be based on a comprehensive and objective analysis of objectives, needs and priorities.

(2) Planning and budgetary process will be coherently linked with each other.

(3) Great cost consciousness among the executives which will induce them to evaluate the cost effectiveness of their operations.

(4) Enlarge the involvement of the executives at all levels in the budget making process.

(5) Enable the managers to make an objective assessment of each programme or activity and stop the programmes which are less productive (or whose utility has diminished) and expand programmes which are of higher value.

(6) Lead to better management of funds.

(7) Make the budget more informative.

The US Experience. ZBB was first used in government budget in 1973 by Jimmy Carter when he was Governor of Georgia. Subsequently a number of other States of USA adopted it. The US experience reveals that although it is not a panacea, if carefully implemented, it can produce significant benefits. It has not led to substantial cuts in budgets but it has certainly succeeded in channelising resources from less productive activities to more productive activities. Professor Musgrave considers it a helpful procedure but it is impracticable in detailed application. According to him, "This is a helpful procedure but, clearly impracticable in detailed application. A more realistic approach would be to apply the Zero-base method to particular departments or programmes on a rotating basis."[9]

Indian Situation. In the context of Indian situation, it is felt that the use of ZBB will be mainly useful in cutting down wasteful use of government resources. It is a common knowledge that our non-plan expenditure (interest payments, subsidies, defence accounts, salaries and dearness allowance form a major portion) is mounting, public savings are falling, public sector undertakings are incurring huge losses and so on. Over the years certain departments and sections have been rendered superfluous. A lot of wasteful expenditure can and should be avoided but no mechanism has been evolved for this purpose. The Government of India undoubtedly feels concerned about it. Its concern can be noted by the fact that as far back as in 1986-87, the then finance minister Shri V.P. Singh announced that a beginning will be made in

9. *Ibid.*

the use of ZBB in the budget of that year and from the following year it will be implemented in full. But so far success has eluded the Government of India. There can be more than one reasons for it. Firstly, it may face a stiff opposition from populist politicians and Employee's Unions. Secondly, the orientation and outlook, skills and exposure necessary for the success of ZBB are very much lacking in the people responsible for implementing it. Thirdly, existing organisational structure suffers from many deficiencies which may impede successful implementation of ZBB, such as multiple tiers of decision making, lengthy and circuitous procedures, lack of efficient means of communication, retrieval of data etc. Fourthly, no department would like to sign its own death warrant, instead it will go all out to justify its expenses and argue for further expansion. Finally, there is the risk that the introduction of ZBB may itself become an item of expenditure in the form of additional department of each ministry and create obstacles in the normal procedure of sanction and flow of expenditure.

Exercises

1. Describe the various techniques of preparing and presenting public budget. Would you prefer a balanced or an unbalanced budget? Give reasons for you answer.
2. Distinguish between performance budgeting and programme budgeting and explain the conditions required for the success of performance budgeting.
3. What is zero-base budgeting ? Explain its benefits.

●●●

Chapter 47

Budgets of the Government of India

In this chapter we explain the main features of the recent budgets of the Government of India. We give the objectives or philosophy of the budget, tax proposals, budget proposals, budget estimates etc. for the years 2006-07 to 2008-09.

Budget—2006-07

The Budget for the year 2006-07 was presented to the Parliament by the F.M. on February 28, 2006. The F.M. stated that according to Central Statistical Organisation (CSO), the growth rate in 2004-05 was 7.5 per cent, with the manufacturing sector growing at 8.1 per cent. More importantly, at current market prices, gross domestic saving increased to 29.1 per cent of GDP and the rate of gross capital formation increased to 30.1 per cent of GDP.

According to the CSO's advance estimates, GDP growth is likely to be 8.1 per cent in 2005-06, with the manufacturing sector expected to grow at 9.4 per cent. Agricultural growth bounced back to 2.3 per cent and, barring mining, all other sectors were performing satisfactorily. Inflation, as on February 11, 2006 was 4.02 per cent. Non-food credit was growing by over 25 per cent.

An Overview of the Budget

In 2005-06, Gross Budgetary Support (GBS) for the Plan was Rs. 143,497 crore. Of this, support to the Central Plan was Rs. 110,385 crore. GBS for 2006-07 had been fixed at Rs. 172,728 crore representing an increase of 20.4 per cent. Out of this, the Central Plan was to receive a support of Rs. 131,285 crore.

For 2006-07, the allocation for education was enhanced by 31.5 per cent to Rs. 24,115 crore and for health and family welfare by 22.0 per cent to Rs. 12,546 crore.

On the eight flagship programme the total allocation in 2005-06 was

Rs. 34,927 crore. In 2006-07, the total allocation was to be Rs. 50,015 crore, representing an additionality of Rs. 15,088 crore or 43.2 per cent, as given below:

			Rs. Crore
1.	Sarva Shiksha Abhiyan	:	10,041
2.	Mid-day-Meal Scheme	:	4,813
3.	Rajiv Gandhi Drinking Water Mission	:	4,680
4.	National Rural Health Mission	:	8,207
5.	Integrated Child Development Services	:	4,087
6.	National Rural Employment Guarantee Scheme	:	11,300
7.	Rural Sanitation Campaign	:	720
8.	J.L. Nehru National Urban Renewal Mission	:	4,595

Women and Children

The statement on gender budgeting was enlarged to include schemes where 100 per cent of the allocation was for the benefit of women as well as schemes where at least 30 per cent of the allocation was targeted towards women. The statement covered 24 demands for grants in 18 Ministries/Departments and five Union Territories and schemes with an outlay of Rs. 28,737 crore.

Scheduled Castes and Scheduled Tribes

Budget, also contained a separate statement on the schemes for the welfare and development of SCs and STs. The allocations for schemes benefiting only SCs and STs had been enhanced by 14.5 per cent to Rs. 2,902 crore and the allocations for schemes with at least 20 per cent allocation for SCs and STs had been enhanced by 13.9 per cent to Rs. 9,690 crore.

The equity contribution to the National SC Finance and Development Corporation was increased to Rs. 37 crore and to the National Safai Karamchari Finance and Development Corporation to Rs. 80 crore in 2006-07.

A contribution of Rs. 16.47 crore was also made to strengthen the equity base of the National Minorities Development and Finance Corporation.

Kasturba Gandhi Balika Vidyalaya Scheme

1,000 New residential scchools for girls from SC, ST, OBC and minority communities will be opened in 2006-07. Rs. 128 crore were provided and an additional sum of Rs. 172 crore was committed for being provided during the year. Further incentive would be given to the girl child who passes the VIII Standard Examination and enrols in a secondary school. A sum of Rs. 3,000 will be deposited in her name, and she would be entitled to withdraw it on reaching 18 years of age.

Investment

Public Sector Enterprises (PSEs) had through internal and extra-budgetary resources, investment plans amounting to Rs. 122,757 crore in 2006-07. Government will provide equity support of Rs. 16,901 crore and loans of Rs. 2,789 crore to Central PSEs (including Railways).

Agriculture

Irrigation

Out of an outlay of Rs. 4,500 crore under AIBP in 2005-06, the grant component was Rs. 1,680 crore. The States were expected to spend about Rs. 2,520 crore from their resources, and 25 projects were expected to be completed before the end of the year. The outlay for 2006-07 was increased to Rs. 7,121 crore, and a grant of Rs. 2,350 crore was committed.

Credit

Farm credit increased to Rs. 125,309 crore in 2004-05 (well above the target) and was expected to cross the target of Rs. 141,500 crore set for 2005-06. It was proposed to ask the banks to increase the level of credit to Rs. 175,000 crore in 2006-07 and also add another 50 lakh farmers to their portfolio.

It was also proposed to grant some relief to the farmers who had availed of crop loans from scheduled commercial banks, RRBs and PACS for Kharif and Rabi 2005-06. Accordingly, an amount equal to two percentage points of the borrower's interest liability on the principal amount up to Rs. 100,000 would be credited to his/her bank account before March 31,2006. A sum of Rs. 1,700 crore was provided for this.

The Rural Infrastructure Development Fund (RIDF) XI sanctions touched a level of Rs. 7,301 crore as on January 31, 2006. The corpus of RIDF XII was increased to Rs. 10,000 crore.

A Separate window under RIDF XII for rural roads with a corpus of Rs. 4,000 crore during 2006-07 was also opened.

In the last two years 801,000 SHGs have been credit linked. The credit disbursed to these SHGs was approximately Rs. 4,863 crore. The proposal was to ask the banking sector to credit-link another 385,000 SHGs in 2006-07.

Manufacturing

In manufacturing, industries which, with appropriate incentives, can throw up huge job opportunities have been identified. These include textiles, food processing, petroleum, chemicals and petro-chemicals, leather, and automobiles. In services, tourism and software can offer a large number of jobs. Incentives will continue to be provided to them and suitable provisions were made in the Budget.

Fiscal Consolidation

Twelfth Finance Commission

The recommendations of the Twelfth Finance Commission (TFC) were being implemented. Cumulatively, State loans amounting to Rs. 103,710 crore have been consolidated. Under the new scheme of tax devolution, Rs. 94,402 crore were to be released as the States' share in 2005-06 compared to Rs. 78,595 crore in 2004-05. As regards grants-in-aid, the amounts granted in 2004-05 and 2005-06 (RE) were Rs. 12,081 crore and Rs. 25,134 crore respectively. In 2006-07, both the tax devolution and the grants would be substantially higher.

Gross Budgetary Support and Gross Fiscal Deficit

The gross tax-GDP ratio, after rising from 9.2 per cent in 2003-04 to 9.8 per cent in 2004-05, had increased further to 10.5 per cent in 2005-06 (RE). It was estimated that, it will increase to 11.2 per cent in 2006-07 (BE).

According to revised estimates, the revenue deficit for 2005-06 will be only 2.6 per cent and the fiscal deficit will be only 4.1 per cent.

Budget Estimates for 2006-07

Plan Expenditure

Plan expenditure for 2006-07 was estimated at Rs. 172,728 crore, up by 20.4 per cent. As a proportion of total expenditure, Plan expenditure had increased from 26.6 per cent in 2004-05 to 28.3 per cent in 2005-06 (RE) and would further increase to 30.6 per cent in 2006-07 (BE).

Non-Plan Expenditure

Non-Plan expenditure in 2006-07 was estimated to be Rs. 391, 263 crore.

Revenue Deficit and Fiscal Deficit

In the Budget Estimates for 2006-07, the total expenditure was estimated at Rs. 563,991 crore, total revenue receipts at Rs. 403,465 crore and the revenue expenditure at Rs. 488,192 crore. Consequently, the revenue deficit was estimated at Rs. 148,686 crore, *i.e.*, 3.8 per cent of the GDP.

Tax Proposals

Indirect Taxes

Customs Duties

In line with the Government's policy of reducing customs duties, the peak rate for non-agricultural products was reduced from 15 per cent to 12.5 per cent.

Accordingly the duty on raw materials and intermediates was also reduced, as given below:

(*i*) On alloy steel and primary and secondary non-ferrous metals from 10 per cent to 7.5 per cent.

(*ii*) On mineral products from 15 per cent to 5 per cent, with a few exceptions.

(*iii*) On ores and concentrates from 5 per cent to 2 per cent.

(*iv*) On refractories and materials required for manufacture of refractories from 10 per cent, or higher rates to 7.5 per cent.

(*v*) On basic inorganic chemicals from 15 per cent to 10 per cent, on basic cyclic and acyclic hydrocarbons and their derivatives to 5 per cent and on catalysts from 10 per cent to 7.5 per cent.

(*vi*) On major bulk plastics like PVC, LDPE and PP from 10 per cent to 5 per cent. Simultaneously, the duty on naptha for plastics will be reduced to nil.

(*vii*) On styrene, EDC and VCM which are raw materials for plastics to 2 per cent.

(*viii*) On 10 anti-AIDS and 14 anti-cancer drugs to 5 per cent, on certain life saving drugs, kits and equipment from 15 per cent to 5 per cent. These drugs will also be exempt from excise duty and countervailing duty (CVD).

(*ix*) On packaging machines from 15 per cent to 5 per cent.

(*x*) The concessional project rate of 10 per cent on pipeline projects for transportation of natural gas, crude petroleum and petroleum products.

A CVD of 4 per cent was imposed on all imports with a few exceptions. Full credit of this duty will be allowed to manufacturers of excisable goods. Duty on vanaspati was increased to 80 per cent, the rate applicable to crude palm oil.

Export oriented units (EOUs) were allowed to clear their goods to the Domestic Tariff Area (DTA) at a concessional rate. The duty rates on clearances by EOUs to the DTA would be adjusted at 25 per cent of basic customs duty plus excise duty on like goods. The excise duty on all man-made fibre yarn and filament yarn was reduced from 16 per cent to 8 per cent. Simultaneously, the import duty on all man-made fibres and yarns was reduced from 15 per cent to 10 per cent. Consequently, the import duty on raw materials such as DMT, PTA and MEG was also reduced from 15 per cent to 10 per cent. The import duty on paraxylene was proposed to be reduced to 2 per cent.

Excise Duty

To converge all rates at the CENVAT rate which is now at 16 per cent, the excise duty on aerated drinks and cars, was reduced to 16 per cent, but only for small cars. A car of length not exceeding 4,000 mm and with an engine capacity not exceeding 1,500 cc for diesel car and not exceeding 1,200 cc for petrol cars.

It was proposed to impose an 8 per cent excise duty on packaged software sold over the counter. Customized software and software packages downloaded from the internet will be exempt from this levy.

DVD Drives, Flash Drives and Combo Drives were fully exempted.

It was proposed to fully exempt from excise duty condensed milk, ice cream, preparations of meat, fish and poultry, pectins, pasta and yeast and to reduce excise duty on ready-to-eat packaged foods and instant food mixes, like *dosa* and *idli* mixes, from 16 per cent to 8 per cent.

It was proposed to exempt from excise duty two vegetable tanning extracts, namely, quebracho and chestnut, and to reduce excise duty on footwear with a retail sale price between Rs. 250 and Rs. 750 from 16 per cent to 8 per cent.

Concessional rate of 8 per cent extended to all LPG stoves without any value limit.

Excise duty on compact fluorescent lamps reduced from 16 per cent to 8 per cent.

Glassware will attract excise duty of 16 per cent on par with ceramicware and plasticware.

Excise duty on specified printing, writing and packing paper reduced from 16 per cent to 12 per cent.

For domestically produced petroleum crude the cess was proposed to be increased from Rs. 1800 to Rs. 2,500 per MT.

The request of domestic manufacturers regarding re-imposition of excise duty on computers at 12 per cent in order to enable them to take CENVAT credit as well as to face competition from imports, was accepted. Similarly, the request to impose excise duty on set top boxes was accepted and an excise duty of 16 per cent was levied and at the same time, the customs duty was reduced from 15 per cent to nil.

The excise duty on cigarettes was increased by about 5 per cent.

It was proposed to remove many exemptions that were granted through notifications.

Service Tax

The new services to be covered included ATM operations, maintenance and management; registrars, share transfer agents and bankers to an issue; sale of space or time, other than in the print media, for advertisements; sponsorship of events, other than sports events, by companies; international air travel excluding economy class passengers; container services on rail, excluding the railway freight charges; business support services; auctioneering; recovery agents; ship management services; travel on cruise ships; and public relations management services.

The service tax rate was increased from 10 per cent to 12 per cent.

Direct Taxes

(*i*) No change was made in the rates of personal income tax or corporate income tax.

(*ii*) No taxes were imposed.

(*iii*) The one-by-six scheme under the Income Tax Act was abolished.

The rate under Minimum Alternate Tax (MAT) increased to 10 per cent.

The rate for the Securities Transaction Tax (STT) increased 25 per cent, across the board.

It was proposed to include investments in fixed deposits in scheduled banks for a term of not less than five years in Section 80C of the Income Tax Act, and to remove the limit of Rs. 10,000 in respect of contribution to certain pension funds in Section 80CCC, subject to the overall ceiling of Rs. 100,000.

Anonymous or pseudonymous donations to wholly charitable institutions to be taxed at the highest marginal rate. Such donations to partly religious and partly charitable institutions/trusts will be taxed only if the donation was specifically for an educational or medical purpose.

Tax proposals on direct taxes were estimated to yield a gain of about Rs. 4,000 crore. On the indirect taxes side, the gain was estimated at Rs. 2,000 crore.

Budget—2007-2008

The Budget was presented to the Parliament by F.M. on February 28, 2007.

A Report on the Economy

The growth rate of GDP had improved from 7.5 per cent in 2004-05 to 9 per cent (Quick Estimate) in 2005-06 and, according to Advance Estimate, to 9.2 per cent in 2006-07. The average growth rate in the last three years was therefore, 8.6 per cent.

The growth rate in manufacturing had accelerated from 8.7 per cent to 9.1 per cent and further to 11.3 per cent. The services sector continued to maintain impressive growth and recorded, in the three years, a growth rate of 9.6 per cent, 9.8 per cent and 11.2 per cent respectively.

On the other hand, the agriculture sector witnessed sharp ups and downs. Average growth during the Tenth Plan period was estimated at 2.3 per cent, which was below the desired level of 4 per cent a year.

Income and Savings

Per capita income in 2005-06, in real terms, increased by 7.4 per cent, and the savings rate had been estimated at 32.4 per cent and the investment rate at 33.8 per cent.

Outlook on Inflation

Until February 2, 2007, bank credit, year on year, had grown by 29.6 per cent. Money supply (M3) had expanded by 21.3 per cent. Foreign exchange reserves stood at US$ 180 billion. These monetary trends put pressure on prices. Global commodity prices also exerted pressure on domestic prices. At the same time, supply constraints emerged in some essential commodities such as wheat, pulses and edible oils. Average inflation in 2006-07 was estimated at between 5.2 and 5.4 per cent, which was higher than 4.4 per cent in 2005-06.

Gross Budgetary Support

In 2006-07, the GBS was fixed at Rs. 172,728 crore and, of this, support to the Central Plan was Rs. 131,284 crore. GBS for 2007-08 will be increased to Rs. 205,100 crore. Out of this, the Central Plan will receive Rs. 154,939 crore.

Allocations for Major Sectors

For Bharat Nirman, as against Rs. 18,696 crore (including the NER component) in 2006-07, Rs. 24,603 crore will be provided in 2007-08, which would mean an increase of 31.6 per cent.

In 2007-08, allocation for education will be increased by 34.2 per cent to Rs. 32,352 crore and for health and family welfare by 21.9 per cent to Rs. 15,291 crore.

Sarva Shiksha Abhiyan and Mid-day Meal Scheme

The allocation for school education will be increased by about 35 per cent from Rs. 17,133 crore in 2006-07 to Rs. 23,142 crore in 2007-08.

Out of this amount, Sarva Shiksha Abhiyan (SSA) will be provided Rs. 10,671 crore. The provision for strengthening teachers training institutions will be increased from Rs. 162 crore to Rs. 450 crore.

The Mid-day Meal Scheme will be provided Rs. 7,324 crore. In addition to covering children in primary classes, beginning 2007-08, children in upper primary classes in 3,427 educationally backward blocks will also be covered.

The provision for secondary education will increase from Rs. 1,837 crore in 2006-07 to Rs. 3,794 crore in 2007-08.

Means-Cum-Merit Scholarships

In order to arrest the drop out ratio and encourage students to continue their education beyond class VIII the proposal was to introduce a National Means-cum-Merit Scholarship Scheme. Selection will be made through a national test from among students who have passed class VIII. Each student will be given Rs. 6,000 per year for study in classes IX, X, XI and XII. The proposal was to award 100,000 scholarships every year. In oder to fund this programme, a corpus fund of Rs. 750 crore has been created to which a like amount will be added to the fund every year over the next three years. Accordingly, a sum of Rs. 750 crore has been placed with the State Bank of India, and the yield from the fund was to be used for awarding the scholarships.

Drinking Water and Sanitation

55,512 habitations and 34,000 schools have been provided drinking water supply till December, 2006 under the Mission. More ambitious targets have been set for 2007-08. It was proposed to enhance the allocation for the Rajiv Gandhi Drinking Water Mission from Rs. 4,680 crore in 2006-07 to Rs. 5,850 crore in 2007-08.

For the Total Sanitation Campaign, the provision will be increased from Rs. 720 crore in 2006-07 year to Rs. 954 crore in 2007-08.

Health Sector; National Rural Health Mission (NRHM)

The allocation for NRHM will be increased from Rs. 8,207 crore in 2006-07 to Rs. 9,947 crore in 2007-08.

HIV/AIDS

For the year 2007-08, the provision for the AIDS control programme will be Rs. 969 crore.

Integrated Child Development Services (ICDS)

The allocation for ICDS will be increased from Rs. 4,087 crore in 2006-07 to Rs. 4,761 crore in 2007-08.

National Rural Employment Guarantee Scheme (NREGS)

The National Rural Employment Guarantee Scheme (NREGS) was launched on February 2, 2006. The proposal was to make an initial allocation of

Rs. 12,000 crore (including NER component) for NREGS. NREGS will be expanded from the current level of 200 districts to 330 districts. In addition, Rs. 2,800 crore will be provided for Sampoorna Gramin Rozgar Yojana (SGRY) for rural employment in the districts not covered by NREGS.

For Swaranjayanti Gram Swarozgar Yojana (SGSY) the allocation will be increased from Rs. 1,200 crore in 2006-07 to Rs. 1,800 crore (including NER component) in 2007-08.

Urban Unemployment

The allocation for Swarna Jayanti Shahari Rojgar Yojana will be increased from Rs. 250 crore in 2006-07 to Rs. 344 crore is 2007-08.

Jawaharlal Nehru National Urban Renewal Mission

The proposal was to enhance the allocation from Rs. 4,595 crore in 2006-07 to Rs. 4,987 crore 2007-08.

Scheduled Castes and Scheduled Tribes

The allocation in 2007-08 for SCs and STs was substantially enhanced. In respect of schemes benefiting only SCs and STs, the allocation was increased to Rs. 3,271 crore. In respect of schemes with at least 20 per cent of the benefits earmarked for SCs and STs, the allocation was increased to Rs. 17,691 crore.

SC and ST students studying in M.Phil and PhD courses are supported by the Rajiv Gandhi National Fellowship Programme for which the allocation was enhanced from Rs. 35 crore in 2006-07 to Rs. 88 crore in 2007-08.

Post-Matric Scholarships

There is a post-matric scholarship programme for SC and ST students. The provision for these scholarships was increased from Rs. 440 crore in 2006-07 to Rs. 611 crore in 2007-08. A separate provision of Rs. 91 crore was made for similar scholarships to be awarded to students belonging to socially and educationally backward classes.

Minorities

A sum of Rs. 63 crore was provided to the share capital of the National Minorities Development and Finance Corporation (NMDFC).

A provision of Rs. 108 crore was also made for a multi-sector development programme in districts, with a concentration of minorities.

For three scholarship programmes being implemented for students belonging to minority communities, following allocations were made:

Pre-matric scholarships	Rs. 72 crore
Post-matric scholarships	Rs. 90 crore
Merit-cum-Means scholarships at graduate and post-graduate levels	Rs. 48.60 crore

Women

There is growing awareness of gender sensitivities of budgetary allocations. 50 ministries/department have set up gender budgeting cells. For 2007-08, the outlay for 100 per cent women specific programmes was Rs. 8,795 crore and for schemes where at least 30 per cent was for women specific programmes it was Rs. 22,382 crore.

North Eastern Region (NER)

The total budget allocation in 2007-08 for the North Eastern Region, culled out from allocations under different ministries/departments, increased from Rs. 12,041 crore in 2006-07 to Rs. 14,365 crore in 2007-08. This included Rs. 1,380 crore provided to the Ministry of Development of North Eastern Region (DONER). The new industrial policy for NER, with suitable fiscal incentives, will be in place before March 31, 2007.

Farm Credit

The goal of doubling farm credit in three years was achieved in two years. The target of Rs. 175,000 crore set for 2006-07 will be exceeded comfortably and was likely to reach Rs. 190,000 crore. Until December 2006, 53.37 lakh new farmers were brought into the institutional credit system. For 2007-08, a target of Rs. 225,000 crore as farm credit had been fixed.

The two per cent interest subvention scheme for short-term crop loans was to continue in 2007-08, for which a provision of Rs. 1,677 crore had been made.

A special plan was being implemented over a period of three years in 31 especially distressed districts in four States of the country involving a total amount of Rs. 16,979 crore. Of this, about Rs. 12,400 crore were for water related schemes. In order to provide subsidiary income to the farmer, the special plan includes a scheme for induction of high yielding milch animals and related activities, Rs. 153 crore were provided for this scheme.

Plantation Sector

A Special Purpose Tea Fund was launched for re-plantation and rejuvenation of tea. Governement was soon to put in place similar financial mechanisms for coffee, rubber, spices, cashew and coconut.

Accelerated Irrigation Benefit Programme

The Accelerated Irrigation Benefit Programme (AIBP) had been revamped in order to complete more irrigation projects in the quickest possible time. 35 projects were likely to be completed in 2006-07 and additional irrigation potential of 900,000 hectares will be created. As against an outlay of Rs. 7,121 crore in 2006-07, the outlay for 2007-08 was increased to Rs. 11,000 crore. Of this, the grant component to State Governments will be Rs. 3,580 crore, an increase from Rs. 2,350 crore.

Rainfed Area Development Programme

The National Rainfed Area Authority was established a few months ago to coordinate all schemes relating to watershed development and other aspects of land use. An allocation of Rs. 100 crore was made for the new Rainfed Area Development Programme.

Agricultural Insurance

The National Agricultural Insurance Scheme (NAIS) was continued in its present form for Kharif and Rabi 2007-08 and a provision of Rs. 500 crore was made for the scheme.

Rural Infrastructure Development Fund

Keeping in view the growing demand for these funds, the corpus of RIDF-XIII in 2007-08 will be raised to Rs. 12,000 crore.

A separate window for rural roads under RIDF was opened with Rs. 4,000 crore. Against this, projects for Rs. 2,311 crore had been sanctioned in 2006-07. The separate window will continue under RIDF-XIII in 2007-08 with a corpus of Rs. 4,000 crore.

Investment

Central Public Sector Enterprises (CPSEs) will, through internal and extra budgetary resources, invest Rs. 165,053 crore in 2007-08. Government will provide equity support of Rs. 16,361 crore and loans of Rs. 2,970 crore to CPSEs.

Further in 2006-07 eight CPSEs were restructured with a cash infusion of Rs. 1,590 crore and non-cash sacrifices of Rs. 1,612 crore.

Infrastructure

Electricity generation had recorded a growth rate of 7.5 per cent in April-December 2008.

The Accelerated Power Development and Reforms Project (APDRP) had reduced significantly Aggregate Technical and Commercial (ATC) losses in 213 towns. APDRP was being restructured to cover all district headquarters and towns with a population of more than 50,000. It was proposed to increase the budgetary support for APDRP from Rs. 650 crore in 2006-07 to Rs. 800 crore in 2007-08.

Having regard to the pace of implementation under the Rajiv Gandhi Grameen Vidyutikaran Yojana and the annual target, it was proposed to increase the allocation from Rs. 3,000 crore in 2006-07 to Rs. 3,983 crore in 2007-08.

National Highways

The provision for the National Highway Development Programme (NHDP) was increased from Rs. 9,945 crore in 2006-07 to Rs. 10,667 crore in 2007-08.

Public Private Partnership and Viability Gap Funding

The Public Private Partnership (PPP) model has enabled greater private sector participation in the creation and maintenance of infrastructure. Under the viability gap funding scheme, 37 proposals had been received of which 21 proposals had been granted 'in-principle' approval with a total project cost of Rs. 9,842 crore and an estimated viability gap funding of Rs. 2,521 crore. The proposal was also to set up a revolving fund with a corpus of Rs. 100 crore.

Industry

Several measures were proposed to provide financial and other incentives to textiles, handloom sector, SMEs and Coir industry.

Other Proposals

Defence Expenditure

The allocation for Defence was fixed at Rs. 96,000 crore, including Rs. 41,922 crore for capital expenditure.

Information Technology

Government had launched an ambitious programme for e-governance. The proposal was to increase the allocation for e-governance from Rs. 395 crore in 2006-07 to Rs. 719 crore in 2007-08. The Central Government supports e-governance action plan at State levels, and it was proposed to increase the allocation for such support from Rs. 300 crore in 2006-07 to Rs. 500 crore in 2007-08, and to provide Rs. 33 crore for a new scheme of manpower development for the software export industry.

Fiscal Responsibility Legislation

Rs. 110,268 crore of States' debt has been consolidated. Twenty States have availed of the benefit of debt waiver to the tune of Rs. 8,575 crore.

In 2006-07, the Centre gave to the States as their share of taxes and duties Rs. 120,377 crore. In 2007-08, this amount will increase to Rs. 142,450 crore. Besides, total grants and loans, both under Plan and non-Plan, to States and Union Territories will increase from Rs. 90,521 crore in 2006-07 to Rs. 106,987 crore in 2007-08.

Revenue deficit for the current year will be 2.0 per cent (against a BE of 2.1 per cent) and the fiscal deficit will be 3.7 per cent (against a BE of 3.8 per cent).

VAT proved to be an unqualified success. VAT revenues of the implementing States increased by 13.8 per cent in 2005-06 and by 24.3 per cent in the first nine months of 2006-07. The CST rate will be reduced from 4 per cent to 3 per cent with effect from April 1, 2007. Rs. 5,495 crore have been provided for compensation for losses, if any, on account of VAT and also on account of CST.

Budget Estimates for 2007-08

Plan Expenditure

Plan expenditure for 2007-08 was estimated at Rs. 205,100 crore. As a proportion of total expenditure (net of the SBI share acquisition), Plan expenditure will be 32.0 per cent.

Non-Plan Expenditure

Non-Plan Expenditure in 2007-08 (net of the SBI share acquisition) was estimated at Rs. 435,421. The increase over 2006-07 was only 6.5 per cent.

Revenue Deficit and Fiscal Deficit

In the Budget Estimates for 2007-08, the total expenditure was estimated at Rs. 680,521 crore (including Rs. 40,000 crore for the SBI share acquisition). The total revenue receipts of the Central Government were projected to be Rs. 486,422 crore and the revenue expenditure to be Rs. 557,900 crore. Consequently, the revenue deficit was estimated at Rs. 71,478 crore which was 1.5 per cent of the GDP. The fiscal deficit was estimated at Rs. 150,948 crore, *i.e.* 3.3 per cent of the GDP.

Tax Proposals

Indirect Taxes

Customs Duties

In order to take one more step towards comparable East Asian rates, the peak rate for non-agricultural products was reduced from 12.5 per cent to 10 per cent.

The Proposal was also to reduce the duties on

(*i*) most chemicals and plastics from 12.5 per cent to 7.5 per cent.
(*ii*) seconds and defectives of steel from 20 per cent to 10 per cent.
(*iii*) polyester fibres and yarns from 10 per cent to 7.5 per cent and consequently, duty on raw-materials such as DMT, PTA and MEG will also be reduced from 10 per cent to 7.5 per cent.
(*iv*) cut and polished diamonds from 5 per cent to 3 per cent; rough synthetic stones from 12.5 per cent to 5 per cent; and unworked corals from 30 per cent to 10 per cent.
(*v*) drip irrigation systems, agricultural sprinklers and food processing machinery from 7.5 per cent to 5 per cent.
(*vi*) medical equipment from 12.5 per cent to 7.5 per cent.
(*vii*) sunflower oil, both crude and refined, by 15 percentage points.
(*viii*) pet foods from 30 per cent to 20 per cent.
(*ix*) watch dials and movements as well as umbrella parts from 12.5 per cent to 5 per cent and
(*x*) 15 specified machinery in the pharmaceutical and biotechnology sector from 7.5 per cent to 5 per cent.

Fully exempt from duty all coking coal irrespective of the ash content and dredgers; and crude as well as refined edible oils from the additional CV duty of 4 per cent.

An import duty of 3 per cent was levied on all private import of aircraft including helicopters. Such import will also attract countervailing duty and additional customs duty.

An export duty of Rs. 300 per metric tonne on export of iron ores and concentrates and Rs. 2,000 per metric tonne on export of chrome ores and concentrates, was imposed.

Exise Duties

No change in the general CENVAT rate or in the service tax rate.

AD valorem component of excise duty on petrol and diesel was reduced from 8 per cent to 6 per cent.

Keeping in mind the special needs of several sectors and the interest of the consumers, relief from excise duty in deserving cases, especially job creating sectors was provided:

(1) Exemption limit for small scale industry (SSI) raised from Rs. 1 crore to Rs. 1.5 crore.

(2) All kinds of food mixes and biscuits whose retail sale price does not exceed Rs. 50 per kilogram fully exempted from excise duty.

Duty reduced on umbrellas and parts of footwear and on plywood from 16 per cent to 8 per cent.

Water purification devices operating on specified membrane based technologies as well as domestic water filters not using electricity, fully exempted from duty and all pipes of diameter exceeding 200 mm used in water supply systems fully exempt from duty.

Duty of Rs. 400 per metric tonne was reduced to Rs. 350 per metric tonne on cement which is sold in retail at not more than Rs. 190 per bag. On cement with a higher MRP, the excise duty will be Rs. 600 per metric tonne.

Specific rates of excise duty on cigarettes were increased by about 5 per cent. Similarly, excise duty (excluding cess) on biris, was raised from Rs. 7 to Rs. 11 per thousand for non-machine made biris and from Rs. 17 to Rs. 24 per thousand for machine made biris.

On pan masala not containing tobacco, the duty was reduced from 66 per cent to 45 per cent.

Service Tax

Exemption limit for small service providers was raised from Rs. 400,000 to Rs. 800,000. The revenue loss will be Rs. 800 crore.

Service tax was extended to :

(*a*) Services outsourced for mining of mineral, oil or gas;

(*b*) Renting of immovable property for use in commerce or business;

(*c*) Development and supply of content for use in telecom and advertising purposes;

(*d*) Asset management services provided by individuals; and

(*e*) Design services;

(*f*) Services involved in the execution of a works contract @ 2 per cent of the total value of the works contract.

Direct Taxes

Personal Income Tax (PIT)

(*a*) the threshold limit of exemption in the case of all assessees was raised by Rs. 10,000, thus giving every assessee a relief of Rs. 1,000;

(*b*) For women assessee, the threshold limit was raised from Rs. 135,000 to Rs. 145,000, giving a relief of Rs. 1,000;

(*c*) The threshold limit of exemption in the case of a senior citizen was raised from Rs. 185,000 to Rs. 195,000, giving him or her a relief of Rs. 2,000; and

(*d*) The deduction in respect of medical insurance premium under Section 80D was increased to a maximum of Rs. 15,000 and, in the case of a senior citizen, a maximum of Rs. 20,000.

Corporate Income Tax (CIT)

The surcharge on income tax on all firms and companies with a taxable income of Rs. 1 crore or less was removed.

A five year holiday from income tax for two, three or four star hotels as well as for convention centres with a seating capacity of not less than 3,000 was proposed. They should be completed and begin operations in the National Capital Territory of Delhi or in the adjacent districts during the period April 1, 2007 to March 31, 2010.

MAT was extended to income in respect of which deduction is claimed under Sections 10A and 10B of the Income Tax Act.

The rate of dividend distribution tax was raised from 12.5 per cent to 15 per cent on dividends distributed by companies.

Dividend distribution tax on dividends paid by money market mutual funds and liquid mutual funds was raised to 25 per cent for all investors.

ESOPs were brought under FBT.

Under the Banking Cash Transactions Tax (BCTT) the exemption limit for individuals and HUFs was raised from Rs. 25,000 to Rs. 50,000.

An additional cess of 1 per cent was levied on all taxes to fund secondary education and higher education and expansion of capacity by 54 per cent for reservation for socially and educationally backward classes.

Tax proposals on direct taxes were estimated to yield a gain of Rs. 3,000 crore. On the indirect taxes side, the proposals were revenue neutral.

Budget—2008-09

The Budget was presented by the FM in the Lok Sabha on February 29, 2008. Following are the notable features of FM's Budget Speech:

An Overview of the Economy

The economy has recorded a growth rate of over 8 per cent. The drivers of growth continue to be services and manufacturing which are estimated to grow at 10.7 per cent and 9.4 per cent respectively.

Agriculture has struck a disappointing note; it grew at 2.6 per cent in 2007-08.

Globbally, there has been a sharp rise in the prices of crude oil, basic metals and food grains and it has caused pressure on domestic prices.

Capital inflows have been far in excess of the current account deficit making monetary management difficult.

The F.M. enumerated a number of initiatives to promote growth in agriculture, women and child development, rural employment, welfare of socially backward classes, development of backward regions, infrastructure and opening of the financial sector in 2008-09.

Budget Estimates

The estimate of Plan expenditure is placed at Rs. 2,43,386 crore—it will be 32.4 per cent of total expenditure. Non-Plan expenditure is estimated at Rs. 5,07,498 crore. Revenue deficit for 2007-08 will be 1.4 per cent against the Budget Estimate of 1.5 per cent and fiscal deficit will be 3.1 per cent against the BE of 3.3 per cent.

Revenue receipts for 2008-09 are projected at Rs. 6,02,935 crore and revenue expenditure at Rs. 6,58,119 crore. Hence, the revenue dificit is estimated at Rs, 55,184 crore *i.e.*, 1 per cent of GDP. The fiscal deficit is estimated at Rs. 1,33,287 crore, which is 2.5 per cent of GDP.

Tax Proposals

Indirect Taxes

Customs Duties

(*i*) No change in the peak rate

(*ii*) Duty on Project Imports reduced from 7.5 per cent to 5 per cent; on steel melting scrap and aluminium scrap from 5 per cent to nil; on life saving drugs and bulk drugs used as raw-material for them from 10 per cent to 5 per cent (as well as total exemption from excise duty and CVD) on vitamin premixes and mineral mixtures used in the manufacturing of cattle and poultry feeds from 30 per cent to 20 per cent; on phosphoric acid from 7.5 per cent to 5 per cent; on bactofuges from 7.5 per cent to nil; on convergence products from 7.5 per cent to 5 per cent; on specified machinery used in manufacturing of sports from 7.5 per cent to 5 per cent; on polished zerconia and rough coral from 10 per cent to 5 per cent; on crude and unrefined sulphur from 5 per cent to 2 per cent.

(*iii*) Duty imposed @ 5 per cent on naptha used in the manufacture of polymer and increased from Rs. 2000 per MT to Rs. 3000 per MT on chrome ore exports:

(*iv*) 4 per cent special CVD levied on a few specified projects in the power sector.

(*v*) Specified parts of set top boxes and specific raw materials used in the IT/electronic hardware industry and helicopter simulators fully exempted from duty.

Excise Duties

(1) General CENVAT rate on all goods reduced from 16 per cent to 14 per cent.

(2) It was proposed to reduce the duty as under:

(*i*) on all goods produced in the pharmaceutical sector from 16 per cent to 8 per cent.

(*ii*) on buses and chessis from 16 per cent to 12 per cent.

(*iii*) on small cars from 16 to 12 per cent and on hybrid cars from 24 to 14 per cent.

(*iv*) on two and three wheelers from 16 to 12 per cent.

(*v*) on paper, paper board and particles made out of non-conventional raw material by units, not having an attached bamboo/wood pulp making plant from 12 to 8 per cent with a further reduction on clearances upto 3500 MT from 8 per cent to nil. Further, on specific varieties of writing, printing and packaging paper from 12 to 8 per cent.

(*vi*) on composting machines, wireless data cards, packaged coconut water, tea and coffee mixes, puffed rice etc from 16 per cent to nil.

(*vii*) on water purification devices, veneers and flush doors, sterile dressing pads, specified packaging materials, breakfast cereals from 16 to 8 per cent.

(3) Total exemption from duty to Anti Aids Drugs and bulk drugs for its manufacture, refrigeration equipment utilizing power of 50 kW and above.

(4) Abolition of ad valorem duty on unbranded petrol and diesel and replacement of the same by an equivalent specific duty of Rs. 1.35 per litre.

(5) Abolition of duty of 1 per cent (called VCCD) imposed on polyester filament of yarn and shifting it to cellular mobile phones.

(6) Increased duty of Rs. 400 per MT on bulk cement and Rs. 450 per MT on cement clinkers and on packaged software from 8 to 12 per cent.

(7) Bringing of non-filter cigarettes on par with filter cigarettes.

Service Tax

(*i*) Four new services, *viz*, Asset management service provided under ULIP; services provided by stock/commodity exchanges and clearing houses, customized software and right to use goods, in cases where VAT is not payable.

(*ii*) threshold limit of exemption for small service providers raised from Rs. 8 lakh to Rs. 12 lakh per year.

Direct Taxes

(*i*) Threshold limit of exemption increased

(*a*) for all assessees—Rs. 1,50,000

(*b*) for women—Rs, 1,85,000

(*c*) for senior citizens—Rs. 2,25,000

(*ii*) Senior citizen savings scheme 2004 and Post Office Time Deposit Account covered under Section 80C of the I.T. Act 1861.

(*iii*) Additional deduction of Rs. 15,000 under Section 80D allowed to an individual who pays medical insurance premium for the parents.

(*iv*) Some minor change in FBT provisions, and STT have been proposed.

(*v*) Rate of tax on short term capital gains raised to 15%.

(*vi*) Commodities Transaction Tax introduced on similar lines as the S.T.T.

(*vii*) Banking Cash Transactions Tax withdrawn w.e.f. 1.4.2009.

Direct tax proposals are revenue neutral while on indirect tax side a loss of Rs. 5,900 crore is estimated.

Exercises

1. Distinguish between revenue budget and capital budget of the Government of India. State the main items on the revenue side of the revenue budget and receipts side of the capital budget.
2. Given your comments on the 2008-09 Budget of the Government of India.
3. Analyse the trends of the finances of the Government of India from the budgetary data during the preceding three years. Have, in your opinion, the budgets been able to achieve the objective 'economic growth'?

•••

Select Bibliography

Money and Banking

Ackley G., *Macroeconomics.*
Basu, A.K., *Fundamentals of Banking Theory and Practice.*
Brooman, F.S., *Macroeconomics.*
Burnstein, M.L., *Money.*
Business Line
Chandler, L.V. and Goldfield, S.M., *The Economics of Money and Banking.*
Chandler, L.V., *Central Banking and Economic Development.*
Clower, R.W., *Monetary Theory.*
Cochran, J.A., *Money; Banking and the Economy.*
Crockett, A., *International Money.*
Croome, H., *Introduction to Money.*
Crowther, G., *An Outline of Money.*
Culbertson, J.M., *Money and Banking.*
Davidson, P., *Money and the Real World.*
Day, A.C.L., *An Outline of Monetary Economics.*
DeCock, M.H., *Central Banking.*
Dcrnberg, T.E, and McDougall, *Macroeconomics.*
Dillard, D., *The Economics of John Maynard Keynes.*
Ellsworth, P.T. and Leith, J.C., *The International Economy.*
Enke, S. and Salera, V., *International Economics.*
Financial Express
Frazer, W.J. and William P.Y., *Analytics and Institutions of Money and Banking.*
Friedman, M., *Studies in the Quantity Theory of Money.*
Ghosh, A., *Financial Intermediaries and Monetary Policy in a Developing Country.*
Gibson, W.E. and Kaufman, G.G., *Monetary Economics.*
Haberler, G.V., *The Theory of International Trade.*
Halm, G.N., *Monetary Theory.*
Hansen, A.H., *A Guide to Keynes.*

Hanson, J.L., *Monetary Theory and Practice.*
Heller, H.R., *International Trade.*
Hicks, J.R., *The Crisis in Keynesian Economics.*
Hodgman, D.R., *Commercial Bank Loan and Investment Policy.*
IMF and the World Bank, *Finance and Development.*
Johnson, H.G., *Macroeconomics and Monetary Theory.*
Johnson, H.G., *Essays in Monetary Theory.*
Kent, R.P., *Money and Banking.*
Keynes, J.M., *A Tract on Monetary Reforms.*
— *A Treatise on Money.*
Kindleberger, C.P., *International Economics.*
Klise, E.S., *Money and Banking.*
Lovell, M.C., *Macroeconomics.*
Makin, J.H., *Macroeconomics.*
Newlyn, W.T. and Bootle, R.P., *Theory of Money.*
Ohlin, B., *Interregional and International Trade.*
Ranlett, J.G., *Money and Banking.*
Robertson, D.H., *Money.*
Robinson, R.S., *The Management of Bank Funds.*
Sayers, R.S., *Modern Banking.*
Schweiter, P.P., *The Role of the International Monetary Fund.*
Sen, S.N., *Central Banking in Underdeveloped Money Markets.*
Shapiro, E., *Macroeconomic Analysis.*
Sirkin, E., *An Introduction to Macroeconomic Theory.*
Snider, D.A., *Introduction to International Economics.*
Sodersten, Bo, *International Economics.*
Thomas, R.G., *Our Modern Banking and Monetary System.*
Timberlake, R.H., *Money, Banking and Central Banking.*
Timlin, M.F., *Keynesian Economics.*
Vanek, J., *International Trade.*
Viner, J., *Studies in the Theory of International Trade.*
Whittlesey, C.R., *Principles and Practice of Money and Banking.*
Wonnacott, P., *Macroeconomics.*
Wrightsman, D., *An Introduction to Monetary Theory and Policy.*
Yeager, L.B., *The International Monetary Mechanism.*

Public Finance

Adam Smith	:	*The Wealth of Nations Book V*
A.P. Lerner	:	*Functional Finance and the Federal Debt*
A.C. Pigou	:	*A Study in Public Finance*
A.T. Peacock	:	*The Economic Analysis of Government and Related Themes*
B.P. Herber	:	*Mordern Public Finance*
B.S. Sahni (Ed)	:	*Public Expenditure Analysis*
B.F. Fliger	:	*Public Finance*
C.F. Bastable	:	*Public Finance*
C.S. Shoup	:	*Public Finance*
E.H. Plank and D.N. Gadhok	:	*Parliamentary Control Over Government Expenditure, 1976.*
David Novic (Ed)	:	*Programme Budgeting.*
E.A.R. Saligman	:	*Essays in Taxation*
F. Shirras	:	*The Science of Public Finance*
K.M. Buchanan	:	*The Public Finance*
NCAER	:	*Management of Public Debt in India, 1965.*
J.W. Jackson	:	*Public Finance*
J.K. Mehta	:	*Public Finance*
J. Stamp	:	*Wealth and Taxable Capacity*
J.S. Mill	:	*Principles of Economics, Book V*
H. Dalton	:	*Public Finance*
H.C. Simons	:	*Personal Income Taxation*
Government of India	:	*Economic Surveys*
Grehard Colm	:	*Essays in Public Finance and Fiscal Policy*
R.A. Musgrave	:	*The Theory of Public Finance*
RBI	:	*Report of Currency and Finance*
V.K. Hicks	:	*Public Finance*